INTERPRETING
QUA DATA

DELETED

DAVID SILVERMAN
INTERPRETING QUALITATIVE DATA

A Guide to the Principles of Qualitative Research

4TH EDITION

Los Angeles | London | New Delhi
Singapore | Washington DC

First edition published 1993
Second edition published 2001. Reprinted 2003, 2004, 2005, 2006
Third edition published 2006. Reprinted 2007, 2008 (twice), 2009 and 2010 (twice)
This fourth edition published 2011

SAGE Publications Ltd
1 Oliver's Yard
55 City Road
London EC1Y 1SP

SAGE Publications Inc.
2455 Teller Road
Thousand Oaks, California 91320

SAGE Publications India Pvt Ltd
B 1/I 1 Mohan Cooperative Industrial Area
Mathura Road
New Delhi 110 044

SAGE Publications Asia-Pacific Pte Ltd
33 Pekin Street #02-01
Far East Square
Singapore 048763

Library of Congress Control Number: 2011921527

British Library Cataloguing in Publication data

A catalogue record for this book is available from the British Library

ISBN 978-0-85702-420-6
ISBN 978-0-85702-421-3 (pbk)

Typeset by C&M Digitals (P) Ltd, Chennai, India
Printed and bound in Great Britain by TJ International Ltd, Padstow, Cornwall
Printed on paper from sustainable resources

For my friends at the Nursery End in the hope (but not the expectation) that Middlesex will finally achieve success in the county championship.

Contents

Companion Website

Be sure to visit the companion website to this book at www.sagepub.co.uk/silvermaniqd to find a range of teaching and learning materials for both lecturers and students, including the following:

- **Methodspace page:** Link to a Methodspace group for the book (www.methodspace.com/group/silverman) where readers can give feedback, discuss issues and pose questions about their research directly to the author.
- **Additional case studies and examples:** Engaging and relevant case studies to help illustrate the main concepts in each chapter.
- **Full-text journal articles:** Full access to selected SAGE journal articles related to each chapter, providing students with a deeper understanding of key topics.
- **Links to useful websites, podcasts and Youtube videos:** An assortment of direct links to relevant websites for each chapter.
- **Student exercises:** Thought-provoking questions for each chapter that are intended to help students think critically about their own research.
- **Helpful tips:** Valuable considerations for students doing their own research.
- **Recommended reading:** Suggestions for further reading.

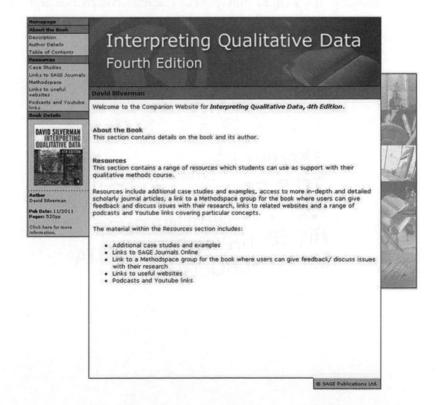

About the Author

David Silverman trained as a sociologist at the London School of Economics and the University of California, Los Angeles. He taught for 32 years at Goldsmiths, University of London. He is interested in conversation and discourse analysis and he has researched medical consultations and HIV-test counselling.

He is the author of *Interpreting Qualitative Data* (Fourth Edition, 2012), *Doing Qualitative Research* (Third Edition, 2010) and *A Very Short, Fairly Interesting, Reasonably Cheap Book about Qualitative Research* (2007). He is the editor of *Qualitative Research* (Third Edition, 2011) and the Sage series Introducing Qualitative Methods. In recent years, he has offered short, hands-on workshops in qualitative research for universities in Europe, Asia, Africa and Australia.

Now retired from full-time work, he aims to watch 100 days of cricket a year. He also enjoys voluntary work in an old people's home where he sings with residents with dementia and strokes.

Preface to Fourth Edition

This new edition has been substantially rewritten. My aim has been to develop the book as an undergraduate introductory qualitative methods text which complements the postgraduate focus of *Doing Qualitative Research*. Rather than attempting to turn this volume into simply an undergraduate research project book, my focus is on introducing first-degree students to the theory, methods and practice of qualitative research. In this way, I have tried to make this book suitable for both taught courses and research projects at the undergraduate level.

Three new chapters have been written for this volume. A chapter on research design seeks to demonstrate the challenges faced by the student in carrying out a small research project and to offer some simple solutions. It is complemented by a chapter on data analysis which deals with the nitty-gritty issues of confronting data for the first time and contains sections on contemporary approaches to data analysis, including grounded theory and narrative analysis. Finally, a new chapter on focus groups offers detailed discussion about how to analyse focus group data.

The rest of the book has been substantially updated with many recent relevant case studies incorporated. The chapter on ethics has been repositioned and expanded, reflecting the need for students at all levels to obtain ethical approval for their projects. The chapter on texts now includes a section on comparative keyword analysis. Also, consonant with the expansion of the use of the Internet as a source of knowledge and research data, the coverage of digital media has been considerably expanded.

Like the Third Edition of *Doing Qualitative Research*, this volume now offers a Companion Website with additional case studies provided by links to Sage journals. It also provides links to useful websites, podcasts and YouTube videos. This Fourth Edition is also accompanied with its own group page on www.methodspace.com where users can give feedback and discuss research-related topics.

I have also consciously tried to make this an interdisciplinary social science text which takes account of the growing interest in qualitative research outside sociology and anthropology from psychology to geography, information systems, health promotion, management and many other disciplines.

Like earlier editions of this book, I aim to demonstrate that qualitative research is not simply a set of techniques to be slotted into any given research problem. That is why this book concentrates on data analysis rather than simply data gathering. Indeed, at the very start of qualitative research, analytic issues should be to the fore.

Contrary to the common tendency simply to select any given social problem as one's focus, I try to demonstrate that research problems, at any level, need to be analytically defined. Indeed, in qualitative research, it often makes sense to begin *without* a clearly defined problem and to gradually work towards a topic by confronting data with the simple question: 'what is going on here?' Here, as elsewhere, my position derives from a *constructionist* stance informed by a refusal to accept taken-for-granted versions of how the world is put together.

Writing a book, like most things we do, is related to our own biography. I say 'related to' because it is both inappropriate and foolish to *reduce* a piece of writing to the personal experiences of its author. Indeed, nothing makes me cringe more than those endless chat shows where the topic is always someone's 'personality' rather than their work. Here, as elsewhere, then, one should trust the tale and not the teller, although my biographical background is sketched out in Chapter 14.

None of this means that the reader should expect to find that this book contains a polemic. My central aim is to show the value of a range of methodologies in social research and to equip the reader with some of the skills necessary to apply these methodologies.

It is the *craft* of social research that this book sets to convey rather than the passive ability to regurgitate appropriate answers in methodology examinations. I believe that knowledge has little to do with rote learning about the advantages and disadvantages of various approaches or methods. To this end, my discussion is illustrated by many detailed examples of qualitative research studies. Technical terms are highlighted and included in the Glossary.

To be effective, a textbook should offer an active learning experience. In ancient Greece, Socrates encouraged understanding by asking his students pointed questions. Much more recently, another philosopher, Ludwig Wittgenstein, filled his book *Philosophical Investigations* with hundreds of provocative questions. Interestingly enough, a period of teaching in an elementary school had shown him how real learning often comes by working through particular examples.

Learning through doing is a wonderful way of appropriating knowledge and turning it into useful skills. The point has not been lost in distance-learning programmes (like those at the Open University in the UK). Thus, I provide many exercises, linked to the surrounding text.

These exercises often involve the reader in gathering and/or analysing data. My aim is that the users of this book will learn some basic skills in generating researchable problems and analysing qualitative data. As I have confirmed through using these materials for assessment on an undergraduate course, the exercises also give students an ability to show the skills of their craft in a way that is not usually possible in the confines of a normal examination method.

I believe that the most challenging of these skills arises in defining research problems and in analysing data. So this present book is not a 'cookbook': it does not discuss in detail many of the practical issues involved in the research process (e.g. how to obtain access, how to present oneself to research subjects). Some of these matters can only be settled by practical experience. Others involve concealed analytic issues (e.g. about the character of observation) which are discussed in this book.

I envisage this reshaped text as a companion volume to the Third Edition of my recent book *Doing Qualitative Research* (2010). That book is a guide to the business of conducting a research project at the graduate level. This book is more introductory and, together with its accompanying volume of key readings (Silverman, 2011), seeks to offer the background undergraduate students need for a methods course or when contemplating their own small-scale qualitative research study.

For my sense of this 'background', I will use the words of Wittgenstein who, in closing his *Tractatus Logico-Philosophicus*, tells us:

> My propositions serve as elucidations in the following way: anyone who understands me eventually recognises them as nonsensical, when he has used them – as steps – to climb up beyond them (he must, so to speak, throw away the ladder after he has climbed up it). He must transcend these propositions, and then he will see the world aright. (1971: 6.54)

It is my hope that this book may serve as something like Wittgenstein's ladder, providing an initial footing for students then to go off to do their own research – charting new territories rather than restating comfortable orthodoxies.

A number of friends have contributed to this Third Edition. I am very grateful for the comments I have received from Kathy Charmaz, Jay Gubrium, Jonathan Potter, Tim Rapley, Cathy Riessman and Sue Wilkinson. I thank Christian Heath, Paul Luff and Cambridge University Press for allowing me to reproduce in Chapter 10 passages from Heath and Luff's book *Technology in Action* (2000). I am also grateful to Clive Seale for giving me permission to mention certain Internet links recommended in his edited textbook (Seale, 2004b) and to Sara Cordell for keeping my back in good enough shape to be able to finish this book.

My editor at Sage, Patrick Brindle, has been a constant source of help. He talked me into this Fourth Edition over an excellent lunch and has been a tower of strength throughout. Katie Metzler at Sage did a very useful survey of responses to the previous edition of this book and made many useful suggestions about how this present volume could be adapted. Naturally, I alone am responsible for any errors or omissions contained in this book.

PART ONE

THEORY AND METHOD IN QUALITATIVE RESEARCH

1

What Is Qualitative Research?

CHAPTER OBJECTIVES

By the end of this chapter, you will be able to:

- understand what is meant by qualitative research
- link your research topic to an appropriate methodology
- recognise the advantages and disadvantages of both qualitative and quantitative methods
- understand the diverse approaches underlying contemporary qualitative research.

1.1 IN SEARCH OF A WORKING DEFINITION

To call yourself a 'qualitative' researcher settles surprisingly little. First, as we shall see at the end of this chapter, 'qualitative research' covers a wide range of different, even conflicting, activities. Second, if the description is being used merely as some sort of negative epithet (saying what we are *not*, i.e. non-quantitative), then I am not clear how useful it is. As Grahame puts it: 'the notion that qualitative research is non-quantitative is true but uninformative: we need more than a negative definition' (1999: 4).

What, then, are the principal differences between quantitative and qualitative research? Table 1.1 sets out some common assumptions.

Unfortunately, as Hammersley (1992) makes clear, each of the assumed differences in Table 1.1 are problematic as follows:

TABLE 1.1   Assumed characteristics of research

Qualitative research	Quantitative research
Uses words	Uses numbers
Concerned with meanings	Concerned with behaviour
Induces hypotheses from data	Begins with hypotheses
Case studies	Generalisations

Source: adapted from Hammersley, 1992

- Quantitative researchers clearly use words as well as numbers. For instance, they usually offer verbal interpretations of their statistical tables. It is also not true that numbers are absent from qualitative research. Having discovered some phenomenon by qualitative means, there is every reason to see how frequently it occurs (see the case study on cancer clinics later in this chapter).
- Quantitative research is often concerned with meanings – questionnaires or surveys are commonly designed to establish how people 'see' themselves or others. Qualitative researchers can be interested in behaviour just as much as how people see things. Many qualitative studies examine how people interact with one another in particular settings like the workplace, a museum or an auction house (see Heath et al., 2010, discussed in Chapter 10).
- The standard, published quantitative study usually does begin with a hypothesis which it then seeks to test. However, it is becoming more common for qualitative researchers to begin with a hypothesis. My research on advice giving in HIV-test counselling (Silverman, 1997), discussed in Chapter 11, was based on a relevant earlier study. After more than a century of qualitative research, we would be in a bad way if we had no findings that were worthy of further study!
- The same applies to generalisations. As I argue later in this book, following Flyvbjerg (2004), we can make certain kinds of generalisations from case studies.

It would be foolish, however, to maintain that there is *no* distinction between qualitative and quantitative research. This can be seen clearly if we compare the format in different journals. Quantitative journals expect their authors to begin with a hypothesis which is then tested using accepted statistical measures on a large number of cases which are often randomly selected. Much of the material consists of tables of numbers. The interpretation of such tables is usually postponed until a final section which is often called 'discussion'.

By contrast, the papers in qualitative journals do not routinely begin with a hypothesis, the 'cases' studied are usually far fewer in number and the authors' interpretation is carried on throughout the writing. There is usually far greater attention paid here to the particular theory or '**model**' of qualitative research which the author is using. This allows me to make some simple, working distinctions set out in Table 1.2.

TABLE 1.2   Qualitative research: some simple characteristics

1	Often begins with a single case, chosen because of its convenience or interest
2	Often studies phenomena in the contexts in which they arise through observation and/or recording or the analysis of printed and Internet material
3	Hypotheses are often generated from the analysis rather than stated at the outset
4	There is no one agreed way to analyse your data. Multiple research models exist (e.g. grounded theory, constructionism, discourse analysis) and sometimes conflict with each other
5	Where numbers are used, these are usually in the form of simple tabulations designed to identify deviant cases and do not lead to statistical correlations or tests

Table 1.2 attempts to paint a realistic picture of what *most* qualitative research looks like – of course, there are exceptions. However, research methods are not always a subject for rational debate. In the next section, you will see how people often make loaded assumptions about different research **methods**.

1.2 LOADED EVALUATIONS OF RESEARCH METHODS

You may have had experience as a student of how different teachers and departments rate qualitative and quantitative methods. Within psychology, for instance, there is a clear split between those who favour quantitative studies, often based on questionnaires or laboratory studies, and those who use qualitative methods to study interaction in the 'field' (see Potter, 2011). However, you also have to bear in mind that these methods are often evaluated differently. This is shown in Table 1.3 which is drawn from the terms used by speakers at a conference on research methods. Unfortunately, little has changed over the decades since then.

Table 1.3 shows how imprecise, evaluative considerations come into play when researchers describe qualitative and quantitative methods. Depending on your

TABLE 1.3   Claimed features of qualitative and quantitative method

Qualitative	Quantitative
Soft	Hard
Flexible	Fixed
Subjective	Objective
Political	Value-free
Case study	Survey
Speculative	Hypothesis testing
Grounded	Abstract

Source: Halfpenny, 1979: 799

point of view, Table 1.3 might suggest that quantitative research was superior because, for example, it is value-free. The implication here is that quantitative research simply objectively reports reality, whereas qualitative research is influenced by the researcher's political values. Conversely, other people might argue that such value-freedom in social science is either undesirable or impossible.

The same sort of argument can arise about 'flexibility'. For some people, such flexibility encourages qualitative researchers to be innovative. For others, flexibility might be criticised as meaning lack of structure. Conversely, being 'fixed' gives such a structure to research but without flexibility.

However, this is by no means a balanced argument. Outside the social science community, there is little doubt that quantitative data rule the roost. Governments favour quantitative research because it mimics the research of its own agencies (Cicourel, 1964: 36). They want quick answers based on 'reliable' **variables** which can be reliably audited. Similarly, many research funding agencies call qualitative researchers 'journalists or soft scientists' whose work is 'termed unscientific, or only exploratory, or entirely personal and full of bias' (Denzin and Lincoln, 1994: 4).

For the general public, there is a mixture of respect and suspicion of quantitative data ('you can say anything you like with figures'; 'lies, damn lies and statistics'). This is reflected by the media. On the one hand, public opinion polls are treated as newsworthy – particularly immediately before elections. On the other hand, unemployment and inflation statistics are often viewed with suspicion – particularly when they appear to contradict your own experience (statistics which show that inflation has fallen may not be credible if you see prices going up for the goods you buy!).

LINK

Ben Goldacre's column in the UK newspaper the *Guardian* (see www.badscience. net/) looks at how the press reports (and distorts) scientific research.

For this reason, by the beginning of the new millennium, in many Western countries, the assumed reliability of quantitative research was starting to be under significant threat. The failure of surveys of voting intention in the British general election of 1992 (almost comparable with the similar failure of US telephone poll studies in the 1948 Truman–Dewey presidential race) made the public a little sceptical about such statistics – even though the companies involved insisted they were providing only statements of current voting intentions and not predictions of the actual result.

The case study below provides a recent example of how one polling company approaches the problem of measuring voting intentions.

CASE STUDY
Why Polls Sometimes Show Different Results

How should you recruit a sample of people in order to ask about their voting intentions? Party identification is usually a good guide. Should you base your sample on the results of the last election? Some pollsters argue that partisan identification is fluid and changes frequently. This approach suggests that whatever partisan mix falls out from the results of a random sample is the 'right' answer. Or should you 'purposively' sample by finding respondents in numbers which fit the ratio of *current* party identification?

[based on *Rasmussen Reports*, Thursday, 26 June 2008]

Part of the public's scepticism about statistics may be due to the way that governments have chosen numbers selectively. For instance, while the US administration kept statistics on US soldiers killed in Iraq, it published no data on the numbers of Iraqi citizens killed since the 2003 Iraq War. Or, to take a second example, in 2005 the British Chancellor of the Exchequer (finance minister) announced a change in the years which constituted the present economic cycle. While this change appeared to be purely technical, it enabled the British Treasury to sanction increasing national debts which, under the previous methods, would have broken the Chancellor's 'golden rule' about public borrowing.

But such concerns may constitute only a 'blip' in the ongoing history of the dominance of quantitative research. Qualitative researchers still largely feel themselves to be second-class citizens whose work typically evokes suspicion, where the 'gold standard' is quantitative research.

It is important to be aware of the environment in which research functions. At the same time, it is important to try to avoid these kind of value-judgements. As I argue in the next section, research methods are rarely intrinsically 'right' or 'wrong'.

1.3 METHODS SHOULD FIT YOUR RESEARCH QUESTION

The term 'qualitative research' seems to promise that we will avoid or downplay statistical techniques and the mechanics of the kinds of quantitative methods used in, say, survey research or epidemiology. The danger in the term, however, is that it seems to assume a fixed preference or predefined evaluation of what is 'good' (i.e. qualitative) and 'bad' (i.e. quantitative) research. In fact, the choice between different research methods should depend upon what you are trying to find out.

TABLE 1.4   Qualitative or quantitative methods?

---

1   Imagine you want to study ambulance crews' responses to emergency calls. One way to do this would be to examine statistics giving the time which such crews take to get to such an emergency. However, such statistics may not tell the whole story. For instance, when does the timing of the emergency services' response begin (when the caller picks up the phone or when the ambulance crew receives the information from the operator)? And isn't it also important to examine how operators and ambulances services grade the seriousness of calls? If so, qualitative research may be needed to investigate how statistics are collected, e.g. when timing starts and what locally counts as a 'serious' incident. Note that this is an issue not just of the statistics being biased (which quantitative researchers recognise) but of the inevitable (and necessary) intrusion of common-sense judgements into practical decision-making (Garfinkel, 1967)

2   Say you are interested in what determines adolescents' diet. So you do a survey which asks them about the influences on their choice of food (e.g. parents, siblings, peer groups, advertisements). But is 'influence' really a suitable way of describing the phenomenon? For instance, a qualitative study may show that eating patterns arise in a variety of contexts including negotiations with parents over such practical matters as who does the cooking and when the food is served. Hence young people's diet is not a simple outcome of different sets of 'influences' (Eldridge and Murcott, 2000)

3   Imagine you want to study decisions by the police to charge juvenile offenders with a crime. It looks like being found with a weapon will lead to a criminal charge. But what kind of weapon? To answer this question, you code official records, giving a code of '1' to the use of a firearm and '2' to the use of a blunt instrument such as a baseball bat. But what are you to do if some offenders used *both* weapons (Marvasti, 2004: 9–10)? Do you just modify your coding system or do you add a qualitative study of meetings where police and public prosecutors grade the 'seriousness' of an offence and the likelihood of obtaining a conviction in deciding whether to charge a juvenile with a crime (Sudnow, 1968b)?

For instance, if you want to discover how people intend to vote, then a quantitative method, like a social survey, may seem the most appropriate choice. On the other hand, if you are concerned with exploring people's life-histories or everyday behaviour, then qualitative methods may be favoured. Table 1.4 gives three more examples of how your research topic should guide your use of quantitative or qualitative methods.

EXERCISE 1.1

Should I use qualitative research?

When planning your research project, try to answer the following six questions suggested by Punch (1998: 244–5):

1   What exactly am I trying to find out? Different questions require different methods to answer them.

2   What kind of focus on my topic do I want to achieve? Do I want to study this phenomenon or situation in detail? Or am I mainly interested in making standardised and systematic comparisons and in accounting for variance?

3 How have other researchers dealt with this topic? To what extent do I wish to align my project with this literature?

4 What practical considerations should sway my choice? For instance, how long might my study take and do I have the resources to study it this way? Can I get access to the single case I want to study in depth? Are quantitative samples and data readily available?

5 Will we learn more about this topic using quantitative or qualitative methods? What will be the knowledge pay-off of each method?

6 What seems to work best for me? Am I committed to a particular research model which implies a particular **methodology**? Do I have a gut feeling about what a good piece of research looks like?

Later in this chapter, we consider whether the kind of issues listed in Table 1.4 may sometimes make it sensible to adopt both quantitative and qualitative approaches.

However, so far we have been dealing with little more than empty terms, apparently related to whether or not researchers use statistics of some kind. If, as I already have argued, the value of a research method should properly be gauged solely in relation to what you are trying to find out, we need now to sketch out the uses and abuses of both quantitative *and* qualitative methods.

LINK

For articles on the qualitative–quantitative debate:

www.qualitative-research.net/fqs/fqs-e/inhalt1-01-e.htm

1.4 THE GOOD SENSE OF QUANTITATIVE RESEARCH

So far we have been assuming that quantitative research always involves studying official statistics or doing a survey. Before you can decide whether to use quantitative research, you need to know the range of options available to you. Bryman (1988) has discussed the five main methods of quantitative social science research and these are set out in Table 1.5.

To flesh out the bare bones of Table 1.5, I will use one example based on the quantitative analysis of official statistics. The example relates to data taken from the General Social Survey (GSS) carried out every year by the US National Opinion Research Center (NORC) and discussed by Procter (1993).

TABLE 1.5   Methods of quantitative research

Method	Features	Advantages
Social survey	Random samples Measured variables	Representative Tests hypotheses
Experiment	Experimental stimulus and control group not exposed to stimulus	Precise measurement
Official statistics	Analysis of previously collected data	Large data sets
'Structured' observation	Observations recorded on predetermined 'schedule'	Reliability of observations
Content analysis	Predetermined categories used to count content of mass media products	Reliability of measures

Source: adapted from Bryman, 1988: 11–12

Procter shows how you can use these data to calculate the relationship between two or more variables. Sociologists have long been interested in 'social mobility' – the movement between different statuses in society either within one lifetime or between generations. The GSS data can be used to calculate the latter as Table 1.6 shows.

In Table 1.6, we are shown the relationship between a father's and son's occupation. In this case, the father's occupation is the 'independent' variable because it is treated as the possible cause of the son's occupation (the 'dependent' variable).

TABLE 1.6   Respondent's occupation by father's occupation

		FATHER'S OCCUPATION	
		Non-manual	**Manual**
SON'S OCCUPATION	Non-manual	63.4%	27.4%
	Manual	36.6%	72.6%

Source: adapted from Procter, 1993: 246

Table 1.6 appears to show a strong association (or 'correlation') between father's and son's occupations. For instance, of the group with non-manual fathers, 63.4 per cent were themselves in non-manual jobs. However, among sons with fathers in manual occupations, only 27.4 per cent had obtained non-manual work. Because the **sample** of over 1000 people was randomly recruited, we can be confident, within specifiable limits, that this correlation is unlikely to be obtained by chance.

However, quantitative researchers are reluctant to move from statements of correlation to causal statements. For instance, both father's and son's occupations may be associated with another variable (say inherited wealth) which lies behind the apparent link between occupations of father and son. Because of such an 'antecedent' variable, we cannot confidently state that father's occupation is a significant *cause* of son's occupation. Indeed, because this antecedent variable causes both of the others to vary together, the association between the occupation of fathers and sons is misleading or 'spurious'.

TABLE 1.7   Club membership and voting in union elections

	POLITICAL INTEREST		
	High	Medium	Low
PRINTER FRIENDS	61%	42%	26%
NO PRINTER FRIENDS	48%	22%	23%
	PERCENTAGE PARTICIPATING IN ELECTIONS		

Source: adapted from Lipset et al., 1962

EXERCISE 1.2

1   Does Table 1.7 show that there is an association between having a printer friend and participating in union elections? Explain carefully, referring to the table.
2   Can we be confident that the degree of political interest of a printer does not make any correlation between friendships and participation into a spurious one?

Along these lines Procter (1993: 248–9) makes the interesting observation that there appears to be a marked correlation between the price of rum in Barbados and the level of Methodist ministers' salaries: that is, in any given year, both go up or down together. However, we should not jump to the conclusion that this means that rum distillers fund the Methodist church. As Procter points out, both the price of rum and ministers' salaries may simply be responding to inflationary pressures. Hence the initial correlation is 'spurious'.

While looking at Tables 1.6 and 1.7, you may have been struck by the extent to which quantitative social research uses the same language that you may have been taught in say physics, chemistry or biology. As Bryman notes:

> Quantitative research is ... a genre which uses a special language ... (similar) to the ways in which scientists talk about how they investigate the natural order – variables, control, measurement, experiment. (1988: 12)

Sometimes, this has led critics to claim that quantitative research ignores the differences between the natural and social world by failing to understand the 'meanings' that are brought to social life. This charge is often associated with critics who label quantitative research as 'positivistic' (e.g. Filmer et al., 1972).

Unfortunately, **positivism** is a very slippery and emotive term. Not only is it difficult to define, but also there are very few quantitative researchers who would accept it (see Marsh, 1982: Ch. 3). Instead, most quantitative researchers would argue that they do not aim to produce a science of laws (like physics) but simply to produce a set of set of cumulative generalisations based on the critical sifting of data, that is a 'science' as defined above.

As I argue, at this level, many of the apparent differences between quantitative and qualitative research should disappear – although some qualitative researchers remain insistent that they want nothing to do with even such a limited version of science (see Section 1.7 below). By contrast, in my view at least, qualitative researchers should celebrate rather than criticise quantitative researchers' aim to assemble and sift their data critically (see Chapter 11). They occasionally also need to reconsider whether qualitative methods might be inappropriate for a particular research question.

Take a research topic which appeared in a recent newspaper job advertisement: how is psycho-social adversity related to asthma morbidity and care? The advert explained that this problem would be studied by means of qualitative interviews.

My immediate question was: how can qualitative interviews help to address the topic at hand? The problem is not that people with asthma will be unable to answer questions about their past, nor, of course, that they are likely to lie or mislead the interviewer. Rather, like all of us, when faced with an outcome (in this case, a chronic illness), they will document their past in a way which fits it, highlighting certain features and downplaying others. In other words, the interviewer will be inviting a retrospective 'rewriting of history' (Garfinkel, 1967) with an unknown bearing on the causal problem with which this research is concerned.

This is not to deny that valuable data may be gathered from such a qualitative study. Rather, that it will address an altogether different issue – **narratives** of illness in which 'causes' and 'associations' work as rhetorical moves. By contrast, a quantitative study would seem to be much more appropriate to the research question proposed. Quantitative surveys can be used on much larger samples than qualitative interviews, allowing inferences to be made to wider populations. Moreover, such surveys have standardised, **reliable** measures to ascertain the 'facts' with which this study is concerned. Indeed, why should a large-scale quantitative study be restricted to surveys or interviews? If I wanted reliable, generalisable knowledge about the relation between these two variables (psycho-social adversity and asthma morbidity), I would start by looking at hospital records.

1.5 THE NONSENSE OF QUANTITATIVE RESEARCH

Procter's attempt to control for spurious correlations was possible because of the quantitative style of his research. This has the disadvantage of being dependent upon survey methods with all their attendant difficulties (see the case study below). As we will see in Chapter 6, what people say in answer to interview questions does not have a stable relationship to how they behave in naturally occurring situations.

CASE STUDY
Are Artists Sex-Crazed Lunatics?

Here is a newspaper report on the results of a questionnaire survey comparing artists with the general public:

> artists are more likely to share key behavioural traits with schizophrenics and (to) have on average twice as many sexual partners as the rest of the population.

This is how this study was carried out:

> The psychologists sent a questionnaire to a range of artists by advertising in a major visual art magazine and writing to published poets ... other questionnaires were passed to the general population by pushing them through letterboxes at random ... another set of questionnaires was filled out by a group of patients diagnosed with schizophrenia. (*Guardian*, 'Mental illness link to art and sex', 30 November 2005)

Of course, the problem with this quantitative approach is that answers to such questionnaires may be highly unreliable. One critic puts it even more strongly:

> What a pile of crap. Those responsible should be shot. Better still, they should be forced to have several thousand sexual partners. Preferably schizoid artists, bad, ugly, psychotic ones. Then shot.

> For a start, they've only polled 425 people by placing adverts and randomly posting questionnaires in artists' whingepapers, read only by those snivelling in the evolutionary foot bath of the artistic gene pool. You should never expect people to tell the truth about their sexual shenanigans. They lie. Always. They lie to themselves – why would they tell the truth to you? (Dinos Chapman, *Guardian*, 1 December 2005)

This is why a dependence on purely quantitative methods may neglect the social and cultural construction of the 'variables' which quantitative research seeks to correlate. As Kirk and Miller argue, 'attitudes', for instance, do not simply attach to the inside of people's heads and researching them depends on making a whole series of analytical assumptions. They conclude: 'The survey researcher who discusses is not wrong to do so. Rather, the researcher is wrong if he or she fails to acknowledge the theoretical basis on which it is meaningful to make measurements of such entities and to do so with survey questions' (1986: 15).

According to its critics, much quantitative research leads to the use of a set of ad hoc procedures to define, count and analyse its variables (Blumer, 1956; Cicourel, 1964; Silverman, 1975). The implication is that quantitative researchers unknowingly use the methods of everyday life, even as they claim scientific objectivity (Cicourel, 1964; Garfinkel, 1967). This is why some qualitative researchers have preferred to describe how, in everyday life, we actually go about defining, counting and analysing.

Let me try to concretise this critique by means of some examples. In what follows, I take a few salient examples of surveys about national identity and briefly review how they have been criticised.

In 1979, 56% of people in Scotland chose being Scottish as their 'best' identity. This compared with 38% who said they were 'British'. By 2001, the proportions were 77% and 16% respectively (Kiely et al., 2005: 66).

Such longitudinal data potentially raise fascinating questions about the direction of change. The data also directly tie in to debates about citizenship and national identity. Unfortunately, robust correlations between variables are only as reliable as the methods which have been used to generate their data. As Fielding and Fielding argue:

> the most advanced survey procedures themselves only manipulate data that had to be gained at some point by asking people. (1986: 12)

Even if we can ask questions in a reliable way, what people say in answer to interview questions may not have a stable relationship to how they behave in naturally occurring situations. In this sense, interview responses may be artefactual.

Again, Fielding and Fielding make the relevant point:

> researchers who generalize from a sample survey to a larger population ignore the possible disparity between the discourse of actors about some topical issue and the way they respond to questions in a formal context. (1986: 21)

Of course, good survey researchers are conscious of the problems involved in interpreting statistical correlations in relation to what the variables involved 'mean' to the participants (see Marsh, 1982: Ch. 5). As the researchers who produced the data on Scottish identity point out, even more nuanced five-point Likert scales would not solve this problem since such scales:

> cannot provide information on what people mean by these categories and what sort of decision-making process they use in plumping for one category over another. (Kiely et al. 2005: 66).

An extreme example of what this means in practice is found in the recent study by a graduate student of residents in a Chicago housing project for the poor (Venkatesh, 2008). Imagine the impact on gun-toting gang members of being confronted by a researcher with a clipboard asking them questions like 'how does it feel to be black and poor?' and offering multiple-choice answers such as 'very bad', 'somewhat bad', 'neither bad nor good', 'somewhat good' or 'very good'!

The surveys I have reviewed are dogged by the problem that their findings might be simply artefacts of the method employed. However, we should not take this argument too far. First, as we know from the uncertainty principle recognised in physics, all data are to some extent an artefact of how they are collected. Second, there are in principle no 'good' or 'bad' research methods and, therefore, the choice between different research methods should depend upon what you are trying to find out.

However, the quantitative desire to establish 'operational' definitions at an early stage of social research can be an arbitrary process which deflects attention away from the everyday sense-making procedures of people in specific milieux. As a consequence, the 'hard' data on social structures which quantitative researchers claim to provide can turn out to be a mirage (see also Cicourel, 1964). This is illustrated by the two examples in Table 1.8.

TABLE 1.8   The limits of quantitative methods

1   Say you are interested in racial discrimination and think of doing a quantitative study. First, you will need an **operational definition** of your topic, e.g. should racial discrimination be defined legally, should you follow the perspective of the victims and potential aggressors or should you yourself define the term? Whatever you decide, your research will be stuck with how you define the phenomenon at the outset (Marvasti, 2004: 11)

2   Imagine you want to discover whether small children who are able to empathise with others will make good teachers. So you administer a psychological questionnaire to a sample of such children. Then you conduct a **laboratory study** to see whether those who score highly on 'empathy' are best at instructing other children on how to complete a simple task such as constructing a toy tower (O'Malley, 2005). However, do your questionnaire answers tell you anything about how 'empathy' is displayed and recognised in everyday life? Moreover, when you watch a video of the lab study, you will need to decide whether or not the instruction was successful in any particular case. But this raises a set of difficulties: if a child being tutored successfully completes the tower, how do you know this was due to the other child's tutoring? Moreover, how did the tutored child define what they were being taught? The very speed at which researchers' coding of the behaviour of the tutor–tutee takes place may underplay how the recipient of the action codes the activity

These brief (non-random!) examples should allow you to understand the kind of criticisms that are often directed at purely quantitative research by more qualitative 'types'. Because space is short, Table 1.9 attempts to summarise these criticisms.

It should be noted that Table 1.9 contains simply complaints made about *some* quantitative research. Moreover, because quantitative researchers are rarely 'dopes', many treat such matters seriously and try to overcome them. So, for instance, epidemiologists, who study official statistics about disease, and criminologists are only too aware of the problematic character of what gets recorded as, say, a psychiatric disorder (Prior, 2003) or a criminal offence (Noaks and Wincup, 2004). Equally, good quantitative researchers are conscious of the problems involved in interpreting statistical correlations in relation to what the variables involved 'mean' to the participants (see Marsh, 1982: Ch. 5).

In the light of this qualification, I conclude this section by observing that an insistence that any research worth its salt should follow a purely quantitative logic would simply rule out the study of many interesting phenomena relating to what

TABLE 1.9 Some criticisms of quantitative research

1 Quantitative research can amount to a 'quick fix', involving little or no contact with people or the 'field'
2 Statistical correlations may be based upon 'variables' that, in the context of naturally occurring interaction, are arbitrarily defined
3 After-the-fact speculation about the meaning of correlations can involve the very common-sense processes of reasoning that science tries to avoid (see Cicourel, 1964: 14 and 21)
4 The pursuit of 'measurable' phenomena can mean that unperceived values creep into research by simply taking on board highly problematic and unreliable concepts such as 'discrimination' or 'empathy'
5 While it is important to test hypotheses, a purely statistical logic can make the development of hypotheses a trivial matter and fail to help in generating hypotheses from data (see my discussion of **grounded theory** in Chapter 3)

people actually do in their day-to-day lives, whether in homes, offices or other public and private places. But, as the next section shows, a balanced view should accept the strengths, as well as the limitations, of quantitative research.

1.6 THE GOOD SENSE OF QUALITATIVE RESEARCH

Qualitative researchers suggest that we should not assume that techniques used in quantitative research are the *only* way of establishing the **validity** of findings from qualitative or field research. This means that a number of practices which originate from quantitative studies may be *inappropriate* to qualitative research. These include the assumptions that social science research can only be valid if based on operational definitions of variables, experimental data, official statistics or the random **sampling** of populations and that quantified data are the only valid or generalisable social facts.

Critics of quantitative research argue that these assumptions have a number of defects (see Cicourel, 1964; Denzin, 1970; Schwartz and Jacobs, 1979; Hammersley and Atkinson, 1995; Gubrium, 1988). These critics note that experiments, official statistics and survey data may simply be inappropriate to some of the tasks of social science. For instance, they exclude the observation of behaviour in everyday situations. Hence, while quantification may *sometimes* be useful, it can both conceal as well as reveal basic social processes.

Consider the problem of counting attitudes in surveys. Do we all have coherent attitudes on any topics which await the researcher's questions? And how do 'attitudes' relate to what we actually do – our practices? Or think of official statistics on cause of death compared with studies of how hospital staff (Sudnow, 1968a), pathologists and statistical clerks (Prior, 1987) attend to deaths. Note that this is *not* to argue that such statistics may be biased. Instead, it is to suggest that there are areas of social reality which such statistics cannot measure.

The main strength of qualitative research is its ability to study phenomena which are simply unavailable elsewhere. Quantitative researchers are rightly concerned to establish correlations between variables. However, while their approach can tell us a lot about inputs and outputs to some phenomenon (e.g. how national identity is correlated with voting behaviour), it has to be satisfied with a purely 'operational' definition of the phenomenon and does not have the resources to describe how that phenomenon is locally constituted (see Figure 1.1). As a result, its contribution to social problems is necessarily lopsided and limited.

FIGURE 1.1   The missing phenomenon in quantitative research

One real strength of qualitative research is that it can use **naturally occurring data** to find the sequences ('how') in which participants' meanings ('what') are deployed. Having established the character of some phenomenon, it can then (but only then) move on to answer 'why' questions by examining the wider contexts in which the phenomenon arises (see Figure 1.2).

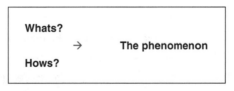

FIGURE 1.2   The phenomenon reappears

Figures 1.1 and 1.2 show that there are gains and losses in quantitative researchers' tendency to define phenomena at the outset through the use of operational definitions. Such definitions aid measurement but they can lose sight of the way that social phenomena become what they are in particular contexts and sequences of action. As we shall see in Chapter 2, what I call **contextual sensitivity** means that qualitative researchers can look at how an apparently stable phenomenon (e.g. a tribe, an organisation or a family) is actually put together by its participants.

LINK
For more on why sequences of action are important, see my paper at:
www.qualitative-research.net/fqs/fqs-e/inhalt3-05-e.htm

> **TIP**
> When researching any phenomenon, try putting it into inverted commas as an aid to thinking about what that phenomenon comes to be in a particular context. This may lead you to see that you are faced with a set of phenomena which can be marked by hyphens, for example the family-in-the-household; the family-in-public; the family-as-depicted-by-the-media; the family-as-portrayed-in-criminal-sentencing. This approach is also a useful way of narrowing down your research problem.

1.7 THE NONSENSE OF QUALITATIVE RESEARCH

Unfortunately, contextual sensitivity is not always shown by qualitative researchers. Sometimes, they forget to put phenomena into inverted commas and chase some 'essential' object often apparently located inside people's heads, like 'meaning' or 'experience'. For instance, some qualitative researchers use open-ended interviews, like TV chat-show hosts, to try to tap directly the perceptions of individuals. This **romantic** approach can make unavailable the situations and contexts to which their subjects' refer (see Figure 1.3).

> **Perceptions → [The phenomenon] → Responses**

FIGURE 1.3 The missing phenomenon in (some) qualitative research

It was bad enough when romanticism was just the basis for some qualitative research and all chat shows. Now it is being used to justify wasting billions of dollars. Despite all the evidence that unmanned space missions give you far more bangs per buck, on BBC World News, a few years ago, I heard a professor at the California Institute of Technology (Caltech) support President Bush's plans for a manned Mars mission by saying: 'Actually having a human being experience being on Mars is important. That means that millions of people on Earth can experience it too.'

This idea of a totally new experience, as we shall see in Chapter 2, is the dream of upmarket tourists. In the context of space travel, it ignores the way in which both astronauts and TV viewers will necessarily draw on pre-existing images (ranging from *Star Wars* to previous visits to strange places) in order to make sense of what they see on a distant planet. Fortunately, President Obama has now frozen plans for such space flights.

It is not just (some) qualitative researchers who misunderstand the potential of what they are doing. Qualitative research is regularly miscategorised by others. For instance, in many quantitatively oriented, social science methodology textbooks, qualitative research is often treated as a relatively minor methodology. As such, it is suggested that it should only be contemplated at early or 'exploratory' stages of a study. Viewed from this perspective, qualitative research can be used to familiarise oneself with a setting before the serious sampling and counting begin.

This view is expressed in the extract below from an early text. Note how the authors refer to 'nonquantified data' – implying that quantitative data is the standard form:

> The inspection of *nonquantified* data may be particularly helpful if it is done periodically throughout a study rather than postponed to the end of the statistical analysis. Frequently, a single incident noted by a perceptive observer contains the clue to an understanding of a phenomenon. If the social scientist becomes aware of this implication at a moment when he can still add to his material or exploit further the data he has already collected, he may considerably enrich the quality of his conclusions. (Selltiz et al., 1964: 435, my emphasis)

Despite these authors' 'friendly' view of the uses of 'nonquantified' data, they assume that 'statistical analysis' is the bedrock of research. A similar focus is to be found, a quarter of a century later, in another mainly quantitative text: 'Field research is essentially a matter of immersing oneself in a naturally occurring … set of events in order to gain firsthand knowledge of the situation' (Singleton et al., 1988: 11).

Note the emphasis on 'immersion' and its implicit contrast with later, more focused research. This is underlined in the authors' subsequent identification of qualitative or field research with 'exploration' and 'description' (1988: 296) and their approval of the use of field research 'when one knows relatively little about the subject under investigation' (1988: 298–9).

These reservations have some basis given the fact that qualitative research is, by definition, stronger on long descriptive narratives than on statistical tables. The problem that then arises is how such a researcher goes about categorising the events or activities described. This is sometimes known as the problem of **reliability**. As Hammersley puts it, reliability 'refers to the degree of consistency with which instances are assigned to the same category by different observers or by the same observer on different occasions' (1992a: 67).

The issue of consistency particularly arises because shortage of space means that many qualitative studies provide readers with little more than brief, persuasive, data extracts. As Bryman notes about the typical observational study: 'field notes or extended transcripts are rarely available; these would be very helpful in order to allow the reader to formulate his or her own hunches about the perspective of the people who have been studied' (1988: 77).

Moreover, even when people's activities are audio- or videotape recorded and transcribed, the reliability of the interpretation of transcripts may be gravely weakened by a failure to note apparently trivial, but often crucial, pauses, overlaps or body movements. This is shown in the following case study.

CASE STUDY
Transcribing Tapes of Cancer Consultations

A study of medical consultations was concerned to establish whether cancer patients had understood that their condition was fatal. When researchers first listened to tapes of relevant hospital consultations, they sometimes felt that there was no evidence that the patients had picked up their doctors' often guarded statements about their prognosis. However, when the tapes were retranscribed, it was demonstrated that patients used very soft utterances (like 'yes' or, more usually, 'mm') to mark that they were taking up this information. Equally, doctors would monitor patients' silences and rephrase their prognosis statements (see Clavarino et al., 1995).

Some qualitative researchers argue that a concern for the reliability of observations arises only within the quantitative research tradition. Because what they call the 'positivist' position sees no difference between the natural and social worlds, reliable measures of social life are only needed by such 'positivists'. Conversely, it is argued, once we treat social reality as always in flux, then it makes no sense to worry about whether our research instruments measure accurately (e.g. Marshall and Rossman, 1989).

Such a position would rule out any systematic research since it implies that we cannot assume any stable properties in the social world. However, if we concede the possible existence of such properties, why should other work not replicate these properties? As Kirk and Miller argue:

> Qualitative researchers can no longer afford to beg the issue of reliability. While the forte of field research will always lie in its capability to sort out the validity of propositions, its results will (reasonably) go ignored minus attention to reliability. For reliability to be calculated, it is incumbent on the scientific investigator to document his or her procedure. (1986: 72)

A second criticism of qualitative research relates to how sound are the explanations it offers. This is sometimes known as the problem of **anecdotalism**, revealed in the way in which research reports sometimes appeal to a few, telling 'examples' of some apparent phenomenon, without any attempt to analyse less clear (or even contradictory) data (Silverman, 1989a). This problem is expressed very clearly by Bryman:

There is a tendency towards an anecdotal approach to the use of data in relation to conclusions or explanations in qualitative research. Brief conversations, snippets from unstructured interviews … are used to provide evidence of a particular contention. There are grounds for disquiet in that the representativeness or generality of these fragments is rarely addressed. (1988: 77)

This complaint of 'anecdotalism' questions the validity of much qualitative research. 'Validity' is another word for truth (see Chapter 11). Sometimes one doubts the validity of an explanation because the researcher has clearly made no attempt to deal with contrary cases. Sometimes, the extended immersion in the 'field', so typical of qualitative research, leads to a certain preciousness about the validity of the researcher's own interpretation of 'their' tribe or organisation. Or sometimes, the demands of journal editors for shorter and shorter articles simply means that the researcher is reluctantly led only to use 'telling' examples – something that can happen in much the same way in the natural sciences where, for instance, laboratory assistants have been shown to select 'perfect' slides for their professor's important lecture (see Lynch, 1984).

EXERCISE 1.3

Review any research study with which you are familiar. Then answer the questions below:

1 To what extent are its methods of research (qualitative, quantitative or a combination of both) appropriate to the nature of the research question(s) being asked?
2 How far does its use of these methods meet the criticisms of both qualitative and quantitative research discussed in this chapter?
3 In your view, how could this study have been improved methodologically and conceptually?

Despite these common problems, doubts about the reliability and validity of qualitative research have led many quantitative researchers to downplay the value of the former. However, as we have seen, this kind of 'damning by faint praise' has been more than balanced by criticisms of quantitative research offered by many qualitative researchers.

I conclude this section, therefore, with a statement which shows the absurdity of pushing too far the qualitative/quantitative distinction:

We are not faced, then, with a stark choice between words and numbers, or even between precise and imprecise data; but rather with a range from more to less precise data. Furthermore, our decisions about what level of precision is appropriate in relation to any particular claim should depend on the nature of what we are trying to describe, on the likely accuracy of our descriptions, on our purposes, and on the resources available to us; not on ideological commitment to one methodological paradigm or another. (Hammersley, 1992a: 163)

EXERCISE 1.4

This exercise requires a group of at least six students, divided into two discussion groups ('buzz groups').

Imagine that you are submitting a proposal to research drug abuse among school pupils. Each buzz group should now form two 'teams' (Team I = QUANTITATIVE; Team II = QUALITATIVE).

1 Team I should formulate a quantitative study to research this topic.
2 Team II should suggests limits/problems in this study (Team I to defend).
3 Team II should formulate a qualitative study to research this topic.
4 Team I should suggest limits/problems in this study (Team II to defend).
5 Both teams should now come to some conclusions.

1.8 VARIETIES OF QUALITATIVE RESEARCH

The methods used by qualitative researchers exemplify a common belief that they can provide a 'deeper' understanding of social phenomena than would be obtained from a purely quantitative methodology. However, just as quantitative researchers would resist the charge that they are all 'positivists' (Marsh, 1982), there is no agreed doctrine underlying all qualitative social research.

Nonetheless, writers of textbooks on qualitative methods usually feel obligated to define their topic and to risk suggesting what qualitative researchers may have in common. Martyn Hammersley has taken a cautious path by arguing that, at best, we share a set of preferences. These are set out in Table 1.10.

TABLE 1.10   The preferences of qualitative researchers

1 A preference for qualitative data – understood simply as the analysis of words and images rather than numbers
2 A preference for naturally occurring data – observation rather than experiment, unstructured versus structured interviews
3 A preference for meanings rather than behaviour – attempting 'to document the world from the point of view of the people studied' (Hammersley, 1992: 165)
4 A rejection of natural science as a model
5 A preference for inductive, hypothesis-generating research rather than hypothesis-testing (cf. Glaser and Strauss, 1967)

Source: adapted from Hammersley, 1992: 160–72

Unfortunately, as Hammersley himself recognises, even such a cautious list is a huge overgeneralization. For instance, to take just item 5 in the table, qualitative research would look a little odd, after a history of over 100 years, if it had no **hypotheses** to test!

Moreover, if we take the list above as a reasonable approximation of the main features of qualitative research, we can start to see why it can be criticised. As already noted, in a world where numbers talk and people use the term 'hard' science, a failure to test hypotheses, coupled with a rejection of natural science methods, certainly leave qualitative researchers open to criticism.

So unless we use the negative criterion of being 'nonquantitative', there is no agreed doctrine underlying all qualitative social research. Instead, there are many 'isms' that appear to lie behind qualitative methods. In the Preface, I referred to my own position as broadly fitting within **constructionism**. In this chapter, we have seen how critics of quantitative research accuse it of positivism. And many readers of this book will have already come across other 'isms' such as **feminism** and **post-modernism**.

The most useful attempt to depict these different approaches within qualitative research is in Gubrium and Holstein (1997a). They use the term 'idiom' to encompass both the analytical preferences indicated by my term model (see Table 2.1) and the use of particular vocabularies, investigatory styles and ways of writing. They distinguish (and criticise) four different 'idioms':

- **Naturalism**: a reluctance to impose meaning and a preference to 'get out and observe the field'.
- **Ethnomethodology**: shares naturalism's attention to detail but locates it in the study of talk-in-interaction.
- **Emotionalism**: desires 'intimate' contact with research subjects and favours the open-ended interview and attempts to understand the impact of the biography of both researchers and subjects.
- Post-modernism: seeks to challenge the concepts of 'subject' and the 'field' and favours pastiche rather than science.

Some development of these ideas is found in Table 1.11.

TABLE 1.11   Four qualitative idioms

Idiom	Concepts	Preferred method
Naturalism	Actors Meaning	Observation Interviews
Ethnomethodology	Members' methods Construction	Audio/video recordings
Emotionalism	Subjectivity Emotion	Interviews Life-histories
Post-modernism	Representation Pastiche Construction	Anything goes

Source: adapted from Gubrium and Holstein, 1997

According to Gubrium and Holstein, qualitative researchers inhabit the 'lived border between reality and representation' (1997a: 102). On this border, in their view, each idiom veers too far to one side as set out below:

- Naturalism: its pursuit of the content of everyday lives offers deep insights into the 'what?' of reality at the price of the 'how?' of reality's representation (by both participants and researchers).
- Ethnomethodology: its focus on common-sense practices gives rewarding answers to 'how?' questions but underplays the 'what' of contextual givens.
- Emotionalism: helps us understand people's experiences but at the cost of privileging a common-sense category ('emotion').
- Post-modernism: reveals practices of representation but can lead to a nihilistic denial of content.

As a way out of this purely critical position, Gubrium and Holstein offer three valuable practical ploys for the qualitative researcher. First, seeking a middle ground to 'manage the tensions between reality and representation' (1997a: 114), they show how we can give voice to each idiom's silenced other. The figure of the insider, so dear to naturalism, can be treated as 'a represented reality' which arises within subjects' own accounts (1997a: 103). The same applies to emotionalism's description of people whose 'feelings' are crucial. Equally, **conversation analysis**'s account of institutionality (see Chapter 9) and Sacks's membership categorisation analysis (see Chapter 8) show how ethnomethodology can put meat on the bare bones of representation. Last, while we must respect what post-modernism tells us about representation, this can be treated as an incentive for empirically based description, not as its epitaph.

EXERCISE 1.5

This exercise will also focus upon drug abuse among school pupils. It can be done in buzz groups or by individuals.

Following Gubrium and Holstein's account of four 'idioms' of qualitative research (Table 1.11), suggest how each idiom might:

1 Define a delimited research problem on this topic.
2 Suggest a particular methodology.

If 'qualitative research' involves many different, potentially conflicting, models or idioms, this shows that the whole 'qualitative/quantitative' dichotomy is open to question.

In the context of this book, I view most such dichotomies or polarities in social science as highly dangerous. At best, they are pedagogic devices for students to obtain a first grip on a difficult field – they help us to learn the jargon. At worst, they are excuses for not thinking, which assemble groups of sociologists into 'armed camps', unwilling to learn from one another.

The implication I draw is that doing 'qualitative' research should offer no protection from the rigorous, critical standards that should be applied to any enterprise concerned to sort 'fact' from 'fancy'. Ultimately, soundly based knowledge should be the common aim of all social science (see Kirk and Miller, 1986: 10–11). As Hammersley argues:

> the process of inquiry in science is the same whatever method is used, and the retreat into paradigms effectively stultifies debate and hampers progress. (1992: 182)

TIP

Quantitative methods are usually the most appropriate if you want to find out social facts or the causes of some phenomenon. Qualitative methods are best suited if you want to ask 'what' and 'how' questions.

KEY POINTS

- When we compare quantitative and qualitative research, we generally find, at best, different emphases between 'schools' which themselves contain many internal differences.
- Qualitative researchers should celebrate rather than criticise quantitative researchers' aim to assemble and sift their data critically.
- Reliability and validity are key ways of evaluating research.
- A dependence on purely quantitative methods may neglect the social and cultural construction of the 'variables' which quantitative research seeks to correlate.
- Qualitative research should not limit itself to the study of perceptions or subjective meanings. Qualitative research has a unique ability to focus on behaviour in naturally occurring situations.

STUDY QUESTIONS

1 What are the main differences between how people have used qualitative and quantitative methods?
2 Are there any similarities in how researchers have used qualitative and quantitative methods?

(Continued)

(Continued)

3 Which comes first: your research question or your choice of methods? Why?
4 What kinds of research questions are most appropriate for quantitative research?
5 What kinds of research questions are best addressed by qualitative methods?
6 What criticisms have been made about (some) quantitative research?
7 What criticisms have been made about (some) qualitative research?
8 What are the main models that inspire qualitative research?

RECOMMENDED READING

Two good chapter-length treatments of the relation between qualitative and quantitative methods are Julia Brannen's 'Working qualitatively and quantitatively' (2004)
and Neil Spicer's 'Combining qualitative and quantitative methods' (2004). The most
useful introductory texts are Alan Bryman's *Quantity and Quality in Social Research*
(1988), Nigel Gilbert's (editor) *Researching Social Life* (1993) and Clive Seale's
(editor) *Researching Society and Culture* (2011). Sensible statements about the
quantitative position are to be found in Marsh (1982) (on survey research) and
Hindess (1973) (on official statistics).

In addition to these general texts, readers are urged to familiarise themselves
with examples of qualitative and quantitative research. Strong (1979) and Lipset
et al. (1962) are classic examples which show respect for both qualitative and
quantitative data.

2

Designing a Research Project

If you are like many readers of this book, you will be scanning these pages looking for some useful advice about the research project that is required for your Research Methods course. In that case, I have some good and bad news for you. It turns out that researching can be a complicated, tricky business. Nonetheless, with a little guidance (and some effort), most students can bring off an acceptable, or even highly graded, project.

Let us begin with a hypothetical case. Imagine that you have 'innocently' decided to gather some interview data for a research project. Making use of the accessibility and good nature of your fellow students, you decide to embark on a study of, say, 'students' perceptions of their future job prospects'.

Because you have read a bit about research design, you decide to 'pre-test' some preliminary questions on a friend to find whether they are easily understood (in the way that you intend). Having sorted out your questions, you find half a dozen students and interview them. Now, you think, all you have to do is to summarise their answers and you will have a legitimate research report on your chosen topic.

Well, maybe. Perhaps, along the way, you failed to ask yourself a number of questions. These include:

- Why (and in what way) is your chosen research topic significant? Does it relate to any **concepts** or **theories** in your chosen discipline? Or is it simply a topic that matters to you and your friends? If so, how, if at all, will your report differ from the kind of story you might find in a newspaper? And why does this matter?
- How far do your topic and findings relate to other research? Have you read the relevant literature or are you in danger of reinventing the wheel? Have you thought laterally, considering, for instance, the variety of contexts in which people's expectations are shaped by a range of institutions (e.g. not just universities but schools, families, churches, peer groups, Internet sites)?
- Why is an interview method appropriate for your topic? Why not simply look at existing records of graduates' first jobs? Maybe this kind of simple quantitative study is the best way of addressing your topic. Or perhaps you should compare such statistics with your interviews?
- Is the size and method of recruitment of your **sample** appropriate to your topic? Should you be worried by what quantitative researchers tell us about the limits of small, non-random samples?
- Did you audio or video record your interviews? How did you transcribe them (if at all)? How can you convince your professor that you did not simply pick out a few extracts to support your preconceived ideas?
- Did you need to interview your respondents face to face? Why not use e-mail? Or find webpages where students discuss such issues and where employers describe what they have to offer to graduates?
- Did you think about using a **focus group** where respondents are offered some topic or stimulus material and then encouraged to discuss it among themselves?
- What status will you accord to your data? For instance, are you seeking objective 'facts', subjective 'perceptions' or simply '**narratives**'?
- How thoroughly have you analysed your data? For instance, have you just reported a few 'telling' extracts? Or have you worked through all your material searching out examples which do not fit your original suppositions (**deviant-case analysis**).

Without answers to these questions, your professor may disappoint you with a surprisingly poor grade for your research project. This book will show you why such questions are important and provide some straightforward ways to answer them.

No doubt you are impatient. Perhaps the submission date for your research plan is approaching and there is little time left to read a whole book. With this in mind, I have set out below a list of common challenges that confront student researchers and offered some simple answers. Since I want you to read more of this book, I do not claim that these answers provide the whole story. But they will give you a rapid take on the issues. These are the challenges:

- selecting a topic
- formulating a researchable question
- fitting your research question into an appropriate theory
- choosing an effective research design
- reviewing the literature effectively.

Two further comments about this chapter. First, I will discuss here the early stages of research design. So very little is said about data analysis. To find out more about how to analyse your data, refer to the relevant chapters of Part Two of this book. Second, the discussion that follows uses terms (like '**methodology**' and '**models**') that are not necessarily familiar to you. So, at the end of this chapter, I show you what these terms mean and indicate how they relate to one another.

2.1 SELECTING A TOPIC

Let us assume that your course requires you to complete a short research report. Where do you begin?

Some people panic and have no idea where to start. If you fall into this category, you have a ready solution at hand. See if you can find research reports by previous cohorts of students on your course. Then scan the topics they chose and see if that gives you any ideas (if you can, try and find out the grades achieved by the reports which interest you). If you are more ambitious, follow up a piece of published research that interests you and get advice on how you might adapt it as a student project.

However, not everybody panics. Some people have a burning interest in a part of the world around them and are enthusiastic about the opportunity to turn their interest into a research project. The enthusiasm is good but you need to beware of two possible unintended consequences of pursuing it:

- inaccessible data
- framing a topic in terms of common-sense assumptions.

2.1.1 Inaccessible data

Time problems are caused not just by having too much data, but by setting your mind on getting certain kinds of data regardless of their accessibility. There are no 'brownie points' given by most disciplines for having gathered your own data. Indeed, by choosing 'difficult' situations to gather data (either because nothing 'relevant' may happen or, for instance, because background noise may mean you have a poor-quality tape), you may condemn yourself to have less time to engage in the much more important activity of data analysis.

Make data collection as easy as possible and beware of complexity. For instance, although video data are very attractive, they are often very complex to work with. So try to keep data gathering simple. Go for a research topic linked to material that is easy to collect. For instance, the Internet is a wonderful source of material. Do not worry if it only gives you one 'angle' on your problem. There are innumerable angles on any topic. So just find one angle on your topic associated with data that are easy to access.

2.1.2 Common-sense assumptions

One has only to open a newspaper or to watch the TV news to be confronted by a host of social problems. In 2005, the British news media were full of references to the disorderly behaviour of young people on city streets – from fights after binge drinking to assaults on respectable citizens. Politicians responded to these reports by talking about a 'culture of disrespect' and by setting a Respect Agenda involving more police on the streets armed with new powers. In the British general election of 2010, some politicians talked about a 'broken society', drawing attention to well-publicised crimes despite the fact that most indicators showed that nearly all types of crime had declined in the previous decade.

The stories and the politicians' speeches have this in common: both assume some sort of moral decline in which families or schools fail to discipline young people. In turn, the way each story is told implies a solution: tightening up 'discipline' in order to combat an assumed 'moral decline'.

However, before we can consider such a 'cure', we need to consider carefully the 'diagnosis'. Has juvenile crime increased or is the apparent increase a reflection of what counts as a 'good' story? Alternatively, might any increase be an artefact of what crimes get reported to the police? Take the scare about paedophiles preying on children through Internet chatrooms. In the case study below, Barry Glassner cuts the media hype to ask: how prevalent is this phenomenon?

CASE STUDY
Online Paedophilia: A Real Problem?

In a decade when the United States had the highest rates of childhood poverty in the developed world and the lowest rates of spending on social services, American journalists and politicians repeatedly portrayed cyberspace as the scariest place a child can be, more menacing than anything young people face in a nonvirtual world. Parents worried that legions of adults would drool over their children's photos on MySpace, the social-networking Web site dating to 2003, and gawk at the videos teens post on YouTube, which was inaugurated in 2005.

The reality is that patterns of abuse have not changed over the past decade. The vast majority of crimes against children and adolescents – sexual and otherwise – continue to be perpetrated by parents, relatives, and other adults the child or teen knows. More than four of five victims are abused by a parent, and another 10 percent by a caregiver, according to the U.S. Department of Health and Human Services. The incidence of actual abuse as a result of an online connection is "vanishingly small," as Mike A. Males, a sociologist who has studied the data, noted.

A group of researchers at the University of New Hampshire put it bluntly: "The publicity about online 'predators' who prey on naïve children using trickery and violence is largely inaccurate. Internet sex crimes involving adults and juveniles more often fit a model of statutory rape – adult offenders who meet, develop relationships with, and openly seduce underage teenagers – than a model of forcible sexual assault or paedophilic child molesting."

When adults do solicit minors online, the researchers found, the young person almost invariably knows that the person at the other computer is an adult. Trickery about the perpetrator's age or intentions is rare. Moreover, as a study in 2009 from Harvard pointed out, youths who are approached and respond are typically teens already at risk because of their own drug abuse or troubled home environments. Many engage willingly with the adult who solicits them.

While adults were being told their kids were endangering their lives online – or at least, wasting them away – studies were finding that the online activities of youths are not only nontoxic, they're productive. For example, a report in 2008 from the John D. and Catherine T. MacArthur Foundation got little attention, but the extensive three-year study showed that youths use online media primarily for self-directed learning and to gain and extend friendships. "The digital world is creating new opportunities for youth to grapple with social norms, explore interests, develop technical skills, and experiment with new forms of self-expression," the researchers wrote.

Source: Barry Glassner, 'Still Fearful After all these Years', The Chronicle of Higher Education [online] 17 January 2010

But apparent 'social' problems are not the only topics that may clamour for the attention of the researcher. Administrators and managers point to 'problems' in their organisations and may turn to social scientists for solutions.

It is tempting to allow such people to define a research problem – particularly as there is usually a fat research grant attached to it! However, we must first look at the terms which are being used to define the problem. For instance, many managers will define problems in their organisation as problems of 'communication'. The role of the researcher is then to work out how people can communicate 'better'.

This means that formulating a student project in terms of 'communication problems' raises many difficulties. For instance, it may deflect attention from the communication 'skills' inevitably used in interaction. It may also tend to assume that the solution to any problem is more careful listening, while ignoring power relations present inside and outside patterns of communication. Such relations may also make the characterisation of 'organisational efficiency' very problematic. Thus 'administrative' problems give no more secure basis for social research than do 'social' problems.

Of course, this is not to deny that there are any real problems in society. However, even if we agree about what these problems are, it is not clear that they directly provide a researchable topic.

Let me turn to another issue which has been at the forefront of our attention since the 1980s: the problems of people infected with HIV. Some of these problems are, quite rightly, brought to the attention of the public by the organised activities of groups of people who carry the infection. What social researchers can contribute are the particular theoretical and methodological skills of their discipline. So economists can research how limited health-care resources can be used most effectively in coping with the epidemic in the West and in the Third World. Among sociologists, survey researchers can investigate patterns of sexual behaviour in order to try to promote effective health education, while qualitative **methods** may be used to study what is involved in the 'negotiation' of safer sex or in counselling people about HIV and AIDS.

As these examples demonstrate, the initial impetus for a study may arise from the needs of practitioners and clients. However, researchers from different disciplines will usually give an initial research topic their own theoretical and methodological 'twist'. For instance, in my research on HIV counselling (Silverman, 1997), the use of tape recordings and detailed transcripts, as well as many technical concepts derived from my interest in **conversation analysis** (CA).

This example shows that it is usually necessary to refuse to allow our research topics to be totally defined in terms of the conceptions of 'social problems' as recognised by either professional or community groups. Ironically, by beginning from a clearly defined social science perspective, we can later address such social problems with, I believe, considerable force and persuasiveness. This issue is discussed in more detail in Chapter 13.

EXERCISE 2.1

Discuss how you might study people who take the law into their own hands ('vigilantes').
Is there any difference between your proposed study and a good TV documentary
on the same subject (i.e. differences in the questions you would ask and how you
would test your conclusions)?

   Now consider: (a) whether this matters and (b) what special contribution, if any,
social science research can bring to such social problems.

2.2 FORMULATING A RESEARCHABLE QUESTION

Say you have avoided the pitfalls described in the previous section. You have
selected a sensible topic. How do you turn it into a researchable question that
you can answer within the constraints of time and available resources? Two tips
may help:

- narrow down your topic
- give focus to your research.

2.2.1 Narrow down your research topic

One merit of the research project that I considered at the start of this chapter is that it concerned a relatively narrow (and hence manageable) topic.
For instance, it has narrowed down the issue of students' perceptions to just
one topic. This is praiseworthy because it is quite common for novice
researchers to take on what turns out to be an impossibly large research
problem.

   Let us look at one example. It is important to find the causes of a social
problem like homelessness, but such a problem is beyond the scope of a single
researcher with limited time and resources. Moreover, by defining the problem
so widely, one is usually unable to say anything at great depth about it. Indeed,
the issues raised may be unanswerable in the sense that it is difficult to see
what data are required to address it or how the data will be obtained (see
Punch, 1998: 49). The next case study shows how one research student discovered that narrowing down his topic to perceptions of people in one homeless
shelter might still lead him up a blind alley if he kept to the assumption that
all homeless people despise the world of work.

CASE STUDY
Are the Homeless Anti-Work?

At the beginning of my ethnography of a homeless shelter, I wanted to organize my dissertation around the notion that the homeless are "the postmodern heroes of our time." The idea was inspired by interviews with homeless men who had said things like "It sucks to be a citizen" or "I feel sorry for the poor bastards who're enslaved by their work. I'm free to sleep where I want and go where I want." I interpreted such statements as clear rejections of the modern, capitalist premise of productive labor. Chatting in coffee shops with fellow students, I championed the cause of the homeless by quoting their anti-work statements, translating my field notes into political slogans. However, when it came to writing the dissertation, aside from a few broad declarations like "It appears that some homeless people reject conventional notions of work," I had little else to write on the topic.

Fortunately, as my writing and analysis progressed, with the help of my peers and dissertation director, I focused on another idea that seemed more in synch with the empirical evidence and my sociological training. In particular, my data seemed to show that the very notion of "the homeless" was problematic. The men and women on the streets and in shelters viewed their circumstances from many different standpoints. Some thought of their situation as a type of personal freedom whereas others said they were "miserable." This way of analyzing and writing about my fieldwork became the foundation of my research and was further polished as the writing went on. (Marvasti, 2011)

As I tell my students, your aim should be to say 'a lot about a little (problem)'. Do not worry if your topic is too small or too narrow. I have never seen a student project assessed in these terms. This is because your professor will commend you for choosing a small-scale and hence manageable topic.

Avoid the temptation to say 'a little about a lot'. Indeed, the latter path can be something of a 'cop out'. Precisely, because the topic is so wide ranging, one can flit from one aspect to another without being forced to refine and test each piece of analysis (see Silverman, 2010: 86–8, 92–5).

TIP
Do not forget that qualitative research is often most effective when it studies how people behave in everyday situations. When studying such behaviour, it is often best to begin without an hypothesis, making your research question simply 'what is going on here?'

2.2.2 Give focus to your research

I have been arguing that it is often unhelpful for researchers to begin their work on a basis of a 'social problem' identified by either practitioners or managers. It is a commonplace that such definitions of 'problems' often may serve vested interests. My point, however, is that if social science research has anything to offer, its theoretical imperatives drive it in a direction which can offer participants new perspectives on their problems. Paradoxically, by refusing to begin from a common conception of what is 'wrong' in a setting, we may be most able to contribute to the identification both of what is going on and, thereby, how it may be modified in the pursuit of desired ends.

The various perspectives of social science provide a sensitivity to many issues neglected by those who define 'social' or administrative 'problems'. Let me distinguish three types of sensitivity:

- historical
- political
- contextual.

I will explain and discuss each of these in turn.

Historical sensitivity

Wherever possible, one should examine the relevant historical evidence when setting up a topic to research. For instance, in the 1950s and 1960s it was assumed that the 'nuclear family' (parents and children) had replaced the 'extended family' (many generations living together in the same household) of pre-industrial societies. Researchers simply seemed to have forgotten that lower life-expectancy may have made the 'extended family' pattern relatively rare in the past.

Again, historical sensitivity helps us to understand how we are governed. For instance, until the eighteenth century, the majority of the population were treated as a threatening 'mob' to be controlled, where necessary, by the use of force. Today, we are seen as individuals with 'needs' and 'rights' which must be understood and protected by society (see Foucault, 1977). But, although oppressive force may be used only rarely, we may be controlled in more subtle ways. Think of the knowledge about each of us contained in computerised databanks and the pervasive video cameras which record movements in many city streets. Historical sensitivity thus offers us multiple research topics which evade the trap of thinking that present-day versions of 'social problems' are unproblematic.

Political sensitivity

Allowing the current media 'scares' to determine our research topics is just as fallible as designing research in accordance with administrative or managerial interests. In neither case do we use political sensitivity to detect the vested interests behind this way of formulating a problem. The media, after all, need to attract an audience. Administrators need to be seen to be working efficiently.

So political sensitivity seeks to grasp the politics behind defining topics in particular ways. For instance, if you set out to research crime today, you should bear in mind that the 'law and order' discourse that politicians use is based, at least in the UK, on a simple formula: 'alcohol plus young men equals violent crime' (Noaks and Wincup, 2004: 34).

This shows how political sensitivity helps in suggesting how 'social problems' arise. For instance, Nelson (1984) looked at how 'child abuse' became defined as a recognisable problem in the late 1960s. She shows how the findings of a doctor about 'the battered baby syndrome' were adopted by the conservative Nixon administration through linking social problems to parental 'maladjustment' rather than to the failures of social programmes.

In case I am misunderstood, political sensitivity does *not* mean that social scientists argue that there are no 'real' problems in society. Instead, it suggests that social science can make an important contribution to society by querying how 'official' definitions of problems arise. To be truthful, however, we should also recognise how social scientists often need tacitly to accept such definitions in order to attract research grants.

Contextual sensitivity

This is the least self-explanatory and most contentious category in the present list. By 'contextual' sensitivity, I mean the recognition that apparently uniform institutions like 'the family', 'a tribe' or 'science' take on a variety of meanings in different contexts. **Contextual sensitivity** is reflected most obviously in Moerman's (1974) study of the Lue tribe in Thailand. Moerman began with the anthropologist's conventional appetite to locate a people in a classificatory scheme. To satisfy this appetite, he started to ask tribespeople questions like 'How do you recognise a member of your tribe?'

He reports that his respondents quickly became adept at providing a whole list of traits which constituted their tribe and distinguished them from their neighbours. At the same time, Moerman realised that such a list was, in purely logical terms, endless. Perhaps if you wanted to understand these people, it was not particularly useful to elicit an abstract account of their characteristics.

So Moerman stopped asking 'Who are the Lue?' Clearly, such ethnic identification devices were not used all the time by these people any more than we use them to refer to ourselves in a Western culture. Instead, Moerman started to examine what went on in everyday situations.

Looked at this way, the issue is no longer who the Lue essentially are, but when, among people living in these Thai villages, ethnic identification labels are invoked and the consequences of invoking them. Curiously enough, Moerman concluded that, when you looked at the matter this way, the apparent differences between the Lue and ourselves were considerably reduced. Only an ethnocentric Westerner might have assumed otherwise, behaving like a tourist craving for out-of-the-way sights.

But it is not only such large-scale collectivities as tribes that are looked at afresh when we use what I have called contextual sensitivity. Other apparently stable social institutions (like the 'family') and identities (gender, ethnicity, etc.) may be insufficiently questioned from a social problem perspective.

For instance, commentators says things like 'the family is under threat'. But where are we to find the unitary form of family assumed in such commentary? And does 'the family' not look different in contexts ranging from the household, to the law courts or even the supermarket (see Section 3.4)? Rather than take such arguments at face value, the researcher must make use of the three kinds of sensitivity, to discover how things actually operate in a social world where, as Moerman shows us, people's practices are inevitably more complex than they might seem.

TIP

Try to avoid thinking of social institutions as unitary phenomena. Get in the habit of considering the various contexts in which such institutions become relevant. By choosing to focus on just one such context, you can help to make your research topic more manageable.

One final point. The three kinds of sensitivity we have been considering offer different, sometimes contradictory, ways of generating research topics. I am not suggesting that all should be used at the beginning of any research study. However, if we are not sensitive to *any* of these issues, then we run the danger of lapsing into a 'social problem' based way of defining our research topics.

EXERCISE 2.2

Return to your interpretation of 'vigilantes' in Exercise 2.1. Now examine how you could generate different research problems using each of the three kinds of 'sensitivity' discussed above:

1 historical
2 political
3 contextual.

2.3 FITTING YOUR RESEARCH QUESTION INTO AN APPROPRIATE THEORY

In some respects, 'common-sense thinking' is the enemy of good research. Research topics which mimic the 'problems' discussed in Internet chatrooms or newspapers usually will not work. What I have called 'sensitivity' refers to the way in which your academic discipline offers you useful theories and concepts which can help you to generate a good research topic.

However, everything is a matter of balance and I will shortly show how we can be over-influenced by theory. These are the topics that follow:

- thinking theoretically
- under-theorised topics
- over-theorised topics.

2.3.1 Thinking theoretically

Some people become qualitative researchers for rather negative reasons. Perhaps they are not very good at statistics (or think they are not) and so are not tempted by quantitative research. Or perhaps they have not shone at library work and hope that they can stimulate their sluggish imagination by getting out into 'the field'.

Unfortunately, as most scientists and philosophers are agreed, the facts we find in 'the field' never speak for themselves but are impregnated by our assumptions. For instance, the initial reports of bystanders in Dallas at the time of the assassination of President Kennedy in 1963 were not of shots but of hearing a car backfiring (Sacks, 1984: 519). Why did people hear it this way?

We all know that people who think they have a heard a shot every time a car backfires may be regarded as unstable or even psychotic. So our descriptions are never simple reports of 'events' but are structured to depict ourselves as particular kinds of people who are usually 'reasonable' and 'cautious'.

But, you may say, surely social scientists are more objective than that? After all, they have scientific methods for making observations more trustworthy.

Well, yes and no. Certainly, social scientists will usually go through a more cautious process of sorting fact from opinion than most of us ever need to do in everyday life (see Chapter 8). However, even scientists only observe 'facts' through the use of lenses made up of concepts and theories.

Sacks has a basic example of this:

> Suppose you're an anthropologist or sociologist standing somewhere. You see somebody do some action, and you see it to be some activity. How can you go about formulating who is it that did it, for the purposes of your report? Can you use at least what you might take to be the most conservative formulation – his name? Knowing, of course, that any category you choose would have the[se] kinds of systematic problems: how would you go about selecting a given category from the set that would equally well characterise or identify that person at hand? (Sacks, 1992, I: 467–8)

Sacks shows how you cannot resolve such problems simply 'by taking the best possible notes at the time and making your decisions afterwards' (1992, I: 468). Whatever we observe is impregnated by assumptions.

EXERCISE 2.3

Sacks (1992) offers a case where you observe a car coming drawing up near you. A door opens and a teenage woman emerges and runs a few paces. Two other people (one male, one female) get out of the car. They run after the young woman, take her arms and pull her back into the car which now drives off.

Now answer these questions:

1 Without using your social science knowledge, prepare at least *two* different interpretations of what you have seen. Focus on whether this is something you should report to the police.
2 Examine at least *two* different interpretations of your behaviour if: (a) you report this matter to the police or (b) you do not report it.
3 Now use any ideas you know from your own discipline to describe and/or explain what you have seen.
4 Consider (a) whether these ideas are likely to give a more 'accurate' picture than your description in 1 and (b) to what extent we need to choose between the descriptions in 1 and 3.

In scientific work, these assumptions are usually given the fancy term 'theories'. But what are 'theories'? O'Brien (1993) has used the example of a kaleidoscope to answer this question. As he explains:

> a kaleidoscope … (is) the child's toy consisting of a tube, a number of lenses and fragments of translucent, coloured glass or plastic. When you turn the tube and look down the lens of the kaleidoscope the shapes and colours, visible at the bottom, change. As the tube is turned, different lenses come into play and the combinations of colour and shape shift from one pattern to another. In a similar way, we can see social theory as a sort of kaleidoscope – by shifting theoretical perspective the world under investigation also changes shape. (O'Brien, 1993: 10–11)

How theory works as a kaleidoscope can be seen by taking a concrete, if crude, example. Imagine that a group of social scientists from different disciplines are observing people at a party through a two-way mirror. The sociologist might observe the gender composition of various conversational groups, while the linguist might listen to how 'small talk' is managed between speakers. The psychologist might focus on the characteristics of 'loners' versus people who are the 'life and soul' of the party and the geographer might observe how the spatial organisation of the room influenced how people conversed.

The point is that none of these observations are more real or more true than the others. For instance, people are not essentially defined in terms of either their social characteristics (like gender) or their personalities (extrovert or introvert). It all depends on your research question. And research questions are inevitably theoretically informed. So we *do* need social theories to help us to address even quite basic issues in social research.

2.3.2 Under-theorised topics

Students commonly assume that the strength of qualitative research is its ability to get under the surface in order to understand people's perceptions and experiences. This particularly applies where the researcher sets out to record faithfully the 'experiences' of some, usually disadvantaged, group (e.g. the homeless, battered women, gay men, the unemployed). However, as we saw in our hypothetical student interview project, it can also involve trying to get inside the heads of any group you find around you.

Trying to understand the other's experiences is very much a feature of the twenty-first century world: not just the topic of (much) student research but also the rationale behind such mass media settings as talk shows and celebrity magazines. However, in a way, this concern with 'experience' also goes back to the nineteenth century. This was the time in which people expected that literature, art and music would express the inner world of the artist and engage the emotions of the audience. This movement was called **romanticism**.

As I argue in Chapter 6, there is more than a hint of this romanticism in some contemporary qualitative research (see also Gubrium and Holstein, 1997a; Atkinson and Silverman, 1997). Yet the romantic approach, although appealing, is also dangerous. It may neglect how 'experience' is shaped by cultural forms of representation. For instance, what we think is most personal to us ('guilt', 'responsibility') may be simply a culturally given way of understanding the world (see my discussion of the mother of a young diabetic person in Section 9.5.2). So it is problematic to justify research in terms of its 'authentic' representation of 'experience' when what is 'authentic' is culturally defined.

This under-theorisation of 'experience' can also be seen when a researcher follows an approach to different cultures which is uncritically 'touristic'. I have in mind the 'upmarket' tourist who travels the world in search of encounters with alien cultures. Disdaining package tours and even the label of 'tourist', such a person has an insatiable thirst for the 'new' and 'different'. The problem is that there are worrying parallels between the qualitative researcher and this kind of tourist. Such researchers often begin without a hypothesis and, like the tourist, gaze rapaciously at social scenes for signs of activities and experiences that appear to be new and different. The danger in all this is that 'touristic' researchers may so focus on cultural and 'sub-cultural' (or group) differences that they fail to recognise similarities between the culture to which they belong and the cultures which they study. For instance, once you switch away from asking 'leading' questions (which assume cultural differences) to observation of what people actually are doing, then you may find certain *common* features between social patterns in the West and East (see Ryen and Silverman, 2000, and my earlier discussion of Moerman's, 1974, study of a Thai tribe).

This discussion of romanticism and tourism has implications for analysing interview data which I discuss fully in Chapter 6. It is a symptom of what I have called 'under-theorisation' not because such research is without a theory but rather because it theorises the world tacitly or unconsciously. Instead, I suggest you try to draw consciously upon the theories and concepts of your discipline.

2.3.3 Over-theorised topics

Any apparent solution, when carried too far, can create a new problem. This is very much the case with theory. Just as some research projects are under-theorised, others carry theory beyond its proper limits. Sometimes the topic is so large and speculative that it is difficult to see how the student will ever get out of the library to gather and analyse some data. Sometimes one finds a quite sensible, well-organised research project dressed up in totally inappropriate theoretical clothes.

The other day I listened to a student giving a talk about his MA project. In most respects, this seemed to be an excellent piece of research. The topic was interesting yet manageable and the analysis was thorough. Unusually for such work, it had been published and its clear policy recommendations had started an important public debate.

I had only one complaint about this research. This was about how the student presented his data analysis. He chose to define his work in terms of **discourse analysis**. As we shall see in Chapter 9, this is a complicated methodology which has a quite specific approach to data. However, it turned out that the student's approach, while thorough, was far less complicated. Basically, he had scanned his interviews without any prior **hypotheses** and sought to develop a set of categories to illuminate his data. This approach, as we shall see in Chapter 3, is associated with **grounded theory**.

So here was a highly worthwhile piece of student research which undercut itself by flirting with an inappropriate theoretical approach. But this is only a minor case of over-theorisation. Far worse instances arise when researchers find it necessary to portray their work in terms of general theories of which they have very little grasp and which often bear little relation to their research. I have lost count of the run-of-the-mill qualitative research papers I have come across which find it necessary to define their work in terms of obscure philosophical positions such as phenomenology or hermeneutics. You will not find either of these terms in the Glossary of this book for one simple reason. In my view, you do not need to understand these terms in order to carry out good qualitative research. Indeed, if you try to understand them, my guess is that you will not emerge from the library for many years!

> **TIP**
> If you have a simple approach that is working well for you, do not try to dress up your work in fancy terms. Do not over-theorise!

2.4 CHOOSING AN EFFECTIVE RESEARCH DESIGN

Let us now assume that you have a workable research topic narrow enough to study and with just the right amount of input from relevant concepts and theories. Now you have to decide how you will study it. This means choosing an effective research design. This revolves around the following issues:

- considering the range of methods of data collection you can use
- making sure that your method is appropriate
- avoiding too many data-collection methods
- making sure you don't collect too much data.

2.4.1 The range of methods

There are four major methods used by qualitative researchers:

- observation
- analysing texts and documents
- interviews and focus groups
- audio and video recording (and other visual material).

These methods are often combined. For instance, many case studies combine observation with interviewing. Moreover, each method can be used in either qualitative or quantitative research studies. As Table 2.1 shows, the overall nature of the research methodology shapes how each method is used.

Table 2.1 shows that methods are techniques which take on a specific meaning according to the methodology in which they are used. (Do not worry if the distinction between 'method' and 'methodology' is unclear to you. Later in this chapter I explain these and other terms that we use in research design.)

TABLE 2.1   Different uses for four methods

| | Methodology | |
Method	Quantitative research	Qualitative research
Observation	Preliminary work, e.g. prior to framing questionnaire	Fundamental to understanding another culture
Textual analysis	Content analysis, i.e. counting in terms of researchers' categories	Understanding participants' categories
Interviews	Survey research: mainly fixed-choice questions to random samples	'Open-ended' questions to small samples
Audio and video recording	Used infrequently to check the accuracy of interview records	Understanding the organisation of talk, gaze and body movements

In quantitative research, observation is not generally seen as a very important method of data collection. This is because it is difficult to conduct observational studies on large samples. Quantitative researchers also argue that observation is not a very 'reliable' data-collection method because different observers may record different observations. If used at all, observation is held to be only appropriate at a preliminary or 'exploratory' stage of research.

Conversely, observational studies have been fundamental to much qualitative research. Beginning with the pioneering case studies of non-Western societies by early anthropologists (Malinowski, 1922; Radcliffe-Brown, 1948) and continuing with the work by sociologists in Chicago prior to the Second World War (see Deegan, 2001), the observational method has often been the chosen method to understand another culture (Chapter 5).

These contrasts are also apparent in the treatment of texts and documents. Quantitative researchers try to analyse written material in a way which will produce reliable evidence about a large sample. Their favoured method is **content analysis** in which the researchers establish a set of categories and then count the number of instances that fall into each category. The crucial requirement is that the categories are sufficiently precise to enable different coders to arrive at the same results when the same body of material (e.g. newspaper headlines) is examined (see Berelson, 1952).

In qualitative research, content analysis is less common (but see Marvasti, 2004: 90–4). The crucial issue is to understand the participants' categories and to see how these are used in concrete activities like telling stories (Propp, 1968; Sacks, 1974), assembling files (Cicourel, 1968; Gubrium and Buckholdt, 1982) or describing 'family life' (Gubrium, 1992). The **reliability** of the analysis is less frequently addressed. Instead, qualitative researchers make claims about their ability to reveal the local practices through which given 'end-products' (stories, files, descriptions) are assembled.

Interviews are commonly used in both methodologies. Quantitative researchers administer interviews or questionnaires to random samples of the population; this is referred to as 'survey research'. 'Fixed-choice' questions (e.g. 'yes' or 'no') are usually preferred because the answers they produce lend themselves to simple tabulation, unlike 'open-ended' questions which produce answers which need to be subsequently coded. A central methodological issue for quantitative researchers is the reliability of the interview schedule and the representativeness of the sample.

For instance, after surveys of voting intention did not coincide with the result of the British general election of 1992, survey researchers looked again at their methodology. Assuming that some respondents in the past may have lied to interviewers about their voting intentions, some companies now provide a ballot box into which respondents put mock ballot slips – thereby eliminating the need to reveal one's preferences to the interviewer. Attention was also given to assembling a more representative sample to interview, bearing in mind the expense of a completely random sample of the whole British population. Perhaps as a result of these methodological revisions, pollsters' final figures of voting intentions fitted much more closely the actual result of subsequent British elections.

'Authenticity' rather than sample size is often the issue in qualitative research. The aim is usually to gather an 'authentic' understanding of people's experiences and it is believed that 'open-ended' questions are the most effective route towards this end. So, for instance, in gathering life-histories or in interviewing parents of handicapped children (Baruch, 1982) people may simply be asked: 'tell me your story'. Qualitative interview studies are often conducted with small samples and the interviewer–interviewee relationship may be defined in political rather than scientific terms (e.g. Finch, 1984).

Finally, audio and video data are rarely used in quantitative research, probably because of the assumption that they are difficult to quantify. Conversely, as we shall see (Chapters 9 and 10), audio and video recordings, as well as other visual images, are an increasingly important part of qualitative research. Transcripts of such recordings, based on standardised conventions, provide an excellent record of 'naturally occurring' interaction. Compared with fieldnotes of observational data, recordings and transcripts can offer a highly reliable record to which researchers can return as they develop new hypotheses.

EXERCISE 2.4

Once more focus on 'vigilantes'. Now suggest what research questions can be addressed by any *two* of the four methods just discussed. Namely:

- observation
- analysing texts, documents and visual images
- interviews
- recording and transcribing.

Now consider: (a) What are the relative merits of each method in addressing this topic? (b) What, if anything, could be gained by combining both methods (you might like to refer forward to my discussion of 'triangulation' in Section 11.3.2)?

2.4.2 Appropriate methods

Both science and everyday life teach us that there is no 'right' method to proceed. Everything depends on what you are trying to achieve.

Despite this truism, students regularly use methods that are quite inappropriate to their research topic. As I noted about our hypothetical student project, how can we be sure that a qualitative approach was appropriate? On the face of it, if you are interested in something as concrete as people's perceptions of their job prospects, surely a quantitative survey of a larger number of students would be more appropriate than a few 'intensive' interviews?

Even if you can convince your professor that a qualitative method is appropriate, are you sure that you have chosen the right method? As I have already suggested, it is possible that many people choose to gather interview data less because they are appropriate to their topic and more because they have unthinkingly assimilated a romantic outlook. Decide the kind of data to use by asking yourself which data are most appropriate to your research problem – for instance, are you more interested in what people are thinking or feeling or in what they are doing? And make an informed choice between the many different kinds of data and methods that are freely available to us in the twenty-first century.

2.4.3 Focus on a single method

Lack of confidence can also manifest itself in an incapacity to choose or to commit oneself. You may be so impressed by the different methods you have learned on your Qualitative Research course that, somehow, you want to use more than one on your student project. Wouldn't it be nice, you ask yourself, to combine your interviews with some observation or, say, a focus group? My response is simple: take this path only if you seriously want to complicate your life and, perhaps, end up having passed the time limit for delivery.

Often the desire to use multiple methods arises because you want to get at many different aspects of a phenomenon. However, this may mean that you have not yet sufficiently narrowed down your topic. Sometimes a better approach is to treat the analysis of different kinds of data as a 'dry run' for your main study. As such, it is a useful test of the kind of data which you can most easily gather and analyse.

'Mapping' one set of data upon another (or data **triangulation**) is a more or less complicated task depending on your analytic framework. In particular, if you treat social reality as constructed in different ways in different contexts (or **constructionism**), then you cannot appeal to a single 'phenomenon' which all your data apparently represent.

Research design should involve careful thought rather than seeking the most immediately attractive option. However, none of the points above exclude the possibility of using multiple means of gathering data. Ultimately, everything will depend on the quality of your data analysis rather than upon the quality of your data. Just make sure you have the time and the ability.

> **LINK**
>
> A very useful website based on Clive Seale's edited book *Researching Society and Culture* (2004b) is:
>
> www.rscbook.co.uk

2.4.4 Make sure you have just the right amount of data

Lack of confidence can create many of the difficulties I have been discussing. For instance, if you are unsure of yourself, you may think it will impress your professor if you set up a huge problem and perhaps define it in grand theoretical terms. Similarly, collecting vast amounts of data may appear to reassure you that you are making progress on your project.

Unfortunately, as generations of PhD students could tell you, until you have analysed your data you have achieved precisely nothing. If depth rather than breadth is the aim of experienced qualitative researchers, how much more so for the beginner!

To make your analysis effective, it is imperative to have a limited body of data with which to work. So, while it may be useful initially to explore different kinds of data, this should usually only be done to establish the data set with which you can most effectively work within the timescale open to you. And do not worry if this means that you will not be able to compare different cases. The comparative method is indeed worthwhile, but it can be used *within* very small data sets.

2.5 AN EFFECTIVE LITERATURE REVIEW

Most people know that research reports should contain a section on the relevant literature. The danger is that you will treat such a literature review as an academic duty rather than as something really relevant to your research project. It is relevant because:

- good research frames its aims in the context of earlier work
- without reading the literature you are in danger of trying to answer questions about research design that have already been answered for you (so you will be trying 'to reinvent the wheel')
- when you write your conclusions, it is important to relate your findings to other studies.

A good discussion of the literature in your area presupposes the sensible recording of what you read. So I will ask first: what is the best way to record your reading?

2.5.1 Recording your reading

During your academic studies, I hope that you will have learned the habit of keeping your reading notes in a word-processed file, organised in terms of (emerging) topics. I stress 'reading notes' because it is important from the start that you do *not* simply collate books or photocopies of articles for 'later' reading but read as you go. Equally, your notes should not just consist of chunks of written or scanned extracts from the original sources but represent your ideas on the *relevance* of what you are reading for your (emerging) research problem. Table 2.2 offers suggestions for sensible note-taking.

TABLE 2.2   Reading and note-taking

1   Never pick up and put down an article without doing something with it
2   Highlight key points, write notes in the margins and summaries elsewhere
3   Transfer notes and summaries to where you will use them in your dissertation
4   Ensure that each note will stand alone without you needing to go back to the original

Source: adapted from Phelps et al., 2007: 175–6

The notes and highlighting mentioned in Table 2.2 should involve your reflections on the material's relevance (to your topic) and on how convincing you find it. This is what is meant by a *critical* reading of the literature. Never just copy chunks of material.

> **TIP**
>
> It goes without saying that you should use a consistent system for referencing authors and other details of the material you are reading. The Harvard method of referencing is usually the system chosen. This involves entering an author's surname, followed by date of publication and any page reference in your main text as below:
>
> Abrams (1984: 2); Agar (1986: 84)
>
> By using this method, you can save footnotes for substantial asides rather than for (boring) references. Detailed references are then appended in a bibliography with the form set out below:
>
> Abrams, P. (1984) 'Evaluating soft findings: some problems of measuring informal care', *Research Policy and Planning*, 2 (2), 1–8.
>
> Agar, M. (1986) *Speaking of Ethnography*, Qualitative Research Methods Series, Volume 2. London: Sage.

I now turn to some practical questions about writing a literature review:

• What should it contain?
• Where will you find what you need to read?
• How should you read?

2.5.2 What should a literature review contain?

In part, a literature review should be used to display your scholarly skills and credentials. In this sense, you should use it:

> To demonstrate skills in library searching; to show command of the subject area and understanding of the problem; to justify the research topic, design and methodology. (Hart, 1998: 13)

Such justification also means that any literature review connected with a piece of research has as much to do with good research design as with displaying your academic credentials.

This involves addressing the questions set out in Table 2.3.

TABLE 2.3 Contents of a literature review

• What do we already know about the topic?
• What do you have to say critically about what is already known?
• Has anyone else ever done anything exactly the same?
• Has anyone else done anything that is related?
• Where does your work fit in with what has gone before?
• Why is your research worth doing in the light of what has already been done?

Source: adapted from Murcott, 1997

Once you start to see your literature review as dialogic rather than a mere replication of other people's writing, you are going in the right direction. Conceived as an answer to a set of questions, your reading can immediately become more directed and your writing more engaging and relevant. Exercise 2.5 gives you an opportunity to test out your skills in using the existing literature to help you in your own research. It emphasises that we should never read such literature without having formulated some prior set of questions.

EXERCISE 2.5

Select what you regard as the two or three most relevant pieces of literature. Now:

1 Make notes on each, attempting to use each one to answer the questions found in Table 2.3.

2 Incorporate these notes in a short literature review section which only refers to these two or three works.
3 Discuss this review with your teacher.

2.5.3 Where will I find the literature?

As Hart (2001: 24) points out, it helps to do some preliminary thinking about what you are doing before you begin the search itself. Below are some issues to think about (drawn from Hart, 2001: 24):

- What discipline(s) relate to my main topic?
- How can I focus my topic to make my search more precise?
- What are main indexes and abstracts relevant to my topic?
- What means of recording will be most efficient for many tasks such as cross-referencing? Hart points out that index cards are useful.

Once you are prepared, it is time to review the many potential sources of information about what literature you need to read and where to find it:

- your supervisor
- the subject librarian in your university library
- bibliographies in the literature you read
- online searches on the World Wide Web
- the Social Sciences Citation Index
- news groups on the Internet
- your fellow students (past and present).

TIP
Excellent discussions of using the Web for literature searches are provided by Phelps et al. (2007: 129–65) and O'Dochartaigh (2007).

LINK
For a template for recording literature searches, go to:
www.sagepub.co.uk/phelps

In literature searches, there is no need to worry about admitting your lack of knowledge. Indeed the American sociologist Gary Marx recommends taking 'short cuts': 'learn how to use computer searches, encyclopaedias, review articles. Ask experts for help' (Marx, 1997: 106).

Once you start looking, you will speedily find that you do not have a problem with too little literature but of too much!. Getting away from the books and towards your data is a leap that most of us need to make as early as possible. As Marx cautions: 'Don't become a bibliophile unless it suits you' (1997: 106). Or, more pointedly, 'know when enough is enough' (Phelps et al., 2007: 176).

2.5.4 There's so much; how will I find the time?

Before you panic, you need to remember that you would not have reached this stage of your academic career without learning the tricks of the reading trade. These tricks go beyond the skills of speed reading (although these help) but also mean that your aim is usually to 'fillet' a publication in terms of your own agenda (not the author's!).

Again, Marx makes the point well:

> Sample! Learn how to read by skimming, attending to the first and last sentence, paragraph or chapter. Read conclusions first, then decide if you want the rest. Most social science books probably shouldn't be books; they have only a few main (or at least original) ideas. (1997: 106)

If these are some answers to the usual 'nuts and bolts' questions, we still need to tackle the underlying principles behind a literature review. As my earlier discussion of 'misconceptions' suggested, these principles are not always obvious or clear cut.

2.5.5 Avoid mere description

This is how the best recent book on the topic defines a literature review:

> The selection of available documents (both published and unpublished) on the topic, which contain information, ideas, data and evidence written from a particular standpoint to fulfil certain aims or express certain views on the nature of the topic and how it is to be investigated, and the effective evaluation of these documents in relation to the research being proposed. (Hart, 1998: 13)

Chris Hart's term 'effective evaluation' means, I believe, that your report should try to avoid simply describing what you have read. Any academic has horror stories of literature reviews which were tediously and irrelevantly descriptive. Rudestam and Newton characterise well such failing reviews:

[they consist of] a laundry list of previous studies, with sentences or paragraphs beginning with the words, "Smith found…", "Jones concluded…", "Anderson stated…", and so on. (1992: 46)

In this vein, Marx recommends avoiding writing 'a literature summary without an incisive critique that will help your peers to view the world differently' (1997: 106). Instead, you need to focus on those studies that are relevant for defining *your* research problem. By the end of the literature review:

the reader should be able to conclude that, 'Yes, of course, this is the exact study that needs to be done at this time to move knowledge in this field a little further along.' (Rudestam and Newton, 1992: 47)

This entails giving different amounts of attention to what you read according to how central they are to your topic. Background literature can just be described in a sentence. By contrast, you need to explain why certain studies contain issues of theory and method that are particularly important for your project.

LINK
For some short tips on literature reviews go to:
www.qmu.ac.uk/psych/RTrek/study_notes/web/sn9.htm

2.6 BASIC TERMS IN RESEARCH DESIGN

I hope the discussion above will offer an initial quick fix on some of the practical problems involved in carrying out a small-scale qualitative research project. The rest of this book will develop and context these themes. However, I recognise that some of the terms I have been using may not be immediately transparent. For instance, how does a 'theory' differ from a 'hypothesis'? And how do we develop both of them?

Questions like this mean that I can no longer postpone the potentially tiresome business of defining my terms. In this chapter, we shall be discussing models, concepts, theories, hypotheses, methods and methodologies. In Table 2.4, I set out how each term will be used.

As Table 2.4 implies, what I call 'models' are even more basic to social research than theories. Models provide an overall framework for how we look at reality. In short, they tell us what reality is like and the basic elements it contains ('ontology') and what is the nature and status of knowledge ('epistemology'). In this sense, models roughly correspond to what are more grandly referred to as 'paradigms' (see Guba and Lincoln, 1994).

TABLE 2.4   Basic terms in research

Term	Meaning	Relevance
Model	An overall framework for looking at reality (e.g. behaviouralism, feminism)	Usefulness
Concept	An idea deriving from from a given model (e.g. 'stimulus–response', 'oppression')	Usefulness
Theory	A set of concepts used to define and/or explain some phenomenon	Usefulness
Hypothesis	A testable proposition	Validity
Methodology	A general approach to studying research topics	Usefulness
Method	A specific research technique	Good fit with model, theory, hypothesis and methodology

In social research, examples of such models are functionalism (which looks at the functions of social institutions), behaviourism (which defines all behaviour in terms of 'stimulus' and 'response'), symbolic interactionism (which focuses on how we attach symbolic meanings to interpersonal relations) and **ethnomethodology** (which encourages us to look at people's everyday ways of producing orderly social interaction). Drawing on Gubrium and Holstein (1997a), I discussed the importance of models further in Chapter 1.

Concepts are clearly specified ideas deriving from a particular model. Examples of concepts are 'social function' (deriving from functionalism), 'stimulus–response' (behaviouralism), 'definition of the situation' (interactionism) and 'the documentary method of interpretation' (ethnomethodology). Concepts offer ways of looking at the world which are essential in defining a research problem.

Theories arrange sets of concepts to define and explain some phenomenon. As Strauss and Corbin put it: 'Theory consists of plausible relationships produced among concepts and sets of concepts' (1994: 278). Without a theory, such phenomena as 'gender', 'personality', 'talk' or 'space' cannot be understood by social science. In this sense, without a theory there is nothing to research.

So theory provides a footing for considering the world, separate from, yet about, that world. In this way, theory provides both:

- a framework for critically understanding phenomena
- a basis for considering how what is unknown might be organised. (J. Gubrium, personal correspondence)

By provoking ideas about what is presently unknown, theories provide the impetus for research. As living entities, they are also developed and modified by good research. However, as used here, models, concepts and theories are self-confirming in the sense that they instruct us to look at phenomena in particular ways. This means that they can never be disproved but only found to be more or less useful.

This last feature distinguishes theories from hypotheses. Unlike theories, hypotheses are tested in research. Examples of hypotheses, discussed later in this book, are:

- how we receive advice is linked to how advice is given
- responses to an illegal drug depend upon what one learns from others
- voting in union elections is related to non-work links between union members.

In many qualitative research studies, there is no specific hypothesis at the outset. Instead, hypotheses are produced (or induced) during the early stages of research. In any event, unlike theories, hypotheses can, and should be, tested. Therefore, we assess a hypothesis by its **validity** or truth.

A methodology refers to the choices we make about cases to study, methods of data gathering, forms of data analysis, etc., in planning and executing a research study. Gobo (2008) suggest that a methodology comprises the following four components:

1 a *preference for certain methods* among the many available to us (listening, watching, observing, reading, questioning, conversing)
2 a *theory of scientific knowledge*, or a set of pre-assumptions about the nature of reality, the tasks of science, the role of the researcher, and the concepts of action and social actor
3 a *range of solutions*, devices and stratagems used in tackling a research problem
4 a systematic sequence of *procedural steps* to be followed once our method has been selected.

So our methodology defines how one will go about studying any phenomenon. In social research, methodologies may be defined very broadly (e.g. qualitative or quantitative) or more narrowly (e.g. grounded theory or conversation analysis). Like theories, methodologies cannot be true or false, only more or less useful.

Finally, methods are specific research techniques. These include quantitative techniques, like statistical correlations, as well as techniques like observation, interviewing and audio recording. Once again, in themselves, techniques are not true or false. They are more or less useful, depending on their fit with the theories and methodologies being used, the hypothesis being tested and/or the research topic that is selected. So, for instance, behaviouralists may favour quantitative methods and interactionists often prefer to gather their data by observation. But, depending upon the hypothesis being tested, behaviouralists may sometimes use qualitative methods – for instance, in the exploratory stage of research. Equally, interactionists may sometimes use simple quantitative methods, particularly when they want to find an overall pattern in their data.

TIP

Get in the habit of thinking about research design in terms of how *useful* a particular approach is for your research topic. Models, concepts, methodologies and methods cannot be right or wrong, only more or less useful.

2.7 CONCLUSIONS

Having explained some basic terms, I want to make two general observations. First, as I have emphasised, no research method stands on its own. So far, I have sought to show the link between methods and methodologies in social research. Second, however, there is a broader, societal context in which methods are located and deployed. As a crude example, texts depended upon the invention of the printing press or, in the case of TV or audio recordings, upon modern communication technologies.

Moreover, such activities as observation and interviewing are not unique to social researchers. For instance, as Foucault (1977) has noted, the observation of the prisoner has been at the heart of modern prison reform, while the method of questioning used in the interview reproduces many of the features of the Catholic confessional or the psycho-analytic consultation. Its pervasiveness is reflected by the centrality of the interview study in so much contemporary social research. For instance, when I reviewed one qualitative journal recently, I found that 16 out of 18 research papers used interview data. One possible reason for this may not derive from methodological considerations. Think, for instance, of how much interviews are a central (and popular) feature of mass media products, from 'talk shows' to 'celebrity interviews'. Perhaps we all live in what might be called an 'Interview Society' in which interviews seem central to making sense of our lives (Atkinson and Silverman, 1997).

All this means that we need to resist treating research methods as mere *techniques*. This is reflected in the attention paid in this book to the analysis of data rather than to methods of data collection.

Part Two of this book sets out each research method in greater detail and Part Three returns to issues of validity and relevance which are touched upon in this chapter.

TIP
Students often err by assuming that 'theory' is best done from the armchair while specu-lating upon great philosophical problems. By contrast, theorising is best accomplished by thinking through the implications of how you have gathered and analysed your data.

KEY POINTS

- The biggest mistake that beginning researchers can make is to attempt too ambitious a research project.
- In both science and everyday life, the facts never speak for themselves. This is because all knowledge is theoretically impregnated.
- Theory provides a framework for critically understanding phenomena and a basis for considering how what is unknown might be organised.
- Research problems are distinct from social problems.
- We can generate valuable research problems by employing three types of sensitivity: historical, political and contextual.
- There are four major methods used by qualitative researchers: observation; analysing texts, documents and images; interviews; recording and transcribing naturally occurring interaction.
- There is a broader, societal context in which research methods are located and deployed.

STUDY QUESTIONS

- Why (and in what way) is your chosen research topic significant? Does it relate to any concepts or theories in your chosen discipline?
- How far do your topic and findings relate to other research?
- Why is your chosen method of data collection appropriate to your research topic?
- Will you have time to analyse all the data you plan to gather?
- What status will you accord to your data? For instance, are you seeking objective 'facts', subjective 'perceptions' or simply people's stories?
- What literature is most relevant to your planned research? Why?

RECOMMENDED READING

The most useful introductory texts are Clive Seale's (editor) *Researching Society and Culture*, Third Edition (2011), Alan Bryman's *Quantity and Quality in Social Research* (1988) and Nigel Gilbert's (editor) *Researching Social Life* (1993). More advanced qualitative analysis is offered by Seale et al.'s *Qualitative Research Practice* (2004), Miles and Huberman's *Qualitative Data Analysis* (1984), Hammersley and Atkinson's *Ethnography: Principles in Practice*, Second Edition (1995) and Denzin and Lincoln's (editors) *Handbook of Qualitative Research*, Third Edition (2006). The essential book on literature reviews is Chris Hart's *Doing a Literature Review: Releasing the Social Science Imagination* (1998). This covers in detail all the issues discussed in this brief chapter as well as addressing the different requirements of literature reviews for BA, MA and PhD dissertations. Hart's later book *Doing a Literature Search* (Sage, 2001) is a helpful guide to planning and executing a literature search.

3

Data Analysis

CHAPTER OBJECTIVES

By the end of this chapter, you will be able to:

- feel confident as you first confront your data
- be familiar with three ways of analysing qualitative data: content analysis, grounded theory and narrative analysis
- know what is shared by all effective methods for analysing data.

If you are new to qualitative research, data analysis can be something of a mystery. You have gathered your interviews, selected your documents or made some observations. Now what do you do?

It appears to be so much easier in quantitative research. Your data usually present themselves as sets of numbers and there are readily available statistical tests which you can apply to see what your numbers 'mean'. This does not imply that your data analysis will be foolproof – you may use an inappropriate statistical test, misinterpret your findings and your primary data may be suspect. But at least you know where to begin.

By contrast, beginning qualitative data analysis can seem like exploring a new territory without an easy-to-read map. When you consult guidebooks, you find a host of competing approaches rather than what appears to be the settled consensus about what constitutes good quantitative research.

This means that, before you begin data analysis, it is crucial to be aware of the key approaches that have been used in qualitative research. Indeed, knowledge of such approaches is crucial in how you go about defining your research problem and reviewing the literature.

Explanations of three widely used approaches – **content analysis**, **grounded theory** and narrative analysis – will follow shortly, illustrated by case studies. However, before I bog you down with detail, I want to provide a short, simplified piece of advice, aimed at the novice. This advice does not directly draw upon any one approach or even very much of what has been written in previous textbooks. Instead, it is based on what I have learned through supervising students grappling with qualitative data. For simplicity's sake, my advice is formulated as a set of rules.

3.1 SOME RULES FOR DATA ANALYSIS

Here are six simple rules:

1   Get down to analysis as early as possible and avoid 'busy' work.
2   Try out different theoretical approaches; see what works for you (and for your data).
3   Avoid too early **hypotheses** and seek to see where your analysis is leading in order to establish an hypothesis.
4   Do not look for telling examples but analyse your data thoroughly and fairly.
5   Initially, focus on a small part of your data and analyse it intensively; there will be time later to test out your findings on your data set as a whole.
6   Try to focus on sequences (of talk, written material or interaction).

I will say some more about each of these rules. Much more detail will be found in Chapter 11 which sets out guidelines for you to use in evaluating other people's research.

3.1.1 Early analysis

It is a commonplace observation that people under stress may often postpone important or difficult tasks. Gathering qualitative data gives you several alibis which mask the fact that you have succumbed to such a temptation:

• Getting access to your data can take ages because of the time it takes to satisfy ethics committee and/or to get access to appropriate subjects or settings.
• Gathering your data can be very time consuming.
• Once you have your data, transcribing them all so that they are ready for analysis can take years.

The sad consequence of taking these facts too seriously is that you have very little, if any, time for data analysis itself. This applies even to PhD students with three or more years to write their dissertation. So imagine how it leaves you as an undergraduate or MA student where start to finish time will, at best, be counted in months!

In fact, if you think sensibly from the start, each of these problems can be avoided. First, when you are designing your study, go for data which offer easy access and are quick to gather. Certain kinds of documents or Internet data are examples. Secondary analysis of other people's data is now much easier with online databanks in use (go to: www.data-archive.ac.uk/home).

Second, never think of transcribing all your material at the start. This is a sure way to delay data analysis. Instead, transcribe one or two examples and analyse those. You will then be in a far better position to decide how much of your material needs to be transcribed in full and how much can be transcribed at particular points of interest.

EXERCISE 3.1

Pick out any research topic that interests you. Then:

- Work out how you could obtain relevant data quickly and easily.
- Consider whether such data could satisfactorily address your original topic.

3.1.2 Try out different theoretical approaches

In reading qualitative research studies, you will speedily discover that authors routinely reference one or another theoretical approach as their point of departure. As Rapley puts it:

> Anyone new to qualitative analysis will be faced with a quandary: what should I do with all this data? You look at various journal articles, and often see the same key phrases again and again. People keep telling you they did 'grounded theory', or conducted a 'phenomenological analysis' and then give you various levels of details about what that did. Some are quite rich descriptions of things done to and with 'raw data'; others just use a couple of phrases and a single reference (often to the same small array of texts). Above all, whatever you read, you realise that it is *de rigeur* to have some kind of tag. You need the right kind of label in your methods section, ideally one that positions you as competent, so that your work can be nicely categorised. (2011: 273)

Rapley rightly injects a cynical note into his comments about theoretical orientations. Too often, labelling your research can be simply a kind of window dressing to obtain status among your peers. It is one thing to 'tag' your work; it is quite another to use theory thoroughly and well.

So why do you need theory when you do data analysis? The simple answer is that *any* analysis depends on the use of certain theory-dependent **concepts**. For instance, even if you claim to be merely reporting how your respondents 'see' things or how things 'are' in the field, I guarantee that you will tacitly be using an unacknowledged theoretical position about what kinds of entities are out there in the 'field'.

So there is no escape from theoretically defined conceptual description. For instance, it is dangerous to assume that the researcher's method of observing 'facts' and then trying to explain them is shared by participants. As Harvey Sacks has pointed out, in everyday life we determine what is a 'fact' by first seeing if there is some convincing explanation around. For instance, coroners may not deliver a verdict of suicide unless there is some evidence that the deceased person had a reason to take their own life (Sacks, 1992, I: 123). In that sense, in everyday life, only those 'facts' occur for which there is an explanation (I: 121).

Sacks made this observation by using a particular theoretical position deriving from **ethnomethodology** (see Section 1.8). Whatever theory you use, concepts will shape your research. Rapley, once again, makes the point:

> all [methods of data analysis] start with a close inspection of a sample of data about a specific issue. This close inspection is used to discover, explore and generate an increasingly refined conceptual description of the phenomena. The resulting conceptual description therefore emerges from, is based on, or is grounded in the data about the phenomena. (2011: 276)

> **TIP**
>
> In theoretically defined data analysis, one shifts the focus from:
>
> what is said by participants, what you've observed them doing or what you read in a text (the level of description and summary) to:
>
> exploring and explaining what is 'underlying' or to 'distil' essence, meaning, norms, orders, patterns, rules, structures etcetera (the level of concepts and themes). (Rapley, 2011: 276)

3.1.3 Avoid early hypotheses

A quick glance at a **sample** of quantitative research articles will show that they commonly contain a section entitled 'hypotheses tested'. Beginning with a hypothesis related to predefined **variables** makes a great deal of sense when you are using a statistical logic. By doing so, you avoid potentially 'sloppy' exploratory research and end up with credible correlations which shed light on your research problem.

By contrast, qualitative researchers usually need to explore the 'field' in depth before they can start to speculate about what elements are most relevant and how they might be related. This does not mean that the early stages of their research are purely descriptive (see Section 3.1.2). Even conceptually driven research needs close familiarity with what is going before it can construct hypotheses to be tested.

Take my research on HIV-test counselling (Silverman, 1997). I collected tapes of counselling sessions in a number of centres. In the context of the AIDS pandemic, it would have been tempting to test an early hypothesis about which centres and what counselling methods were most effective in preventing HIV transmission among their clients. However, this would have ignored tricky questions about what was actually happening in these counselling interviews. Such questions could not be answered by consulting the centres' officially stated philosophy or even the practices in which their counsellors were trained (see Silverman, 2010: 125–31). Instead, the hypotheses I eventually generated and then tested were based on detailed analysis of how counsellors and their clients actually communicated with each other.

CASE STUDY

In a study of HIV-test counselling (Silverman, 1997), I examined the relationship between the different formats used by counsellors to give advice and how the advice was received by their clients. Based on 50 advice sequences, I showed how personalised advice, offered after clients had been asked to specify their concerns, was associated with a 'marked acknowledgement' (e.g. a comment on the advice or a further question from the client). Conversely, counsellors who gave generalised advice, without first getting their clients to specify a particular problem, generally received only 'unmarked acknowledgements' (e.g. 'mm', 'right', 'yes').

However, the availability of detailed transcripts meant that I could go beyond this predictable finding. The problem was that, if asked, many counsellors would have recognised that generalised advice-giving is likely to be ineffective. So I generated and tested hypotheses about two *functions* of generalised advice-giving in HIV-test counselling:

- managing potentially disruptive minimal client uptakes by marking them as appropriate receipts to information-giving rather than advice-delivery
- speeding up the interview since advice did not need to be based on prior elicitation of clients' perspectives.

I sought, thereby, to make a constructive input into policy debates by examining the *functions* of communication sequences in a particular institutional context.

3.1.4 Avoid telling examples

An all too common way of reporting qualitative research findings is to present a slab of data (for instance, an interview transcript) prefaced with a comment like 'an interesting example of this is …'. To my mind, such use of materials works far better in, say, journalism than in scientific research. This is because journalists want to write lively stories with telling examples. They do not usually have the time, the space or the incentive to worry about whether their interpretation fits all their material.

By contrast, scientific research, whether quantitative or qualitative, must convince readers that the claims being made fit all the data and that negative instances have not been discounted. This involves actively searching for deviant cases to test emerging hypotheses and the use of the constant comparative method (see Chapter 11).

So, rather than using a few telling examples, one must seek to demonstrate that one's findings are robust even when subjected to the hardest of tests. This involves procedures described in Sections 3.1.5 and 3.1.6.

3.1.5 Focus initially on a small part of your data

As we saw in Section 3.1.1, early data analysis tends to be associated with good qualitative research. Because it usually needs to be carried out before all your data are available, this generally means that you will be seeking to analyse only a small part of your eventual data corpus.

However, even if you have all your data to hand (perhaps because you are doing secondary analysis of someone else's data), it makes sense to begin by trying to develop a detailed analysis of a very limited amount of data (**intensive analysis**). This should provide a good initial grasp of the phenomena with which you are concerned. These can then be tested by looking at relevant features of your whole data set (**extensive analysis**).

My counselling research followed exactly this pattern (Silverman, 1997; 2010: 125–31):

- At the start, I transcribed just a few counselling interviews which were analysed in depth.
- From such intensive analysis, I developed some provisional hypotheses about the patterns of communication between counsellors and their clients.
- I then transcribed parts of the other interviews that were relevant to these hypotheses.
- This material was then examined and my initial hypotheses revised accordingly.

3.1.6 Try to focus on sequences

One further reason why brief data extracts are usually unreliable is that they tend to pull out material from the sequences of actions in which they are embedded. So, for instance, it should be unacceptable for interview researchers to offer only an interviewee's comment without prefacing it with the interviewer's question, comment or response token (e.g. 'mm, mm') that preceded it, followed up with some attention to how the former shaped the latter. Just this issue arises later in this chapter when I compare grounded theory with narrative analysis.

In everyday life, we constantly attend to where an utterance is positioned in order to find its sense. For example, try saying 'hello' to someone half-way through a conversation! These are exactly the kinds of things that qualitative research has shown and it is incumbent upon good researchers to locate the sequences in which utterances and actions are embedded.

Two final comments about sequence are in order. The specialised approach of **conversation analysis** (CA) has been central to this argument about the relevance of sequence to action (see Section 9.4). However, this is not a veiled recommendation that the only way to do credible qualitative research is via CA. On the contrary, a range of qualitative approaches take on board the idea of sequence. And, long before CA, linguists recognised how meaning is always tied to the order in which things happen or are presented. For instance, think of how, when you are ordering a meal in a Western restaurant, the waiter will not expect you to order your dessert before your soup (see my discussion of Saussure in Section 10.4).

The second comment is that, of course, you must, at some point elect to narrow down the sequence on which you focus – otherwise you could only make observations about, say, one whole interview or document. However, at least try to retain the immediate surroundings of whatever data you are analysing. And bear in mind that there may well be evidence that the participants indicate to another where one part of their interaction is concluded and another is about to begin (in conversation, think of how we use such markers as 'turning to (another topic)' to move the agenda on, or 'as you say' to link our talk to what has preceded it).

TIP

Ultimately, the most satisfactory way to develop good research skills is through writing (see Chapter 12). As Rapley puts it:

(Continued)

(Continued)

The practices of good (or even adequate) qualitative data analysis can never be adequately summed up by using a neat tag. They can also never be summed up by a list of specific steps or procedures that have been undertaken. Above all, you need to develop a working, hands-on, empirical, tacit knowledge of analysis. This should enable you to develop, what I can only think to call, 'a qualitative analytic attitude'. (2011: 274)

What Rapley calls 'a qualitative analytic attitude' is, in the final instance, more important than any set of rules. So use the rules I have just offered as a kind of ladder to give you access to the level at which qualitative researchers operate. Once you start to write up your research and become confident in what you are arguing, you can throw the ladder away.

As we have seen, there is no such thing as theory-free research. In the rest of this chapter, I want to explore three ways of exploring qualitative data:

- content analysis
- grounded theory
- narrative analysis.

These are just examples of how to analyse qualitative data. Later on in this book, I will discuss others (**discourse analysis** and conversation analysis in Chapter 9 and **semiotics** in Chapter 10).

I have deliberately not attempted to cover *every* approach as this would have produced a very long, indigestible chapter. At this stage, it is more important that you get some sense of the ways in which we can analyse qualitative data.

3.2 CONTENT ANALYSIS

Content analysis involves establishing categories and then counting the number of instances when those categories are used in a particular item of text, for instance a newspaper report. Because it is a very familiar method in quantitative research, it is important to distinguish how content analysis is used in qualitative studies.

Content analysis is an accepted method of **textual** investigation, particularly in the field of mass communications. In content analysis, researchers establish a set of categories and then count the number of instances that fall into each category. The crucial requirement is that the categories are sufficiently precise to enable different coders to arrive at the same results when the same body of material (e.g. newspaper headlines) is examined (see Berelson, 1952). In this way, content analysis pays particular attention to the issue of the **reliability** of its measures – ensuring that different researchers use them in the same way – and to the **validity** of its findings – through precise counts of word use (see Selltiz et al., 1964: 335–42). Table 3.1 shows the sequence of steps involved in quantitative content analysis.

TABLE 3.1   Doing quantitative content analysis

1   Select particular texts relevant to your research problem
2   Sample texts if there are too many to analyse completely
3   Construct a coding frame (categorisation scheme) that fits both the theoretical considerations and the materials
4   Pilot and revise the coding frame and explicitly define the coding rules
5   Test the reliability of codes, and sensitise coders to ambiguities
6   Code all materials in the sample, and establish the overall reliability of the process
7   Set up a data file for the purpose of statistical analysis
8   Write a codebook including (a) the rationale of the coding frame; (b) the frequency distribution of all codes; and (c) the reliability of the coding process

Source: adapted from Bauer, 2000: 149 and Marvasti, 2004: 94

CASE STUDY
Bilingualism in Florida

Amir Marvasti gives an example of the use of this kind of content analysis in his study of newspaper content (Marvasti, 2004: 91–2). He was interested in South Floridians' attitudes towards bilingualism, which in this case referred to the official recognition and use of the Spanish language in addition to English. In 1980, a conservative political group in Dade County (a large municipality in South Florida with a sizeable Hispanic population) organised a referendum vote to declare the county officially monolingual. This 'English-only' proposal, which was eventually voted into law, was intended to reverse earlier legislation that had declared the area officially bilingual in 1973.

Marvasti's research question was: What is the public's rationale for supporting the anti-bilingual initiative? To collect data for his analysis, he went through the archives of a local newspaper, *The Miami Herald*, in search of editorials, letters to the editor and articles that argued in favour of the proposed law. In doing so, he unearthed the following kind of letter:

> The ordinance is not a hate thing … The American, the English-speaking people would like to have this community back the way it was. They would like to have their language back. (South Florida resident: Marvasti, 2004: 91)

Thirty-five letters to the editor were then analysed in search of themes that Marvasti thought served as rhetorical explanations for supporting anti-bilingualism. These themes are displayed in Table 3.2.

TABLE 3.2 Classification of *Miami Herald* articles, editorials and letters to the editor published in 1980 in support of anti-bilingualism in Dade County, Florida

Theme	Example	Number	Percentage
Patriotism	To be *true* Americans immigrants must speak English	6	17%
Assimilation	America is a "melting pot" and English is the "common element"	11	31%
Polarization	Bilingualism polarizes members of society	5	14%
Voters' rights	Voters have the right to vote on anything they choose including anti-bilingualism	4	11%
Public nuisance	Immigrants who speak Spanish in public places disturb native English speakers	4	11%
Job discrimination	Employers might discriminate against English-only speakers by hiring bilinguals	3	9%
Non-official bilingualism	Bilingualism could exist, but it shouldn't be officially recognized	2	6%
		35	100%

Source: Marvasti, 2004: 92

Marvasti comments that his study:

> serves as an example of a very simple content analysis project aimed at revealing public opinion about a particular issue by summarizing related texts into explanatory categories. Using a small sample, it shows seven ways in which South Floridians accounted for their desire to make the area officially monolingual. (2004: 92)

Marvasti's newspaper study involved simple tabulations of instances of particular categories. Undoubtedly, content analysis has advantages for qualitative researchers. As Marvasti points out, the method offers 'convenience … in simplifying and reducing large amounts of data into organized segments' (2004: 91). But these advantages are gained at a cost. Instead of examining the participants' deployment of categories within their interactions, it uses pre-designed categories prior to data analysis. This seems to tie it back inexorably to the theoretical approach of quantitative research, following the latter's dependence upon operational definitions at the beginning stage of a piece of research (see Chapter 2).

So the theoretical basis of qualitative content analysis is at best unclear and this means that, unfortunately, its conclusions can often seem trite. As Atkinson points out, one of the disadvantages of the coding schemes used in such enterprises as content analysis is that, because they are based upon a given set of categories, they furnish 'a powerful conceptual grid' (Atkinson, 1992: 459) from which it is difficult to escape. While this 'grid' is very helpful in organising the data analysis, it also deflects attention away from uncategorised activities (see my discussion of fieldnotes in Section 5.2.6).

In part, Atkinson's critique vitiates the claims of many quantitative researchers who attempt to produce reliable evidence about a large sample of texts. The meat of the problem with content analysis (and its relatives) is not simply Atkinson's point about overlooked categories but how analysts usually simply trade off their tacit everyday knowledge in coining and applying whatever categories they do use.

EXERCISE 3.2

Look at the letters page of any newspaper (select one topic about which there are at least two letters) or at today's comments on any Internet chatroom. Now:

- Identify the main categories that are used.
- Count the frequency with which these categories are used.
- Consider what conclusions you can draw from your findings.

3.3 GROUNDED THEORY

As we have seen, one of the problems with content analysis is that it appears to fit most neatly into a quantitative version of how to analyse data. By contrast, grounded theory is firmly rooted in an assumption common to qualitative researchers: do not begin with a prior hypothesis but induce your hypotheses from close data analysis. As Charmaz and Bryant put it: 'Grounded theory is a method of qualitative inquiry in which researchers develop inductive theoretical analyses from their collected data and subsequently gather further data to check these analyses. The purpose of grounded theory is theory construction, rather than description or application of existing theories' (2011: 292).

This leads to a number of practical questions:

- In the midst of a field setting, how do you go about codifying your observations?
- How can you develop hypotheses from your observations?
- How can you go on to build a theory?

CASE STUDY

Glaser and Strauss's (1967) famous account of grounded theory sought to provide answers to such questions and, by doing so, has become by far the most influential approach to methodology in qualitative work. The approach emerged after the authors' study of dying on a hospital ward (Glaser and Strauss, 1968). This revealed the different contexts in which terminal patients became aware of their fate. As Glaser and Strauss recognised, such 'awareness contexts' must be a more general phenomenon which extend beyond hospital wards and into a range of settings (from schools, universities to prisons) where people learn what is expected of them.

In the rest of this section, I examine three crucial aspects of grounded theory:

- coding through memo-writing
- theoretical **sampling**
- generating **theories** grounded in your data.

3.3.1 Coding through memo-writing

Doing grounded theory involves close inspection of data leading to memos using tentative codes which may form the basis of a later theory. As Charmaz puts it:

> As grounded theorists, we study our early data and begin to separate, sort, and synthesize them through qualitative coding. Coding means that we attach labels to bits of data to distil it and give us a handle for comparing data. Our nascent ideas point to areas to explore during subsequent data-collecting. (2006: 3)

What are the practicalities of coding?

- You can highlight a word, line, sentence or paragraph and then give it a label.
- Your labels can range from the quite descriptive to the abstract and conceptual.
- You can pick out single 'key words' that do some nice summing up, or can select a few words, phrases or even sentences.
- These labels can emerge from using the specific words that people use, as well as modifying, somewhat, those phrases. This is often referred to as '*in vivo* coding' and is used at any early stage of analysis. (adapted from Rapley, 2011: 282)

The following case study is an example of how Kathy Charmaz started to code an interview with Bessie, a handicapped woman in a wheelchair.

CASE STUDY
Bessie and her Daughter

Bessie sat bent over in her wheelchair at the kitchen table and tells me of her rapid descent into life-threatening illness. When she began her tale of her risky surgery, her middle-aged daughter, Thelma, who had been tidying kitchen counters in the adjoining room, stops and joins us. Bessie tells of her near-death experience when her heart stopped. Thelma listened with rapt attention and awe. Though she had heard the tale many times before, it transformed the moment anew. Bessie told of being in the long dark tunnel, then seeing a beautiful bright light. Bessie believed that the light emanated from the face of God. As Thelma heard her mother's tale again, she gazed upon her with reverence. Afterwards, Thelma emphasized how this event had lifted Bessie's spirits and improved her attitude toward her illness. (Charmaz, 2006: 74)

Kathy reflected upon what she had heard and seen during her interview with Bessie. Afterwards, she wrote a memo in which she picked out the categories used by Bessie and her daughter and started to build a grounded theory from them.

WRITING A MEMO

Suffering as a Moral Status

Suffering is a profoundly <u>moral status</u> as well as a physical experience. Stories of suffering reflect and redefine that moral status.

With suffering come **moral rights** and **entitlements** as well as **moral definitions – when suffering is deemed legitimate.** Thus, the person can make certain moral claims **<u>and</u>** have certain moral judgments conferred upon him or her.

- Deserving
- Dependent
- In need

Suffering can bring a person an elevated moral status. Here, suffering takes on a sacred status. This is a person who has been in sacred places, who has seen known what ordinary people have not. Their stories are greeted with awe and wonder. The self also has elevated status. This person is special; the compelling story casts an aura of compelling qualities on the storyteller. This is a person who has been in sacred places, who has seen and known what ordinary people have not. Their stories are greeted with awe and wonder. (Charmaz, 2006: 73–4)

Writing memos like this involves walking a particular kind of tightrope. At one extreme, you could simply list the categories used by the participant ('*in vivo*' coding). While this might be useful at an early stage, if you do nothing else, then it will start to look like mere content analysis and any link to theory generation will be uncertain.

Tim Rapley offers some wise words of advice about this:

> Despite repeated warnings in the literature to retain 'the participant's voice', when it comes to the words you choose for your labels you really don't have to take this too far. Don't feel that you need to stick to exactly the phrase used, that to modify it, say by changing the tense or taking out an utterance, you are somehow being disrespectful to that person's 'lived experience'. This can lose the point of good analysis and can cause confusion. First, you need to remember that creating a list of key verbatim descriptions is not the end stage of analysis, it is the start. Second, it confuses the analytic phase with the phase of presentation of your argument to others. In notes to yourself and in publications, you will probably end up using verbatim quotes, and so give others access to these 'voices'. (2011: 282)

By contrast, it is tempting to code in terms of technical concepts drawn from your discipline. However, if this is done too early, you may lose touch with the fine detail of what you are hearing and seeing. In this case, you tend to exclude the possibility of being surprised by the complexities of your data and the sophistication of participants' skills in doing whatever they are doing. Again, Rapley puts it nicely:

> grouping relatively large chunks of text together, using large theoretical labels like 'power' or 'identity work' is rarely a good way to start. Such grand, off-the-shelf, labels are clearly the mainstay of a lot of academic writing and discussion, and such issues may be present, shaping, or clearly visible in your data. However, this can easily close down the analysis far too quickly, in the sense that you've already decided that the specific focus is on issues such as this, and that these are the key examples that inform you about its properties or essential make-up. As such it can overly-determine the shape and possibilities of your data. Such broad concepts are actually the end-point of a careful process of analytic work. By starting with and only working with such theory driven macro-labels, you often fail to grasp the specifics of the phenomena. The point is to try to make sense of how, when and why specific processes, practices, and structures happen. (2011: 282).

So did Charmaz introduce the concept of 'moral status' too early into her analysis? Here is her response to Rapley's implied criticism of using labels too eagerly:

> As Rapley might have put it, there are numerous off the shelf analyses of stigma in medical sociology and disabilities studies. Like his example of using 'identity work,' I long thought stigma too general, too easy, to paste the concept of stigma on data and call it an analysis. The memo that I wrote on suffering as a moral status was only partly based on the interview with Bessie. More of my earliest framing of it consisted of an analysis of an interview with Christine Danforth. I didn't pick out categories used by Bessie but did try to interpret and conceptualize what she said. For many years before the specific interview with Christine Danforth, I had many codes about interviewees' descriptions of being devalued and stories and codes about loss. It was apparent that the stories spoke to interviewees' accounts of feeling diminished, but it was while doing line-by-line coding of this particular interview with Christine (I had interviewed her three or four times before) that I came up with the code of 'suffering as a moral status,' and begin to trace out its implications. The interview with Bessie provided more comparative data for the code and for my larger category of a 'hierarchy of moral status in suffering.' (K. Charmaz, personal correspondence)

3.3.2 Theoretical sampling

A defining strategy of grounded theory is theoretical sampling. In quantitative research, we sample in order to achieve numbers that appropriately represent various demographic characteristics of the population (e.g. gender, age, health status). By contrast, in grounded theory, we use theoretical sampling in order to flesh out the properties of a tentative category. As Charmaz and Bryant put it:

> Theoretical sampling involves gathering new data to check hunches and to confirm that the properties of the grounded theorist's theoretical category are filled out. Researchers may also use it to define variation in a studied process or phenomenon or to establish the boundaries of a theoretical category. When these properties are saturated with data, the grounded theorist ends data collection and integrates the analysis. (2011: 292)

Returning to Charmaz's memo about Bess and her daughter, we can ask questions which provide answers about how theoretical sampling might develop Charmaz's categories. For instance:

- If suffering is viewed as a moral status, in what other settings might 'suffering' be displayed? This suggests sampling, say, pain clinics, daytime television talk shows or popular autobiographies.
- How can we use lateral thinking to develop the concepts of 'suffering' and 'morality'? As Charmaz points out (2006: 76), she attempted to move on from her memos describing Bessie's and Thelma's accounts to build a grounded theory based on Erving Goffman's ideas about how we present ourselves and Emile Durkheim's older account of the place of the 'sacred' and 'profane' in the moral order. Using Goffman, we might theoretically sample from among the many situations in which people present versions of who they are, for example job selection interviews. Using Durkheim, we might look at settings where 'sacredness' was made an issue, for example not just religious sermons but also political speeches as politicians define the limits of the acceptable.

3.3.3 Developing grounded theories

Theoretical sampling helps develop grounded theories based on situations and concepts which are progressively widened by:

- including social situations very different from those with which one began
- linking concepts to broader theories.

This reflects two key features of the grounded theory approach:

- the constant comparative method as the analyst seeks out settings which may modify or broaden their initial categories
- a continual movement between data, memos and theory so that data analysis is theoretically based and theory is grounded in data.

As Charmaz and Bryant put it:

> Grounded theorists engage in data collection and analysis simultaneously in an iterative process that uses comparative methods. They compare data with data, data with codes, codes with codes, codes with tentative categories, and categories with categories. This method fosters analyzing actions and processes rather than themes and topics. Grounded theorists code their data for actions and study how these actions might contribute to fundamental processes occurring in the research site or in the research participants' lives. Through comparing data with codes and codes with codes, grounded theorists can decide which codes to treat and test as tentative theoretical categories. (2011: 292)

The constant movement between data, coding and theory can be quite daunting to the apprentice researcher. The simplified model in Table 3.3 breaks down the process into a number of easy-to-understand steps.

TABLE 3.3   The stages of building grounded theory

1   *Initial coding and memo writing* (line-by-line coding, compare new codes with old, evaluate, alter, adjust, write notes)
2   *Focused coding and memo writing* (select and then code key issues, keep comparing, write notes to refine ideas)
3   *Collect new data via theoretical sampling* (strategically sample to further develop categories and their properties)
4   *Continue to code, memo and theoretical sampling* (develop and refine categories until no new issues emerge)
5   *Sort and integrate memos* (refine links between categories, develop concepts, write a initial draft of a theory) (Rapley, 2011: 274–5)

How does this back and forth movement between data and theory ever end? When should you stop gathering data or developing theories from it? The answer to these questions is suggested by the grounded theory concept of **theoretical saturation**. When fresh data or new settings no longer produce new insights, your research circle is finally closed. As Charmaz puts it:

> Categories are saturated when gathering fresh data no longer sparks fresh theoretical insights, nor reveals new properties of your core theoretical categories. (2006: 113)

As we have seen, Glaser and Strauss use their research on death and dying as an example. They show how they developed the category of 'awareness contexts' to refer to the kinds of situations in which people were informed of their likely fate. They call this a grounded **substantive theory**. The category was then saturated and finally related to non-medical settings where people learn about how others define them (e.g. schools). This is now called a grounded **formal theory**.

TIP

Theoretical Saturation

Boredom can be your friend ... you are seeing the same issues again and again and certain labels seem to be emerging as dominant. Discovering repetition can be a good thing. Qualitative research is in part about finding and describing patterns and structures, observing routines. When you've seen the same thing, again and again, you may be onto something. In the early stages of analysis, seeing repetition can be useful. However, in these early stages, it can also mean that your labels are just too large, that you are not thinking with your data at an adequate level of detail. In the later stages, when you're trying to verify your ideas, being bored can be quite useful as it may signify that you've potentially hit gold. (Rapley, 2011: 284–5)

3.3.4 Summary

A simplified model of the grounded theory approach is set out in Table 3.4.

TABLE 3.4   Grounded theory models

1   Try to generate theories through data rather than through prior hypotheses
2   Instead of identifying a single site at the outset, use a process of 'theoretical sampling' of successive sites and sources, selected to test or to refine new ideas as they emerge from the data (as in the refocusing of my hospital research from a single clinic to a comparison of private and NHS clinics, see Section 5.3)
3   Start by coding data line by line to show action and process
4   Raise significant codes into analytic categories for purposes of comparison
5   Check and fill out categories through theoretical sampling and integrate categories into a theoretical framework
6   Stop data collection when categories reach 'theoretical saturation', for example when a 'core category' emerges around which the researcher can integrate the analysis
7   Develop these categories into more general analytic frameworks with relevance outside the setting ('formal theories')

Source: adapted from Strauss and Corbin, 1990: 61, 96, 116; Dey, 2004: 80–1; Charmaz and Mitchell, 2001: 162

3.3.5 Conclusion

At its best, grounded theory offers an approximation of the creative activity of theory-building found in good qualitative work, compared with the dire abstracted empiricism present in the most wooden statistical studies. Grounded theory has been criticised for its failure to acknowledge implicit theories which guide work at an early stage. It also is clearer about the generation of theories than about their test. Used unintelligently, it can degenerate into simplistic interview research based on a fairly empty building of categories (aided by some computer programs) or into a mere smokescreen used to legitimise purely empiricist research (see Bryman, 1988: 83–7; Silverman, 2010: 297–302).

One way to save 'grounded theory' from being a trite and mistaken technique is to treat it as a way of building theories from a particular **model** of social reality. As Charmaz (2006) has pointed out, a **constructionist** will use grounded theory in a very different way to those ethnographers who believe that their categories simply reproduce nature. In Charmaz's terms: a 'constructivist would emphasize eliciting the participant's definitions of terms, situations, and events and try to tap his or her assumptions, implicit meanings, and tacit rules. An objectivist would be concerned with obtaining information about chronology, events, settings, and behaviors' (2006: 32).

While Charmaz's point about how models shape analysis is welcome, her version of constructionism focuses only on people's *perceptions* of reality. This suits her emphasis on analysing interview data which, as she comments, fit 'grounded theory methods particularly well' (2006: 28). Whether grounded theory can adequately cope with the analysis of **naturally occurring data** remains unclear (for a recent exception based on a study of children's use of school rules, see Thornberg, 2008). A useful start would be to abandon Charmaz's assumption about which topics fit within the 'objectivist' realm and allow constructionists to study what she calls 'chronology, events, settings and behaviour' (see Gubrium, 2010).

LINKS

www.groundedtheory.com/

http://sbs.ucsf.edu/medsoc/anselmstrauss

EXERCISE 3.3

This is part of the life story of a Finnish man attending an alcohol clinic:

When I was a child, the discipline was very strict. I still remember when my younger brother broke a sugar cup and I was spanked. When my father died, my mother remarried. The new husband did not accept my youngest brother. When I was in the army, my wife was unfaithful to me. After leaving the army, I didn't come home for two days. I started to drink. And I began to use other women sexually. I drank and I brawled, because I was pissed off and because her treacherousness was in my mind.

When I came to the alcohol clinic, it made me think. I abstained for a year. There was some progress but also bad times. I grew up somewhat. When the therapist changed, I was pissed off and gave it all up.

Source: adapted from Alasuutari, 1990

Following what you have read about grounded theory:

- Code the terms which this person tells his story.
- Try to turn your codes into categories.
- What other situations might you sample in order to build a grounded theory (about what?)?

3.4 NARRATIVE ANALYSIS

We have just seen how Kathy Charmaz sought to develop a theory by beginning from the way Bess, a disabled woman, described her situation. Bess's account was in the form of a story. NA offers a way to describe the structures of stories. Like grounded theory, many of these stories are elicited by interviews (see my discussion below of Catherine Riessman's demonstration of how stories work).

For narrative analysis (NA), Charmaz's version of grounded theory analysis of interview data is deficient in three ways:

1 Although Charmaz acknowledges the importance of pauses and overlaps in the interview, her analysis pays little attention either to such features of talk or to how interviewees' comments are tied to the utterances of the interviewer.
2 What interviewees say tends to be treated as offering a more or less transparent picture of their internal meanings. This ignores the way in which talk performs a range of *actions* which can be comprehended without reference to speakers' inner states [see Chapter 9].
3 In her pursuit of categories which can build formal theories, Charmaz may lose some of the fine details of particular cases. If GT [Grounded Theory] is category-based, NA is case-based. (Riessman, 2009: 391–2)

If you think about it, however, we do not necessarily need to interview people in order to discover stories. Thomas and Znaniecki's (1927 [1918–20]) study of the immigration experience of Polish Americans in Chicago, titled *The Polish Peasant in Europe and America*, is largely based on letters that the authors collected from Polish family members written to each other between Europe and America.

The authors show how the letter writers' identities are displayed as they reflect on who they were in Europe and what they have become in the New World. Like Charmaz, this kind of NA uses a constructionist approach to demonstrate how we actively construct a version of who we are.

The Polish Peasant was based on letters. Around the same time, V.I. Propp was using published stories, another kind of naturally occurring document, to show how we can analyse the structure of folktales.

Propp argues that the fairy tale establishes a narrative form which is central to all story-telling. The fairy tale is structured not by the nature of the characters that appear in it, but by the function they play in the plot. Despite its great detail and many characters, Propp suggests that 'the number of functions is extremely small' (1968: 20). This allows him to attend to a structuralist distinction between appearances (massive detail and complexity) and reality (a simple underlying structure repeated in different ways).

Propp suggests that fairy tales in many cultures share similar themes, for example 'a dragon kidnaps the king's daughter'. These themes can be broken into four elements, each of which can be replaced without altering the basic structure of the story. This is because each element has a certain function. This is shown in Table 3.5.

TABLE 3.5   'A dragon kidnaps the king's daughter'

Element	Function	Replacement
Dragon	Evil force	Witch
King	Ruler	Chief
Daughter	Loved one	Wife
Kidnap	Disappearance	Vanish

Source: adapted from Culler, 1976: 207–8

Following this example, we could rewrite 'A dragon kidnaps the king's daughter' as 'A witch makes the chief's wife vanish', while retaining the same function of each element. Thus a function can be taken by many different roles. This is because the function of a role arises in its significance for the structure of the tale as a whole.

Using a group of 100 tales, Propp isolates 31 'functions' (actions like 'prohibition', 'violation', or, as we have seen above, 'disappearance'). These functions are played out in seven 'spheres of action': the villain, the provider, the helper, the princess and her father, the despatcher, the hero and the false hero.

Functions and 'spheres of action' constitute an ordered set. Their presence or absence in any particular tale allows their plots to be classified. Thus plots take four forms:

1 Development through struggle and victory
2 Development through the accomplishment of a difficult task
3 Development through both 1 and 2
4 Development through neither.

Thus, although any one character may be involved in any sphere of action, and several characters may be involved in the same sphere, we are dealing with a finite sequence:

> the important thing is to notice the number of spheres of action occurring in the fairytale is infinite: we are dealing with discernible and repeated structures. (Hawkes, 1977: 69)

Writing in 1966, Greimas agrees with Propp about the need to locate narrative form in a finite number of elements disposed in a finite number of ways. However, he modifies Propp's list of each elements (Greimas, 1966). This is set out below.

1 Propp's list of seven spheres of action can be reduced into three sets of structural relations: subject versus object (this assumes 'hero' and 'princess' or 'sought-for person'); sender versus receiver (includes 'father' and 'dispatcher'); And helper versus opponent (includes 'donor', 'helper' and 'villain'). This reveals the simple structure of many love stories, that is involving relations between both subject and objects and receivers and senders.
2 Propp's 31 functions may be considerably reduced if one examines how they combine together. For instance, although Propp separates 'prohibition' and 'violation', Greimas shows that a 'violation' presumes a 'prohibition'. Hence they may be combined in one function: 'prohibition versus violation'. Hawkes points out that this allows Greimas to isolate several distinctive structures of the folk narrative. These include:

- contractual structures (relating to establishing and breaking contracts)
- performative structures (involving trials and struggles)
- disjunctive structures (involving movement, leaving, arriving, etc.).

EXERCISE 3.4

Return to the interview with the Finnish man in Exercise 3.2.

- Using what you have read about Propp and Greimas, identify the following elements in this story:

  a Functions (e.g. 'prohibition' or 'violation')
  b Spheres of action (e.g. the villain, the provider, the helper, the princess and her father, the dispatcher, the hero and the false hero).

c Structures (e.g. subject versus object (this includes 'hero' and 'princess' or 'sought-for person'); sender versus receiver (includes 'father' and 'dispatcher'); and helper versus opponent (includes 'donor', 'helper' and 'villain').

- What can be said about the sequence of actions reported?
- Having done this analysis, what features would you look for in other life stories?

This summarised presentation of the work of Propp and Greimas has underlined two useful arguments. First, the structuralist method reminds us that 'meaning never resides in a single term' (Culler, 1976) and consequently that understanding the articulation of elements is our primary task. Second, more specifically, it shows some aspects of how narrative structure works.

When one reflects how much of qualitative data (interviews, documents, conversations) takes a narrative form, as indeed do research reports themselves, then the analysis of the fairy tale stops to look like an odd literary pursuit.

Catherine Riessman further develops the approach by analysing stories not only for the way plots depict social life, but for how distinctive themes and the internal shape of accounts construct experience. Her book *Divorce Talk* (1990) shows how 'women and men make sense of personal relationships', in this case divorce, through story-telling. As the back cover of the book points out:

To explain divorce, women and men construct gendered visions of what marriage should provide, and at the same time they mourn gender divisions and blame their divorces on them. Riessman examines the stories people tell about their marriages – the protagonists, inciting conditions, and culminating events – and how these narrative structures provide ways to persuade both teller and listener that divorce was justified.

As Gubrium and Holstein note:

the reference to 'narrative structures' echoes Propp's pioneering functional analysis of Russian folk tales … Whether it is the function of a witch or a dragon, the true-to-life representation of a social world, or the construction of a form of experience by those differentially positioned in it, the internal features of stories have generalizable characteristics that move us beyond the idiosyncrasies of individual accounts. Fairy tales and reports of neighborhood experience have discernable narrative contours, in other words, suggesting that narrativity can be examined on its own terms for the manner it shapes what is known about its subject matter. (2008: 245).

The following case study from a medical encounter demonstrates the kind of features which Riessman's focus on narrative can reveal. However, it should be emphasised that this excerpt is not from Riessman's own data, but from a corpus of medical interviews collected and analysed by Clark and Mishler (1992).

CASE STUDY
Using Narrative Analysis

A middle-aged African-American man with a seizure disorder comes to a scheduled appointment with a primary care physician, a third year male resident in an outpatient clinic of a large public teaching hospital in the northeastern US. In the conversation the patient and doctor each try to make coherent sense of a recent seizure. The physician's pause during his opening question ("Okay so you said you ha: d a-seizure.......yesterday?", line 1), which he follows with "Hmm" (2), a long pause and then another question: "At work?" (5). This opening invites the story. The patient then begins with an abstract – he is not "really worried" because it is another instance of "gettin upset and aggravated" (9–10) – a precipitant apparently leading to seizures that the parties share. The patient then develops a detailed account of a challenging brake job on an Audi that required several days to complete – "you get right up on the caliper." (21–2) He hit his eye on the caliper, got a black eye and headache, his boss failed to secure the necessary parts and the next day he had to move onto a second car. The repeated frustrations ("It never took me that long before to finish up a brake job", 32–3) led to aggravation to the point of having a seizure (Riessman, 2011: 318–18).

1R: Okay so you said you ha: d a-seizure yesterday?
2[pause]
3P: Uh u yesterday yesterday about
4 about eleven o'clock yeah
5R: Hmm. . At work?
6P: (h)um hum
7R: Okay, uh
8 [pause]
9P: Well I'm not really worried itz same thing you told me not gettin
10ya-know not upset and aggravated and . I couldn't have-ta uhm my
11[pause]
12?: hh.hh
13boss give me a car Tuesday right? . . . . and I workin-on it was an
14Audi I never did brakes on an Audi before, ya-know front wheel drive?
15[pause]
16/?: hh.hh
17R: Yeah
18P: And it was a problem, ya-know and I was down all day long you know
19w – back like this-here. Like the car's on a lift,
20R: Yeah
21P: But it's two bolts ya-know ya just can't get to-em unless you get right up

(Continued)

(Continued)

22on the caliper and ah twis- jus can twist a little bit with a
23screwdriver. And I was going like (gangbust) when (it) ya see I got a
24black e(h)ye .hhuh
25R: (O-)Oh from the "seizure
26P: No. From the caliper. One of em fell, to the eye
27?: Oh I see
28[pause]
29P: And it hit me there so Tuesday night and I had this terrible
30headache and all. So I slept with a ya-know with a ice pack
31over-it all night to keep- tryin to keep it from swelling and all.
32. . And then I went back in yesterday to try to finish it up. It
33never took me that long before to finish up a brake job
34R: .hhhh.
35P: And my boss hadn't got all the parts for it so I start working
36on another car-ya-know? That's when I ended up having the seizure.
37R: Okay uhm .hh so: did your boss or someone else see the seizure happen

Source: Clark and Mishler, 1992: 349, as cited by Riessman, 2011 (I have simplified the transcription and added line numbers)

Here are Riessman's observations on how this narrative is constructed between the doctor and patient:

- The story is invited and interactionally built, becoming a situated interactional accomplishment. The physician's long pauses cede the floor to the patient, creating the space to narrate. The patient then takes up the active role, developing a plot sequence embedded in his life world as an auto mechanic. (Riessman, 2011: 317)
- The conversation allows the patient [to] make an identity claim, developing the theme of his personal responsibility. More than merely a report of a seizure, the patient can position himself in a story as the diligent and responsible worker who was frustrated in his attempt to meet a challenge at work. His experience becomes the center of attention; the story functions, as personal stories often do, to make an explanatory argument and presentation of 'self.' He can construct a positive identity in the face of what might have been a stigmatizing illness episode on the job. He can ward off the stigma of epilepsy and any possible blame for precipitating the seizure by his behavior.
- For the physician, the story provides something different: the historically connected facts needed to evaluate a clinical problem in a way that takes account of the life world of the patient.
- Shaped by the constraints of the medical setting, the story is recipient-designed; it provides the detail and specificity needed to make clinical sense of a problem. (Riessman, 2011: 318)

This case study shows how, in answering someone's questions about something that happened to us, we construct a version of ourselves full of moral claims. Moreover, such questions are always situated in some social context – from everyday conversation to some institutional setting (here a doctor–patient interview).

There appear to be similarities with Charmaz's account of Bessie and her daughter. Both are concerned with how people present their identities and both use a constructionist model.

Yet Riessman claims that there are differences between narrative analysis (NA) and constructionist grounded theory (GT). In particular:

- GT is primarily concerned with perception and focuses on how 'meaning' is constructed in talk. By contrast, NA is concerned with action and examines the activities that are performed when people talk with one another.
- GT wants to move beyond particular cases to make broader generalisations about social processes. By contrast, NA seeks to preserve and interrogate particular instances. In GT terms, NA does not aim to construct formal theories which move beyond particular cases. As Charmaz puts it: 'narrative analyses emphasize stories and their structure, grounded theory emphasizes processes and actions. Grounded theorists use stories in service of analyzing processes' (C. Riessman, personal correspondence).
- NA is more concerned than GT with the local context of a narrative. So, in the case study just cited, it is important to understand the way in which the patient and doctor shape their remarks to the context of a medical setting.
- In research interviews all the speakers (participant, listener/questioner) shape the interaction to suit the setting and their perceptions of the evolving research relationship.
- NA examines how stories make use of cultural discourses and accounting practices. This is illustrated in the following case study.

CASE STUDY
A Turn to Narrative Practice

As plentiful and detailed as stories might be, they are always more than accounts; they are accounts that have been conveyed and stand to be reconveyed in concrete circumstances, Stories are constructed with an audience in view and, for that reason, are eventful. Their eventfulness draws attention to the actual, not just the reported, sites of their social lives .... Organizational researchers, from those in management studies to those in organizational sociology, have seen the analytic importance of turning narrative inquiry to the sites of narrative practice (Boje, 1991; Czarniawska, 1997; Gabriel, 2000). Sites of narrative practice are not confined to the formally established, like schools and businesses, but now extend to sites in transition or under construction, such as storytelling in times of social crises or in political protests ... In fact, it's the business of some organizations to offer guidelines, if not directives, for fashioning one's story in a particular way. The question of narrative ownership is pertinent here and is hardly just a matter of personal property. In practice, ownership extends to the myriad and diverse sources of narrative construction. In a complex world of stories, it is useful to imagine that the little stories we hear day-in and day-out relate to bigger stories, some of which may be *the* big story of the experience in view, bringing on board issues of discourse, power, influence, and globalization. (Gubrium, 2010: 390–1)

3.4.1 Summary

I conclude my discussion of NA by summarising some key questions it suggests we ask about **narratives**:

- In what kind of a story does a narrator place herself?
- How does she position herself to the audience, and vice versa?
- How does she position characters in relation to one another, and in relation to herself?
- How does she position herself to herself, that is, make identity claims? (Bamberg, 1997, quoted by Riessman, 2011)

Riessman offers a number of suggestions about how we should answer these questions and I have set these out in Table 3.6.

TABLE 3.6   Working with narrative analysis

- adopt a constructionist framework and be precise in your use of an appropriate narrative vocabulary
- in analyzing particular narrative segments, think about form and function – the way a segment of data is organized and why
- don't neglect the local context in your analysis, including the questioner/listener, setting, and position of an utterance in the broader stream of the conversation

Source: adapted from Riessman, 2011: 328–9

TIP

If you want to do NA, the following questions are useful to ask (see Cortazzi, 2001, and also Riessman, 1993):

- What is the content of the story you are examining?
- Who are the principal agents?
- How is the story told (structure and sequence)?
- What purposes does the story serve (functions)?
- In what place or setting is the story told (context)?
- Does the story have a clear culmination with a moral, as in a fairy tale, or does it follow a different pattern (issues of genre)?

LINK

Summary and review of Catherine Kohler Riessman (2008) *Narrative Methods for the Human Sciences*, R. Lyle Duque (2010), 'Forum: Qualitative Social Research': www.qualitative-research.net/index.php/fqs/article/view/1418

EXERCISE 3.5

Return again to the interview with the Finnish man in Exercise 3.2 and answer these questions:

- In what kind of a story does the narrator place himself?
- How does he position himself to the audience, and vice versa?
- How does he position characters in relation to one another, and in relation to himself?
- How does he position himself to himself, that is, make identity claims? (Bamberg, 1997, quoted by Riessman, 2011)

3.5 CONCLUSION

I appreciate that my presentation of three different ways of doing data analysis may have been difficult to digest if you are new to the field. But do not worry if you did not follow every nuance of each approach. You will only fully understand these three approaches (and the others which follow in later chapters) when you try them out yourselves on some data.

My main concern has been to give you a taste of how we can rigorously analyse data. And, as I tried to show at the start of this chapter, *all* effective ways of working have much in common.

Tim Rapley has offered some wise advice about what this involves and his suggestions are reproduced in Table 3.7.

TABLE 3.7   Good practice in qualitative data analysis

- *Always start by engaging in some kind of close, detailed, reading of a sample/section/bit of your archive of data:*

  ○ Close, detailed, reading means looking for key, essential, striking, odd, interesting things people or texts say or do as well as repetition
  ○ You should make notes, jottings, markings etcetera, either on the pages or somewhere else
  ○ Always distinguish participants' categories [emic] from your own categories [etic]

- *Always read and systematically label your archive of data:*

  ○ Label key, essential, striking, odd, interesting things
  ○ Label similar items with the same label
  ○ These labels can be drawn from ideas emerging from your close, detailed, reading of your data archive, as well as from your prior reading of empirical and theoretical works
  ○ With each new application of a label, review your prior labelling practices and see if what you want to label fits what has gone before. If yes, use that label. If no, create a new one. If it fits somewhat, you may want to modify your understanding of that label to include this

(Continued)

TABLE 3.7   (Continued)

- *Always reflect on why you've done what you've done:*

  o Come up with a document that lists your labels. It might be useful to give some key examples, to write a sentence or two that explains what you are try to get at, what sort of things should go together under specific labels

- *Always review and refine your labels and labelling practices:*

  o For each label, collect together all the data you've given that label to. Ask yourself whether the data and ideas collected under this label is coherent, ask yourself what are the key properties and dimensions of all the data collected under that label
  o Try to combine your initial labels, look for links between them, look for repetitions, exceptions and try to reduce them to key ones. This will often mean shifting from more verbatim, descriptive, labels to more conceptual, abstract and analytic labels
  o Keep evaluating, adjusting, altering and modifying your labels and labelling practices
  o Go back over what you've already done and re-label it with your new schema or ideas

- *Always focus on what you feel are the key labels and the relationship between them:*

  o Make some judgments about what you feel are the central labels and focus on them
  o Try to look for links, patterns, associations, arrangements, relationships, sequences etcetera

Source: adapted from Rapley, 2011: 277–8

One final word: just as you will only really understand any approach by trying it out yourself, so you will only start to do qualitative analysis when you start to write it up in your own words. You may think you have made great mental leaps but data analysis can only take off when you commit yourself to print (see Chapter 12).

> **TIP**
> Qualitative data analysis can seem very complex. Here are some ideas which simplify matters:
>
> - The constant comparative method is a feature of all good research and comparison can be made between the elements in a single case. Therefore, you do not necessarily need data from more than one setting
> - Constructionist qualitative researchers reject the assumption that there is some total picture of any phenomenon which can be obtained by multiple data sets and multiple methods. Since, according to this view, there are only **hyphenated phenomena,** just make what you can of what you have.
> - It follows that the navigational logic of **triangulation** (where you compare different readings to get at the truth) does not apply. Rather than, say, comparing interviewees' responses with their actions, look at one aspect or the other and marvel at what they achieve.

KEY POINTS

- Get down to analysis as early as possible and avoid 'busy' work.
- Try out different theoretical approaches; see what works for you (and for your data).
- The theoretical basis of qualitative content analysis is at best unclear and this means that, unfortunately, its conclusions can often seem trite.
- Grounded theory involves coding through memo-writing, theoretical sampling and generating theories grounded in your data,
- Narrative analysis usually adopts a constructionist framework and uses an appropriate narrative vocabulary; consider the way a segment of data is organised (and why) and examine the local context in which the data arise.

STUDY QUESTIONS

1 Why is it usually important to avoid formulating an early hypothesis?
2 What considerations arise in deciding how much data to transcribe before you begin analysis?
3 What is meant by 'telling examples' and why should you generally avoid them in writing up your research?
4 What is meant by 'content analysis'? What are its advantages and limitations?
5 What is meant by 'grounded theory'? What are its advantages and limitations?
6 What is meant by 'narrative analysis'? What are its advantages and limitations?
7 What does Rapley mean by 'close, detailed reading' of data?

RECOMMENDED READING

This chapter draws heavily on the chapters by Kathy Charmaz (on grounded theory), Catherine Riessman (on narrative analysis) and Tim Rapley (on doing qualitative data analysis) in my edited collection *Qualitative Research* (Third Edition, 2011). I strongly recommend reading these chapters. You might also look at Charmaz's *Constructing Grounded Theory* (2006) and Riessman's *Narrative Methods for the Human Sciences* (2008). Gubrium and Holstein's *Analyzing Narrative Reality* (2009) offers an approach to analysing actively constructed narratives, including

(Continued)

(Continued)

those produced by interviewing. Gubrium's 'A turn to narrative practice' (2010) is a marvellous brief introduction to how narrative analysis can go beyond the contents of stories to analyse the resources and contexts upon which story-tellers draw.

I discuss qualitative analysis for PhD students in my book *Doing Qualitative Research* (2010). I consider further the importance of looking at sequences in data in my *A Very Short, Fairly Interesting, Reasonably Cheap Book about Qualitative Research* (2007).

4

Research Ethics

CHAPTER OBJECTIVES

By the end of this chapter, you will be able to:

- understand why ethics matter
- recognise the pitfalls that confront the ethical researcher
- understand key guidelines to ethical practice
- recognise the limits of these guidelines in the varying contexts of social research.

Beginners as well as some experienced researchers sometimes view getting ethical approval as just another box that has to be ticked. For them, the real business of social research is research design and data analysis. This chapter will try to show you why such a view is mistaken.

If we ignore ethical issues or treat them simply as a matter of routine form-filling, we start to go down a slippery slope where 'doing a good job' is all that matters. For instance, we should remember that this was the defence of the doctors who conducted horrific 'experiments' in the Nazi concentration camps. To think of ourselves as mere 'technicians' disconnects us from two sets of crucial questions:

- Why are we researching this topic? Will our findings contribute in some way to what we value as the common good (even if this is 'basic research' and that good is, at the moment, unclear)? Or are we just interested in furthering our educational or research career?

- Do we want to help and, at the very least, protect the people we study? Or are we using them simply as research fodder?

In a lecture delivered in the early years of the twentieth century, the German sociologist Max Weber addressed both sets of questions. Weber (1946) pointed out that all research is influenced to some extent by the values of the researcher. Only through those values do certain problems get identified and studied in particular ways. Even the commitment to scientific (or rigorous) method is itself, as Weber emphasises, a value. Finally, the conclusions and implications to be drawn from a study are, Weber stresses, largely grounded in the moral and political beliefs of the researcher.

From an ethical point of view, Weber was fortunate in that much of his empirical research was based on documents and texts that were already in the public sphere. In many other kinds of social science research, ethical issues are much more to the fore. When you are studying people's behaviour or asking them questions, not only the values of the researcher but also the researcher's responsibilities to those studied have to be faced. Ryen shows how complex these responsibilities can be:

> At times we come across delicate situations that involve hidden or problematic information that someone may be harmed or put at risk (like crimes being planned), or that certain findings may be discomforting (like job evaluations or health information) or even dangerous to some subjects (like some kinds of illegal activities). These issues call for decisions on whether we should do such projects (alone or with someone) or not at all, when to decide there are data we do not want to get (is it ok just to turn off the tape recorder, to get the conversation on to another track or do we need more explicit strategies?) or if we simply need to shut down the whole project. (2011: 420)

The possible decisions that Anne Ryen mentions derive from a recognition that, when we involve people in our research, we enter a *relationship* with them. As Marvasti has noted:

> The ethics of social research have to do with the nature of the researcher's responsibilities in this relationship, or the things that should or should not be done regarding the people being observed and written about. This is not significantly different from what we do in other relationships. We try to be polite, treat people with respect, and don't do or say anything that will harm them. Good manners are a good beginning, but actual research scenarios may require guidelines that go beyond common courtesy. (2004: 133)

The following case study, drawn from Amir Marvasti's own PhD research, serves to give us an initial example of how ethical issues can confront you in fieldwork.

CASE STUDY
Ethics in Fieldwork

My own fieldwork at a homeless shelter presented a number of ethical dilemmas. Gregory was a middle-aged white man who lived on the streets near the shelter. Gregory was a talented poet and author who suffered from alcoholism. As we became more familiar with each other, he began asking me to buy him beer. So as a matter of courtesy, from time to time I paid for his bar tab. Unfortunately, Gregory's drinking became worse and his requests for money to support his habit became more frequent and direct. He started leaving messages on my home answering machine begging me to meet him at a bar to pay his tab. I finally decided that it was unethical for me to support his addiction and stopped helping him. The next phone call I received from Gregory was from a local jail where he was being held for shoplifting a bottle of beer from a convenience store. He wanted me to make arrangements for his legal defence. I went to visit Gregory at the jail and told him there was very little I could do for him. Several weeks later he was released and subsequently left for New York City. I did not hear from him again. (Marvasti, 2004: 132–3)

EXERCISE 4.1

Marvasti comments about the example of his dealings with Gregory: 'Thinking about these stories may cause you to wonder if you would have handled these situations differently. Perhaps I was too involved with Gregory and should have severed my ties with him much earlier' (2004: 133).

- Do you agree with Marvasti's self-criticism?
- Was the only choice, as Marvasti suggests, to break off contact earlier?

This chapter is organised into three interlinked sections which discuss:

- ethical pitfalls in qualitative research
- ethical safeguards
- ethical complications which show that guidelines always need to be interpreted within particular contexts.

4.1 ETHICAL PITFALLS

In this section, I will review a number of ethical pitfalls that are a particular feature of qualitative research:

- exploitation
- deception
- researching vulnerable people
- revealing people's identities when they might not want it or not revealing people's identities when they expect it
- fraternising with groups we dislike
- participating in dubious bargains.

I will consider each issue in turn, illustrating my argument with case studies.

4.1.1 Exploitative social research

It is really only in the past two decades that researchers have seriously faced up to the ethical dimensions of their research. As Marvasti has noted, until the 1970s, highly unethical social and medical studies were common. Marvasti gives the frightening example set out in the case study below.

CASE STUDY
Not Treating Syphilis

In what Marvasti refers to as 'one of the most troubling examples of unscrupulous research', a group of 399 African American men afflicted with syphilis unknowingly became participants in a medical experiment:

From the 1930s to 1970s, the physicians assigned to these men deliberately did not treat them for their ailment, even after penicillin was developed and could have been used as a cure. Instead, the patients were secretly experimented on to examine the effects of untreated syphilis. By the time this US Public Health Service study was exposed and subsequently terminated, many of the patients whose condition had gone untreated for years had either died horribly or become more severely ill. (Marvasti, 2004: 135)

Another US study has, somewhat unfairly, achieved even more notoriety than this case. In the 1960s, Milgram (1963) conducted a laboratory experiment using university students. The students were divided into interviewers and interviewees. The interviewers were told that it was important that people answered their questions correctly. When an interviewee failed in his performance, the supervisor was instructed to press a switch which he was told would administer a slight electric shock to the under-performing interviewee. Milgram reported that interviewers obeyed this instruction and were prepared to increase the shock up to quite high levels.

In fact, the student interviewers had been deceived. The interviewees were not students but Milgram's confederates. Nor were they actually exposed to electric shocks (they just pretended to be in pain when appropriate).

Although Milgram's study appears to exploit the student interviewers, it reveals an important point. Like the Nazi concentration camp guards, ordinary people may be prepared to obey horrific orders if the order appears to emanate from a 'legitimate' source (in this case, a university professor). Similarly, in 1971 a planned two-week investigation into the psychology of prison life had to be ended prematurely after only six days because of what the situation was doing to the college students who participated. In only a few days, the guards became sadistic and the prisoners became depressed and showed signs of extreme stress.

LINK
For details of this study, go to:
www.prisonexp.org/

4.1.2 Deception

Deception in research is most likely to be a problem when it causes the subjects to unknowingly expose themselves to harm. A key problem with Milgram's study is that subjects were essentially lied to about a situation that could have been emotionally damaging to them (A. Marvasti, personal correspondence).

Covert observation, where the observer does not inform subjects about the study, can lead to severe ethical problems about the lack of consent that such people have given to being observed. It can also lead to physical danger to the researcher. For example, Fielding (1982) obtained permission to research a far Right British political party but still felt it necessary to supplement official access with covert observation. In this new situation, he put himself at some potential risk as well as creating ethical dilemmas relating to how much he revealed to his subjects and to outside authorities.

One famous observational study of gay men, discussed by Amir Marvasti, involved a clear invasion of personal privacy. It is described in the case study below.

CASE STUDY
Tearoom Trade

Laud Humphreys' book *Tearoom Trade* (1970) reports research on anonymous homosexual encounters in semi-public places. After positioning himself in a restroom in a city park, Humphreys gained the trust of the men who frequented it by acting as a lookout for them while they engaged in sexual activities. Humphreys secretly recorded their license plate numbers, and with the help of the police discovered who they were and where they lived. Months later, he visited the men in their homes disguised as a survey researcher. He gathered additional information about these men and their families and subsequently published his research in a book that was widely praised before questions were raised about its ethics.

Humphreys was interested in the background of men who had sex with other men in public restrooms. He found that many of the men in his study were married and of middle class background. However, this finding was at the cost of deception and achieved through the covert invasion of the subjects' privacy. (Discussed by Marvasti, 2004: 135)

However, we should not assume that 'covert' access always involves possible offence. For instance, on a course I used to teach, students were asked to engage in a small exercise where they observed people exchanging glances in an everyday setting (see Sacks, 1992, I: 81–94). Providing the students were reasonably sensitive about this and refrained from staring at others, I did not envisage any problems arising.

4.1.3 Researching vulnerable groups

A more obvious case of exploitation can arise when we carry out studies of vulnerable people ('underdogs'). Despite the physical and ethical dangers that may arise in studying groups who may be defined as on the edge of the law, the researcher must remember that relatively easy access to such groups also suggests their vulnerability (even if they may welcome our interest). The behaviour of 'underdog' groups like these is sometimes open to inspection by closed circuit television (CCTV) and other forms of official surveillance. This is hardly the case with the activities of 'topdogs' (unless, like President Nixon, they are foolish enough to preserve audio recordings of their conversations!). So the ethnographer who studies sub-cultures may unthinkingly be preying upon groups who are least able to protect themselves.

Issues of consent become even more complicated when you want to study vulnerable people such as children or adults with disabilities. A set of complex issues arise:

- How can young children or people with limited mental capacity realistically give informed consent to your research?
- Is it satisfactory for parents, other family members or carers to give consent?

Here is the guidance of a British research council.

RESEARCH ETHICS AND VULNERABLE PEOPLE

In cases where research involves vulnerable groups such as children, older persons or adults with learning difficulties, every effort should be made to secure their informed consent. However, in cases where this is seen as impossible or where the research subjects are considered not competent to give their assent to the research, the issue of honesty and consent may need to be managed via proxies, who should be either those with a duty of care or who can provide disinterested independent approval depending on the individual circumstances. In the case of research on children, one cannot expect parents alone to provide disinterested approval on their children's behalf. In such cases, every effort should be made to deal with consent through dialogue with both children and their parents (or legal equivalent). Again, there may be circumstances where this could jeopardise the research (again in some areas of deviance, such as research into teenage sexuality or teenage pregnancy). In such circumstances, researchers will need to regard the potential risk to the principal subjects of the research as a priority. (Research Ethics Framework (Economic and Social Research Council, July 2005), pp. 23–5)

The ESRC's advice shows how difficult ethical practice can be if one wants to research vulnerable people. For instance, the idea of a 'dialogue with both children and their parents' may be unattainable or even unfair to all parties. The next case study illustrates the complexities of researching vulnerable older people.

CASE STUDY

I welcomed the idea that colleagues should research the old people's home where I do voluntary work. They wanted to video my singing sessions with residents with Alzheimer's disease. However, the ethical issues involved in studying people with dementia are vast and apparently intractable, particularly if you want to use video data. Families, carers and care managers will all have to be consulted. But what happens when the camera accidentally includes a resident or carer for whom you have no permission to record? Moreover, how satisfactory is it to use family permission to record intimate details of somebody's daily life?

4.1.4 Identification of subjects

When we report our observations or interviews, it is common sense to protect the identities of the people we have researched and to ensure that they understand and consent to our research. Such protection is required even when, unlike Laud Humphreys' research, we are not dealing with matters that seem, on the face of things, to be particularly delicate or intimate. The following case study illustrates how upset somebody can be when they read about themselves in a research report.

CASE STUDY
Unmasking Emotions

The ethnographer Sue Estroff received a phone call at 3 a.m. from an irate woman, who had just read what Estroff had written about her many years before. The informant felt 'wounded by the images of herself in the past … exploited … misunderstood … unmasked.' The ethnographer's gift of the book – the final product of intensive fieldwork among a group of chronic mental patients – had opened up unspeakable pain for one informant: she recognized herself and was deeply troubled by the representation. Estroff uses the incident to raise a series of compelling questions about ethnographic authority, voice, and responsibility in field research. She asks: 'Was it possible for this person to consent to a process whose product [ethnography] she could not imagine?'(Estroff, 1995: 98, reported by Riessman, 2004: ms5)

Riessman's report makes it clear that we should never assume that people have understood our research sufficiently in order to give truly *informed* consent to describing their accounts or behaviour in our reports.

However, as always, social context is crucial. Certain people, in particular contexts, may actually want to be identified in your research report and feel let down if their identity is concealed. In my research on HIV-test counselling (Silverman, 1997), several of the counsellors told me that they not only wanted to be identified but expected to be listed as a co-author of some of my publications. Working in a medical setting linked to a university, these people recognised that (certain kinds of) social research could help their careers.

Moreover, this desire to be identified may not be confined to highly educated Western professionals. Ryen notes that in African countries such as Tanzania:

> there is an established and well-accepted procedure that interviewees' names and titles are given in the appendix … To deviate from this procedure may be perceived as either confusing or arrogant. This dilemma partly stems from experiences with donor projects like Western projects in local villages whose aim it is to alleviate poverty by offering grants or loans. To be selected for funding demands that your name is put on a list. (2004: 233)

TIP
You should not make assumptions about what your research subjects expect or want. Moreover, as Ryen's comments suggest, thinking about the social contexts which people inhabit is not only the basis of good ethical practice but also the basis of good research.

4.1.5 Fraternising with groups we dislike

Social research can take you to what appear to be strange places and place you among people whose values clash with yours. For instance, like Fielding (1982), Les Back researched members of an extreme right-wing British political party. As Back asks:

> There has been some concern to connect sociology to the process of empowering research participants but how is this different when you are studying people who use ideologies like racism to empower themselves? Also … what should we do as researchers when we encounter views that are politically and morally offensive? How are our own biographies and social positions implicated in the research act and in the process of understanding and analysis? (2004: 263)

Back gives us a vivid account of interviewing Nick Griffin, the leader of the British National Party, and subsequently attending his trial. Simple acts, such as a handshake or small talk over a meal, become imbued with layers of meaning. Back raises two important questions about interactions with people whose views you may find repellent:

> How are the ethics of investigating racial power implicated in these strange acquaintances – necessitated by the research act itself – and the desire to understand the advocates of intolerance and racism? What issues does this extreme case where one is almost literally researching political opponents raise in relation to wider concern of sociological practice and particular the place from which we make interpretations and strive for understanding? (2004: 263-4)

There are no easy answers to Back's questions. They raise a crucial ethical dilemma: do you salve your conscience by avoiding studying such people or do you enter a potential minefield and try to do the best you can without compromising your beliefs?

Amir Marvasti (personal correspondence) suggests that one reason to fraternise with groups we dislike is to gain intellectual flexibility; simple us–them dichotomies are rarely intellectually fruitful or useful for progressive social change. He notes that research on white identity shows, for example, that many racists see themselves as 'victims' rather than 'aggressors'. We can learn a lot about fighting the social ill of racism by learning from the racists themselves. So 'fraternising with groups we dislike' may be necessary for researchers and social activists.

4.1.6 Participating in dubious bargains

Informed consent should mean that you do not pressure people into agreeing to participate in your study. But what about poor or disadvantaged people who plea to be rewarded for participation? Catherine Riessman points out that it is now common practice in the United States to pay respondents for their time ($25–$50). In one case financial incentives kept rising (beyond $100) until the final respondents in a panel study agreed to participate. This seems like clear coercion (C. Riessman, personal correspondence).

Amir Marvasti gives the example of his research on homelessness where he might give someone living on the streets a few dollars for an interview. He wonders whether this is ethical:

> Many would argue that asking the poor to participate in a study in exchange for money is the moral equivalent of asking a starving person to answer a few questions in exchange for a plate of food. What is the solution? One possibility is to solicit interviews without any rewards. Another approach is to contact their service providers and ask if they know of anyone who is willing to be interviewed for a research project. (2004: 136)

Marvasti's dilemma is common to researchers who work with poor people in the Third World. As Ryen observes: 'I have frequently met expectations that I will reciprocate in one way or another in African settings … These have been of different kinds, from expecting me to cope with local poverty and offering grants, to gift exchanges and sexual offers' (2004: 238).

In the following case study below (from Ryen's Tanzanian data recorded in the aftermath of a research interview), we see Eke making what may turn out to be a sexual approach.

CASE STUDY
Emotions in the Bush

Extract 4.1 [Ryen, 2004: 230]

Eke: What do you do (2.0) I mean (1.0) do you never do anything when out travelling? You're always travelling alone.
Anne: I am here to work.
Eke: Yeah, but you can't be working all the time.
Anne: (laughing) That's true. So, what do you offer?
Eke: What do you want?

This byplay between Eke and Anne shows that establishing 'rapport' with research subjects can leak over into delicate territory. As Ryen comments:

> there is nothing sensational about this extract. The sensation rests with the peculiar situation that the issue of delicate emotions in fieldwork is conspicuous in its absence from methodological textbooks or field reports. Why are these fairly frequent experiences treated as non-data, how do we handle 'field offers', does the effort to get close by building rapport imply that we are cheating, and would it be ethically acceptable (and probably methodologically interesting) to follow up invitations? (2004: 230)

These examples reveal clearly the kind of ethical problems that can confront the social researcher. In the next section, I present some guidelines designed to deal with them. However, as we shall see, since we are dealing with real dilemmas, technical answers (like ethical rules) are unlikely always to provide a clear answer.

4.2 ETHICAL SAFEGUARDS

There are a number of goals which we aim to achieve in ethical research:

- ensuring that people participate voluntarily
- making people's comments and behaviour confidential
- protecting people from harm
- ensuring mutual trust between researcher and people studied.

Two ways of achieving such ethical goals will be noted:

- ethical guidelines
- thoughtful and ethically responsible research practice.

4.2.1 Ethical guidelines

Central to most ethical guidelines is the idea of *informed consent*. A straightforward statement of this idea is provided by Ryen:

> Informed consent ... means that research subjects have the right to know that they are being researched, the right to be informed about the nature of the research and the right to withdraw at any time ... In general, deception is only acceptable if discomfort is believed to vanish by itself or removed by a debriefing process after the study. (2004: 231)

The right to be informed means that potential research subjects should be given a detailed but non-technical account (in a format that they can understand) of the nature and aims of your research. As Ryen remarks, people should be able to withdraw from your research at any time. For instance, in my research on HIV-test counselling, both counsellors and their clients were told that they could ask for the tape recorder to be turned off at any time without offering a reason.

Perhaps informed consent is seen best as a process of negotiation, rather than a one-off action. Some investigators ask again for consent as an interview is ending, others come back to respondents with pieces of text they want to use to see if the excerpt is sufficiently disguised (C. Riessman, personal correspondence).

EXERCISE 4.2

In my research on HIV-test counselling (Silverman, 1997), despite my offer, no counsellors or clients ever asked for the tape recorder to be switched off during their interview.

- Does this mean that my offer to them to switch off was insufficient?
- In what other ways could I offer them a sound ethical basis to participate in my research?

Ethical procedures can be clarified by consulting the ethical guidelines of one's professional association. All such guidelines stress the importance of 'informed consent' where possible (see Punch, 1994: 88–94). The nature of 'informed consent' is set out in Table 4.1.

TABLE 4.1   What is informed consent?

- Giving information about the research which is relevant to subjects' decisions about whether to participate
- Making sure that subjects understand that information (e.g. by providing information sheets written in subjects' language)
- Ensuring that participation is voluntary (e.g. by requiring written consent)
- Where subjects are not competent to agree (e.g. children and even adolescents), obtaining consent by proxy (e.g. from their parents)

Source: adapted from Kent, 1996: 19–20

Kelly and Ali (2004) have suggested that an accessible way to present information is through providing answers to a number of questions that people might ask about your research. These questions are listed in Table 4.2.

TABLE 4.2 Questions for an information sheet

- Why do you think I am suitable to take part in this research?
- How did you get my name or find out that I was suitable for this study?
- Why is this study important?
- How will this study be done?
- What does this study involve?
- Will this study benefit me?
- Are there any risks or hazards involved?
- Will people be able to find out my details because of this study?
- What if I change my mind or don't want to be involved?
- Can I get a summary of the findings of your research?

Source: Kelly and Ali, 2004: 121, and C. Riessman, personal correspondence

The following case study is an example of a typical consent letter, sent to counsellors on a child protection helpline.

CASE STUDY
Sample Permissions Letter

I am writing to ask if you will help me with my research. I am a lecturer in psychology at Loughborough University. I am studying the process of counselling on telephone help lines ...

My aim is to highlight the rich and complex set of discursive and conversational practices that are used by both counsellors and young people. This kind of study has been especially useful in family therapy, social work and relationship counselling, and I have good links with some of the key analysts in this field. The research will not involve extra work for you or your team in the form of questionnaires or interviews [explains the use of tape recorders in the research] ...

The research will be conducted fully within BPS ethical guidelines ... I can (also) offer ... to share my results with you in the form of a feedback report and workshop. (Hepburn and Potter, 2004: 184)

For reasons of space, this permissions letter has been considerably shortened. However, it will give you some idea of the sort of information about your research that busy people will expect.

However, maybe for once, the issue of consent is less complicated than it seems. It is important to recognise that people want information they can understand; they are usually not interested in the often technical and theoretical research questions you want to address.

It is true that researchers who study human subjects ponder over the dilemma of wanting to give full information to the people they study but seeking not to 'contaminate' their research by informing subjects too specifically about the research question to be studied. As Gobo points out:

In some kinds of research (for example with alcoholics, drug addicts, the mentally ill, the handicapped, former prisoners) it is not always possible to tell the subjects why and how they have been selected for interview. How can we say to someone 'you interest me because you're an alcoholic' or 'I want to interview you because you've been in jail'? And if we did say so, would not this induce the person to behave according to the stereotype given to him or her by society?' (2008: 138)

There is a further twist to this problem. If, like Hepburn and Potter, you are recording what people say, *initial* consent may not be enough. In such cases, it often is proper to obtain further consent to how the data may be used, as in the following case study.

CASE STUDY
A Sample Consent Form for Studies of Language Use

As part of this project, we have made a photographic, audio and/or video recording of you ... We would like you to indicate below what uses of these records you are willing to consent to. This is completely up to you. We will only use the records in ways that you agree to. In any use of these records, names will not be identified.

- The records can be studied by the research team for use in the research project.
- The records can be used for scientific publications and/or meetings.
- The written transcript and/or records can be used by other researchers.
- The records can be shown in public presentations to non-scientific groups.
- The records can be used on television or radio.

This form has been adapted from ten Have (1998: Appendix C) and is based on a form developed by Susan Ervin-Tripp, Psychology Department, University of California at Berkeley.

However, as always, ethical guidelines depend on the context. Even informed consent of participants may not be required in every form of research. Marvasti gives the example of a study where you are observing people in public places such as malls or restaurants. As he asks:

Do you need to approach each patron for permission to observe them? The general consensus is that what people do in public places is by definition there for all to observe. The same guideline applies to public statements. If in a published newspaper editorial I refer to my personal experiences, you don't need my permission to use words that are already public domain (obviously, you have to cite the author and the source). What if the interviewee is a child or someone who is mentally incapacitated? In these cases, the recommendation is to gain consent from a parent or a guardian before proceeding with the research. (2004: 136)

Marvasti raises some important issues about when and how consent to research should be obtained. However, it would be wrong to assume that ethical matters are confined to how you deal with research subjects. As the next section will show, it is wise to think about ethical issues at all stages of a research study.

4.2.2 Ethically responsible research practice

In this section, I consider three different stages of research:

- framing your research topic
- analysing data
- when the study is completed.

Framing your research topic

Research topics rarely come out of the blue. Sometimes you will choose a particular topic because it seems strange or exotic; sometimes because it is close and familiar. Practical matters such as ease of access and the speed with which you can gather detail may be important. Inevitably, your personal biography will be involved in topic selection.

Jennifer Mason suggests that one way to confront your mixed motives is to try to clarify your intentions while you are formulating your research problem. Table 4.3 contains her advice on ethical matters at this early stage of your research.

TABLE 4.3 Ethical questions for the researcher

1 What is the purpose(s) of your research, e.g. self-advancement, political advocacy?
2 Which individuals or groups might be interested or affected by your research topic?
3 What are the implications for these parties of framing your research topic in the way you have done?

Source: adapted from Mason, 1996: 29–30

Analysing data

Although you may claim that your study is meant to improve public understanding of your chosen group's situation and perspective, your motives can also be criticised. For instance, Dingwall (1980) has noted how studying underdogs (disadvantaged people) 'undoubtedly furnishes an element of romance, radical chic even, to liven the humdrum routine of academic inquiry'. He then goes on to note that a concern to champion the 'underdog' is 'inimical to the serious practice of **ethnography**, whose claims to be distinguished from polemic or investigative journalism must rest on its ability to comprehend the perspectives of top dogs, bottom dogs and, indeed, lap dogs' (1980: 874).

Dingwall concludes that social research, whatever its methods, must seek to produce valid generalisations rather than 'synthetic moral outrage' (1980: 874). So, when it comes to data analysis, you need to show your readers that you have dealt even-handedly with the people whose lives and experiences you describe. To this end, Dingwall suggests an ethic of 'fair dealing'. This implies that we should ask of any study:

> Does it convey as much understanding of its villains as its heroes? Are the privi-leged treated as having something serious to say or simply dismissed as evil, cor-rupt or greedy without further enquiry? (1992: 172)

After the study

When your research is completed, ethical issues remain. For instance, should you be satisfied with the *initial* consent that you may have obtained from informants? Or should you ask them for further permission before you publish (this is known as *process consent* according to A. Ryen, personal correspondence)?

These questions concerned Sarah Pink after she had interviewed informants in their homes using videos of their homes:

> (At the start) I asked each informant to sign a form agreeing to take part in the study and to the confidentiality of the materials I would produce. Later when I produced visual projects about the study I wrote to my informants asking if they would allow me to use their images in my visual projects and to confirm if they would like to re-view and approve the images I selected before these were screened publicly. Working this way I intended to ensure that both my informants and I were comfortable with the way they were represented. (2004: 395)

Pink reports that only half of her informants agreed to allow her to use their video interviews. By asking them for their views of her research, Pink suggests that researchers can also gain vital new information because 'informants do not always agree with our analyses of them and their comments can provide important new insights' (2004: 395).

Here Pink raises the issue of **respondent validation** discussed in Section 11.3.2. Although I question its methodological usefulness, there is no question that attempts at some kind of feedback to the people you study is a proper *ethical* goal.

For instance, following my research on hospital clinics for children (Silverman, 1987), I gave a talk to the Parents' Association at one of the hospitals I had studied. In this talk, I discussed new facts from my research about doctor–parent commu-nication. I also examined the implications of my findings for reform of current hospital practices. Subsequently, I was invited to write a short piece on my research for the newsletter of a British organisation called the Patients' Association. In this article, I covered much the same ground as well as adding guidelines for how to manage better or get better service from hospitals that treat sick children. Finally,

I spoke at a meeting of parents of children with diabetes. My aim here was to stress what my research had revealed about the painful dilemmas experienced by such parents. In this way, I sought to assure them that others share their own experience and that there is no need for them to reproach themselves.

However, as I have already implied, ethical issues can turn out to be a minefield in which apparently clear guidelines do not straightforwardly settle real dilemmas. In the final section of this chapter, I discuss ethical complications.

TIP

Before you begin any research study, it is wise to think about its ethical implications. On rare occasions, this may lead you to abandon the study. More commonly, it will help you to design a study with proper ethical safeguards.

Always discuss such issues with your teachers. Also consult the guidelines of the professional association of your discipline. However, do not assume that these guidelines will cover every contingency and so be open to the emerging ethical challenges that may confront you at any stage of your research.

LINKS

US Office of Human Subjects Research:
ohsr.od.nih.gov (go to Regulations and Ethical Guidelines)

The Social Research Association Ethical Guidelines at:
www.the-sra.org.uk/documents/pdfs/ethics03.pdf

The US National Institute of Mental Health:
http://ohsr.od.nih.gov/guidelines/belmont.html

EXERCISE 4.3

Select any published account of qualitative research. Re-read it in order to answer the following questions:

1 In what way(s), if at all, did the author(s) address ethical matters arising in this research?
2 Were there any unacknowledged ethical issues? If so, how might they have been addressed?
3 In what way(s), if at all, did the author(s) discuss the contribution of this research for non-academic audiences including the people researched?
4 What unacknowledged relevance for the wider community might this research have? Explain this (in no more than 200 words) without using any specialist jargon.

4.3 SOME ETHICAL COMPLICATIONS

Things do not always work out in the way that ethical guidelines would suggest. I discuss below a small selection of issues that can complicate ethical decision-making:

- the limitations of the informed consent model
- researching 'strange' cultures
- ethics online
- ethics and the unexpected.

4.3.1 The limitations of the informed consent model

Amir Marvasti has observed that the standard model of informed consent approach derives from quantitative survey research, where questions are asked from a known **sample** with very little variation from one respondent to another. As he comments about interview studies:

> The problem is that in qualitative research sometimes the interview questions and the focus of the project itself changes in the course of the study. Depending on the circumstances, one interview may be very different from another. This is especially true for in-depth interviews in which follow-up questions emerge spontaneously in reaction to respondent's comments. Since one cannot anticipate the exact direction the interview will take, it is impossible to fully inform the respondent about the focus of the study in advance. (2004: 141)

Similar problems arise in ethnographic studies (see Chapter 5), where in the course of your observations, you come into contact with people in to many different settings and may want to change the focus of your research. As Marvasti notes, such challenges have led some qualitative researchers to raise fundamental questions about the feasibility of informed consent. To illustrate these questions, Marvasti reports a study by Julia Lawton of dying patients at a hospice (a medical/residential facility designed for the care of the terminally ill). According to Marvasti, Lawton (2001) asks:

> 'How informed is informed consent? … many of the dying patients (Lawton) studied were not alert enough to fully understand the purpose of her research. (Lawton asked herself) is (it) necessary to continually remind research participants of the informed consent agreement since in prolonged studies, such as ethnographies, the participants may be observed many times in many situations for different purposes? (2004: 141)

It may appear to be unfortunate that there are no hard and fast solutions to such dilemmas. However, it reminds us that the very act of being alert to such potential issues is a hallmark of the ethical researcher.

4.3.2 Researching 'strange' cultures

How we define the 'strangeness' of other cultures is highly problematic. As I remarked in Section 2.3.2:

> (an) under-theorisation of 'experience' can ... be seen when a researcher follows an approach to different cultures which is uncritically 'touristic'. I have in mind the 'upmarket' tourist who travels the world in search of encounters with alien cultures. Disdaining package tours and even the label of 'tourist', such a person has an insatiable thirst for the 'new' and 'different'. The problem is that there are worrying parallels between the qualitative researcher and this kind of tourist.

The problematic analytic (and ethical) character of defining the Other also has a purely practical side. As Ryen notes, on the basis of her research in East Africa:

> For many poor third-world interviewees, local norms make it difficult to turn down a request from a visitor to be interviewed or they do not know the potential implications of participating in research. (This means that) the general ethical correctness of informed consent irrespective of the location of the field may be questionable with reference to the North–South dimension in Third World projects. (2004: 232)

Riessman builds on Ryen's observations by reminding us of 'the inherent and practical risks associated with ethical universalism – the problematics of applying "universal" moral principles that have been constructed (that is, derived) in one cultural context and exporting them, without modifications, in another' (2004: ms24). The following case study gives us a sense of these issues.

CASE STUDY
Informed Consent and Ruptured Understandings

Riessman conducted research in villages in Kerala, South India, between 1993 and 1994. Her interest was in the meaning and management of infertility which, she remarks, was 'an invisible problem in the Indian context'. Here is a shortened account of how she describes her ethical dilemmas:

> My research proposal ... included procedures for obtaining informed consent from childless women. But ... the very language of Western research practice – 'obtaining' informed consent – indicates who will be in control.

> The first hint of trouble happened shortly after I joined my host institution, the research unit of a small college in Kerala. (My) research assistant, Liza – a 26 year old Malayali graduate level social worker, educated in Kerala ... was surprised ... by my consent form: 'we don't do that

(Continued)

(Continued)

here,' she told me gently ... I persisted, and asked her to translate into Malayalam the form I had prepared according to my University's guidelines ...

Because women in Kerala are educated and literate, many informants read along as we communicated the contents of the consent form. Most women signed it. A significant number, however, were reluctant to affix their names. They were suspicious, not about interviewing or taping, but about the form. Perhaps they thought it a government document.

Reflecting now on the refusal of some women, I hear their worry. The consent form *was* a government document – an import from the West, designed to meet my University's Institutional Review Board requirement ... Signing documents in the Indian context carries a history of well-deserved suspicion: government intrusion into property rights, inheritance, marriage customs, and reproductive health. Strangers seeking information and bearing forms are not easily trusted, especially in rural villages. (2004: ms 8–9)

In her research on business in East Africa, Ryen reports that, like Riessman, she sometimes used local people as helpers (in Ryen's case, she used civil servants to find and inform interviewees). However, as she notes, this 'simply replaces the foreign, Western authority with the local, and thereby introduces us to another ethical dilemma' (2004: 233).

Another example from Ryen's fieldwork shows that these sort of issues need not be specific to the Western researcher in developing countries. Ryen writes:

In a couple of interviews with poor female employees, the interviewees seemed mentally stressed. Rather then seeing the (oral) informed consent as a licence to go on, I dropped the interviews and took the role of a friend. It is definitely easier for me as a woman to hold the hand of a poor woman compared to a rich businessman (my interviewees in another project). Ethical challenges do not deprive actions of their symbolic value. (2004: 233)

4.3.3 Ethics online

Some of Ryen's research was conducted online with Asian entrepreneurs operating in East Africa. The Internet has provided a valuable resource for qualitative researchers but, like any source of data, it contains many ethical dilemmas. Once again, Ryen raises a set of crucial questions:

How do we relate to research subjects without bodies, what about identities in a world fit for masquerade, are real-time chatrooms like the public square or does conversational chat need written consent to be used in research, have the research subjects now turned into authors, and if so, what are the ethical consequences for researchers? (2004: 236)

The following case study is an example of how Ryen tried to handle ethical issues when using material gained from e-mail messages with an East African businessman whom she refers to as Sachin.

CASE STUDY
Analysing Emails

I suggested to Sachin that each e-mail should consist of two parts – one private and one interview. This worked perfectly. Eventually, also the private sections of his e-mail responses turned out to have wonderful data. My dilemma was that I had told him that I would publish from the interview part only. However, in one publication we ended up also using 'private' data in our draft (Ryen and Silverman, 2000). I explained the situation to Sachin, and was very happy indeed, when close to the deadline for a conference, I got his consent. The question is what I would have done without this consent. I had earlier asked Sachin if he wanted me to send him copies of publications. He never responded. I saw his non-response as a sign that my invitation was irrelevant to his business focus and of no interest. He was fully familiar with research and publications as implicitly indicated by his response to his pseudonym, that of an international cricket player: "…and calling me "SACHIN" is quite an honour.!!!!!!!" (22.02.99). On those bases I would have drawn the conclusion that it was ethically acceptable to use the data without Sachin's explicit consent apart from extracts of more private character. His consent was implicit in the sense that I earlier had made it clear that I saw the communication as part of my research. I had promised him that I would be in control of this data, and being the only one to see and select data in case of co-publications that I invited to. None of these conditions had been violated. (Ryen, 2004: 243)

Online research is not, however, limited to e-mails. With the emergence of online tools like blogs for conducting research come new and challenging ethical dilemmas and controversies. At the centre of this emerging dialogue is the issue of the adequacy of conventional 'offline' ethical guidelines for conducting research in online contexts. This raises a number of questions:

- What do the conventional notions of private and public mean in online research venues?
- Do blog researchers need to gain authorial permission from bloggers when recording their posts?
- Is blog material academic fair game or is informed consent needed?

There is no consensus among social scientists' responses to the broader question of what is private and what is public online. Hookway (2008) has noted three different positions:

1 There are researchers who argue that archived material on the Internet is publicly available and therefore participant consent is not necessary. This position often rests on an analogy between online forums and public space, where the observation and recording of publicly accessible Internet content is treated like research on television content, a piece of art in a public gallery or letters to the editor.
2 Some researchers claim that online postings, though publicly accessible, are written with an expectation of privacy and should be treated as such.
3 There are those who argue that online interaction defies clearcut prescription as either public or private; they warn online researchers of mistaking public accessibility of online forums for the public nature of the interactions, instead emphasizing how actors themselves construe their participation in online environments.

Hookway's response to these arguments is to suggest that:

> There is a strong case for blog researchers to adopt the 'fair game–public domain' position. Blogs are firmly located in the public domain and for this reason it can be argued that the necessity of consent should be waived. Further, blogs are public not only in the sense of being publicly accessible but also in how they are defined by users. Blogging is a public act of writing for an implicit audience. The exception proves the rule: blogs that are interpreted by bloggers as 'private' are made 'friends only'. Thus, accessible blogs may be personal but they are not private. (2008: 104–5).

4.3.4 The unexpected

No set of guidelines or principles of good practice can foresee every eventuality. As Marvasti argues:

> In theory, researchers should take every reasonable measure to protect their subjects from harm, but in reality, it is impossible to anticipate every risk. One reason for this is that your study might affect respondents in different ways … Even if your respondents voluntarily take part in your study, they may not be in a position to fully appreciate the potential harm they could suffer from their participation. (2004: 136–7)

Marvasti gives the hypothetical example of a research study of a support group for people with chronic depression. In the study, a researcher conducts interviews where people are asked about what they think are the sources of their mental illness:

One of the questions that comes up during the interview is whether or not the respondent has been a victim of child abuse. Specifically, the researcher asks, 'Have you been sexually or physically abused by a relative or an acquaintance? If so, please describe how this happened and when?' Suppose the respondent tries to answer this question and in the process has to recall a very painful past. After the interview, the respondent becomes even more depressed and tries to commit suicide. Is the researcher to blame for this unfortunate event, given that the participation was completely voluntary? (Marvasti, 2004: 137)

Although this tragic outcome could not have been predicted, Marvasti suggests that two additional precautions might have led to a better outcome:

- The research participants should have been informed in advance about the types of questions they would be asked and reminded that they have the option not to answer certain questions or to end the interview whenever they wish.
- Given the sensitive nature of child abuse, perhaps our researcher should have taken precautionary steps to terminate the interview if the respondent appeared overly emotional. (2004: 137)

TIP

If respondents get upset in interviews, ask if they want to talk with someone further about issues/memories that came up, and provide a list of mental health practitioners and/or clinics. When studying divorce, Riessman called several respondents the day after the interview to ask if they had any further thoughts, indirectly enquiring if they were all right (C. Riessman, personal correspondence).

LINKS

For the ethical guidelines provided by the Economic and Social Research Council (UK), go to:
www.esrc.ac.uk

US ethical guidelines are provided by an Institutional Review Board. See:
www.fda.gov/oc/ohrt/irbs/default.htm

KEY POINTS

- At every stage of the research process, from study design to data gathering to data analysis and writing your report, you need to be aware of ethical issues.

- Ethical guidelines are usually available from your university department and from the professional associations that recruit within your discipline.

- The varying social contexts of action mean that such guidelines cannot cover every situation that will arise. This means that you should always be alert to emerging ethical issues and confront them as best you can.

STUDY QUESTIONS

1 Why do research ethics matter?
2 What kind of ethical problems can arise in social research?
3 What special ethical issues arise in researching vulnerable people?
4 What safeguards can we put in place to try to maintain ethical integrity?
5 What is informed consent? How can it be achieved in practice?
6 What ethical issues arise in using online material such as blogs?

RECOMMENDED READING

Hay and Israel (2006) provide a valuable textbook on research ethics. Ryen's (2011) chapter 'Ethics in qualitative research' is a key source which includes fascinating material on her ethnographic research in East Africa. The special issue on research ethics in *Qualitative Social Work: Research and Practice*, guest edited by Ryen (http://qsw.sagepub.com/content/vol7/issue4/), offers an overview article and some good illustrations on ethical governance, informed consent, trust, etc.

For more details of some of the case studies discussed in this chapter, see Back (2004) and Riessman (2004). For a discussion of the ethics of interviews, look at Gatrell (2009).

PART TWO

Methods

5

Ethnographic Observation

CHAPTER OBJECTIVES

By the end of this chapter, you will be able to:

- understand the meanings and aims of ethnography, observation and fieldwork
- recognise the methodological choices that face the ethnographer
- locate the different theoretical positions that animate ethnographic work
- understand the basics of analysing field data including how to make field-notes.

Employing one's eyes and ears to understand what is going on in any setting is a major method of qualitative research. Put crudely, while the quantitative researcher uses methods like surveys or laboratory experiments to get an overall picture of society, we try to get inside the fabric of everyday life. As Eberle and Maeder put it:

> Doing ethnography means using multiple methods of data gathering, like observation, interviews, collection of documents, pictures, audio-visual materials as well as representations of artefacts. The main difference from other ways of investigating the social world is that the researcher does 'fieldwork' and collects data herself through physical presence. In contrast to survey research, ethnographic research cannot be done solely from a desk. An ethnographer enters a field with all of his or her senses, and takes into account the architecture, the furniture, the spatial arrangements, the ways people work and interact, the documents they produce and use, the contents of their communication, the timeframe of social processes, and so on. (2011: 54)

But observation, of course, is not just the province of social scientists. Physicists, engineers and police officers all make their 'observations'. More tellingly, in our everyday lives, we depend upon making observations of each other – for instance, about whether to categorise a stranger's question as 'genuine' or a 'pick-up line' (see Sacks, 1992, I: 49, 103 and 130–1). Indeed, as Giampietro Gobo has suggested, observation is part of the very fabric of the society in which we live – an 'observation society'.

CASE STUDY
The Observation Society

The clues that we are living in an 'observation society' are many: wherever we go there is always a television camera ready to film our actions (unbeknownst to us). Camera phones and the current fashion for making video recordings of even the most personal and intimate situations and posting them on the Internet; or logging on to webcams pointed at city streets, monument, landscapes, plants, birds nests, coffee pots, etc. to observe movements, developments and changes. Then there is the trend of webcams worn by people so that they can lead us virtually through their everyday lives. These are not minor eccentricities but websites visited by millions of people around the world. (Gobo, 2011: 25)

Of course, the status of social science observations versus what we observe in everyday life is a big issue (see Section 5.3.3). A common terminological solution is to say that social scientists do something extra with their observations – they write ethnographies. **Ethnography** puts together two different words: 'ethno' means 'folk' while 'graph' derives from 'writing'. Ethnography refers, then, to social science writing about particular folks. This simple definition is expanded below.

DEFINITIONS

Ethnography is the study of people in naturally occurring settings or 'field' by methods of data collection which capture their social meanings and ordinary activities, involving the researcher participating directly in the setting, if not also the activities, in order to collect data in a systematic manner. (Brewer, 2000: 6)

Participant observation, ethnography and fieldwork are all used interchangeably ... they can all mean spending long periods watching people, coupled with talking to them about what they are doing, thinking and saying, designed to see how they understand their world. (Delamont, 2004: 218)

LINK
www.qualitative-research.net/fqs/fqs-eng.htm
Use the search facility with the words 'ethnography' and 'participant observation'.

EXERCISE 5.1

An instructor begins an Introductory Sociology course with the following statement:

> The problem with everyday talk is that it is so imprecise. For instance, sometimes we say: 'too many cooks spoil the broth'. On other occasions, we say: 'many hands make light work'. On this course, based on scientific research, I will demonstrate which of these proverbs is more accurate.

The instructor now reports on laboratory data from an experiment where students have been assigned tasks and then work either in teams or on their own. This experiment seems to show that, all things being equal, teamwork is more efficient. Therefore, the instructor claims, we can have more confidence in the validity of the proverb 'many hands make light work'.

1   Are you convinced by the instructor's claim? (For example, what assumptions does the experiment make? Can proverbs be equally appropriate in different contexts?)
2   Outline how you might do *observational* work on people's use of such proverbs. (For example, what settings would you look at? What sort of things would you be looking for?)
3   Examine *either* newspaper advertisements *or* advertisements on radio or TV. Make a note when proverbs are used. What *functions* do these proverbs seem to have? Do they make the advertisement more convincing? Why?

An illustration of one observational study may bring to life how social science observers try to watch people in the field. This is shown in the case study below.

CASE STUDY
Restaurant Work

More than half a century ago, William Foote Whyte carried out over a year's participant observation in a number of Chicago restaurants. He points out (Whyte, 1949) how, in a service trade, like a restaurant, the organisation of work differs from other settings. Instead of the industrial pattern,

(Continued)

(Continued)

whereby a supervisor gives orders to a worker, in a restaurant work originates from a customer's order. Whyte shows this difference generates a number of problems for restaurant workers:

- Who originates action?
- For whom?
- How often?
- With what consequences?

The social structure of the restaurant functions as an organised response to these problems. This can be seen in the following three patterns:

1 Many of us will have had the experience of a member of staff snatching away a menu which we have innocently picked up on sitting down at a restaurant table. Whyte argues that this occurs because the skilful waitress/waiter attempts to fit customers into *her* pattern of work (e.g. her need to ensure that the table has been cleared before she takes an order). So, by not passively responding to the initiatives of customers, serving staff preserve their own work routines.
2 Back in the 1940s, widespread gender inequalities caused a particular problem for waitresses because they were expected to transmit orders to mainly male cooks. A structure emerged which concealed this initiation of work by waitresses: rather than shout out orders to the cooks, the women wrote out slips which they laid on the counter to be dealt with in the cooks' own time.
3 Barmen also engaged in informal behaviour to distance themselves from the initiation of orders by waitresses. When they had lots of orders, they would not speed up and so waitresses (and their angry customers) would just have to wait. Moreover, at busy times, they would not mix one cocktail until they had several orders for it which could be mixed together.

Half a century later, Whyte's work remains impressive. His restaurant study shows the importance of *context* and *process* in understanding behaviour (see item 3 of Table 5.1 below). Thus Whyte shows the skills of staff in reproducing occupational and gender hierarchies by modifying the flow of work and, thereby, redefining apparently simple acts. Moreover, Whyte does not let a preference for an unstructured research design lead to a study which merely tells anecdotes about a few choice examples. For instance, the restaurant study uses powerful *quantitative* measures of the number of times different types of people initiate actions.

EXERCISE 5.2

When you are next in a restaurant, make observations about how the staff interact with customers. Using Whyte's findings as a guide, examine:

1 Who originates action?
2 For whom?
3 How often?
4 With what consequences?

If you had an audio or video recording of what you heard and saw, how might that have improved the quality of your analysis?

The origins of ethnography are in the work of nineteenth-century anthropologists who travelled to observe different pre-industrial cultures (see Section 5.1.1). Today, 'ethnography' encompasses a much broader range of work from studies of groups in one's own culture to experimental writing to political interventions (see Section 5.1). Moreover, ethnographers today do not always 'observe', at least directly. They may work with cultural artefacts like written texts or study recordings of interactions they did not observe firsthand. For this reason, in what follows I will use 'ethnography' to refer to a general approach and reserve 'observation' to talk about specific issues of ethics and technique.

Some contemporary researchers share the early anthropologists' belief that in order to understand the world 'firsthand', you must participate yourself rather than just observe at a distance. This has given rise to what is described as the method of **participant observation** (see Section 5.3.2). Indeed, in a very general sense, participant observation is more than just a method but describes a basic resource of all social research: 'in a sense, *all* social research is a form of participant observation, because we cannot study the social world without being part of it. From this point of view, participant observation is not a particular research technique but a mode of being-in-the-world characteristic of researchers' (Atkinson and Hammersley, 1994: 249).

How does this 'mode-of-being' impact on the specifics of ethnographic research? Bryman (1988) has provided a useful list of the principal characteristics of qualitative research. As adapted in Table 5.1, they stand as a simple guide for the ethnographer.

Bryman's list provides a useful orientation for the novice. Item 2 is particularly important: Description: 'attending to mundane detail'. One way to understand the import of 'mundane detail' is to say that the ethnographer attempts to answer Agar's (1986: 12) question 'what is going on here?' However, the reader should proceed with caution about uncritically accepting all the items in this table.

As I suggested in Chapter 1, any attempt to base observation on an understanding of how people 'see' things (item 1) can speedily degenerate into a

TABLE 5.1   Aims of observational research

1   'Seeing through the eyes of': 'viewing events, actions, norms, values, etc. from the perspective of the people being studied'

2   Description: 'attending to mundane detail … to help us to understand what is going on in a particular context and to provide clues and pointers to other layers of reality'

3   'Contextualism': 'the basic message that qualitative researchers convey is that whatever the sphere in which the data are being collected, we can understand events only when they are situated in the wider social and historical context'

4   Process: 'viewing social life as involving interlocking series of events'

5   Flexible research designs: 'qualitative researchers' adherence to viewing social phenomena through the eyes of their subjects has led to a wariness regarding the imposition of prior and possibly inappropriate frames of reference on the people they study'. This leads to a preference for an open and unstructured research design which increases the possibility of coming across unexpected issues

6   Avoiding early use of theories and concepts: rejecting premature attempts to impose theories and concepts which may 'exhibit a poor fit with participants' perspectives'

Source: adapted from Bryman, 1988: 61–6

commonsensical or psychologistic perspective. To put the argument in its most extreme form, I believe that the ethnographer should pursue what people actually do, leaving what people say they 'think' and 'feel' to the skills of the media interviewer. This will often involve a focus on the most mundane activities in everyday settings (see my discussion of making 'ordinary' activities 'extraordinary' in Silverman, 2007: Ch. 1).

CASE STUDY
Photographing Everyday Things

Many years ago, the American photographer Diane Arbus wrote this brief note about her interests entitled 'American rites, manners and customs':

> I want to photograph the considerable ceremonies of our present because we tend, while living here and now, to perceive only what is random and barren and formless about it. While we regret that the present is not like the past, we despair of its ever becoming the future, its innumerable inscrutable habits lie in wait for their meaning. I want to gather them like somebody's grandmother putting up preserves because they will have been so beautiful. (Successful application for Guggenheim Fellowship, 1963)

Arbus goes on to describe the importance of observing ceremonies (e.g. celebrations and competitions) and ceremonial places (e.g. beauty and funeral parlours). Her project is precisely that of good ethnographers like Erving Goffman (see Section 5.1.4).

TIP

Do not assume that ethnography is simple to do. It involves defining a research problem, adopting a theoretical orientation and having rigorous methods to record and analyse your data. See Section 5.2 below, Hammersley and Atkinson (1995) and Noaks and Wincup (2004: 91–3).

However, I run ahead of myself. Let us slow down and provide more background. In the rest of this chapter, I will attempt to illuminate three crucial aspects of ethnographic and observational work:

- the 'focus' of the study (including 'tribes', 'sub-cultures', the 'public realm' and organisations)
- methodological choices (including access, identity, defining a research problem, methods of recording data, looking as well as listening, developing analysis of ethnographic data and feedback to participants)
- theoretical issues (the theoretically derived nature of ethnographic analysis and the main contemporary theoretical approaches including '**grounded theory**', '**naturalism**' and '**ethnomethodology**').

5.1 THE ETHNOGRAPHIC FOCUS

Just as, according to Bryman, the qualitative researcher seeks to see things in context, so the student needs some basic knowledge of the historical tradition from which observational studies arose. This is because 'Qualitative research is an empirical, socially located phenomenon, defined by its own history, not simply a residual grab-bag comprising all things that are "not quantitative"' (Kirk and Miller, 1986: 10).

In this section, we shall consider four different topics on which ethnographic studies have focused: tribes, sub-cultures, the public realm and organisations.

5.1.1 Studies of 'tribes'

The initial thrust in favour of observational work was anthropological. Anthropologists usually argue that, if one is really to understand a group of people, one must engage in an extended period of observation. Anthropological fieldwork routinely involves immersion in a culture over a period of years, based on learning the language and participating in social events.

An important early study arose out of Malinowski's (1922) research on the everyday social life of the Trobriand Islanders in the Western Pacific. Like Radcliffe-Brown (1948), Malinowski was committed to rigorous scientific description of the beliefs and practices of 'native' peoples (see Atkinson and Hammersley, 1994: 249–50).

However, in the early twentieth century, the idea of 'native' populations with 'primitive' beliefs was already familiar to the colonial rulers of the British Empire. Indeed, these rulers employed administrators with the explicit task of reporting on the ways of colonial subjects. In this sense, it could be argued that these early anthropologists adopted a 'colonial methodology' (Ryen and Silverman, 2000).

Both anthropologist and colonial civil servant seem to have perceived the foreigner as someone who was outside and different from the white middle class. So the 'foreign' becomes something they can discover, research and understand (of course, most of the middle-class persons involved in and writing about foreign cultures were men).

This focus on the difference between foreign and Western culture appears in different ways in both novels and academic works. Daniel Defoe's story about Robinson Crusoe shows how the middle class saw travel to 'the foreign', with Crusoe as the representative of the civilisation transforming nature into culture. Joseph Conrad's Mr Kurtz's anxiety for the dark and wild Africa is revealed when fever fantasies make his office-holder mask crack.

In general, however, exotic cultures studied by anthropologists like Malinowski and Evans-Pritchard very often turned out to be folk groups of the Third World countries, or former colonial states far away from the Western world and academic institutions. Though anthropologists have recognised for a long time that cultural positions are relative, their insistence on the anthropologist as a cultivated European based within classic science seemed to be more long-lived. This perception of the researcher was not challenged until the group of anthropologists itself became more diverse in respect of gender, age, experience and methodological background.

However, while we may today have freed ourselves from most of the earlier assumptions of effortless superiority, not everything has changed. Like the early anthropologists, it is tempting to attempt to fix a boundary around 'native' populations. Like them, we may unreflectively distinguish the 'exotic' by what appears to be 'familiar'. So the early anthropologist may have shared with modern 'upmarket' tourists a belief in the irreplaceable intrinsic value of every culture still not affected by Western influence (see Section 2.3.2).

Contemporary anthropologists do not, however, limit themselves to criticising the 'colonial' or 'touristic' impulses of their forebears. Providing we can rid ourselves of a colonial mentality, it is both practically and analytically important to attempt to understand other cultures in the context of an increasingly 'globalised' world.

One important contemporary example of such an attempt is to be found in **cognitive anthropology**. As its name suggests, cognitive anthropology seeks to understand how people perceive the world by examining how they communicate. This leads to the production of ethnographies, or conceptually derived descriptions, of whole cultures, focused on how people communicate. For instance, Basso (1972) discusses the situations in which native American Apache people prefer to remain silent and Frake (1972) shows how the Subanun, a people living in the Philippines, assign social status when talking together during drinking ceremonies.

While cognitive anthropology is usually content with single case studies of particular peoples, **structural anthropology** is only interested in single cases insofar as they relate to general social forms. Structural anthropologists draw upon French social and linguistic theory of the early twentieth century, notably Ferdinand de Saussure and Emile Durkheim. Their main building blocks are Saussure's account of sign-systems (see Section 10.4) and Durkheim's insistence that apparently idiosyncratic forms of behaviour can be seen as 'social facts' which are embedded in forms of social organisation. In both cases, behaviour is viewed as the expression of a 'society' which works as a 'hidden hand' constraining and forming human action (see Levi-Strauss, 1967).

A classic case of an anthropologist using a case study to make such broader generalisations is found in Mary Douglas's work on a Central African tribe, the Lele. Douglas (1975) noticed that an anteater, what Western zoologists call a 'pangolin', was very important to the Lele's ritual life. For the Lele, the pangolin was both a cult animal and an anomaly.

In part, this was because it was perceived to have both animal and human characteristics – for instance, it tended only to have one offspring at a time, unlike most other animals. It also did not readily fit into the Lele's classification of land and water creatures, spending some of its time on land and some time in the water. Curiously, among animals that were hunted, the pangolin seemed to the Lele to be unique in not trying to escape but almost offering itself up to its hunter.

True to her structuralist perspective, Douglas resisted a 'touristic' response and moved beyond curiosity to systematic analysis. She noted that many groups who perceive anomalous entities in their environment reject them out of hand. To take an anomalous entity seriously might cast doubt on the 'natural' status of your group's system of classification.

The classic example of the rejection of anomaly is found in the Old Testament. Douglas points out that the reason why the pig is unclean, according to the Old Testament, is that it is anomalous. It has a cloven hoof which, following the Old Testament, makes it clean but it does not chew the cud – which makes it dirty. So it turns out that the pig is particularly unclean precisely because it is anomalous. Old Testament teachings on inter-marriage work in the same way. Although you are not expected to marry somebody of another tribe, to marry the offspring of a marriage between a member of your tribe and an outsider is even more frowned upon. In both examples, anomaly is shunned.

However, the Lele are an exception: they celebrate the anomalous pangolin. What this suggests to Douglas is that there may be no *universal* propensity to frown upon anomaly. If there is variability from community to community, then this must say something about their social organisation.

Sure enough, there is something special about the Lele's social life. Their experience of relations with other tribes has been very successful. They exchange goods with them and have little experience of war.

What is involved in relating well with other tribes? It means successfully crossing a frontier or boundary. But what do anomalous entities do? They cut across boundaries. Here is the answer to the puzzle about why the Lele are different.

Douglas is suggesting that the Lele's response to anomaly derives from experiences grounded in their social organisation. They perceive the pangolin favourably because it cuts across boundaries just as they themselves do. Conversely, the ancient Israelites regard anomalies unfavourably because their own experience of crossing boundaries was profoundly unfavourable. Indeed, the Old Testament reads as a series of disastrous exchanges between the Israelites and other tribes.

By means of this historical comparison, Douglas has moved from a single-case explanation to a far more general theory of the relation between social exchange and response to anomaly. In their discussion of grounded theory, Glaser and Strauss (1967) have described this movement towards greater generality as a move from **substantive** to **formal theory** (see Section 3.3). In their own research on hospital wards caring for terminally ill patients, they show how, by using the comparative method, we can develop accounts of people's own awareness of their impending death (i.e. a substantive theory) to accounts of a whole range of 'awareness contexts' (formal theory).

5.1.2 Studies of sub-cultures

A crude (and sometimes inaccurate) way to distinguish sociology from anthropology is to say that, unlike anthropology, sociology's 'tribe' is the people around them.

Sociological ethnography is usually assumed to have originated in the 1920s when students at the University of Chicago were instructed to put down their theory textbooks and get out onto the streets of their city and use their eyes and ears. As Robert Park told undergraduate students at the University of Chicago in the 1920s (note his reference to 'men' and 'gentlemen'; gender issues are discussed in Section 5.3.2):

> You have been told to go grubbing in the library thereby accumulating a mass of notes and a liberal coating of grime. You have been told to choose problems wherever you find musty stacks of routine records. This is called 'getting your hands dirty in real research'. Those who counsel you thus are wise and honourable men.

But one thing more is needful: first hand observation. Go sit in the lounges of the luxury hotels and on the doorsteps of the flop-houses; sit on the Gold Coast settees and the slum shakedowns; sit in the orchestra hall and in the Star and Garter Burlesque. In short, gentlemen, go get the seat of your pants dirty in real research. (Park, quoted by Brewer, 2000: 13)

The **Chicago School**, as it became known in the 1930s, had two strands. One was concerned with the sociology of urban life, represented by the work of Park and Burgess on the social organisation of the city into different 'zones' and the movement of population between zones over time. The second strand, associated with Everett Hughes, provided a series of vivid accounts of urban settings, particularly focused on 'underdog' occupations and 'deviant' roles (see Deegan, 2001).

> **LINK**
> For a brief assessment of Hughes's work by another master ethnographer, Howard Becker, go to Becker, H.S. (2010). 'The art of comparison: lessons from the master, Everett C. Hughes', *Sociologica*, 2:
> www.sociologica.mulino.it/main

This tradition continued for two decades after the Second World War – sometimes known as the Second Chicago School. In the 1950s, Becker (1953) conducted a classic observational study of drug use. He was particularly concerned with the relationship between marihuana smokers' own understandings and the interactions in which they were involved. He discovered that people's participation in groups of users taught them how to respond to the drug. Without such learning, novices would not understand how to smoke marihuana nor how to respond to its effects. Consequently, they would not get 'high' and so would not continue to use it.

CASE STUDY
Drug Use

Becker (1953) outlines a number of stages through which novices pass on their path to become a regular smoker. These include:

1 *Direct teaching* – for example, being taught the difference between how to smoke marihuana and how to smoke tobacco; learning how to interpret its effects and their significance.
2 *Learning how to enjoy the effects* – through interaction with experienced users, the novice learns to find pleasure in sensations which, at first, may be quite frightening.

(Continued)

(Continued)

3　*Resocialisation after difficulties* – even experienced users can have an unpleasant or frightening experience through using either a larger quantity or different quality of marihuana. Fellow users can 'cool them out', explaining the reasons for this experience and reassuring them that they may safely continue to use the drug.

4　*Learning connoisseurship* – through developing a greater appreciation of the drug's effects, becoming able to distinguish between different kinds and qualities of the drug.

Becker stresses that it is only in the context of a social network, which provides a means of interpreting the effects of the drug, that people become stable marihuana users. It is unlikely, however, that such a network could have been identified by, say, survey research methods concerned with the attitudes of marihuana users.

Studies of different sub-cultures are the bread and butter of contemporary ethnography (see my discussion of studies of drug use in adolescent cultures and of female members of youth gangs in Section 6.7). However, as most ethnographers recognise, the ethics of observing such potentially vulnerable groups are complicated (see Section 4.1.3).

5.1.3 Studies of the public realm

Many studies of sub-cultures take place in public areas like streets, shopping malls and parks. However, ethnographers who observe the public domain sometimes have a wider interest than the sub-culture of particular groups. Instead, their aim is to observe how people in general behave in certain public contexts; for example while using public transport (see Adler and Adler, 1994: 384–5, and also Nash, 1975; 1981).

Three sociologists, Simmel, Goffman and Sacks, gave the impetus to this focus on public space. In the nineteenth century, the German sociologist Georg Simmel (1950) developed propositions about the basic forms of human interaction according to the number in a group – for example, what happens in 'dyads' (groups of two) compared with 'triads' (groups of three). From these formal propositions, Simmel derived compelling accounts of the 'stranger' and of urban life.

Judging by the number of references to his work by others, Erving Goffman was probably the most influential sociologist working on face-to-face behaviour in the twentieth century.

Goffman's early work, based on a study of the Shetland Islanders in the 1950s, set out the arts of what Goffman (1959) referred to as '**impression management**'. This involved people managing their own appearances by controlling the impressions they gave by, for instance, organising what guests might see in their home. Goffman further distinguished 'face work', which smoothed interaction by maintaining a ceremonial order, from 'character work', which served to maintain or challenge the moral standing of particular individuals.

Goffman shows us two recurrent kinds of rule used to organise social interaction:

- Rules of courtesy, manners and etiquette (who is able to do and say what to whom and in what way).
- Rules of what is relevant or irrelevant within any setting depending upon the definition of the situation.

As Goffman points out, these rules give us a clue to understanding what is going on in definitions of situations in face-to-face encounters. For, 'instead of beginning by asking what happens when this definition of the situation breaks down, we can begin by asking what perspectives this definition of the situation *excludes* when it is being satisfactorily sustained' (Goffman, 1961b: 19, my emphasis).

Harvey Sacks's lectures to undergraduates at the University of California between 1965 and 1972 showed the influence of Goffman's insights in studies of the public realm. For instance, Sacks offers a Goffmanesque discussion of how 'excuse me' rather than 'hello' works as an effective 'ticket' to talk to strangers (Sacks, 1992, II: 195: see also Goffman, 1981: Ch. 1).

Equally, Sacks's discussion of how appearances are organised when your private space becomes public is very close to that of Goffman (1959). It is routine, for instance, to arrange your living area in a particular way when guests are about to call: 'the magazines on somebody's coffee table are routinely seen to be intended to suggest that they are intellectuals, or whatever else' (Sacks, 1992, I: 329).

Moreover, Sacks develops this example by trading off Goffman's (1959) discussion of how a visitor can contrast such appearances to the appearances they were unable to control but 'gave off'. As Sacks puts it: 'And you can walk out of a house and say that somebody's a phoney by virtue of some lack of fit between what you figured you could infer from various things in their house, and what you've found out about them other than that' (1992, I: 329).

Observations like these can be made in the course of everyday life, thereby resolving the ethnographer's problem of access (see Section 5.2.1 below). Curiously, however, very few novice researchers think about using the public realm as a data source.

5.1.4 Studies of organisations

We study and work in organisations like universities and businesses. Often, we spend our leisure time in organised social groups. It is, therefore, hardly surprising that organisations should prove to be a fertile field for the ethnographer. Indeed, most of my research data have been drawn from organisations including a personnel department in local government (see Section 5.4.1), outpatient consultations in hospitals and private clinics (Silverman, 1987) and public and private organisations offering HIV-test counselling (see Section 1.2.4).

Useful discussions of ethnographic studies of organisations may be found in Boden (1994) and Czarniawska (1998), while Smith (1996) provides an important account of what she calls 'institutional ethnography' which seeks to link what happens to individuals to larger frameworks of institutional practices. The following case study is a good example of what ethnographers can discover about organisations.

CASE STUDY
Gender Roles in a French Trade Union

Unlike survey researchers, who treat gender as a variable that shapes attitudes and behaviour, Marie Buscatto wanted to use observation to study how gender relations are constructed in a particular setting. She observed how union activity was conducted, by whom and with what consequences. In doing so, she discovered three major social processes that combine over time and work together to produce and legitimate the marginalisation of women employees in union structures, especially at relatively high levels in the union hierarchy:

- The model of the 'union career,' which requires having a great deal of time and personal energy to devote to the activity, turns out to be strongly 'male.' The internal process of union promotion corresponds to a role that has been socially constructed as 'male': total commitment to an external activity and delegation of household tasks to the spouse. This means that it is harder for women to attain and remain in these positions.
- It turned out that union activism is a way of 'changing occupations' for men (but not for women) who wish to devote themselves fully to an activity and are unable to do so in their current occupational activity due to a lack of educational, social or occupational resources.
- The 'maleness' of union activity – as reflected in areas of interest, networks, behavioural norms – makes it fairly unattractive to most women. This also means that women who get into such activity 'anyway' are likely to be judged less favourably than men, to appear less legitimate in the eyes of their peers and the people they mix with, regardless of the level at which they practice that activity. (Buscatto, 2011: 38)

Buscatto draws upon the trailblazing American ethnographer Erving Goffman. Goffman's (1961a) book *Asylums* is probably the only sociological monograph ever to have become widely read by the general public. *Asylums* even entered (usually misunderstood) into the recent debate about the 'community care' of mental patients. The 'character work' that he observed among the Shetland Islanders was very much to the fore in Goffman's ethnographic study of what he called 'the moral career of the mental patient', which is discussed in the case study below.

CASE STUDY
Mental Hospitals

Goffman (1961a) suggests that mental hospitals, like other 'total institutions', such as barracks, prisons, monasteries and boarding schools, break down the usual boundaries between work, rest and play through using various strategies to strip people of their non-institutional identities, for example dressing inmates in uniforms, calling them by a number or institutional nickname.

Faced with what he called a 'mortifying process', Goffman argued that inmates were by no means passive. In particular, they engaged in various 'secondary adjustments' which served to preserve a non-institutionally defined identity. These adjustments ranged from minor infringements of rules ('make-dos') to actively 'working the system' for their own benefit by making skilful use of 'free places' and establishing private and group 'territories'.

Like Goffman, Sacks had no interest in building data-free grand theories or in research methods, like laboratory studies or even interviews, which abstracted people from everyday contexts. Above all, both men marvelled at the everyday skills through which particular appearances are maintained.

We can catch sight of Sacks's use of Goffman's ideas in his article 'Notes on police assessment of moral character' (Sacks, 1972b) which was originally written as a course paper for Goffman's course at Berkeley in the early 1960s (Sacks, 1972a: 280n.). For Sacks, police officers face the same kind of problem as Goffman's Shetland Islanders: how are they to infer moral character from potentially misleading appearances?

To solve this problem, police 'learn to treat their beat as a territory of normal appearances' (Sacks, 1972a: 284). Now they can treat slight variations in normal appearances as 'incongruities' worthy of investigation, working with the assumption of the appearances of 'normal' crimes (cf. Sudnow, 1968a).

So observational data can contribute a great deal to understanding how organisations function. However, as Sacks realised, a problem of such ethnographic work is that its observations may be based upon a taken-for-granted version of the setting in question. For instance, Strong's (1979) powerful analysis of the 'ceremonial order' of doctor–parent consultations undoubtedly depends, in part, upon our readiness to read his data extracts in the context of our shared knowledge of what medical consultations look like.

Consequently, ethnographic work can only take us so far. It is able to show us how people respond to particular settings. It is unable to answer basic questions about how people are constituting that setting through their talk (see my discussion of ethnomethodology in Section 5.2.3). As Maynard and Clayman argue:

> using terms such as 'doctor's office', 'courtroom', 'police department', 'school room', and the like, to characterise settings ... can obscure much of what occurs within those settings ... For this reason, conversation analysts rarely rely on ethnographic data and instead examine if and how interactants themselves reveal an orientation to institutional or other contexts. (1991: 406–7)

By not relying on ethnographic data, Maynard and Clayman imply that observational fieldnotes must be wedded to more reliable data such as audio or video recordings of actual organisational (or institutional) behaviour (see Section 5.2.4 below). The precise methods and concerns of what he calls **conversation analysis** will be discussed in Section 9.4.

5.2 METHODOLOGICAL ISSUES

Atkinson and Hammersley (1994: 248) have suggested that ethnographic research usually involves the following four features:

1   A strong emphasis on exploring the nature of particular social phenomena, rather than setting out to test **hypotheses** about them.
2   A tendency to work primarily with 'unstructured' data, that is, data that have not been coded at the point of data collection in terms of a closed set of analytic categories.
3   Investigation of a small number of cases, perhaps just one case, in detail.
4   Analysis of data that involves explicit interpretations of the meanings and functions of human actions, the product of which mainly takes the form of verbal descriptions and explanations, with quantification and statistical analysis playing a subordinate role at most.

Atkinson and Hammersley's list implies ethical issues regarding access to particular cases and theoretical concerns (e.g. point 4's focus on 'the meanings and functions of human actions'). In Section 5.3, I will examine how theory enters into ethnography. Chapter 4 of this book is devoted to ethical issues.

At first sight, however, Atkinson and Hammersley's characterisation of ethnography appears to deal primarily with **methodology**, that is the choices that confront us in planning and executing a research study. In this section, we shall examine the following methodological issues in conducting an ethnography:

• defining a research problem
• choosing a research site

- gaining access
- finding an identity
- looking as well as listening
- recording observations
- developing analysis of field data.

5.2.1 Defining a research problem

In Section 1.6, I argued that the premature definition of '**variables**' was dangerous in field research. Early 'operational' definitions offer precision at the cost of deflecting attention away from the social processes through which the participants themselves assemble stable features of their social world. So, for instance, the qualitative social scientist may be reluctant to begin by defining, say, 'depression' or 'efficiency'. Instead, it may be preferable to examine how, in different contexts, 'depression' and 'efficiency' come to be defined.

The assumption that one should avoid the early specification of definitions and hypotheses has been common to ethnographers since the 1930s. As Becker and Geer argued many years ago:

> a major part of … research must consist of finding out what problems he [*sic*] can best study in this organisation, what hypotheses will be fruitful and worth pursuing, what observations will best serve him as an indicator of the presence of such phenomena as, for example, cohesiveness or deviance. (1960: 267)

However, this does not mean that the early stages of an observational study are totally unguided. The attempt to describe things 'as they are' is doomed to failure. Without *some* perspective or, at the very least, a set of animating questions, there is nothing to report. Contrary to crude empiricists, the facts *never* speak for themselves (see the discussion of foreshadowed research problems by Delamont, 2004: 224).

Gobo (2008: 78) refers to 'decomposing the topic' as the process by which an ethnographer narrows down the processes to be studied. To illustrate this, he invents the following imaginary conversation between two colleague researchers.

CASE STUDY

A   I want to study the doctor/patient relationship …
B   Why precisely that relationship and not something else, like health policies, hospital bureaucracy, the lobbies of doctors and pharmaceutical companies?

(Continued)

(Continued)

A   Because I'm interested in interactions.

B   So you've got a specific theoretical approach in mind, have you?

A   Yes, I'm interested in interactional approaches.

B   What do you mean by interaction? What interactions do you want to observe? Those between the doctor and the patient or also those between the patient and the doctor's secretary, those between the doctor and his secretary, or also the interactions among the patients in the waiting room?

A   Er ... I don't know ... I'll have to think about it ...

B   But what aspect of the doctor/patient interaction do you want to observe? What particular details interest you? Welcome rituals, presentation rituals, the doctor's rhetorical strategies, misunderstandings between the doctor and the patient, the patient's difficulties in describing his symptoms, the power relation and asymmetry between them ...

A   I don't know ... I don't know ... I've still got to think about all that ...

(Gobo, 2008: 79)

As Gobo notes: 'Although B's insistent questioning might seem rude (and reminiscent of Garfinkel's breaching studies), these research questions are in fact extremely useful for A because they prompt him to reflect on his research topic and to specify and circumscribe it' (2008: 80).

Gobo shows us that ethnography should not consist of simply going out into the field and making some observations. Indeed, this assumption can be an excuse for sloppy, unfocused research. So Mason (1996: 6) rejects the suggestion that qualitative research can just 'describe' or 'explore' the social world. As Miles and Huberman point out, such unfocused research can be a recipe for disaster:

> the looser the initial design, the less selective the collection of data; *everything* looks important at the outset to someone waiting for the key constructs or regularities to emerge from the site, and that wait can be a long one. (1984: 28)

So the ethnographer must get beyond the initial experience of fieldwork when every issue seems so fascinating, each aspect seems interconnected and each piece of reading that you do only adds further ideas (and suggests further readings).

Narrowing down is often the most crucial task when fieldworkers are tempted to throw the kitchen sink at their data. As Wolcott puts it, the answer is to 'do less, more thoroughly' (1990: 62). This means strictly defining your research problem, using **concepts** drawn from a particular **model** (see Section 5.3). It also means limiting the amount of data you gather to what you can readily analyse.

You can decide which data to use by asking yourself which data are most appropriate to your research problem – for instance, are you more interested in what people are thinking or feeling or in what they are doing?

TIP

To make your analysis effective, it is imperative to have a limited research problem with which to work. Indeed, ethnographers often begin research by simply asking: 'what is going on here?' While it may be useful initially to explore different kinds of problems, this should usually only be done to establish the research topic with which you can most effectively work. Does this mean that your data and its analysis will be partial? Of course it does! But this is not a problem – unless you make the impossible claim to give 'the whole picture'. So celebrate the partiality of your topic and data and delight in the particular phenomenon that it allows you to inspect (hopefully in detail).

5.2.2 Choosing a research site

Having worked out a research topic, you need to decide the best place to do your field-work. Marvasti (2004: 44) gives the example of a researcher interested in the shopping patterns of people who live in suburbs. Should you study a department store, supermarket or a whole shopping mall? Moreover, are you more interested in shoppers or salespeople, or both? Alternatively, should you instead look at things that might precede shopping and, say, examine how people discuss the family budget in their household?

There can be no clear answer to these questions until you have narrowed down your research problem. Perhaps the best way to do this is to combine armchair thought with a little observation. 'Casing the joint' at an early stage can aid the sluggish analytical imagination. It may reveal phenomena of which you were unaware. It can also tell you about the time required for observation of different matters and the financial (and perhaps emotional) costs involved. For instance, one of the reasons I chose to observe hospital outpatient consultations was that they were scheduled events (Silverman, 1987). So I knew that, if I turned up at the heart hospital at 11 a.m. on a Wednesday, I could get several hours of 'good' data. By contrast, casing the joint revealed that observation on the ward or in the parents' room, while potentially revealing, might mean hours and days without 'good' data. With my busy teaching schedule, these pragmatic issues determined my choice of research site.

5.2.3 Gaining access

Textbooks (e.g. Hornsby-Smith, 1993: 53; Walsh, 2004: 230–2) usually distinguish between two kinds of research setting:

- 'Closed' or 'private' settings (organisations, deviant groups) where access is controlled by **gatekeepers**.
- 'Open' or 'public' settings (e.g. vulnerable minorities, public records or settings) where access is freely available but not always without difficulty either practical (e.g. finding a role for the researcher in a public setting) or ethical (e.g. should we be intruding upon vulnerable minorities?).

Depending on the contingencies of the setting (and the research problem chosen) two kinds of research access may be obtained:

- 'Covert' access without subjects' knowledge (for the ethical issues involved here, see Chapter 4).
- 'Overt' access based on informing subjects and getting their agreement often through gatekeepers.

The impression you give may be very important in deciding whether you get overt access:

> Whether or not people have knowledge of social research, they are often more concerned with what kind of *person* the researcher is than with the research itself. They will try to gauge how far he or she can be trusted, what he or she might be able to offer as an acquaintance or a friend, and perhaps also how easily he or she could be manipulated or exploited. (Hammersley and Atkinson, 1995: 78)

Of course, gatekeepers' responses to your approach should not be regarded as merely being a stage through which you need to pass, but as providing you with valuable data on the very setting which you want to study. The terms on which you gain entry also tell you something about the setting you want to study. For instance, I have found that medical staff often require access to be coupled with an agreement that their names will appear on publications arising from the research. This tells you something about the professional needs of hospital doctors (who are often connected to university medical schools) to publish.

CASE STUDY
'Acceptable' Research Topics

Buscatto tells how she managed to get access to two French insurance companies by proposing a topic which was fashionable in management circles:

Getting such open access is often difficult since most top managers experience this presence at best as an investment to be made profitable, at worse as a risk to be tightly controlled. How does one get top management's interest in one's work while being allowed to observe as freely as possible over time? … It gradually appeared that I had been accepted in this organization mainly because my research goal had been considered to be interesting by both Human Resources and operational managers. This had supposed that I transform my academic research interest – *'organizational socialisation in big private companies using a comparative approach'* – into acceptable and understandable managerial terms … When sending letters to big organizations, I had first translated my academic research question into operational terms: *'organizational learning conditions at work'*. I presented my research as *'easy to lead'* and as *'an experimental research'*. To my big surprise, three insurance companies showed interest, including Hermes and Mercure! Other letters got lost in recruiting services or were filed without even being answered. As I found out later, once inside [these organisations], my problematization work was successful in companies which were already sensitive to such a question: I was part of a fashion trend … *'Organizational learning'* had become a trendy topic in the French business literature. (Buscatto, 2008: 30–1)

LINK

You can find Marie Buscatto's study at:

www.qualitativesociologyreview.org/ENG/archive_eng.php

Even once you are 'inside', confidantes or informants in a social setting may be entirely unrepresentative of the less open participants. So the factory managers who were keenest to speak to Dalton (1959) turned out to be the most socially isolated and least powerful in the managerial clique structure.

TIP

Delamont (2004: 225) refers to three golden rules in relation to access negotiations:

1 Every aspect needs to be meticulously recorded because vital features of the setting are made visible during the access stages.
2 Failed access attempts are data just as much as successful attempts.
3 The harder it is to gain access, the more likely the research will be rewarding once 'inside'.

This clearly brings us on to how the ethnographer finds an identity in the field.

5.2.4 Finding an identity

Observers may change the situation just by their presence and so the decision about what role to adopt will be fateful. Alternatively, observers may 'go native', identifying so much with the participants that, like a child learning to talk, they cannot remember how they found something out or articulate the principles underlying what they are doing. More frequently, faced with moving between your identity in the field and your other identities at home and at work, you have to make difficult choices.

CASE STUDY
Field Identities at a Homeless Hostel

Marvasti shows, in his research on a homeless shelter, that he had to face a difficult balancing act between his theoretical preferences, personal characteristics and the practical contingencies of the field. The comment below also reveals that it is usually wrong to assume that, even in the field, the observer has only one identity: 'I might have begun a day with the peripheral role of just listening to the clients' conversations in the parking lot. I could then go on to the more active role of a volunteer. The day could have ended with me assuming the completely participant role of the shelter's night manager' (Marvasti, 2004: 52).

Czarniawska (2007) has shown the value of **shadowing** people during the course of their everyday activities. This is a frequently used method in studying organisations. However, in the case study below, the 'shadower' is interested in family dynamics, using a set of concepts deriving from Erving Goffman.

CASE STUDY
Shopping Together

Gary Miller (personal correspondence reported in Czarniawska, 2007) followed a married couple, Sheila and Bob, when they shopped together. In his reading, they both held conservative notions of gender differences, which provided grounds for a constant comic banter between the spouses when they were shopping:

> A key element within this comic banter is her constant criticism of his lack of shopping skills … Taken in context, however, these criticisms are a mechanism she uses to affirm that as a man, although he may shop, he is not a natural shopper. He is thereby able to receive such 'criticisms' as praise for his natural manliness, something which he recognizes. (2007: 25)

The complications of impression management became even more obvious when Miller shadowed a couple-to-be, a young divorced woman and her boyfriend:

At this stage the crucial factor in shopping was my [Miller's] presence. This was an occasion to learn about each other's taste and forge a relationship in terms of shopping compatibility. But there was also a question as to how they appeared as a couple to an outsider. The sheer effort that I felt they were putting into showing me how happy they were together should not be seen as thereby false. It reflected their own question as to whether, when revealed in the reflected gaze of the anthropologist, they would find themselves to be in love. (2007: 29)

This is Czarniawska's insightful comment about Miller's observation:

This was indeed an interesting situation, because the young woman and her boyfriend, unlike Sheila and Bob, did not rehearse their common impression management many times before. Theirs was a double trial: to perform together an act of acting together. One could venture a guess that the anthropologist's presence was beneficial to the couple, setting this double test for them. Eventually, the anthropologist managed to see more in their performance than they themselves knew. Although this was, upon their own declaration, a couple that aimed at equality, the woman was trying to learn as much as possible about her boyfriend's habits and desires, while he was establishing his right to have the last word on everything, which she could accept as long as he did not force her to acknowledge this fact (they did become engaged, however). (2007: 38)

Does such shadowing change the situation that the shadower observes? Undoubtedly, if we assume that there is a single 'truth' about any couple's behaviour. But, if we follow Goffman's focus on impression management, we do not need to assume that we are 'distorting' observed behaviour. As Czarniawska comments:

A potential criticism would be that the banter was produced for the benefit of the shadow, as it were. [But] impression management is a methodological problem only under the assumption that deeds and utterances of people under study should correspond one-on-one to a reality hidden behind appearances, to be revealed in the course of research. If this assumption is replaced by the Goffmanian premise that life is a theatre, however, then that which is played is of central importance. (2007: 37–8)

Table 5.2 follows the conventional assumption that fieldwork 'distorts' behaviour.

Following Czarniawska and Goffman, however, we can treat the relationship between fieldworker and participants less as a distorting mechanism and more as a fruitful source of additional data. Take item 3 in Table 5.2 which relates the observer's behaviour to how the researcher is defined by research subjects.

In a study of a ward for terminally ill patients, Peräkylä (1989) has shown how staff can use four different ways to define themselves and their patients. Following

TABLE 5.2   Problematic features of fieldwork identity

1 Whether the researcher is known to be a researcher by all of those being studied or only by some, or by none
2 How much, and what, is known about the research by whom
3 What sorts of activities are and are not engaged in by the researcher in the field, and how this locates the researcher in relation to the various conceptions of category and group membership used by participants
4 The orientation of the researcher; how completely the researcher consciously adopts the orientation of insider or outsider

Source: adapted from Atkinson and Hammersley, 1994: 249

Goffman (1974), how people treat what is currently relevant and irrelevant defines the **frame** through which a setting is constituted. Using what Peräkylä calls a *psychological* frame, staff define themselves as objective surveyors of the emotional reactions of patients; patients are both subjects (who feel and experience) and objects (of the knowing psychological gaze). The psychological frame is a powerful means of resolving the identity-disturbances found in other frames – where a patient is resisting practical or medical framing, for instance, this can be explained in terms of their psychological state.

But the psychological frame was also relevant to how staff defined the researcher's own identity. This frame seemed to be a convenient means for the staff to talk about their activities to Peräkylä himself and to define his presence to each other and to patients. So, although Peräkylä was actually a sociologist, staff found it convenient to define him as a psychologist.

CASE STUDY
Identity in the Field

In a comparative study of public and private cancer clinics (Silverman, 1984), I saw how the emphasis on privacy in British 'private' medicine creates a special problem of identity for the researcher. While at the National Health Service (NHS) clinics I sheltered happily behind a name-tag, at the private clinic my presence was always explained, if ambiguously ('Dr Silverman is sitting in with me today if that's all right?'). Although identified and accepted by the patient, I remained uncomfortable in my role in this setting. Its air of quiet seclusion made me feel like an intruder.

Like the doctor, I found myself dressing formally and would always stand up and shake hands with the patient. I could no longer merge into the background as at the NHS clinics. I regularly experienced a sense of intruding on some private ceremony.

Finding an identity in the field may not, of course, just be about your professional affiliation. Your gender in relation to the gender of the people you are studying may turn out to be very important in relation to how you are defined and, therefore, what you find out. Although, as we have seen, in his study of restaurants, Whyte (1949) treated gender as a topic, it was not until 20 years later that social scientists began to think systematically about the impact of gender on the fieldwork process as a whole.

In part, this reflected an interest in the interplay between gender and power. For instance, almost all the 'classics' of the Chicago School were written by men, as were those researchers who rose up the academic hierarchy to become full professors (see Warren, 1988: 11). Increasingly, the gender of fieldworkers themselves was seen to play a crucial factor in observational research. Informants were shown to say different things to male and female researchers.

For instance, in a study of a nude beach, when approached by someone of a different gender, people emphasised their interest in 'freedom and naturalism'. Conversely, where the researcher was the same gender as the informant, people were far more likely to discuss their sexual interests (Warren and Rasmussen, 1977, reported by Warren, 1988).

In studies which involved extended stays in 'the field', people have also been shown to make assumptions based upon the gender of the researcher. For instance, particularly in rural communities, young, single women may be precluded from participating in many activities or asking many questions. Conversely, female gender may sometimes accord privileged access.

For instance, Oboler (1986) reports that her pregnancy increased her rapport with her Kenyan informants, while Warren (1988: 18) suggests that women fieldworkers can make use of the sexist assumption that only men engage in 'important business' by treating their 'invisibility' as a resource. Equally, male fieldworkers may be excluded or exclude themselves from contact with female respondents in certain kinds of situation (see McKeganey and Bloor, 1991).

One danger in all this, particularly in the past, was that fieldworkers failed to report or reflect upon the influence of gender in their fieldwork. For instance, in a study of a large local government organisation, mentioned in Section 8.3.1, we discussed but did not report the different kinds of situations to which the male and female researchers gained easy access (Silverman and Jones, 1976). These are important issues which have been taken up by feminist ethnographers (for summaries, see Brewer, 2000: 99–101; Noaks and Wincup, 2004: 96–8). However, even as the role of doing fieldwork as a woman has become more addressed, hardly any attention has been paid by researchers to questions of male gender (McKeganey and Bloor, 1991: 198).

Nonetheless, as fashions change, it is possible to swing too far and accord gender issues too much importance. As McKeganey and Bloor (1991: 195–6) argue, there are two important issues relevant to the significance of gender in fieldwork. First, the influence of gender may be negotiable with respondents and not simply ascribed. Second, we should resist 'the tendency to employ gender as an explanatory catch-all' (1991: 196).

For instance, McKeganey and Bloor suggest other variables than gender, like age and social class, may also be important in fieldwork. Equally, I would argue, following Schegloff (1991), we need to demonstrate that participants are actually attending to gender in what they are doing, rather than just work with our intuitions or even with statistical correlations (see Section 2.1 and Frith and Kitzinger, 1998).

None of this should imply that it would be correct to swing full circle and, like an earlier generation, ignore gender issues in research. It is incumbent upon field-workers to reflect upon the basis and status of their observations. Clearly, how the researcher and the community studied respond to their gender can provide crucial insights into field realities. Indeed, we would do well to become conscious that even taken-for-granted assumptions may be culturally and historically specific. For instance, Warren suggests that: 'The focal gender *myth* of field research is the greater communicative skills and less threatening nature of the female fieldworker' (1988: 64, my emphasis).

As Warren notes, the important thing is to resist treating such assumptions as 'revealed truths' but as 'accounts' which are historically situated.

5.2.5 Looking as well as listening

In his study of the social organisation of a restaurant, Whyte (1949) reaped rich rewards by using his eyes to observe the spatial organisation of activities. However, ethnographers have not always been as keen to use their eyes as well as their ears. Notable exceptions are Humphreys' (1970) *Tea Room Trade* (a study of the spatial organisation of gay pick-up sites) and Prior's (1988) work on hospital architecture. Michel Foucault's *Discipline and Punish* (1977) offers a famous example of the analysis of prison architecture, while Edward Hall's *The Hidden Dimension* (1969) coined the term 'proxemics' to refer to people's use of space – for instance, how we organise an appropriate distance between each other.

However, these are exceptions. For instance, Stimson (1986: 641) has noted how 'photographs and diagrams are virtually absent from sociological journals, and rare in sociological books' (but see Prior, 2003).

But, when it comes to treating what you *see* as data, all is not doom and gloom (see Chapter 10). In a study of interaction in hospital wards, Peräkylä (1989) notes how spatial arrangements differentiate groups of people. There are the wards and patient rooms, which staff may enter anytime they need to. Then there are patient lounges and the like, which are a kind of public space. Both areas are quite differ-ent from areas like the nurses' room and doctors' offices where patients enter only by invitation. Finally, if there is a staff coffee room, you never see a patient there.

As Peräkylä points out, one way to produce different categories of human beings in a hospital is the allocation of space according to categories. At the same time, this allocation is reproduced in the activities of the participants. For instance, the percep-tive observer might note the demeanour of patients as they approach the nurses' room. Even if the door is open, they may stand outside and just put their heads round the door. In doing so, they mark out that they are encroaching on foreign territory.

In the early 1980s, like Peräkylä, I tried to use my eyes as well as my ears in a study of medical practice already mentioned in Section 5.2.2 above. First, I obtained access to a number of clinics treating cancer patients in an NHS hospital. Following Strong's (1979) account of the 'ceremonial order of the clinic', I was interested in how doctors and patients presented themselves to each other. For instance, Strong had noted that NHS doctors would adhere to the rule 'politeness is all' and so rarely criticise patients to their faces.

While at the hospital, I noticed that one of the doctors regularly seemed to 'go missing' after his morning clinics. My curiosity aroused, I made enquiries. I discovered that most afternoons he was conducting his 'private' practice at consulting rooms in a salubrious area of London's West End.

Nothing ventured, nothing gained, so I tried asking this doctor if I could 'sit in' on his private practice. To my great surprise, he consented on condition that I did not tape record. I happily agreed, even though this meant that my data were reduced to (what I saw as) relatively unreliable fieldnotes (see Section 5.2.6). A brief account of what I saw is contained in the case study below.

CASE STUDY
Viewing Private Medicine

Both NHS clinics were held in functional rooms, with unadorned white walls, no carpets, simple furniture (a small desk, one substantial chair for the doctor and a number of stacking chairs for patients, families and students). Like most NHS hospitals, heating pipes and radiators were very obtrusive.

To enter the consulting rooms of the private clinic is to enter a different world. The main room has the air of an elegant study, perhaps not unlike the kind of room in a private house where a wealthy patient might have been visited by an eighteenth-century doctor. The walls are tastefully painted and adorned with prints and paintings. The floor has a fine carpet. The furniture is reproduction antique and includes a large, leather-topped desk, several comfortable armchairs, a sofa, a low table covered with coffee table books and magazines, and a bookcase which holds ivory figures as well as medical texts. Plants are placed on several surfaces and the room is lit by an elegant central light and a table lamp. To add an executive touch, there are three phones on the desk, as well as a pen in a holder.

This room establishes an air of privacy as well as luxury. At the NHS clinics, patients are nearly always examined in curtained-off areas. Here, however, the examination couch is in a separate room which can only be entered through the consulting room. Although more functional than the latter, it is nonetheless carpeted and kept at a high temperature to keep patients warm. Even the doctor himself may knock before entering this examination room while the patient is dressing or undressing.

Such observations were a very important resource in understanding the character of 'private' medicine at this British clinic. Unfortunately, we have all become a little reluctant to use our eyes as well as our ears when doing observational work. However, there are exceptions. Stimson (1986) discusses a room set out for hearings of a disciplinary organisation responsible for British doctors. The Professional Conduct Committee of the General Medical Council sits in a high-ceilinged, oak-panelled room reached by an imposing staircase. There are stained-glass windows, picturing 16 crests and a woman in a classical Greek pose. As Stimson comments:

> This is a room in which serious matters are discussed: the room has a presence that is forced on our consciousness … speech is formal, carefully spoken and a matter for the public record. Visitors in the gallery speak only, if at all, in hushed whispers, for their speech is not part of the proceedings. (1986: 643–4)

In such a room, as Stimson suggests, even without anything needed to be said, we know that what goes on must be taken seriously. Stimson aptly contrasts this room with a McDonald's hamburger restaurant:

> Consider the decorations and materials – plastic, paper, vinyl and polystyrene, and the bright primary colours. [Everything] signifies transience. This temporary character is further articulated in the casual dress of customers, the institutionally casualised dress of staff and the seating that is constructed to make lengthy stays uncomfortable. (1986: 649–50)

Stimson and Peräkylä show that ethnographers who fail to use their eyes as well as their ears are neglecting a crucial source of data. This lesson is most readily learnt if you imagine a sighted person being forced to make sense of the world while blindfolded! The importance of such visual data is discussed at length in Chapter 10.

EXERCISE 5.3

This is a research exercise to improve your observational skills in the public realm. These are your instructions:

1   Select a setting in which you regularly participate – good examples would be a student cafeteria, a bus or train or a supermarket checkout queue.
2   Make a sketch map of the site. What sort of activities does the physical layout encourage, discourage or is neutral towards? (Refer to Section 5.2.5 for Stimson's comparison of the room for medical hearings and McDonald's).
3   How do people use the space you are studying? What do they show they are attending to? How do they communicate with one another or avoid communication? Do they look at one another or avoid it? What distance do they keep between one another?

4   In what ways are people using the space to co-operate with one another to *define* themselves (e.g. as a restaurant crowd but not bus passengers)?

5   Is there any difference between how people organise their activities when they are on their own, in pairs or in a crowd?

6   How do people use the setting as a resource for engaging in activities not specifically intended (but not necessarily inappropriate) in that setting (e.g. displaying particular personal characteristics such as wanting to communicate or not wanting to communicate)?

5.2.6 Recording observations

Even if you are using both eyes and ears, you will still have to decide how to record your data. Let us assume that you are not using electronic recordings (audio- or videotapes) or that you wish to supplement such recordings with observational data. (Working with transcripts deriving from recordings is discussed in Chapter 9.) In this case, you must rely on contemporary fieldnotes. How should you write fieldnotes?

The greatest danger is that you will seek to report 'everything' in your notes. Not only does this overlook the theory-driven nature of field research (see Section 5.4), but also it gives you an impossible burden when you try to develop a more systematic analysis at a later stage. As Wolcott puts it: 'The critical task in qualitative research is not to accumulate all the data you can, but to "can" (get rid of) most of the data you accumulate. This requires constant winnowing' (1990: 35).

At the outset, however, it is likely that you will use broad descriptive categories 'relating to particular people or types of people, places, activities and topics of concern' (Hammersley and Atkinson, 1995: 167). Moreover, items may be usefully assigned to more than one category in order to maximise the range of hypotheses that can be generated. To do this, it may help to make multiple copies of each segment of data, filed under several categories (1983: 170).

TIP

Emerson et al. suggest five sets of questions which you should try to answer when making fieldnotes:

1   What are people doing? What are they trying to accomplish?

2   How exactly do they do this?

3   How do people characterise and understand what is going on?

4   What assumptions do they make?

5   Analytic questions: What do I see going on here? What did I learn from these notes? Why did I include them? (1995: 146)

One useful aid in filing and indexing is provided by a computer program in computer-assisted qualitative data analysis (CAQDAS). What Seale (2010) has called 'mainstream' CAQDAS software allows the user to see these materials in the same way that a word processor allows a user to see a document. The software will also support the user in searching through documents for particular features, for example a particular word or phrase. Sometimes each instance of a word or phrase can be inspected in its context. Additionally, and this is perhaps the most commonly used core feature, such software allows the user to code segments of data (e.g. some text) according to some conceptual scheme. Coded segments can then be searched for and retrieved. Together, this is known as the 'code and retrieve' element of such software.

LINK
NVIVO   www.qsrinternational.com
MAXqda   www.maxqda.com
ATLAS.ti www.atlasti.com

In order to make this discussion of note-taking more concrete, I want to give an example from a piece of research I carried out in the early 1980s (see Silverman, 1987). The study was of a paediatric cardiology unit. Much of my data derived from tape recordings of an outpatient clinic that lasted between two and four hours every Wednesday.

Secure in the knowledge that the basic data were being recorded, I was free to use my eyes as well as my ears to record more data to help in the analysis of the audiotapes. Gradually, with the help of my co-worker Robert Hilliard, I developed a coding sheet to record my observations.

As an illustration of how I coded the data, Table 5.3 shows the full coding sheet used in this study. In order to explain how we derived the categories, I have included explanations of some of the categories in square brackets.

I ought to stress that this coding form was only developed after observation of more than ten outpatient clinics and after extensive discussions between the research team. During this time, we narrowed down what we were looking for.

Increasingly, we became interested in how decisions (or 'disposals') were organised and announced. It seemed likely that the doctor's way of announcing decisions was systematically related not only to clinical factors (like the child's heart condition) but to social factors (such as what parents would be told at various stages of treatment).

For instance, at a first outpatients' consultation, doctors would not normally announce to parents the discovery of a major heart abnormality and the necessity for life-threatening surgery. Instead, they would suggest the need for more tests and only hint that major surgery might be needed. They would also collaborate with

TABLE 5.3   Outpatient coding form

1   Name of patient

2   Age

3   Clinic and date

4   Doctor

5   Family present

6   Non-family present

7   Length of co-presence of doctor and family [we wanted to record the time of the encounter not including periods when the doctor was out of the room]

8   Diagnosis

9   Stage of treatment:

   1st consultation

   Pre-inpatient

   Post-catheter [test requiring inpatient stay]

   Post-operation

10   Outcome of consultation:

   Discharge or referral elsewhere

   Non-inpatient follow-up

   Possible eventual catheter or surgery

   Catheter

   Surgery

   No decision

11   Consultation stages [this derived from Robert Hilliard's attempt to identify a series of stages from a greeting exchange to elicitation of symptoms, through to examination and diagnosis statement (see Silverman, 1985: 265–9)]:

   Stage

   Questions asked

   Topics covered

   Notes/Markers

(Continued)

TABLE 5.3   (Continued)

12 Does doctor invite questions?

   No

   Yes (When:)

13 Use of medical terminology:

   Stage

   Doctor/Family

14 Scope of consultation:

	Family	Doctor
Prior treatment history		
Extra-cardiac physical states		
Child development		
Child behaviour		
Family's practicalities of treatment or attendance		
Doctor's practicalities of treatment or attendance		
Anxieties and emotional problems of family		
Social situation of family		
External treatment agencies		

15 Family's presentation of a referral history

16 Format of doctor's initial elicitation question [e.g. how is she? Is she well?]

17 Patency [this referred to whether symptoms or diseases were visible or 'patent' to the family]:

   Family's presentation of problems/symptoms

   Doctor's mention of patent symptoms

   Family's assent to problems/symptoms

   Not patent?

18 Location of examination:

   Desk

   Couch

   Side-room

TABLE 5.3   (Continued)

19 Diagnosis statement:

    a) Use of 'well' (Doctor/Family/Both)

    b) Use of 'normal' (Doctor/Family/Both)

    c) Possible diagnoses mentioned (0/1/>1)

20 Decisions:

    a) Possible disposals mentioned (0/1/>1)

    b) Medical preference stated (Yes/No)

    c) Medical intention stated (Yes/No)

    d) Family assent requested (Yes/No)

    e) Family allowed to make decision (Yes/No)

    f) Family wishes volunteered (Yes/No)

    g) Family dissent from doctor's proposed disposal (Yes/No)

21 Uncertainty expressed by doctor:

    a) Over-diagnosis

    b) Over-treatment

parents who produced examples of their child's apparent 'wellness'. This step-by-step method of information-giving was avoided in only two cases. If a child was diagnosed as 'healthy' by the cardiologist, the doctor would give all the information in one go and would engage in what we called a 'search and destroy' operation, based on eliciting any remaining worries of the parent(s) and proving that they were mistaken.

In the case of a group of children with the additional handicap of Down's syndrome, as well as suspected cardiac disease, the doctor would present all the clinical information at one sitting, avoiding a step-by-step method. Moreover, atypically, the doctor would allow parents to make the choice about further treatment, while encouraging parents to focus on non-clinical matters like their child's 'enjoyment of life' or friendly personality (Silverman, 1981).

The coding form shown in Table 5.3 allowed us to identify these patterns. For instance, by relating item 14 on the scope of the consultation to the decision format (item 20), we were able to see differences between consultations involving Down's children and others. Moreover, it also turned out that there were significant differences between these two groups in both the form of the elicitation question (item 16) and the diagnosis statement (item 19).

The coding form in Table 5.3 followed a practice which derives from

> that well-established style of work whereby the data are inspected for categories and instances. It is an approach that disaggregates the text (notes or transcripts) into a series of fragments, which are then regrouped under a series of thematic headings. (Atkinson, 1992: 455)

Obviously, in making fieldnotes, one is not simply recording data but also analysing them. The categories you use will inevitably be theoretically saturated – whether or not you realise it! So the coding form shown as Table 5.3 reflected my interest in Goffman's (1974) concept of 'framing'. This meant that I tried to note down the activities through which the participants managed their identities. For instance, I noted how long the doctor and patient spent on social 'small talk' and how subsequent appointments were arranged.

These concerns show how theoretically defined concepts drive good ethnographic research (see Section 5.3). They also demonstrate how one can develop analysis of field data after a research problem has been carefully defined.

However, as Atkinson points out, one of the disadvantages of coding schemes is that, because they are based upon a given set of categories, they furnish 'a powerful conceptual grid' (1992: 459) from which it is difficult to escape. While this 'grid' is very helpful in organising the data analysis, it also deflects attention away from uncategorised activities. In these circumstances, it is helpful to return occasionally to the original data.

In our research, we had our tapes and transcripts which offered endless opportunities to redefine our categories. By contrast, lacking tapes of his data on medical education, Atkinson returned to his original fieldnotes. He shows how the same, original data can be re-read in a quite different way. Atkinson's earlier method had been to fragment his fieldnotes into relatively small segments, each with its own category.

For instance, a surgeon's description of post-operative complications to a surgical team was originally categorised under such headings as 'unpredictability', 'uncertainty', 'patient career' and 'trajectory'. Later, when Atkinson returned to his data, it was re-categorised as an overall narrative which sets up an enigma ('unexpected complications') resolved in the form of a 'moral tale' ('beware, unexpected things can always happen'). Viewed in this way, the surgeon's story becomes a **text** with many resemblances to a fairy tale, as we shall see in Section 5.3.

There is a further 'moral tale' implicit in using Atkinson's story. The field researcher is always torn between the need to narrow down analysis through category-construction and to allow some possibility of reinterpretation of the same data. So, while the rush to categorise is laudable, it should always occur in the context of a solid body of original data. The ideal form for this is a tape recording or original document. Where these cannot be used, the field researcher must attempt to transcribe as much as possible of what is said and done – and the settings in which it is said and done.

In such transcription, R. Dingwall (personal correspondence) notes how important it is to record *descriptions* rather than mere impressions. In practice, this means that we should always try to note concrete instances of what people have said or done, using verbatim quotations and 'flat' (or unadorned) descriptions.

EXERCISE 5.4

Return to your fieldnotes in Exercises 5.2 and 5.3 and answer the following questions:

1 How were your notes organised (did you just write down verbatim what you saw or heard or did you use some organising principle, e.g. 'frames')?
2 If there was an organising principle, which one was it? Why did you choose it? And how did it help or hinder you?
3 If there was no organising principle, how did you move from description of what you observed to its analysis?
4 In what ways were your notes dependent on your common-sense knowledge of what was going on?
5 How can that dependence be treated as a problem but also as a help?

5.2.7 Developing analysis of field data

One of the strengths of observational research is its ability to shift focus as interesting new data become available. For instance, as already noted, during a study of two cancer clinics at a British NHS hospital, I unexpectedly gained access to a 'private' (fee-paying) clinic run by one of the doctors in his spare time. I was thus able to change my research focus towards a comparison of the 'ceremonial orders' of public and private medicine (Silverman, 1984). This process of interweaving different aspects of research is well described by using an analogy with a funnel:

> Ethnographic research has a characteristic 'funnel' structure, being progressively focused over its course. Progressive focusing has two analytically distinct components. First, over time the research problem is developed or transformed, and eventually its scope is clarified and delimited and its internal structure explored. In this sense, it is frequently only over the course of the research that one discovers what the research is really 'about', and it is not uncommon for it to turn out to be about something quite remote from the initially foreshadowed problems. (Hammersley and Atkinson, 1995: 175)

For instance, my research on the two cancer clinics unexpectedly led into a comparison of fee-for-service and state-provided medicine (Silverman, 1984). Similarly, my observation of a paediatric cardiology unit moved unpredictably in the direction of an analysis of disposal decisions with a small group of Down's syndrome children (Silverman, 1981).

We may note three features which these two cases had in common:

1 The switch of focus – through the 'funnel' – as a more defined topic arose.
2 The use of the comparative method as an invaluable tool of theory-building and testing.
3 The generation of topics with a scope outside the substantive area of the research. Thus the 'ceremonial orders' found in the cancer clinics are not confined to medicine, while the 'democratic' decision-making found with the Down's children had unexpected effects of power with a significance far beyond medical encounters.

However, shifts of focus in ethnographic research can sometimes resemble not so much a funnel as a rubbish dump! Some ethnographies seem like a disorganised stumble through a mass of data, full of 'insightful' observations of a mainly 'anecdotal' nature. For instance, in a survey of qualitative papers in two journals in the area of health and social science, I was struck by the number of articles based on one or two 'convincing' examples (Silverman, 2005: 232–5).

There is absolutely no reason why observational research cannot combine insight with rigour. In other words, it is right to expect that such research should be *both* original *and* valid. This will involve testing hypotheses that we have generated in the field. Increasingly, however, as our knowledge of micro-social processes expands, it will mean that we can enter the field with an hypothesis we already want to test. So, in my comparative study of medical practice, Strong's (1979) work on the 'ceremonial orders' of doctor–patient interaction gave me a clear hypothesis which became testable when I gained access to a private clinic. For more on testing hypotheses in qualitative research, see Chapter 11.

5.3 THE THEORETICAL CHARACTER OF ETHNOGRAPHIC OBSERVATIONS

> any researcher, no matter how unstructured or inductive, comes to fieldwork with *some* orienting ideas, foci and tools. (Miles and Huberman, 1984: 27)

As we have already seen, even the apparently simple act of describing what you see in the field can be highly complicated. Arguing that subjects' meanings are always part of a wider system of signs or webs of significance, Geertz (1973) has called for **thick description** based on a study of systems of signs (see the discussion of **semiotics** in Chapter 10). However, given that one always has to select from a large data corpus, researchers have to seek a balance between 'thick' description of some phenomena at the cost of 'thin' description of others (see

Brekhus et al., 2005). So no research can ever be 'theory-free'. We only come to look at things in certain ways because we have adopted, either tacitly or explicitly, certain ways of seeing. This means that, in observational research, data collection, hypothesis construction and theory-building are not separate things but are interwoven with one another.

Three 'ways of seeing' are outlined in Table 5.4.

TABLE 5.4   Three views of ethnographic descriptions

1 Faithful representation of subjects' worlds – achieved by minimising the researcher's presuppositions. This is usually referred to as naturalism
2 A focus on participants' practices in which participants' accounts are treated as narrative accomplishments rather than as true or false reports on reality. This is the constructionist approach
3 A specialised version of the constructionist approach is ethnomethodology. This studies folk ('ethno') methods ('methodology') for assembling any social phenomenon. The researcher's task is to study members' descriptive work as it locally assembles some phenomenon (see my discussion of how traffic works in Section 5.3.3)

5.3.1 The naturalist model

As Gubrium and Holstein note, the apparently atheoretical position of some ethnographers itself derives from a theory: 'The directive to "minimize presuppositions" in order to witness subjects' worlds on their own terms is a key to *naturalistic* inquiry' (1997a: 34, my emphasis)

So the idea of just 'hanging out' with the aim of 'faithfully representing subjects' worlds ('telling it like it is') is a convenient myth derived from a theory that Gubrium and Holstein term naturalism. Of course, without some conceptual orientation, one would not recognise the 'field' one was studying. So the problem is that many closet naturalists fail to come clean about the theory dependence of their research. As two ethnographers put it:

> Telling it like it is implies presenting an account of the social world from the perspective of those being researched; telling the story as they would tell it (based on the unlikely assumption that they would all tell the same story). This is an overly *simplistic* view because if an ethnographer were to do this, he or she would have 'gone native', in other words become so immersed in the culture they were studying that they had left their academic culture behind. (Noaks and Wincup, 2004: 92)

I only have space for one example of the problems of naturalism (see Silverman, 2010: 297–308, for more discussion of this and other examples). Engebretson (1996) reports a participant observation and interview study of three groups of healers who 'heal' through the laying on of hands. She locates her findings in terms of three 'dimensions' (setting, interaction and cognitive process) and finds, unsurprisingly, that such healing differed from biomedicine on each of these dimensions.

Unfortunately, Engebretson mentions no explicit model or theory. So, although her descriptions of how healing was organised and how the sessions were opened and closed have at least the potential to suggest practical relevance, they lack the coherence that a theoretically defined study might offer. Such a theory would, for instance, inform how data are recorded. Yet Engebretson makes no mention of the system used for recording fieldnotes and its impact on the **reliability** of her data (see Section 11.2).

Second, her account of her data is presented just as a simple description. Without a discussion of the analytic basis for the researcher's account, her report once more can only have a journalistic status. As I point out in Chapter 14, this is not to criticise journalism which, at its best, can be highly illuminating. It is simply intended to distinguish between journalism and social science. Third, although Engebretson groups her interview respondents' accounts into a number of categories (physical sensations, emotional experiences and visual images), there is nothing to suggest that these are anything but ad hoc labels without a clear analytical basis.

I should add two qualifications to this critique. First, it is unfair to single out just one study when even respected academic journals are overflowing with research reports that refuse to recognise the theoretically guided character of ethnographic description. Second, it would be foolish to deny that naturalism (even when unacknowledged) has been the source of any insights. Even one of naturalism's fiercest critics, Harvey Sacks, nonetheless found much to admire in the naturalistically informed Chicago School's attention to detail. As Sacks put it:

> Instead of pushing aside the older ethnographic work in sociology, I would treat it as the only work worth criticizing in sociology; where criticizing is giving some dignity to something. So, for example, the relevance of the works of the Chicago sociologists is that they do contain a lot of information about this and that. And this-and-that is what the world is made up of. (1992, I: 27)

However, the ethnographers' praiseworthy attention to detail rarely satisfied Sacks's rigorous methodological demands. For Sacks, the ethnographer needs to go beyond naturalism in order to analyse the most basic details of interaction. The ethnographer cannot rely on glosses of what everyone knows. What this might entail will be illustrated in the following discussion of **constructionism**.

5.3.2 The constructionist model

Maynard (1989) notes how ethnographers are still trying to picture how people see things rather than focusing on what is observable. As he puts it:

In doing ethnography, researchers attempt to draw a picture of what some phenomenon 'looks like' from an insider's account of the phenomenon and for some audience who wants to know about it. The ethnographer, in general, is in the business of describing culture from the members' point of view. (1989: 130)

Maynard shows how such concerns have shaped research in one part of the sociology of law. 'Plea bargaining' has been identified as a process by which defendants plead guilty to a 'lesser' offence, thereby minimising their punishment and speeding up the work of the courts (evidence does not need to be heard if the defendant pleads guilty). Ethnographers have assumed that this process works on the basis of shared perceptions held by prosecution and defence lawyers.

However, Maynard suggests that such ethnographic work, based on the identification of people's perceptions, has at least three deficiencies:

1   It depends upon common-sense knowledge: 'ethnographers rely on unnoticed abilities to record and recognise such features, just as participants rely on basically uninvestigated abilities in producing them (1989: 130).
2   It glosses over what 'plea bargaining' actually is – the diversity of discourse that gets called 'plea bargaining'.
3   It fails to treat the common orientation of the parties concerned as an outcome of their interaction, preferring to make such 'mutuality appear to be a matter of cognitive consensus' (1989: 134).

Instead, following Sacks's emphasis on what is observable, Maynard studies 'how a sense of mutuality is accomplished' (1989: 134). This involves examining how plea-bargaining sequences are introduced into the talk. For instance, a bargaining proposal can be solicited or it can be announced, as shown in Table 5.5.

Maynard's study draws attention to how the phenomenon of 'plea bargaining' is itself locally constituted in the activities of the participants. If we follow naturalism and reduce social life merely to the definitions of the participants, there is a danger that we lose sight of social interaction.

TABLE 5.5 Two forms of plea bargaining

PD = Public Defender, DA = District Attorney	
Solicitation	
(solicit)	PD: Is there an offer in this case?
(proposal)	DA: I would say in this case a fine, seventy five dollars
Announcement	
(announcement)	PD: I'll propose a deal to you
('go-ahead' signal)	DA: Tell me what ya got
(proposal)	PD: If ya dismiss the 242, I might be able to arrange a plea to 460 for a fine

Source: Maynard, 1989: 134

Instead, the point is to narrow the focus to what people are *doing*. As Maynard puts it:

> The question that ethnographers have traditionally asked – 'How do participants see things?' – has meant in practice the presumption that reality lies outside the words spoken in a particular time and place. The … (alternative) question – 'How do participants do things?' – suggests that the microsocial order can be appreciated more fully by studying how speech and other face-to-face behaviours constitute reality within actual mundane situations. (1989: 144)

James Holstein and Jaber Gubrium clearly show how constructionism departs from naturalistic ethnography based on the study of how people see things. As they put it:

> The naturalistic goal in ethnography is to understand social reality on its own terms, 'as it really is,' to describe what comes naturally, so to speak. It seeks rich descriptions of people and interaction as these exist and unfold in their native habitats … Whereas the naturalistic impulse in fieldwork is typically to ask '*What* is going on?' with, and within, social reality, constructionist sensibilities provoke questions about *how* social realities are produced, assembled, and maintained. (2008: 374–5)

Table 5.6 sets out these differences in more detail.

TABLE 5.6   Two models compared

Naturalism	Constructionism
Getting inside social reality	Studying how 'reality' is assembled
Understanding 'meanings'	Examining narrative construction
Asking 'what is going on?'	Studying everyday procedures
Fieldnotes as snapshots of the field	Transcripts reveal unexpected practice

Source: adapted from Holstein and Gubrium, 2008: 375, 385

The following case study shows how I used a constructionist approach in an ethnography of cleft-palate clinics.

CASE STUDY

Cleft-palate clinics treat children born with hare lips and/or cleft palates. Cleft-palates can stop babies feeding and so are usually repaired in the first few months of life. A hare lip is treatable by routine, low-risk, cosmetic surgery usually carried out when the patient is in their teens. The rationale for delaying cosmetic surgery in the cleft-palate clinic is that, since appearance is a matter of personal judgement, it is best left until somebody is of an age when they can decide for themselves rather than be influenced by the surgeon or their parents. This is how things panned out in an Australian cleft-palate clinic I studied in 1986:

Extract 5.1 [Silverman, 1987: 182]

(D = Doctor, S = Simon, an 18-year-old patient)

D: Do you worry at all about your appearance?
S: Oh I really notice it but I um if it could be improved, I'd like to get it done. I really worry about it.
D: *Really*?
S: Yes
D: Not really but *really*?
S: But *really* yes.

In one leap, Simon (S) seems to have overcome the communication difficulties that a question about your appearance usually generates in these clinics. He freely admits that he 'notices' and 'worries' about his looks and, consequently, would 'like to get it done'.

What is going on in Extract 5.1? Why is Simon's apparently straightforward response subject to further questioning? To answer these questions, I noted comments made by a doctor before Simon had entered the room. These are shown in Extract 5.2:

Extract 5.2 [Silverman, 1987: 180]

D: He's er (0.5) it's a matter of deciding whether he should have an operation. And, er, what we are concerned about is his degree of maturity which it will be very interesting for you [D turns towards me] to make a judgement on when he comes in.

We see from Extract 5.2 that, even before Simon enters the room, his 'degree of maturity' will be an issue. We are advised that Simon's answers should not stand alone as expression of his wishes but should be judged as mature or immature and, perhaps, discarded or reinterpreted.

After Simon leaves, this doctor worries some more about what Simon's answers 'really' mean:

Extract 5.3 [Silverman, 1987: 186]

D: It's very difficult to assess isn't it? Because he's pretty sophisticated in some of his comments and it's er (1.0) it's just the, you know, continuously sunny nature that's troubling me a little bit about the problem as to whether it should be done.

Eventually, this doctor concludes that Simon's relaxed manner is merely 'a cover-up' for his self-consciousness about his appearance. Although this is rather an odd conclusion since Simon has freely admitted that he is concerned about his appearance, it generates general consent and all the doctors present agree that Simon is 'motivated' and should have his operation.

EXERCISE 5.5

Referring to Table 5.6, show why my analysis of the cleft-palate clinic had a constructionist flavour. How might my approach have differed if I had been a naturalist?

5.3.3 The ethnomethodological model

Just because something seems 'pretty routine', we cannot assume that it is not difficult to explain. As Sacks pointed out in one of his lectures: 'the activities that molecules are able to engage in quickly, routinely, have not been described by enormously brilliant scientists' (1992, I: 115).

To understand humans' routine activities, Sacks followed his teacher Harold Garfinkel in attempting to make common sense a 'topic' not just a tacit 'resource'. It follows that how societal members (including social researchers) 'see' particular activities is, for Sacks, the central research question.

In this respect, together with Garfinkel (1967), he offers a unique perspective in social science. This perspective is ethnomethodology (or the study of folk – or members' – methods) which 'seeks to describe methods persons use in doing social life' (Sacks, 1984: 21).

For Garfinkel and Sacks, when ethnographers 'describe' and 'question', the problem is that they are tacitly using members' methods. If we are to study such methods, it is, therefore, crucial that we do not take for granted what it is we appear to be 'seeing'. As Sacks says:

> In setting up what it is that seems to have happened, preparatory to solving the [research] problem, do not let your notion of what could conceivably happen decide for you what must have happened. (1992, I: 115)

Here Sacks is telling us that our 'notion of what could conceivably happen' is likely to be drawn from our unexamined members' knowledge. Instead, we need to proceed more cautiously by examining the methods members use to produce activities as observable and reportable.

Sacks suggests that people should not be seen as 'coming to terms with some phenomenon' (I: 437) but as actively *constituting* it. The phenomenon of 'speeding' on the roads is considered in the next case study.

CASE STUDY

How does one know one is speeding? One solution is to look at the car's speedometer. However, another well-used method is to compare the car's movement relative to other traffic. And 'traffic' is a phenomenon that is actively organised by road users. As Sacks suggests:

> persons can be seen to clump their cars into something that is 'a traffic', pretty much wherever, whenever, whoever it is that's driving. That exists as a social fact, a thing which drivers do ... [so]

by 'a traffic' I don't mean that there are some cars, but there is a set of cars that can be used as 'the traffic', however it's going; those cars that are clumped. And it is in terms of 'the traffic' that you see you're driving fast or slow. (1992, I: 437)

Sacks here is arguing that, rather than being a natural fact, 'the traffic' is a self-organising system, in which people adjust their speed by reference to how they define 'the traffic'. The traffic thus serves as a metaphor for how social order is constructed by reference to what can be inferred. It also shows how the ability 'to read other people's minds' (in this case, the minds of other drivers) is not a psychotic delusion but a condition for social order. For Sacks, then, 'traffic' and 'speed' are not natural facts but locally assembled phenomena (see also Pollner, 1987).

As Sacks notes, the selfsame features can be seen in medical consultations, where what is 'normal' is attended to by doctors on the basis of their elicitation of what is normal for you (I: 57–8). Moreover, while illnesses may be 'erasable', this does not usually apply to speeding fines or suicide attempts – and the latter is seen in people's reluctance to identify themselves when calling an emergency psychiatric service (I: 61).

Put at its simplest, researchers must be very careful how they use categories. For instance, Sacks quotes from two linguists who appear to have no problem in characterising particular (invented) utterances as 'simple', 'complex', 'casual' or 'ceremonial'. For Sacks, such rapid characterisations of data assume 'that we can know that without an analysis of what it is (they) are doing' (I: 429). Over 20 years on, his comments stand as a criticism of the rapid coding of data that sometimes passes as grounded theory.

TIP

Before you code any data extract, ask yourself what common-sense knowledge you are using to see it in the way that you do. Treat this as a way to try to get at how participants 'code' (constitute) particular phenomena.

5.3.4 Constructionism and ethnomethodology compared

You may now wonder how ethnomethodology differs from constructionism. After all, both are concerned with how social phenomena from medical interviews to 'speeding' are constructed. I like to see the differences between the two approach as a matter of emphasis. To explain this further, I will look at another case study.

CASE STUDY

Around the time I was observing the cleft-palate clinics, Gubrium (1988) was doing an ethnographic study of Cedarview, a US residential treatment centre for emotionally disturbed children. Extract 5.4 below involves three boys (aged 9–10) who are talking in their dormitory room. Gubrium reports that he overheard this conversation from an adjacent room while reading comics with other boys.

Extract 5.4 [Gubrium, 1988: 10]

Gary: can you really get firecrackers from your brother?
Tom: really!

[Gary produces 'a chain of accusatory exchanges that play on the word "really"']
[Gary and Bill press Tom to tell the truth 'or else' asking Tom whether he was just kidding]

Tom: really, really, really
Gary and Bill: [jostling Tom] no you didn't … you're lying

In this extract, Gary and Bill are challenging Tom about his access to firecrackers. Compare what is said to what we have just seen in the Australian cleft-palate clinic:

Extract 5.5 [Extract 5.1 repeated]

S: I really worry about it.
D: *Really*?
S: Yes
D: Not really but *really*?
S: But *really* yes.

Despite two very different settings and participants (a peer group and a professional–client interview), note how participants systematically search for what 'really' is the case, using that term to frame questions and to provide answers. In formal terms, both extracts look like the kind of charge–rebuttal sequences that are common in courts of law. Is it appropriate to say that we are dealing with a single phenomenon which happens to be located in a variety of contexts?

Yes and no. An analysis of the features of charge–rebuttal sequences is indeed a useful exercise since it can identify the various strategies available to people to make or rebut charges. However, we must not exclude the different agendas the participants bring to different contexts and the resources they can draw upon in, say, medical clinics, peer group interaction and law courts. Without this further step, our analysis runs the danger of becoming purely formalistic and, thereby, likely to lack the kind of practical relevance in which I am interested.

Gubrium (1988) suggests how we can reframe this argument to mark out the limits of three different kinds of ethnography:

1 *Structural ethnography* simply aims to understand participants' subjective meanings. It makes great use of open-ended interviews and, as such, is the most common approach. It is associated with naturalism.
2 By contrast, *articulative ethnography* seeks to locate the formal structures of interaction. It is usually based on audio- or videotapes of naturally occurring interaction and identifies sequential structures like charge–rebuttal sequences. It is associated with ethnomethodology.
3 *Practical ethnography* recognises that members' interpretations are neither limitless nor purely formal. For example, in Gubrium's residential home, staff members would construct particular versions of children in different contexts, for example a treatment review team versus a meeting with the child's family. Again, charge–rebuttal sequences may look very different in children's talk versus a clinic or courtroom. Such actions are, as Gubrium (1988) puts it, 'organisationally embedded', that is different settings may provide the participants with differing meanings and interactional resources. This approach is associated with Gubrium's version of constructionism.

Gubrium is arguing that, although both structural and articulative ethnography answer important questions, they cannot, even in combination, define the whole of the ethnographic enterprise. To do this, we need to understand the context in which the parties generate their meanings and interactions.

5.4 CONCLUSION: THE UNITY OF THE ETHNOGRAPHIC PROJECT

It would be entirely mistaken to believe that all the certainties in observational work derive from constructionist and/or ethnomethodological insights. In fact, as I have argued already, a number of ethnographers have either taken on board many of these insights or reached them independently. For instance, a recognition that social phenomena are locally constituted (through the activities of participants) is not confined to Sacks and Maynard. Using the example of studies of the 'family', I want to show another direction from which one can draw the same conclusion.

In a paper on methodological issues in family studies, Gubrium and Holstein (1987) show how much sociological work assumes that 'family life' is properly depicted in its 'natural' habitat – the home. Conversely, they argue that the 'family' is not a uniform phenomenon, to be found in one setting, but is 'occasioned' and 'contexted'. We can see more clearly what they are saying in Table 5.7 which contrasts the 'conventional understanding' with Gubrium and Holstein's alternative.

Gubrium and Holstein's alternative direction for family studies closely fits Sacks's approach, while opening up a number of fascinating areas for family studies, as set

TABLE 5.7 Two ways of describing 'family life'

The conventional understanding

1 Families have 'inner' and 'outer' sides
2 The 'inner' side is located in the household
3 Outside households we obtain only a 'version' of this 'prime reality'
4 Members of the household have a privileged access to family order
5 Participant observation is required to obtain 'authentic understanding' of family life

An alternative

1 Family is a way of interpreting, representing and ordering social relations
2 The family is not private but inextricably linked with public life
3 The household does not locate family life
4 The household is not 'trivial' because it is often appealed to by laypeople and professionals alike as the determinant of family life

---

Source: adapted from Gubrium and Holstein, 1987

out below. Once we conceive of the 'family' in terms of a researchable set of descriptive practices, we are freed from the methodological and ethical nightmare of obtaining access to study families 'as they really are', that is in their own households. This means that:

1 We can now study how the structures of family organisation are depicted in different milieux (e.g. employment agencies, schools, clinics).
2 This links to studies of the social distribution of 'knowledge' about the family (e.g. when, where and by whom theories of the nature and consequences of 'broken homes' are employed).
3 It also ties in with the study of how different organisational routines constrain particular depictions of family order.

As already noted, issues of household location and privileged access now become re-defined as topics rather than troubles – for example, we might study the claims that professionals make for such access. This underlines Gubrium and Holstein's point that family knowledge is never purely private. Family members themselves appeal to collective representations (like maxims and the depictions of families in soap operas) to explain their own behaviour. Family members also present the 'reality' of family life in different ways to different audiences and in different ways to the same audience (see Gubrium and Holstein, 1990, for a fuller discussion).

EXERCISE 5.6

This exercise encourages you to use the 'alternative' version of describing family life proposed by Gubrium and Holstein.

Imagine that you wish to do an observational study of the family. Now consider the following questions:

1 What are the advantages and disadvantages of obtaining access to the family household?
2 In what ways may families be studied outside the household setting? What methodology might you use and what questions could you ask?
3 What might observation tell you about the 'family' in each of the following settings:

   • law courts
   • doctor–patient consultations
   • TV soap operas?

(*Either* do a study of *one* of these settings *or* write hypothetically about all *three*.)

4 What does it mean to say you are studying the 'family' (i.e. within inverted commas)?

Gubrium and Holstein offer an exciting prospectus for family studies and an appropriate way to conclude this chapter on observation. For this kind of work (termed 'practical ethnography' by Gubrium, 1988), together with ethnomethodology, offers three crucial insights for observational studies:

1 It switches attention away from a more psychological orientation around what people are thinking towards what they are doing.
2 It shows the analytic issues that lie behind methodological puzzles.
3 It firmly distinguishes social science observational work from journalism and common sense, thus, in a certain sense, fulfilling Durkheim's project.

As Moerman once commented: 'Folk beliefs have honourable status but they are not the same intellectual object as a scientific analysis' (1974: 55).

KEY POINTS

There are three crucial aspects of observational research:

• the focus of the study

• methodological decisions

• theoretical choices.

Naturalism, constructionism and ethnomethodology provide very different ways of defining observational research. Each offers a 'toolbox' providing a set of concepts and methods to select appropriate data and to illuminate data analysis.

STUDY QUESTIONS

1 What is ethnography?
2 Why should qualitative research study behaviour as well as perceptions?
3 What methodological issues arise in doing an ethnography? How can they best be resolved?
4 What is 'shadowing'? How can it be used in ethnographic research?
5 What problems and insights arise in negotiating an identity for the fieldworker?
6 What can ethnographers learn by using their eyes as well as their ears?
7 What are fieldnotes and how can they be organised?
8 What do we gain by obtaining audio or video recordings of events in the field?
9 What are the different theoretical underpinnings of ethnography? What are the advantages and disadvantages of each approach?

RECOMMENDED READING

Introductions to observational and ethnographic work are given by Gobo (2011) and Buscatto (2011). On the ethnography of organizations, see Eberle and Maeder (2011) and Nick Llewellyn and Jon Hindmarsh's edited collection *Organization, Interaction and Practice* (2010).

Gubrium and Holstein (1997a) provide an important account of four current models used in observational research. Harvey Sacks's lectures offer marvellous insights on the current relevance of the Chicago School (Sacks, 1992, I: 26–31). Buscatto (2008) has written an online article which is full of methodological insights about participant observation:

www.qualitativesociologyreview.org/ENG/archive_eng.php

6
Interviews

CHAPTER OBJECTIVES

By the end of this chapter, you will be able to:

- distinguish the different kinds of interview
- understand what skills are used in doing an interview
- recognise the various theoretical bases of interview research
- conduct a simple analysis of interview data in a way which is appropriate to your research problem.

If you have been thinking about doing a research project, the likelihood is that the first method you considered is the open-ended interview. In this chapter, we examine the uses and pitfalls of interview data. Working through a number of examples, I will show the key role played by basic theoretical assumptions about how we treat interview data.

However, first we must understand the method. The 'unstructured' or 'open-ended' interview is most common in qualitative research. How does it differ from other kinds of interview? And what kinds of skills does it involve?

6.1 WHAT IS AN 'OPEN-ENDED' INTERVIEW?

Noaks and Wincup (2004) have sketched out the characteristics of three different interview formats and of the **focus group**, in which the researcher acts more as

TABLE 6.1 Typology of interview strategies

Type of interview	Required skills
Structured interview	Neutrality; no prompting; no improvisation; training to ensure consistency
Semi-structured interview	Some probing; rapport with interviewee; understanding the aims of the project
Open-ended interview	Flexibility; rapport with interviewee; active listening
Focus group	Facilitation skills; flexibility; ability to stand back from the discussion so that group dynamics can emerge

Source: adapted from Noaks and Wincup, 2004: 80

the facilitator of a group discussion rather than as a questioner. Table 6.1 shows the skills expected in each format.

Chapter 7 examines focus groups. I will concentrate here on the open-ended interview which, as Noaks and Wincup note, is commonly used to elicit life-histories. In such interviews, in order to achieve 'rich data', the keynote is 'active listening' in which the interviewer 'allows the interviewee the freedom to talk and ascribe meanings' while bearing in mind the broader aims of the project (Noaks and Wincup, 2004: 80).

These aims have been described as 'understanding the language and culture of the respondents' (Fontana and Frey, 2000: 654). In order to achieve such an under-standing, according to Fontana and Frey, the open-ended interviewer must resolve these problems:

• deciding how to present yourself, e.g. as a student, as a researcher, as woman-to-woman or simply as a humble learner
• gaining and maintaining trust, especially where one has to ask sensitive questions
• establishing rapport with respondents, i.e. attempting to see the world from their viewpoint without 'going native'. (2000: 655)

Lists like these can look pretty empty without any concrete illustrations. Let us look at how issues like 'rapport' turn out in practice. Extract 6.1 is an excerpt discussed by Tim Rapley. It comes from a qualitative interview with a teenager (Dan) who has trained as a drug peer–educator. After some ice-breaking questions, the interviewer (IR) shifts to the 'official' topic of the interview – discovering Dan's motivations for doing his job. Note that the transcript conventions used in Extract 6.1 are shown in the Appendix, for example (0.4) indicates a pause in parts of a second. However, at this stage, if you prefer, you can ignore these conventions and just focus on the bare text.

CASE STUDY

Extract 6.1 [Rapley, 2004: 21, simplified]

```
11    IR:    all right (.) okay hh so can you tell me why why did you
12           put yourself forward at that stage
13    dan:   erm phh Well it is the sort of thing erm (0.4) I like to do
14           and I do I enjoy you know (.) learning things I didn't
15           know before and then you know teaching it its
16           things that I do you know I teach a lot of other things
17           as well as drama and so forth so um .hh quite used to doing
18           it and I come from a medical family so er (0.3)
19           [you k]now drugs and so forth we do
20    IR:    [m m]
21    dan:   it we discuss quite a lot and er
22    IR:    yeah
23    dan:   and it is something it doe- did interest me really
24    IR:    okay was there any other particular interest in the
25           fact that it was drugs I mean is that something
26           that is meaningful to you pa   [rticularly or not
27    dan:                                 [well-
28           yeah well it is I mean cause it's everywhere
29           I think is mean- its got to be meaningful t- t- to
30           you know a greater or lesser extent to everyone
31           [because there is so] much of it around and
32    IR:    [ r i g h t ]
33    dan:   er you know it's good to know things as well
34           I think its er simply because its you know its so much
35    IR:    mm
36    dan:   you know in the news and everything it's er
```

Rapley asks us to notice how, in this extract, IR may be seen to produce some of the skills listed in Table 6.1. For instance:

> IR works to 'just' follow-up on Dan's talk [lines 24–6], to facilitate his talk [through the displays of understanding and interest at lines 22, 32 and 35] without asserting his opinions or making any appreciative or critical comments. IR is doing being neutral towards the topic while displaying interest. He is engaged in 'neutral*istic*' conduct *but* he is not 'being neutral' in any conventional sense. (Rapley, 2004: 21, with my comments added in brackets)

As Rapley suggests, this extract 'demonstrates some key interactional practices of qualitative interviewing … [aimed] at gaining *very detailed and comprehensive talk* – which I take it is a central rationale to qualitative interviewing' (2004: 22). To this end, interviewers follow up on aspects of interviewees' answers but, above all, 'allow them the space to talk' (2004: 25).

I conclude this section with four observations that follow from Rapley's suggestions:

1 *No special skills are required*: qualitative interviewing

> does not involve extra-ordinary skill, it involves just trying to interact with that specific person, trying to understand their experience, opinion and ideas … [This may involve] initially introducing a topic for discussion [lines 11–12 of Extract 6.1]; listening to the answer and then producing follow-up questions [lines 24–6]; asking them to unpack certain key-terms … And whilst listening going 'mm', 'yeah', 'right' [lines 20, 22, 32 and 35] alongside nodding, laughing, joking, smiling, frowning. (Rapley, 2004: 25–6; I have added line numbers)

We do not need to be trained in these skills. The activities that Rapley describes are used by all of us all the time in everyday conversations. Even if we are the kind of person who, unlike the qualitative interviewer, tries to monopolise a conversation, we still use these skills to gain the floor.

2 *The interview is collaboratively produced*: both interviewer *and* interviewee use their mundane skills. The interviewee is not a passive 'vessel waiting to be tapped' (Gubrium and Holstein, 2004: 151). For instance, look at how Dan, in Extract 4.1, line 27 onwards, nicely manages the potentially damaging implications of his avowed interest in drugs (line 23). So Dan is not passively 'offering *the* truth of his experience; in other interactions, with other questions, other … truths would emerge' (Rapley, 2004: 21–2). Later in this chapter, we shall show how Rapley analyses this extract in detail. For the moment, it is worth noting that, from this perspective, 'the respondent is transformed from a repository of opinions and reason or a wellspring of emotions into a productive source of either form of knowledge' (Gubrium and Holstein, 2004: 150).

3 *Interviewers are active participants*: while qualitative interviewers do not attempt to monopolise the conversation, neither do they fade into the background. So, in Extract 6.1, without IR's 'mm's, Dan might not have expanded on his answers. As Gubrium and Holstein put it: 'while the respondent … actively constructs and assembles answers, he or she does not simply "break out" talking. Neither elaborate narratives, nor one-word replies emerge without provocation' (2004: 152). This means, as Rapley points out, that interviewing is never just 'a conversation': the interview 'may be conversation*al*, but you as the interviewer do have some level of control. You routinely decide which bit of talk to follow-up, you

routinely decide when to open and close various topics and the interaction as a whole' (Rapley, 2004: 26).

4 *No one interviewing style is 'best'*: interviewers can choose to be more or less passive or active (even, as Rapley argues, choosing to disclose information about themselves in order to provoke further talk). However, there are no principled grounds to assume that 'passivity' or 'activity' works best: '*no single ideal gains "better data" than the others*. You cannot escape from the *interactional* nature of interviews. Whatever "ideals" interviewers practice, their talk is central to the trajectories of the interviewees' talk' (Rapley, 2004: 26, author's emphasis).

Points 1–4 above show that the issues at stake in deciding what is a qualitative interview transcend purely technical matters. So, in this section, we have moved from normative issues of what is 'good' and 'bad' interview practice to key theoretical assumptions about what is involved in 'the active interview' in which both interviewer *and* interviewee participate actively in making sense together. As Gubrium and Holstein put it:

> *all* interviews are active, regardless of how neutral the interviewers and how co-operative the respondents. No matter how hard interviewers try to restrain their presence in the interview exchange and no matter how forthright interviewees are in offering their views, these are interactional accomplishments rather than neutral communicative grounds. (2011: 150)

TIP

Always try to record your interviews. When you have completed your first interview, transcribe it using one of the existing methods (see the Appendix). Remember that if Rapley had not followed this approach, his analysis would have been poorer (and probably plain wrong!).

LINK

www.qualitative-research.net/fqs/fqs-eng.htm (in the 'Search' box, enter 'Interview')

We will now see that similar theoretical matters arise in a second, basic question: why interview?

6.2 WHY INTERVIEW?

This may seem like a surprising question. After all, the majority of published qualitative research articles use interviews (Silverman, 2005: 238–9). In a recent survey of one qualitative journal, I found that, of the 18 research papers published in 2008–9, 16 were based on interview data.

Of course, compared with other **methods**, interviews are relatively economical in terms of time and resources. However, as we have already seen, one of the strengths of qualitative research is its ability to access directly what happens in the world, that is to examine what people actually do in real life rather that asking them to comment upon it. Given the availability of the other methods discussed in Part Two of this book, why should we ever depart from **naturally occurring data** and use contrivances like interviews and focus groups (Potter, 2002)?

There are two simple answers to this question. First, as pointed out in Chapter 1, everything depends upon your research topic; methods in themselves have no intrinsic value. Second, we should be wary of an oversimplistic distinction between methods that are contrived and those that are 'natural' (see Atkinson and Coffey, 2002; Speer, 2002). The world never speaks directly to us but is always encoded via recording instruments like fieldnotes and transcripts. Even if we use audio or video recorders, what we hear and see is mediated by where we place our equipment.

Although this is an important caveat, following Potter (2002), I argued in Chapter 2 that it is incumbent upon qualitative researchers to justify using contrivances like interviews and focus groups. However, it must be stressed that such justifications are by no means the norm. When qualitative researchers justify using interviews, they tend to forget other qualitative methods and simply stress the advantages of the open-ended interview compared with the quantitative fixed-choice interview or questionnaire. The following case study is an example of this.

CASE STUDY
Unsafe Sex

Peter Weatherburn et al.'s research was part of Project SIGMA, which is a British longitudinal study of a non-clinic-based cohort of over 1000 gay men. Like other qualitative researchers, they distrusted explanations of behaviour which reduced social life to a response to particular 'stimuli' or 'variables'. Many such studies assert that there is an association between alcohol and drug 'misuse' and 'risky' sexual behaviour. Conversely, Weatherburn et al. suggest the following: 'the link is asserted but not proven; that the evidence is at best contradictory and that this assertion is informed by a puritanical moral agenda' (1992: 119).

In their own research, we find two assumptions which are absent from these earlier, generally quantitative, research studies:

1 No assumption is made about a strong interrelation between alcohol use and engagement in unsafe sex.
2 Psychological traits (like defects of character or weakness of resolve under the influence of alcohol) are held to be an inadequate explanation of enduring unsafe sexual practices. (1992: 122–3)

Consequently, they favoured 'open-ended' questions to try to understand the meanings attached to alcohol use by their sample. For instance: 'The first question asked respondents: "Would you say alcohol plays a significant role in your sex life?"' Those respondents who said 'yes' were probed in detail about its exact nature. Respondents were also asked 'whether alcohol had ever influenced them to engage in unsafe sexual behaviours' (1992: 123). Typically, in an open-ended interview study, respondents were encouraged to offer their own definitions of particular activities, 'unsafe sex' for example.

The findings of the study reflect the complexity of the attempt to explain the 'causes' of social behaviour. The effects of alcohol were found to depend upon 'the context of the sexual encounter and the other party involved in the sexual negotiation' (1992: 129). Only in a minority of reports was alcohol treated as the 'cause' of unsafe behaviour. In the majority of cases, although people might report themselves as 'fairly drunk', they described their sexual activities as the outcome of conscious deliberation.

This interview study highlights the advantages of open-ended interviews in offering an apparently 'deeper' picture than the variable-based correlations of quantitative studies. However, it also implies why it can be difficult to get funding or acceptance for qualitative research. While quantitative research may make questionable assumptions, it tends to deliver apparently reliable and valid correlations between 'variables' that appear to be self-evident. Moreover, these correlations usually lead in clear-cut policy directions.

Indeed, how justified is it to suggest that open-ended interviews offer a 'deeper' picture than survey research? What meaning should we should attach to descriptions of using alcohol, given that people may recall those features that depict their behaviour as socially desirable? As Weatherburn et al. put it, 'it is recognized that asking people retrospective questions about alcohol use may well be problematic, both because of social desirability phenomena and because alcohol itself impairs recall' (1992: 123).

This observation goes to the heart of an unresolved debate about the status of interview accounts; namely are such accounts:

- true or false representations of such features as attitudes and behaviour?
- simply 'accounts' where the researcher's interest is in how they are constructed rather than their accuracy?

Bridget Byrne follows the logic of the alcohol study in recommending open-ended interviews to overcome the inadequacies of survey research. As she puts it:

> qualitative interviewing is particularly useful as a research method for accessing individuals' attitudes and values – things that cannot necessarily be observed or accommodated in a formal questionnaire. Open-ended and flexible questions are likely to get a more considered response than closed questions and therefore provide better access to interviewees' views, interpretation of events, understandings, experiences and opinions ... (qualitative interviewing) *when done well* is able to achieve a level of depth and complexity that is not available to other, particularly survey-based, approaches. (2004: 182, my emphasis)

Notice how Byrne confines her comparisons to the survey or questionnaire. However, although she finds such quantitative methods wanting, she shares a common assumption with survey researchers. Like them, she emphasises the importance of interviewer skills in bringing off an effective interview (one 'done well') as seen in Table 6.1.

For the moment, however, I want to focus on one further aspect of Byrne's defence of the qualitative interview. Drawing upon feminism, she suggests that 'qualitative interviewing has been particularly attractive to researchers who want to explore voices and experiences which they believe have been ignored, misrepresented or suppressed in the past' (Byrne, 2004: 182). Many researchers follow Byrne and use interviews because they feel they can employ them to 'explore voices and experiences'.

However, this assumes that what people say in interviews can be treated as a direct expression of their 'experience'. As we shall see shortly, this **emotionalist** argument, while very common in qualitative research, makes several problematic assumptions. Later in this chapter, I return to the issue of the analysis of interview data. First, however, we must come to grips with the theoretical issues, hinted at by Byrne, that lie behind how we approach interview data.

6.3 IMPLICATIONS: THREE VERSIONS OF INTERVIEW DATA

Two troubling issues arise from what Rapley and Weatherburn et al. say about their data:

- Interviews do not appear to give us direct access to the 'facts' (e.g. why Dan became a drug educator) or to events (e.g. becoming an alcoholic).
- Interviews do not tell us directly about people's 'experiences' but instead offer indirect 'representations' of those experiences. As Byrne herself recognises, 'few researchers believe that in the course of the interview, you are able to "get inside someone's head". What an interview produces is a particular *representation* or *account* of an individual's views or opinions' (2004: 182).

The lack of stability of such apparent 'realities' as 'facts' and 'experiences' resembles my discussion of the family in Chapter 5. As we saw, Gubrium's research on the 'family' points to the way in which idealised conceptions of social phenomena can, on closer examination, become like a will-o'-the-wisp, dissolving into sets of practices embedded in particular settings. The methodological import of this for interview data has been made clear by Carolyn Baker. As she writes:

> When we talk about the world we live in, we engage in the activity of giving it a particular character. Inevitably, we assign features and phenomena to it and make it out to work in a particular way. When we talk with someone else about the

world, we take into account who the other is, what that other person could be presumed to know, 'where' that other is in relation to ourself in the world we talk about. (Baker, 1982: 109)

Here Baker, like Rapley, is questioning the attempt to treat interview questions and answers as passive filters towards some truths about people's identities (for instance, as a lesbian who has 'come out'). Instead, she is telling us, interviewer and interviewee actively *construct* some version of the world appropriate to what we take to be self-evident about the person to whom we are speaking and the context of the question.

Baker is raising a number of issues about the status of interview data, including:

1 What is the relation between interviewees' accounts and the world they describe? Are such accounts potentially 'true' or 'false' or is neither concept always appropriate to them?
2 How is the relation between interviewer and interviewee to be understood? Is it governed by standardised techniques of 'good interviewing practice'? Or is it, inevitably, as Rapley shows us, based on conversational practices we all use in everyday life?

There are three different ways in which most social scientists would answer Baker's questions, as follows.

According to **positivism**, interview data have the potential to give us access to 'facts' about the world; the primary issue is to generate data which are **valid** and **reliable**, independently of the research setting; the main ways to achieve this are the random selection of the interview **sample** and the administration of standardised, questions with multiple-choice answers which can be readily tabulated.

According to **emotionalism**, interviewees are viewed as experiencing subjects who actively construct their social worlds; the primary issue is to generate data which give an authentic insight into people's experiences; the main ways to achieve this are unstructured, open-ended interviews.

According to **constructionism**, interviewers and interviewees are always actively engaged in constructing meaning. Rather than treat this as standing in the way of accurate depictions of 'facts' or 'experiences', the researcher's topic becomes how meaning is mutually constructed. Because of this, research interviews are not treated as specially privileged and other interviews (e.g. media or professional–client interviews) are treated as of equal interest, that is interviews are treated as *topics* rather than as a research *resource*. A particular focus is on how interviewees construct **narratives** of events and people (see Riesmann, 1993, and Section 5.2) and the turn-by-turn construction of meaning (see the discussion of **conversation analysis** in Section 6.3).

These three positions are set out in Table 6.2.

Let me now describe these three different approaches in greater detail, looking at the type of knowledge each pursues and the different research tasks they set themselves.

TABLE 6.2   Three versions of interview data

	Status of data	Methods
Positivism	Facts about behaviour and attitudes	Random samples Standardised questions Tabulations
Emotionalism	Authentic experiences	Unstructured, open-ended interviews
Constructionism	Mutually constructed	Any interview treated as a topic

6.4 POSITIVISM

In survey research, which is geared to a statistical logic, interview data give access to 'facts' about the world. Although these facts include both biographical information and statements about beliefs, all are to be treated as accounts whose sense derives from their correspondence to a factual reality. Where that reality is imperfectly represented by an account, checks and remedies are to be encouraged in order to get a truer or more complete picture of how things stand.

6.4.1 Type of knowledge

Positivists treat people as collections of attributes and use interviews as a means to tap into who respondents are. As Holstein and Gubrium put it: 'In conventional approaches, respondents are basically conceived as passive *vessels of answers* to whom interviewers direct their questions. They are repositories of facts, reflections, opinions, and other traces of experience' (2011: 152).

Here are the six kinds of topics to which, according to a standard text on survey research, interview questions are addressed. Notice how these writers envisage problems and recommend remedies in relation to each topic:

1 *Facts*: these relate primarily to biographical information about the respondent, to statements from informed sources about the structures, policies and actions of organisations, and to descriptions of an event or a community. In this last case, it is possible to weed out 'inaccurate' descriptions by comparing different people's statements:

> If respondents occupying widely different positions in the community agree on a statement, there is much better ground for accepting it as true than if only one of these respondents makes the statement. On the other hand, contradictions between the reports of apparently reliable informants provide important leads for further investigation. (Selltiz et al., 1964: 245)

2 *Beliefs about facts*: in questions about beliefs or attitudes, no inter-personal cross-checking of statements is appropriate. However, Selltiz et al. (1964: 246) point

out that it is always important to check first whether the respondent has any beliefs about the topic in question, otherwise the researcher may put words into the respondent's mouth.

3   *Feelings and motives*: here, 'because emotional responses are frequently too complex to report in a single phrase' (1964: 248), Selltiz et al. recommend the use of open-ended questions, allowing the respondents to choose their own terms.

4   *Standards of action*: these relate to what people think should or could be done about certain stated situations. Here it helps to link such standards to people's experiences. Where someone has actually faced a situation of the type described, their response is likely to be more reliable.

5   *Present or past behaviour*: again, specific questions related to actual rather than hypothetical situations are recommended.

6   *Conscious reasons* (for 1 to 5): rather than simply ask 'Why?', Selltiz et al. (1964: 253) recommend that the researcher should examine broad classes of considerations that may have determined this outcome (e.g. 'the history of the actor's feeling', or 'the characteristics in a given entity that provoke a given reaction').

For each of these six topics, the task of the interviewer is to elicit a body of facts 'out there' in the world. For positivists, an observation that interview responses might be an outcome of the interview setting would be heard as a charge against the reliability of the technique. As Kitzinger has noted:

> Positivist social scientists … have shown that a great deal of what people say about their lives and experiences is (either deliberately or inadvertently) at variance with the facts. Discrepancies between objective measures and subjective reports have been well-documented (e.g. between the number of beer cans in dustbins and interviewee reports of household beer consumption, Rathje and Hughes, 1975) and people cannot, apparently, be relied upon to report accurately even such an uncontroversial fact as their height (Cherry and Rodgers, 1979). Retrospective accounts are particularly unreliable, being subject to 'conventionalisation' (Baddeley, 1979) and influenced by subsequent events and by theories current at the time of interview (Yarrow et al., 1970). People contradict their own words within a single interview session, and talk about their lives in line with culturally constructed implicit theories of self narration (Neisser, 1994). (Kitzinger, 2004: 128)

Because they recognise such difficulties in matching interviewees' responses to the 'facts', positivists build in various checks and remedies into their research designs as is shown in the following section. As Holstein and Gubrium point out, in the positivist approach:

> Interviewing is likened to 'prospecting' for the true facts and feelings residing within the respondent (cf. Kvale 1996). The image of the researcher/prospector casts the interview as a search-and-discovery mission, with the interviewer intent

on detecting what is already there inside variably cooperative respondents, undertaken for scientific reasons. The challenge lies in extracting information as directly as possible, without contaminating it. Highly refined interview techniques streamline, systematize, and sanitize the process. (2011: 153)

6.4.2 Research task

We have seen that the aim of interviews for positivists is to generate data which hold independently of both the research setting and the researcher or interviewer. One way of achieving this is by attempting to standardise interviews. Table 6.3 shows how this standardisation is built into instructions to interviewers administering structured sets of questions.

TABLE 6.3   Guidelines for structured interviews

1   Never get involved in long explanations of the study; use the standard explanation provided
2   Never deviate from the sequence of questions or question wording
3   Never let another person interrupt the interview or let another person answer for the respondent or offer their opinions
4   Never suggest an answer (other than reading out the fixed-choice answers if provided); never agree or disagree with an answer or give the respondent any idea of your personal opinions on the topic
5   Never interpret the meaning of a question; just repeat it and/or give instructions or clarifications provided in training
6   Never improvise such as by adding answer categories or making wording changes

Source: adapted from Fontana and Frey, 2000: 649–50

These guidelines emphasise the need to follow a standardised interview protocol. So Selltiz et al. offer an Appendix entitled 'The Art of Interviewing' which provides a set of rules and taboos. Interviewers should ask each question precisely as it is worded and in the same order that it appears on the schedule. They should not show surprise or disapproval of an answer, offer impromptu explanations of questions, suggest possible replies, or skip certain questions. Similarly, Michael Brenner offers a list of 'do's' and 'don'ts' ('basic rules of research interviewing', Brenner, 1981: 129–30), which are defended in terms of the necessity of standardisation:

In order to ensure adequacy of measurement in a data collection programme it is of primary importance to secure, as much as is possible, the equivalence of the stimulus conditions in the interviews. If these are not equivalent, measurement may be biased, and it may be unwarranted to group responses together for the purposes of statistical analyses. (1981: 115)

Although Brenner is more sceptical than Selltiz et al. about the prospects of obtaining 'literal measurement' in the interview situation (Brenner, 1981: 156), the statement quoted indicates that he shares with them the same statistical and behaviouralist (or stimulus–response) logic. Following that logic, he calls for more research on social interaction in interviews as a means of: 'improving the quality of research interviews … and increasing the degree of social control over the measurement process' (1981: 156).

Given this concern for accurate measurement, Selltiz et al. are rather suspicious of unstructured interviews which they see as inherently unreliable research instruments. Although they concede that unstructured or open-ended interviews are more flexible than pre-scheduled interviews and can allow more intensive study of perceptions and feelings, they have inherent problems for positivists:

> The flexibility frequently results in a lack of comparability of one interview with another. Moreover, their analysis is more difficult and time-consuming than that of standardised interviews. (1964: 264)

EXERCISE 6.1

This exercise gives you an opportunity to think through the debate about whether it is appropriate to assess whether interview accounts are true or false. The following extract is taken from a study in which scientists were interviewed about the factors that influence changes in scientific theories:

(S = Scientist)

1 S: To make changes you have to be highly articulate, persuasive, and devastating.
2   You have to go to the heart of the matter. But in doing this you lay yourself open
3   to attack. I've been called fanatical, paranoid, obsessed … but I'm going to win.
4   Time is on my side

(quoted by Gilbert and Mulkay, 1983, 10).

1 How might this extract be used to support the view that scientific research is largely influenced by scientific politics?
2 Why might you *not* be convinced by this view on the basis of this extract?
3 Why might it be important to understand the different *social contexts* in which scientists give an account of their work?
4 Can it be said *definitively* whether or not science is *essentially* a political process? If not, why not?

6.4.3 The limits of positivism

For many years, positivist survey research provided the main source of data for sociology. For instance, Brenner (1981) reports studies which indicate that, during the 1960s, around 90 per cent of all the papers in the two leading American sociology journals were based on data derived from interviews and questionnaires.

From a critical position, Per Maseide has summarised the most significant assumptions of the positivist approach to interview data. These are shown in Table 6.4.

TABLE 6.4 Positivist assumptions

1 The aim of social science is to discover unknown but actual social facts or essentials
2 Reality is supposed to be 'out there'. Thus it is a matter of finding the most effective and unbiased methods that, as precisely and objectively as possible, could bring out information about this reality
3 The existence of typical respondents is explicitly presupposed. These respondents are implicitly supplied with standardised mental structures that match the analyst's reasoning and use of language
4 Methodological problems are more technical than theoretical or interpretative

Source: adapted from Maseide, 1990: 4

As Maseide points out, positivists' 'belief in standardized forms of interviewing relies on an exclusive emphasis on the referential functions of language' (1990: 9). However, interview responses 'are delivered at different descriptive levels. The informant does different things with words and stories' (1990: 11).

We can extend Maseide's critique of positivism. As Rapley (2004) shows, *both* informant *and* interviewer do many 'different things with words and stories'. To what extent can we understand these 'things' if we switch away from the standardised interview forms of positivism towards more open-ended interviews or even conversations? To answer this question, we must review the arguments of emotionalists.

6.5 EMOTIONALISM

For positivists, interviews are essentially about ascertaining facts or beliefs out there in the world. Emotionalists switch this focus but only slightly. Their concern is not with obtaining objective 'facts' but with eliciting authentic accounts of subjective experience. To do so, emotionalists believe that interviewers should try: 'to formulate questions and provide an atmosphere conducive to open and undistorted communication' (Gubrium and Holstein, 1997b: 116).

The key here is to obtain rapport with respondents and to avoid manipulating them. So, while positivists regard departure from an interview schedule as a possible source of bias, emotionalists may actively encourage it. For instance, feminist interviewers are sometimes advised to take the opportunity to tell their own stories to respondents (Oakley, 1981).

6.5.1 Type of knowledge

Emotionalist interviewers want to access the *subject* behind the person given the role of interview respondent. As we saw above in the case study Hearing Women's Voices, the particular concern is with *lived experience*. Emotions are treated as central to such experience.

A further example of this approach will show what this involves in practice. Schreiber (1996) describes an interview study with a snowball sample of 21 women who identified themselves as having recovered from depression. She sets out to establish an account of the depression experience which, she claims, is 'grounded in the real world of the participant' (1996: 471). This 'real world', we are told, contains six 'phases' of '(re)defining the self', each with between three and five 'properties' or 'dimensions'.

In this way, the author attempts to put her readers (and herself) in touch with what she calls 'the depression experience'. However, as Schreiber points out, this was a retrospective study, based on what her respondents told her on being invited to look back at their past. For instance, as she notes, what she calls the first phase of this experience ('My Self Before') 'is only seen upon reflection' (Schreiber, 1996: 474).

For positivists, this would cast doubt on the reliability of Schreiber's data and the validity of her claim to access the depression experience. But instead, true to her emotionalist position, Schreiber is less concerned with 'bias' than with 'authenticity'. From this point of view, 'there is merit in hearing the women's understandings of the people they were at the time' (1996: 474).

6.5.2 Research task

Emotionalists aim to access emotions by describing respondents' inner experiences, by encouraging interviewers to become emotionally involved with respondents and to convey their own feelings to both respondents and readers (see Gubrium and Holstein, 1997a: 58).

This means that emotionalists reject the positivist assumption that both interviewer and interviewee are properly treated as 'objects'. Instead, they depict both as (emotionally involved) subjects. This is set out in Table 6.5.

If interviewees are to be viewed as subjects who actively construct the features of their cognitive world, then one should try to obtain intersubjective depth

TABLE 6.5   Two versions of the interview relationship

	Positivism	Emotionalism
Interviewer	Object – following research protocol	Subject – creating interview context
Interviewee	Object – revealing items relevant to the research protocol	Subject – complying with or resisting definition of the situation

between both sides so that a deep mutual understanding can be achieved. As Reason and Rowan argue:

> Humanistic approaches favour 'depth interviews' in which interviewee and interviewer become 'peers' or even 'companions'. (1981: 205)

In this 'humanistic' version of the interview, both the type of knowledge gained and the validity of the analysis are based on 'deep' understanding. This is because 'the humanistic framework' supports 'meaningful understanding of the person … and wholeness in human inquiry' (1981: 206).

Similarly, in Burgess (1980), in his chapter significantly entitled 'The unstructured interview as a conversation', the interview is seen to give greater depth than other research techniques. This is because, Burgess claims, it is based on 'a sustained relationship between the informant and the researcher' (1980: 109).

For this reason, most emotionalists tend to reject pre-scheduled standardised interviews and to prefer open-ended interviews. In an early work, Denzin (1970: 125) offered three reasons for this preference:

1   It allows respondents to use their 'unique ways of defining the world'.
2   It assumes that no fixed sequence of questions is suitable to all respondents.
3   It allows respondents to 'raise important issues not contained in the schedule'.

6.5.3 The limits of emotionalism

These positions might seem to be a welcome alternative to the purely technical version of interviews espoused by positivists. After all, is it not both more valid and more ethical to recognise that interviews are encounters between human beings trying to understand one another?

This 'humanistic' position is seductive. It seems to blend a self-evident truth about humanity with political correctness about the need for mutual understanding and dialogue. A nice review of emotionalist interview studies and a critique from a constructionist perspective is provided by Donileen R. Loseke and Margarethe Kusenbach. As they show (Loseke and Kusenbach, 2008), emotionalists *neglect* three issues:

- the assumptions made in preferring open-ended interviews
- the difference between a 'humanistic' and a social science position
- the role of common-sense knowledge, rather than 'empathy', in allowing us to conduct and analyse interviews.

I will consider each issue in turn.

Open-endedness: As Hammersley and Atkinson (95: 110–11) point out, it is somewhat naive to assume that open-ended or non-directive interviewing is not in itself a form of social control which shapes what people say. For instance, where the researcher maintains a minimal presence, asking few questions and offering only the occasional 'mm hmm', this can create an interpretive problem for the interviewee about what is relevant. Indeed, the very passivity of the interviewer can create an extremely powerful constraint on the interviewee to talk (as seen in 'non-directive' styles of psychotherapy and counselling – see Peräkylä, 1995).

I would also add that this preference for a particular form of interview can be defined in terms of avoiding bias which is entirely appropriate to a positivist approach. Conversely, in certain feminist writings, where value-freedom is rejected, structured interviews are criticised on political grounds as maintaining a hierarchical relationship in research (see Stanley and Wise, 1983).

Humanism: Why are interviews so self-evidently based on an exchange of unique human experiences and emotions? Indeed, may not this self-evident 'truth' derive not from social science but from a widespread cultural assumption? The well-meaning 'humanistic' social scientist may thus have uncritically taken on board a common-sense assumption about the immediacy and validity of accounts of human experience.

Think of our fascination with interviews with celebrities on TV news or chat shows. Or consider the way in which sporting events or even Nobel Prize ceremonies are now incomplete without 'pre-match' and 'post-match' interviews. Do the latter give us insights into 'unique' experiences or do they simply reproduce predictable forms of how it is appropriate to account for sporting or academic success or failure (see Mulkay, 1984; Emmison, 1988)?

Only occasionally do sportsmen and women resist their depiction as heroes or villains. For instance, the British decathlete Daley Thompson was well known for nonplussing the media by producing the 'wrong' account – claiming he was 'over the moon' when he had failed and 'sick as a parrot' when he had won. Again, in this vein, a British boxer was recently termed 'arrogant' by a reporter because he had refused to engage in the usual pre-fight slanging-match with his next opponent.

This, of course, is the irony. The media aim to deliver us immediate 'personal' experience. Yet what they (we) want is simple repetition of familiar tales. Perhaps this is part of the post-modern condition. Maybe we feel people are at their most authentic when they are, in effect, reproducing a cultural script. The well-meaning 'humanistic' social scientist may thus have uncritically taken on board a common-sense assumption about the immediacy and validity of accounts of human experience and emotion (Atkinson and Silverman, 1997).

CASE STUDY
Murder in the Outback

A few years ago, the newspapers were running a big story about a British backpacker, Joanne Lees, who narrowly escaped from a roadside attack in the Australian outback during which her boyfriend was murdered. It turns out that, despite her horrific experience, her character was pilloried by the media shortly afterwards. The main reason given was that her account of what happened was strangely 'unemotional'. At the trial of her alleged attacker, she showed that she has learned her 'mistake'. This time round, the prosecution counsel asked her several questions about how she felt at the time and Lees is reported to have given very emotional answers, even breaking down in tears.

Where are Lees's emotions? Are they outpourings of how she felt at the time or right now? Or was Lees co-operating with the lawyer in producing a display of emotion appropriate to her situation? And isn't this how emotions usually work? For instance, Heath (2004) shows how a cry of 'pain' in a medical consultation is closely tied to the interaction between doctor and patient – it does not recur when a 'painful' part of the body is touched by the doctor a second time.

Taking 'emotions' or 'experiences' as self-evidently present in what people say leads to analytic laziness in considering the status of interview data. It also raises many questions. If you can see uniformity in even the most intimate kind of account, this surely creates plenty of room for analysis of what may be the cultural resources used in answering interviewers' questions. This is something I take up when I consider constructionism below.

Common sense: Although positivists and emotionalists seek to document different orders of reality (respectively, 'facts' and 'emotions'), there is a surprising degree of tacit agreement between them about one issue. Both are aware of 'traps' in their path which must be overcome if their preferred order is to be properly documented.

So, in an early text, Denzin lists a number of 'problems' which can 'distort' interviewees' responses (Denzin, 1970: 133–8):

Respondents possessing different interactional roles from the interviewer.

The problem of 'self-presentation' especially in the early stages of the interview.

The problems of 'volatile', 'fleeting' relationships to which respondents have little commitment and so 'can fabricate tales of self that belie the actual facts' (1970: 135).

The difficulty of penetrating private worlds of experience.

The relative status of interviewer and interviewee.

The 'context' of the interview (e.g. home, work, hospital).

However, to speak of 'distortions' is to play the positivist's game. For positivists are equally concerned with 'misunderstandings' between interviewer and interviewee (or respondent).

By contrast, as Rapley's analysis showed us earlier, interviews can be seen to possess basic properties of all social interaction. These properties derive from both parties' employment of their everyday, common-sense knowledge of social structures to engage in such business as recognising a question and providing an answer which will be heard as 'appropriate' for a particular identity (see my discussion below of the study by Baruch). It follows that such properties should be *investigated* rather than treated as a 'problem' standing in the way of accurate reporting of 'facts' or 'experiences'.

In fact, in Denzin's later work, he recognises this very point and abandons the emotionalist assumptions about 'lived experience' found in his earlier writings. As he puts it:

> The subject is more than can be contained in a text, and a text is only a reproduction of what the subject has told us. What the subject tells us is itself something that has been shaped by prior cultural understandings. Most important, language, which is our window into the subject's world (and our world), plays tricks. It displaces the very thing it is supposed to represent, so that what is always given is a trace of other things, not the thing – lived experience – itself. (1991: 68)

6.5.4 Emotionalism: Summary

For the emotionalist, the open-ended interview apparently offers the opportunity for an authentic gaze into the soul of another, or even for a politically correct dialogue where researcher and researched offer mutual understanding and support. The rhetoric of interviewing 'in depth' repeatedly hints at such a collection of assumptions. Here we see a stubbornly persistent **romantic** impulse in contemporary social science: the elevation of the experiential as the authentic – the selfsame gambit that can make the TV chat show or news interview so appealing.

There are also real methodological doubts about the emotionalist project which relate to emotionalists' claims to depict the 'authentic' reality they want to access. These doubts have been forcefully presented by Gubrium and Holstein:

> Do we have any evidence of emotion other than its expression? Can researchers give us access to "real" emotion simply by re-presenting or reenacting subjects' *expressions* of these emotions? Do emotions exist apart from culturally available modes of expression? (1997a: 74, emphasis in original)

EXERCISE 6.2

Below is an extract from an interview with an adult daughter who is caring for her mother – a victim of senile dementia – at home. The daughter is employed part-time, and shares the household with her employed husband and their two sons. The extract begins when the interviewer (**I**) asks the adult daughter (**R**) to describe her feelings about having to juggle so many needs and schedules:

1 **I:**   We were talking about, you said you were a member of the, what did you
2   call it?
3 **R:** They say that I'm in the sandwich generation. You know, like we're sandwiched
4   between having to care for my mother…and my grown kids and my husband.
5   People are living longer now and you've got different generations at
6   home and, I tell ya, it's a mixed blessing.
7 **I:**   How do you feel about it in your situation?
8 **R:** Oh, I don't know. Sometimes I think I'm being a bit selfish because I
9   gripe about having to keep an eye on Mother all the time. If you let down
10   your guard, she wanders off into the back yard or goes out the door
11   and down the street. That's no fun when your hubby wants your attention
12   too. Norm works the second shift and he's home during the day a lot. I
13   manage to get in a few hours of work, but he doesn't like it. I have pretty
14   mixed feelings about it.
15 **I:**   What do you mean?
16 **R:** Well, I'd say that as a daughter, I feel pretty guilty about how I feel sometimes.
17   It can get pretty bad, like wishing that Mother were just gone, you know
18   what I mean? She's been a wonderful mother and I love her very much,
19   but if you ask me how I feel as a wife and mother, that's another matter.
20   feel like she's [the mother], well, intruding on our lives and just making
21   hell out of raising afamily. Sometimes I put myself in my husband's
22   shoes and I just know how he feels. He doesn't say much, but I know
23   that he misses my company, and I miss his of course. [Pause] So how
24   do you answer that?

(Gubrium and Holstein, 1997b: 124).

1 What do we learn here about **R**'s feelings?
2 How do **R** and **I** together construct a story? What you learn from that? [TIP: think about **R**'s framing her comments 'as a daughter' (line 16).]
3 What have you learned from your analysis about the uses and limitations of emotionalism?

6.6 CONSTRUCTIONISM

While positivists acknowledge that interviewers interact with their subjects, they demand that such interaction should be strictly defined by the research protocol. Consequently, positivists only become seriously interested in interviewer–interviewee interaction when it can be shown that interviewers have departed from the protocol (Brenner, 1981).

Conversely, for emotionalists, interviews are inescapably encounters between subjects. As Denzin has put it: 'I wish to treat the interview as an observational encounter. An encounter … represents the coming together of two or more persons for the purpose of focused interaction' (1970: 133).

What distinguishes constructionists from emotionalists is the former's attempt to treat what happens in what Denzin terms 'focused interaction' as a *topic* in its own right, not as something which can stand in the way of 'authentic' understanding of another's experience. This has a direct impact on the type of knowledge which constructionists want to access.

6.6.1 Type of knowledge

> accounts are not simply representations of the world; they are part of the world they describe. (Hammersley and Atkinson, 1995: 107)

Emotionalists help us to see that interviewee respondents are active sense-making subjects. However, they persist in the positivist rhetoric in which accounts are 'simply representations of the world'. By contrast, constructionists are interested in documenting the way in which accounts 'are part of the world they describe'. As Kitzinger puts it:

> Constructionism … disputes the possibility of uncovering 'facts', 'realities' or 'truths' behind the talk, and treats as inappropriate any attempt to vet what people say for its 'accuracy', 'reliability', or 'validity' – thereby sidestepping altogether the positivist problems raised above. From this perspective, what women say should not be taken as evidence of their experience, but only as a form of talk – a 'discourse', 'account' or 'repertoire' – which represents a culturally available way of packaging experience. (2004: 128)

Kitzinger adds:

> This approach is valuable insofar as it draws attention to the fact that experience is never 'raw', but is embedded in a social web of interpretation and re-interpretation.

Women's 'experience' does not spring uncontaminated from an essential inner female way of knowing, but is structured within, and in opposition to, social (heterosexist, patriarchal etc) discourses. (2004: 128)

What does this mean in practice? The type of knowledge we are concerned with here is concerned with how interview participants actively create meaning. This lies behind Gubrium and Holstein's idea of 'the active interview':

Construed as active, the subject behind the respondent not only holds facts and details of experience, but, in the very process of offering them up for response, constructively adds to, takes away from, and transforms the facts and details. The respondent can hardly 'spoil' what he or she is, in effect, subjectively creating. (1997b: 117)

The implication is that **methodology** texts which advise on 'good' interview technique should only be taken seriously if we are positivists. If not, we need to recognise that the skills involved in bringing off a successful interview are, as Rapley shows, shared by both interviewer *and* interviewee. Ultimately, whatever these methodology texts say, both are ultimately drawing upon common-sense knowledge.

The earliest attempt to set out this version of interview data was made by Cicourel (1964). For Cicourel, previous advice about good interview technique offers a revealing insight into our dependence on everyday knowledge of social structures. As he writes:

The subtleties which methodologists introduce to the novice interviewer can be read as properties to be found in the everyday interaction between members of a society. Thus the principles of 'good and bad interviewing' can be read as basic features of social interaction which the social scientist presumably is seeking to study. (1964: 68)

For Cicourel, the remedies recommended by methodologists derive from the very knowledge of the social world which should be made problematic. Moreover, the 'errors' they detect are not really obstacles to social research but rather exhibit basic properties of social interaction revealed as people make sense together. For Cicourel, then, there is no distinction between the practical skills of methodologists, researchers and interviewers. All are uniformly concerned with what he calls 'the synchronisation of meaning'. All use 'rules of evidence' deriving from a single conceptual scheme based on assumed common relevances, stocks of knowledge, typifications, recipes, rules for managing one's presence before others, and so on. As Rapley shows us, these shared 'commonsense devices for making sense of the environment' (Cicourel, 1964: 100) are presupposed in conducting or analysing interviews. We must, therefore, learn to 'conceive of the error as evidence not only of poor reliability but also of "normal" interpersonal relations' (1964: 74).

6.6.2 Research tasks

Cicourel's position derived from **ethnomethodology**, an approach we have already encountered in earlier chapters of this book (most notably in Chapter 5).

Constructionists share ethnomethodologists' focus on how people assemble sense in situations like interviews. This is seen in Gubrium and Holsteind's constructionist account of 'the active interview':

> Respondents' answers and comments are not viewed as reality reports delivered from a fixed repository. Instead, they are considered for the ways that they construct aspects of reality in collaboration with the interviewer. The focus is as much on the assembly process as on what is assembled. (1997b: 127)

Note this concern with *both* the assembly of meanings and with what gets assembled. Like most constructionists, Gubrium and Holstein want to preserve a concern with *what* interviewees are saying as well as with *how* they get to say it. As they put it:

> The goal is to show how interview responses are produced in the interaction between interviewer and respondent, without losing sight of the meanings produced or the circumstances that condition the meaning-making process. The analytic objective is not merely to describe the situated production of talk, but to show how what is being said relates to the experiences and lives being studied. (1997b: 127)

Gubrium and Holstein's comments raise two important questions:

- By reinstating a reference to 'the experiences and lives being studied' are Holstein and Gubrium taking us back to the emotionalist position?
- Can interview data tell us anything beyond how the participants locally assemble recognisable interview talk?

Such questions have led to a very lively debate about how constructionists want to treat interviews. This debate is discussed in Section 6.6.3.

EXERCISE 6.3

The extract below is taken from Carolyn Baker's study of 'adolescents':

(I = Interviewer; V = Victor, age 12)

1	I:	Are there any ways in which you consider yourself still to be a child, or to
2		have child-like interests or habits or attitudes?
3	V:	Yeah I still like doin' things that I did when I was a kid you know like,
4		y'know, Lego 'n that just building stuff you know like when I, I was a kid
5		you know.
6	I:	Yeah. You still take pleasure in that kind of thing.
7	V:	Yeah, I get a friend over and we just build a, great big house 'n that, it's
8		still just like doing it.
9	I:	Do you feel at the same time that you're too -really too old for it or do you
10		not feel it's too
11	V:	Well when people say 'ah, he's still doin' that stuff' I don't really care. I just
12		do it in the living room 'n that, 'n it's still fun. Pretty soon I'll, I'll stop doin'
13		it but, when I get too old for it.
14	I:	Or when you no longer think it's fun.
15	V:	Yeah.
16	I:	Which one?
17	V:	How do you mean?
18	I:	What would make you stop, feeling you were too old for it or
19	V:	Yeah, like everyone buggin' me too much y'know 'n, it's not really that bad
20		just building a house or something y'know like, just show my mom it'n everything
21		just take it apart y'know, sort of something to do on a rainy day

(Baker, 1984: 308–9).

1 In what sense does this interview give us reliable information about how Victor seems himself?
2 With close attention to the text, show:

- How Victor accounts for potentially child-like activities.
- How the interviewer identifies child-like activities.
- How both Victor and the interviewer attend to the implications of what the other is saying.

6.6.3 Criticisms of Constructionism

Narrowness: although the constructionist critique of both positivism and emotionalism may appear to be convincing, its own position seems to have problems and inconsistencies. Cicourel's ethnomethodological concern with the basic properties of social interaction would seem to deny the value of treating interview data as saying anything about any other reality than the interview itself.

This means that many interview researchers would complain that, if we follow Cicourel's ethnomethodologically inspired position, we would simply focus on the conversational skills of the participants rather than on the content of what they are saying and its relation to the world outside the interview.

In reply to this criticism, two responses have been made. Those sympathetic to ethnomethodology argue that such content is only to be found through how it is made available by the participants to an interview. Therefore, by focusing closely on the co-production of interview talk, we can say a great deal about content without *importing* our own sense of what content is important. So rather than looking for preconceived 'topics' in the talk, we need to see *when* and *how* the participants make certain features of their worlds visible to each other – and to us (see Schegloff, 1997).

By contrast, many constructionists accept that there is some justification for the alleged 'narrowness' of ethnomethodology and claim that it is possible to combine a concern with both form (how?) and content (what?). Gubrium and Holstein have been the principal exponents of this position claiming that it is necessary to treat interview data as reporting on both what they call *how* and *what* questions.

In a project on the quality of care and quality of life of nursing home residents (Gubrium, 1997), interview responses were, in part, analysed to address 'what' questions. Here the researcher attempted to: 'link … the topics to biographical particulars in the interview process, and thus produce … a subject who responds to, or is affected by, the matters under discussion' (Gubrium and Holstein, 1997b: 121).

But such a focus on 'what' did not, it was claimed, mean that 'how' questions were neglected:

> The standpoint from which information is offered is continually developed in relation to ongoing interview interaction. In speaking of the quality of care, for example, nursing home residents, as interview respondents, not only offer substantive thoughts and feelings pertinent to the topic under consideration, but simultaneously

and continuously monitor who they are in relation to the person questioning them. For example, prefacing her remarks about the quality of life in her facility with the statement 'speaking as a woman,' a nursing home resident informs the interviewer that she is to be heard as a woman, not as someone else—not a mere resident, cancer patient, or abandoned mother. (1997b: 122)

So, in what Gubrium and Holstein call 'the active interview', 'data can be analyzed to show the dynamic interrelatedness of the *whats* and the *hows*' (1997b: 127, emphasis in original).

Inconsistency? Gubrium and Holstein's answer to the charge of 'narrowness' leaves them open to a different criticism. Are not 'what' questions precisely the concerns of emotionalists and positivists? If so, are not constructionists who want to use interview data to answer such questions simply taking us back to earlier positions?

This is an important and complex issue with no easy answer. So that you can try to make up your own mind, most of the rest of this chapter will be used to give telling examples. Each example takes a different position on the appropriateness of using interview data to answer 'what' questions.

> TIP
>
> Holstein and Gubrium (1995: 33–4) cite tell-tale phrases which respondents use to signal shifts in roles, for example 'speaking as a mother now'; 'thinking like a woman'; 'wearing my professional hat'; 'if I were in his shoes'; and 'now that you ask'. When analysing your interview data look for prefaces of this kind and try to identify the range of subject positions your respondents invoke.
>
>   Note that this approach is a useful antidote to the assumption that people have a single identity waiting to be discovered by the interviewer. By contrast, it reveals that we are active narrators who weave skilful, appropriately located, stories.

6.7 ADOLESCENT CULTURES: COMBINING 'WHAT' AND 'HOW' QUESTIONS

Miller and Glassner (1997; 2004) describe a study involving in-depth, open-ended interviews with young women (aged 12 to 20) who claim affiliation with youth gangs in their communities (Miller, 2001). These interviews follow the completion of a survey interview administered by the same researcher.

Here is how they describe the purposes of each form of data:

While the survey interview gathers information about a wide range of topics, including the individual, her school, friends, family, neighborhood, delinquent involvement, arrest history, sexual history, and victimization, in addition to information about the gang, the in-depth interview is concerned exclusively with the roles and activities of young women in youth gangs, and the meanings they describe as emerging from their gang affiliation. (Miller and Glassner: 2004: 131)

So far Miller and Glassner are focusing on how we can use interviews to understand the meaning of these young women's identity. To see how this works out in practice, let us focus on the data that Miller obtained from her in-depth interviews. This is one example:

Describing why she joined her gang, one young women told Miller, 'well, I didn't get any respect at home. I wanted to get some love and respect from somebody somewhere else'. (1997: 107)

Here is another respondent's explanation of why she joined a gang: 'I didn't have *no* family ... I had nothin' else' (1997: 107).

Another young woman, when asked to speculate on why young people join gangs, suggested:

Some of 'em are like me, don't have, don't really have a basic home or steady home to go to, you know, and they don't have as much love and respect in the home so they want to get it elsewhere. And, and, like we get, have family members in gangs or that were in gangs, stuff like that. (1997: 107)

Let us assume that you have gathered these data and now want to begin analysis. Put at its starkest, what are you to do with the data?

In line with the positivist or emotionalist approach, you may start by coding respondents' answers into the different sets of reasons that they give for participation in gangs (perhaps using qualitative software such as Ethnograph or NUD*IST; see Silverman, 2010: Ch. 14). From these data, two reasons seem to predominate: 'push' factors (unsupportive families) and 'pull' factors (supportive gangs).

Moreover, given the availability of survey data on the same respondents, you are now in a position to correlate each factor with various background characteristics that they have. This seems to set up your research in good shape. Not only can you search for the 'subjective' meanings of adolescent gangs, but also you can relate these meanings to 'objective' social structures.

Both positivist and emotionalist approaches thus have a high degree of plausibility to social scientists who theorise the world in terms of the impact of (objective) social structures upon (subjective) dispositions. Moreover, the kind of research outputs that it seeks to deliver are precisely those demanded by 'users' in the community, seeking immediate practical pay-offs from social science research.

However, Miller and Glassner are not satisfied by the apparent plausibility of emotionalism. Drawing on constructionism, they recognise that their respondents are not simply individuals with their own unique experiences. Instead, as members of a variety of cultures, their gang members use culturally available resources in order to construct their stories. As Richardson suggests: 'Participation in a culture includes participation in the narratives of that culture, a general understanding of the stock of meanings and their relationships to each other' (1990: 24).

How, then, can the data above be read in these terms? The idea is to see respondents' answers as *cultural stories*. This means examining the rhetorical force of what interviewees say as

> interviewees deploy these narratives to make their actions explainable and understandable to those who otherwise may not understand. (Miller and Glassner, 1997: 107)

TIP
Treating interview responses as cultural stories fits with narrative analysis discussed in Chapter 3.

In the data already presented, Miller and Glassner note that respondents make their actions understandable in two ways. First, they do not attempt to challenge public views of gangs as bad. But, second, they do challenge the notion that the interviewee herself is bad.

However, Miller and Glassner note that not all their respondents glibly recycle conventional cultural stories. As they put it: 'Some of the young women go farther and describe their gang involvement in ways that directly challenge prevailing stereotypes about gangs as groups that are inherently bad or antisocial and about females roles within gangs' (Miller and Glassner, 1997: 108).

Here are some of their gang members' accounts which challenge stereotypes (drawn from Miller and Glassner, 2004: 132–5):

> Girls at school … was like, 'well you probably got sexed in. You probably got sexed in.' … Like, 'oh, you a ho. How'd you get put in?' I was like, 'none of your business.' They was like, 'you probably got sexed in.' I was like, 'no, I really didn't.'

> Some people stereotype, they just stereotype gang members to be hardcore and to always be shootin' at somebody. They don't stereotype people that that could be a gang member but still they could go to school and get straight A's. That's stereotyping because I know, I know a few gang-bangers who go to school, get straight A's, hit the books but still when they on the street, you know, they take good care of theirs. They takin' care of theirs in school and they takin' care of theirs on the street and I don't think that's right to stereotype people.

In accounts like these, Miller and Glassner argue that there is an explicit challenge to what the interviewees know to be popular beliefs about youth gangs – note how the respondent in the last extract actually uses the word 'stereotype'. So instead of accepting the conventional definition of their behaviour as 'deviant', the girls attempt to convey the normalcy of their activities. Indeed, their narratives directly challenge stereotypical cultural stories of the gang. Following Richardson, Miller and Glassner refer to such accounts as 'collective stories' which 'resist the cultural narratives about groups of people and tell alternative stories' (Richardson, 1990: 25).

However, Miller and Glassner also show how these female gang members not just are rebels who resist society's stereotypes but also, at times, *rely upon* certain cultural stories. For instance, they label and denigrate young women they themselves deem sexually loose. Talking about those girls who had been 'sexed in', one girl explained:

> They know that they was getting' looked at as ho's. We just look at 'em. Sometimes we tell 'em too, we be like, 'ooh y'all look, y'all some little ho's,' or 'why y'all do that?' (Miller and Glassner, 2004: 135)

So these young women tended to accept society's judgement on 'promiscuous behaviour' and to imply that it is always the girl's own 'fault'. As Miller and Glassner comment:

> Though extremely judgemental of girls who were sexually abused by male gang members, girls did not negatively evaluate young men's sexual behaviours. In this way, gang girls drew from familiar cultural stories that single out and blame female victims of mistreatment. Women continue to be held responsible for their victimization in both popular discourses about violence against women and legal response; gang girls culled from these cultural traditions when they described and evaluated the exploitation of young women around them. (Miller and Glassner, 2004: 135)

At the same time, gang girls did recognise the potential threat from male gang members and showed how they skilfully resisted it. As one girl said:

> We just like dudes to them. We just like dudes, they treat us like that 'cause we act so much like dudes they can't do nothing. They respect us as females though, but we just so much like dudes that they just don't trip off of it. (Miller and Glassner, 2004: 136)

Miller and Glassner bring out the ambivalence these young women show to conventional social mores. However, as they imply, this ambivalence need not be seen as an inconsistency or failing. Instead, like all of us, these young gang members are not cultural dummies but are able to use cultural stories as resources to tell the stories they want to tell.

Miller and Glassner's sensitive address of the narrative forms from which perspectives arise suggests that interview analysis can, as Holstein and Gubrium suggest, be used to answer both *what* questions (concerned with identity) and *how* questions (concerned with matters such as narrative construction). In doing so, they show that constructionists do not need to choose between form and content:

> Instead, we argue against the dualistic imperative to classify them (interviews) as one or the other. All we sociologists have are stories. Some come from other people, some from us, some from our interactions with others. What matters is to understand how and where the stories are produced, which sort of stories they are, and how we can put them to honest and intelligent use in theorizing about social life. (Miller and Glassner, 2004: 138)

Rapley's analysis of interviews with drug educators shows us further how we can analyse the stories that interviewees tell us. In lines 28–36 of Extract 6.1 above, Rapley (2004: 17) notes that Dan says drugs are meaningful to him by way of the 'fact' that they are *meaningful to everyone* – drugs are 'everywhere', 'so much of it around' and it's 'so much … in the news'.

Rapley shows how Dan's answer works to rebut one possible account of his interest in drugs: that he is himself involved in drug use. He notes that:

> The interviewee's account – that *drugs are an 'inescapable' part of our culture* – is intimately tied to his prior talk, his identity as someone who was trained to con- duct drug peer-education and the interviewer's question. The interviewee has already noted that drugs are only 'meaningful to him' as he comes from a 'medical family', so any interest in drugs has *only* entered his life through *legitimate and ordinary* ways. (Rapley, 2004: 17)

The interviewer then asks whether there was any other 'particular interest' in the fact the training would be about drugs. At this point:

> The interviewee … produces the account that *drugs are an 'inescapable' part of our culture*. So that specific account is intimately tied to that specific interactional context, that the interviewee is arguing that 'I don't do drugs and I didn't become a drug peer-educator because I'm either pro or anti-drugs' – and 'good' peer- educators should not be overtly pro or anti drugs. (2004: 17)

So far, Rapley has shown us the *moral work* that Dan does to portray himself as someone with a purely professional interest in drugs. However, like Miller and Glassner, he also shows how we can move beyond such local identity work to examine the *cultural stories* from which our respondents draw. As Rapley puts it:

(Dan's) account – that *drugs are an 'inescapable' part of our culture* – emerges from and is shaped by the broader social context of the *contemporary debate about drugs*. The interviewee, in the very act of drawing on that account, is demonstrating (and reinforcing) that broader social norm. The interviewee is demonstrating *one of the possible ways* that are available to understand, experience and talk about drugs. These can be contrasted with the *other possible ways*, be it in the context of other interviews, government reports, newspapers. (2004: 17)

Like Miller and Glassner, Rapley reveals the danger of assuming that interview talk is only about the official topic of the interview. Instead, interview talk always reveals two interlinked phenomena:

1 *Identity work*:

> The talk in an interview may be as much about the person producing themselves as an '*adequate interviewee*', as a '*specific type of person in relation to this specific topic*'. In this sense, interview data may be more a reflection of the social encounter between the interviewer and the interviewee than it is about the actual topic itself. (Rapley, 2004: 16)

2 *Cultural stories*:

> A focus on interview-talk as locally and collaboratively produced does not deny that the talk is reflexively situated in the wider cultural arena … In this sense, interview-talk *speaks to* and *emerges from* the contemporary ways of understanding, experiencing and talking about that specific interview topic. (2004: 16)

However, we should never separate our analysis from the turn-by-turn production (by both interviewee and interviewer) of these identities as stories. Once more, Rapley makes the point succinctly: 'these ways of understanding, experiencing and talking about that specific interview topic are contingent on the specific local interactional context and should be analysed, at least initially, from the circumstances of their production' (2004: 16).

> **TIP**
> Never conduct a research interview until you have sorted out two issues:
>
> - your precise research topic
> - your analytical framework.
>
> Then, as soon as you have completed your first interview, try to analyse it in terms of your topic and analytic framework. Do not delay analysis while your interviews pile up!

I will give a final example of how we can treat the interview-as-local-accomplishment. The example is taken from a study of 'parenthood'.

6.8 MORAL TALES OF PARENTHOOD

Baruch (1982) notes that, when parents of handicapped children are first interviewed, they often offer 'atrocity' stories, usually about the late discovery or inadequate treatment of their child's condition. These stories reveal both local identity work and cultural tales.

It is tempting to compare what parents say with observations of what has happened and with medical workers' accounts. However, as Baruch suggests, such a comparison is based on the positivist assumption that interview responses are to be valued primarily because of their accuracy as objective statements of sets of events. Conversely, we might address the moral forms that give force to 'atrocity' stories, whatever their accuracy. Right or wrong, biased or unbiased, such accounts display vividly cultural particulars about the moral accountability of parenthood.

Baruch begins by looking at data extracts from Burton's (1975) study of parents of children with cystic fibrosis. In Extract 6.2 below, one such parent tells about an early experience at a baby clinic.

Extract 6.2 [quoted by Baruch, 1982: Appendix Two]

Parent: I went to the baby clinic every week. She would gain one pound one week and lose it the next. They said I was fussing unnecessarily. They said there were skinny and fat babies and I was fussing too much. I went to a doctor and he gave me some stuff and he said 'You're a young mother. Are you sure you won't put it in her ear instead of her mouth?' It made me feel a fool.

Baruch compares these data with a data extract from his own study, as follows.

Extract 6.3 [Baruch, 1982: Appendix Two]

(Int = interviewer)

Parent: When she was born, they told me she was perfectly all right. And I accepted it. I worried about her which most mothers do, you know. Worry about their first child.
Int: Hm
Parent: She wouldn't eat and different things. And so I kept taking her to the clinic. Nothing wrong with her my dear. You're just making yourself … worrying unnecessarily, you see.

Despite the different illnesses, there are striking similarities in the content of what each mother is saying. Both mothers report their concern about the baby's eating habits. Both complain that the clinic doctor dismissed their worries as groundless.

Nonetheless, Baruch notes that each account is treated very differently by each researcher. More specifically:

> Burton treats her findings as an accurate report of an external event and argues that parents' early encounters with medical personnel can cause psychological damage to the parents as well as lasting damage to the relationship with doctors. On the other hand, I see parents' talk as a situated account aimed at displaying the status of morally adequate parenthood. In this instance, the display is produced by the telling of an atrocity story. (Baruch: 1982: Appendix Two, 2)

Following positivist assumptions, Burton treats parents' answers as deriving from the social structure of mother–doctor interactions, coupled with a given psychological reality to do with parents' feelings of guilt and responsibility. For Burton, then, the interview is a technique used by social scientists to get closer to such 'facts'.

Conversely, Baruch is arguing that mothers are trading on common-sense knowledge of 'what everyone knows' about the concerns of young mothers. Treating the interview as a local accomplishment, he invites us to see how the construction of an 'atrocity story' is an effective way for mothers to display their identity as morally responsible.

It might appear that Burton and Baruch are offering *competing* versions of mothers' behaviour. Burton seems to be stressing the mothers' goodwill in difficult circumstances, while Baruch appears to be offering a more cynical account which seems to argue that mothers are mainly concerned with how they will look in the eyes of others. However, it must be stressed that, for Baruch at least, the two accounts are *not* competitive.

This is because Baruch is not treating what his mothers tell him as either true or false accounts of what actually happened to them when they took their babies to the clinics. Consonant with his view of these interviews as 'local accomplishments', he is instead focusing on how, in telling their story to a stranger, mothers skilfully produce demonstrably 'morally adequate' accounts.

Notice how, in both extracts, the mothers report that they noticed that their babies had eating problems prior to the disease diagnosis specifically implies and contradicts the possible identity 'mother-who-did-not-monitor-her-baby-sufficiently'. Coupled with their reports that doctors had, at first, played down their fears, this effectively produces the identity of 'mother-who-thoroughly-monitored-her-baby-but-was-spurned-by-the-doctor'.

So Baruch is asking about the *functions* of the mothers' accounts rather than casting doubt on their motives. He is not competing with what Burton says about the reality of what happens in mother–doctor encounters because he is refusing to treat interviewees' accounts as simple *reports* on such an external reality.

If anything, however, Baruch's analysis offers a more human account than Burton of the capacities of his respondents. While Burton's mothers' responses seem determined by social and psychological structures, Baruch reveals that human subjects actively participate in the construction of social and psychological realities.

So far, however, we have been depending on brief extracts to show how such an analysis works. As I argued in Chapter 2, a danger of depending on such extracts is that one can use them to support a preconceived argument rather than to test it.

Baruch (1982) overcomes such dangers by two effective strategies:

- tabulating many cases
- investigating deviant cases.

Let me briefly review each strategy in turn.

Baruch used only the parents' initial responses to the interviewer's opening question: 'So could you just tell me the story?' Following Sacks, Baruch was interested in the identity categories or **membership categorisation devices** (MCDs) employed by respondents. The MCDs used by Baruch's parents were mainly 'parent', 'child' and 'medical professional'. Baruch then tabulated these responses in terms of pairs of MCDs. His analysis showed that these MCDs were grouped in various pairs at different parts of the account according to who had a duty towards the other (e.g. parent–child, professional–parent). Table 6.6 indicates the pairs identified – in each case, the category mentioned first is described by the parent as having an implied duty towards the second category.

TABLE 6.6   Membership categories

Categories	Number	%
Parent–child	160	51
Parent–professional	86	28
Professional–child	49	16
Professional–parent	16	5
Total	311	100

Source: Baruch, 1982: Appendix 2, 17

Baruch notes that earlier studies (e.g. Voysey, 1975) have stressed the perceived importance of parental responsibilities towards their children. Table 6.6 supports this finding showing that:

Parent–child norms are central to parents' accounts and, on their own, amount to all the other norms put together. Thus, when parents provide an account of their responses, they are heard to attend to their duties, rights and obligations towards their child, even though they might have been expected to emphasise the medical aspect's of their child's career, e.g. professional–child relationships. (Baruch, 1982: Appendix 2, 18)

In Sacks's terms, each of these pairs of MCDs implies common expectations about what sort of activities are appropriate. For instance, the parent–child pairing implies a standard obligation of parental responsibility such that we can describe the collection 'parent–child' as a **standardised relational pair** (SRP).

Looking just at the SRP 'parent–child', Baruch finds the following kinds of activities described in the interviews (as shown in Table 6.7).

TABLE 6.7   Parent–child activities

Type of activity	Number	%
Emotional responses to the child's illness and treatment	101	63
Action taken in relation to the child's illness	38	24
Taking responsibility for the child's illness	11	7
Showing knowledge about the child's development and illness	10	6
Total	160	100

Source: Baruch, 1982: Appendix 2, Table 3

We see from Table 6.7, as Baruch puts it, that: 'One of the central features of these stories is the way parents appeal to their emotionality as a normal, moral response of anyone who is in their situation' (1982: Appendix 2, 21).

This emotional response (described in 63 per cent of all such descriptions of parents and children) appears to set the backdrop for the other accounts of action taken (24 per cent) in the context of responsibility (7 per cent) and knowledge (6 per cent). Thus parents describe their relationship to their children as primarily grounded in emotion but leading to actions embodying the more cognitive dimensions of responsibility and knowledge.

Using such tabulations, Baruch demonstrates that the construction of what he calls 'moral tales' (see also Baruch, 1981) not just is an isolated feature of one or two extracts but runs throughout his corpus of data. When grounded on MCD analysis, Baruch's tabulation of data is possible without violating the recognition of the interview as a situated encounter.

Nonetheless, as in all data sets, there are always exceptions. As already mentioned, Baruch stringently seeks to identify such exceptions and, through the method of **deviant-case analysis**, uses them to refine his analysis. The most important deviant case is discussed briefly below.

One set of parents, when asked to tell their story, responded entirely in terms of descriptions of what medical professionals had done for their child. They made no mention of their own emotional responses, nor of their own actions as parents. The following extract gives a brief taste of their response:

Extract 6.4 [Baruch, 1982: Appendix 2, 28]

(P = Parent)

1   P: Well the story really started with him going in for a minor op last year and the
2   anaethetist just er investigations discover a murmur which she wasn't very happy
3   about and referred us to a paediatrician after the op who agreed that it was an unusual
4   sight and um murmurs are commonplace really
5   I: um
6   P: But on the sight and nature of it, it sort of wanted further investigation

---

While Baruch's other interviews contained several descriptions of parent–child SRPs, they are totally absent here where the tale is told simply in terms of professional–child activities. If you compare Extract 6.4 with the ones given earlier, the absence here of references to parents' worries is quite striking.

Baruch suggests that the key to understanding this deviant case lies in P's statement on line 4 that 'murmurs are commonplace really'. As he notes, this involves: 'the use of a technical language … which is never heard in other parents' accounts at this stage of the child's career' (1982: 29).

It turns out that these parents are themselves medical professionals and are treating the interviewer's question as a request for a reasonably 'objective' account of events seen from a medical point of view. This 'deviant case' thus highlights the way in which, for parents without these medical resources, the request for a story is heard as an opportunity to display that one is still an adequate parent.

Two points of clarification perhaps need to be made. First, this extract is being viewed as deviant purely in a statistical sense. As Baruch argues:

> we are not viewing [the parent's] account as deviant in terms of pre-conceived assumptions about what constitutes adequate parenthood. Rather, the claims we are making about its status are based on a comparison of the considerable differences between its normative character and that of the rest of the sample. As Strong (1979) has argued, such limiting cases are extremely valuable in illuminating consistent features of social life. (1982: 30)

The second point derives from this: it might be suggested that Baruch is arguing that the occupation of these parents is the *cause* of why they give their account in this way. If so, Baruch would be treating the interviewees' account as stemming from their place in the social structure and, thereby, be reverting to a positivist version of the interview.

However, although Baruch is not explicit on this matter, his method would suggest that this is *not* his argument at all. Following Rapley, Kitzinger, Miller and Glassner, and Holstein and Gubrium, we must recognise that any person can describe themselves (or be described) in a multiplicity of ways. These parents could have elected to have heard the interviewer's request for 'the story' to be addressed to them purely as 'parents' rather than as 'health-care-professionals-who-happen-to-be parents'. By choosing the latter format, they display other, equally moral, qualities, for example as people who are, for the moment, able to put their feelings on one side and seek to offer an admirably 'objective' account.

In neither case do we have to see an external, pre-given social structure as the determinant of the account. Rather, all the interviewees invoke a sense of social structure in order to assemble recognisably 'sensible' accounts which are adequate for the practical purposes at hand.

EXERCISE 6.4

This exercise gives you an opportunity to work with some of Baruch's data and to compare his approach with others. Here are some extracts from interviews with mothers of children with congenital heart disease:

1

Well um … the first thing the nurse who delivered him said was: 'Don't worry, it's alright. Everything's alright.' And I didn't even realise there was anything wrong with him to start with

2

When she was born they told me everything was perfectly alright. And I accepted it.

3

He was very breathless and I kept saying to midwives and doctors and various bods that came round, um I said to the midwife look, I said, he's breathing so fast

4

He was sitting in his buggy just looking absolutely lifeless. So I thought right up to the doctor's and see what she says

> Now answer the following questions:
>
> 1 Is it helpful to check the accuracy of what these mothers are saying (e.g. by comparing them to case-notes, medical accounts)? Explain your answer.
> 2 Attempt a psychological interpretation of what these mothers are saying (refer to the discussion of Burton in Section 6.8).
> 3 Now attempt to show how these mothers construct their own moral adequacy using Baruch's concept of 'atrocity stories'. Is the same strategy used in every story?

The implications are clear cut. First, in studying accounts, we are studying displays of identities which arise as part of participants' artful practices (e.g. in telling a particular kind of 'moral tale'). Second, there is no necessary contradiction in seeking to study *both* identities and practices. Sacks himself, for instance, seeks to establish the norms at work in children's stories in order to give an account of the artful practices through which they are assembled. It is equally possible, as Baruch has shown, to study the cultural norms at work within a narrative and to understand how their power derives from *both* their cultural base and the local skills of participants in invoking 'culture'.

Following Kitzinger, Rapley, Gubrium and Holstein, and Miller and Glassner, Baruch's research reveals that, for analytic purposes and in real life, form and content depend upon each other. In this way, the debate between different kinds of constructionism (focused on either *what* or *how* questions) may be resolvable.

6.9 THE THREE MODELS: A SUMMARY

6.9.1 The value of interview data

Positivists argue that interviews based upon pre-tested, standardised questions are a way of increasing the reliability of research. However, both emotionalism and constructionism bring into question the value of data derived from standardised, survey-research-style interviews.

Constructionists, like Miller and Glassner, assume that people's cultural worlds are more complex than most positivists will allow. Consequently, it is insufficient simply to 'pre-test' an interview schedule by asking questions of a few respondents. Instead, for Miller and Glassner, it is more appropriate to engage in systematic observation *before* any interviewing takes place.

Ethnomethodologists take the argument far further, rarely using interview methods as a way of gathering data. Instead, ethnomethodologists tend to concentrate on purely 'naturally occurring' settings which are observed and/or recorded firsthand.

However, it should at once be noted that the critique of the value of interview data shares an assumption with more traditional approaches. As Hammersley and Atkinson (1995) have pointed out, an attachment to **naturally occurring data** is a kind of **naturalism**. Naturalism, they argue, unwittingly agrees with positivism that the best kind of data are somehow 'untouched by human hands' – neutral, unbiased and representative. In some senses, then, naturalists are the inheritors of the positivist programme, using different means to achieve the same unquestioned ends.

So, despite the power of naturally occurring data, it does not follow that it is illegitimate to carry out our own research interviews. Everything depends on the status which we accord to the data gathered in such interviews.

6.9.2 The 'truth' of interview data

One important dimension which distinguishes both positivists and emotionalists from constructionists is whether interviews are treated as straightforward reports on another reality or whether they merely report upon, or express, their own structures.

According to the former position, interviews can, in principle, be treated as reports on external realities. The only condition for positivists is that strict protocols are observed. For emotionalists, the condition is that the interviewer should seek to overcome the presumed power imbalance with their interviewees.

For constructionists, interviews also present interesting data. But these data express interpretive procedures or conversational practices present in what both interviewer and interviewee are **doing** through their talk and non-verbal actions (see Baker, 1997). This means that we need not hear interview responses simply as true or false *reports* on reality. Instead, we can treat such responses as *displays* of perspectives and moral forms which draw upon available cultural resources.

The need to preserve and understand the local accomplishment of the interview account is central to the argument of many constructionists. Indeed, the ethnographic tradition (see Section 5.1) contains a way of looking at respondents' accounts which goes beyond categorising them as 'true' or 'false'. Whyte has observed:

> In dealing with subjective material, the interviewer is, of course, not trying to discover the *true attitude or sentiment* of the informant. He should recognise that ambivalence is a fairly common condition of man – that men can and do hold conflicting sentiments at any given time. Furthermore, men hold varying sentiments according to the situations in which they find themselves. (1980, 117)

Unlike positivists, but like Rapley, Kitzinger, Miller and Glassner, and Holstein and Gubrium, Whyte shows us how it is not always necessary to treat respondents' accounts as if they were scientific statements and subject them to possible refutation. This leads Whyte to ask questions about the causes of respondents' accounts ('the events and interpersonal relations out of which [they] arise'; 1980: 117).

Of course, this pays scant attention to the form and structure of such accounts. For instance, following Gilbert and Mulkay (1983), we can treat interviews as giving us access to the *repertoire* of narratives that we use in producing accounts (see Exercise 6.1 and my discussion of **discourse analysis** in Section 9.4). However, in a paper first published in 1960, we can forgive Whyte neglecting the study of the interview as a narrative.

Indeed, it may sometimes be appropriate to address issues of truthfulness in what interviewees tell us. As I have argued throughout this book, everything depends on your purposes at hand. For instance, in quantitative studies of voting intentions or patient satisfaction, it becomes appropriate to treat what interviewees say as potentially 'true' reports. At the other extreme, as in Baruch's work, it makes sense consistently to concentrate on the local or situated character of interview talk. And again, sometimes, it is appropriate to ask broader questions about the cultural resources upon which interviewees draw to do their inevitably 'local' work. For it rarely makes sense to privilege form over content.

By analysing how people talk to one another, one is directly gaining access to a cultural universe and its content of moral assumptions. As Rapley puts it, 'we are never interacting in a historico–socio–cultural vacuum, we are always *embedded in* and *selectively* and *artfully* draw on broader institutional and organisational contexts' (2004: 26).

TIP

Always study both *how* the narrative process unfolds and *what* is said in an interview. As Holstein and Gubrium suggest:

> researchers need to pay explicit attention to both the practical *hows* and the substantive *whats* of interviewing, taking care to give them equal status in both the research process and in reporting results ... The *whats* always reflect the circumstances and practices conditioning the interview. A dual interest in the *hows* and *whats* of interview narratives makes visible the animated parameters of the interview process. (2011: 151)

6.10 SUMMARY: BASIC ISSUES

Astute readers may have noticed that my argument in this chapter has moved between two different positions. What I might call the *minimalist* position addresses deficiencies in interview research and offers remedies to improve it. My *maximalist*

TABLE 6.8   How to improve interview research

- Do not delete interviewers' talk. At minimum it should include the relevant interview questions, the topic initial question as well as any follow-ups or 'prompts'. If you just report what interviewees say, their talk is rendered as an abstract statement rather than a specific answer to a specific question put by a specific interviewer
- Avoid tidied up transcripts that provide a reconstructed, simplified and distorted version of the interview. Include such basic features as pauses, repairs and overlaps
- Analysis should not simply pick out 'themes' from what interviewees say. You need to show how your claims can account for the specifics of the talk, not just its broad themes
- Report the 'set-up' of the interview. First, what category have the participants been recruited under? Are they taking part in the research on the basis that they are a 'lesbian mother', an 'adolescent male', a 'recreational drug user', or something less explicit? Interview research typically recruits participants under categories of this kind. After all, this is a feature of proper attention to sampling. How are these categories constructed in the various parts of the recruitment (including the introduction to the research, ethics procedures, administrative arrangements, and so on)? Second, what is the task understanding offered to the participant? This involves questions such as: what are they told that the interview will be about, what will it be for, and what will be the task of the interviewee?

Source: adapted from Potter and Hepburn, 2005: 281–91

TABLE 6.9   Do we need interviews at all?

- Interviews flood what happens with social science agendas and categories. Question construction with its informality and candidate answer carefully coaches the participant in the relevant social science agenda
- Qualitative interviews make the problematic assumption that what interviewees say can be treated as a report on events, actions, social processes and structures, and cognitions
- Naturally occurring data avoid flooding the interaction with psychology and social science agendas and avoids cognitivism by collecting material where participants are not required to offer abstract conceptual rumination on some aspect of their lives

Source: adapted from Potter and Hepburn, 2005: 291–301

position questions the way in which interviews have become central to such qualitative research and dares to pose the question: do we need interviews at all? These two positions are set out in Tables 6.8 and 6.9.

6.11 THREE PRACTICAL QUESTIONS – AND ANSWERS

In the light of the discussion above, I suggest below three questions that interview researchers might ask themselves:

1 What status do you attach to your data?
    Many interview studies are used to elicit respondents' perceptions. How far is it appropriate to think that people attach a single meaning to their experiences?

May not there be multiple meanings of a situation (e.g. living in a community home) or of an activity (e.g. being a male football fan) represented by what people say to the researcher, to each other, to carers and so on (Gubrium, 1997)?

This raises the important methodological issue about whether interview responses are to be treated as giving direct access to 'experience' or as actively constructed 'narratives' involving activities which themselves demand analysis (Holstein and Gubrium, 1995). Both positions are entirely legitimate but the position taken will need to be justified and explained.

2   Is your analytic position appropriate to your practical concerns?

Some ambitious analytic positions (e.g. ethnomethodology, discourse analysis) may actually cloud the issue if your aim is simply to respond to a given social problem like 'students' perceptions of their future job prospects (see Chapter 1). If so, it might be simpler to acknowledge that there are more complex ways of addressing your data but to settle on presenting your research as a *descriptive* study based upon a clear social problem.

3   Do interview data really help in addressing your research topic?

If you are interested in, say, what happens in school classrooms, should you be using interviews as your major source of data? Think about exactly why you have settled on an interview study. Certainly, it can be relatively quick to gather interview data but not as quick as, say, texts and documents. How far are you being influenced by the prominence of interviews in the media (see Atkinson and Silverman, 1997)?

In the case of the classroom, could you not observe what people do there instead of asking them what they think about it? Or gather documents that routinely arise in schools, for example pupils' reports, mission statements, and so on?

Of course, you may still want to do an interview study. But, whatever your method, you will need to justify it and show you have thought through the practical and analytical issues involved in your choice. Now look at the tip below which shows one way of addressing the practical issues in doing interview research.

> **TIP**
>
> Rapley gives a very practical example of how to work with interview data:
>
> As soon as I become interested in a specific topic, I'll start to collect some literature on the topic – both 'academic' and 'non-academic'. This reading, alongside conversations, past experiences and 'bizarre bolts from the blue' (often over a strong coffee) gives me an initial clue as to possible interviewees, interview questions and analytic themes. These sources of knowledge often

become analytic themes that I explore with interviewees in interviews. I'll then try and recruit the interviewees, making notes on this process – these notes cover both the successes and the failures, the kinds of accounts people provide for not taking part (again providing more 'data' and more possible questions). Once I've got some interviews lined up, I'll prepare a brief topic guide. In choosing those specific interviewees and in producing that specific topic guide (that is shaped for that specific interviewee) I am already making some specific analytic choices about what types of people, what *voices or identities*, are central to the research (and which ones will remain silenced) alongside what sorts of topics of discussion might be important. I then go to the interview.

During the interview, I often try to raise some of the themes I've been thinking through either by asking interviewees specific questions about them or, sometimes, telling them about my thoughts and letting them comment on them. So in one sense, the actual interview interactions are a space in which I seek to test 'my' analysis of these specific themes by asking interviewees to talk about them. Or to put it another way, *interview interactions are inherently spaces in which both speakers are constantly 'doing analysis' – both speakers are engaged (and collaborating in) 'making meaning' and 'producing knowledge'*.

After the interviews I write up my notes on the encounter, noting both pre and post-tape talk alongside my reactions and observations about the interview itself (another moment of analysis). I then re-think about the trajectory of the research, refine the kinds of themes and ideas I want to think through with interviewees, and go and interview someone else.

In the past, I used to always transcribe the interview tapes myself. In this way, I got to repeatedly listen to the tapes, and so generate, check and refine my analytic hunches whilst simultaneously producing a *textual* version of the interaction that could be used both for further analysis and reports. Increasingly, my tapes have been sent to transcribers, which means I always check the transcript against the tape and add the sort of detail I'm often interested (pauses, stress, overlapping speech). However, when it comes to sustained periods of analysis, I always prefer to re-listen to the tapes alongside re-reading the transcript. This allows me to get a sense of the interactional, collaborative, work of the speakers. I then try and write up the research (and re-write it, and re-write …). (2004: 26–7)

6.12 CONCLUSION

Interviews share with any conversation an involvement in moral realities. They offer a rich source of data which provide access to how people account for both their troubles and good fortune. In the words of Atkinson and Coffey:

We need … to divorce the use of the interview from the myth of inferiority: the essentially romantic view of the social actor as a repository of "inner" feelings and intensely personal recollections. Rather, interviews become equally valid ways of capturing shared cultural understandings and enactments of the social world. (2002: 811)

Or, as Charmaz and Bryant put it:

Interviews are, of course, retrospective accounts that often explain and justify behaviour. Yet they may also be special social spaces in which research participants can reflect on the past and link it to the present and future in new ways. An interview is a performance, whether stories tumble out or are strategically calculated and enacted, but that does not disqualify interviews from providing rich data and sparking analytic insights. (2011: 299)

Such observations are hardly surprising since the evidence for them is immediately before our eyes in our everyday experience. Only by following misleading correspondence theories' truth could it have ever occurred to researchers to treat interview statements as only potentially accurate or distorted reports of reality.

TIP
Do not think of the role of the interviewer as just asking questions. Consider the variety of your other actions, for example saying 'hmm, mm', re-formulating a question, agreeing and remaining silent. Always assess how these influence what an interviewee says.

TIP
If you are interested in understanding people's experiences, do not assume that the interview is the only appropriate research method.

TIP
Apparent 'contradictions' in your data depend on the model you are employing. For constructionists, such contradictions may reflect the different discourses that are being used by participants.

TIP
Potter and Hepburn introduce the anthropological terms 'emic' and 'etic'. 'Emic' refers to the categories that participants use. 'Etic' refers to an analyst's categories.

KEY POINTS

- There are three different **models** relevant to interview data: positivism, emotionalism and constructionism.

- Each model provides different answers to questions about whether we should gather interview data and, if so, how to analyse these data.

- Unlike the other models, constructionism allows us to see the local, inter-actional work carried out by both interviewer and interviewee, without losing sight of the cultural resources which they draw upon.

STUDY QUESTIONS

1 What are the different types of qualitative interview?
2 Assess the relevance of guides about how to conduct an interview.
3 Why is it important to audio-record research interviews?
4 Give three different versions of what interview answers 'represent'. Why does this matter?
5 Can interview data tell us anything beyond how the participants locally assemble recognisable interview talk?
6 Do we have to analyse interviews in terms of either form or content?
7 Explain the uses of asking 'when?', 'how?' and 'what?' questions about interview data.

RECOMMENDED READING

The *Handbook of Interview Research* edited by Jaber F. Gubrium and James A. Holstein (2002) is both a thematic and encyclopaedic collection of state-of-the-art descriptions of different approaches to interviewing. The handbook covers theoretical, technical, analytic and representation issues relating to interview research. The best short introduction to analysing interview data, written from a constructionist perspective, is Holstein and Gubrium (1995). It provides extensive illustration of the interactional, interpretive activity that is part and parcel of all interviewing.

Silverman (2011) includes important chapters by Miller and Glassner, Holstein and Gubrium, Charmaz and Bryant, and Riessman. Seale et al. (2004) is an edited collection covering qualitative research in general and contains the work by Rapley and Kitzinger discussed in this chapter. Potter and Hepburn's (2005) excellent paper 'Qualitative interviews in psychology: problems and possibilities' provides a detailed

(Continued)

(Continued)

overview of many of the issues raised in this chapter. Fontana and Frey (2000) offer a survey of the literature which is sympathetic to many of the issues raised in this chapter.

Interviews have always been used to elicit autobiographical tales. For an introduction to the life-history approach, see Miller (2000). The advent of the Internet now means that researchers need no longer be face to face with interviewees (see the chapter on Internet communication by Markham, 2011). Mann and Stewart (2000) provide a collection of papers on this issue and Ryen and Silverman (2000) provide an example of research based on e-mail interviews.

7

Focus Groups

CHAPTER OBJECTIVES

By the end of this chapter, you will be able to:

- understand what focus groups are, how they are organised and what they are used for
- recognise the different ways you can analyse focus group data
- identify the advantages and disadvantages of content analysis, thematic analysis and constructionist analysis
- recognise how focus group data may be used to contribute to our understanding of social problems.

7.1 WHAT ARE FOCUS GROUPS?

Wilkinson has described focus group **methodology** when used in social science research as 'deceptively simple' (2011: 168). It is a way of collecting qualitative data, which usually involves:

- Recruiting a small group of people (often between six and eight) who usually share a particular characteristic (e.g. mothers of children under two; sufferers of a particular illness).
- Encouraging an informal group discussion (or discussions) 'focused' around a particular topic or set of issues. This could be, for example, young women sharing experiences of dieting, single parents evaluating childcare facilities, or fitness instructors comparing and contrasting training regimes.

- The discussion is usually based on the use of a schedule of questions. This is sometimes followed by use of some kind of stimulus material (visual or otherwise) for discussion. A wide range of more structured 'exercises', including ranking, rating, card sorting or use of vignettes are sometimes used.
- Although **focus groups** are sometimes referred to as 'group interviews', the moderator does not ask questions of each focus group participant in turn but, rather, facilitates group discussion, actively encouraging group members to interact with each other.
- Focus groups may be reconvened at a later date (a 'longitudinal' design) or a series of focus groups may be held, using the outcome of an earlier focus group to specify the subjects under discussion.
- Typically, the discussion is recorded, the data transcribed, and then analysed using conventional techniques for qualitative data, most commonly content or **thematic analysis**. (Adapted from Bloor et al., 2000 and Wilkinson, 2011)

CASE STUDY
Perceptions Of AIDS

Kitzinger and Miller (1992) were interested in the role of the media in changing, reinforcing or contributing to ideas about AIDS, Africa and race. They began by analysing three years of TV news reports on these topics. In one such report, statistics on HIV infection were given for the whole of Africa and a map of Africa was shown with the word 'AIDS' fixed across the continent. The map was also stamped with the words '3 Million Sufferers'.

To see how these media images impacted upon their audience, many focus groups were established among people with particular occupations (e.g. nurses, police, teachers), perceived to have a 'high involvement' in the issue (e.g. gay men, prisoners) and 'low involvement' (e.g. retired people, students).

Members of all groups were sceptical about media coverage of news issues although it is possible that this scepticism might have reflected the prompting of the focus group moderator with their presumably liberal opinions (P. Brindle, personal correspondence). Despite this, most accepted the general assumption that AIDS came from Africa and is prevalent there. White people usually began from the assumption that Africa is a hot bed of sexually transmitted diseases. This was based on the belief that sexual intercourse typically begins at an early age and that sexual diseases are spread through polygamy.

However, not all individuals shared these beliefs. Kitzinger and Miller refer to several factors which led people to doubt the media treatment. Among these were the following: personal contact with alternative information from trusted individuals or organisations, personal experience of being 'scapegoated', personal experience of conditions in Africa and being black yourself. The authors conclude:

Our research shows both the power of the media and the pervasiveness of stock white cultural images of black Africa; it is easy to believe that Africa is a reservoir of HIV infection because 'it fits'. Journalists draw on these cultural assumptions when they produce reports on AIDS and Africa. But, in so doing, they are helping to reproduce and legitimize them. (1992: 49)

Focus groups as a research method originated in the work of the Bureau of Applied Social Research at Columbia University in the 1940s. Its leader, the sociologist Paul Lazarsfeld, was conducting commercial market research on audience responses to soap operas. The US government requested the Bureau to assess the impact of its wartime radio propaganda and Lazarsfeld asked another famous sociologist, Robert Merton, to join the project. Until then, focus group members had simply responded to what they heard by pressing buttons to express approval or disapproval. At Merton's suggestion, the groups were now given questions about the broadcasts and asked to discuss them among themselves (Bloor et al., 2001: 1–2).

Since then, focus groups have continued to be a key tool in commercial market research. For instance, an episode of the fourth TV series of *Mad Men* shows a focus group on skincare products being held in a Madison Avenue advertising agency in 1964.

In commercial qualitative research, focus group 'findings' are directly related to the business goals of the client. This is explained in the comment below by Jonathan Potter, a social scientist who studied commercial focus groups.

CASE STUDY
Commercial Focus Group Research

The companies or organizations who commission the group pay for three kinds of output. First, they may have a representative who watches the interaction from behind a one-way mirror. Second, they will be given a video of the interaction. Third, they will be given a report of the interaction written by the moderator (which typically summarizes themes and gives sample quotes of people's views).

Typically, none of these forms of output takes priority over the others. This means that the moderator is the central part of the data production. He or she can, for example, display the importance of something by drawing attention (for example, by repeating it) or display its irrelevance to the business of the group by ignoring it. This will be apparent to the client whether through the one-way mirror or on the video, or in what is quoted in the report. The visibility of the data in market research groups is a much more direct issue than in a social science focus group where considerable sifting and coding may go into the production of a data set for analysis. And there would be no expectation that a research article, say, would include the raw interaction as its data and finding. By contrast, in commercial focus group research, there is a special sense of visibility at work where the unedited record of the focus group is itself the result of the research. (J. Potter, personal correspondence; see also Puchta et al., 2004)

To understand what Potter calls 'sifting and coding' and the study of 'raw interaction', we must consider how focus group data have been analysed in social science research.

EXERCISE 7.1

The following is an extract from a focus group discussion (M = the moderator). What features of the moderator's talk suggests that this is a commercial focus group?

M: Rick　　And the characteristics of this↑pe: rson
　　　　　　　(.) if you can imagine them,
　　　　　　　(.)

Mary　　　　Powerful,
　　　　　　　(.)

M: Rick　　°Powerful,°
Hannah　　DOMIN↓ANT
　　　　　　　(.)

M: Rick　　Dominant,

(Puchta et al., 2004).

7.2 ANALYSING FOCUS GROUP DATA IN SOCIAL SCIENCE

As Sue Wilkinson notes, it was not until the 1990s that focus groups became a popular method of research across a broad range of disciplines – including education, communication and media studies, feminist research, sociology and social psychology. She adds:

> In qualitative research, focus groups, initially only used in consumer and voting studies, are now just as popular as interviews. The popularity of focus group research continues to rise, with almost 6000 focus group studies published across the social sciences in the last five years, more than a quarter of these in 2009 alone. (Wilkinson, 2011: 168)

In social science, focus groups tend not to be a stand-alone method. Instead, they are usually employed within a multi-method research design in three ways:

- To clarify, extend or qualify findings produced by other **methods**.
- To feed back research findings to study participants (Bloor et al., 2001: 90).
- To identify research foci or develop research questions *prior to* the conduct of the main study (particularly in questionnaire studies, where they often inform question design and terminology) (S. Wilkinson: personal correspondence).

As with many research methods, more information is available about how to *collect* data than how to *analyse* them. As Wilkinson notes:

Focus groups are distinctive … primarily for the method of data *collection* (i.e. informal group discussion), rather than for the method of data *analysis*. It is this, perhaps, which leads most accounts of the method to emphasize how to run an effective focus group, rather than how to analyze the resulting data. (2011: 169)

In line with the rest of this book, this chapter will focus on *data analysis*.

Three main methods have been used to analyse focus group data:

- Quantitative **content analysis**
- Qualitative thematic analysis
- **Constructionist** methods.

Before we look at each method in detail, it is worth noting that nearly all qualitative focus group studies use one form or another of thematic analysis. Constructionist methods, including **discourse analysis** (DA) and **conversation analysis** (CA) are barely represented (but see Wilkinson, 2011).

The following case study illustrates a conventional way of analysing focus group data. It then shows how constructionist methods may be used on the same data.

CASE STUDY
Focus Groups on Genetically Modified Food

Phil Macnaghten and Greg Myers were interested in how the scientific debate about genetically modified food was reflected in popular feelings about the subject. Through focus groups, they sought to elicit 'the different ways people relate to animals and … the ways their beliefs and values about animals relate to implicit beliefs about what is natural (Macnaghten and Myers, 2004: 67).

Below is one extract from their data (see the Appendix for the transcription symbols used). The extract begins with a leading question from the moderator:

Extract 7.1 [Macnaghten and Myers: 2004, 75, adapted]

(M = moderator; X and Y = participants)

M: Can I just say, so in what ways do you think these animals are natural?

(1.0)

X: well, they won't be natural will they=
Y: = they're not natural, they're   [man-made aren't they?
M: [they'd be engineered
Y: engineered

(Continued)

(Continued)

How can social scientists (as distinct from commercial researchers) analyse such data? Very helpfully, Macnaghten and Myers discuss two different strategies based, in part, on practical contingencies. Working to a tight timescale, Macnaghten paid more attention to setting up the focus groups than to data analysis. His strategy involved the following three simple steps:

1 Finding 'key passages' quickly (in 200,000 words of transcript).
2 Choosing quotations that made a relevant (and repeated) point briefly and in a striking way.
3 Marking 'quotable themes' with a highlighter (ending up with eight groups of quotes on each of the topics in which he was interested).

The authors note that this simple method offers a rapid way of sorting out data to bear on a particular research topic. When we begin data analysis, we may be in an unknown terrain. In this sense, Macnaghten and Myers' method allows us, as they put it, to 'map the woods'.

The kinds of rapid answers that can arise through 'mapping the woods' undoubtedly have an appeal to social-problem-oriented research. However, this method of identifying repeated themes overlooks the fact that the focus group participants are not isolated individuals but are engaged in a conversation. To understand the conversational character of the data, Myers suggests that we need to look at how meaning gets constructed in the interactions between moderator and participants and between the participants themselves.

In Extract 7.1, he notes:

1 X pauses for one second and uses a preface of 'well' which presents his response as unexpected and dispreferred (for a discussion of preference organisation, see Heritage, 1984).
2 Y enters very quickly and M overlaps with him, both of which display preferred actions.
3 Y modifies his term ('man-made') to fit M's term ('engineered'). In this way, Y ratifies the term produced by M, by repeating it.

This detailed analysis, the authors suggest, is more like 'chopping up trees' than 'mapping the woods'. Unlike the latter approach, it rejects the assumption that there is a one-to-one link between utterances in focus groups and people's 'views' on animals and genetically modified research. Instead, it shows how 'a focus group transcript is a way of recovering, as far as is now possible, a moment-to-moment situation, and the shifting relations of people in that situation' (Macnaghten and Myers, 2004: 75).

This case study illustrates two ways of analysing focus group data which derive from different traditions:

- Mapping the woods, as we shall see, approximates to qualitative thematic analysis.
- Chopping up trees is the path chosen by constructionists, particularly those influenced by DA or CA.

However, like any method of data analysis, 'chopping up trees' presents potential problems. First, it is clearly a much slower method than if we proceed by identifying 'key passages'. Second, its linguistic approach may run the risk of losing sight of the research problem with which we began. In this example, critics may justly argue that Myers' sequential analysis has little bearing on the debate about genetically modified food.

Experienced qualitative researchers will recognise that the alternative approaches posed by Macnaghten and Myers exemplify two widely used (and very different) methods for analysing our data. 'Chopping up trees', with its fine-grained sequential analysis, seems a more soundly grounded research method (offering depth) than the scattergun approach of simply quoting favourable instances. However, at least 'mapping the woods', whatever its limitations, tells us directly about a substantive phenomenon and thus offers breadth.

By contrast, we can only make an indirect link between Myers' sequential analysis and the debate about genetically modified food. If Y may be seen to be ratifying the term produced by M (and − before that − as aligning with him in taking issue with the terms of the moderator's question), we get a sense that these focus group participants share a view of genetically modified animals as 'engineered/not natural', as opposed to 'natural' (S. Wilkinson, personal correspondence).

I now present each of these methods in greater detail.

7.2.1 Quantitative content analysis

As we saw in Section 3.2, content analysis is based on examination of the data for recurrent instances of some kind. These instances are then systematically identified across the data set, and grouped together by means of a coding system. Wilkinson notes that:

> The majority of published focus group studies use some type of content analysis. At its most basic, content analysis simply entails inspection of the data for recurrent instances of some kind. This is irrespective of the type of instance (e.g. word, phrase, some larger unit of 'meaning'); the preferred label for such instances (e.g. 'items', 'themes', 'discourses'); whether the instances are subsequently grouped into larger units, also variously labelled (e.g. 'categories', 'organizing themes', 'interpretive repertoires'); and whether the instances − or larger units − are counted or not. (2011: 171)

It involves the following stages:

- deciding on a unit of analysis (the whole group, the group dynamics, the individual participants, or, more usually, the participants' utterances)
- developing a coding system

- applying the codes systematically across a transcript (or transcripts)
- (sometimes) using simple tabulations of instances of codes. (Adapted from Wilkinson, 2011: 170)

We shall shortly see an example of quantitative content analysis, using Wilkinson's own focus group data.

7.2.2 Qualitative thematic analysis

In quantitative content analysis, participants' talk is taken as providing a transparent window to something that lies behind or beyond it, for example participants' experiences, life-histories or social situations. By contrast, qualitative methods are designed to give access to how the social world is lived, not simply how people talk about it to researchers (see Chapter 1). Nonetheless, as Wilkinson points out, many qualitative focus group studies, which aim to provide contextual, interpretive accounts of people's social worlds, end up having much in common with quantitative content analysis:

> For example, in Lyons et al.'s (1995) study of women with multiple sclerosis, and Agar and McDonald's (1995) study of ex-users of LSD, research participants' talk is taken to provide a 'transparent' window onto the circumstances of their lives outside the focus group (to which the focus group moderator has no independent access), inferred from self-report. What people say in the context of the focus group discussion is taken as 'revealing', for example, the nature of daily life for people with chronic physical illness, or as flagging up a 'significant issue' in the life 'territory' of the drug-experienced young. In other words, talk is used as a 'means of access' to something that lies behind or beyond it, rather than treated as of interest in its own right. (2011: 174)

This tendency to cut across methods is reflected in the following features of qualitative thematic analysis:

- It tries to find out about participants' lives through what they say within the focus group.
- It aims to ground interpretation in the particularities of the situation under study, and in participants' (rather than analysts') perspectives.
- Its data are generally presented as accounts of social phenomena or social practices, substantiated by illustrative quotations from the focus group discussion. (Adapted from Wilkinson, 2011: 170)

The following case study illustrates how focus group data are often coded in qualitative research. Like the earlier study on genetically modified foods, it also reveals the problems of thematic analysis.

CASE STUDY
Adolescents Who Smoke

In a focus group study of adolescent smoking behaviour, the analysis centred on perceived pressures on the decision to quit:

- 'Peer pressure' was frequently discussed and became a central code.
- Participants talked of different kinds of peer pressure, including 'bullying' and 'exclusion from the group'. These categories were used as sub-categories of 'peer pressure'.
- 'Exclusion' was further sub-categorised between 'real' friends and 'instrumental' friends (e.g. people who were only friendly with you if you got them cigarettes).

This is an example of how a comment from the group was coded, with codes in square brackets:

Extract 7.2 [Bloor et al., 2001: 63–4]

Simon: you know, like some people don't pressure people into smoking, [**PEER PRESSURE**] people just if, say like, say somebody was smoking and I was gonna give up, I don't think these (indicating his friends) would bully me [**BULLYING**] because they're like my friends, aren't they, [**TYPE OF FRIEND**] and they're not gonna just come up to me, punching me, 'you've stopping smoking so you're not my friend', are they? [**EXCLUSION**].

As these authors note, this type of thematic analysis can 'lose sight of where the data [coded] sit within the whole [transcript]' (Bloor et al., 2001: 64). As we saw in the Macnaghten and Myers study, our third method, constructionism, attempts to remedy these shortcomings by looking at process as well as content within the focus group.

Table 7.1 sets out the key issues involved in attempting a qualitative thematic analysis of focus group data. In practice, the questions in Table 7.1 are usually answered by selective quotations from what participants say. Although this seems to satisfy the ethnographer's demand for 'depth', it usually preserves very little of the social processes involved in the focus group discussion.

TABLE 7.1   Qualitative thematic analysis: three key issues

1   How to select the material to present?
2   How to give due weight to the specific context within which the material was generated?
3   How best to prioritize participants' orientations in presenting an interpretive account?

Source: Wilkinson, 2011: 170

EXERCISE 7.2

Examine when Simon refers to 'friends' in Extract 7.2 and consider what interactional 'work' is achieved by these references in these places. For instance, show what other interpretations of his smoking Simon's references to his friends may exclude.

Sue Wilkinson has provided us with an insight into how such coding works. She uses a segment of a focus group in which three women who share a breast cancer diagnosis are talking about possible causes of the disease.

Extract 7.3 [Wilkinson, 2011: 176]

(SW = Sue Wilkinson)

01	SW:	D'you have any idea what <u>caused</u> your breast cancer[pause] any of you.
02	Fre:	No- What <u>does</u> cause breast cancer do you think.
03	SW:	What do you think it <u>might</u> be?
04	Ger:	[cuts in] There's a lot of <u>stories</u> going about.=I was once told that
05		if you use them aluminium pans that cause cancer. .hh I was also told
06		that if you- if you eat tomatoes and plums at the same meal that-
07	Dor:	[laughs]
08	Ger:	[to Doreen] Have you heard all these those things?
09	Dor:	[laughs] No
10	Ger:	Now that's what <u>I</u> heard and-
11	Dor:	[laughs] Mm
12	Ger:	Oh there's several things that if you <u>listen</u> to people [pause] we::ll-
13	Dor:	Mm
14	SW:	[to Gertie, laughingly] What else have they told you?
15	Ger:	Pardon?
16	SW:	[to Gertie, laughingly] What else have they told you?
17	D/SW:	[laughter]
18	Ger:	I can't think off hand I knew a- I knew a <u>lot</u> that I've heard over the
19		years from people who've passed on 'Oh yeah well that causes cancer'.
20	Dor:	Mm
21	Ger:	But I don't know but-
22	Dor:	[cuts in] I mean uhm-
23	Ger:	Now <u>I've</u> no views on this [To Doreen] have you?

Wilkinson helpfully provides two different analyses – one quantitative, one qualitative – of these data. As she explains:

> The 'results' of the quantitative content analysis are presented as frequency counts, while the 'results' of the qualitative thematic analysis are presented as illustrative quotations. Both analyses take the 'mention' of a cause as the unit of analysis, and organize these 'mentions' using a category scheme derived from Blaxter's (1983) classic study of talk about the causes of health and illness. However, the first analysis systematically records the *number* of 'mentions' within each category (including null categories), summarizing what these 'mentions' are; while the second records the *words* in which these 'mentions' are couched, presenting them as quotations under each category heading. (2011: 171)

Wilkinson's content analysis gives us an overall sense of the distribution of different lay **theories** of the causes of breast cancer (Table 7.2). However, by depriving these women's talk of the local context in which it was said, it makes the problematic assumption of 'relatively stable "cognitions" (beliefs, attitudes or opinions) assumed to underlie people's talk (and – at least sometimes – to inform their subsequent behaviour)' (Wilkinson, 2011: 174).

TABLE 7.2   Content analysis (causes of breast cancer)

1   *Infection:* 0 instances
2   *Heredity or familial tendencies:* 2 instances family history (×2)
3   *Agents in the environment:*

   (a)   *'poisons', working condition, climate:* 3 instances aluminium pans; exposure to sun; chemicals in food
   (b)   *drugs or the contraceptive pill:* 1 instance taking the contraceptive pill

4   *Secondary to other diseases:* 0 instances
5   *Stress, strain and worry:* 0 instances
6   *Caused by childbearing, menopause:* 22 instances not breast feeding; late childbearing (×3); having only one child; being single/not having children; hormonal; trouble with breast feeding – unspecified (×4); flattened nipples (×2); inverted nipples (×7); nipple discharge (×2)
7   *Secondary to trauma or to surgery:* 9 instances knocks (×4); unspecified injury; air getting inside body (×4)
8   *Neglect, the constraints of poverty:* 0 instances
9   *Inherent susceptibility, individual and not hereditary:* 0 instances
10 *Behaviour, own responsibility:* 1 instance mixing specific foods
11 *Ageing, natural degeneration:* 0 instances
12 *Other:* 5 instances 'several things'; 'a lot'; 'multi-factorial'; everybody has a 'dormant' cancer; 'anything' could wake a dormant cancer

Source: Wilkinson, 2011: 171–2.

EXERCISE 7.3

Return to Extract 7.3 and answer the following questions:

- What 'stake' does Gertie show in her account of the possible causes of breast cancer; that is, does she wholeheartedly assert these things or does she seek to distance herself from what she has heard?
- Does Gertie change her stake in what she is saying during the course of the discussion? If so, point out what features may lead her to change her position?

As Wilkinson shows, the same data may be analysed qualitatively, by identifying relevant themes from what respondents say in a manner found in much **naturalist** ethnographic research (and in **emotionalist** interview studies). This kind of thematic analysis is presented in Table 7.3.

TABLE 7.3   Thematic analysis (causes of breast cancer)

Heredity or familial tendencies

- 'I mean there's no family <u>history</u>'

Agents in the environment

(a) 'poisons', working condition, climate

- 'I was once told that if you use them aluminium pans that cause cancer'
- 'Looking years and years ago, I mean, everybody used to sit about sunning themselves on the beach and now all of a sudden you get cancer from sunshine'
- 'I don't know (about) all the chemicals in what you're eating and things these days as well, and how cultivated and everything'

(b) drugs or the contraceptive pill

- 'You know, obviously I took the pill at a younger age'

Caused by childbearing, menopause

- 'Inverted nipples, they say that that is one thing that you could be wary of'
- 'Until I came to the point of actually trying to breast feed I didn't realise I had flattened nipples and one of them was nearly inverted or whatever, so I had a lot of trouble breast feeding, and it, and I was several weeks with a breast pump trying to get it right, so that he could suckle on my nipple, I did have that problem'
- 'Over the years, every, I couldn't say it happened monthly or anything like that, it would just start throbbing, this leakage, nothing to put a dressing on or anything like that, but there it was, it was coming from somewhere and it were just kind of gently crust over'
- 'I mean, I don't know whether the age at which you have children makes a difference as well because I had my eight year old relatively <u>late</u>, I was an old mum'
- 'They say that if you've only had <u>one</u> that you're more likely to get it than if you have a <u>big</u> family'

TABLE 7.3   (Continued)

Secondary to trauma or to surgery

- 'Sometimes I've heard that <u>knocks</u> can bring one on'
- 'I then remembered that I'd <u>banged</u> my breast with this … you know these shopping bags with a wooden rod thing, those big trolley bags?'
- 'I always think that people go into hospital, even for an exploratory, it may be all wrong, but I do think, well the <u>air</u> gets to it, it seems to me that it's not long afterwards before they simply find that there's more to it than they thought, you know, and I often wonder if the <u>air</u> getting to your inside … brings on cancer in any form'

Behaviour, own responsibility

- 'I was also told that if you eat tomatoes and plums at the same meal'

Other

- 'He told them nurses in his lectures that <u>every</u>body has a cancer, <u>and</u> it's a case of whether it lays dormant'
- 'I don't think it could be one cause, can it? It must be multi-factorial'

Source: Wilkinson, 2011: 172–3

As Wilkinson notes, despite the apparent differences between the analyses presented in Tables 7.2 and 7.3, they share the same assumptions. Both treat what people say as providing a 'window' into their perceptions and neither reveals the local context of what these women say. This is because both analyses ignore 'the interactive quality of the focus group data' (Wilkinson, 2011: 174). This is how they both differ from an analysis inspired by constructionist methods.

7.2.3 Constructionist methods

These seek to analyse the process of interaction within a focus group. Rather than inferring meaning from what one person says, the aim is to expose the local and sequential construction of meaning. The case study which follows shows how Wilkinson attempted a constructionist analysis of her focus group data presented as Extract 7.3.

CASE STUDY
Constructing Meaning in a Breast Cancer Focus Group

The extract opens with my question (as moderator) about causes, and the responses from Freda and Gertie to this question. A content analysis (of the kind presented earlier) might code Freda's

(Continued)

(Continued)

initial response (line 2) as 'I don't know'; and Gertie's subsequent response (lines 4–6) as items in the categories 'agents in the environment' (aluminium pans) and 'behaviour, own responsibility' (choosing to eat tomatoes and plums at the same meal) … by contrast, [I now] focus on the immediate interactional context. Talk about causes can be interactionally tricky – particularly when a presumed 'expert' is asking questions, or in settings in which potentially equally knowledgeable others might have different or even conflicting opinions. Conversation analysts (e.g. Sacks, 1992: 340–7) have noted the asymmetry between being the first to express an opinion and being second: going first means you have to put your opinion on the line, whereas going second offers an opportunity either for agreement or for potential challenge. Consequently, speakers often try to avoid first position, and this is precisely what Freda does in response to the moderator's question: she declines to gives an opinion, and bounces the question right back to the moderator, as a 'counter' (Schegloff, 2007: 16–19). It is not simply then, as a content analysis (within an essentialist framework) might suggest, that Freda 'doesn't know' what causes breast cancer: from the perspective of … a social constructionist framework, she is not here reporting a state of mind, but is engaged in a piece of local interactional business.

The moderator (SW) avoids answering Freda's direct question: instead she reformulates it (in the manner typically recommended for interviewers and focus group moderators), making clear she is interested in what the participants themselves 'think it <u>might</u> be' (line 3), rather than in any purported 'actual' (i.e. scientific) causes of breast cancer. It is with this reassurance that Gertie offers some 'stories' (i.e. folk wisdom, labelled as such), thereby putting herself in the vulnerable first speaking position, and attracting just the kind of second speaker disagreement that Freda's counter enabled her to avoid: Doreen, the third member of the group, <u>laughs</u> at Gertie's response.

Note that within most other approaches, Gertie's references to 'stories', and to what she has 'heard over the years', would be taken as transparent reports of the <u>source</u> of her ideas about cause: i.e. as indicating a reliance on folk knowledge. Within a social constructionist framework, however, this attribution of ideas about cause to folk knowledge is seen an *interactional device* seeking to protect the speaker from challenge (although, here, it fails to avert ridicule).

Gertie's candidate causes, then, are presented as 'stories'. However, only moments later, even these 'stories' are retracted. By the end of Doreen and Gertie's subsequent exchange (at line 23), Gertie, like Freda before her, is claiming to have 'no views' on the causes of breast cancer.

Again (within this approach to data), this not simply a straightforward report of a cognitive state: it arises out of the interactional sequence within which it is embedded, in the course of which both Doreen and the moderator have implied, through their laughter, that Gertie's candidate causes are rather implausible; indeed, the moderator's probe (line 14) can be heard as 'positioning' (Wilkinson and Kitzinger, 2003) Gertie as the sort of gullible person who believes anything she is told. Gertie responds first by reminding everyone that she is not reporting her own views, but those of others, and then she flatly refuses to offer further candidate answers, explicitly handing the floor to Doreen at (line 23). (Wilkinson, 2011: 177)

Wilkinson has demonstrated the local positioning and fate of Gertie's 'stories'. These are generated within a cautious environment and subsequently withdrawn when challenged. Rather than being a reflection of how Gertie views the world, these stories make sense within the turn-by-turn organisation of this conversation.

However, Wilkinson is *not* claiming that focus group talk is the product of some external social mechanism and that the participants are puppets. Instead, she demonstrates:

- how focus group speakers skilfully attend to the constraints and opportunities presented by the positioning of what they say within a sequence of turns
- how we can establish participants' own understandings as displayed directly in the talk.

This is a distinct advance on content and thematic analysis. In both approaches, researchers have to *infer* participants' understandings by using their own common-sense knowledge of what focus group members' talk 'means'.

However, if we follow Wilkinson's constructionist approach and treat focus group talk as constitutive of social and psychological 'realities', how much can we say about the original topic of our research? In Wilkinson's case, what can we say about women's attitudes towards breast cancer? In the next section, I will try to answer this question referring to a paper based on the same data.

EXERCISE 7.4

Compare the findings of Wilkinson's approach to the Macnaghten and Myers (2004) 'chopping up trees' approach:

- Do you find these constructionist approaches to focus group data more convincing than the alternatives?
- Can you find any ways in which these two studies can help answer substantive questions about the topics which the participants discussed?
- Should we prefer content or thematic analysis since they seem to offer clear answers to policy-relevant questions?

7.3 FORM OR SUBSTANCE?

My earlier discussion of the work of Macnaghten and Myers (2004) on attitudes towards genetically modified food raised issues about form versus substance. Can a constructionist concern with sequential organisation tell us about more than con-versational structures? To obtain an initial answer to this question, I will discuss further research on this breast cancer data in which such substantive matters are more clearly highlighted.

Wilkinson and Kitzinger (2000) were interested in the way in which both lay-people and many medical staff assume that 'positive thinking' helps you cope better with cancer. They point out that most of the evidence for this belief derives from questionnaires in which people tick a box or circle a number.

By contrast, Wilkinson and Kitzinger follow a constructionist approach in which statements about 'thinking positive' are treated as actions and we seek to understand their functions in particular sequences of talk. Put simply, they seek to insert 'scare marks' around 'positive thinking' and to examine when and how it is used.

Let us look at one data extract that they use from a focus group of women with breast cancer:

Extract 7.4 [Wilkinson and Kitzinger, 2000: 807]

Hetty: When I first found out I had cancer, I said to myself, I said right, it's not gonna get me. And that was it. I mean (Yvonne: Yeah) obviously you're devastated because it's a dreadful thing

Yvonne: (overlaps): yeah, but you've got to have a positive attitude thing, I do

Betty: (overlaps): but then, I was talking to Dr.Purcott and he said to me the most helpful thing that <u>any</u>body can have with <u>any</u> type of cancer is a positive attitude

Yvonne: a positive outlook, yes

Betty: because if you decide to fight it, then the rest of your body will st-, will start

Yvonne: motivate itself, yeah

Betty: to fight it

In this extract, Hetty's account of feeling 'devastated' by a cancer diagnosis is met by appeals to a 'positive attitude' by both Yvonne and Betty. On the surface, then, Extract 7.4 seems to support the idea that 'positive thinking' is an internal, cognitive state of people with cancer. However:

> this overlooks the extent to which these women are discussing 'thinking positive' not as a natural reaction to having cancer (the natural reaction [mentioned by Hetty] is that, 'obviously you're devastated because it's a dreadful thing'), but rather as a moral imperative: 'you've got to have a positive attitude'. (Wilkinson and Kitzinger, 2000: 806–7)

So Wilkinson and Kitzinger's analysis suggests two different ways in which these women formulate their situation:

Positive thinking is presented as a moral imperative, part of a moral order in which they *should* be thinking positive.

Other reactions (including fear and crying) are simply described as what 'I did' not as 'what you have got to do'.

This distinction shows the value of looking at how talk is organised and not just treating it 'as providing a transparent "window" on underlying cognitive processes' (2000: 809). By contrast, Wilkinson and Kitzinger's constructionist focus on sequences of talk allows us to get a quite different, more processual, grasp of the phenomenon.

As already noted, the close attention to detail shown here is similar to the work of Macnaghten and Myers (2004) on attitudes towards genetically modified food. So, in this version of 'chopping up trees', do we lose sight of the substantive phenomenon? To answer this question, we need to consider the limits of what other approaches to focus group data can tell us.

Wilkinson and Kitzinger's findings are simply not available from answers to questionnaires or, more relevantly, from conventional qualitative analysis of their focus group data which, no doubt, would find multiple instances of 'positive thinking' within these women's talk. This is because content and thematic analysis are both ultimately dependent upon analysts using their common-sense knowledge of what participants' words 'mean'. So, while their coding has the air of scientific respectability, their results depend upon taken-for-granted knowledge of the world we live in.

In this case, such analyses can do little more than confirm lay or medical beliefs about the usefulness of certain mental responses to life-threatening illness. By contrast, this research reveals that expressions of 'positive thinking' may have more to do with public displays of one's moral position than with how people actually respond to their illness. As in much scientific research, such a negative finding can be treated as an opportunity for researchers to advance our knowledge of the field through asking different questions. Moreover, it suggests that neither patients nor health workers need to worship at the shrine of 'positive thinking' nor feel guilty when they do not enact it. Such a conclusion provides new insights of potentially great value to both patients and health workers.

EXERCISE 7.5

The following is an extract from a focus group with Danish women in their forties. The participants have sorted pictures and recipes cut from women's magazines, and they are now in the middle of discussing what good and bad cooking is to them.

- What themes can you find in the talk?
- What interactional processes can you discover as the participants come to a conclusion about what fried food signifies?

Extract 7.5 [Halkier, 2010: 75]

Sonja:	When I was a child, when we had fish it was these frozen fish fingers…
Karen [interrupts]:	Yes, THAT is disgusting [Sonja: He, he…] … that is bad cooking.
Dorte:	Yes, it is.
Sonja:	That is simply YUKKY.
Birgit:	Yes, my kids love them…
Dorte [interrupts]:	No, nobody likes fish fingers.
Birgit:	Yes, I like them.
Karen:	It's the same with that breaded fish you can buy, it's only breading.
Birgit:	No, that depends on which ones you buy … some of it is okay to buy…
Karen [interrupts]:	I will rather buy it without breading, and then… [pause]
Birgit [interrupts]:	…where there is a lot of fish… [pause] [Karen: do it myself] but that is [Sonja: You don't know what's in there] obvious…
Karen:	No.
Sonja:	It looks like such stuff.
Karen:	Yep.
Sonja:	Oh yes, that's bad cooking too. To me bad cooking is doing it with deep-frying.
Birgit:	Yes, all right I can only admit that [Karen: Yes] to you … we don't use that either.
Karen:	I also think…
Sonja [interrupts]:	But then again, it's that fat.
Karen:	I actually used it, I used it to deep-fry those camembert cheeses for dessert, but I have begun to make that in the oven … that's actually the only deep-fry…
Dorte:	It's a long time since you have made that dessert for us.

Conventional analyses of both focus groups and interviews sometimes have the aim of 'giving voices' to people who are often silenced. For instance, as we saw in Chapter 6, Byrne, drawing upon feminism, has suggested that 'qualitative interviewing has been particularly attractive to researchers who want to explore voices and experiences which they believe have been ignored, misrepresented or suppressed in the past' (2004: 182). Unfortunately, this attempt to give substantive relevance to qualitative research falls short where it simply abstracts talk from the local context in which participants embed it.

The case study below, based upon Celia Kitzinger's research, shows the complex issues involved in trying to use focus groups to explore potentially suppressed voices.

CASE STUDY
Hearing Women's Voices

Kitzinger notes certain key methodological assumptions used by feminist researchers who seek to treat focus groups' (or interviewees') responses as giving access to previously silenced 'voices':

In practice, most qualitative feminist social science research equates women's voices with women's experience. That is, the researcher collects data (e.g. from interviews or focus groups) in which women talk about experiences (or that subset of them of interest in the context of any given research project) and treats them as more or less 'accurate' reports of the experiences the women have described … Access to experience is gained through the talk. (2004: 128)

To show how researchers make this link between talk and experience, Kitzinger examines the following extract from a focus group discussion.

Extract 7.6 [Duncombe and Marsden, 1993]

I think I always loved him too much. I didn't really have a 'falling in love' … but I had a deep love for him, but it was all very unequal … I never felt really very loved and I think that for every one of the sixteen years of my marriage, it was a struggle to make him love me more and to get the relationship equal.

Kitzinger notes that Duncombe and Marsden claim that 'the dominant pattern of our female respondents' experience of coupledom was an asymmetry of emotional response' (1993: 225) and this extract is 'presented as an example of how women "experience" (rather than, for example, "describe" or "talk about") coupledom as asymmetrical' (Kitzinger, 2004: 134). This involves two big assumptions:

- *Transparency*: 'this research participant's description of her marriage is taken as a transparent window through which the analysts are able to see what the marriage was "really" like'. What she *says* is taken as pretty much accurately reflecting what her marriage was actually like and as revealing the existence of her emotional labour within this marriage.
- *Lack of context:* Although she is speaking in a group discussion, there is no explanation of why the woman is telling her story at this particular point, how her listeners react, or to which of their expectations and previous statements she may be orienting in telling her story. (2004: 134)

Kitzinger adds that these kinds of assumptions are common in feminist writing on another topic: women who 'come out' as lesbian or bisexual. She notes that:

The entire literature on 'coming out' is based on interviews or other self-report data in which people *talk about* coming out, and as such it raises all the problems about the relationship between 'voice' and 'experience' which has been discussed here. How do we know that their retrospective account is what it was really like? Are they telling the story of how they came out to their parents, or friends, or colleagues, in a 'slanted' way to impress the interviewer, or to display their own victimisation? (2004: 135)

To show what an alternative approach might look like, Kitzinger examines an extract from the same focus group on women's experience of breast cancer. She remarks that: 'Sue [Wilkinson] knew I

(Continued)

(Continued)

was collecting instances of "coming out" and remarked casually one evening: "What a pity it was that I didn't come out in the breast cancer group today or you could have had it for your collection" (2004: 135). Here is the extract:

Extract 7.7 [Kitzinger 2004: 135, simplified]

```
36   Eve:   I mean he ain't sex-mad my 'usband but [I mean] a::ll me: n:
37   Jill:                                          [No::::]
38   Eve:   (0.2) like boobs don't they?
39          (0.5)
40   Sue:   [°I believe so°]
41   Eve:   [So there you a:re.]=If 'he didn't- = Wh::y?=Aren't you married¿
42          (0.5)
43   Eve:   hu::h [hu:h ]
44   Sue:   [Divo: r]ced.
45   Eve:   [Di(h)vo(h)rced huh huh]
46   Jill:  [(huh huh ]
47   Eve:   A::h we(h)ll.
48          (0.5)
49   Eve:   °Ah well.° ((sadly))
```

Kitzinger focuses on Eve's question 'aren't you married?' (line 41) and asks why this question is positioned there. She looks at the previous sequence of talk (lines 36–40) to find an answer.

Note that Eve has just made a statement about men's sexual tastes and that her utterance is in the form of a maxim ('all men like boobs'). As Sacks (1992) shows, the recipient of a maxim can do little else with it but agree. And this is, indeed, what Sue does at line 40. But notice that her agreement is delayed by half a second, is said softly and somehow from a distance (°I believe so°).

As Kitzinger points out:

> Eve asks her question not out of a dispassionate interest in Sue's marital status, but in order to solve the problem as to why Sue has just distanced herself from this bit of folk wisdom about what all men are like. Sue's 'answer' (although it deals with the format of Eve's question) does not really engage with the action Eve is concerned with, and in this sense it's a kind of evasion. (2004: 137)

Of course, Sue could have answered differently. For instance: 'some answer such as "No, I'm not married because I'm a lesbian and what would I know or care about men's interest in boobs?" would have engaged with Eve's reason for asking her question'. However, as Kitzinger observes, such a reply 'would also, of course, have caused major disruption to the otherwise ongoing activity of the group – activity for which Sue, as the researcher facilitating the group discussion, is responsible' (2004: 137). So Sue's turn at line 44 ('divorced') which implies, at the very least, a heterosexual past, represents a 'stepping back from the "coming out" process she has initiated, and Eve has pursued' (2004: 137).

Like Wilkinson's earlier constructionist analysis, Kitzinger's focus on locating utterances in sequences of talk derives from conversation analysis. This allows her to show precisely how 'not coming out' happens through Eve's making available 'an interactional slot in which "coming out" could be, but is not done' (Kitzinger, 2004: 136).

The moral that Kitzinger draws from this fascinating material is that we should not rely too much on respondents' self-reports, taken from focus groups or interviews, to identify social phenomena such as 'coming out'. As she pointedly puts it:

> My own view is that the emphasis on 'voice' has led to an over-reliance on self-report methods, to the detriment of approaches which involve the researcher in direct observation of the phenomenon of interest. So, for example, if 'coming out' is the research topic, data in which research participants *talk about* coming out (or not coming out) as lesbian or gay require the researcher to make an interpretive leap from these retrospective accounts to the experience they purport to represent – with all of the problems associated with such a leap. By contrast, data in which people actually do (or don't) come out as lesbian or gay give the researcher direct access to this topic. (Kitzinger, 2004: 138)

What Kitzinger says here parallels my argument in Chapter 2 about how a reliance on interview data can allow phenomena to 'escape'. By reinstating the phenomenon of 'coming out' as something which is locally enacted, Kitzinger demonstrates how constructionists attention to form can lead to findings of considerable relevance to issues of substance.

7.4 CONCLUDING COMMENTS

Kitzinger and Wilkinson show how we can analyse focus groups as interactions and not lose sight of substance. However, focus groups, like interviews, are **manufactured data** in the sense that they only arise through the intervention of the researcher. Given the wealth of **naturally occurring data**, the question that then arises is whether, if you are interested in interaction, it makes sense to contrive a manufactured situation like a focus group.

However, as already noted, we would be wrong to assume that this means that we should delete focus groups from qualitative research. Everything must depend both on your research topic and on how you analyse your data (from whatever method the data derives).

KEY POINTS

- Focus groups are a deceptively simple method which usually involves recruiting a small group of people who usually share a particular characteristic and encouraging an informal group discussion (or discussions) 'focused' around a particular topic or set of issues.

- Quantitative content analysis involves counting instances of categories established by the researcher.

- In qualitative thematic analysis, we seek to understand focus group participants' meanings and illustrate our findings by extracts which depict certain themes.
- Constructionist analysis of focus groups pays attention to how particular utterances are always positioned within an unfolding sequence of a focus group discussion. It reveals participants' own understandings as displayed directly in their talk.
- Content and thematic analyses appear to have more to say about substantive topics. However, on closer inspection, constructionist analysis can make a sophisticated and vital contribution to issues of substance.

STUDY QUESTIONS

1 Describe how focus groups are organised in social science research.
2 What is involved in doing a content analysis of focus group talk? What are the advantages and limitations of this method?
3 What does thematic analysis involve? Is it more or less effective than content analysis?
4 How would you do a constructionist analysis of focus group talk? What are its uses and limitations?
5 'Content analysis and thematic analysis may be relatively crude methods but at least they allow us to use focus group data to say something about the *content* of what participants say and, thereby, to contribute to debate about substantive topics. Constructionist methods, whatever their analytic merit, do not allow this.' Do you agree?

RECOMMENDED READING

There is a plethora of advice on the methodological and procedural choices entailed in setting up and conducting a focus group – see, for example, Bloor et al. (2000) and Barbour (2007). Wilkinson (2011) provides a valuable discussion of the theoretical and epistemological choices entailed in analysing and interpreting focus group data. Puchta et al.'s paper (2004) shows what happens in commercial focus group discussions and uses a constructionist method to analyse their data. This is treated at book length in Puchta and Potter (2004). A recent paper by Halkier (2010) shows how a focus group where women are asked to talk about cooking can be analysed from a constructionist perspective.

8

Texts

CHAPTER OBJECTIVES

By the end of this chapter, you will be able to:

- understand how you can analyse blogs, e-mails, official documents, lonely hearts advertisements and other texts
- treat texts as representations of reality rather than as simply true or false
- learn about comparative key-word analysis
- appreciate the questions that ethnographers ask about texts
- analyse how people use categorisation devices to make sense of texts.

Having a separate chapter on 'texts' may look a little artificial. After all, to treat an interview as a narrative (see Section 3.4) can mean looking for the same **textual** features as researchers working with printed material. Indeed, the mere act of transcription of an interview turns it into a written **text**.

To make things clearer, in this chapter, I use text to identify data consisting of words and/or images which have become recorded without the intervention of a researcher (e.g. through an interview). For presentational purposes, the chapter will focus on written texts such as blogs, e-mails or documents produced by organisations. The analysis of images will be discussed in Chapter 10.

Written texts and interviews have one more thing in common. Both underline the linguistic character of much qualitative data. Even if our aim is to search for supposedly 'external' realities in our data (e.g. class, gender, power), our raw material is inevitably the words written in documents or spoken by interview respondents.

As Table 8.1 shows, texts are marvellous data for even novice researchers to analyse.

TABLE 8.1   The advantages of textual data

1   *Richness*: Close analysis of written texts reveals presentational subtleties and skills
2   *Relevance and effect*: Texts influence how we see the world and the people in it and how we act – think of advertisements and CVs!
3   *Naturally occurring*: Texts document what participants are actually doing in the world – without being dependent on being asked by researchers
4   *Availability*: Texts are usually readily accessible and not always dependent on access or ethical constraints. Because they may be quickly gathered, they encourage us to begin early data analysis

Yet British and American social scientists have never been entirely confident about analysing written texts. Perhaps, in (what the French call) the Anglo-Saxon cultures, words seem too ephemeral and insubstantial to be the subject of scientific analysis. It might seem better, then, to leave textual analysis to literary critics and to concentrate on definite social phenomena, like actions and the structures in which they are implicated.

This uncertain attitude to language is also reflected in the way in which quantitative researchers sometimes begin with fairly arbitrary but measurable definitions of their '**variables**'. The classic model is Durkheim's suicide which offers a 'conclusive' definition of the phenomenon in its first few pages and then rushes off to investigate it in these terms. As Atkinson (1978) has pointed out, this method rules out entirely any analysis of the very social processes through which suicide is socially defined – particularly in the context of death certificates or of coroners' investigations.

Even in qualitative research, texts are sometimes only important as 'background material' for the 'real' analysis. Where texts are analysed, they are often presented as 'official' or 'common-sense' versions of social phenomena, to be undercut by the underlying social phenomena apparently found in the qualitative researcher's analysis of their interviewees' stories. The model is: the documents claim X, but we can show that Y is the case. According to this approach, documents are to be used as a resource for social scientists in order to get a better overall picture of how a social institution operates.

The problem with this position is that, in some respects, it replicates how ordinary participants in society use documents. Think, for instance, what happens when an insurance company decides whether to pay out on a claim for accidental damage to the contents of a house. In order to make a decision, insurance assessors will then examine documents like the houseowner's claim form and any accompanying builders' estimates. In doing so, the documents will be treated as a resource in order to establish the facts of the case.

By contrast, constructionist qualitative researchers are not specifically interested in working out what 'really' happened (in this example, we can safely leave that to the

TABLE 8.2 Constructionist research questions

- Documents, as other forms of data, do not speak for themselves, but must be made to speak by the analyst
- This means that we must determine *who* the participating actors are, *how* they go about constructing or contesting the aspect of reality we are interested in, what the interpretive *content* of their activities and claims are, and what documentary *venues* for identifying these processes we might consult
- Although constructionists do not ultimately evaluate texts in terms of their truth-value, they address truth-related issues such as (1) how particular biases push reality constructions in distinct directions, (2) which particular aspects of reality, if any, are subject to conflicting interpretations (or, in the absence of conflict, which are generally agreed upon), and (3) where the sources of interpretive divergence are located (e.g. in collective interests, in documentary conventions, or in the setting in which documents are produced)

Source: adapted from Linders, 2008: 469

insurance assessors who are likely to be more expert in this field than we can ever be!). Our concern is rather with how such documents are assembled and evaluated.

Table 8.2 implies that constructionists are interested in texts as topics but not as resources (for further discussion of this issue in textual analysis, see Noaks and Wincup, 2004: 107–10). The following case study illustrates this point.

CASE STUDY
Studying 'Livejournal', a Weblog

Nicholas Hookway chose weblogs as his research data. He points out (Hookway, 2008) that weblogs, or 'blogs' as they are more commonly known:

> refer to a website which contains a series of frequently updated, reverse chronologically ordered posts on a common web page, usually written by a single author. Blogs are characterized by instant text/graphic publishing, an archiving system organized by date and a feedback mechanism in which readers can 'comment' on specific posts. Blogs are typically housed by software programs that enable users of low technical competence to present attractive and regularly updated online material.

> LiveJournal became [my] main data source. LiveJournal was deemed to be the most appropriate because it had the following features: (1) user-friendly interface; (2) systematic search engine which enabled identification of blogs by location (country, state, city) and age; (3) a sizeable share of the blog market in Australia and (4) a reputation as a site purely for online diaries

> The online diaries of LiveJournal vary greatly in degrees of self-reflection and analysis. At one end of the 'self-reflection continuum' are purely descriptive blogs, which non-reflexively recount the events of the day, from what the blogger has eaten for breakfast to who they have seen that day.

(Continued)

(Continued)

At the other end of the continuum, are highly confessional and self-analytical blogs in which bloggers make sense of their identity and relationships with others. For my purposes, I trawled for the latter style of blog as they were more likely to be of a morally reflective nature. The following quotations illustrate these two extremes:

32-year-old male: Things i've done recently: been to ikea, been to my local furniture shop, been to ikea again, been to ikea yes i know, … again … bought a rug, bought a lamp, bought a bigger lamp … dug my lawn up, re-sown lawn, bought some shredded bark … walked along the beach, moved the shelving unit from the lounge to the kitchen, paid for my flight, cut my hair … had a performance review at work, asked for a pay rise, got laid, filed a years worth of bill … thats all for now.

36-year-old male: I wish i had the magic to give Janine the life i stole from her. of all the people i've hurt in my life, it's her that i feel most dreadful about. she put so much trust and faith in me … and i really loved her. i still do. yet i screwed her over and tore that wonderful heart in two. if only i had some way to make it so i'd never happened to her life … if i could just patch up my era [*sic*] with a big sander bandaid … so that it had been him that she'd met and not me. admittedly, i'd lose a part of my life that means a lot to me … but i'd really rather never to have hurt her. and no matter how sorry i am, and how deeply i feel the grief, the apologies i give her can never unhurt her. (2008: 102–3)

Hookway says that the first questions he is asked when he tells people that he is using blogs as a data source are: 'How trustworthy are the expressions of self that bloggers provide? How do you know what bloggers are telling you is true? They could be an elaborate fiction' (2008: 97).

This is his answer to such questions:

> While I do not – and cannot believe that I can definitely answer this question – what I can do instead is animate a series of questions that are worth considering in response to *this* question. The first question is 'does it really matter?' Even if bloggers do not tell the 'truth', these 'fabrications' still tell us something about the manner in which specific social and cultural ideas such as morality are constructed. Here issues of 'truth' are not really at stake as the emphasis is on how the constitutive elements of blogs work to produce 'particular effects'. (2008: 97)

EXERCISE 8.1

1 What features seem to differentiate the blogs of the two males in their thirties provided by Hookway?
2 Attempt to use any one data analysis method discussed in this book (e.g. content analysis, narrative analysis or membership categorisation device analysis) on these extracts. What further features can you see?

Hookway underlines the point that, from a constructionist viewpoint, documents such as blogs are properly used as a topic but not as a resource. However, this is by no means always the case, even in qualitative research. Take a further example. In the UK, academic disciplines in higher education are subjected to external scrutiny and inspection of their research. The Research Assessment Exercise (RAE) is a system of peer review of every academic department's national and international reputation for high-quality research. As part of this exercise, every four or five years, each academic department prepares a long and detailed statement of its research achievements.

Of course, what might be called the 'politics' of this process is deeply fascinating to academics. For instance, how do departments present themselves to the world and what influences the judgements of their peers?

Because of my interest in these matters, I recently attended a presentation of some research on this very topic. The research data consisted of interviews with members of several departments as well as the documents these departments had submitted for the RAE. Yet the paper I heard dealt only with what these academics said when interviewed about this topic. When I asked about the written material, I was told this was only being used as 'background' material.

Here we see how qualitative researchers can sometimes privilege the accounts people give of themselves over data drawn from what they actually do (when not being pestered by an interviewer's questions). Yet this is not the only way to proceed. A constructionist way of looking at documents from the RAE is demonstrated in the case study below.

CASE STUDY
Claiming Academic Distinction

Below is part of the document submitted by the Cardiff University Education Department for the 2001 RAE (cited by Atkinson and Coffey, 2011: 81, my emphasis):

Educational research at Cardiff has for some time adopted an explicit analytical perspective that views education as a '*cradle-to-grave*' process, within which schooling constitutes only one, albeit very important, part. Learning is seen as taking place in a variety of social contexts; in schools, colleges and universities certainly, but also within homes, work-places and wider community settings. The impacts of educational change are understood not simply within the educational system itself, but also in relation to other elements of the social structure, such as families, labour markets and political and cultural institutions. This approach necessitates situating educational research within a *strong social scientific framework*, which fosters the *development of interdisciplinary work*. This counters any tendencies for educational research to be both *intellectually isolated and dominated by its predominantly teacher education environment*.

(Continued)

(Continued)

It also facilitates contribution to the improvement of policy and practice in an era of increasingly 'joined-up' government and collaborative initiatives between professional disciplines.

The creation of the School of Social Sciences has boosted *capacity to deliver* this ambitious research agenda. The School brings together almost 100 *research-active staff* in education, sociology, social policy, social work and criminology.

Atkinson and Coffey (2011: 81–4) indicate three lines of enquiry which help us to look at this document as a topic:

1 How the use of terms like 'cradle to grave', learning taking place in a 'variety of contexts' and 'interdisciplinarity' invites the reader to see what is distinctive about this department.
2 How these and other terms (e.g. 'a strong social scientific framework', 'capacity to deliver' and 'research-active staff') serve as linguistic building blocks which will be familiar to the audience of academic assessors who will read this document.
3 How the document draws upon the genre of other such document and is constructed in terms recognisably appropriate to a situation in which claims are being evaluated by peers.

By raising these issues, we recognise that this document:

is not a transparent description … This is not because the author(s) set out to deceive in some way. The issue here is not about honesty, or even about accuracy, in any simple sense. It reflects the extent to which documentary realities constitute distinctive levels of *representation*, with some degrees of autonomy from other social constructions. (Atkinson and Coffey, 2011: 84, my emphasis)

Analysing material like this RAE document shows that qualitative researchers are quite wrong to neglect textual data.

TIP

There is one obvious trap in analysing documents. Just as we may be tempted to treat interview responses as true or false depictions of inner 'experience', so we may scan texts in terms of their correspondence to 'reality'. If this tempted you when reading the last case study, remember that this is the way that the RAE assessors themselves will have read the Cardiff document. By contrast, the role of textual researchers is not to criticise or to assess particular texts in terms of apparently 'objective' standards. It is rather to analyse how they work to achieve particular effects – to identify the elements used and the functions these play.

8.1 STRUCTURE OF THIS CHAPTER

Three commonly used ways of analysing texts are: **content analysis** (discussed in Sections 3.2 and 7.2.1); **thematic analysis** (discussed in Section 7.2.2); and narrative analysis (discussed in Section 3.3).

In this chapter, I will consider three other ways in which textual researchers have analysed how texts represent reality. Each is set out below with a brief definition:

- *Comparative keyword analysis (CKA)*: CKA is based on corpus linguistics (Seale et al., 2006). This method uses the computational power of modern personal computers and WordSmith Tools software (www.lexically.net/wordsmith/), which supports the creation and comparison of lists of words appearing in different texts, to perform a conjoint 'quantitative' and 'qualitative' analysis of text. Hence it is a method that breaks free of the division between these forms of research that underlies much debate about qualitative secondary analysis, and indeed **methods** in general.
- *Ethnography*: as we saw in Chapter 5, ethnographers seek to understand the organisation of social action in particular settings. Most ethnographic data are based on observation of what people are saying and doing (and of the territories in which this talk and action take place). However, in literate societies, written accounts are an important feature of many settings (Hammersley and Atkinson, 1995: 128). Therefore, ethnographers must not neglect the way in which documents, tables and visual material like advertisements and cartoons (see Chapter 10) exemplify certain features of those settings. Notable attention has been paid to the common-sense practices involved in assembling and interpreting written records. This work has refused to reduce texts to a secondary status and has made an important contribution to our understanding of the everyday practices of organisations.
- *Ethnomethodology*: following Garfinkel (1967), ethnomethodology attempts to understand 'folk' (ethno) methods (methodology) for organising the world. It locates these methods in the skills ('artful practices') through which people come to develop an understanding of each other and of social situations. Drawing on an important paper by Sacks (1974), a major focus of ethnomethodology has been on the skills we all use in producing and understanding descriptions – from a remark in a conversation to a newspaper headline. I will, therefore, conclude this chapter by an account of Sacks's concept of membership categorisation.

I now turn to a closer description of each of these three approaches.

8.2 COMPARATIVE KEYWORD ANALYSIS (CKA)

CKA counts the frequencies with which participants use particular words. One of the disadvantages of the coding schemes used in other enterprises concerned with word counts, such as content analysis, is that, because they are based upon a given set of categories, they furnish 'a powerful conceptual grid' (Atkinson, 1992: 459) from which it is difficult to escape. While this 'grid' is very helpful in organising the data analysis, it also deflects attention away from uncategorised activities (see my discussion of fieldnotes in Section 5.2.6).

In part, Atkinson's critique vitiates the claims of many quantitative researchers who attempt to produce reliable evidence about a large **sample** of texts. The meat of the problem with content analysis (and its relatives) is not simply Atkinson's point about overlooked categories but how analysts usually simply trade off their tacit members' knowledge in coining and applying whatever categories they do use.

For instance, in a lecture given in the 1960s, Harvey Sacks compared the social psychologist Bales's (1950) tendency to produce immediate categories of 'interaction process' with the relatively long time taken by experienced physicians to read the output of electroencephalographs (EEGs). For Sacks, you should not 'categorize … as it comes out' (1992, I: 28). Indeed, as we shall see in my later discussion of what Sacks called membership categorisation, our ability to categorise quickly is properly treated as a research topic rather than a research resource.

By contrast, in some qualitative research, small numbers of texts and documents may be analysed for a very different purpose. The aim is to understand the participants' categories and to see how these are used in concrete activities like telling stories (Propp, 1968; Sacks, 1974), assembling files (Cicourel, 1968; Gubrium and Buckholdt, 1982) or describing 'family life' (Gubrium, 1992).

Although CKA appears similar to content analysis, its word counts are not based on researchers' categories. CKA has the advantage of rapidly identifying points of key difference in large bodies of text. Unlike content analysis, it removes the preexisting preferences of the researcher from the initial identification of features of interest, as keywords are identified purely because of their relative frequency rather than that they catch the researcher's eye. Features can be identified that might otherwise go unnoticed in conventional content or thematic analysis (for instance, in the study that follows, unexpected features such as superlatives, or the focus of men on localised body regions were identified).

In this sense, CKA is a more purely inductive approach than conventional qualitative thematic analysis (see Section 7.2.2). As such, it fits other qualitative methods of data analysis such as **grounded theory** (see Section 3.4).

The following case study shows how Clive Seale used CKA to study gender differences in the content of a web forum for people with cancer.

CASE STUDY
Gender in a Cancer Web Forum

Web forums are a rich source of data about illness experience and gender differences. Forums and message boards provide online support, enabling individuals to post and respond to messages over time. CKA was used to compare the language of men and women with cancer in two popular Internet-based support groups for people with cancer. A complete retrieval (on 20 April 2005) was made of all current and archived postings to the online forums/message boards of the two most popular UK-based breast and prostate cancer websites. Messages were converted into text files and grouped according to name of author. The content of messages was inspected to determine the gender of the author, whether the author was a person with cancer (PWC), a person investigating symptoms that they felt might be cancer, the relative or friend of a PWC, or some other type of person. Only postings by PWCs were analysed, comprising 12,757 posts and 1,629,370 words. Marked gender differences were evident. These differences followed linguistic and other behavioural patterns (such as social network differences) established in other contexts:

- Men used a somewhat greater number and range of key words concerning the disease and its actual and potential progression, such as 'spread', rate', 'enlarged', 'doubling' than did women (28 such words for men; 15 for women).
- Key words associated with research and the Internet featured more in men's than women's text, a difference not evident in the interview text. Thus men were frequently found citing other websites that contained information about aspects of cancer, reflected in the key words 'www', 'http', '.com', 'htm', '.org' and '.asp'. Women's key words involving Internet-related terms contained no such website references, being references to the forums themselves (e.g. '[chat] room' and 'forums'). While women's text contained no key words associated with research, men's contained four that were unambiguously categorised under this heading: 'study', 'data', funding' and 'median'. 'Cases' was also a key word in the men's text, though this word was 'split' in being categorised both under 'research' and 'people'.
- Women's forum postings orient much more towards the exchange of emotional support, including concern with the impact of illness on a wide range of other people. Women's use of superlatives as well as words referring to feelings indicate their enactment of greater emotional expressivity.
- Lifestyle key words differed between men and women on the web forums, with men being more concerned with 'wine', 'running', '[red] meat', 'cranberry [juice]', 'exercise', 'fitness', 'golf', 'drinking', 'intake' and in '[running a] mile'. Women's 'lifestyle' key words were 'birthday', 'party', 'organic', 'job', 'pay', 'chocolate' and 'Xmas'.
- Direct expressions of support and interpersonal greetings were present in the web forums. But their nature differed between men and women: women's expressions were effusive, with a higher emotional content ('love', [take] care, 'x', 'xx', 'hugs') whereas men's were more restrained ('regards', 'hello', 'welcome', [all the] best', 'regs' (regards), 'hi', 'bless [you]'). Additionally, the quantitative difference in words categorised as being about 'feelings' was, if anything, more extreme on the web forums than in the interviews (40 keywords in women's web text, as opposed to 21 in their interview text). (Adapted from Seale, 2006, 2011)

Seale (2006) notes that CKA has potential for application in areas outside that of illness experience, for example in comparisons of the leadership styles of politicians (see e.g. Charteris-Black, 2005). But Seale also identifies some disadvantages of CKA:

- It is suited to the detection of differences rather than similarities. It is possible that this leads to a greater sense of difference than is justified.
- Differences at the level of phrases or sentences may be missed. For example, journey metaphors are commonly used to describe cancer experience (Seale, 2002) and these may be differentiated by gender.
- Interactive and sequential features of communication (such as one speaker contradicting, praising or criticising another) may be missed. The detection of some of these features, though, can be assisted by concordance software, as has been shown by Skelton et al. (2002) who have used this to identify usage of metaphors in transcripts of medical consultations.

> **TIP**
>
> Think long and hard before you categorise and code data. In particular:
>
> - make sure your categories fit an appropriate model
> - consider the relationship between your categories and those of the persons involved in producing your data.

8.3 ETHNOGRAPHY

Like other constructionists, ethnographers are more concerned with the processes through which texts depict 'reality' rather than with whether such texts contain true or false statements. As Atkinson and Coffey put it:

> In paying due attention to such materials, however, one must be quite clear about what they can and cannot be used for. Documents are 'social facts', in that they are produced, shared and used in socially organised ways. They are not, however, transparent representations of organizational routines, decision-making processes, or professional diagnoses. They construct particular kinds of representations using their own conventions. (2004: 58)

The implications of this are clear:

> Documentary sources are not surrogates for other kinds of data. We cannot, for instance, learn through records alone how an organization actually operates day by day. Equally, we cannot treat records – however 'official' – as firm evidence of

what they report … This recognition or reservation does not mean that we should ignore or downgrade documentary data. On the contrary, our recognition of their existence as social facts (or constructions) alerts us to the necessity to treat them very seriously indeed. We have to approach documents for what they are and what they are used to accomplish. (2004: 58)

How do ethnographers approach texts 'for what they are'? Table 8.3 provides some answers to this question.

TABLE 8.3 Ethnographic questions about texts

1	How are texts written?
2	How are they read?
3	Who writes them?
4	Who reads them?
5	For what purposes?
6	On what occasions?
7	With what outcomes?
8	What is recorded?
9	What is omitted?
10	What is taken for granted?
11	What does the writer seem to take for granted about the reader(s)?
12	What do readers need to know in order to make sense of them?

Source: Hammersley and Atkinson, 1995: 142–3

Table 8.3 shows many interesting ethnographic questions that can be asked about texts. Some of these questions (e.g. how are texts read and for what purposes?) take us beyond Seale's concern with the internal structures of **narratives** and moves us towards a concern with the social contexts in which narratives are articulated. As Gubrium has argued:

Much narrative analysis has centered on the internal organization of stories. Less attention has been paid to their production, distribution, and circulation in society. This requires that one step outside of narrative material itself and consider questions such as who produces particular kinds of stories, what interests publicize them, how do they gain popularity, where are they likely to be encountered, what are the consequences, and how are they challenged? … I have found that the internal organization of stories, while important to understand in its own right, does not tell us very much about the relation of stories to the worlds in which they circulate. (2005: 525)

Gubrium reveals how his own research on dementia support groups in the United States (Gubrium, 1986) illustrates this very point:

The Alzheimer's disease movement transformed, virtually overnight, the way professionals, families, the senile, and significant others narrated their relation to the aging brain and its associated cognitive functions. As the senile became victims of a disease, the aging enterprise – from the new National Institute of Aging to local caregivers – went into high gear to construct the associated social problems that became issues of national and international importance. It became evident that what was new and what was being affirmed were interwoven. (2005: 527)

Gubrium is concerned with spoken narratives (e.g. in support groups) as well as with written texts. Similarly, Prior (2011) has shown how medical staff at a cancer genetics clinic discuss their understanding of the degree to which a given patient is at risk of inheriting a certain type of cancer mutation by drawing upon documents such as referral letters and drawings of families' medical histories.

In this chapter, however, I will focus just upon the internal organisation of written texts. Such texts may include novels, newspapers and magazines, blogs, e-mail messages and official documents. In this section, I will focus on documents because they have been a fruitful area for ethnographic research. Subsequently, I will examine how newspapers, e-mail messages and diaries have been analysed using other approaches.

I discuss below different kinds of documents, taken in the following order:

- files
- statistical records
- records of official proceedings.

It should be stressed that this is not a hard and fast or an all-embracing list of every kind of document. It is organised in this way purely for ease of presentation. Nonetheless, the discussion that follows tries consistently to pursue the analytic issues involved in dealing with textual data. Although there are always practical problems which arise in data analysis and techniques that can offer assistance, methodological problems should never be reduced to merely practical issues and 'recipe' solutions.

> **TIP**
> Remember that people who generate and use such documents are concerned with how accurately they represent reality. Conversely, ethnographers are concerned with the construction or social organisation of documents, irrespective of whether they are accurate or inaccurate, true or biased.

8.3.1 Files

Like all documents, files are produced in particular circumstances for particular audiences. Files never speak for themselves. The ethnographer seeks to understand both the format of the file (for instance, the categories used in blank printed sheets) and the processes associated with its completion.

Selection interviews provide a good example of a setting where an interaction is organised, at least in part, by reference to the categories to be found on some document that will later constitute a 'file'. For instance, a large British local government organisation used the following record of job-selection interviews with candidates in their final year at university (Silverman and Jones, 1976):

- name
- appearance
- acceptability
- confidence
- effort
- organisation
- motivation
- any other comments.

Following Hammersley and Atkinson's set of questions in Table 8.3, the ethnographer can immediately ask about which items are represented on this list and which are omitted. For instance, the fact that 'appearance' and 'acceptability' are cited and located at the top of the list, while 'ability' is omitted, gives us clues about the culture of the organisation. So:

> successful candidates will be recognised in their preparedness to defer to 'commonsense' and to the accumulated wisdom of their seniors; to 'sell themselves' without implying that a university degree provides any more than a basis for further training. (Silverman and Jones, 1976: 31)

Some of this is seen in the completed file of one (unsuccessful) applicant to whom we gave a fictitious name. This is set out in Table 8.4.

TABLE 8.4 A completed selection form

Name:	Chadwick
Appearance:	Tall, slim, spotty-faced, black hair, dirty grey suit
Acceptability:	Non-existent. Rather uncouth
Confidence:	Awful. Not at all sure of himself
Effort:	High
Organization:	Poor
Motivation:	None really that counts
Any other comments:	Reject

Source: Silverman and Jones, 1976: 31–2

It is tempting to treat such completed forms as providing the causes of selection decisions. However, two important points must be borne in mind before we rush to such a conclusion. First, such forms provide 'good reasons' for any selection decision. This means that we expect the elements of the form to 'fit' the decision recorded. For instance, we would be surprised if the 'reject' decision had been preceded by highly favourable comments about the candidate.

Thus the language of 'acceptability' provides a rhetoric through which selectors define the 'good sense' of their decision-making. It does not determine the outcome of the decision.

EXERCISE 8.2

The following is a completed selector's report using the same form as found in Table 8.4.

Name:	Fortescue
Appearance:	Tall, thin, straw-coloured hair. Neat and tidy
Acceptability:	High. Pleasant, quite mature sensible man
Confidence:	Very good. Not conceited but firm, put himself across very well
Effort:	Excellent academic record
Organization:	Excellent, both at school and university
Motivation:	Keen on administration and very well informed on it. Has had considerable experience. Quite well informed about both organization and its functions generally.
Any other comments:	Call for interview. First-rate.

1 What conclusions may be drawn from how the selector has completed this form (e.g. what sort of features does the selector find praiseworthy or not needing comment?).
2 Does the completed form help us in understanding why certain candidates are selected at this organisation? If so, how? If not, why not?
3 If you were told that this selector came to a different decision when played a tape recording of the same interview some months later, what would you make of this fact? What research questions could be asked now?

A telling example of this was provided when we played back tapes of selection interviews to selectors several months later without meeting the selectors' request to remind them of their decision. Predictably, on hearing the tapes, selectors often made a different decision than they had made at the time. Nevertheless, when told of their earlier decision, they were able to adjust their comments to take account of it. The 'acceptability' criterion (and its converse 'abrasiveness') thus served more as a means to **rewrite history** (Garfinkel, 1967) than as a determinant of a particular selection decision.

The second point is that the files themselves are not simple 'records' of events but are artfully constructed with a view to how they may be read. For instance, in a study of a promotion panel at the same organisation, I showed how the committee organised its discussion in a way which made its eventual decision appear to be sound. In particular, I identified a three-stage process:

1 Beginning with premises all can accept (e.g. 'facts' everyone can agree upon).
2 Appealing to rules in ways which make sense in the present context.
3 Reaching conclusions demonstrably grounded in the rules as applied to the facts. (Silverman, 1973)

In order to produce 'sound' decisions, committees attend to relevant background circumstances which shape how 'facts' are to be seen. For instance, in the case of one candidate who had not made much progress, the following was said.

Extract 8.1 [extracts adapted from Silverman and Jones, 1976: 157–8]

Chair: and, um, is no doubt handicapped in, you know, his career development by the fact that that Department suddenly ha, ha
?: yes, yes
Chair: came to an end and he was, had to be pitched forth somewhere

---

Even when the facts are assembled, they ask themselves further questions about what the facts 'really mean'. For instance:

Extract 8.2

May: He's been there a long while in this job has he not? Does he do it in exactly the same way as when he started?

Or again:

Extract 8.3

May: supposing he had people under his control who needed the softer form of encouragement
        (…) assistance rather than pushing and driving; could he handle that sort of situation?
?:   Yes, and not only could he, but he has done
May: He has, ah good

Gubrium and Buckholdt's (1982) study of a US rehabilitation hospital shows that a concern to assemble credible files may be a common feature of organisational activities. The authors examine how hospital staff select, exchange and present information about the degree of physical disability and rehabilitation of patients and potential patients. Like reports of selection interviews, such descriptions are never context-free but are assembled or 'worked up' with reference to some audience: 'staff members work up descriptions of activities … using their knowledge of audience relevance in organizing what they say and write' (Gubrium and Buckholdt, 1982: ix).

The case study below illustrates such 'working up' in the context of what the authors call 'third-party description'. This refers to descriptions assembled for insurers and government agencies rather than for patients or their families.

CASE STUDY
Third-party Description at a Hospital

Gubrium and Buckholdt (1982) show that rehabilitation at a US hospital was paid for through government funds (via Medicare and Medicaid programmes) and insurance companies. An essential constraint, established by the US Congress in 1972, was a review agency called the Professional Standards Review Organization (PSRO). The PSRO looks at decision-making over patient intake and discharge with a view to limiting costs. For instance, the acceptable average stay for a rehabilitation patient had been calculated at 38 days.

A further constraint on the organisation of patient care was two rules of insurance companies. First, the hospital's charges would not be paid if a patient could not have rehabilitation because of additional medical problems (e.g. pneumonia). Second, if a patient's stay is very short, the insurance company may decide, retrospectively, that the patient should not have been admitted in the first place. These constraints shape how admissions are organised and how patient 'progress' is described.

Admissions staff have to make an initial decision about whether or not a potential patient is suitable for rehabilitation or needs other services involving chronic or acute care. A rule of thumb when considering whether a patient should be admitted is that the patient should be able to benefit from at least three hours of therapy per day. However, staff recognise that the files they are sent are not conclusive and may 'shade the truth'. For instance, another institution may wish to discharge the patient or the family may have exerted pressure for a transfer to the rehabilitation hospital. Consequently, admissions staff appeal to 'experience' and 'professional discretion' in working out what a potential patient's notes 'really mean'.

Appealing to these kinds of grounds, staff establish a basis for deciding what is 'really' meant by any file. Thus, in sorting out 'facts' from 'fancy', participants use a body of interpretive and rhetorical resources to define what will constitute 'reality' or 'the bottom line'.

Once a patient is admitted, the 'work up' of descriptions continues. 'Progress Notes' are prepared at regular intervals and staff work at making them internally consistent and appropriate to the recommendation (just like selectors). For instance, staff talk about 'the need to make sure that the figures tell the right story' and regularly try out their accounts on colleagues by asking 'how does that sound?'

The institutional interest is to show some sort of progress which will be sufficient to satisfy the funding agencies. Consequently, there is a pressure to identify simple problems where progress can readily be made and to seek patient statements which accord with the therapist's version of progress.

Gubrium and Buckholdt's work shows that hospital files can be treated as the outcome of a series of staff decisions grounded in the contingencies of their work. Similarly, Silverman and Jones reveal how records of selection interviews satisfy organisational conceptions of what is appropriate.

Both studies confirm that qualitative researchers are not primarily concerned with whether files are factually 'true' or 'false'. Instead, they focus on how such files reveal the practical decision-making of employees in the context of the constraints and contingencies of their work.

EXERCISE 8.3

In a discussion of how records are assembled on 'juvenile delinquents' in the US justice system, Cicourel (1968) considers the case of Linda, aged 13. Linda first came to the attention of the police when she reported that she had been kidnapped by four boys. She said that she had been coaxed away from a party by them and admitted that she had told them that she would get drunk and then have sexual intercourse with one of them. After stealing some alcohol, the boys took her to a club where they all got drunk and she had sex with the youngest boy. Although the boys sought to depict Linda as a 'slut', the police viewed Linda as an 'attractive' victim with no prior record. However, some weeks later, acting on information from Linda's parents, the police saw Linda in a drunken state and obtained an admission that she had had sex with ten boys. She was now charged as in danger of leading a lewd and immoral life. Extract 8.3 is from an interview between Linda (L) and a female Probation Officer (PO) after Linda's arrest:

PO: You're not pregnant?

L: No

PO: Have you used anything to prevent a pregnancy?

L: Once X (one of her boyfriends) used one of those things

PO: Did you ever feel scared about getting pregnant?

L: No, I was always trying to get even with my parents

PO: You sort of wanted to get even with them?

L: Yes. I always wanted to get even with other people. My mother gets mad at me. I love my father. I know that's what's wrong with me. I talk about this with my parents. I don't know why.

The PO's report suggests that Linda needs psychotherapy and suggests that she be institutionalised for three to six months' treatment.

1 How does the PO organise her questioning to support her eventual recommendation?

2 Is there any evidence that Linda is colluding with the PO in a particular interpretation of her past behaviour?

8.3.2 Statistical records

Until the 1960s, official statistics, like files, were treated as a more or less accurate representations of a stable reality. Of course, this did not mean that their **reliability** or **validity** were taken for granted. Particular statistics or measures were often found to be of dubious scientific status. However, it tended to be assumed, in these cases, that such data or measures could always be improved.

The 1960s saw a massive shift of focus among sociologists as documented below:

- Cicourel and Kitsuse (1963) showed how school statistics on educational performance depended upon the organised, practical judgements of school staff.
- Garfinkel revealed how coroners writing death certificates formulated accounts 'of how death really (for-all-practical-purposes) happened' (1967: 12). As Garfinkel noted, 'really' in these cases, referred, unavoidably, to common-sense understandings in the context of organisational contingencies.

- Sudnow (1968a) showed how hospital 'death' was recognised, attended to and disattended to by hospital staff.
- Sudnow (1968b) revealed that US criminal statistics depended, in part, on a socially organised process of 'plea bargaining' through which defendants were encouraged to plead guilty.

Now, of course, many of these processes had already been recognised by sociologists and demographers. The difference was that such processes were no longer viewed as 'problems' which distorted the validity or reliability of official statistics. Instead, they were now treated in their own right, not as distortions of the phenomena they ostensibly measured but as constitutive of those phenomena. In other words, inspired by these studies, many sociologists now treated such phenomena ('death', 'guilt, 'ability') as arising within the very record-keeping activity which was supposed passively to record them.

This shift of focus did not mean that demography, based on official statistics, suddenly became worthless. As Hindess (1973) showed, one can pay attention to the social context of statistical production and still make use of statistics for both practical and analytical purposes. So the work that developed out of the insights of the 1960s is properly seen as having taken a divergent but non-competitive path to the continuing studies based on the use of official statistics.

For instance, Prior (1987) follows Garfinkel by looking at how 'deaths' are investigated by coroners. Prior puts it this way:

> men are more likely to have their deaths investigated, and to have their deaths regarded as 'unnatural', than are women. The same is true of the middle class as against the working class, the married as against the unmarried, widowed or single, and the economically active as against the inactive. (1987: 368)

However, in the case of decisions to do a post-mortem (autopsy) after 'violent' deaths, Prior finds that the figures go in the other direction: manual workers and the single, widowed or divorced are more likely to have an autopsy than the middle class or married.

Prior suggests that coroners use their 'common-sense knowledge' to treat sudden and violent death as more suspicious among the former groups. Although autopsy is generally more common after a death defined as 'violent', Prior notes that: 'in its search for the origins of death, forensic pathology tends to reserve the scalpel as an investigatory instrument for distinct and specific segments of the population' (1987: 371).

The implication is that statistical tables about causes of death are themselves the outcome of a decision-making process which needs to be described (see also Prior, 2003, 2004).

Consequently, for the qualitative researcher, statistics, like files, raise fundamental questions about the processes through which they are produced.

8.3.3 Official proceedings

Public or official records are not limited to statistical tables. A common feature of democracies is a massive documentation of official business covering legal proceedings, certain business meetings and the work of parliaments and parliamentary committees.

Such public records constitute a potential goldmine for sociological investigation. First, they are relevant to important issues – revealing how public and private agencies account for, and legitimate, their activities. Second, they are accessible; the field researcher does not have the problem, so common in observational work, of negotiating access.

Despite the potential of such work, it has been sadly neglected by field researchers. However, an important source of studies in this area has been provided by the journal *Discourse and Society*.

I will take just one example: a study of the 1973 Watergate Hearings in the US Congress. Molotch and Boden (1985) show how their work on the text of these hearings arises in the context of a debate about the nature of power. They are not concerned with explicit power battles or with the ability to set agendas. Instead, they are concerned with a 'third face of power': 'the ability to determine the very grounds of the interactions through which agendas are set and outcomes determined … the struggle over the linguistic premises upon which the legitimacy of accounts will be judged' (1985: 273).

As they show, a problem resolved in all talk is that, while accounts are context-bound, a determinate account has 'somehow' to be achieved (see Garfinkel, 1967). Molotch and Boden apply this insight to the interrogation of President Nixon's counsel (John Dean) by a pro-Nixon senator (Sen. Gurney). Dean had made public charges about the involvement of the White House in the Watergate 'cover-up'. Gurney's strategy is to define Dean as someone who avoids 'facts' and just relies upon 'impressions'. This is seen in the following extract:

Extract 8.4 [Molotch and Boden, 1985: 280, adapted]

(G = Sen. Gurney; D = John Dean)

[Transcription conventions are given in the Appendix]

G: Did you discuss any aspects of the Watergate at that meeting with the President? For example, did you tell him anything about (1.4) what Haldeman knew of or what Ehrlichman knew?

D: Well, given the- given the fact that he told me I've done a good job I assumed he had been very pleased with what ha- what had been going on…

G: Did you discuss what Magruder knew about Watergate and what involvement he had?
D: No, I didn't. I didn't get into any – I did not give him a report at that point in time
G: Did you discuss cover-up money money that was being raised and paid?
D: No, sir…
G: Well now how can you say that the President knew all about these things from a simple observation by him that Bob tells me you are doing a good job?

As Molotch and Boden show, Gurney's strategy is to insist on literal accounts of 'facts' not 'impressionistic' ones. Throughout Extract 8.4, for instance, Gurney demands that Dean state that he actually discussed the cover-up with Nixon. When Dean is unable to do this, Gurney imposes limits on Dean's ability to appeal to a context (Dean's 'assumptions') which might show that Dean's inferences were correct.

However, as Gurney knows, all accounts can be defeated by demonstrating that at some point, since they depend upon knowing the context, they are not 'really objective'. Hence:

> Demands for 'just the facts', the simple answers, the forced-choice response, preclude the 'whole story' that contains another's truth … [consequently] Individuals can participate in their own demise through the interactional work they do. (1985: 285)

EXERCISE 8.4

Here is a further extract from the Watergate Hearings. At this point, Dean is trying to implicate Nixon in the 'cover-up' operation:

1   D: When I discussed with him (Nixon) the fact that I thought he ought to be
2   aware of the fact I thought I had been involved in the obstruction of justice …
3   He told me, John, you don't have any legal problems to worry about…
4   G: Did you discuss any specific ob- instances of obstruction of justice?
5   (1.3)
6   D: Well, I'd- Senator, from- based on conversations I'd had with him- I had
7   worked from-I am talking about this meeting.
8   D: Yes, I understand. I'm answering your question. Uh- the- eh-you c- y- I
9   can tell when-when uh I am talking with somebody if they have some
10   conception of what I am talking about- I had the impression that the
11   President had some conception of what I was talking ab[out
12   G: [But I am not
13   talking about impressions. That is what I am trying to get away from. (0.8)
14   I am talking about specific instances

1 Using this material, show what strategies Sen. Gurney is using to discredit John Dean's evidence.

2 Show how Dean tries to sustain the credibility of what he is saying.

3 Why might Dean's appeal to what 'I can tell when I am talking with somebody' be seen as 'a risky strategy' by Molotch and Boden?

So far we have been dealing with documents assembled within organisations. However, ethnographers have also shown how we can fruitfully examine textual material generated in more mundane settings. This is illustrated in my next two examples: diaries and Internet communication.

8.3.4 Diaries

Diaries can be rich sources of data which detail how people make sense of their everyday lives. In contemporary society, handwritten diaries have almost entirely been replaced by the kind of weblogs discussed earlier in this chapter. Like organisational documents, blogs are **naturally occurring data** which vividly represent how people represent their activities and experiences.

Haldar and Wærdahl (2009) have mined some marvellous diary data from Norwegian and Chinese schools. Following Gubrium and Holstein (1987), they are interested in family life within a constructionist framework. As the following case study shows, teddy diaries show how 'families need to be "displayed" as well as "done"' (2009: 1141).

CASE STUDY
Teddy Diaries

Norway has used 'teddy diaries' as a common tool to bridge the transition between family and school for pupils entering school for the very first year. A teddy carrying a diary is circulated between the children's homes and the school. The diary entries are written by the children and their parents. As Haldar and Wærdahl put it:

The child is encouraged to be the author of the diary on behalf of the bear. Given the young age of the child, he/she naturally enlists the aid of adult family members in making the entries. Regardless of the actual author, the child or the bear are understood to be the voice of the story. Even if the adult members of the family do the actual writing, it is very likely that the content of the story is discussed with the child before it is written. After all, it is the child

who is going to bring the story back to the classroom to talk about. The family representations in these books can thus be seen as a child–adult negotiated perspective on family life.
(2009: 1144)

The written stories from the teddy's experiences in the children's home are shared with the others
in class, as well as with the school and the next families to receive the book. In other words, they
are not produced for research, and usually not even initiated by researchers. In this sense, they are
naturally occurring data.

Teddy diaries provide rich data on how family life is represented:

The diaries allow for multiple authors to create stories of the teddy bear's home visits. Likewise,
the voice of the narrator in the diary can be the product of many voices. In this way, the singular
voices often weakening family studies can be avoided (Gubrium and Holstein, 1987). For each
visit by the teddy, it is the child, the child together with the parents or the parents alone that
make an entry telling the other children in the class what the bear has been up to while it has
been away from the classroom. (2009: 1143-4)

To provide comparative data, ten schools in the centre of Beijing, China, were asked to introduce a
teddy and a diary for their first-grade school classes. Around 250 teddy diaries were collected from
each country. For each teddy-visit, the child, the child with its parents or its parents make an entry
in the book telling the other children in class what the teddy has been up to while gone from the
classroom. The diary usually has a greeting page with a greeting from the teddy written by the
teacher, sometimes with a photo of the teddy. The greeting page would be written in the teddy's
voice and say something like:

Hello, my name is Bobby and I am a special friend of this class. This is my book. I will be very happy
if you write and draw in my book about the things you and I experience together. I am sure that your
Mama or your Papa can help you.

Warm regards,

Bobby

Here is a child entry from one of the Chinese books:

October 28th 2006 [Sunny].

In the morning, I and [Bangbang] slept/took a bath together, brushed our teeth, washed our faces,
played together. I did homework together with [Bangbang].

Before noon, I and [Bangbang] [skipped rope] and slept/took a nap.

In the afternoon, I and [Bangbang] went outside to play/went to do outdoors activities. Together we
jumped high, jumped long, spun around. Bangbang and I played quite happily together. Di. (Chinese
entry 2.1)

This is a typical child entry, and it is fair to say that they look trivial and maybe insignificant at first
sight. But remember that this is not just any list of daily activities. It is a list of the activities worth

(Continued)

(Continued)

mentioning, an image of what an ideal day should look like. In this entry Bangbang gets to take part in the hygienic routines, in doing homework and in play activities. The togetherness in play is also described as happy. Among other possible interpretations, the entry shows a balance between duty and play, and also gives a sense of the expectations of how these tasks are to be performed. This is not just a repetition of 'what we did today', but a list of 'what we did today for others to read and judge'.

One could read the Chinese children's brushing of teeth and keen reference to homework as explicit norms. These things are mentioned because they are of true and explicit value. Explicit norms build character and carry tradition. In the Norwegian sample, washing is not mentioned but the other relations and activities mentioned can also be read as narratives of what are considered good things to do or good places to be. Being with your grandparents, outdoor life, baking wheat buns, and trips to the cabin or feeding ducks are all considered good and healthy activities for children.

In sum, teddy diaries provide answers to questions that researchers never think to ask and provide exactly the sort of data that a constructionist approach demands.

8.3.5 The Internet

It is now commonplace to remark that communication is increasingly mediated by information technology. Originally, telephone calls were a great impetus to research. Somehow, without visual cues, people managed to communicate with each other. Researchers investigated how we create an orderly structure here with stable expectations of the rights and obligations of, for instance, 'caller' and 'called' (see Section 9.3).

More recently, as we saw with Hookway's blog data earlier in this chapter, the Internet has been a crucial medium of largely text-based communication. Dependent upon ethically appropriate access, this has opened up a whole new field for ethnographic investigation of textual data including homepages, chatrooms and e-mail correspondence.

Markham (2004) has argued that three different frameworks can help illustrate how the Internet is typically conceptualised in qualitative research. These frameworks are presented in Table 8.5. They show the qualitative researcher might use or study it as a context in itself or use it as a tool in a traditional study.

The three frameworks shown in Table 8.5 can, as Markham shows, be collapsed into two different ways of analysing the Internet. The qualitative researcher can use it as a *resource* or can treat it as a *topic*, studying it as a social and technological context in itself.

TABLE 8.5   Frameworks for conceptualising the Internet

- As a *medium for communication*, the Internet provides new channels for people to communicate with each other, new channels for researchers to communicate with participants and new venues for conducting research
- As a *network of computers*, the Internet collapses physical distances between people, thus creating the potential for collectives and collaborations not heretofore available. This network extends the potential reach of the researcher to a more global scale. Understanding and utilising time and notions of space in creative ways can significantly augment research practice, particularly in terms of collecting information for study
- As a *context of social construction*, the Internet is a unique discursive milieu that facilitates the researcher's ability to witness and analyse the structure of talk, the negotiation of meaning and identity, the development of relationships and communities, and the construction of social structures as these occur discursively

Source: adapted from Markham, 2004: 96–7

TIP

Before you set out to gather new data using research instruments (such as interviews or **focus groups**), consider whether the kind of material you need is available on the Internet. If it is, not only will you save a lot of time but your data will be naturally occurring.

To give a taste of what such topicalising of the Internet can reveal, I will use a case study drawn from a fairly recent piece of research in which I participated (Ryen and Silverman, 2000).

CASE STUDY
Asian Businessmen on the Internet

The data set used in this study consisted of face-to-face interviews and e-mail exchanges between a Norwegian researcher (Ryen) and Asian businessmen. The interviewees reported clear boundaries between Tanzanian African and Asian 'culture'. Broadly speaking, these Asian entrepreneurs travelled widely, used the latest technologies and were risk-takers. According to a conventional interpretation, in terms of an appeal to 'culture', our data show how Asian Tanzanian entrepreneurs constitute themselves as different from Tanzanian Africans and similar to Western Europeans.

By contrast, analysis of e-mails between Anne Ryen and one Asian businessman (to whom we gave the name Sachin) suggest the limits of an analyst's appeal to such use of 'culture' as an explanation. In particular, this Norwegian researcher's relative ease in communicating with Asian businessmen

(Continued)

(Continued)

needs further investigation. Rather than explain it away in terms of cultural similarities, it is worth examining how both parties achieve mutual understanding.

For instance, we examined how Anne Ryen (AR) and Sachin work at achieving agreed forms of 'sign-off' greetings at the end of their mutual e-mails. Sachin's first message ends as follows:

Extract 8.5 [extracts from Ryen and Silverman, 2000]

tell me more about yourself in your next email…
love Sachin [ending of first message 26 October 1998]
AR replies among other things:

Extract 8.6

I am married and have two small children [30 October 1998]

Presumably, even if she were married, AR might not have mentioned it. Note how in categorising yourself, you categorise the other person (e.g. in this case as a 'friend' or something 'more'). Moreover, AR does not use 'love' as a greeting but 'hilsen' (Norwegian for 'greetings'). Sachin monitors the category-bound implications here. His next message now ends:

Extract 8.7

regards Sachin [5 November 1998]

In his later messages, 'love' is again not used by Sachin but: 'Well regards' [17 November 1998], 'well cherio' [10 December 1998] and 'cheeeers' [26 December 1998].

In her later correspondence [23 November 1998], AR modifies her somewhat impersonal 'hilsen' to 'Beste hilsen' and then 'Kjaere (= dear) Sachin!' [22 December 1998].

Despite her self-identification as 'non-available', AR responds to Sachin's information that he intends to get married soon by writing:

Extract 8.8

Lucky woman to marry you – tell me more! [10 November 1998]

Such banter is used by AR to maintain a 'friendly' relationship with a respondent who is, after all, giving his time freely to help her. As we see above, flattery ('lucky woman') is another reward that can be offered to research subjects. Later AR will refer to Sachin's 'energy' and 'vigour' (e.g. 23 November 1998, data not shown). By the next month, after describing her work activities, AR adds:

Extract 8.9

And the most interesting, is an e-mail interview with an Asian businessman!!! [10 December 1998]

Such 'friendly', non-instrumental framing can be used for a whole message. So one of AR's e-mails begins:

Extract 8.10

Sachin, this time I have no research questions [30 November 1998]

In the same message, she uses a reference to the weather to issue a lighthearted invitation:

Extract 8.11

So if you send me a mild summer wind and loads of sunshine, I'll invite you for dinner.

In these ways, AR and Sachin negotiate the parameters of their relationship, invoking a range of paired identities: researcher–researched; female–male; married woman–single man; friend–friend.

So AR begins by implying her sexual unavailability and this is recognised by Sachin's modification of his sign-off greetings. However, conscious of the rewards that research subjects rightly may expect, AR later shows her respondent that, just because she is 'unavailable', does not mean that she cannot treat him as a friend or that, indeed, she is unaware of his attractiveness to other women.

Like other ethnographic work on texts, this research shows how, despite their relative newness, e-mails are yet another site, like files, statistical records and records of official proceedings, where identities are actively produced.

EXERCISE 8.5

Select a series of past e-mail messages between yourself and another person. To satisfy ethical issues, ask the permission of your correspondent to use their messages for research purposes. To simplify analysis, limit your data to messages which total no more than 20 lines.

Now identify the identities invoked and the activities described in these messages. Examine how the meanings of these identities and activities are maintained or change over the course of the correspondence.

The issue of identity takes us full circle back to my earlier critique of other approaches to textual analysis. My problem with content analysis was that its numerical outcomes were achieved through counting in terms of analysts' categories. While such categories can be well defined, they have an unknown relation to how participants themselves categorise (and count) (see Section 3.2).

By contrast, narrative analysis does claim to access the active story-telling formats of participants (see Section 3.4). However, it usually reverts once again to an analyst's set of categories (e.g. hero/villain; leader/led).

Such forms of textual analysis leave themselves open to exactly the same charge that can be made about some observational research. This is why, as we saw in

Chapter 3, Sacks made the following comment about much sociological research, whether qualitative or quantitative: 'All the sociology we read is unanalytic, in the sense that they simply put some category in. They may make sense to us in doing that, but they're doing it simply as *another Member*' (1992, I: 41–2, my emphasis).

Fortunately, the kind of ethnographic work we have just been discussing does attempt to identify the categories used by ordinary participants ('members'). In my view, however, ethnography lacks a well-developed model to describe these categories. To find such a model, we must turn to ethnomethodology and, more particularly, Sacks's account of **membership categorisation devices**.

8.4 ETHNOMETHODOLOGY: MEMBERSHIP CATEGORISATION ANALYSIS

As we saw in Chapter 3, the work of the sociologist Harvey Sacks has raised some vital methodological questions for ethnographers and anyone else attempting to construct the social sciences as a set of 'observational' disciplines.

Sacks puts the issue succinctly:

Suppose you're an anthropologist or sociologist standing somewhere. You see somebody do some action, and you see it to be some activity. How can you go about formulating who is it that did it, for the purposes of your report? Can you use at least what you might take to be the most conservative formulation – his name? Knowing, of course, that any category you choose would have the(se) kinds of systematic problems: how would you go about selecting a given category from the set that would equally well characterize or identify that person at hand. (1992, I: 467–8)

The classic statement of this problem is found in Moerman's (1974) self-critical treatment of his attempt to do a standard ethnography upon a Thai tribe (see Section 1.2.3). But the message has also been taken by intelligent ethnographers who, like Gubrium (1988), are centrally concerned with the descriptive process (see Section 3.4).

Sacks shows how you cannot resolve such problems simply 'by taking the best possible notes at the time and making your decisions afterwards' (1992, I: 468). Instead, our aim should be to try to understand when and how members do descriptions, seeking thereby to describe the apparatus through which members' descriptions are properly produced.

Consider this description in which the identities of the parties are concealed:

The X cried. The Y picked it up.

Why is it that we are likely to hear the X as, say, a baby but not a teacher? Furthermore, given that we hear X as a baby, why are we tempted to hear Y as an adult (possibly as the baby's mother) (Sacks, 1992, I: 248–9)?

In fact, Sacks looks at the first two sentences of a story written by a child: 'The baby cried. The mommy picked it up.' Why do we hear the 'mommy' as the mother of this 'baby' (I: 236)? Why do we hear the baby's cries as the 'reason' why the mommy picks him up?

Not only are we likely to hear the story this way, but we hear it as 'a possible description' without having observed the circumstances which it characterises. Sacks asks: 'Is it some kind of magic? One of my tasks is going to be to construct an apparatus for that fact to occur. That is, how we come to hear it in that fashion' (I: 236).

No magic lies behind such observations. Instead: 'What one ought to seek is to build an apparatus which will provide for how it is that any activities, which members do in such a way as to be recognizable as such to members, are done, and done recognizably' (1992, I: 236).

Returning to the way we read the children's story, Sacks observes that our reading is informed by the way we infer that the categories 'baby' and 'mommy' come from a collection of such categories which we call 'family' (I: 238). While the 'family' connection can include many categories (i.e. not just 'baby' and mommy' but also 'daddy', 'daughter', 'grandmother', etc.), some categories are or can be built as two-set collections (e.g. gender, race) (I: 47–8).

Of course, not any set of categories will be heard as a collection. As Sacks says:

> We only talk about a collection when the categories that compose it are categories that members do in fact use together or collect together, as 'male' and 'female' go together. (I: 238)

Sacks notes that, as here, younger children's stories may have just one collection of categories – the 'family'. Young children apply this collection to virtually everyone, for example parents' friends become called 'aunt' and 'uncle' (I: 368).

However, for children, like any population, there are always at least two collections of categories available (1972b: 32). This means that young children can at least choose between, say, 'auntie' and 'woman' as a way of categorising a female.

Of course, one only has to read accounts of the 'same' event in two different newspapers to realise the large number of categories that can be used to describe it. For instance, as feminists have pointed out, women, but not men, tend to be identified by their marital status, number of children, hair colour and even chest measurement. Such identifications, while intelligible, carry massive implications for the sense we attach to people and their behaviour. Compare, for example:

    A: Shapely, blonde, mother of 5
    B: 32-year old teacher.

Both descriptions may 'accurately' describe different aspects of the same person. But each constitutes very definitely how we are to view that person (for instance, in A, largely in terms of certain ways of constructing gender).

Each identity is heard as a category from some collection of categories. For instance, in A and B above, we hear 'mother' as a category from the collection 'family'. By contrast, 'teacher' is heard as located in a collection of 'occupation'. The implication is that to choose one category from a collection excludes someone being identified with some other category from the same collection.

Sacks calls such a collection a 'Membership Categorisation Device' (or MCD). This device consists of a collection of categories (e.g. baby, mommy, father = family; male, female = gender) and some rules about how to apply these categories. Sacks gives the definition of an MCD as follows:

> Membership categorization device: 'any collection of membership categories, containing at least a category, which may be applied to some population containing at least a member, so as to provide, by the use of some rules of application, for the pairing of at least a population member and a categorization device member. A device is then a collection plus rules of application'. (1972b: 332)

What are these 'rules of application' to which Sacks refers? First, returning to the child's story, we can note that the characters are described by single categories ('baby', 'mommy'). So we are not told, as we might be, about, say, the baby's age or gender or the mommy's occupation or even hair colour. And this did not cause us a problem when we first saw 'The baby cried. The mommy picked it up.'

The intelligibility of single category descriptions gives us what Sacks calls the 'Economy Rule' as defined below:

> *The Economy Rule:* 'a single category from any membership categorization device can be referentially adequate'. (I: 246)

Of course, single category descriptions are not confined to children's stories – sometimes categories like 'man', 'nurse' or 'pop star' are entirely referentially adequate. Nonetheless, the Economy Rule gives us a very interesting way of addressing how children's socialisation may occur. First, children seem to learn single names ('mommy', 'daddy'). Then they learn how such single categories fit into collections ('family') and come to understand various combinatorial tasks (e.g. man = daddy or uncle). So, even at this early stage of their lives, say before they are two years old, children have already learned 'what in principle adequate reference consists of' (1972b: 35) and, in that sense, entered into society/been 'socialised'.

A second rule of application of MCDs suggests that once one category from a given collection has been used to categorise one population **member**, then other categories from the same collection may be used on other members of the population. Sacks refers to this as the 'Consistency Rule'. It is formally defined below:

> *The Consistency Rule:* 'If some population of persons is being categorized, and if some category from a device's collection has been used to categorize a first

Member of the population, then that category or other categories of the same collection *may* be used to categorize further members of the population'. (1972b: 33, my emphasis; see also 1992, I: 225, 238–9 and 246)

The import of the Consistency Rule may be seen in a simple example. If we use an abusive term about someone else, we know that a term from the same collection can be used on us. Hence one of the reasons we may avoid name-calling is to avoid the development of this kind of slanging-match.

However, any category can belong in more than one collection. For instance, as Sacks points out, 'baby' can belong to the collection 'stage of life' ('baby', 'child', 'teenager', adult') as well as the 'family' collection (I: 239). 'Baby' also used to be a term of endearment heard in Hollywood movies; here it belonged to a different collection ('romance'?).

Sacks suggests a 'hearing rule' (I: 239) or 'Consistency Rule Corollary' (I: 248) which provides a way for members to resolve such ambiguities. When a speaker uses two or more categories to describe at least two members of a population and it is possible to hear the categories as belonging to the same collection, we hear them that way. That is why, in the story with which Sacks begins, we hear 'baby' and 'mommy' in relation to the collection 'family'.

> *Consistency Rule Corollary*: 'If two or more categories are used to categorize two or more Members to some population, and those categories can be heard as categories from the same collection, then hear them that way'. (I: 247)

The Consistency Rule and its Corollary have explained why we hear 'mommy' and 'baby' as part of the same 'family' collection but it remains to be seen 'how "the mommy" is heard as "the mommy of the baby"' (I: 247). The answer stems from the way in which 'the family' is one of a series of collections that may be heard as constituting a 'team', that is as part of the same 'side'. In this respect, 'mommy' and 'baby' belong together in the same way as, say, 'defender' and 'striker' in a football team. Sacks suggests that one of the central properties of teams is what he calls 'Duplicative Organization':

> *Duplicative Organization*: means that we treat any 'set of categories as defining a unit, and place members of the population into cases of the unit. If a population is so treated and is then counted, one counts not numbers of daddies, numbers of mommies, and numbers of babies but numbers of families – numbers of "whole families", numbers of "families without fathers", etc.' (1972b: 334; see also 1992, I: 225, 240, and 247–8)

Duplicative Organization helps us in seeing that 'mommy' and 'baby' are likely to be heard as part of the same 'unit'. But a further rule suggests that this is not just likely but required (in the sense that if you saw things differently then your seeing would appear to other Members to be 'odd'). This rule is the 'Hearers' Maxim for Duplicative Organization' as set out below:

> *The Hearers' Maxim for Duplicative Organization*: 'If some population has been categorized by use of categories from some device whose collection has the "duplicative organization" property, and a Member is presented with a categorized population which can be heard as co-incumbents of a case of that device's unit, then hear it that way'. (I: 248)

Given that the MCD 'family' is duplicatively organised, the Hearer's Maxim shows us how we come to hear 'the mommy' as not anyone's 'mommy' but as 'the mommy of this baby' in the children's story (I: 248).

However, 'mommy' and 'baby' are not only more than co-incumbents of a team but a pair of positions with mutual rights and obligations (e.g. the baby's right to be fed but, perhaps, obligation not to cry all the time). In this respect, mothers and babies are like husband–wife, boyfriend–girlfriend and even neighbour–neighbour. Each party has certain standardised rights and obligations; each party can properly expect help from the other.

Sacks refers to such groupings as standardised relational pairs (SRPs). SRPs, in turn, are found in 'Collection R' which is defined below:

> *Collection R*: a collection of paired relational categories 'that constitutes a locus for a set of rights and obligations concerning the activity of giving help'. (1972b: 37)

One aspect of the relevance of such paired **relational** categories is that they make observable the absence of the second part of any such pair. In this way, we come to observe that a player in a sporting team is 'missing' or, more seriously, treat non-incumbency of, say, a spouse as being a criterion of suicidalness (see the discussion of suicide at the beginning of this chapter and Sacks, 1972b: 38-40).

Such absences reveal what Sacks calls the 'Programmatic Relevance' of Collection R:

> *Programmatic Relevance*: 'if R is relevant, then the non-incumbency of any of its pair positions is an observable, i.e. can be proposedly a fact'. (1972b: 38)

Just as Collection R consists of pairs of categories who are supposed to offer each other help, there are also categories of 'experts' who offer specialised help with particular 'troubles'. When paired with some 'troubled' person (e.g. a client), they constitute what Sacks refers to as 'Collection K'.

> *Collection K*: 'a collection constructed by reference to special distributions of knowledge existing about how to deal with some trouble'. (1972b: 37)

Collection R and its Programmatic Relevance allow someone to analyse their situation as, say, properly 'suicidal'. Collection K then allows such a person to know who can offer dispassionate 'advice'.

Collection K implies something about the proper activities of particular categories of people like professionals and clients. This helps to resolve one further issue in our reading of the children's story. Why do we have no trouble with the description: 'The baby cried. The mommy picked it up'? To put it more pointedly: why might it look odd if the story read: 'The mommy cried. The baby picked it up'?

The answer, of course, lies in the way in which many kinds of activities are commonsensically associated with certain membership categories. So, if we know what someone's identity is, we can work out the kind of activities in which they might engage. Similarly, by identifying a person's activity (say, 'crying'), we provide for what their social identity is likely to be (in this case, a 'baby').

Sacks refers to activities which imply identities as 'Category-Bound Activities'. His definition is set out below:

> *Category-Bound Activities (CBAs)*: 'many activities are taken by Members to be done by some particular or several particular categories of Members where the categories are categories from membership categorization devices'. (I: 249)

CBAs explain why, if the story had read 'The X cried. The Y picked it up', we might have guessed that X was a baby and Y was a mommy. Crying, after all, is something that babies do and picking up (at least in the possibly sexist 1960s) is something that mothers did. Of course, as Sacks points out, no description is ever completely unambiguous. For instance, 'crying' is not confined to 'babies' and an adult can themselves sometimes be called a 'baby' (I: 584).

Members employ their understandings of CBAs to recognise and to resolve such ambiguities. Above all, everyday understanding is based on the assumption that, as Sacks puts it, 'they (i.e. some category of people) do such things' (I: 179). As Sacks shows, through this means, you can do 'racism' while avoiding the use of explicitly ethnic or religious categories.

Moreover, what we know about CBAs allows us to construct what he calls 'a search procedure' when some problematic occurrence appears to have occurred. For instance, Sacks shows how, at the end of 1963, the claim that the assassin of President Kennedy was a 'communist' clinched the case for many people – after all assassination of capitalist leaders appears to be category bound to the category 'communist infiltrator'. In this way, CBAs allow us to 'tie' certain activities to particular categories. As Sacks puts it:

> if somebody knows an activity has been done, and there is a category to which it is bound, they can damn well propose that it's been done by such a one who is a member of that category. (I: 180)

So, even though we know people other than babies do cry, we are unlikely to say 'the baby cried' if we mean 'the baby of the family'. In this way, the selection of a category makes many potential ambiguities 'non-arisable' (I: 585).

However, on the face of it, when we observe an activity, it could be ambiguous to find the right category to which the activity is bound. Take the case of a 'confession'. As Sacks points out, we know that both Catholics and criminals often 'confess'. Have we observed a Catholic or a criminal?

We see at once that, in everyday life, there is rarely such an ambiguity. For, of course, we all know that a Catholic confessional 'looks' very different from a criminal confessing (I: 584–5). So, if we read about a 'confession', the surrounding features of the story (e.g. as part of a 'criminal' story) will tell us immediately how we are to understand it. And all this happens without any sense of problem or ambiguity.

For instance, we do not have any problem of seeing a struggle between two adults (a man and a woman) and a younger person as a 'family fight' (I: 90–1). Ambiguity about this interpretation is much more likely to appear when parties subsequently review an incident. So in a legal context, what unambiguously appeared to be merely a 'family fight' can be transformed into a 'kidnap'. At the time of the incident, however, witnesses properly treat things as 'normal' partly because they assume it is not your job but the police's to note crimes (I: 92). Thus we invoke our knowledge of CBAs and SRPs as ways of resolving incongruity.

Returning to our children's story, 'baby' is also a member of a class which Sacks calls 'Positioned Categories' (i.e. baby ... adolescent ... adult) in which the next category is heard as 'higher' than the preceding one. This creates the possibility of praise or complaint by using a higher or lower position to refer to some activity. So an adolescent can be described as acting in a very 'adult' way or as acting just like a 'baby':

> *Positioned Categories*: a collection has positioned categories where one member can be said to be higher or lower than another (e.g. baby ... adolescent ... adult). (I: 585)

The fact that activities are category bound also allows us to praise or complain about 'absent' activities. For instance, a baby that does not cry where it might (say at a christening) can be properly praised, while an older child that does not say 'thank you' when passed some food or given a present is properly blamed (I: 585).

In both these cases, certain activities become remarkable because of the way their presence or absence is tied to a stage of life. Stage of life is important not only, say, around the dinner table, but also in the compilation of official statistics. As Sacks points out, statisticians, like the rest of us, know that, for instance, being unmarried or unemployed are not usually descriptors appropriate to school-age children (I: 68).

As we have seen, because of the category-bound character of many activities, we can establish negative moral assessments of people by describing their behaviour in terms of performing or avoiding activities inappropriate to their social identity. For instance, it may be acceptable for a parent to 'punish' a child, but it will usually be unacceptable for a child to 'punish' a parent.

Notice that, in both cases, 'punish' serves as a powerful picture of an activity which could be described in innumerable ways. Social life, unlike foreign films, does not come with subtitles attached. Consequently, how we define an activity is morally constitutive of it. So if, like other sociologists, Sacks is talking here about norms, unlike them (and members) he is not treating norms as descriptions of the causes of action. Instead, he is concerned with how 'viewers use norms to provide some of the orderliness, and proper orderliness, of the activities they observe' (1972b: 39).

How viewers use norms takes us back to the way we read 'the baby cried'. For instance, babies can be boys or girls. Why, then, might not a 'cry' be reported as, say, 'the boy cried'? The answer, says Sacks, lies in a 'Viewer's Maxim' for CBAs which is set out below:

> *Viewer's Maxim*: 'If a Member sees a category-bound activity being done, then, if one sees it being done by a member of a category to which the activity is *bound*, see it that way'. (I: 259, my emphasis)

Through the Viewer's Maxim, we can understand why we would see a 'baby' rather than 'a boy' crying, since a 'baby' is a category that we treat as having 'a special relevance for formulating an identification of its doer' (I: 259).

Finally, why do we treat it as unremarkable that the story reports as the next activity: 'The mommy picked it up'? As we have already seen, part of the answer lies in the way in which we hear 'mommy' and 'baby' as part of a 'team'. In this respect, Duplicative Organization is relevant here.

In addition, however, picking a baby up is likely to be heard as a norm such that where a baby cries, a mother properly picks it up. In this regard, we have, therefore, a 'Second Viewer's Maxim' as defined below:

> *Second Viewer's Maxim*: 'If one sees a pair of actions which can be related by the operation of a norm that provides for the second given the first, where the doers can be seen as members of the categories the norm provides as proper for that pair of actions, then (a) see that the doers are such Members, and (b) see the second as done in conformity with the norm'. (I: 260)

Through using this Second Viewer's Maxim, viewers provide for the 'proper orderliness of the activities they observe' in at least two ways:

1 by explaining the occurrence of one activity given the occurrence of the other; and
2 by explaining the sequential order of the two activities (first one, then the other). (I: 260)

Until now, you may have got the impression that because Membership Categorisation allows people to make sense of people and events, Sacks is implying that everything always proceeds smoothly in the best of all possible worlds. Far from it. First, we have already seen how categorisation can just as easily serve to maintain racism as to preserve harmony. Second, the use of quite innocent knowledge of CBAs can unintentionally allow horrible crimes to be committed.

For instance, in the case of the young British boys who murdered the child Jamie Bulger, witnesses who had seen Jamie holding the hands of his two assassins reported that they had assumed they were watching a child with his two elder brothers. Similarly, as Sacks notes, people working in organisations, faced with possibly life-threatening events, do not take remedial action themselves but report what they have seen to the next person up the hierarchy (I: 64). This is because in organisations categories are organised into hierarchies. So people assume that they need to refer to another category to confirm some act or to take some action.

> **LINK**
>
> The International Institute for Ethnomethodology and Conversation Analysis:
>
> www.iiemca.org
> Ethno/CA news

Most readers, I suspect, will by now be pretty sated with **concepts**. I therefore want to slow up the pace somewhat and offer three illustrations and applications of these concepts here. The first comes from one of Sacks's own lectures.

8.4.1 The Navy Pilot Story

Given that many categories can be used to describe the same person or act, Sacks's task was 'to find out how they [members] go about choosing among the available sets of categories for grasping some event' (1992, I: 41).

Of course, Sacks does not mean to imply that 'society' determines which category one chooses. Instead, he wants to show the active interpretive work involved in rendering any description and the local implications of choosing any particular category.

A particularly telling example of this is to be found in Sacks's analysis of a *New York Times* story about an interview with a navy pilot about his missions in the Vietnam War (I: 205–2, 306–11).

CASE STUDY
The Navy Pilot Story

Sacks is specially interested in the story's report of the navy pilot's reported answer to a question in the extract below:

How did he feel about knowing that even with all the care he took in aiming only at military targets someone was probably being killed by his bombs?

'I certainly don't like the idea that I might be killing anybody,' he replied. 'But I don't lose any sleep over it. You have to be impersonal in this business. Over North Vietnam I condition myself to think that I'm a military man being shot at by another military man like myself.' (I: 205)

Sacks invites us to see how the pilot's immediate reply ('I certainly don't like the idea …') shows his commitment to the evaluational scheme offered by the journalist's question. For instance, if the pilot had instead said 'Why do you ask?', he would have shown that he did not necessarily subscribe to the same moral universe as the reporter (and, by implication, the readers of the article) (I: 211).

Having accepted this moral schema, Sacks shows how the pilot now builds an answer which helps us to see him in a favourable light. The category 'military man' works to defend his bombing as a CBA which reminds us that this is, after all, what military pilots do. The effect of this is magnified by the pilot's identification of his co-participant as 'another military man like myself'. In this way, the pilot creates an SRP (military man/military man) with recognisable mutual obligations (bombing/shooting at the other). In terms of this pair, the other party cannot properly complain or, as Sacks puts it:

there are no complaints to be offered on their part about the error of his ways, except if he happens to violate the norms that, given the device used, are operative. (I: 206)

Notice also that the pilot suggests 'you have to be impersonal in this business'. Note how the category 'this business' sets up the terrain on which the specific SRP of military men will shortly be used. So this account could be offered by either pair–part.

However, as Sacks argues, the implication is that 'this business' is one of many where impersonality is required. For:

if it were the case that, that you had to be impersonal in this business held only for this business, then it might be that doing this business would be wrong in the first instance. (I: 206)

Moreover, the impersonality involved is of a special sort. Sacks points out that we hear the pilot as saying not that it is unfortunate that he cannot kill 'personally' but rather that being involved in this 'business' means that one must not consider that one is killing persons (I: 209).

However, the pilot is only proposing an SRP of military man–military man. In that sense, he is inviting the North Vietnamese to 'play the game' in the same way as a child might say to another 'I'll be third base'.

(Continued)

(Continued)

However, as Sacks notes, in children's baseball, such proposals can be rejected:

if you say 'I'll be third base', unless someone else says 'and I'll be …' another position, and the others say they'll be the other positions, then you're not that thing. You can't play. (I: 307)

Of course, the North Vietnamese indeed did reject the pilot's proposal. Instead, they proposed the identification of the pilot as a 'criminal' and defined themselves as 'doing police action'.

As Sacks notes, these competing definitions had implications which went beyond mere propaganda. For instance, if the navy pilot were shot down then the Geneva Conventions about his subsequent treatment would only properly be applied if he indeed were a 'military man' rather than a 'criminal (I: 307).

EXERCISE 8.6

The following is an extract from a speech made by an English Member of Parliament in the late 1960s. The topic was a Race Relations Bill then going through the British Parliament. The MP was Enoch Powell and the speech because (in)famous as the 'Rivers of Blood' speech because Powell concludes his argument against laws on racial discrimination by saying: 'Like the Roman, I see the River Tiber foaming with much blood.' The extract below occurs earlier in the speech (Mercer, 1990):

1 Nothing is more misleading than comparison between the Commonwealth
2 immigrant in Britain and the American Negro. The Negro population of the
3 United States, which was already in existence before the United States
4 became a nation, started literally as slaves and were later given the franchise
5 and other rights of citizenship … The Commonwealth immigrant came to
6 Britain as a full citizen, to a country which knew no discrimination between
7 one citizen and another, and he entered instantly into the possession of the
8 rights of every citizen, from the vote to free treatment under the National Health
9 Service … But while to the immigrant entry to this country was admission to
10 privileges and opportunities eagerly sought, the impact upon the existing
11 population was very different. For reasons which they could not comprehend,
12 and in pursuit of a decision by default, on which they were never consulted,
13 they found themselves made strangers in their own country. They found their

14 wives unable to obtain hospital beds in childbirth, their children unable to
15 obtain school places, their homes and neighbourhoods changed beyond
16 recognition … At work they found that employers hesitated to apply to
17 the immigrant worker the standards of discipline and competence required
18 of the native-born worker; they began to hear, as time went by, more and
19 more voices which told them that they were now the unwanted. On top of
20 this, they now learn that a one-way privilege is to be establish by Act
21 of Parliament: a law, which cannot, and is not intended to, to operate to
22 protect them or to redress their grievances, is to be enacted to give the stranger,
23 the disgruntled and the agent-provocateur the power to pillory them for their
24 private actions.

Source: Kobena Mercer (1990) 'Powellism as a political discourse', PhD thesis,
Goldsmiths College, University of London

1   What MCDs and CBAs does Powell use here?
2   On this basis, why was Powell's speech so powerful? (Here is a clue: look at
    how the term 'strangers', first used on line 13, takes on a different meaning in
    line 22.)
3   How could the same descriptive strategies be used to oppose his arguments?

Having used one of Sacks's own examples, I now turn, briefly, to two of
my own.

8.4.2 A Newspaper Headline

Father and Daughter in Snow Ordeal

This headline appeared in the inside pages of *The Times*. I want to examine how
we can understand the sense it makes using MCD analysis. A schematic reading of
this headline, using MCD analysis, is set out in Table 8.6.

TABLE 8.6   'Father and Daughter in Snow Ordeal'

Concept	Explanation	Headline
Category	Any person can be labelled in many 'correct' ways	Persons later described as 'supermarket manager' and 'student'
Membership Categorisation Device (MCD)	Categories are seen as grouped together in collections	MCD = 'family'
Economy Rule	A single category *may* be sufficient to describe a person	Single categories are used here
Consistency Rule	If one person is identified from a collection, then a next person *may* be identified from the same collection	'Daughter' is from same MCD as 'father'
Duplicative Organization	When categories can be heard as a 'team' hear them that way	'Daughter' is the daughter of *this* 'father'
Category-Bound Activities (CBAs)	Activities may be heard as 'tied' to certain categories	'Snow ordeal' is *not* heard as tied to 'father–daughter' categories; this is why the story is newsworthy
Standardised relational pairs (SRPs)	Pairs of categories are linked together in standardised, routine ways	'Father' and 'daughter' assumed to be linked together through 'caring' and 'support'; how could 'snow ordeal' have happened?

EXERCISE 8.7

I want to develop Table 8.6 by asking you a series of questions. In answering them, you will see the skill involved in constructing headlines which encourage us to read the story beneath the headline.

First, note that the persons are described as 'father' and 'daughter'. Given that people can be described in many 'correct' ways, what are the implications of choosing these categories? For instance, the story below the headline tells us that the 'father' is also a 'supermarket manager' and the 'daughter' is a 'school student':

- How would we have interpreted the story if the headline had read as follows? 'Supermarket Manager and School Student in Snow Ordeal'
- Given that headline, would we have felt like reading the rest of the story and, if so, why?
- What are implications of the chosen categories being derived from the MCD 'family'? And what does it tell us about the saliency of this MCD, that single categories will do (remember that the Economy Rule is not obligatory)?
- Why do we not doubt that this is not any daughter but the daughter of this 'father'?
- Why is 'snow ordeal' newsworthy in the context of the MCD 'family'?

8.4.3 A Lonely Hearts Advertisement

> Move over Nigella. Funky F.26, a whizz with spaghetti and meatballs & music-mad WLTM M, 25-33, with a wicked SOH. (*Guardian*, 22 October 2005)

Like the headline, this advertisement was chosen at random in order to show how MCD analysis can fruitfully analyse any material of this kind. Now I take it that, while successful newspaper headlines make you want to read the story, the success of a lonely hearts advertisement is judged by the number of appropriate responses that it elicits.

Let us begin by focusing upon the category 'Nigella' to see what function it serves. Sacks points out that when you just use a first name like this, the hearer is expected to use it to find some person that they already know (1992, II: 445). This means that the reader of this ad must try to work out a person whom they know in common with a stranger. The implication is that Nigella can only be a celebrity – somebody whom everybody knows.

Nigella is a pretty unusual name and the only celebrity who uses it is Nigella Lawson (a British TV cook and partner of the advertising mogul Charles Saatchi). In this context, to say 'move over Nigella' will be heard to claim something like 'I can do anything better than her'. However, this claim cuts two ways. Although it might suggest a very attractive person (with more spark than a celebrity), like any such claim about oneself it can be heard as tied to the category of 'boasting'.

Now note how the advertiser next refers to herself as 'a whizz with spaghetti and meatballs'. By choosing such an everyday meal, she works to downplay the (implied) category of 'boasting'. Now she is claiming neither great cooking skills nor, by implication, celebrity.

So the reference to spaghetti serves as a category-modifier which retrospectively recasts the reference to Nigella as ironic. As a consequence, we now hear the advertiser not to be claiming celebrity status but simply to be someone with an ironic sense of humour. Moreover, this explains and justifies her search for a man with 'a wicked SOH'.

EXERCISE 8.8

Here is another 'lonely hearts' advertisement:

> Good looking (so I am told!) Englishman, 35, tall, professional, seeks very attractive lady, preferably non-smoker, to wine, dine and make her smile. Age unimportant. Photo appreciated.

1 What does this advertisement imply about the advertiser or the 'lady' sought even though it does not tell us these things directly?

2 Show how we can see this by examining how this advertisement uses the following devices:

- categories
- MCDs
- Economy Rule
- Consistency Rule
- Category-Bound Activities
- category-modifiers
- standardised relational pairs
- Positioned Categories.

8.4.4 Summary

The examples that we have just been considering demonstrate that membership categories are far from being the inert classificatory instruments to be found, say, in the more rigid forms of content analysis or in Bales's categorisations of 'interaction process'.

By contrast, MCDs are local members' devices, actively employed by speakers and hearers to formulate and reformulate the meanings of activities and identities. Unlike more formalistic accounts of action found in content analysis and some versions of narrative analysis, Sacks shows us the nitty-gritty mechanisms through which we construct moral universes 'involving appropriate kinds of action and particular actors with motives, desires, feelings, aspirations and sense of justice' (J. Gubrium, personal correspondence).

TIP

How to Choose (the Right) Documents

The determination of which kinds of documents to choose as data sources is first and foremost linked to the research questions asked ... The selection and or/ sampling of document types, as well as the selection of subsets or sub-segments of those documents, go hand in hand with the evaluation of how, by whom, for what purpose, and with what audience in mind particular documents are produced, all of which impact the content and structure of documents in various ways ... For constructionists, one of the most prominent challenges is to ensure that our findings are not artifacts of the particular documents we have chosen to interrogate (unless that is a purpose of the study).

How to Select Document Types

Given that different document types constrain the information contained in them in more or less distinct ways, it is important to consider the ramifications of such variations for our ability to reconstruct a process of social construction ... analyses of the news (or other documents) should ideally be based in an understanding of how the news (or other documents) are produced ... As a distinct document type, institutionally generated data, especially in the form of statistics, warrant special consideration.

How to Select Documents within a Type

The strategy most commonly used among constructionists is *targeted sampling* of documents pertaining to the emergence, persistence and/or evolution of a particular social construction. The challenges involved in drawing a good targeted sample are linked to the constructionist aim of placing the analytical spotlight on a particular process of social construction in conjunction with the requirement that the findings are not predetermined by the particular selection of documents and the conclusions not foregone in the sense that we pick only documents that fit. *Anything-you-can-lay-your-hands-on* is sometimes the only possible strategy for locating enough information pertaining to research involving marginal, obscure, delicate, or clandestine topics, either because the pool of data itself is so scarce as to make any example an important find (e.g., authentic slave narratives) or because a particular content is only rarely addressed directly in the documents we are searching (e.g., interviews with clients in news reports about prostitution).

When do you have enough data?

As a general methodological rule of thumb for projects that do not rely on a predetermined sample size, which few constructionist projects do, we have enough data when we learn nothing new by adding additional items. (Drawn from Linders, 2008: 469–76)

8.5 CONCLUSION

I hope that, by the end of this chapter, the reader is not feeling punch-drunk! We have indeed covered an enormous amount of ground.

The wide scope of the chapter arose for two reasons. First, I am convinced that qualitative sociologists make too little of the potentialities of texts as rich data. Second, I am also convinced that there are several powerful ways of analysing such data.

Three threads have run through my presentation of different ways to analyse such textual data (for a development of this argument, see Silverman, 2010: 52–5).

The importance of a clear analytic approach

Successful textual studies recognise the value of working with a clearly defined approach. Having chosen your approach (e.g. narrative analysis, ethnography or Sacks's analysis of Membership Categorisations), treat it as a 'tool box' providing a set of concepts and methods to select your data and to illuminate your analysis.

The relevance of theory to textual analysis

The distinctive contribution that qualitative research can make is by utilising its theoretical resources in the deep analysis of small bodies of publicly shareable data. This means that, unlike much quantitative research, including content analysis, we are not satisfied with a simple coding of data. Instead, we have to work to show how the (theoretically defined) elements we have identified are assembled or mutually laminated.

The importance of detailed data analysis

Like many other qualitative approaches, textual analysis depends upon very detailed data analysis. To make such analysis effective, it is imperative to have a limited body of data with which to work. So, while it may be useful initially to explore different kinds of data (e.g. newspaper reports, scientific textbooks, magazine advice pages), this should usually only be done to establish the data set with which you can most effectively work. Having chosen your data set, you should limit your material further by only taking a few texts or parts of texts (e.g. headlines).

In the course of this chapter, we have rapidly moved between several complex and apparently different **theories** – all the way from narrative analysis to ethnomethodology. However, if the reader has grasped at least one useful way of thinking about textual analysis, then I will have achieved my purpose.

KEY POINTS

- Texts provide rich, naturally occurring, accessible data which have real effects in the world.

- I considered three ways in which textual researchers have analysed how texts represent reality: comparative keyword analysis, ethnography and Membership Categorisation Device analysis

- From a constructionist perspective, the role of textual researchers is not to criticise or to assess particular texts in terms of apparently 'objective' standards. It is rather to treat them as representations and to analyse their effects.

STUDY QUESTIONS

1 What are the advantages of working with textual data?
2 Can texts be analysed in the same way as interviews?
3 What questions do constructionists ask about texts?
4 What does the topic/resource distinction imply?
5 How does comparative keyword analysis analyse texts? What are its advantages and disadvantages?
6 List *three* research questions that you might ask about one kind of Internet data (e.g. blogs, e-mails, company reports).
7 Select any lonely heart advertisement (in a newspaper or on the Internet). Show how you can analyse it in terms of members' categorisations.
8 On what basis can you select documents to study?
9 When do you know that you know have enough material?

RECOMMENDED READING

The most useful texts on narrative analysis and ethnography are: Alasuutari (1995), Coffey and Atkinson (1996) and Czarniawska (1998; 2003). More advanced texts are Atkinson (1990) and the chapters on analysing texts in my edited collection *Qualitative Research* (2011). Linders (2008) offers a useful chapter-length discussion of how constructionists use documents.

My book *Harvey Sacks and Conversation Analysis* (1998) is an introduction to the ideas of Harvey Sacks (Chapters 5 and 7 deal with MCD analysis). Volume 1 of Sacks's *Lectures on Conversation* (1992) is a marvellous resource. See especially his discussions of Category-Bound Activities (I: 179–81, Lecture 8, Fall 1965); (I: 301–2, Lecture 4, Spring 1966); (I: 333–40, Lecture 8, Spring 1966); (I: 568–96, Lectures 11–14, Spring 1967). See also:

The Consistency Rule (I: 326–7, Lecture 7, Spring 1966)
The hotrodders example (I: 169–74; Lecture 7, Fall 1965); (I: 396–403)
The navy pilot example (I: 205–22; Research Notes, Fall 1965); (I: 306–7, Lecture 5, Spring 1966)
The child's story (I: 223–31; Appendix A and B, Fall 1965); (I: 236–66; Lectures 1–2(R), Spring 1966)

9

Naturally Occurring Talk

CHAPTER OBJECTIVES

By the end of this chapter, you will be able to:

- recognise the advantages of analysing naturally occurring talk
- see why it is important to record talk and to transcribe it using standardised conventions
- understand the basic principles of conversation analysis (CA) and discourse analysis (DA)
- recognise the similarities, as well as the differences, between them and realise the contribution that both can make to understanding the world around us.

When social science researchers begin to design a research study, they encounter a series of choices about how narrowly to define their research problem and which method or methods of data collection are appropriate to its study (see Chapter 2). If we consider the methods so far discussed in this book – observation, interviews, **focus groups** and **texts** – our choice appears to be very clear cut.

Using research interviews (or focus groups) involves actively creating data which would not exist apart from the researcher's intervention (**researcher-provoked data**). By contrast, observation or the analysis of written texts, audio-tapes or visual images deals with activities which seem to exist independently of the researcher. This is why we call such data **naturally occurring** – they derive from situations which exist independently of the researcher's intervention.

However, like most social science concepts, the opposition between naturally occurring and researcher-provoked data should not be taken too far. Indeed, no data are ever untouched by human hands. If we choose to observe, our data do not speak for themselves but have to be recorded (and transformed) into fieldnotes. Equally, audio and video recordings usually end up being transcribed using particular researcher-designed interventions which are never 'perfect' but only more or less useful. Moreover, the character of such data will be crucially affected by where you position your recording equipment and/or point your camera.

All this suggests that here, as elsewhere, we should treat appeals to 'nature' (as in the term 'naturally occurring') with considerable caution (an alternative, with fewer assumptions, would be *naturalistic* data). Nonetheless, providing we do not push it too far, it can still be helpful to make use of the distinction between two kinds of data: naturally occurring and researcher provoked. Indeed, if we can, at least to some extent, study what people are actually doing in 'naturally occurring' situations, why should we ever want to work with 'researcher-provoked' data (Potter, 2002)?

Most quantitative researchers have a straightforward answer to this question. Data gathered from naturally occurring settings often appear horribly messy and unreliable to quantitative types. If you want to measure things reliably, then, they argue, it helps to create carefully controlled settings and to use well-tested research instruments like questionnaires or laboratory experiments.

By contrast, qualitative researchers who work with researcher-provoked data do not always seem to have thought through their choices. Certainly, open-ended interviews and focus groups can give you data much more quickly than observation and/or recording – although more slowly than texts. Moreover, many researchers claim that it is often not possible to obtain access to naturally occurring settings appropriate to a given research topic – even though this sometimes shows a lack of imagination on their part (see my discussion of methods for studying 'the family' in Section 5.4).

Such instrumental factors (speed, lack of alternatives), however, conceal the appeal of methods like the interview and the focus group to a particular research model (**emotionalism**) and more generally to a set of mass-media-driven assumptions deriving from what I have called the 'Interview Society' (Section 2.7).

Asking people what they think and feel appears to have an immediacy, even 'authenticity', which curiously is believed to be absent in naturally occurring data. So, even when you have tapes or observations of behaviour, you are tempted to 'complete the picture' by interviewing the people concerned about what they were thinking or feeling at the time. The arguments for and against researcher-provoked data are summarised in Table 9.1.

By contrast, some qualitative researchers prefer to work with 'naturally occurring' data although their reasons may differ. For the ethnographers of the **Chicago School**, the real form of immediacy was out on city streets and they wanted to 'tell it like it is' by observing life as it happened. However, their **naturalistic** focus meant that they usually sought to combine observation with interviews with key informants.

TABLE 9.1   Why work with researcher-provoked data?

For	Against
Speed	What about texts?
Easy access	Public data usually available
Authenticity of interviews	Reflects temptations of the 'Interview Society'
Interviews help you to understand behaviour	Participants can predict someone's intentions without access to their thoughts

For a later generation of researchers, influenced by **constructionism** and **ethnomethodology**, audiotapes of naturally occurring conversation provided marvellous data to analyse how people actually went about constructing a social world together.

Although you may be inclined to think of conversation as trivial ('merely' talk), it is worth reflecting that conversation is the primary medium through which social interaction takes place. In households and in more 'public' settings, families and friends relate to one another through talk (and silence!). At work, we converse with one another and the outcome of this talk (as in meetings or job selection interviews) is often placed on dossiers and files. As Heritage argues:

> the social world is a pervasively conversational one in which an overwhelming proportion of the world's business is conducted through the medium of spoken interaction. (1984: 239)

Indeed, what Heritage calls 'the world's business' includes such basic features as a child learning how to converse with its mother and adults telling news, getting into conversation with a stranger and even deciding to commit suicide (see Sacks, 1992; Maynard, 2003; Silverman, 1998: Ch. 1). As we shall also see, in a powerful case study provided later in this chapter, the world's business also includes men being acquitted from rape charges on the grounds that a woman did not clearly say 'no'.

TIP

'[P]eople studying (talk and) discourse see language as performative and functional: *language is never treated as a neutral, transparent, means of communication.* [For example] two reporters see a man being shot. The next day one headline reads "Freedom fighter kills politician" and the other headline reads "Terrorist kills politician".

Some of the questions you could ask are:

- Which one is true?
- Which one is correct?
- Which was is factual?

And this is not just a philosophical or abstract question. We have seen this being explored in our recent history through the debates about the status of the people moved from Afghanistan to the American enclave in Cuba and interned in Guantanamo Bay. One of the debates has centred on whether these people are to be understood as "prisoners of war" – and therefore they have specific sets of legally binding human rights – or as "unlawful combatants". Similarly, Pervez Musharraf, Pakistan's president, is one of many political leaders that have commented on the contemporary difficulties in defining just who is a "freedom fighter" and who is a "terrorist". So as these examples begin to show, language is constructive, it is constitutive of social life. As you speak and write you produce a world. So the interest for those analysing discourse is on *how* language is used. The focus is on what specific version of the world, or identity or meaning is produced by describing something in just that way over another way; what is made available and what is excluded by describing something this way over an alternative way.' (Rapley, 2007: 2).

Even if you are unconvinced by the argument that conversation is central to making the social world the way it is, there is still a strong methodological argument which suggests that audiotapes of naturally occurring talk are useful data. To understand why, we must return to the work of Harvey Sacks.

9.1 WHY WORK WITH TAPES?

> the kind of phenomena I deal with are always transcriptions of actual occurrences in their actual sequence. (Sacks, 1984: 25)

Sacks stresses that one should work with 'actual occurrences' of talk. So, even though twentieth-century philosophers like Wittgenstein (1968), Austin (1962) and Searle (1969) have had important things to say about the things we do in conversation, they do not study actual talk but work with invented examples and their own intuitions about what it makes sense to say. For Sacks, on the contrary:

> One cannot invent new sequences of conversation and feel happy with them. You may be able to take 'a question and answer', but if we have to extend it very far, then the issue of whether somebody would really say that, after, say, the fifth utterance, is one which we could not confidently argue. One doesn't have a strong intuition for sequencing in conversation. (1992, I: 5)

Unlike philosophers, ethnographers do not usually invent conversations. Instead, they observe and record their observations through fieldnotes (see Section 5.2.6). Why did Sacks prefer to use an audio recorder?

Sacks's answer is that we cannot rely on our notes or recollections of conversations. Certainly, depending on our memory, we can usually summarise what different people said. But it is simply impossible to remember (or even to note at the time) such matters as pauses, overlaps, in-breaths and the like.

> Now whether you think these kinds of things are important will depend upon what you can show with or without them. Indeed, you may not even be convinced that conversation itself is a particularly interesting topic. But, at least by studying tapes of conversations, you are able to focus on the 'actual details' of one aspect of social life. As Sacks put it: My research is about conversation only in this incidental way, that we can get the actual happenings of on tape and transcribe them more or less, and therefore have something to begin with. If you can't deal with the actual detail of actual events then you can't have a science of social life. (1992: II, 26)

Tapes and transcripts also offer more than just 'something to begin with'. They have three clear advantages compared with other kinds of qualitative data:

1 Tapes are a public record.
2 Tapes can be replayed and transcripts improved.
3 Tapes preserve sequences of talk.

Let me expand a little on this list. In the first place, tapes are a public record, available to the scientific community, in a way that fieldnotes are not. Second, they can be replayed and transcriptions can be improved and analyses take off on a different tack unlimited by the original transcript. As Sacks told his students:

> I started to play around with tape recorded conversations, for the single virtue that I could replay them; that I could type them out somewhat, and study them extendedly, who knew how long it might take … It wasn't from any large interest in language, or from some theoretical formulation of what should be studied, but simply by virtue of that; I could get my hands on it, and I could study it again and again. And also, consequentially, others could look at what I had studied, and make of it what they could, if they wanted to disagree with me. (1992: I, 622)

A third advantage of detailed transcripts is that, if you want to, you can inspect sequences of utterances without being limited to the extracts chosen by the first researcher. For it is within these sequences, rather than in single turns of talk, that we make sense of conversation. In this way, tapes and transcripts preserve sequences of talk. As Sacks points out, 'having available for any given utterance other utterances around it, is extremely important for determining what was said. If you have available only the snatch of talk that you're now transcribing, you're in tough shape for determining what it is' (1992, I: 729).

There remains the potential charge that data based mainly on audio recordings are incomplete. We see Sacks's response to this issue when a student on his lecture course asked a question about 'leaving out things like facial expressions' from his analysis (II: 26). Sacks at once conceded that 'it would be great to study them [such things]. It's an absence.' Nonetheless, he constructs a two-part defence of his data.

First, the idea of 'completeness' may itself be an illusion. Surely, there cannot be totally 'complete' data any more than there can be a 'perfect' transcript? Second, Sacks recognised some of the undoubted technical problems involved in camera positioning and the like if you were to use videos (II: 26–7). These are the very issues that have been addressed, if not resolved, by more recent work based on video-recorded data (see Heath et al., 2010; Heath, 2011). I will return to this work in Chapter 10.

However, as always in science, everything will depend on what you are trying to do and where it seems that you may be able to make progress. As Sacks put it, 'one gets started where you can maybe get somewhere' (I: 26).

Getting started, in Sacks's sense, means repeated, careful listening to your tapes. As you listen, you build an improving version of a transcript. In Section 9.2 below, I discuss why you need to transcribe your tapes and what you need to put into your transcripts.

TIP

Working with a cassette tape can be very slow. For instance, it takes a long time to find two segments of a tape that are several minutes apart. Using digital sound, the recording can be made with PC software and turned into a file that can be listened to, edited and emailed between researchers. Hepburn and Potter (2004: 186) recommend the use of CoolEdit (from www.syntrillium.com) for sound recording, manipulation and transcription.

9.2 TRANSCRIBING AUDIOTAPES

As already noted, even if some people are able to remember conversations better than others, we are unlikely to be able to recall such potentially crucial details as pauses and overlaps. Indeed, even with a tape recording, transcribers may 'tidy up' the 'messy' features of natural conversation such as length of pauses or overlapping or aborted utterances.

Features like pauses matter to all of us, not just to analysts of conversations. Indeed, they are one basis on which, as Sacks (1992) has pointed out, reading somebody else's mind, far from being some paranoid delusion, is both routine and necessary in everyday life. Look at Extract 9.1 below.

Extract 9.1 [Levinson, 1983: 320, simplified]

1   C: So I was wondering would you be in your office on Monday by any chance?
2   (2.0)
3   C: Probably not

The numbers in brackets on line 2 indicate a two-second pause. The presence of this pause gives us a clue to how C can guess that the person he is questioning might indeed not be in his office on Monday (line 3). This is because when there is a pause when it is someone's turn to speak, we can generally assume the pause will foreshadow some difficulty. Hence C is able to read the pause as indicating that the other person is unlikely to be in his office on Monday and say 'Probably not' in line 3.

Now consider Extract 9.2 below. This is taken from an interview between a health adviser (H) and a patient who has requested an HIV test. H is offering a piece of advice about condom use and her patient is a young woman who has just left school.

Extract 9.2 [Silverman, 1997: 6.3]

1   H: it's <u>important</u> that you tell them to (0.3) use a condom (0.8) or to practise
2   safe sex that's what using a condom means.
3   (1.5)
4   H: okay?

In line 4, H asks 'okay?' which may be heard as a request for the patient to indicate that she has understood (or at least heard) H's advice about condom use. As with Extract 9.1, we can see that a pause in a space where a speaker might have taken a turn at talk (here at line 3) has indicated some difficulty to the previous speaker.

Indeed, it is likely that H heard an earlier difficulty. Note that in line 1 there is a pause of 0.8 seconds. It is not unreasonable to assume that since the patient has not used this space to indicate some understanding of what H has just said (for instance, by saying 'mm'), H's explanation of what 'using a condom means' (lines 1–2) is given precisely in (what turns out to be) an unsuccessful attempt to overcome this difficulty.

At this point you may be wondering how these transcripts can give such precise lengths of pauses. In fact, you do not need any advanced technology for this. Although transcribers may use complicated timing devices, many others get into the habit of using any four-syllable word which takes about a second to say. If you then say this word during a pause, you can roughly count each syllable as indicating a pause of one-quarter of a second.

> **TIP**
>
> Peräkylä (2004b: 169) notes that when transcribing your 'ear' develops through experience as you gradually hear things that were originally inaudible and learn how to time overlapping talk, etc. He suggests that it helps to have another person check your transcription. Not only will that lead to a more reliable transcript, but it will help you to hear things that you did not hear at first.

However, pauses are not the only features that you may need to record. In the Appendix, I provide a simplified set of transcription symbols. As we have seen, **conversation analysis**'s concern with the *sequential* organisation of talk means that it needs precise transcriptions of such (commonsensically) trivial matters as overlapping talk and length of pauses. Close, repeated listening to recordings often reveals previously unnoted recurring features of the organisation of talk. Such listening can most fruitfully be done in group data sessions. As described by Paul ten Have, work in such groups usually begins by listening to an extract from a tape with a draft transcript and agreeing upon improvements to the transcript. Then:

> the participants are invited to proffer some observations on the data, to select an episode which they find 'interesting' for whatever reason, and formulate their understanding or puzzlement, regarding that episode. Then anyone can come in to react to these remarks, offering alternatives, raising doubts, or whatever. (ten Have, 1998: 124)

However, as ten Have makes clear, such group data sessions should be rather more than an anarchic free for all:

> participants are, on the one hand, *free* to bring in anything they like, but, on the other hand, *required* to ground their observations in the data at hand, although they may also support them with reference to their own data-based findings or those published in the literature. (1998: 124)

EXERCISE 9.1

This is a task designed to help you familiarise yourself with the transcription conventions used in conversation analysis. As a consequence, you should start to understand the logic of transcribing this way and be able to ask questions about how the speakers are organising their talk.

You are asked to tape-record no more than five minutes of talk in the public domain. One possibility is a radio call-in programme. Avoid using scripted, drama productions as these may not contain recurrent features of natural interaction (such as overlap or repair). Do not try to record a TV extract as the visual material will complicate both transcription and analysis. Now go through the following steps:

1 Attempt to transcribe your tape using the conventions in the Appendix to this book. Try to allocate turns to identified speakers where possible but do not worry if you cannot identify a particular speaker (put ? at the start of a line in such cases).
2 Encourage a friend to attempt the same task independently of you. Now compare transcripts and listen to the tape recording again to improve your transcript.
3 Using this chapter as a guide, attempt to identify in your transcript any features in the organisation of the talk (e.g. adjacency pairs, preference organisation, institutional talk).

However, without a way of defining a research problem, even detailed transcription can be merely an empty technique. Thus we need to ask: what sort of features are we searching for in our transcripts and what approach lies behind this search?

TIP

The level of detail you need in your transcripts will depend upon your research problem and your preferred analytical approach. Practical issues, such as time and resources, are also relevant: you may only be able to transcribe in detail certain parts of your data. The main thing is that you 'consider carefully the reasons for (your) style of transcription and be explicit about (your) rationale for the format adopted' (Noaks and Wincup, 2004: 130).

It should not be assumed that the preparation of transcripts is simply a technical detail prior to the main business of the analysis. As Atkinson and Heritage (1984) point out, the production and use of transcripts are essentially 'research activities'. They involve close, repeated listenings to recordings which often reveal previously unnoted recurring features of the organisation of talk. The convenience of transcripts for presentational purposes is no more than an added bonus.

As an example, the reader might examine Extract 9.3 below, based on the transcribing conventions listed in the Appendix, which report such features as overlapping talk and verbal stress as well as pauses (in parts of a second):

Extract 9.3 [Her: OII: 2: 4: ST]

(S's wife has just slipped a disc.)

```
1   H:    And we were wondering if there's anything we can do to help
2   S:    [Well 'at's
3   H:    [I mean can we do any shopping for her or something like tha:t?
4         (0.7)
5   S:    Well that's most ki:nd Heatherton .hhh At the moment
6         no: . because we've still got two bo: ys at home
```

In Extract 9.3, we see S refusing an offer made by H. Heritage shows how S's refusal (lines 5–6) of H's offer displays three interesting features. First, when S does not take an early opportunity to accept H's offer (after 'anything we can do to help', line 1), H proceeds to revise it. Second, S delays his refusal via the pause in the slot for his turn at line 4. Third, he justifies it by invoking a contingency about which H could not be expected to know.

Why should S and H bother with these complexities? The answer lies in the way in which they end up by producing an account which blames nobody. In an early work, Goffman (1959) similarly suggested that a persistent consideration of interactants is to protect one another's public self-esteem, or 'face'. In doing whatever people are doing, they take into consideration the moral standing of themselves and their co-interactants that their doings project. In the ordinary course of events, this consideration entails the *protection* of the positive moral standing of the self and of others.

We can develop Goffman's observation by noting that certain actions – typically actions that occur in response to other actions, such as invitations, offers or assessments – can be marked as *dispreferred*: that is, problematic in one way or another. Thus, rejections of invitations or offers, or disagreements in response to assessments, can be performed in such a way that encodes their problematic status. Conversely, an acceptance of an invitation or offer, or an agreement with an assessment, can be performed in a way that does not exhibit such problematic status.

Subsequent research has identified a number of practices through which the *dispreferred* status of an action can be marked. According to Heritage (1984: 265–80), these practices include:

1 The action is delayed within a turn or across a sequence of turns.
2 The action is commonly prefaced or qualified within the turn in which it occurs.
3 The action is commonly accomplished in mitigated or indirect form.
4 The action is commonly accounted for.

These actions together constitute what has been called *preference organisation*. But note that the concept of 'preference', when used in this sense, does not refer to inner experiences of the actors about 'problems' or the lack of them involved in performing certain actions (Levinson, 1983). Furthermore, the distinction between preferred and dispreferred actions does not involve an a priori categorisation of actions as problematic or non-problematic. Rather, the distinction between 'preferred' and 'dispreferred' action format involves a resource for the interactants, through the use of which they can portray their actions as problematic, or, alternatively, as ones that do not involve problems in the interaction at hand.

We can see how conversationalists can prevent problems arising if we return to Extract 9.1.

Extract 9.4 [Levinson, 1983: 320, simplified]

1   C: So I was wondering would you be in your office on Monday by any chance?
2   (2.0)
3   C: Probably not

C's question (at line 1) is one of those kinds of questions that we hear as likely to precede some other kind of activity. For instance, we all know that, if somebody asks if we will be free on Saturday night, an invitation is in the offing. Here we can guess that if C had got a positive reply, he would then have gone on to offer a request or an invitation.

Why should speakers proceed in this indirect way? The answer is to do with what Goffman called 'face' and what we have called 'preference organisation'. By asking a question about someone's whereabouts or plans, speakers avoid others having to engage in the 'dispreferred' act of turning-down-an-invitation. If we reply that we are busy, the invitation need never be offered. The prior question thus helps both parties: the recipient is not put in the position of having to turn down an invitation and, if the question elicits negative information or a meaningful pause (as in Extract 9.1), the questioner is saved from losing face by being able to avoid offering an invitation doomed to be declined.

9.3 WHY TALK MATTERS

Readers new to this kind of work may be wondering if they are being introduced to a highly technical approach with little if any relevance to the real world. The following case study shows why features like preference organisation really matter.

CASE STUDY
So What?

Date rape prevention programmes often provide 'assertiveness training' to encourage women to respond to unwanted sex through a direct and straightforward 'no'. However, conversation analysis shows that refusals are complex conversational interactions, incorporating delays, prefaces, palliatives, and accounts. In focus groups run by Kitzinger and Frith, 'although young women do not, of course, use the term, they know that refusals are *dispreferred* conversational actions' (1999: 293); that is, that they necessitate a great deal more interactional work than do, for example, acceptances. Their young women display sophisticated knowledge about talk-in-interaction by describing feelings akin to wrongness, rudeness or foolishness which accompany the unvarnished 'no', and by insisting on the need to explain and justify their refusals.

Extract 9.5 (Kitzinger and Frith, 1999: 303)

Liz: It just doesn't seem right to say no when you're up there in the situation.
Sara: It's not rude, it's not rude – it sounds awful to say this, doesn't it.
Liz: I know.
Sara: It's not rude, but it's the same sort of feeling. It's like, 'oh my god, I can't say no now, can I?'

Refusal skills training often ignores and overrides these with its simplistic prescription to 'just say no'. It should not in fact be necessary for a woman to say 'no' in order for her to be understood as refusing sex. (1999: 293)

Kitzinger uses research of the kind mentioned in this case study to examine criticisms of CA for having 'too narrow and restrictive a scope for politically engaged research … It is dismissed as jargon-ridden and impenetrable, and (despite its claims to fidelity to participants' own orientations) as divorced from speakers' own understandings of what is going on in interactions' (2007: 134).

She goes on to note how each of these criticisms is rejected by her students who use CA because they believe that it gives them the opportunity to understand the world – and, through understanding, to change it for the better. Rose Rickford, an undergraduate student at York, puts it like this:

> For me the most important thing about CA is that it's inherently political. It politicizes the everyday. It completely overturns the notion that politics belongs in a separate space – that it's something you do when you vote, or go on a demonstration, or write a letter of protest. I believe that by changing the everyday we can change the world. For me, CA is fundamental in that. Micro-interactions are not tiny insignificant little things that happen underneath the big umbrella of macro-structures. The macro-structure is – in part – something we create through our moment-by-moment micro-interactions. And we could do them differently! (Quoted by Kitzinger, 2007: 134)

The rest of this chapter will outline the two main social science traditions which inform the analysis of transcripts of tapes: conversation analysis (CA) and **discourse analysis** (DA). I will begin with CA.

9.4 CONVERSATION ANALYSIS

CA is based on an attempt to describe people's methods for producing orderly social interaction. In turn, CA emerged out of Garfinkel's (1967) programme for ethnomethodology and its analysis of 'folk' (ethno) methods. Sacks's MCD analysis, discussed in Section 8.5, also derives from this programme.

9.4.1 Four fundamental assumptions

I will begin by summarising Peräkylä's account (2004b: 166–8) of four fundamental assumptions of CA:

1 *Talk is action*: in CA, talk is understood first and foremost as a vehicle of human action; the capacity of language to convey ideas is seen as derivative from this more fundamental task. In CA, treating talk as action does not involve philosophical considerations, but very concrete research practice. Some CA studies have as their topics the organisation of actions that are recognisable *as* distinct actions even in an everyday sense, e.g. opening and closing conversations, making assessments, telling stories and receiving news.

2 *Action is structurally organised*: in the CA view, the practical actions that comprise the heart of social life are thoroughly structured and organised. In pursuing their goals, the actors have to orient themselves to rules and structures that only make their actions possible. These rules and structures concern mostly the relations between actions. Single acts are parts of larger, structurally organised entities. These entities can be called sequences. We shall examine some basic sequences in Sections 9.4.2 and 9.4.3.

3 *Talk creates and maintains intersubjective reality*: CA is not a mechanical approach. For instance, rather than overlooking 'meaning' and 'experience', CA offers a tool for studying them in a rigorous empirical way. In CA studies, talk and interaction are examined as a site where intersubjective understanding about the participants' intentions is created and maintained. Thereby, CA gives access to the construction of meaning in real time.

4 *Understanding is publicly displayed*: CA focuses exclusively on meanings and understandings that are made public through conversational action, and it remains 'agnostic' regarding people's intra-psychological experience (Heritage, 1984). The most fundamental level of intersubjective understanding concerns

the understanding of preceding turn displayed by the current speaker. Just as any turn of talk is produced in the context shaped by the previous turn, it also displays its speaker's understanding of that previous turn (Atkinson and Drew, 1979: 48). Thus, in simple cases, in producing a turn of talk that is hearable as an answer, the speaker also shows that they understood the preceding turn as a question. Sometimes these choices can be crucial for the unfolding of the interaction and the social relation of its participants (see my discussion of *preference organisation* in Section 9.2). Moreover, if the first speaker considers the understanding concerning their talk, displayed in the second speaker's utterance, as incorrect or problematic, the first speaker has an opportunity for correcting this understanding in the 'third position' (Schegloff 1992b), for example by saying 'I didn't mean to criticize you but just to tell about the problem', or the like.

> **TIP**
>
> When you analyse your data, always try to understand how the positioning of a particular utterance or action relates to how the participants make sense of what is going on. This means that you should try to avoid analysing single turns of talk in, say, an interview as interviewees' answers are always related to what interviewers do. For examples of this, refer back to the beginning of Chapter 6 in which Rapley (2004) discusses interviewer–interviewee talk and Kitzinger's case study 'hearing women's voices' in Section 7.3 in which she discusses how 'coming out' in terms of your sexual preference is related to available 'interactional slots'.

It is important to understand that these are not purely theoretical assumptions but are strongly linked to the practicalities of how we do research. As Heritage puts it:

> Specifically, analysis is strongly 'data-driven' – developed from phenomena which are in various ways evidenced in the data of interaction. Correspondingly, there is a strong bias against *a priori* speculation about the orientations and motives of speakers and in favour of detailed examination of conversationalists' actual actions. Thus the empirical conduct of speakers is treated as the central resource out of which analysis may develop. (1984: 243)

In practice, Heritage adds, this means that it must be demonstrated that the regularities described 'are produced and oriented to by the participants as normatively oriented-to grounds for inference and action' (1984: 244). Further, deviant cases, in which such regularities are absent. must be identified and analysed (see Section 11.3.2 for a further discussion of the role of **deviant-case analysis** in relation to the **validity** of field research).

For reasons of space, I will briefly describe just three features of talk with which CA is concerned. These are:

1 turn-taking and repair
2 conversational openings and 'adjacency pairs'
3 how 'institutional' talk builds upon (and modifies) the structures of ordinary conversation.

All three features relate to what Sacks calls 'sequencing in conversation'.

9.4.2 Turn-taking and repair

Turns at talk have three aspects (Sacks et al., 1974). They involve:

- How a speaker makes a turn relate to a previous turn (e.g. 'Yes', 'But', 'Uh huh').
- What the turn interactionally accomplishes (e.g. an invitation, a question, an answer).
- How the turn relates to a succeeding turn (e.g. by a question, request, summons).

Where turn-taking errors and violations occur, 'repair mechanisms' will be used. For instance, where more than one party is speaking at a time, a speaker may stop speaking before a normally possible completion point of a turn. Again, when turn transfer does not occur at the appropriate place, the current speaker may repair the failure of the sequence by speaking again. Finally, where repairs by other than the current speaker are required (for instance, because another party has been misidentified), the next speaker typically waits until the completion of a turn. Thus the turn-taking system's allocation of rights to a turn is respected even when a repair is found necessary.

There are three consequences of this which are worth noting:

1 *Needing to listen*: the turn-taking system provides an 'intrinsic motivation' for listening to all utterances in a conversation. Interest or politeness alone is not sufficient to explain such attention. Rather, every participant must listen to and analyse each utterance in case they are selected as next speaker.
2 *Understanding*: turn-taking organisation controls some of the ways in which utterances are understood. So, for instance, it allows 'How are you?', as a first turn, to be usually understood not as an enquiry but as a greeting.
3 *Displaying understanding*: when someone offers the 'appropriate' form of reply (e.g. an answer to a question, or an apology to a complaint), they display an understanding of the significance of the first utterance. The turn-taking system is thus the means whereby actors display to one another that they are engaged in *social* action – action defined by Weber as involving taking account of others.

Thus CA is an empirically oriented research activity, grounded in a basic theory of social action and generating significant implications from an analysis of previously unnoticed interactional forms. As the next section shows, one such unnoticed form is the structure of questions and answers.

9.4.3 Conversational openings and adjacency-pairs

In the 1960s, the American sociologist Emmanuel Schegloff studied data drawn from the first five seconds of around 500 telephone calls to and from an American police station. Schegloff began by noting that the basic rule for two-party conversation, that one party speaks at a time (i.e. providing for a sequence a–b–a–b–a–b where a and b are the parties), 'does not provide for the allocation of the roles "a" and "b"' (1968: 350). Telephone calls offer interesting data in this regard because non-verbal forms of communication – apart from the telephone bell – are absent. Somehow, despite the absence of visual cues, speakers manage an orderly sequence in which both parties know when to speak. How?

Schegloff suggests: 'A first rule of telephone conversations which might be called "a distribution rule for first utterances"' is: *the answerer speaks first*' (1968: 351, original emphasis).

In order to see the force of the 'distribution rule', consider the confusion that occurs when a call is made and the phone is picked up, but nothing is said by the receiver of the call. Schegloff cites an anecdote by a women who adopted this strategy of silence after she began receiving obscene telephone calls. Her friends were constantly irritated by this practice, thus indicating the force of the rule 'the answerer speaks first'. Moreover, her tactic was successful: 'however obscene her caller might be, he would not talk until she had said "hello", thereby obeying the requirements of the distribution rule' (1968: 355).

Although answerers are expected to speak first, it is callers who are expected to provide the first topic. Answerers, after all, do not normally know who is making the call, whereas callers can usually identify answerers and answerers will assume that callers have initiated a call in order to raise a topic – hence the embarrassment we feel when somebody we have neglected to call calls us instead. Here we may convert ourselves from answerers to hypothetical callers by using some formula like: 'Oh, I'd been trying to reach you.' Having reallocated our roles, we are now free to introduce the first topic.

On examining his material further, Schegloff discovered only one case (out of 500) which did not fit the rule: answerer speaks first. He concluded that the person who responds to a telephone bell is not really answering a *question*, but responding to a *summons*. A summons is any attention-getting device (a telephone bell, a term of address – John? – or a gesture, like a tap on the shoulder or raising your hand). A summons tends to produce answers. Schegloff suggests that summons–answer

(SA) sequences have the following features which they share with a number of other linked turns (e.g. questions–answers, greetings) classed as *adjacency pairs*:

1   *Non-terminality* They are preambles to some further activity; they cannot properly stand as final exchanges. Consequently, the summoner is obliged to talk again when the summoned completes the SA sequence.
2   *Conditional relevance* Further interaction is conditional upon the successful completion of the SA sequence.
3   *Obligation to answer* Answers to a summons have the character of questions (e.g. 'What?', 'Yes', 'Hello'). This means that, as in question–answer (QA) sequences, the summoner must produce the answer to the question (s)he has elicited. Furthermore, the person who has asked the question is obliged to listen to the answer (s)he has obligated the other to produce. Each subsequent nod or 'uh huh' recommits the speaker to attend to the utterances that follows. Through this 'chaining' of questions and answers: 'provision is made by an SA sequence not only for the coordinated entry in a conversation but also for its continued orderliness'. (1968: 378–9)

Schegloff was now able to explain his deviant case as follows: summons (phone rings) – no answer; further summons (caller says 'Hello'). The normal form of a phone call is: summons (phone rings) – answer (recipient says 'Hello'). In the deviant case, the absence of an answer is treated as the absence of a reply to a summons. So the caller's use of 'Hello' replaces the summons of the telephone bell. The failure of the summoned person to speak first is heard as an uncompleted SA sequence. Consequently, the caller's speaking first makes sense within the 'conditional relevance' of SA sequences.

The power of these observations is suggested by two examples. The first is mentioned by Cuff and Payne: 'The recipient of a summons feels impelled to answer. (We note that in Northern Ireland, persons still open the door and get shot – despite their knowledge that such things happen.)' (1979: 151).

The second example arises in Schegloff's discussion of a child's utterance: 'You know what, Mommy?' (first discussed by Sacks, 1974). The child's question establishes an SA sequence, where a proper answer to the summons (Mommy) is 'What?' This allows the child to say what it wanted to at the start, but as an obligation (because questions must produce answers). Consequently, this utterance is a powerful way in which children enter into conversations despite their usually restricted rights to speak.

EXERCISE 9.2

Examine Extracts 9.6 and 9.7 below (drawn from Atkinson and Drew, 1979: 52, and discussed in Heritage, 1984: 248–9).

Extract 9.6

```
1   A:    Is there something bothering you or not?
2         (1.0)
3   A:    Yes or no
4         (1.5)
5   A:    Eh?
6   B:    No.
```

Extract 9.7

```
1   Ch:   Have to cut the:se Mummy.
2         (1.3)
3   Ch:   Won't we Mummy
4         (1.5)
5   Ch:   Won't we
6   M:    Yes
```

1 Why does Heritage argue that these extracts demonstrate that 'questioners attend to the fact that their questions are framed within normative expectations which have sequential implications' (1984: 249)? Use the concept of 'adjacency pairs' in your answer.
2 What are the consequences of the child (in Extract 9.5) naming the person to whom the child's utterance is addressed? Why might children often engage in such naming? Use the concept of 'summons–answer'.

As Heritage points out, this should not lead us to an over-mechanical view of conversation: 'conversation is not an endless series of interlocking adjacency pairs in which sharply constrained options confront the next speaker' (1984: 261).

Instead, the phenomenon of adjacency works according to two non-mechanistic assumptions:

1 An assumption that an utterance which is placed immediately after another one is to be understood as produced in response to or in relation to the preceding utterance.
2 This means that, if a speaker wishes some contribution to be heard as *unrelated* to an immediately prior utterance, they must do something special to lift Assumption 1 – for instance, by the use of a prefix (like 'by the way') designed to show that what follows is unrelated to the immediately prior turn at talk.

9.4.4 Institutional talk

Contrary to some critics (e.g. Goffman, 1981: 16–17), who accuse conversation analysts of depicting a mechanical system, CA takes very seriously the contexts of interaction. For instance, in the classic statement of CA, it is noted very early on that 'conversation is always "situated" – it always comes out of, and is part of, some real sets of circumstances of its participants' (Sacks et al., 1974: 699).

However, although such matters as place, time and the identities of the participants are undoubtedly relevant to speakers, we are reminded that we must be cautious about how we invoke them: 'it is undesirable to have to know or characterize such situations for particular conversations in order to investigate them' (1974: 699).

Two decades later, this position was clearly laid out by Maynard and Clayman:

> Conversation analysts ... (are) concerned that using terms such as 'doctor's office', 'courtroom', 'police department', 'school room', and the like, to characterise settings ... can obscure much of what occurs within those settings ... For this reason, conversation analysts rarely rely on ethnographic data and instead examine if and how interactants themselves reveal an orientation to institutional or other contexts. (1991: 406–7)

As already noted, talk is a feature of both 'formal' and 'informal' interactions, ranging from a courtroom to a casual 'chat'. In a courtroom, for instance, who can speak when is usually clearly defined and, unlike casual chatter, one can be ruled to be speaking 'out of order' and even held to be 'in contempt of court'.

However, it is dangerous to assume that just because talk is occurring in some 'formal' setting, it necessarily has a different structure to ordinary conversation. As we all know, people still chatter in the course of doing their jobs and some formal move may be needed for the talk to take on a formal (or institutional) character, for instance by the chair of a meeting calling the meeting to order.

In any event, as Sacks et al. (1974) suggest, ordinary conversation always provides a baseline from which any such departures are organised and recognised. This means that, in the study of institutional talk, we need carefully to examine how the structures of ordinary conversation 'become specialised, simplified, reduced, or otherwise structurally adapted for institutional purposes' (Maynard and Clayman, 1991: 407).

I will use research on the organisation of TV news interviews as an example before attempting a brief summary of what is known so far about institutional talk.

CASE STUDY
TV News Interviews

Clayman (1992) characterises TV news interviewing as a site for much caution given that news interviewers are supposed to be neutral or objective. How is this achieved?

When interviewers (IVs) come onto relatively controversial opinion statements, they distance themselves, creating what Clayman calls a different 'footing'. This is seen in Extract 9.8 below.

Extract 9.8 [Clayman 5] (Meet the Press 12/8/85)

```
1   IV:   Senator, (0.5) uh: President Reagan's elected thirteen months ago: an enormous
2         landslide.
3         (0.8)
4   IV:   It is s::aid that his programs are in trouble
```

In lines 1–2, a footing is constructed whereby IV is the author of a factual statement. However, at line 4, the footing shifts to what 'it is said' – hence, here IV is no longer the author and the item is marked as possibly 'controversial'.

Footing shifts are also *renewed* during specific 'controversial' words and IVs avoid affiliating with or disaffiliating from the statements they report. They also may comment on the authoritateveness of the source of an assertion or comment on the range of persons associated with it.

However, the achievement of 'neutrality' is a locally accomplished and co-operative matter. Thus interviewees (IEs) 'ordinarily refrain from treating the focal assertion as expressing the IV's personal opinion' (1992: 180). For instance, they do this by attributing the assertion to the same third party.

As Clayman remarks, this is unlike ordinary conversation, where it seems unlikely that speakers are expected to be neutral. As he says, minimal responses to such things as invitations or advice are *not* usually taken as evidence of the recipient's neutrality but are hearable as constituting actual or possible rejection (as we saw in Extract 9.1).

Like Clayman, Greatbatch (1992) notes the specific ways in which participants produce their talk as 'news interview' talk. He shows how the maintenance of IRs' neutrality ties in with the mutual production of the talk as aimed at an overhearing *audience*. Both parties maintain a situation in which it is not problematic that IEs properly limit themselves to responses to IR questions, while IRs:

- confine themselves to asking questions
- avoid a range of responsive activities which would make them a report-recipient rather than just a report-elicitor (e.g. acknowledgment tokens like mmm hm, uh huh, yes and news-receipt objects like oh, really, did you). (1992: 269-270)

In this context, 'neutrality' is not the only feature which contrasts with talk in other settings. Greatbatch shows that 'disagreements' have features specific to news interview talk. In ordinary conversation, 'whereas agreements are normally performed directly and with a minimum of delay, disagreements are commonly accomplished in mitigated forms and delayed from early positioning within turns and/or sequences' (1992: 273). This suggests, as we saw in Section 9.1, that agreements, like acceptance of invitations or advice, are marked as preferred objects.

Greatbatch shows how disagreements arise in the following two ways in multi-party news interviews. First, following a question repeated to the second IE, they can disagree immediately with the opinion of the first IE. As Greatbatch notes, however, this disagreement is *mitigated* since it is *mediated* by the IR's question. As Greatbatch suggests:

> The structure of turn taking in news interviews ... means that disagreements between IEs are ordinarily elicited by and addressed to a third party, the IR, with whom neither party disagrees. Disagreements which are produced in this manner are not systematically mitigated or forestalled by the use of the preference features that are associated with disagreement in conversation. (1992: 279–80)

(Continued)

(Continued)

Second, however, IEs may disagree in other turn positions, for instance following a co-interviewee's turn or during such a turn. This is seen in Extract 9.9.

Extract 9.9 [Greatbatch (12)]

```
1   IE1:   the government advertising campaign is h highly irresponsible. h It's being
2          given [under huge
3   IE2:        [Utter rubbish
```

Note how this extract departs from the conversational rules of 'preference organisation' (which, as we have seen, mark disagreements as dispreferred and hence delayed objects). It also seems to clash with the normal production of a news interview format (because they are not produced as an answer to an IR's question). However, Greatbatch argues, such disagreements display an underlying adherence to the news interview format. Namely:

- IE2 can still be heard as responding to the question that produced IE1's answer.
- IE2 directs his answer to the IR *not* to IE1 and this is quite different from ordinary conversation where the person being disagreed with is also the addressee of the disagreement – such disagreements are routinely followed (data not shown here) by IR intervening to manage an exit from the disagreement without requiring them to depart from their institutional roles as IEs but not, for instance, combatants, mutual insulters, etc.

Greatbatch summarises his findings as follows:

1 In news interviews, many of the features of preference organisation are rendered redundant, replaced by the interview turn-taking system.
2 Within news interviews, 'the structure of turn taking and its associated expectancies provide simultaneously for the *escalation and limitation* of overt disagreement' (1992: 299, my emphasis). As Greatbatch suggests, this may explain why panel interviews are so common and assume to produce 'lively' broadcasting.

Basic features of institutional talk

Drew and Heritage (1992: 22–5) distinguish some dimensions according to which we can analyse institutional talk including TV news interviews:

- It is usually goal oriented in institutionally relevant ways; thus people design their conduct to meet various institutional tasks or functions, e.g. emergency calls to the police need to be rapidly but accurately accomplished (Zimmerman, 1992); alternatively, the goals of interactions can be ill-defined, creating a need for the participants to fashion a sense of what the interaction will be about (Peräkylä and Silverman, 1991; Heritage and Sefi, 1992).

- It is usually shaped by certain constraints, e.g. what can be done in a court of law or news interview; however, in other situations, like counselling or doctor–patient interaction, participants may negotiate or ignore such constraints.
- It is associated with particular ways of reasoning or inference-making, e.g. meaning of not giving response tokens in news interviews; hearing a charge in health–visitor–mother (Heritage and Sefi, 1992) or doctor–mother (Silverman, 1987: Ch.10) interactions.

EXERCISE 9.3

Below is an extract from an HIV-test counselling interview. Read it through carefully in terms of the transcriptions set out in the Appendix.

Extract 9.10 [Excerpt no.: SS/2/16: DG]

```
 1   C:   Okay. (0.7) It may sou:nd (0.5) perhaps a dumb question but if you did
 2        have HIV how: might you have got it.
 3        (1.0)
 4   P:   I'm sorry?
 5   C:   If you did have HIV how might you have gotten it.
 6   P:   How might I have er gotten it.
 7   C:   Mm=
 8   P:   =er: Through gay se:x.
 9   C:   Okay:.
10        (0.5)
11   C:   [Uh:m:
12   P:   [How I- exactly how I don't know:, (0.5) uh::: (3.0) I am (.) really not sure.
13        (.)
14   C:   Okay. .hhh When you say through gay sex I mean how long have you
15        bee:n (0.4) having relationships with other guys for.
16   P:   Okay: er:::: (1.0) s-well (0.3) since I was a little kid.=As long as I c(h)an
17        reme(h)mbe(h)r. .hhhh er::: (1.5) Bu:t (0.4) before I got my jo:b I: (0.3)
18        started seeing someone, (0.4) a:nd it was the only relationship for two
19        and half years.
20   C:   Mm hm
21   P:   And might add a stormy relationship so: (0.2) I was not (.) the faithful
22        lover.
23        (.) The entire two and a half year:s.
24   C:   Both of you [were unfaithful or you weren't.
```

```
25   P:   [er::
26   P:   I: (0.6) I was no:t. I'm sure he wa:s (0.5) er::: (0.2) I mean we had several
27        periods of falling ou:t. (0.6) er::
28        (0.6)
29   C:   Mm hm
30        (1.0)
```

- List the devices from ordinary conversation that C and P use to monitor each other's talk.
- In what ways do C and P produce their talk as 'institutional'?

The issue of context

As Drew and Heritage have pointed out, while one can do 'institutional work' on a home telephone, not everything said at work is specifically 'institutional':

> Thus the institutionality of an interaction is not determined by its setting. Rather, interaction is institutional insofar as participants' institutional or professional identities are somehow made relevant to the work activities in which they are engaged. (1992: 3–4)

The question that then arises is how we demonstrate what is 'relevant'. Schegloff (1992a) has suggested that this is a basic methodological issue. It causes two problems which he calls 'relevance' and 'procedural consequentiality'. These two problems are set out below:

1 *Relevance*: this is the problem of 'showing from the details of the talk or other conduct in the materials that we are analyzing that those aspects of the scene are what the parties are oriented to' (Schegloff, 1992a: 110). The problem arises because, as we saw in Chapter 5, Sacks reveals how people can describe themselves and others in multiple ways. This problem, Schegloff insists, is simply disregarded in social science accounts which rely on statistical correlations to 'demonstrate' the relevance of some such description. Instead, we need to demonstrate that participants are currently oriented to such descriptions.

2 *Procedural consequentiality*: a demonstration that our descriptions of persons and settings are currently relevant for participants is not enough. We must also consider:

> How does the fact that the talk is being conducted in some setting (e.g. 'the hospital') issue in any consequence for the shape, form, trajectory, content, or character of the interaction that the parties conduct? And what is the mechanism by

which the context-so-understood has determinate consequences for the talk? (1992a: 111)

Schegloff gives two examples relevant to such 'procedural consequentiality'. First, he looks at how a particular **laboratory study** sought to demonstrate something about how people 'repair' mistakes in talk. He shows that, in this study, only the subject was allowed to talk. Hence many features which arise in whether such repairs should be done by self or other (given that there is a preference for self-repair) were unavailable. Thus it will not do to characterise the context as a 'laboratory setting' because other features (only one person talking) can be shown to have more procedural consequentiality.

Schegloff's second example is taken from an interview between George Bush and Dan Rather in the 1988 US election campaign. The interview became famous because of the apparent 'row' or confrontation between the two men. Schegloff shows that such features were noticeable because Bush refused to co-operate in producing a central feature of 'interviews': that is, that they consist of question–answer sequences where one party asks the questions and the other holds off speaking until a recognisable question has been posed (Silverman, 1973).

The implication is that we cannot describe what went on as occurring in the context of an 'interview'. Instead, interactions only become (and cease to be) 'interviews' through the co-operative activity of the participants. As Schegloff shows, this may make some of the claims relating gender to interruption (Zimmerman and West, 1975) somewhat premature.

These examples show that the issue of determining context is not a once-and-for-all affair because parties have to continue to work at co-producing any context. Equally, we cannot explain people's behaviour as a simple 'response' to some context when that context is actively constructed (and reconstructed).

This means that we should not assume that what we find in talk is necessarily a feature of the institutional setting or other social structural element that our intuitions tell us is relevant. Since 'not everything said in some context … is relevantly oriented to that context' (Schegloff, 1991: 62), we must not risk characterising a conversational structure possibly found across a range of contexts as institutionally specific.

This point is made elegantly in the Editor's Introduction to a collection of studies of 'institutional talk':

CA researchers cannot take 'context' for granted nor may they treat it as determined in advance and independent of the participants own activities. Instead, 'context' and identity have to be treated as inherently locally produced, incrementally developed and, by extension, as transformable at any moment. Given these constraints, analysts who wish to depict the distinctively 'institutional' character of some stretch of talk cannot be satisfied with showing that institutional talk exhibits aggregates and/or distributions of actions that are distinctive from ordinary conversation. They must rather demonstrate that the participants constructed their conduct over its course − turn by responsive turn − so as progressively to constitute … the occasion of their talk, together with their own social roles in it, as having some distinctively institutional character. (Drew and Heritage, 1992: 21)

However, this does *not* mean that such work treats institutional talk as a closed system cut off from the wider society. By contrast, without making any prior assumptions about 'context', these studies are able to examine how members themselves invoke a particular context for their talk. As we have seen, Clayman and Greatbatch show how TV news interviewers produce their talk as 'neutral' or 'objective', thereby displaying their attention to an overhearing audience's presumed expectations.

Elsewhere, I have argued (Silverman, 1997: 34–5) for the value of respecting CA's assertion that one's initial move should be to give close attention to how participants locally produce contexts for their interaction. By beginning with this question of 'how', we can then fruitfully move on to 'why' questions about the institutional and cultural constraints to which the parties demonstrably defer. Such constraints reveal the functions of apparently irrational practices and help us to understand the possibilities and limits of attempts at social reform.

> TIP
> The issue of context is crucial for qualitative social research. Quantitative research-ers establish a statistical version of context and seem to assume that, if one variable correlates with another, that is sufficient context. Some qualitative researchers implicitly go along with this position by assuming that some context is self-evident in what people do (see Kitzinger's critique of the use of 'gender' as a self-evident context, discussed in Section 7.3).
>
>   When you analyse data, try to be attentive to how the participants together pro-duce some context for their actions. Do not make assumptions about contextual factors. For a good debate on these issues see Holstein and Gubrium (2004).

9.4.5 Doing CA

Despite the battery of concepts found in this chapter, doing CA is not an impossibly difficult activity. As the founder of CA, Harvey Sacks once pointed out that in doing CA we are only reminding ourselves about things we already know. Sacks remarks:

> I take it that lots of the results I offer, people can see for themselves. And they needn't be afraid to. And they needn't figure that the results are wrong because they can see them … As if we found a new plant. It may have been a plant in your garden, but now you see its different than something else. And you can look at it to see how it's different, and whether it's different in the way that somebody has said. (1992, I: 488)

However, the way in which CA obtains its results is rather different from how we might intuitively try to analyse talk. Peräkylä (2004b: 170–1) depicts the careful inductive method used in CA in terms of the following stages:

- Explore your data in an 'unmotivated' way (without any initial **hypotheses**).
- Identify some phenomenon worthy of further study.
- Establish how this phenomenon occurs in varying ways in your data.
- Try to account for this variation.

Given the extent to which CA is counter-intuitive in a common-sense world in which actions are usually understood psychologically rather than interactionally, it may be helpful, therefore, if I conclude this section by offering a crude set of pre-scriptions about how to do CA. These are set out in Tables 9.2 and 9.3.

TABLE 9.2 How to do CA

1 Always try to identify sequences of related talk
2 Try to examine how speakers take on certain roles or identities through their talk (e.g. questioner–answerer or client–professional)
3 Look for particular outcomes in the talk (e.g. a request for clarification, a repair, laughter) and work backwards to trace the trajectory through which a particular outcome was produced

TABLE 9.3 Common errors to avoid when doing CA

1 Explaining a turn at talk by reference to the speaker's intentions
2 Explaining a turn at talk by reference to a speaker's role or status (e.g. as a doctor or as a man or woman)
3 Trying to make sense of a single line of transcript or utterance in isolation from the surrounding talk

If we follow these rules, as Sacks suggests, the analysis of conversations does not require exceptional skills. As he puts it, all we need to do is to 'begin with some observations, then find the problem for which these observations could serve as … the solution' (1992, II: xlviii).

TIP
Doing CA involves putting on one side both our common-sense knowledge (of what speakers may mean) and social science concepts like 'culture':

The task is to avoid bringing to the analysis what, as cultural members, we already know and instead to discover the taken-for-granted practices of the

(Continued)

(Continued)

> culture *in the interaction itself*. As a conversation analyst I believe that if cultural norms can be shown to be interactionally relevant in any given interaction, then their existence elsewhere (in a speaker's psychological make-up, or in the broader society) is rendered beside the point so far as the data analysis is concerned; and if they *cannot* be shown to be interactionally relevant, then it is not analytically useful to invoke them. (Kitzinger, 2006: 75)

LINKS

Conversation analysis.net
Ethnomethodology and conversation analysis newsletter 'Ethno/CA News'

Emanuel A. Schegloff's transcription training module:
www.sscnet.ucla.edu/soc/faculty/schegloff/TranscriptionProject/

Loughborough University CA site:
www-staff.lboro.ac.uk/~ssca1/sitemenu.htm

9.5 DISCOURSE ANALYSIS

DA describes a heterogeneous range of social science research based on the analysis of interviews and texts as well as recorded talk. It shares with CA a common intellectual ancestor in the Oxford philosopher J.L. Austin. In his book *How To Do Things with Words*, Austin (1962) showed that many utterances do not simply describe a state of affairs but perform an action. For instance:

'Help'
'I thee wed'

In both cases, the speakers are not heard to describe the state of their mind nor to picture reality but to perform some action ('asking for help', 'getting married'). Uttering such 'performatives', as Austin calls them, commits speakers to their consequences. For instance, when people come to give you help and find nothing amiss, it is no defence to say that you were not calling for assistance but simply singing a song. Alternatively, Austin points out, you will not escape a charge of bigamy by saying that you had all kinds of mental reservations when you uttered 'I thee wed' for the second time.

Like nearly all linguistic philosophers, Austin worked with *invented* examples, relying on his native intuition. Social scientists prefer to understand the complexities of naturally occurring talk. What they take from Austin is his concern with the activities performed in talk.

9.5.1 What is Discourse Analysis?

At first sight, compared with CA, DA looks like conventional social science. This arises for two reasons:

1 DA is concerned with a range of topics which are often much closer to conventional social science concerns (e.g. gender relations, social control) than is the case in CA.

> Take gender inequalities for example. [DA] Studies have considered both the way in which such inequalities are constructed, made factual, and justified in talk, and they have also considered the resources ('interpretative repertoires', identities, category systems) that are used to manufacture coherent and persuasive justifications that work to sustain those inequalities. (Potter, 1997: 148)

2 Unlike CA, DA can be quite catholic about what kind of data are acceptable. So, although some DA studies use transcripts of talk from everyday or institutional settings, others are based on transcripts of open-ended interviews, or on documents of some kind. Sometimes these different materials are even combined together in the same study (Potter: 1997, 147). However, not all DA researchers are entirely happy with using non-naturally occurring data such as interviews (see Potter, 1996: 134–5).

These two features mean that DA is quite heterogeneous and it is, therefore, difficult to arrive at a clear definition of it. Here is one authoritative version:

> DA has an analytic commitment to studying discourse as *texts and talk in social practices* … the focus is … on language as … the medium for interaction; analysis of discourse becomes, then, analysis of what people do. One theme that is particularly emphasised here is the rhetorical or argumentative organisation of talk and texts; claims and versions are constructed to undermine alternatives. (Potter, 2004: 203, emphasis in original)

Potter suggests that this Austinian concern with the rhetorical organisation of talk and texts has given DA three unifying assumptions:

1 *Anti-realism*: DA is resolutely against the assumption that we can treat accounts as true or false descriptions of 'reality'. As Potter puts it: 'DA emphasises the way versions of the world, of society, events, and inner psychological worlds are produced in discourse.'

2 *Constructionism*: DA is concerned with 'participants' constructions and how they are accomplished and undermined' (see the tip that follows).

3 *Reflexivity*: DA considers 'the way a text such as this is a version, selectively working up coherence and incoherence, telling historical stories, presenting and, indeed, constituting an objective, out-there reality'. (Potter, 2004: 202)

TIP

Discourse analysis is based on the constructionist model that we have encountered in earlier chapters of this book. As Potter and Hepburn explain:

Discursive constructionism works with two senses of construction. On the one hand, discourse is construct*ed* in the sense that it is assembled from a range of different resources with different degrees of structural organization. Most fundamentally these are words and grammatical structures, but also broader elements such as categories, metaphors, idioms, rhetorical commonplaces and interpretative repertoires. For example, how is a description manufactured in a way that presents something that has been done as orderly and unproblematic? On the other hand, discourse is construct*ive* in the sense that these assemblages of words, repertoires and so on put together and stabilize versions of the world, of actions and events, of mental life and furniture. For example, how does one party in a relationship counselling session construct a version that presents the breakdown of a long term relationship as primarily the responsibility of the other party, who might be the one most in need of counselling and under most pressure to change? (2008: 277)

To put some meat on these bare bones, the following case study may be helpful.

CASE STUDY
Calls to a Child Protection Hotline

Alexa Hepburn and Jonathan Potter describe the data they gathered of calls reporting cases of abuse to a hotline set up by the UK child welfare charity. Among the 50 calls recorded, the following began in this way:

Extract 9.11 [Hepburn and Potter, 2004: 189]

(CPO = child protection officer)

1 CPO: Hello NSPCC Helpline can I help you?
2 Caller: Good afternoon >I wonder if you
3   could<

```
4   CPO:     Yes [ certainly, ]
5   Caller:  [I'm concerned] about
6            [a- ] about a child that lives
7   CPO:     [Yeh]
8   Caller:  next door to me.
9   CPO:     Ri:ght, could- before you go on can I
10           ((NPO reads ethics script))
```

Hepburn and Potter became interested in the way in which callers began with a reference to being 'concerned' (as in line 5 above). They started to note the functions served by such 'concern constructions' in 'unpacking' a complaint:

- it works as a pre-sequence to the complaint itself.
- it orients to asymmetries in the interaction – it treats the actionable status of what is to be reported as not yet established, allowing it to be established in the interaction with the CPO. The other side of this coin is that it heads off a problem that might arise with direct opening announcements ('a child next door has been sexually abused'), which is that the next turn from the CPO would likely be about the basis of that knowledge.
- 'concerns constructions' display the caller's stance to the abuse – it is serious, critical, and, well, concerned. They are managing their own stake as reporters.
- such constructions allow the CPOs to treat abuse claims as serious without having to assume that they are true, accurate or actionable. The concern opening can evolve into a discussion of specific things in the world – injuries, times, family relationships – or into a discussion of, broadly, the psychology of the caller – their heightened anxieties, confusions or misperceptions. (2004: 189)

Among the 20 calls in which callers did not use such constructions, several were from institutional callers who, presumably, did not need to attend to asymmetries in the interaction. In the other cases, the CPOs would themselves use the language of 'concerns' (2004: 190–2).

I present below three **concepts** used in DA research:

- interpretive repertoires
- stake
- scripts.

This is not meant to be an exhaustive list. In particular it leaves out DA work concerned with rhetoric and ideology (e.g. Billig, 1991, 1995; Wetherell and Potter, 1992) and with issues relating to the construction of scientific texts (e.g. Ashmore, 1989; Potter, 1996b).

9.5.2 Interpretive repertoires

Early DA studies attempted to identify broad 'discourses' which participants use to define their identities and moral status. As Potter puts it:

Interpretive repertoires are systematically related sets of terms that are often used with stylistic and grammatical coherence and often organized around one or more central metaphors. (1996a: 131)

Two examples will indicate how this concept has been used.

Science as a repertoire

Nigel Gilbert and Mike Mulkay were concerned with scientists' accounts of scientific practice. As they point out (Gilbert and Mulkay, 1983), one way of hearing what scientists say is as hard data which bear on debates in the philosophy of science about the character of scientific practice. It is then tempting to treat such accounts as 'inside' evidence ('from the horse's mouth', as it were) about whether scientists are actually influenced by 'paradigms' and community affiliations more than by sober attempts to refute possible explanations as in Popper's **critical rationalism** (see Section 11.1.4).

Confusingly, Gilbert and Mulkay's scientists used both quasi-Kuhnian and quasi-Popperian explanations of scientific practice. Understandably, however, they were much keener to invoke the Popperian ('sober refutation') account of how they worked and the Kuhnian ('community context') account of how certain other scientists worked.

Were these accounts to be treated as a direct insight into how scientists do their work or how they experience things in the laboratory? Not at all, given the anti-realist posture of DA. Instead, this interview data gave Gilbert and Mulkay access to the *vocabularies* that scientists use. These vocabularies were located in two very different **interpretative repertoires**:

- a *contingent* repertoire, in which scientists used a political vocabulary of 'influence' and 'interest' to talk about each other's institutional affiliations and ability or inability to get big research contracts, etc.
- an *empiricist* repertoire, in which scientific activity was described as a response to data 'out there' in 'nature'.

Neither repertoire conveyed the 'true' sense of science – for DA, there is no more an essential form of scientific practice than there is a single reality standing behind 'atrocity stories' told by mothers of handicapped children (see Section 6.8). Everything is situated in particular contexts. So scientists, Gilbert and Mulkay note, are much more likely to use a 'contingent' repertoire in a discussion at a bar than in a scientific paper.

In this way, the research question ceases to be 'What is science?' and becomes 'How is a particular scientific discourse invoked? When is it invoked? How does it stand in relation to other discourses?'

Gilbert and Mulkay's focus on interpretative repertoires leads us to see that 'science', like other social institutions, is a **hyphenated phenomenon** which takes on different meanings in different contexts (see Section 1.6).

Motherhood as a repertoire

As just noted, it is not only sober institutions like 'science' which dissolve into a set of repertoires. The same process can be seen when we look at how women invoke the identity of 'motherhood'. My example of this will be drawn from a clinic for young diabetics (Silverman, 1987: Ch. 10).

Extract 9.12 involves a consultation between a mother of a diabetic child aged 16 and her paediatrician. It takes place when her daughter is in another room having her blood taken and the mother has asked specially if she can see the doctor. This extract comes a little way into the consultation.

Extract 9.12

(D = Doctor; M = Mother of June, aged 16)

1 M: She's going through a very languid stage ( ) she won't do anything unless you push her
2 D: so you're finding you're having to push her quite a lot?
3 M: mm no well I don't (.) I just leave her now

At line 3, there is evidence to suggest that M hears the doctor's question as a charge against her parenting. Notice how she withdraws from her initial depiction about 'pushing' her daughter when the doctor, through repeating it, makes it accountable. One way to look at what is happening here, then, is as a *charge–rebuttal* sequence.

Now why would she want to withdraw from her depiction of her daughter and herself in line 1 of this extract? It seems that M hears D's question as depicting her as potentially a 'nagging' mother (it is interesting that only women can nag!). So, when the doctor topicalises 'pushing', the mother withdraws into an account which suggests that she respects her daughter's autonomy.

Shortly after, June's mother produces another worry about how her daughter is coping with her diabetes. This time her concern is her daughter's diet:

Extract 9.13

1 M: I don't think she's really sticking to her diet (.) I don't know the effects this will have on
2   her (.) it's bound to alter her sugar if she's not got the right insulin isn't it? I mean
3   I know what she eats at home but [outside
4 D: [so there's no real consistency to her diet? It's sort [of
5 M: [no well I
6   keep it as consistent as I can at home

Now look at what the doctor says this time. Unlike Extract 9.12, he does not topicalise M's 'pushing' her child. Instead, he produces what M hears as a charge against her responsibility towards June (there 'is no real consistency to her diet'). In response, the mother now uses the very thing she denied earlier in order to rebut what she hears as the charge of 'irresponsibility' in what the doctor is saying.

This brings us to the issue of interpretive repertoires: in this case a repertoire of 'parental responsibility' and one of 'young adults' autonomy'. M is skilfully operating with two repertoires that apparently are quite contradictory. In purely logical terms, you cannot on the one hand say 'I watch everything my child does' and at the same time 'I leave my child to do anything she wants to do'. However, by using each repertoire when situationally appropriate, the mother is able to detect and rebut possible traps in the way the doctor is responding to what she is saying.

Consonant with DA's anti-realist and constructionist position, this naturally occurring material reveals that this mother is not *intrinsically* 'nagging' or 'irresponsible'. Instead, both depictions are *locally* available and *locally* resisted. Conversely, if we had interviewed mothers, the temptation would have been to search for idealised conceptions of their role.

EXERCISE 9.4

Extract 9.14

(D = doctor; M = mother)

1   D: It sounds as if generally you're having a difficult time
2   M: Her temper is vile
3   D: She with you and you with her
4   M: Yes. And her control of the diabetes is gone, her temper then takes control
5   of her

Using the analysis already given of Extracts 9.12 and 9.13, consider the following:

1   What *interpretative repertoires* do M and D use to organise their talk?
2   How is D's interpretation on line 3 of M's utterance on line 2 hearable as a charge?
3   How does M's utterance on line 4 respond to D's interpretation? Is it hearable as a rebuttal?
4   Can we learn anything from this extract about:

   a   M's attitude to her daughter?
   b   Cultural assumptions about motherhood?

The reader will note that the gain of this analysis is that, like many DA studies, it addresses a conventional social science topic (conceptions of gender and mother-hood). Moreover, it seems to have an immediate practical application. For instance, doctors were interested to learn about the double-binds present in their attention to the autonomy of their young patients. Likewise, parents' groups (largely mothers) of diabetic children found it very helpful to go through material of this kind. It brought out the way in which things they may feel personally guilty about in their relationships with their teenage children are not something that relates to their individual failings. Instead, such problems arise in our culture in the double-binds built into the parent–adolescent relationship.

Uses and Limitations of Interpretative Repertoires

Both studies identify the cultural resources that participants bring to institutional settings. At the same time, as we have seen, these resources are not treated as simple determinants of their behaviour but used locally and skilfully. As Potter puts it:

> these resources have a ... 'bespoke' flexibility, which allows them to be selectively drawn upon and reworked, according to the setting. (1996a: 131)

However, as Potter himself recognises, the concept of interpretive repertoires does present certain difficulties. Let me mention two:

1 Although the concept may help in understanding communication in well-defined settings like medicine or science, it is 'difficult to make clear and consistent judgments concerning the *boundaries* of particular repertoires outside constrained institutional settings' (1996a: 131).
2 Appealing to interpretative repertoires may fail to bring out more basic conversational rules to which participants are attending. Consequently, it lays itself open to the charge of basing its analysis upon taken-for-granted knowledge about the basic structures of talk (e.g. how charges or accusations are hearable by conversationalists). As Potter writes: '(a) problem is that the generality of the notion of a repertoire may obscure local interactional "business" that is being achieved by particular forms of discourse' (1996a: 131).

Because of these difficulties, Potter (1996a) argues that the concept of 'repertoire' is being replaced in DA by rather less broad-brush concepts. One such concept is 'stake'.

9.5.3 Stake

> How is a particular type of blaming achieved? How is a particular version of the world made to seem solid and unproblematic? How are social categories constructed and managed in practice? (Potter, 1996a: 131–2)

These kinds of questions can only be answered by different concepts which allowed a more fine-grained attention to conversational detail. The concept of 'stake' attempts to satisfy this need. 'Stake' is explained by Potter in this way:

> People treat each other as entities with desires motives, institutional allegiances and so on, as having a stake in their actions. Referencing stake is one principal way of discounting the significance of an action or reworking its nature. (2004: 210)

The case study below gives an example of the use of 'stake' in DA.

CASE STUDY
The Princess Di Interview

Princess Diana was interviewed by the British TV reporter Martin Bashir not long before her death. Part of the interview went as follows:

Extract 9.15 [adapted from Potter, 2011: 193–4]

1	Bashir:	Did you (.) allow your friends, >your close friends,<
2		to speak to Andrew Morton?
3	Princess:	Yes I did. Y[es, I did
4	Bashir:	[Why?
5	Princess:	I was (.) at the end of my tether (.)
6		I was (.) <u>desperate</u> (.)
7		>I think I was so fed up with being< (.)
8		seen as someone who was a ba:sket case (.)
9		because I am a very strong person (.)
10		and I <u>know</u> (.) that causes complications, (.)
11		in the system (.) that I live in.
12		(1.0) (smiles and purses lips)
13	Bashir:	How would a book change that.
14	Princess:	I dunno. ((raises eyebrows, looks away))
15		Maybe people have a better understanding (.)
16		maybe there's a lot of women out there
17		who <u>suffer</u> (.) on the same level
18		but in a different environment (.)
19		who are unable to: (.) stand up for themselves (.)
20		because (.) their self-esteem is (.) cut into two.
21		I dunno ((shakes head))

Potter focuses on Princess Diana's two 'I dunno's' (lines 14 and 21). Utterances like this, he says, work as 'uncertainty tokens' (words or expressions that people use to report states of uncertainty). So, by using 'I dunno', Princess Diana invites us to minimise her *stake* and *interest* in what she is saying. In this way, she discounts the significance of her actions or reworks their nature (Potter, 2011: 192–5).

Potter compares this case with an interview with Salman Rushdie. In the extract below, David Frost is asking about the fatwah – the religious death sentence on Rushdie.

Extract 9.16 [Potter, 2011: 196]

1	Frost:	And how could they cancel it now? Can they cancel it –
2		they say they can't.
3	Rushdie:	Yeah, but you know, they would, wouldn't they,
4		as somebody once said. The thing is, without going into the kind of arcana of
5		theology, there is no technical problem. The problem is not technical. The
6		problem is that they don't want to.

Potter draws our attention to Rushdie's comment 'they would, wouldn't they' (line 3). This treats Frost's suggestion that the fatwah cannot be cancelled as a claim which is motivated by special interests:

> The familiar phrase 'they would, wouldn't they' treats the Iranians' claim as something to be expected: it is the sort of thing that people with that background, those interests, that set of attitudes *would* say; and it formulates that predictability as shared knowledge. This extract illustrates the potential for invoking stake to discount claims. (Potter, 2011: 196)

The concept of '**script**', like that of 'stake', helps us to understand the ways in which participants attend to the normative character of their actions.

9.5.4 Scripts

As used in DA, 'script' refers to the ways in which participants construct events 'as "scripted", as instances of some general pattern, or as anomalies and exceptions' (Edwards, 1997: 144).

As Derek Edwards points out, the DA use of this concept is quite different from that found in cognitive psychology in which 'script' refers to a more or less fixed mental schema which people learn to associate with certain activities or settings (e.g. a 'restaurant script' involving a series of roles and props, see Edwards, 1997: 143).

By contrast, in DA, a *script* is a way of invoking the *routine* character of described events in order to imply that they are features of some (approved or disapproved) general pattern. Through this device, participants assemble descriptions that attend to matters of appropriateness, responsibility and blame and 'build a picture of what kind of person the actor is – that is, his or her personality, disposition or mental state' (Edwards, 1997: 144).

Extract 9.17 below shows how 'script' is used as a participant's device. It is an extract from a counselling session in which Mary and Jeff are talking to a counsellor about their marital problems.

Extract 9.17 [Edwards, 1997: 142, simplified transcription]

1   Mary: I went out Friday night (.) and Jeff was working (.) on call (.) and (.) um (2.2) the
2   place that I went to (.) like (.) <u>cl</u>osed at half past tw<u>e</u>lve and I got home about one
3   o'cl<u>ock</u>

Edwards draws attention to Mary's mention of what time the 'place' she went to closed. Her description attends to her earlier account of an argument with Jeff about the time that she had arrived home and the fact that she had met her ex-lover while out (data not shown).

Edwards argues that Mary's simple narrative (the 'place' '<u>cl</u>osed at half past tw<u>e</u>lve and I got home about one o'cl<u>ock</u>') presents what happened as merely a routine set of events (a 'script') in which nothing extraordinary or morally reprehensible happened. As Edwards puts it, through scripting what happened, Mary diverts attention from other kinds of interpretations, for instance that:

> she was enjoying herself and did not *want* to come home, let alone that she was enjoying the attentions of men, or even of the man with whom she had had the affair. Mary's getting home at one o'clock (a.m.) is provided as part of a narrative sequence of going somewhere that happened to close at 12.30. (1997: 142–3)

Mary also says: 'I went out Friday night (.) and Jeff was working'. Note how this part of Mary's description allows us to add to Edwards's account. In this passage,

Mary chooses to account for the fact that she went out without Jeff. We are now to hear her evening out not as some wilful action of a woman ignoring her partner but as something that was unavoidable ('scripted') and, therefore, morally acceptable. The following case study shows how a man attends to such issues of moral acceptability.

CASE STUDY
Telling a Story about Sex

In my own data, taken from a counselling session about a possible HIV test, a male client who had not accompanied his girlfriend on holiday also attended to the matter of his (and her) accountability. I will use Edwards's concept of *script* to analyse one extract from this data (a fuller discussion, addressed in terms of other, related concepts is to be found in Silverman, 1997: 78–84).

Extract 9.18 below is at the very beginning of a pre-test counselling interview held at the sexually transmitted disease department of a hospital in a provincial British city. When asked by the counsellor (C) about why he wants an HIV test, this male patient (P) tells a story about what happened on his girlfriend's holiday (I have disguised the country concerned):

Extract 9.18 [Silverman, 1997: 78–9]

```
 1   C:   righty ho (0.2) could you tell us (.) why you've come for an HIV test today=
 2   P:   =well basically (.) because I'm: worried that I might have AIDS (0.2) er: (0.2)
 3        when my girlfriend (.) like she was on holiday in: (.) [X] (0.2) in April with her
 4        friend
 5   C:   mm hm
 6   P:   I didn't go because I was busy (1.0) er:: (0.6) she came back but she was away
 7        for three weeks she came back (0.6) er: April (  ) May (.) April (.) May June July
 8        August September October November (0.8) and it's now November she's just
 9        told me (.) that she had sex with (.) a [Xian] when she was out there well not
10        actually had sex with but this she said that this guy (0.2) this is what she told me
11        this guy had (.) forced herself (.) hisself upon her you know (0.6) er::
```

As with Edwards's extract, the matter of who goes away from home with whom is made accountable here. 'With her friend' (line 4) tells us that his 'girlfriend' had not gone away on her own, where going away on your own *may* be heard as implying a problem with a relationship. 'Her friend' does not tell us the gender of the 'friend'. However, we know that, if that gender had been male, it would have massive implications for the story that is being told and, therefore, P would have been obliged to tell us. Given that he doesn't, we must assume that 'her friend' is 'female'. Moreover, we can also assume, for the same reason, that it is not a sexual relationship.

(Continued)

(Continued)

But P also leaves a question hanging about why he had not accompanied his girlfriend given that 'going on holiday together' can be heard as a script appropriate to the relationship girlfriend/boyfriend.

'I didn't go because I was busy' (line 6) attends to this question, Here P shows that he analyses these inferences in exactly this way. First, he underlines what we had implied in his original description: 'I didn't go'. Second, he shows that this 'not going' is accountable and provides its warrant: 'because I was busy'. Just as Mary accounts for her husband's absence because 'Jeff was working', so P makes accountable that he did not accompany his girlfriend on her holiday. In both cases, we have accounts which invoke the *routine* character of described events and, thereby, function to constitute the accounts as *scripts* which describe some morally acceptable 'business as usual'.

Further scriptlike elements in P's account can be seen in the way he begins his answer to C's question. Note how being 'worried' about 'AIDS' (line 2) is appropriate to the implied category 'patient' who, in C's words, has 'come for an HIV test today'. When produced as scripts, descriptions construct a profoundly *moral* universe of 'reasonable' activities conducted and perceived by 'reasonable' people. So, for instance, coming today for an HIV test is not only an 'appropriate' activity if you are 'worried', but also sensible and reasonable, serving to protect yourself (against further 'worry') and the community (because it shows you are aware of the dangers of receiving and transmitting the virus).

However, P's account also provides a description of events that may be heard in terms of another *script*. 'She was on holiday' (line 3) conjures up the category 'holidaymaker' which can be heard to imply innocent enjoyment but may also be associated with other activities (e.g. holiday 'romances', holiday 'flings'). Because we know that holidays may be a time when moral inhibitions may be temporarily lifted, the upcoming description of potentially 'promiscuous' behaviour is potentially downgraded or at least made comprehensible.

'She's just told me (.) that she had <u>sex</u> with (.) a [Xian] when she was out there' (line 9) consists of a series of highly implicative descriptions of activities. Having 'sex' with a third party implies 'being unfaithful'. Although the earlier description 'on holiday' (confirmed by the place-locater 'when she was out there') may make this description understandable, it may not make it excusable. As we shall see, P engages in considerable interpretive work to preserve the moral status of P's girlfriend in a way that does not threaten his own status as a 'reasonable' person.

'Well not actually had sex with' (lines 9–10): here the damaging description 'having sex (with a third party)' is immediately repaired by B. Thus we have to suspend the implied category 'unfaithful girlfriend'.

But this repaired description is ambiguous. For instance, are we to hear 'not actually sex' as a physical or social description of the activity?

'She said that this guy (0.2) this is what she told me this guy had (.) forced herself (.) hisself upon her you know' (lines 10–11). It is clear from his next utterance that P is attending to this ambiguity as something in need of further explication. If 'he forced … hisself upon her', then we are given a description which implies the categories rapist/victim where 'victim' implies the activity of not giving consent.

So P re-works his original category 'having sex', with its damaging implications, by positing the absence of consent and thus a withdrawal of the warrant of the charge 'unfaithful girlfriend' and a return to a description of the events as scripted.

However, there is a further nice feature embedded in P's description. It arises in its preface: 'she said that this guy (0.2) this is what she told me'. P's story of these events is thus doubly embedded (both in 'she said' and in 'this is what she told me'). How does 'this is what she told me' serve to repair 'she said'?

We can unpick the nature of this repair by recognising that when somebody offers an account the upshot of which puts them in an unfavourable light, we may suspect that they have organised their description in order to put themselves in a more favourable light. So, if P had simply reported what his 'girlfriend' had said about this incident, then, although he would be implying that he was a 'trusting partner', he could be seen as 'too trusting', that is as a dope.

Now we see that 'this is what she told me' makes him into an astute witness by drawing attention to the potential credibility problem about his girlfriend's account – just, as in Extract 9.14, Salman Rushdie's observation 'they would, wouldn't they' functions to minimise the credibility of a reported statement. However, note that, unlike this comment, P is *not* directly stating that his girlfriend is to be disbelieved. Rather her story is offered just as that – as her *story* without implying that P knows it to be true or false.

The beauty of P's repair into 'this is what she told me' is that it puts him in a favourable light (as an astute observer), while not making a direct charge against his girlfriend's veracity (an activity which would allow us to see him as a 'disloyal partner'). This allows a hearer of his story to believe or disbelieve his girlfriend's account and allows him to go along with either conclusion.

P's elegantly crafted story leaves it up to the hearer to decide which script best describes these 'events'. Is this the story of an unfaithful girlfriend or of someone who has been shamefully assaulted? However we decide, P fits into the script of a 'loyal partner' and so is in the clear.

EXERCISE 9.5

Lindsay Prior has studied the ways in which people who work in and use a cancer genetics clinic in the UK talk about the 'gene for cancer'. His first source of talk (Prior, 2007) relates to clinic consultations between cancer genetics specialists (CG) and patients of the cancer genetics service. The following talk was directed to a male patient at risk of colorectal cancer.

Extract 9.19 (Prior, 2007: 990)

```
237  CG3:   [So] the correct building block doesn't follow. So then, sort of, quality
238          control comes along and looks at this protein and says, 'you've made a
239          terrible mess up here' and it destroys it.
```

The second type of talk arises from exchanges between laboratory scientists (LS) and a social scientist concerning the identification of genetic mutations in the laboratory. In the following extract, LS is talking about a slide:

> **Extract 9.20 (Prior, 2007: 992)**
>
> 320 LS3: This one here which is 14. She [the image of the mutation in a patient's
> 321   DNA] is faint. The reason that she is faint is that she [the patient] is
> 322   dead, and we have extracted DNA from a paraffin block. So it's less high
> 323   quality. And she does work eventually if you change the PCR conditions
> 324   and things. And then she is beautiful. We do have to go back and do
> 325   her on her own. Always fails; [Mary]. [Mary] fails all the time.
> 326   We do them [the gels] in blocks of 30. And this I will have to do again
> 327   because I didn't run it long enough
>
> - Using the DA concepts of 'stake' and 'script' how can you analyse these two extracts? In what ways are they organised differently or similarly?
> - How far does it matter that these two extracts do not show any response by a hearer?

9.6 CONVERSATION ANALYSIS AND DISCOURSE ANALYSIS COMPARED

The difference between DA and CA is a matter for debate. Some DA researchers find CA's refusal to engage directly with cultural and political context disconcerting (see Wetherell, 1998). Equally, CA specialists question the validity of some DA researchers' appeals to their own sense of context (see Schegloff, 1997).

CA gains by mobilising information about the structures of ordinary conversation in the context of very detailed transcripts. Following CA, Edwards has called for a DA which draws from Sacks the assumption that 'no hearable level of detail that may not be significant, or treated as significant by conversational participants' (Edwards, 1995: 580).

At first glance, as Edwards implies, this seems to represent an accurate reading of Sacks's programme. However, as Schegloff points out, in practice, DA has not always been responsive to the relevance of all aspects of talk to the local production of sense. For instance, some DA researchers may treat particles like 'mm' and 'uh huh' as 'conversational "detritus" apparently lacking semantic content, and not contributing to the substance of what the discourse ends up having said' (Schegloff, 1982: 74).

For Schegloff, then, DA can ignore a basic aspect of CA by treating talk:

> as the product of a single speaker and a single mind; the conversation-analytic angle of inquiry does not let go of the fact that speech-exchange systems are involved, in which more and more than one co-participant is present and relevant to the talk, even when only one does the talking. (1982: 72)

However, DA-based research studies do provide important insights into institutional talk based on pressing sociological and practical concerns (like doctor–patient and teacher–pupil communication). Equally, like CA, it can be attentive to the sequential embeddedness of talk – as, for instance, in Extracts 9.12 and 9.13, when the mother's changes of tack are interpreted in terms of the doctor's glosses on what she has just said.

It is for the reader to judge whether any DA study is susceptible to Schegloff's criticisms. Certainly, there is some evidence in recent work (e.g. Potter, 2011) that at least some DA researchers pay considerable attention to the turn-by-turn organisation of talk. Moreover, we cannot assume that transcripts which do not record such details as length of pause are necessarily imperfect. There cannot be a *perfect* transcript of a tape recording. Everything depends upon what you are trying to do in the analysis, as well as upon practical considerations involving time and resources.

Table 9.4 presents a reasonably balanced account of the similarities and differences of CA and Potter's style of DA.

TABLE 9.4   DA and CA compared

- *Detail*: DA follows the CA assumption that any order of detail in talk and text is potentially consequential for interaction, and for that reason high-quality transcript are used in conjunction with audio or video recordings
- *Assumptions*: DA avoids trading on analysts' prior assumptions about ethnographic particulars (e.g. participants' status, the nature of the context, the goals of the participants), preferring to see these as things that are worked up, attended to and made relevant in interaction rather than being external determinants
- *Rhetoric*: whereas CA work is focused on sequential organisation, discursive psychology is also focused on rhetorical organisation – the way versions are put together to counter alternatives. Often an understanding of sequential organisation is a prerequisite for understanding rhetorical organisation
- *Cognition*: DA, like most CA, is anti-cognitivist. That is, it rejects the goal of explaining action by reference to underlying cognitive states or entities
- *Interviews*: much of the earlier work in DA was done using interviews (Billig, 1992; Wetherell and Potter, 1992). CA has largely rejected interviews as a research tool (although they have been treated as a topic of study – see Rapley, 2004, discussed in Chapter 6). This difference is less pronounced now as discourse researchers have started to accept some of the implications of the critique of interviews (e.g. in Widdicombe and Wooffitt, 1995), and there is an increasing focus on naturally occurring materials
- *Resources*: DA has had a focus on the resources drawn on in practices as well as the practices themselves. This is seen particularly in early work that studied interpretive repertoires (Potter and Wetherell, 1987). One of the issues at stake is how far such resources can be studied independently of the practices they are a part of. There is no easy resolution of this. A similar tension is apparent in the early Sacks's interest in membership categorisation analysis and the later emphasis on sequential analysis
- *Epistemology*: DA has been strongly influenced by work in the sociology of scientific knowledge, and has often adopted a methodologically relativist position. CA has tended to take a more robust view of science and knowledge

Source: adapted from Hepburn and Potter, 2004: 192–3 and Potter, 2011: 191–2

In my view, Hepburn and Potter point to more convergence than divergence between DA and CA. Above all, it is important that we do not end up in a pointless debate about whether a particular study is 'really' DA or CA! Indeed, in some cases, this distinction has more to do with whether the author pays their disciplinary dues to, respectively, psychology or sociology.

LINKS
DA online:
www.shu.ac.uk/daol

The Loughborough Discourse and Rhetoric Group website includes an up-to-date bibliography, information about methods and examples of transcription alongside sound and video files. Many articles can be downloaded directly.:
www.lboro.ac.uk/departments/ss/centres/darg/dargindex.htm

9.7 CONCLUSION

The last thing I want to do is to impose conversation or discourse analysis as the only acceptable ways of doing qualitative research. As noted elsewhere in this volume, everything will depend upon the research problem being tackled. Moreover, thoughtful researchers will often want to use a combination of methods.

However, my benevolent neutrality towards the varying logics of qualitative research co-exists with an appeal to two very strong principles. First, researchers always need to address the analytic issues that may lie concealed behind apparently straightforward issues of method. Second, qualitative research's concern for an 'in-depth' focus on people's activities (or representations of those activities) is no warrant for sloppy thinking or anecdotal use of 'telling' examples. We owe it to ourselves and our audiences to generate reliable data and valid observations.

If there is a 'gold standard' for qualitative research, it should only be the standard for any good research, qualitative or quantitative, social or natural science. That is, have the researchers demonstrated successfully why we should believe them? And does the research problem tackled have theoretical and/or practical significance?

TIP
Like so many activities when doing qualitative research, choosing a transcription method is never a purely technical matter. Transcription is saturated with theoretical assumptions.

KEY POINTS

- If we can study what people are actually doing in *naturally occurring* situations, why should we ever want to work with *researcher-provoked* data?

- Tapes and transcripts have three clear advantages compared with other kinds of qualitative data: tapes are a public record; they can be replayed and transcripts improved; and they preserve sequences of talk.

- CA attempts to describe people's methods for producing orderly social interaction; it identifies these methods in the sequential organisation of talk-in-interaction.

- DA studies discourse as texts and talk in social practices; it is particularly concerned with rhetorical or argumentative organisation.

- The differences between CA and DA are becoming smaller.

- Both CA and DA are not simply technical exercises; they have much to contribute to our understanding of how the world is organised including the social problems around us.

STUDY QUESTIONS

1 Explain the distinction between 'researcher-provoked' and 'naturally occurring' data. What are the advantages and disadvantages of each?
2 What does it mean to say language is 'performative'?
3 In what sense might it be said that audio data are 'incomplete'? Does it matter?
4 What assumptions does CA make about conversation?
5 Explain any *two* features of turn-taking or repair.
6 How does 'institutional' talk different from an everyday conversation?
7 Does CA ignore the context of talk?
8 What is DA? How does it differ from CA? In what ways are CA and DA similar?
9 Explain DA's use of any *two* of the following concepts: interpretive repertoires, stake, scripts.

RECOMMENDED READING

For advice on working with talk aimed at undergraduate readers, see Rapley (2007). Kitzinger's (2007) article shows how CA has been used by her undergraduate and

(Continued)

(Continued)

PhD students researching issues related to gender and feminism. For a book-length introduction to CA, see ten Have (2007) and Schegloff (2007); for a single-chapter treatment, see Heritage (2011). For DA, see Potter (1996a; 2011), Potter and Hepburn (2008) and Hepburn and Potter (2004). Sacks's work on CA is found in his collected lectures (Sacks, 1992, I and II). These lectures are introduced in my book *Harvey Sacks: Social Science and Conversation Analysis* (Silverman, 1998). The diabetic clinic data discussed here are taken from my book *Communication and Medical Practice* (Silverman, 1987: Chs 9–10).

10
Visual Images

CHAPTER OBJECTIVES

By the end of this chapter, you will be able to:

- identify the different kinds of visual data
- understand how analysis of visual images relates to a research strategy
- recognise three different ways of collecting and analysing visual data.

In Chapter 9, we considered how we can transcribe and analyse conversations. As I noted, however, audio recordings will not tell us about such potentially relevant interactional matters as who is looking at whom and their body posture. Similarly, in Chapter 8, we concentrated on written texts to the exclusion of the visual images which co-exist with words (as in most advertisements and highway signs) and sometimes replace them (as in traffic lights).

Up to this point, my avoidance (or downplaying) of the visual image follows a tendency in much qualitative research. As I noted in Chapter 5, even ethnographers who gather observational data have sometimes been curiously reluctant to use their eyes as well as their ears. In defence of this position, it is sometimes argued that an attention to the image alone can detract attention from the social processes involved in image production and image reception. For instance, Slater (1989) suggests that a focus on the images used in advertisements has neglected the way in which such images are shaped by the economic logic and social organisation of the relationship between advertising agencies and their clients. A similar argument lies behind the switch of film analysis in recent years away from the analysis of film images and towards understanding the logic of movie production in terms of the studio system.

Whatever the strength of these arguments, perhaps our focus on the verbal may, in part, reflect something altogether more mundane. Unlike artists, architects, engineers or craftspeople, academic researchers learn to prioritise verbal products ('publish or perish' as the slogan goes). So what we *see* is taken for granted and our first thought tends to associate social research with what we can *read* (texts, statistics) or *hear* (interviews, conversations).

However, our reluctance to consider using our eyes as a research tool points, I think, to something far deeper than academic politics. In societies where TV and cinema are central to leisure, there are grounds to believe that, somewhat ironically, we have become lazy with our eyes. Perhaps our learned appetite for 'action' blinds us to the possibility of a slower, more reflective viewing.

In any event, as I have found to my own cost, sit a bunch of students in front of a movie and they will tend to switch off their brains and just let the experience wash over them. So the likely output will not be close-grained analysis but mental popcorn.

However, it is not just a matter of recognising the importance of visual phenomena. The analysis of images raises complex methodological and theoretical issues. We can appreciate this point by using a concrete example taken from Eric Livingston. Livingston (1987) asks us to imagine that we have been told to carry out some social research on city streets. Where should we begin? Some alternatives are set out in Table 10.1.

TABLE 10.1   Viewing a street: data possibilities

1   Official statistics (traffic flow, accidents)
2   Interviews (how people cope with rush hours)
3   Observation from a tower (viewing geometric shapes)
4   Observation/video at street level (how people queue/organise their movements)

Source: adapted from Livingston, 1987: 21–7

As Livingston points out, each of these different ways of looking at the street involves theoretical as well as methodological decisions. Very crudely, if we are attached to social **theories** which see the world in terms of correlations between social facts (think of demography or macroeconomics), we are most likely to consider gathering official statistics (option 1 in Table 10.1). By contrast, if we think that social meanings or perceptions are important (as in certain varieties of sociology and psychology), we may be tempted by the interview study (option 2). Or if we are anthropologists or those kinds of sociologists or students of organisational behaviour who want to observe and/or record what people actually do *in situ*, we might elect options 3 or 4. But note the very different views of people's behaviour we get from looking from on high (3), where people look like ants forming geometrical shapes like wedges, or from street level (4), where behaviour seems much more complex.

The point is that none of these data are more real or more true than the others. For instance, people are not really more like ants or complex actors. It all depends on our research question. And research questions are inevitably theoretically informed.

EXERCISE 10.1

This exercise asks you to use some ideas from Table 10.1 about viewing a street. You will need to spend time observing a local street in order to define a researchable topic.

1 What is your topic? What **models** and **concepts** can you use to understand it?
2 What data will you use? Which kind of people or objects will you observe?
3 Which position will you choose to observe from? Why? Would you like to use a video camera? If so, where would you position it? Why?
4 What conclusions about which topics do you think you will be able to derive from your analysis?

TIP

All this means that visual data are not intrinsically better or worse than any other kind of data. We need social theories to help us to identify what is important in the world around us and then, by analysis, to make something of it.

I will shortly introduce some of the theories that we can use to analyse visual images. First, however, I want to raise the three basic questions discussed in this chapter:

- What kind of visual data can we use?
- What role can visual data play in our research strategy?
- How can we analyse visual data?

10.1 KINDS OF VISUAL DATA

Following Emmison (2011), it is important to distinguish two kinds of visual data:

- artefacts (e.g. photographs, movies, advertisements and cartoons)
- how people actually use what they see to navigate the world (e.g. as pedestrians walking on busy city streets, as employees carrying out tasks by looking at the screens of PCs, as museum-goers gazing at exhibits or actually looking at the kinds of artefacts listed above).

10.1.1 Artefacts

Much of the history of visual research is associated with artefacts such as photographs. Marvasti (2004) notes that, more than a hundred years ago, the *American Journal of Sociology* published a number of articles that used photos as data. Yet, this early interest in the visual waned as the written word accompanied with numerical analysis became the dominant mode of sociological analysis. As Marvasti suggests: 'In a way, statistical figures, charts, and tables became the visual centerpieces of professional sociological publications' (2004: 67). However, anthropologists retained their interest in photography. Bateson and Mead's (1942) study of Balinese culture juxtaposed text and the visual in a complementary way so that one would enhance the meaning of the other.

Following in their footsteps, a number of sociologists in recent decades have revived the interest in visual artefacts in their discipline, notably Becker (1981) who follows a visual presentation style similar to that of Bateson and Mead, Goffman (1979) who looks at how gender roles and expectations are reflected in magazine advertisements, and Denzin (1991; 1995) who argues that we can understand and express ourselves and our social settings through Hollywood films. For instance, Denzin treats the movie *When Harry Met Sally* as a 'Field Guide to Single Yuppies' (1995: 117).

10.1.2 What people see

Emmison notes that this focus on cultural products has meant that researchers have tended to neglect 'the places and settings – the actual environments or locales – in which humans conduct their lives' (2004: 260). An exception has been what Heath (2004: 267) refers to as *interaction analysis* which works with video recordings of everyday activities. For instance, important studies on how we move our bodies in social spaces were carried out by Scheflen (1964), Birdwhistell (1970) and Kendon (1991).

In other research, video recordings have been used to examine the *in situ* organisation of social actions and activities in face-to-face interaction. As Heath notes, this includes work on the place of gaze and gesture in everyday interaction and studies of human–computer interaction in workplace settings. This kind of research, which draws upon **conversation analysis**, is discussed later in this chapter.

I now move on to my second question: the place of visual data in our research strategy.

10.2 RESEARCH STRATEGIES

It is helpful to distinguish three ways in which visual data have been incorporated into such strategies:

- as quasi-experimental data
- as a supplement to **researcher-provoked data**
- as **naturally occurring** material to be analysed in its own right.

10.2.1 Quasi-experimental data

Sometimes researchers generate data by giving a camera or VCR to a group of people and then observing how they use it. This is a kind of experiment insofar as it involves introducing a new variable into a given setting. For instance, by showing a series of photos of a given native ritual on one page and related text on the opposite page, Bateson and Mead (1942) encouraged their readers to see and read the story simultaneously.

A more recent example of the quasi-experiment is Sharples et al.'s (2003) study of photographs made by children, where 180 children of three different ages (7, 11 and 15) were given single-use cameras by researchers and asked to use them in any way they pleased over a weekend. Over 4300 photographs were generated by this means and the following issues were investigated:

- What is the content of each photograph?
- Are the people or objects shown posed?
- Who are the people shown?
- How do each of these features vary by the age of the photographer?

The analysis showed significant variation by the age of the child. For instance, 7-year-old children were more likely to take photographs of toys and other possessions. They also took more photographs of their home and family. By contrast, the 11-year-olds concentrated on outdoor and/or animal photographs (usually their pets), while the 15-year-olds mainly took photographs of their friends, usually of the same sex and often in 'informal and striking poses' (2003: 316–17).

Such experiments are often supplemented by more conventional kinds of researcher-provoked activity. In this case, the researchers followed up their quasi-experiment with qualitative interviews with their child photographers.

10.2.2 Supplements to researcher-provoked data

Pink (2004: 395) writes about 'mixing the visual with other perhaps more established qualitative methods'. In this strategy, researcher-provoked **methods** such as interviews may be photographed or recorded on video. Pink claims that video interviews allow informants to tell us about their lives using not only words but also visual images, gestures and body movements.

Reflecting upon her interview study of students asked to recall their first few weeks at university, Pink writes:

> at such times in modern western cultures … we might make great use of photographs to tell new friends, families about our lives at home. Video and photographic interviews are especially suitable for both encouraging and recording this type of behaviour. Visual interviews allow informants to tell us about their lives using not only words, but visual images, gestures and body movements. When I interviewed informants in their homes they often enacted or performed certain ideas or activities they wanted to express, they led me to and talked me through their photographic collections, the paintings they had on their walls, their ornaments and their furniture. In doing so they were telling me stories about themselves, their lives and their experiences. (2004: 395)

CASE STUDY
Evoking and Participating in People's Sensory Worlds

Like Pink, Jennifer Mason and Katherine Davies used photographs in interviews. The Living Resemblances Project involved a set of around 30 qualitative interviews with 'ordinary' people in their homes, with the aim of exploring how they experienced family resemblances in their own lives. The interviews incorporated some ethnographic elements, including observation of the environment of the home, exploring the meaning of objects and pictures, working with interviewees on drawing family trees, and participation in family interactions including discussions and demonstrations of, and negotiations about, resemblance. This is how they describe their study:

> Our interviews involved talking to people about themselves and their relatives, and we decided as part of that process to ask to see any photographs that people had that might be relevant so that we could use these to elicit or evoke reflection on resemblances. Sometimes, either in response to our request or spontaneously to help them make a point, interviewees would refer to photographs that were on display already. At other times they would go and fetch an album, a laptop, or an old shoebox full of pictures … Looking at photographs with interviewees helped to establish the sometimes enormous emotional significance of resemblance and the connections it expresses between people, as well as some of the social conventions and etiquette around not simply viewing people's personal pictures, but also affirming and negotiating resemblances interactively. (Mason and Davies, 2009: 590–1)

LINK

For more information on the Living Resemblances Project go to:

www.reallifemethods.ac.uk/research/resemblances/

and then click on Realities (www.manchester.ac.uk/realities).

Following Pink, Mason and Davies ask interviewees to talk about existing objects like photographs. By contrast, Lesley Murray gave video cameras to young people. Her research is presented in the next case study.

CASE STUDY
Filming Mobile Spaces

Twenty-five young people filmed their journey to or from school, often describing their feelings and responses to mobile space as they travelled The use of video enabled a glimpse of mobile space through the eyes of the participants, providing a clearer view of what is more or less important to them. It illuminated the particular issues experienced in the moment, the sequence of visual images that form a narrative and represent a mobile practice in a way that it is most easily understood. To some extent, I was able to look at their journeys through their eyes, both through the camera lens and through exploring these visual images with them. (Murray, 2009: 482)

Videoing was followed by film-elicitation interviews where the young people's footage acted as a focus of discussion. The young people's films, the film-elicitation interviews, and the in depth interviews carried out with the young people's mothers, provided an insight into:

- the role of personal biography in mobility
- decision-making
- the importance of social networking and local cultures of risk
- the impacts of life-stage on risk landscapes
- the inextricable links between risk and cultures of mothering and blame. (2009: 476)

10.2.3 Naturally occurring images

The first two research strategies just discussed represent interesting ways to gather visual material. Nonetheless, they run up against the problems that are faced by any researcher working in artificial settings with researcher-provoked data (such as interviews or quasi-experiments). In particular, how does one know the relation (if any) between what research subjects do in those settings and what they do in everyday life? As Emmison observes when discussing the future use of visual methods:

> The use of still photographic images will no doubt continue to figure in visual inquiry, both as illustrative ends in themselves and as ingredients of other modes of inquiry such as photo-elicitation in ethnography or interviews but the prospects here appear relatively stagnant ... only when researchers also come to appreciate the value of direct observation of the social world, harnessed with a powerful theoretical imagination, will visual research come to enjoy the centrality throughout the social and cultural fields which it deserves. (2011: 246)

Following Emmison, some researchers have employed naturally occurring data to try to understand the visual element in everyday interaction. For instance, Rod Watson has described some research he carried out with John Lee on video recordings of people at bus stops and shelters in an inner suburb of Paris:

> People formed a cluster in and around the shelter. A bus came with the sign '16' on its side. On the front was another '16' plus the name of the destination. Some people in the cluster self-selected for the bus and formed a queue in order to board it. Others 'disqualified' themselves for this bus, often pulling back to let past those visibly wishing to board. The bus route (and destination) sign served to 'partial out' or partition those passengers wishing to board that particular bus and those wanting a bus for another destination. In addition, there were some young people 'hanging around' the outside of the shelter for a considerable time with no apparent intention of boarding any bus, and it is arguable that the sign on the bus helped to 'partial out' 'waiting passengers' as opposed to 'non-passengers'. (Watson, 1997: 92)

Watson suggests that you can identify 'a variety of courses of action' that follow from how these people responded to the bus sign. These actions include:

- people who incorporated themselves as part of a queue waiting for the number 16 bus
- people who showed that they were waiting for other buses on different routes but who still manifested 'waiting behaviour'
- people whose activities were those of a non-travelling spectatorship, including the researchers. (1997: 92)

Only the first two groups actively displayed that they were monitoring the signs on approaching buses. Even then, before they boarded, some passengers were observed to put questions to the driver, to other passengers getting onto the bus, or to consult the bus timetable perhaps, through the consultation of another text, the route description-cum-timetable. As Watson notes:

> These courses of action resulted in the re-formatting of the configuration of persons in and around the bus shelter in somewhat the same way as a kaleidoscope re-formats patterns. (1997: 92)

Following what we have learned from Livingston (Table 10.1), Watson's approach leads him to interpret pedestrians as forming self-constituting shapes or patterns. So waiting at a bus stop is analysed as:

> a … self-administered sorting system. That is, the re-configuration of the people at the shelter, e.g. the formation of some of them into a queue upon the arrival

of the 'bus, where before there had simply been a cluster of waiting persons, was their own collaborative, textually-mediated accomplishment'. (Watson, 1997: 93)

Watson's research was based on video recording naturally occurring interactions using an **ethnomethodological** approach. Later in this chapter, we shall look at approaches to naturally occurring data deriving from conversation analysis.

> **TIP**
> All research strategies have advantages and disadvantages. Therefore it is important not to worry that the strategy you adopt may not be able to cover *every* issue. Seasoned researchers simply choose a strategy that has the least disadvantages when dealing with their research problem.

> **LINKS**
> Visual methods in social research, by Marcus Banks:
> http://sru.soc.surrey.ac.uk/SRU11/SRU11.html
>
> International Visual Sociology Association:
> www.visualsociology.org/

The rest of this chapter is now devoted to explanations and examples of three widely used ways of analysing visual images:

- content analysis
- semiotics
- workplace studies.

10.3 CONTENT ANALYSIS

This approach was explained in Section 3.2 so the following account will be brief. Marvasti (2004: 73) suggests that **content analysis** follows the steps listed below:

1 Define the research problem.
2 Decide where the source of the visual material will be.
3 Identify the categories or features that will be the focus of your research.
4 Sample documents from the sources previously defined.
5 Measure or count the occurrence of the pre-established categories

An example of the content analysis of images is contained in the next case study.

CASE STUDY
Gender in Soap Operas

Ali (2004: 271) suggests that content analysis of visual images in TV soap operas can answer the following kind of questions:

- How prevalent are sexist images of women?
- How often are women depicted as mothers, workers or sex objects?
- Are older women less important in soap operas?

As noted by Ali, Cantor and Pingree (1983) studied soap operas in order to answer these sorts of questions.

However, as Marvasti (2004: 272) points out, content analysis of visual data suffers the major shortcoming of primarily dealing with what is visible on the surface – the image itself. As he says, this leaves out of account two important questions:

- How such images get produced (e.g. day-to-day practices at TV stations which commission or buy soap operas).
- How such images are used and/or received.

Full answers to these questions may be provided by approaches outside the scope of this chapter. For instance, **ethnography** (discussed in Chapter 5) can examine environments such as how TV programmes are produced and study how programmes are received in the home (e.g. who gets to hold the remote control). In terms of the latter issue, quantitative audience surveys are also important.

Of the two other approaches we now consider, conversation analysis can help us to understand the receipt of visual images. As we shall now see, **semiotics**, although not equipped to examine how visual images are received, does offer a valuable way of understanding the mechanisms through which images produce a particular meaning and does so in a more sophisticated way than content analysis.

10.4 SEMIOTICS

One of the difficulties in working with images is the range of complex theoretical traditions available. One tradition that has been used to considerable effect in this area is concerned with the analysis of sign-systems or *semiotics*. Semiotics was briefly discussed early in Chapter 7 in the context of systems of narration, within literature and elsewhere.

Semiotics is the science of 'signs'. It shows how signs relate to one another in order to create and exclude particular meanings. Semiotics arose in the early years of the last century out of the lectures of the Swiss linguist Ferdinand de Saussure (see Culler, 1976; Hawkes, 1977).

To understand what Saussure was saying (like Harvey Sacks, most of Saussure's work is only available in transcripts of his lectures), we must know a little about the concerns of linguistics. Before the twentieth century, linguistics viewed language as an aggregate of units (words), each of which had a separate meaning attached to it (Stubbs, 1981). Linguistic research was mainly **etymological**, that is it concentrated on historical changes in the meanings of words.

In the early 1900s, Saussure revolutionised this approach. Hawkes (1977) has identified the two crucial aspects of Saussure's reform of linguistic research:

1 His rejection of a substantive view of language – concerned with the correspondence between individual words and their meanings – in favour of a **relational** view, stressing the system of relations between words as the source of meaning.
2 His shift away from historical or **diachronic** analysis towards an analysis of a language's present functioning (a **synchronic** analysis). No matter what recent change a language has undergone, it remains, at any given point in time, a complete system. As Hawkes puts it: 'Each language has a wholly valid existence apart from its history as a system of sounds issuing from the lips of those who speak it now' (1977: 20).

Saussure makes a distinction between *language* and *speech*. We need to distinguish the system of language (in French, *langue*) from the actual speech acts (*parole*) that any speaker actually utters. The latter are not determined by language which only provides the system of elements in terms of which speech occurs.

Saussure uses the analogy of a chess game to explain this. The rules and conventions of chess constitute a language (*langue*) within which actual moves (*parole*) take place. For Saussure, the linguist's primary concern is not to describe *parole* but to establish the elements and their rules of combination which together constitute the linguistic system.

Having identified *la langue* as the concern of linguistics, Saussure now notes that language is comparable with other social institutions like systems of writing, symbolic rites and deaf-sign-systems. All these institutions are systems of signs and can be studied systematically.

Signs have the four characteristics set out in Table 10.2.

Saussure's focus on language may make you wonder why his work is included in this chapter. A visual example should help to show the relevance of looking at images in terms of what Saussure says about signs. Think of traffic lights:

TABLE 10.2   Four characteristics of signs

1   Signs bring together an image or word (the 'signifier') and a concept (the 'signified'). For example, in a road sign, a picture of a deer is the signifier and 'take care, animals about' is signified

2   Signs are not autonomous entities – they derive their meaning only from the place within a sign system. What constitutes a linguistic sign is only its difference from other signs (so the colour red is only something which is not green, blue, orange, etc.)

3   The linguistic sign is *arbitrary* or unmotivated. This, Saussure says, means that the sign 'has no natural connection with the signified' (Saussure, 1974: 69). Different languages simply use different terms for concepts. Indeed they can generate their own concepts – think, for instance, how difficult it is to translate a game into another culture where, because the game is not played there, they lack the relevant terms

4   Signs can be put together through two main paths. First, there are possibilities of combining signs (e.g. the order of a religious service or the prefixes and suffixes that can be attached to a noun – for example, 'friend' can become 'boyfriend', 'friendship', 'friendly'). Saussure calls these patterns of combinations *syntagmatic relations*. Second, there are contrastive properties (e.g. choosing one hymn rather than another in a church service; saying 'yes' or 'no'). Here the choice of one term necessarily excludes the other. Saussure calls these mutually exclusive relations *paradigmatic oppositions*

- They bring together concepts ('stop', 'start') with images ('red', 'green').
- These images are not autonomous: red is identifiable by the fact that it is not green, and vice versa.
- Traffic lights have no natural connection with what they signify: red has simply come to mean 'stop' and green to mean 'start'.
- Traffic lights express *syntagmatic* relations (the order in which the traffic lights can change: from red to green and back again but much more complicated in countries where there is also an amber light).
- Traffic lights are also interpreted by means of *paradigmatic* oppositions: imagine the chaos created if red and green lights up simultaneously!

This means that signs derive their meaning only from their relations with and differences from other signs. This further implies that the meaning of signs cannot be finally fixed. It is always possible to extend the signifying chain.

EXERCISE 10.2

This is an exercise to help you to use Saussure's abstract concepts. Imagine you are given a menu at a restaurant. The menu reads as follows (for convenience we will leave out the prices):

Tomato soup
Mixed salad
***

Roast beef
Fried chicken
Grilled plaice
***

Ice cream (several flavours)
Apple pie

Your task is to work out how you can treat the words on the menu as a set of related signs. Try to use all the concepts above: for example, *langue*, *parole*, syntagmatic relations and paradigmatic oppositions.

Here are some clues:

1 What can you learn from the *order* in which the courses are set out?
2 What can you learn from the *choices* which are offered for each course?

CASE STUDY
Cartoons as Sign-systems

Emmison and McHoul (1987) gathered a set of cartoons about economic issues that appeared in English-language newspapers and periodicals between roughly 1920 and 1980 (see also Emmison and Smith, 2000: 86–90). According to their analysis, it turns out that there are at least three phases in how 'the economy' is represented:

1 Before the 1930s, 'economy' refers only to the classical notion of 'economising' through cutting back unnecessary expenditure.
2 In the 1930s, Keynesian ideas about a national economic structure, able to be modified by government intervention, start to be represented. Thus a contemporary cartoon shows 'Slump' as a half-ghost, half-scarecrow figure, while a jaunty Father Christmas dismisses the slump with a wave of his hand. For the first time, then, the 'economy' becomes embodied (as a sick person) and collective solutions to economic problems are implied (Father Christmas dispensing gifts via government spending).
3 By the 1940s, the economy is understood as a fully collective, embodied being. Often cartoons of that period use animals to represent both the economy and economic policy. One cartoon depicts the economy as a sea-monster. Another shows the Budget as a box of snakes charmed by a finance minister.

Emmison and McHoul give us a way to think about the interplay between words and images in cartoons. As they would recognise, we can apply their approach to how the world is represented in a wide range of media products (see my discussion of newspaper headlines and lonely hearts columns in Section 8.2.3).

Semiotics continues to provide a vital apparatus for the analysis of texts – both verbal and visual. For instance, Vladimir Propp's influential analysis of the narrative organisation of fairy stories (see Section 3.4) clearly draws upon Saussure's concept of the *synchronic* organisation of system of signs.

Thirty years after Propp, the French writer Roland Barthes also followed Saussure by arguing that semiotics was a science of *differences*, focused, like economics, on the *value* of different elements in relation to one another. To illustrate this point, Barthes (1967) uses a visual example drawn from one of Saussure's lectures.

Think of a sheet of paper. Imagine that we cut this paper into a number of shapes. Each shape has a 'value' in relation to the others (for instance, it is bigger or smaller than they are); it also has a back and a front. If we imagine that the sheet of paper corresponds to a system of signs (language), semiotics' task is to discover how the different shapes (signs) into which it is cut establish a particular set of meanings. This means that we must observe any given systems of signs 'from the inside', using a finite corpus of shapes. As Barthes argues: '[we must not] add anything to it [the corpus] during the course of the research, [we must] exhaust it completely by analysis, every fact included in the corpus having to be found in the system' (1967: 96–7).

However, like many later researchers, Barthes is critical about Saussure's insistence (taken up in **structural anthropology**) that we should focus only on sign-systems (what Saussure called *langue*) not on how signs are actually used (*parole*). How signs are actually used (*parole*) is not, for Barthes, the kind of trivial, psychological domain that Saussure indicated. For Barthes and most later semioticians, the work of signs is not reducible to the mechanics of a given sign-system. Indeed, how signs are actually used sets into play and potentially challenges (as well as sustains) the codes of language.

Some examples may help to explain this. Following Saussure, colours are *relational* – constituted by their differences. Hence red is not orange (or any other colour). Now think of the way in which some great artists use palettes which make us rethink the way particular colours stand in relation to others. Although the spectrum of colours is fixed, the *relation* between particular colours can be endlessly rearticulated. This process is, however, not limited to aesthetics.

Think of the symbolic potential of a cut-price airline's advertising slogans in the 1980's: 'People's Airline'. Here the signifier 'People' is being used to signify that flying is everybody's right. We only have to compare the slogan 'People's Airline' with the term 'People's Republic' (still used to describe the Chinese state) to see that how signs are articulated with each other is not a trivial matter. And, of course, these examples reflect only some of the myriad connections that have been made between these elements.

EXERCISE 10.3

This exercise is designed to help you to think about how sign-systems work in visual images.

1 Select two Internet advertisements which contain visual images for different makes of the same product (e.g. a mobile phone).
2 List the signifiers present in each advert.
3 Now consider how these signifying elements are related (or articulated) to each other and the meaning (or 'message') that is, thereby, signified in each advert.
4 Do the two adverts use the same or different strategies to convey their message?

The use of 'nationalism' and 'patriotism' underlines the political implications of how signs are articulated with each other and puts some further meat on Saussure's somewhat bare and abstract bones. What Saussure called a *relational* view of language shows how nationalism only gets a meaning in relation to other terms – hence the Nazi success in identifying a relation between nationalism or patriotism and fascism (e.g. national socialism). Conversely, as Laclau (1981) has shown, during the Second World War, communist Italian politicians successfully appealed to the apparently indissoluble links between being a patriotic Italian and supporting a party opposed to the Germans.

Since terms have no fixed meaning derived from their past use, populist politicians will try to incorporate popular signs (such as 'patriotism') into their vocabulary. Think, for instance, of how politicians like to stand in front of their national flag (as I write, the British Prime Minister, David Cameron, is holding a press conference with two Union Jacks displayed behind him).

Following Saussure, these examples show that the meaning of a sign is never totally fixed. However, Saussure's insistence on the 'arbitrary' character of any sign need not mean that we should follow him in downplaying the creative way in which signs can be used to establish a favoured set of meanings.

Let me provide a famous *visual* example of how signs are used in this way.

CASE STUDY
The Colonial Soldier

Barthes (1973) discusses a photograph in a French magazine taken at the time when France still possessed an African empire. The photo shows a black man who is wearing the uniform of the French Army. This man is depicted saluting the French national flag.

(Continued)

(Continued)

To understand the layers of meaning we can read into this image, Barthes (1967: 89ff.) introduces the concept of *denotation*. Denotation, according to Barthes, is the surface meaning of signs. In these terms, we note the sign of the salute, formed between the movement of the soldier's arm and the flag upon which his gaze is fixed, and the sign of colour ('black' being selected from the *paradigmatic* opposition of primary colours).

However, Barthes tells us, there is a deeper level of meaning to be found in this image. The sign as a whole connotes the free participation of 'subject' peoples in the French Empire. At this level, the surface meaning is used to signify a system of *connotation*. This system unconsciously informs the viewer about what the surface meaning of this image implies – the naturalness and hence unquestionability of French imperialism.

Barthes claims to have identified how this image works to sustain what he terms a 'myth' (indeed his book of essays on different images is called *Mythologies*). Conceived as a 'narrative' (Section 3.4), the myth re-created in this image is, for Barthes, 'true' because it expresses an ideology actually used to sustain French imperialism. But it is also 'false' because it conceals a particular system of connotation.

Barthes' identification of the semiotic analyst as a 'reader of myths' has an impressive intellectual pedigree. In the nineteenth century, Karl Marx had suggested that we treat textbooks of political economy not as sober academic treatise but as 'adventure stories'. And, as we have seen, in the twentieth century, Saussure, followed by structural anthropology, exhibited the structuralist urge to locate 'deep structures' behind particular signs.

However, as Barthes himself was later to recognise, such ploys have at least two limitations:

1 By looking behind and underneath signs, they fail to analyse properly the complex internal workings of relations between signs.
2 Accounts of underlying structures or 'myths' create the illusion of an all-knowing analyst who somehow remains outside sign-systems.

Barthes' later work was an attempt to recant much of his position in *Mythologies*. In his collection of essays called *Image/Music/Text* (Barthes, 1977), the concept of 'myth' disappears. It is replaced by an insistence on what Barthes terms a 'play of signifiers'. If there is anything 'ideological' about signs, Barthes now finds it not in ironic contrasts between 'appearance' and 'reality' but wherever this potentially 'indefinite' play of signifiers is terminated or closed off. Barthes' later position was important in the emergence of **post-modernism** and its treatment of signification as a pastiche of insecure and changing elements.

LINK

Semiotics for beginners, by David Chandler:

www.aber.ac.uk/media/Documents/S4B/semiotic.html

The rest of this chapter is taken up with an account of research on images taken from a very different tradition: conversation analysis.

10.5 WORKPLACE STUDIES

In Section 9.3, I outlined the approach of conversation analysis (CA). As noted there, CA involves the recording and detailed transcription of talk in order to analyse how the participants orient to the sequential organisation of turns. Since the 1980s, the use of video recorders has allowed researchers influenced by ethnomethodology and CA to analyse such features as gaze and body movements and see how they are tied into talk and other actions.

The analysis of talk in organisational settings ('institutional talk') has become increasingly important within CA. This approach has become known as workplace studies. As Christian Heath notes, workplace studies have carried out the programme of the early ethnographers (the **Chicago School** and their post-war followers such as Everett Hughes and Howard Becker), while using methods which, until recent decades, were unavailable or unknown. As Heath puts it:

> in sociology the conceptual and theoretical resources which have informed a substantial corpus of rich ethnographic work since the 1950s, do not readily lend themselves to the analysis of the details of social actions and activities captured on video. In contrast however, ethnomethodology and conversation analysis, with their commitment to the local in situ organisation of human conduct, and their interest in taking talk and interaction seriously, as topics in their own right, provide an analytic orientation which can take advantage of the opportunities afforded through video. (2004: 273)

Within the workplace, the institutional talk programme has paid a great deal of attention to how people use information on computer screens. For instance, Zimmerman (1992) has shown the unintended consequences of the use of PCs in emergency call centres. In particular, callers can be confused by the silence on their phone while, unbeknown to them, the operator is typing on their computer keyboard.

TIP

To make recordings of visual data you have the choice between:

* Analogue devices – recording onto VHS or Hi8 tapes.
* Digital devices – recording onto Mini DV tapes, memory cards or DVDs.

Although some cameras have quite good microphones it is generally necessary to use some form of external microphone as well. In some situations, you may want to use an additional wide-angled lens (which you thread onto the lens of your camera) and a tripod. To transcribe (and analyse) the recording you can either use the appropriate video-player or download the images onto the computer. If using a video-player you often need to be able to produce a stable freeze frame (i.e. not fuzzy or jerky) and have good slow motion facilities. Digital video cameras have recently become a lot more affordable and offer a better quality of recording and more stable image when viewing freeze frames or playing the tape in slow motion. (Rapley, 2007: 36)

Table 10.3 gives you some idea of how to analyse your video data. Following that, I outline some examples of workplace studies.

TABLE 10.3   How to do video analysis

1   Catalogue your data (e.g. list the contents of each recording)
2   Find an activity that occurs several times in your data
3   Select one data fragment to see in detail how this activity is carried out
4   Transcribe this fragment in detail
5   Examine the organisation of this activity and the sequence of actions which precede and follow it and how the participants attend to what precedes and follows it
6   Throughout, analyse *visible* conduct; do not speculate upon what participants may be thinking but analyse what they are doing (in their speech, actions and gazes)

Source: adapted from Heath et al. 2010: 61–85

TIP

Rapley offers his own, more informal, version of Table 10.3:

When I'm working with audio or video-recordings, I initially just listen and/or watch the recordings once through as soon as I have time. I'll make some notes and if any moments really stand out I might even very roughly transcribe that section of talk. So again, my coding and analysis is both ongoing and refined and guided by what I feel is 'interesting' or 'noticeable'. When

I've got more time, I'll then repeatedly listen/watch the tapes, and so generate, check and refine my analytic hunches. If I'm working with a very small number of recordings or if I think a specific recording is vital, I might transcribe them all – to whatever level of detail I think is useful. With larger archives or recordings, I generally only transcribe those sections that are key – either because they are really good examples of what *typically goes on* or because they are *atypical* and therefore reflexively show what is routine. (2007: 127)

In the rest of the chapter, I give some more examples of how visual data have been used in workplace studies.

10.5.1 Communicating with patients: the body in action

As Heath (2004) demonstrates, the growing use of PCs by general practitioners has also had an unexpected impact on their communication with patients. To understand this further, we need to see how Heath used his videos of medical consultations to examine how doctors and patients organise their gaze. It turns out that even the simple act of writing a prescription has important interactional consequences.

Heath (2004) discusses a medical consultation with a female patient complaining of pain in her knee. Towards the end of the consultation, the doctor begins to prepare a prescription. As he starts to write, the patient, who is still standing following the physical examination, begins to tell a story.

Extract 10.1 shows how she tells her story. Her words are transcribed using the CA conventions explained in the Appendix. In addition, however, Extract 10.1 shows both body movements and the direction of the participants' gaze (marked as 'up' or 'down' below).

Extract 10.1 [Heath, 2004: 274: Fragment 1 (adapted)]

walks

up   *down*   *up*   *down up down*   *up down*

P: I was coming up the steps li:ke this all the way up I felt

Dr: *writes*   *turns to*   *turns to*   *nods and*

prescription   *P's face*   *P's legs*   *smiles*

Here is how Heath describes this extract:

> As the patient begins to describe the difficulties she had walking up the stairs at Debenhams, she starts to walk up and down on the spot, illustrating the problems she experienced. More particularly she places her hand on the doctor's desk and balancing her weight, shows the way in which she distorted her hip and leg movement to actually climb the stairs. The movements give sense to the talk they accompany. They lucidly reveal the problems she experienced and provide a vivid picture of the suffering that she incurred. The story points to the difficulties and provides a framework in which the movements embody, literally, the patient's difficulties and suffering. (2004: 274)

As Heath points out, however, we should not treat these movements as simply to do with the patient herself. It turns out that P has a problem: how to encourage the doctor to look as well as listen to her story. For, as this extract begins, Dr is looking down, while writing a prescription. By its end, however, Dr is looking at his patient. As Heath comments:

> The patient's success in encouraging the doctor to watch the performance and thereby achieving the sequential relevance of the story derives from the ways in which she designs her bodily conduct. As she begins to step up for the second time, she swings her hips towards the doctor. In particular, she swings her hips towards his visual field, an area midway between the prescription pad and his face. Just as her hips move towards the doctor he looks up, turning to the face of the patient. The patient's movement, a component of the overall demonstration, engenders the reorientation by doctor, encouraging him to abandon the prescription temporarily and transform the ways in which he is participating in the delivery of the story. On turning to the patient's face, he finds her looking at her own legs as she utters 'like this'. He looks down and watches her dramatic performance as she steps up and down. And, as she beings the performance to completion with 'terribly' and the doctor utters 'yeh', 'yes' and nods, the patient successfully transforms the participation of the doctor and has him temporarily abandon his current activity to witness the difficulties that she experienced walking up the steps at Debenham's. (2004: 276–7)

By including video data in his analysis, Heath has elegantly revealed the interplay between words, gaze and bodily movements. As he puts it, P's bodily conduct is both 'part of her story' but functional in gaining Dr's gaze and, thereby, 'establish an audience for her performance and thereby achieve the sense and sequential significance of the story' (2004: 277). Now that doctors' activities include not only prescription-writing but, like Zimmerman's emergency service telephone operators, looking at the screens of their PCs, Heath's address of the visual elements of conduct could not be more practically relevant.

10.5.2 Communicating with a photocopier

Like Heath, Lucy Suchman is concerned with the interaction between people and machines. However, in this case (Suchman, 1987), the communication is not mediated through a caller or client. Instead, she takes the example of a computer-based system attached to a photocopier and intended to instruct the user in the photocopier's operation.

Suchman focuses on how rules function in human–computer interaction. She draws upon Gladwin's (1964) account of the navigation methods of a South East Asian tribe – the Trukese – with no 'rational' Western theory of navigation. Instead, the Trukese navigate via various ad hoc methods (e.g. responding to the wind, waves, stars, clouds). Suchman asks how real is the contrast between Western and Trukese methods of navigation? Theories and plans do not *determine* the actions of either Western or Trukese navigators. Rather Western navigators *invoke* a plan when asked to account for their navigation which, inevitably, depends on ad hoc methods (e.g. accounting for disasters like the *Exxon Valdez* oil spill off Alaska).

This creates a problem in artificial intelligence systems which are 'built on a *planning model* of human action. The model treats a plan as something located in the actor's head, which directs his or her behaviour' (Suchman, 1987: 3).

As Suchman notes, plans neither determine action nor fully reconstruct it. Thus she argues that 'artifacts built on the planning model confuse *plans* with *situated actions*' and proposes 'a view of plans as formulations of antecedent conditions and consequences that account for actions in a plausible way' (1987: 3).

Conversely, she suggests, the successful navigation of the Trukese shows that 'the coherence of situated action is tied in essential ways not to … conventional rules but to local interactions contingent on the actor's particular circumstances' (1987: 27–8).

This implies that, in designing computers that can interact with humans, the system of communication 'must incorporate both a sensitivity to local circumstances and resources for the remedy of troubles in understanding that inevitably arise' (1987: 28).

This will mean that: 'Instead of looking for a structure that is invariant across situations, we look for the processes whereby particular, uniquely constituted circumstances are systematically interpreted so as to render meaning shared and action accountably rational' (1987: 67).

There is a methodological basis behind Suchman's focus on 'processes [of] … systematic interpretation' that is worth noting. Although we have not reproduced her data here, like Zimmerman and Heath, her analysis is concerned with the sequential organisation of verbal and non-verbal interaction.

Suchman's data derive from videos of four sessions, each of more than an hour, involving first-time users of this 'expert system'. In each session, two novices worked together in pairs. She is particularly concerned with how interactional 'troubles' arise and are resolved.

TABLE 10.4   The basic interactional sequence

1   *Machine presents instruction*
    User reads instruction
    interprets referents
    and action descriptions
2   *User takes action*
    Design assumes that the action means that the user has understood the instruction
3   *Machine presents next instruction*

Source: based on Suchman, 1987: 107

In Suchman's study, the computer used in the photocopier 'project(s) the course of the user's actions as the enactment of a *plan* for doing the job, and then use(s) the presumed plan as the relevant context for the action's interpretation' (1987: 99, my emphasis). However, the problem is that 'plans' have a different status for computers and users: 'While the (design) plan directly *determines* the system's behaviour, the user is required to *find* the plan, as the prescriptive and descriptive significance of a series of procedural instructions' (1987: 101, my emphasis).

This is shown in Suchman's model of how the computer is supposed to 'instruct' a user set out in Table 10.4.

Despite this rational model, much of the user's behaviour is unavailable to the system, for instance: 'the actual work of locating referents and interpreting action descriptions' (1987: 107). This means that if an instruction is *misunderstood* by the user, the error will go unnoticed.

Predictably, Suchman's study reveals many conflicts between the design assumptions (DAs) built into the machine and user assumptions (UAs). Some examples of this are set out in Table 10.5.

TABLE 10.5   Design assumptions (DAs) and user assumptions (UAs)

DA: treat the question 'what next?' as a request for the next step – attended to by presentation of the next instruction

UA: can ask 'what next?' sometimes in order to know how to abort or repair an activity (e.g. where only one photocopy obtained instead of the five desired).

DA: repeat instructions either (a) where task needs to be repeated or (b) where user's action in response to the instruction is in error such as to return the system to a state prior to the instruction being given (a loop)

UA: in the case of repeated instructions, (b) does *not* occur in human interaction. Instead, the repetition of an instruction indicates that the action taken in response to the instruction in some way fails to satisfy its intent and needs to be remedied

DA: users will follow instructions; where they do not, this will be detected by the machine

UA: can sometimes ignore instructions because of preconceptions about what is appropriate, based on prior experience

Source: based on Suchman, 1987: 148–67

As Table 10.5 shows, a faulted action can go unnoticed at the point where it occurs. This is because 'what is available to the system is only the action's effect and that effect satisfies the requirements for the next instruction' (1987: 167).

As a consequence, while, from the point of view of the design, users have achieved precisely what they want, this is not how users actually perceive their situation. Because of these kinds of conflicts between the assumptions of designers and users, Suchman concludes that users often fail to get what they want from the photocopier:

> Due to the constraints on the machine's access to the situation of the user's inquiry, breaches in understanding that for face-to-face interaction would be trivial in terms of detection and repair become 'fatal' for human–machine communication. (1987: 170)

Like many studies concerned with the mechanics of our interaction with the objects around us, Suchman's findings are both analytically and practically rich. Among the practical implications of her study, we may note that:

- It reveals the character of practical decision-making in a way relevant to the design of expert systems.
- It suggests the constructive role of users' troubles in system design, that is troubles arise not by departing from a plan but in the situated contingencies of action. She notes how such systems may not seek to eliminate user errors but 'to make them accessible to the student, and therefore instructive'. (1987: 184)

Suchman's work is important because it uses video recordings to focus on the precise mechanics of institutional interaction. In particular, Suchman, following a tenet of CA, begins by using everyday interaction as a baseline and then seeing how far human–computer interaction departs from it. This means that she avoids starting with the common-sense assumption that there is a stable organisational or institutional order separate from everyday interaction. The same approach is taken in my final example of workplace studies in Section 10.5.3.

EXERCISE 10.4

This exercise invites you to build upon Lucy Suchman's work. Before you attempt it, you must get the permission for filming of all the photocopier users and of the university authorities responsible for the photocopying room (for a sample consent form, see the relevant case study in Chapter 4: ten Have, 1998).

1 Take a video camera into a photocopying room in your university.
2 Film the instructions that each user gives to the photocopier, the message that then follows and the user's response to each message, and audio record the comments that each user makes during these activities.

3 Carefully transcribe your data, using Heath's transcription symbols found earlier in his data.
4 What are the similarities and differences evident between user assumptions (UAs) and design assumptions (DAs)?
5 What does your research suggest about (i) how the photocopier could be better designed; and (ii) how photocopier users could be better trained?

10.5.3 Teamwork in London Underground control rooms

Christian Heath and Paul Luff studied videos of staff working at a control room which oversees the Bakerloo Line on the London Underground. The four staff who work there oversee traffic movement and deal with problems and difficulties when they arise. Heath and Luff (2000) argue that the flexibility and emergent character of the staff's activities is far more complex and interactionally co-ordinated than could be formally prescribed in documents or training manuals.

The Line Control Room houses a line controller, who co-ordinates the day-to-day running of the railway, a divisional information assistant (DIA) whose responsibilities include providing information to passengers through a public address (PA) system and communicating with station managers, and two signal assistants who oversee the operation of the signalling system on the busiest section of the line. To show how the control team work, I will take one episode discussed by Heath and Luff (2000: 108ff.). It takes place during a minor crisis when, in a few hours, the personnel within the control room have had to deal with a station closure, a fire on a train, a mechanical failure and a missing driver. These problems have meant that two controllers have become involved in managing the traffic on the line. These problems have also meant that personnel in the control room, including the signal assistants, have lost the location of particular trains, and are trying to maintain an adequate service irrespective of the timetable and the scheduled running times.

The following fragment begins approximately 15 seconds before Cii's request to the DIA. Cii is having a heated discussion with his colleague (Ci) concerning the failure of a signalman (located outside the Line Control Room) to undertake various changes to the running times of the trains. During this discussion the telephone rings. Cii picks up the handset, but delays taking the call until an opportune moment arises in the discussion. On his colleague uttering 'Oh for fucks sake' (frame 7.4), Cii responds to the call.

The call informs Cii of the difficulties at Oxford Circus. Cii then grabs the radio phone and attempts to contact the driver, through which he tries to do three times. While Cii is attempting to intervene, the DIA and the other signal assistant (Si) have been trying to identify the train at Baker Street. The DIA switches the CCTV

.
.
.

Ci: How could he have done it
      if he's taken the only

      (one round it)
      (0.4)

Cii: said he (would not have) and then swapped
      them around behind the (Beeb)
      (0.5)

Ci: Well (.) I just spoke to Mickey (.) Knight
      and I said (then) why

      didnt you do tha:t and he said he wouldnt
      (0.4)

Cii: He (interferes a lot)
      (0.6)

Ci: Oh f   [or fucks sake

Cii: [Controller
                  (1.5)

            Cii: Ye:s:
                  (0.6)

IMAGE 10.1

monitor to Baker Street South and attempts to read the number from the front of train as it enters the platform. The DIA utters 'all the two::s' and Si returns to his own desk, calling out to his fellow signal assistant 'two two two' (frames 7.5 and 7.6).

Heath and Luff note that at least two parallel and independent activities are now taking place. Cii is attempting to free the hold-up at Oxford Circus and the DIA, signal assistants and Ci are, in various ways, concerned with the number of the train at Baker Street.

As the DIA utters 'all the two::s', he turns from the CCTV monitor (showing Baker Street) to the fixed line diagram. The alignment of gaze from the one representation to the other serves to mark not only the completion of the previous activity, but the onset of another, namely an assessment of a particular aspect of the operation of the service. In realigning his gaze, the DIA adopts a parallel orientation to the fixed line diagram to Cii, looking towards Oxford Circus just as the latter is uttering 'do you receive: over' (frame 7.2). As the DIA aligns his gaze towards the diagram, Cii momentarily adjusts his own orientation towards the area of mutual regard. The position of the DIA's alignment of gaze, at the point at which Cii voices the potential location of the 'problem', coupled with its orientation towards the domain in question, suggests that as the one activity is brought to completion, the DIA is already sensitive to the attempts by Cii to contact the driver and intervene in the operation of the service. Moreover, Cii's reorientation may suggest that he is also sensitive to the DIA's alignment towards his own attempts to contact the driver at Oxford Circus.

As Cii begins his second attempt to contact the driver, he turns from the diagram to his desk. The DIA simultaneously turns from the diagram towards the console (frame 7.7). As Cii produces the word 'Oxford' in 'Oxford Circus South', the DIA moves his hand forward towards the key controls of the PA system in readiness for a public announcement.

Heath and Luff comment upon how the video data have displayed teamwork in fine detail:

> The juxtaposition of the DIA's actions with components within Cii's utterances which identify the locale of the problem, coupled with the ways in which his physical alignment and realignment parallels the actions of his co-participant, suggests and displays that the emergent activity of the DIA is convergent with the problem with which Cii is attempting to address. Moreover, moving his hand to the PA controls serves to confirm, retrospectively, that the initial alignment by the DIA towards the fixed line diagram is indeed a first action within an emergent trajectory of conduct ... Through the use of particular tools at successive stages within Cii's attempts to deal with the problem, the DIA's actions become visible and intelligible as part of a routine and recurrent activity – the delivery of an announcement following an intervention by a controller. Cii's actions not only provide the resources to enable the DIA to examine the fixed line diagram and infer the reasons for the upcoming intervention, but allow him to prepare to undertake a series of public announcements as soon as the problem is solved. (2000: 111)

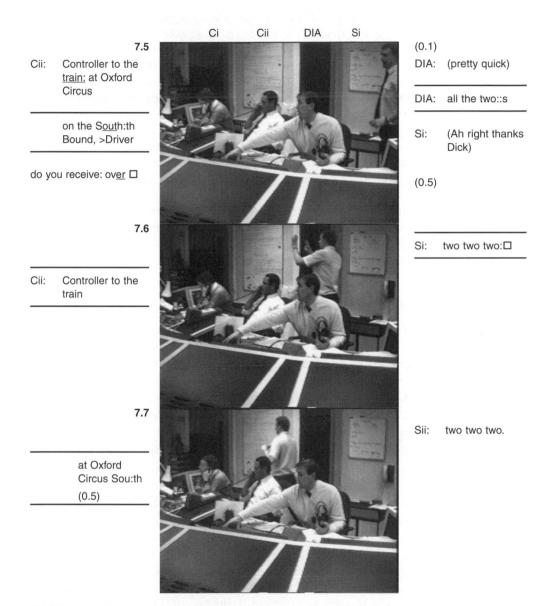

IMAGE 10.2

I conclude my discussion of this highly sophisticated analysis of video data by noting how it develops the tradition of the sociology of work and occupations associated with Hughes (1958, 1971). We can understand this point in Heath and Luff's discussion of organisational learning. They state:

The difficulty faced by trainee Controllers, Information Assistants and Signalmen is not simply learning to undertake a body of relatively complex and specialised tasks, but rather learning to accomplish those activities with respect to the real-time contributions and demands of personnel both within and outside the Line Control Room. Following the classic essays of Hughes … we might think of the trainee's problem as one of becoming familiar with an unexplicated and tacit organisational culture which might consist of skills, collective representations, defences, mandates, ideologies and the like. Whilst such features may well inform occupational performance within the Line Control Rooms, and perhaps in other work environments, the difficulties faced by the trainees derive from the ways in which tasks are systematically coordinated in real-time with the actions and activities of colleagues. Indeed, it appears that individual tasks and activities are inseparable from, and thoroughly embedded in, ongoing concerted interaction with colleagues within the local milieu. (2000: 116–17)

10.6 CONCLUSION

The observant reader may remark that this is rather an unbalanced account of how qualitative researchers have used visual data. For instance, I have barely discussed certain kinds of data, such as photographs or movies, and I have underplayed the dominant role of post-modernism in the analysis of the image.

I plead 'guilty' to this charge of imbalance. However, I would enter a plea in mitigation.

With the burgeoning of cultural studies within social science, the study of visual images has become a highly fashionable topic. Although this rediscovery of the visual is welcome, it has occurred at some cost.

First, as Emmison and Smith (2000: viii–ix, 22) suggest, cultural studies' usual focus on commercially produced images (like advertisements and TV news bulletins) has led to a relative neglect of research on how everyday participants use the visual and mechanical resources in their environment. Second, I have reservations about the quality of analysis that passes as adequate in many areas of cultural studies. Rather than cautious, rigorous research on visual images, we tend to find either the kind of politically driven 'demythologising' seen in the early work of Roland Barthes (see Section 10.2) or a post-modernist pastiche where 'anything goes'.

Of course, these are big generalisations. And even I would exclude from my charge sheet certain kinds of research which accepts the post-modernist banner (see, for example, Kendall and Wickham's, 1999, argument that we treat Foucault's work as a toolbox for empirical research rather than as an impetus to woolly theorising).

Nonetheless, this helps to explain why I have given so much attention to how everyday participants use the visual and mechanical resources in their environment. Emmison and Smith elegantly make this point:

> In giving up the idea that visual research is only the study of photographs, advertisements, etc. ... a far broader range of data becomes available for investigation. From our vantage point, visual inquiry is no longer just the study of the image, but rather the study of the seen and the observable. (2000: ix)

This change of focus to 'the seen and the observable' also serves to reconnect visual research to lively *models* of social research forgotten in the post-modern fashion parade. These include the approaches discussed in this chapter, as well as the models considered in Chapter 5: the **naturalism** of the Chicago School and Erving Goffman's analysis of **framing**.

KEY POINTS

- The aim of researching visual images is to examine the 'work' that they do and to understand how they do that work.
- Content analysis counts the occurrence in images of the pre-established categories.
- Semiotics is the science of 'signs'. It shows how signs relate to one another in order to create and exclude particular meanings.
- Workplace studies inspect videos to show how participants actually attend to visual elements in their environment, for example the bodily presence and gaze of others and/or the technologies through which people communicate.

STUDY QUESTIONS

1 What kinds of visual artefacts can we study?
2 What are the advantages of studying how people use visual cues in everyday situations?
3 How can content analysis be used to analyse visual images?
4 What is meant by semiotics?
5 Explain *three* semiotic terms and show how they can help you analyse visual images.
6 What is meant by 'workplace studies'?
7 List *three* strategies helpful in the collection or analysis of videos of people in everyday situations.

RECOMMENDED READING

The most recent, systematic and accessible discussion of the significance of visual images is *Researching the Visual* (Emmison and Smith, 2000). Christian Heath, John Hindmarsh and Paul Luff's marvellous textbook *Video in Qualitative Research* (2010) provides the student with all the resources necessary to do video analysis – from gathering data to analysing it. Christian Heath and Paul Luff's book, *Technology in Action* (2000) offers a more advanced example of workplace studies. The research reported there ranges from newsrooms to architects' offices to London Transport control rooms.

Famous examples of semiotic readings of images are to be found in Barthes' collection of essays called *Mythologies* (Barthes, 1973). For Barthes' semiotic analysis of photographs see his essay 'The photographic message' (Barthes, 1977) and his book *Camera Lucida: Reflections on Photography* (1981).

A difficult but rewarding semiotic treatment of cinema is found in Stephen Heath's *Questions of Cinema* (1981). For an attempt to apply some of Stephen Heath's concepts to a movie, see my paper 'Unfixing the subject: viewing "*bad timing*"' (Silverman, 1991).

Two of Harvey Sacks's lectures give stunning examples of analysing visual data from an ethnomethodological model: glances (1992, I: 81–94) and traffic (1992: 435–440). For a short treatment of the methodological issues involved when students use video data, see Silverman (2005: 57–60).

PART THREE

RESEARCH PRACTICE

11

Credible Qualitative Research

CHAPTER OBJECTIVES

By the end of this chapter, you will be able to:

* assess whether qualitative research studies are credible
* distinguish sound and unsound claims to credibility
* recognise what it means to describe a study as 'scientific'
* understand the nature and basis of 'reliability'
* see how 'validity' may be achieved.

So far in this book we have been describing the different ways in which qualitative researchers gather and analyse their data. When a study is finished, it is, of course, turned over to its readers (and, in the case of students, examiners). What are they to make of it?

C. Riessman (personal correspondence) has suggested a number of pertinent questions that such readers can ask: 'Is the investigator's interpretation of data (stories told in field interviews, for example) persuasive and plausible, reasonable and convincing?' Riessman comments that: 'Every reader has had the experience of encountering a piece of research and thinking "but of course..." even when the argument an author was making was counterintuitive.' Where does that 'of course' response come from? As Riessman puts it:

> Persuasiveness is strengthened when the investigator's theoretical claims are supported with evidence from informants' accounts, negative cases are included, and alternative interpretations considered. The strategy forces investigators to document their claims for readers who weren't present to witness stories as they unfolded, or beside the investigator who tried to make sense of them. (Personal correspondence)

If you think about it, any form of writing involves some sort of attempt to make your audience want to stay with you. Qualitative researchers need to decide, however, if they are satisfied simply with keeping their audience sufficiently interested that they will want to turn the page. Is qualitative research any different, as Riessman suggests, from good journalism or novel writing? Should we want to achieve anything more?

Based on these doubts, in this chapter, I will examine two questions:

1 Does it matter whether qualitative research findings are credible?
2 If so, how might that credibility be sustained and recognised?

I will begin with the 'does it matter?' question. For, if our answer is no, then this can be a very short chapter!

> **TIP**
>
> Riessman notes some techniques which can be used to increase the 'plausibility' of a research study:
>
> > I insist, whenever possible, that students tape record conversations so they can represent what was said with greater accuracy. I also teach students to keep a diary or log of decisions and inferences made during the course of a research project. The practice encourages … critical self-awareness about how the research was done, and the impact of critical decisions made along the way. A log also helps when writing up a project, jogging memory and encouraging truthfulness. (Personal correspondence)

11.1 DOES CREDIBILITY MATTER?

The array of suggestive **theories** and contrasting **methodologies**, reviewed in the last part of this book, may tempt us to believe that credibility does not matter and that the maxim 'anything goes' applies to qualitative research. Such a reading gains support in high places. In Denzin and Lincoln's Introduction to the Second Edition of their influential *Handbook*, they refer to a 'legitimation crisis' which 'makes problematic the traditional criteria for evaluating and interpreting qualitative research' (2000a: 17). Among the sources of this crisis, they cite:

• the linguistic turn which, in principle, could include scientific texts within the category of social construction
• feminist critiques which seek to identify the sexist basis of certain claims to 'objectivity'
• the post-modern turn in which ethnographies are read as 'tales from the field' which unthinkingly construct the 'other'.

Taking up these claims, I will first refer to the position of the ethnographer Michael Agar and then touch upon some feminist critics of how scientists normally claim credibility.

11.1.1 Critics of scientific credibility

Agar (1986: 11) has criticised what he calls 'the received view' of science, based on the systematic test of explicit **hypotheses**. This view, he argues, is inappropriate to research problems concerned with 'What is going on here?' (1986: 12) which involve learning about the world firsthand.

So far, this is not contentious. As you will have gathered from Chapter 5 of this book, it does not always make sense for people doing observational work, like Agar, to begin with prior hypotheses. However, Agar draws a contestable implication from this truism. The implication, according to Agar, is a rejection of the standard issues of credibility in favour of 'an intensive personal involvement, an abandonment of traditional scientific control, an improvisational style to meet situations not of the researcher's making, and an ability to learn from a long series of mistakes' (1986: 12).

Since it is very difficult for any reader to check the extent of what Agar calls the researcher's 'intensive personal involvement', he is, in effect, asking us to take on trust any research findings based on such claims. Yet, as Hammersley and Atkinson point out, it is paradoxical to assert that the qualitative research community cannot or should not check findings: 'This is a paradoxical conclusion. While culture members freely and legitimately engage in checking claims against facts … the social scientist (claims to be) … disbarred from this on the grounds that it would "distort reality"' (1995: 13).

Moreover, negative practical consequences for social science would, I believe, follow from the kind of anarchy that Agar implies. First, by minimising the credibility of qualitative research findings (at least in conventional terms), it would play into the hands of our quantitative critics. Second, by downplaying the cumulative weight of evidence from social science research, it lowers our standing in the community.

While Agar writes about the 'personal involvement' of the *researcher*, many qualitative researchers also want to emphasise the involvement and experiences of their research *subjects*. This can encourage some to go even further than Agar in rejecting conventional versions of scientific credibility. For instance, Stanley and Wise describe 'objectivity' as:

> an excuse for a power relationship every bit as obscene as the power relationship that leads women to be sexually assaulted, murdered and otherwise treated as mere objects. The assault on our minds, the removal from existence of our experiences as valid and true, is every bit as questionable. (1983: 169)

Like many feminist sociologists, Stanley and Wise argue that the **validity** of 'experiences' should replace supposedly male-dominated versions of 'objectivity'. Thus, although qualitative **methods** are held to be most appropriate for understanding women's experience, such experiences are seen as valid or 'true' in themselves. In any event, it is argued, the goal of research is not to accumulate knowledge but to serve in the emancipation of women.

For purposes of exposition, I have chosen an extreme position – readers wanting a less dogmatic feminist approach might turn to Cain (1986) or to Kitzinger (2007). However, Stanley and Wise's argument has the merit that it reveals a methodological assumption which many feminists share.

Nonetheless, from my point of view, all these writers too readily abandon any reference to the credibility of qualitative research findings. First, it simply will not do to accept any account just on the basis of the researcher's political credentials (see my discussion of the researcher as partisan in Section 12.1). As Seale has noted:

> Some, in searching for new ideals … seek to substitute moral values and political positions as guarantors of standards: promoting dialogue, emancipating the oppressed, empowering the weak become the purposes of social research. But the epistemological relativism that these writers often claim stands in marked contrast to their political absolutism My view is that such attempts to resolve the problem of criteria by resort to political values are frighteningly weak – the kind of thing that, as European history has shown, can be swept away in a few nights of concentrated book burning. I am also impressed by the general observation that one person's liberation may be another's oppression, and that 'emancipatory' positions too often involve closed minds. (2004a: 409)

Second, we should not be all that impressed if a researcher makes very much of their 'intensive personal involvement' with their subjects. Immediacy and authenticity may be a good basis for certain kinds of journalism but qualitative researchers must make different claims if we are to take their work seriously.

Not only are the effects of these positions potentially dangerous, but the position itself is based on what I take to be somewhat misleading assumptions which I criticise below (for another relevant critique, see Hammersley, 1992a):

1 The assumption that 'experience' is paramount is not at all new. Indeed, it was a primary feature of nineteenth-century **romantic** thought (see Silverman, 1989b). As I have argued in this book, to focus on 'experience' alone undermines what we know about the cultural and linguistic forms which structure what we count as 'experience'. As we saw in the last case study of Chapter 7, Celia Kitzinger, who writes as a feminist, nonetheless is highly critical of many attempts to treat people's accounts as direct windows to their experience.

2 Rather than being a male standard, the attempt to generate credible knowledge lies at the basis of *any* dialogue. Without the ability to choose between the

truth-claims of any statement, we would be reduced to name-calling along the lines of 'you would say that, wouldn't you?' Against certain current fashions, we ought to recognise how, when eighteenth-century 'Enlightenment' thinkers emphasised the power of reason, they were seeking just such a way out from prejudice and unreason.

3 To assume that emancipation is the goal of research conflates yet again 'fact' and 'value'. How research is used is a value-laden, political question (see Chapter 12). To my mind, the first goal of scientific research is valid knowledge. To claim otherwise is, as Seale implies, to make an alliance with an awful dynasty that includes 'Aryan science', under the Nazis, and 'Socialist science' under Stalin.

If qualitative research is to be judged by whether it produces valid knowledge, then we should properly ask highly critical questions about any piece of research. And these questions should be no less probing and critical than we ask about any quantitative research study.

11.1.2 Key Questions for Evaluating Research

Any systematic attempt at description and explanation, whether quantitative or qualitative, needs to answer many critical questions. Moisander and Valtonen (2006) have argued that research reports should demonstrate the following features:

- the importance of the topics and issues to the field of inquiry
- their contribution to existing research and theoretical debates
- their conceptual rigour through explicit specification of concepts and theoretical perspectives, clarity of objectives, appropriate treatment of relevant literature, logical reasoning, etc.
- their methodological rigour through the use of appropriate methods, appropriate and sufficient data, rigorous and innovative analysis
- clarity of writing and argumentation.

This list may be recast as a set of questions that we can ask of any piece of research. These questions are set out in Table 11.1 which emerged out of a conference between American social scientists drawn from political science, anthropology, sociology and law.

Although Table 11.1 was prepared as a set of criteria for the evaluation of *qualitative* research papers, I believe that the criteria I have selected are equally appropriate for quantitative studies. This shows that, in principle, there is no reason to prefer any form of data.

Table 11.1 offers a guide to the criteria that research findings must satisfy if they are to be regarded as credible. All research reports must find a way of blending data

TABLE 11.1   Criteria for designing and evaluating qualitative research

- Situate the research in appropriate literature; that is, the study should build upon existing knowledge
- Clearly articulate the connection between theory and data
- Describe and explain case selection: why particular sites, participants, events, or cases are chosen
- Pay attention to alternative explanations and negative cases
- Operationalize constructs and describe expected findings
- Provide clear and detailed descriptions of both data collection and anticipated data analysis techniques: specify what counts as data, how the researcher will go about obtaining data and analyzing it
- Describe the intellectual, social, and political significance of the research
- Discuss generalizability or significance beyond the specific cases selected
- Specify the limitations of the research and anticipate potential reviewer objections

Source: Lamont and White, 2005: 4

extracts with research findings in order to claim credibility. In doing so, three particular issues stand out:

- How are data extracts presented? Is the detail of the transcription or of the fieldnotes appropriate to the claims being made?
- Are data extracts positioned within the local context from which they arose? For instance, in an interview or **focus group** study, are we given what precedes and/or follows a particular utterance?
- Is any attempt made to establish that the data extracts selected are representative of the data as a whole? For instance, are simple tabulations used or **deviant cases** followed up?

EXERCISE 11.1

Select a qualitative research study in an area you know something about. Now go through the following steps:

1 Review the study in terms of the quality criteria set out in Table 11.1.
2 If the study fails to satisfy all these criteria, consider how it could have been improved to satisfy them.
3 Consider to what extent these criteria are appropriate to your area. Are there additional or different criteria which you would choose?

As Mehan points out, the very strength of qualitative research – its ability to give rich descriptions of social settings – can also be its weakness. Mehan identifies three such weaknesses:

1 conventional field studies tend to have an anecdotal quality. Research reports include a few *exemplary* instances of the behavior that the researcher has culled from field notes.

2 researchers seldom provide the criteria or grounds for including certain instances and not others. As a result, it is difficulty to determine the typicality or *representativeness* of instances and findings generated from them.

3 research reports presented in tabular form do not preserve the materials upon which the analysis was conducted. As the researcher abstracts data from raw materials to produce summarized findings, the original form of the materials is *lost*. Therefore, it is impossible to entertain alternative interpretations of the same materials. (Mehan, 1979: 15, my emphasis)

In the light of Mehan's arguments, even a brief perusal of published articles using qualitative methods can be profoundly disturbing (Silverman, 2010: 297–302). Much too frequently, the authors created two problems identified by Fielding and Fielding:

- a tendency to select their data to fit an ideal conception (preconception) of the phenomenon;
- a tendency to select field data which are conspicuous because they are exotic, at the expense of less dramatic (but possibly indicative) data. (1986: 32)

These problems have been succinctly diagnosed by Bryman:

> There is a tendency towards an anecdotal approach to the use of data in relation to conclusions or explanations in qualitative research. Brief conversations, snippets from unstructured interviews … are used to provide evidence of a particular contention. There are grounds for disquiet in that the representativeness or generality of these fragments is rarely addressed. (Bryman, 1988: 77)

This complaint of **anecdotalism** implies that qualitative researchers cannot exempt themselves from the standard demands that must be met by any research that claims to be 'scientific'. However, before we take an unyielding stand on this issue, we need to bear in mind two caveats:

- Your research strategy must always depend upon what you are trying to find out and the resources you have available to do this; for some kinds of research problems, the very general approach of 'mapping the woods' may be highly appropriate.
- 'Science' is a highly loaded term which can mean many things.

The first of these issues has already been dealt with extensively in this book (see Chapter 2). So I will now discuss the second issue: what is a 'scientific' approach and how does it relate to what we can recognise as credible qualitative research?

11.1.3 What is social science?

Agar and Stanley and Wise share a common assumption with some social scientists with whom they might otherwise disagree. Many qualitative researchers assume that there is a huge gulf not only between natural science and social science but between qualitative and quantitative social research.

However, we must not make too much of the differences between qualitative research and other research styles (see also Chapter 2). For instance, as Hammersley (1990) points out, although replication of an ethnographic study in the same setting may be difficult, we need to understand that replication is not always a straightforward process even in the natural sciences. Hence where research findings are not replicated this is often put down to variation in laboratory conditions and procedures (this relates to the **reliability** of the research instruments used – see Section 11.2). Moreover, only hardcore laboratory scientists would assume that the controlled experiment offers an appropriate or indeed useful model for social science.

It is an increasingly accepted view that work becomes scientific by adopting methods of study *appropriate* to its subject matter. Social science is thus scientific to the extent that it uses appropriate methods and is rigorous, critical and objective in its handling of data. As Kirk and Miller argue: 'The assumptions underlying the search for objectivity are simple. There is a world of empirical reality out there. The way we perceive and understand that world is largely up to us, but the world does not tolerate all understandings of it equally' (1986: 11).

Following Kirk and Miller, we need to recognise that 'the world does not tolerate all understandings of it equally'. This means that we must overcome the temptation to jump to easy conclusions just because there is some evidence that seems to lead in an interesting direction. Instead, we must subject this evidence to every possible test. This implies that qualitative research can be made credible (and hence resistant to the charge of anecdotalism) if we make every effort to falsify our initial assumptions about our data.

The critical method implied here is close to what Popper (1959) calls **critical rationalism**. This demands that we must seek to falsify our initial hunches about the relations between phenomena in our data. Then, only if we cannot falsify (or refute) the existence of a certain relationship are we in a position to speak about 'objective' knowledge. Even then, however, our knowledge is always provisional, subject to a subsequent study which may come up with disconfirming evidence. Popper puts it this way:

> What characterises the empirical method is its manner of exposing to falsification, in every conceivable way, the system to be tested. Its aim is not to save the lives of untenable systems but, on the contrary, to select the one which is by comparison the fittest, by exposing them all to the fiercest struggle for survival. (1959: 42)

Of course, qualitative researchers are not alone in taking Popper's critical method seriously. One way in which *quantitative* researchers attempt to satisfy Popper's demand for attempts at 'falsification' is by carefully excluding 'spurious' correlations (see Section 1.4).

To do this, the survey researcher may seek to introduce new **variables** to produce a form of 'multivariate analysis' which can offer significant, non-spurious correlations (see Mehan, 1979: 21). Through such an attempt to avoid spurious correlations, quantitative social scientists can offer a practical demonstration of their orientation to the spirit of critical enquiry that Popper advocates. Later in this chapter, in Section 8.3, we shall examine the methods, both numerical and non-numerical, that qualitative researchers can use to satisfy Popper's criterion of 'falsifiability'.

One of the most contentious issues in Popper's account of science is his claim that we can appeal to 'facts' to test our findings despite recognising that we only see such facts through particular theoretical lenses. This relates to my discussion of **models** and theories (see Table 2.1).

Hammersley (1990; 1992a) has suggested that qualitative researchers can manage the kind of circularity implied by Popper through adopting what he calls a 'subtle form of realism'. This has the following three elements:

1 validity is identified with confidence in our knowledge but not certainty of its truth;
2 reality is assumed to be independent of the claims that researchers make about it;
3 reality is always viewed through particular perspectives; hence our accounts *represent* reality they do *not* reproduce it. (Hammersley, 1992a: 50–1)

This is very close to Popper's account of falsification rather than verification as the distinguishing criterion of a scientific statement. Like Popper, Hammersley also argues that claims to validity, based on attempts at refutation, are ultimately sustained by a scientific community prepared 'to resolve disagreements by seeking common grounds of agreement' (1990: 63).

TIP

'Truth' is an exceptionally tricky term which can land us in a philosophical minefield. However, this does not mean that everything depends upon someone's opinions. When evaluating research papers, do not ask whether what they say is true but whether it is credible. As Seale puts it:

> Commitment to the revelation of truth always had that 'big' quality. Maybe all we have got now is a general sense of the value of careful scholarship, commitment to rigorous argument, attending to the links between claims and evidence, consideration of all viewpoints before taking a stance, asking and answering important rather than trivial research questions. (2004a: 409–10)

The two central **concepts** in any discussion of the credibility of scientific research are 'validity' and 'reliability'. *Reliability* refers to the stability of findings, whereas *validity* represents the truthfulness of findings (Altheide and Johnson, 1994). In the rest of this chapter, I will now discuss each in turn, examining what each concept means in practice in both quantitative and qualitative research.

11.2 RELIABILITY

> refers to the degree of consistency with which instances are assigned to the same category by different observers or by the same observer on different occasions. (Hammersley, 1992a: 67)

Reliability usually refers to the degree to which the findings of a study are independent of accidental circumstances of their production (Kirk and Miller, 1986: 20). It deals with replicability, the question whether or not some future researchers could repeat the research project and come up with the same results, interpretations and claims. In quantitative research, for example, reliability usually refers to the extent to which an experiment, test or measurement yields the same result or consistent measurements on repeated trials. In this context, Kirk and Miller cite the example of using a thermometer:

> A thermometer that shows the same reading of 82 degrees each time it is plunged into boiling water gives a reliable measurement. A second thermometer might give readings over a series of measurements that vary from around 100 degrees. The second thermometer would be unreliable but relatively valid, whereas the first would be invalid but perfectly reliable. (1986: 19)

Obviously, in qualitative research, we are unlikely to use a thermometer! So how can we make our research more reliable? Moisander and Valtonen (2006) suggest two ways to satisfy reliability criteria in non-quantitative work:

- by making the research process *transparent* through describing our research strategy and data analysis methods in a sufficiently detailed manner in the research report
- paying attention to 'theoretical transparency' by making explicit the theoretical stance from which the interpretation takes place and showing how this produces particular interpretations and excludes others.

However, writers who contest the applicability of scientific standards of credibility to qualitative research predictably also deny the relevance of reliability. Let us examine their arguments before going on to consider, in more detail, how reliability criteria can be applied to different kinds of qualitative data.

11.2.1 Reliability not a problem?

Some social researchers argue that a concern for the reliability of observations arises only within the quantitative research tradition. Because such **positivist** work sees no difference between the natural and social worlds, it wants to produce reliable measures of social life. Conversely, it is argued, once we treat social reality as always in flux, then it makes no sense to worry about whether our research instruments measure accurately.

This is an example of such a critical argument:

> Positivist notions of reliability assume an underlying universe where inquiry could, quite logically, be replicated. This assumption of an unchanging social world is in direct contrast to the qualitative/interpretative assumption that the social world is always changing and the concept of replication is itself problematic. (Marshall and Rossman, 1989: 147)

But is this so? It is one thing to argue that the world is processual, it is much more problematic to imply, as Marshall and Rossman seem to do, that the world is in infinite flux (appropriate to the pre-Socratic Greek philosopher Heraclitus, perhaps, but not a comfortable position for social scientists).

Such a position would rule out any systematic research since it implies that we cannot assume any stable properties in the social world. However, if we concede the possible existence of such properties, why should other work not replicate these properties? As Kirk and Miller argue:

> Qualitative researchers can no longer afford to beg the issue of reliability. While the forte of field research will always lie in its capability to sort out the validity of propositions, its results will (reasonably) go ignored minus attention to reliability. For reliability to be calculated, it is incumbent on the scientific investigator to document his or her procedure. (1986: 72)

Following Kirk and Miller, I consider below how reliability can be addressed in qualitative studies. Central to my argument is the assumption that high reliability in qualitative research is associated with what Clive Seale calls **low-inference descriptors**. As Seale puts it, this involves 'recording observations in terms that are as concrete as possible, including verbatim accounts of what people say, for example, rather than researchers' reconstructions of the general sense of what a person said, which would allow researchers' personal perspectives to influence the reporting' (1999: 148).

I will now look at the methodologies discussed in Part Two of this book: observation, **textual** analysis, the interview, the focus group and the transcription of naturally occurring talk and visual data. Using such data, how can we achieve low-inference descriptions and thereby satisfy the criterion of reliability?

11.2.2 Reliability and observation

Observational studies rarely provide readers with anything other than brief, persuasive, data extracts. As Bryman notes about the typical ethnography: 'field notes or extended transcripts are rarely available; these would be very helpful in order to allow the reader to formulate his or her own hunches about the perspective of the people who have been studied' (1988: 77).

Although, as Bryman suggests, extended extracts from fieldnotes would be helpful, the reader also should require information on how fieldnotes were recorded and in what contexts. As Kirk and Miller argue:

> he contemporary search for reliability in qualitative observation revolves around detailing the relevant context of observation. (1986: 52)

Spradley (1979) suggests that observers keep four separate sets of notes:

1 short notes made at the time
2 expanded notes made as soon as possible after each field session
3 a field-work journal to record problems and ideas that arise during each stage of field work
4 a provisional running record of analysis and interpretation (discussed by Kirk and Miller, 1986: 53).

Spradley's suggestions help to systematise fieldnotes and thus improve their reliability. Implicit in them is the need to distinguish between **etic analysis** (based on the researcher's concepts) and **emic analysis** (deriving from the conceptual framework of those being studied). Such a distinction is employed in the set of fieldnote conventions set out in Table 11.2.

TABLE 11.2   Some fieldnote conventions

Sign	Convention	Use
" "	Double quotation marks	Verbatim quotes
' '	Single quotation marks	Paraphrases
( )	Parentheses	Contextual data or fieldworker's interpretations
< >	Angled brackets	Emic concepts
/	Slash	Etic concepts
____	Solid line	Partitions time

Source: adapted from Kirk and Miller, 1986: 57

The case study below seeks to put some meat on the bare bones of this discussion of reliable observation.

CASE STUDY
Adolescent Drug Users

In their ethnographic study of adolescent drug users, Barry Glassner and Julia Loughlin carefully tape recorded all their interviews. These tapes were then transcribed and coded by 'identifying topics, ways of talking, themes, events, actors and so forth … Those lists became a catalogue of codes, consisting of 45 topics, each with up to 99 descriptors' (Glassner and Loughlin, 1987: 25).

On the surface, such tabulation appears to involve the counting for the sake of counting found in some quantitative research. However, the authors make clear that their approach to data analysis is different from positivistic, survey research studies:

> In more positivistic research designs, coder reliability is assessed in terms of agreement among coders. In qualitative research one is unconcerned with standardizing interpretation of data. Rather, our goal in developing this complex cataloguing and retrieval system has been to retain *good access to the words of the subjects*, without relying upon the memory of interviewers or data analysts. (1987: 27, my emphasis)

By retaining this access to subjects' own categories, Glassner and Loughlin satisfy the theoretical orientation of much qualitative research while simultaneously allowing readers to retain some sort of direct access to raw data. In this way, they satisfy Seale's criterion of using *low-inference descriptors*. Moreover, Glassner and Loughlin suggest that their analysis fits two criteria of reliability more commonly found in quantitative studies, namely:

1 The coding and data analysis was done 'blind' – both the coding staff and the analysts of the data 'conducted their research without knowledge of (the) expectations or hypotheses of the project directors' (1987: 30).

2 The computer-assisted recording and analysis of the data meant that one could be more confident that the patterns reported actually existed throughout the data rather than in favourable examples. This follows the argument of Maynard and Clayman (1991) that observational fieldnotes must be wedded to more reliable data such as audio or video recordings of actual behaviour (see Section 11.2.5).

EXERCISE 11.2

This exercise asks you to use the fieldnote conventions set out in Table 11.2. You should gather observational data in any setting with which you are familiar and in which it is relatively easy to find a place to make notes (you may return to the setting you used for Exercise 5.2). Observe for about an hour. Ideally, you should carry out your observations with someone else who is using the same conventions.

1 Record your notes using these fieldnote conventions. Compare your notes with your colleague's. Identify and explain any differences.

2 What conventions were difficult to use? Why was this so (e.g. because they are unclear or inappropriate to the setting)?

3 Can you think of other conventions that would improve the reliability of your fieldnotes?

4 What have you gained (or lost) compared with earlier observational exercises (e.g. Exercise 3.2)?

5 Which further fields of enquiry do your fieldnotes suggest?

11.2.3 Reliability and texts

When you are dealing with a **text**, the data are already available, unfiltered through the researcher's fieldnotes. For this reason, textual data are, in principle, more reliable than observations. Of course, I say 'in principle' because it is possible that any text can be forged – think of the example of the so-called 'Hitler diaries'.

Providing there is no evidence of forgery, issues of reliability now arise only through the *categories* you use to analyse each text. It is important that these categories should be used in a *standardised* way, so that any researcher would categorise in the same way.

A standard method of doing this is known as 'inter-rater reliability'. It involves giving the same data to a number of analysts (or raters) and asking them to analyse those data according to an agreed set of categories. Their reports are then examined and any differences discussed and ironed out. In order to see how this method works, you should find a colleague who worked on the same exercise in Chapter 5. Compare your analysis of the same data and see if you can iron out any differences.

TIP

Just because you and a colleague agree about the use of a category, it does not mean that the category itself stands up to any scrutiny. As we saw in Section 3.2, **content analysis** can involve a relatively arbitrary imposition of categories upon data. So always ensure that how you categorise fits the analytic model with which you are working.

11.2.4 Reliability and interviews

The reliability of interview schedules is a central question in quantitative methods textbooks. According to these books, it is very important that each respondent understands the questions in the same way and that answers can be coded without the possibility of uncertainty. This is achieved through a number of means, including:

- thorough pre-testing of interview schedules
- thorough training of interviewers
- as much use as possible of fixed-choice answers
- inter-rater reliability checks on the coding of answers to open-ended questions.

In Chapter 6, I argued that a concentration on such matters tended to deflect attention away from the theoretical assumptions underlying the meaning that we attach to interviewees' answers. Nonetheless, this does not mean that we can altogether ignore conventional issues of reliability, even if we deliberately avoid treating interview accounts as simple 'reports' on reality. So even when our analytic concern is with narrative structure or **Membership Categorisation**, it is still helpful to pre-test an interview schedule and to compare how at least two researchers analyse the same data.

Interview studies must also satisfy the criterion of using *low-inference descriptors*. When we do e-mail interviews, we can readily satisfy this criterion because the participants have already done their own transcribing. When reporting other interviews or focus groups, we can satisfy the need for low-inference descriptors by:

- tape recording all interactions
- carefully transcribing these tapes according to the needs of reliable analysis (not handing the problem over to an audio-typist!)
- presenting long extracts of data in the research report – including, at the very least, the question that provoked any answer.

EXERCISE 11.3

This exercise gives you the opportunity to assess the reliability of your analysis of the data used in earlier exercises, using the method of inter-rater agreement.

You should find a colleague who carried out the same data-analysis exercise in Chapter 5. Return to your answers to that exercise and now consider:

1 What are the major differences and similarities in the way in which you used concepts and categories in this exercise?
2 Which part of either person's analysis needs to be revised or abandoned?
3 Do similarities in your analysis mean that the concepts and categories you have used are good ones (distinguish issues of reliability and usefulness?).
4 Do any differences mean that the concepts and categories you have used are badly designed and/or that you have used them inappropriately?
5 What have you learned from this comparison? How would you redo your analysis in the light of it?

11.2.5 Reliability and transcripts of audio and video data

Kirk and Miller's argument for the conventionalisation of methods for recording fieldnotes can be applied to transcripts. For we need only depend upon fieldnotes in the absence of audio or video recordings. The availability of transcripts of such recordings, using standard conventions (see the Appendix), satisfies Kirk and Miller's proper demand for the documentation of procedures.

In the case of video recordings, standard transcription conventions are gradually emerging (see Chapter 10). In addition, readers of printed papers can be given prints of still pictures, so-called 'frame grabs' (see ten Have, 1998: 93). With the advent of Internet technologies, we may see a quantum leap where readers and viewers have access to audio- and videotapes while reading the researcher's transcripts.

Although this would go a long way to satisfying the need for low-inference descriptors, we should not make the assumption that it totally overcomes reliability issues. For instance, video researchers still have to make potentially fallible decisions about where to place their camera(s) and when to stop filming (see Heath et al., 2010).

At a more basic level, when people's activities are tape recorded and transcribed, the reliability of the interpretation of transcripts may be gravely weakened by a failure to transcribe apparently trivial, but often crucial, pauses and overlaps. This was revealed when I participated in a study of medical consultations which sought to establish whether cancer patients had understood that their condition was fatal

In this study (Clavarino et al., 1995), we attempted to examine the basis upon which interpretive judgements were made about the content of a series of audio-taped doctor–patient interviews between three oncologists and their newly referred cancer patients. It was during this interview that the patients were supposedly informed that their cancer was incurable.

Two independent transcriptions were performed. In the first, an attempt was made to transcribe the talk 'verbatim', that is without grammatical or other 'tidying up'. Using the first transcription, three independent coders, who had been trained to be consistent, coded the same material. Inter-coder reliability was then estimated. Inconsistencies among the coders may have reflected some ambiguity in the data, some overlap between coding categories, or simple coding errors.

The second transcription was informed by the analytic ideas and transcription symbols of **conversation analysis** (CA). This provided additional information on how the parties organised their talk and, we believe, represents a more objective, comprehensive and therefore more reliable recording of the data because of the level of detail given by this method.

By drawing upon the transcription symbols and concepts of CA, we sought to reveal subtle features in the talk, showing how both doctor and patients produced and received hearable ambiguities in the patient's prognosis. This involved a shift of focus from coders' readings to how participants demonstrably monitor each other's talk. Once we pay attention to such detail, judgements can be made that are more convincingly valid. Inevitably, this leads to a resolution of the problem of inter-coder reliability.

For instance, when researchers first listened to tapes of relevant hospital consultations, they sometimes felt that there was no evidence that the patients had picked up their doctors' often guarded statements about their prognosis. However, when the tapes were retranscribed, it was demonstrated that patients used very soft utterances (like 'yes' or, more usually, 'mm') to mark that they were taking up this information. Equally, doctors would monitor patients' silences and rephrase their prognosis statements.

In CA, as discussed in Chapter 9, a method similar to inter-rater comparison is used to strengthen reliability. Wherever possible, group data analysis sessions are held to listen to (or watch) audio or video recordings. It is important here that we do not delude ourselves into seeking a 'perfect' transcript. Transcripts can always be improved and the search for perfection is illusory and time consuming. Rather the aim is to arrive at an agreed transcript, adequate for the task at hand. A further benefit arising from such group sessions is that they usually lead to suggestions about promising lines of analysis.

As already noted, the credibility of qualitative research studies rests not just on the reliability of their data and methods but also on the validity of their findings. I now turn, therefore, to the nature of validity in qualitative research and the means through which we can approach it.

11.2.6 Reliability: A Summary

I have suggested that both reliability and validity are important issues in field research. I went on to suggest that reliability can be addressed by using standardised methods to write fieldnotes and prepare transcripts. In the case of interviews, focus groups and textual studies, I also argued that reliability can be improved by comparing the analysis of the same data by several researchers. Let us now turn to validity.

11.3 VALIDITY

> By validity, I mean … the extent to which an account accurately represents the social phenomena to which it refers. (Hammersley, 1990: 57)

Proposing a purportedly 'accurate' statement involves the possibility of two kinds of *error* which have been clearly defined by Kirk and Miller (1986: 29–30):

- *Type 1* error is believing a statement to be true when it is not (in statistical terms, this means rejecting the 'null hypothesis', i.e. the hypothesis that there is no relation between the variables).
- *Type 2* error is rejecting a statement which, in fact, is true (i.e. incorrectly supporting the 'null hypothesis').

Because the idea of validity originated in quantitative research, I will begin by considering what it means in that context and how applicable it is to more qualitatively oriented studies.

11.3.1 Validity in quantitative research

In quantitative research, a common form of Type 1 error arises if we accept a 'spurious' correlation. For instance, just because X seems always to be followed by Y, it does not mean that X necessarily *causes* Y. There might be a third factor, Z, which produces both X and Y. Alternatively, Z might be an 'intervening variable' which is caused by X and then influences Y (see Selltiz et al., 1964: 424–31 and my discussion of Procter's 1993 data in Section 1.4).

As we saw in Chapter 1, the quantitative researcher can use sophisticated means to guard against the possibility of spurious correlations. However, the survey methods discussed there are not without problems. As Fielding and Fielding argue: 'the most advanced survey procedures themselves only manipulate data that had to be gained at some point by asking people' (1986: 12).

As I suggested in Chapter 6, what people say in answer to interview questions does not have a stable relationship to how they behave in naturally occurring situations. Second, as we saw in Chapter 1, researchers' claims may sometimes be credible merely because they rely on common-sense knowledge which stands in need of explication rather than passive acceptance.

Again, Fielding and Fielding make the relevant point: 'researchers who generalize from a **sample** survey to a larger population ignore the possible disparity between the discourse of actors about some topical issue and the way they respond to questions in a formal context' (1986: 21).

So quantitative methods offer no simple solution to the question of validity:

> ultimately all methods of data collection are analysed 'qualitatively', in so far as the act of analysis is an interpretation, and therefore of necessity a selective rendering. Whether the data collected are quantifiable or qualitative, the issue of the *warrant* for their inferences must be confronted. (Fielding and Fielding, 1986: 12, my emphasis)

We shall now examine how qualitative researchers may claim, in Fielding and Fielding's terms, that they have a 'warrant for their inferences' and that their work is valid.

11.3.2 Claims to validity in qualitative research

As I have argued, the issue of validity is appropriate whatever one's theoretical orientation or use of quantitative or qualitative data. Few contemporary social scientists are satisfied by **naturalism**'s assumption that credibility is guaranteed provided one 'hangs out' with one's tribe or sub-cultural group and returns with an 'authentic' account of the field.

However, I shall not discuss here many standard criteria of assessing validity, either because they are available in other methodology texts or because they are commonsensical and/or inappropriate to the theoretical logic of qualitative research as discussed in Section 1.6. These criteria include:

- the impact of the researcher on the setting (the so-called 'halo' or 'Hawthorne' effect) (see Landsberger, 1958; Hammersley, 1990: 80–2)
- the values of the researcher (see Weber, 1949, and this volume, Chapter 12)
- the truth status of a respondent's account (see Chapters 6 and 7).

Two other forms of validation have been suggested as particularly appropriate to the logic of qualitative research:

1 Comparing different kinds of data (e.g. quantitative and qualitative) and different methods (e.g. observation and interviews) to see whether they corroborate one another. This form of comparison, called **triangulation**, derives from navigation, where different bearings give the correct position of an object.
2 Taking one's findings back to the subjects being studied. Where these people verify one's findings, it is argued, one can be more confident of their validity. This method is known as **respondent validation**.

Each of these methods is discussed below. In my discussion, I show why I believe these methods are usually *inappropriate* to qualitative research.

Triangulating data and methods

Triangulation usually refers to combining multiple theories, methods, observers and empirical materials, to produce a more accurate, comprehensive and objective representation of the object of study. The most common application of triangulation in qualitative research is the use of *multiple methods*. For instance, one may try to combine interviews with observation or qualitative analysis with surveys. The assumption is that, if the findings obtained with all these methods correspond and draw the same or similar conclusions, then the validity of those findings and conclusions has been established (see Moisander and Valtonen, 2006).

However, this is to assume that:

> by looking at an object from more than one standpoint, it is possible to produce a more true and certain representation of the object. In natural sciences, particularly with concrete physical objects, this may well make sense. But in cultural research, which focuses on social reality, the object of knowledge *is* different from different perspectives. And the different points of view cannot be merged, into a single, 'true' and 'certain' representation of the object. (Moisander and Valtonen, 2006: 45)

A major early advocate of the method of triangulation was Denzin (1970) who suggested that 'method triangulation' can serve to overcome partial views and present something like a complete picture. However, as Denzin elsewhere notes, actions and accounts are 'situated' in particular contexts. This implies, contrary to Denzin's early work about triangulation, that methods, often drawn from different theories, cannot give us an 'objective' truth (Fielding and Fielding, 1986: 33). So:

> multiple theories and multiple methods are … worth pursuing, but not for the reasons Denzin cites … The accuracy of a method comes from its systematic application, but rarely does the inaccuracy of one approach to the data complement the accuracies of another. (Fielding and Fielding, 1986: 35)

However, Fielding and Fielding remind us that it may not be sensible to throw the baby out with the bathwater. Accordingly, they suggest that the use of triangulation should operate according to ground rules. Basically, these seem to operate as follows:

- begin from a theoretical perspective or model (e.g. naturalism, emotionalism or **constructionism**)
- choose methods and data which will give you an account of structure and meaning from within that perspective (e.g. emotionalists will want to generate data which give an authentic insight into people's experiences, while constructionists will prefer to reveal how particular social phenomena are put together through particular interactions).

Yet, even when we use a single analytical model, it can be tricky to aggregate data in order to arrive at an overall 'truth'. As Hammersley and Atkinson point out: 'one should not adopt a naively "optimistic" view that the aggregation of data from different sources will unproblematically add up to produce a more complete picture' (95: 199).

Of course, this does not imply that the qualitative researcher should avoid generating data in multiple ways. Even for constructionists, data triangulation can serve as an assembly of reminders about the situated character of action. For instance, R. Dingwall (personal correspondence) has suggested that triangulation has some value where it reveals the existence of public and private accounts of an agency's work. Here 'interview and field data can be combined ... to make better sense of the other'. Triangulation, from this perspective, is not a way of obtaining a 'true' reading but 'is best understood as a strategy that adds rigor, breadth, complexity, richness and depth to any inquiry' (Denzin and Lincoln, 2000a: 5).

The 'mistake' only arises in using data to adjudicate between accounts. For this reduces the role of the researcher to what Garfinkel (1967) calls an 'ironist', using one account to undercut another, while remaining blind to the sense of each account in the context in which it arises.

To conclude: the major problem with triangulation as a test of validity is that, by counterposing different contexts, it ignores the context-bound and skilful character of social interaction and assumes that members are 'cultural dopes', who need a social scientist to dispel their illusions (see Garfinkel, 1967; Bloor, 1978).

EXERCISE 11.4

This exercise is concerned with method triangulation. You should select any *two* of the methods discussed in Chapters 5–10 (i.e. observation, texts, interviews, focus groups transcripts and visual images). Then you should choose a research topic where these two methods can be applied. For example, you might want to compare your observations of a library with interviews with library users and staff. Alternatively, you could obtain official documents about the academic aims of your university and compare these with your observations, interviews or audio recordings of a teaching session (subject to everyone's agreement).

Now do the following:

1 Briefly analyse each of your two sources of data. What does each source tell you about your topic?
2 Identify different themes emerging in the two data sources. How far are these differences relevant for an overall understanding of the topic?
3 Using your data, assess the argument that evidence is only relevant in the context of the situation in which it arises.
4 In the light of the above, explain whether, if you had to pursue your topic further, you would use multiple methods.

Respondent validation

If you privilege 'experience' as 'authentic', as is **emotionalism**'s preference, you will probably want to try to validate your research findings by taking them back to the people you have studied to see whether the findings conform to their own 'experience'. Along these lines, Reason and Rowan (1981) criticise researchers who are fearful of 'contaminating their data with the experience of the subject'. On the contrary, they argue, good research goes back to the subjects with tentative results, and refines them in the light of the subjects' reactions.

Bloor (1978) incorporates Reason and Rowan's preferred approach (item 3 in the list below) in his discussion of three procedures which attempt respondent validation (see also Frake, 1964):

1 The researcher seeks to predict members' classifications in actual situations of their use.
2 The researcher prepares hypothetical cases and predicts respondents' responses to them.
3 The researcher provides respondents with a research report and records their reactions to it.

Bloor (1978; 1983) used the third procedure in his study of doctors' decision-making in adeno-tonsillectomy cases, hoping that doctors would validate his descriptions of their practice – what he calls 'a sort of self-recognition effect' (1978: 549). Although Bloor reports that he was able to make some useful modifications as a result of the surgeons' comments, he reports many reservations. These centre around whether respondents are able to follow a report written for a sociological audience and, even if it is presented intelligibly, whether they will (or should) have any interest in it (1978: 550). A further problem, noted by Abrams (1984: 8), is that 'overt respondent validation is only possible if the results of the analysis are compatible with the self-image of the respondents'.

However, Bloor concludes, this need not mean that attempts at respondents' validation have *no* value. They do generate further data which, while not validating the research report, often suggest interesting paths for further analysis (Bloor, 1983: 172). This is shown in the case study which follows.

Bloor's point has been very effectively taken up by Fielding and Fielding (1986) (respondent validation is also criticised by Bryman, 1988: 78–9). The Fieldings concede that subjects being studied may have additional knowledge, especially about the context of their actions. However:

> there is no reason to assume that members have privileged status as commentators on their actions ... such feedback cannot be taken as direct validation or refutation of the observer's inferences. Rather such processes of so-called 'validation' should be treated as yet another source of data and insight. (1986: 43)

CASE STUDY
Drinkers' Talk

In his ethnographic study of Finnish drinkers in a bar, Pertti Alasuutari reports that he raised the issue of why participants were always so eager to compete for the title of heaviest drinker and at the same time to belittle the drinking of others. This was the conversation:

Extract 11.1 (Alasuutari)

PA: Somehow I feel there's this feeling in this group that there's someone here who hasn't drunk as much as the others or who's been down and out for a shorter while than others, that you tend to belittle that person's drinking, that, you know that's nothing really, I drank a lot more than he did.

A: Where've you heard that?

PA: I have you know.

B: I see.

PA: Even during these sessions right here.

C: It's always better the sooner you have the sense to go and get help isn't it.

A: That's right.

C: The longer you drink the more stupid you are, there's no doubt about that.

PA: But do you brag about being more stupid?

C: You tend to color things a bit, like I've been drinking longer than you have. You've only been drinking for year but I've been there two years. So the one has been drinking a year realizes that this is the point where I need to go and get help for myself. I'm so stupid that I didn't have the sense to come and get help, I had to carry on. So this is how I describe the situation so that there you are, I'm a bit better, *I know these things*, a bit better. (1995: 170–1)

This is Alasuutari's account of the conversation:

When I raised this question the members of the group first wanted to deny my interpretation, even though I had clear examples of these sorts of situations in my field notes. When at long last it is admitted that the phenomenon really exists, member C [in the italicized section of his speech] renders further support to my interpretation that the emphasis on the seriousness of one's earlier alcohol problems is associated with the respect that members show for practical experience. (1995: 171)

Kathy Charmaz (personal correspondence) has suggested that this example displays a subtle version of respondent validation:

In this instance, Alasuutari offered his interpretation and pushed for a dialogue about it. He gained confirmation of his view then pushed further later in the same conversation … Interestingly, Alasuutari did not take the men's support for his interpretation at face value. Rather he took it a few analytic steps further. He located his confirmed idea in the context of the group culture and concluded that it reflected the group members' contradictory relationships with staff and lack of trust in professionals.

If we are not fully convinced by either triangulation or members' validation, how, then, are we to overcome the anecdotal quality of much qualitative research in order to claim validity? To answer this question, I will review what I believe to be more appropriate methods for validating studies based largely or entirely upon qualitative data. These include:

- analytic induction
- the constant comparative method
- deviant-case analysis
- comprehensive data treatment
- using appropriate tabulations.

Analytic Induction (AI)

As I remarked in Section 1.6, qualitative researchers need not accept the assumption that their work can only be exploratory or descriptive. As Glaser and Strauss (1967) argue, **grounded theory** demands that we often avoid prior hypotheses; this does not mean that we cannot (or should not) generate and test hypotheses 'grounded' in our data. This is done through **analytic induction**.

> The purpose of analytic induction is to uncover causal relations through identification of the essential characteristics of the phenomenon studied. To this end, the method starts not with a hypothesis but with a limited set of cases from which an initial explanatory hypothesis is then derived. If the initial hypothesis fails to be confirmed by one case, it is revised. Additional cases of the same class of phenomena are then selected. If the hypothesis is not confirmed by these further cases, the conceptual definition of the phenomenon is revised. The process continues until the hypothesis is no longer refuted and further study tells the researcher nothing new. (Gobo, 2009: 198)

Using AI in qualitative research, we seek to identify some 'phenomenon' and to generate a provisional hypothesis. We can then go on to take a small body of data (a 'case') and examine it as follows:

> one case is ... studied to see whether the hypothesis relates to it. If not, the hypothesis is reformulated (or the phenomenon redefined to exclude the case). While a small number of cases support practical certainty, negative cases disprove the explanation, which is then reformulated. Examination of cases, redefinition of the phenomenon and reformulation of hypotheses is repeated until a universal relationship is shown. (Fielding, 1988: 7–8)

AI is the equivalent to the statistical testing of quantitative associations to see if they are greater than might be expected at random (random error). However: 'in qualitative analysis ... there is no random error variance. all exceptions are eliminated by revising hypotheses until all the data fit. The result of this procedure is that statistical tests are actually *unnecessary* once the negative cases are removed' (Fielding and Fielding, 1986: 89).

CASE STUDY
Decision-Making in the Clinic

An example of AI being used in a field research study will be helpful. In Bloor's study of surgeons, already discussed, he tried 'to inductively reconstruct each specialist's own standard "decision rules" which he normally used to decide on a disposal' (Bloor, 1978: 545). These rules were then compared with each doctor's procedures for searching through relevant information.

Bloor draws upon the distinction between 'necessary' and 'sufficient' conditions for an outcome. 'Necessary' conditions are conditions without which a particular outcome is impossible. 'Sufficient' conditions are conditions which totally explain the outcome in question. For instance, a necessary condition for me to give a lecture is that I should be present at a particular time and place. Sufficient conditions may include me knowing about the subject, having my notes with me, finding an audience awaiting me, and so on. This is how Bloor reports his inductive method:

1　For each specialist, cases were provisionally classified according to the disposal-category into which they fell.
2　The data on all a specialist's cases in a particular disposal-category were scrutinized in order to attempt a provisional list of those case-features common to the cases in that category.
3　The 'deviant cases' (i.e. those cases where features common to many of the cases in the disposal-category were lacking) were scrutinized in order to ascertain whether (a) the provisional list of case-features common to a particular category could be modified as to allow the inclusion of the deviant cases; or, (b) the classificatory system could be so modified as to allow the inclusion of the deviant cases within a modified category.
4　Having thus produced a list of case-features common to all cases in a particular category, cases in alternative categories were scrutinized to discover which case-features were shared with cases outside the first category considered. Such shared case-features were thus judged *necessary* rather than *sufficient* for the achievement of a particular disposal.
5　From the necessary and sufficient case-features associated with a particular category of cases sharing a common disposal, the specialist's relevant decision rules were derived'. (1978: 546, my emphasis)

This case study provides a shortened version of Bloor's list. He adds two further stages where cases are rescrutinised for each decision rule and then the whole process is re-enacted in order to account for the disposals obtained by all the specialists in the study.

Bloor recognises that his procedure was not *wholly* inductive. Before beginning the analysis, he already had general impressions, gained from contact in the field (1978: 547). We might also add that no hypothesis-testing can or should be theory-free. Necessarily, then, AI depends upon both a model of how social life works and a set of concepts specific to that model.

AI may appear to be rather complicated. However, it boils down to two simple techniques which I shall now consider:

- the use of the constant comparative method
- the search for deviant cases.

The constant comparative method

The comparative method means that the qualitative researcher should always attempt to find another case through which to test out a provisional hypothesis. In a early study of the changing perspectives of medical students during their training, Becker and Geer (1960) found that they could test their emerging hypothesis about the influence of career stages upon perceptions by comparing different groups at one time and also comparing one cohort of students with another over the course of training. For instance, it could only be claimed with confidence that beginning medical students tended to be idealists if several cohorts of first-year students all shared this perspective.

Similarly, when I was studying what happened to Down's syndrome children in a heart hospital, I tested out my findings with tape recordings of consultations from the same clinic involving children without the congenital abnormality (see later in this section). And, of course, my attempt to analyse the ceremonial order of private medical practice (Chapter 5) was highly dependent on comparative data on public clinics.

In the case study that follows, the great ethnographer, Howard Becker, reflects on what the comparative method can offer us.

CASE STUDY
The Comparative Method

Comparison has always been the backbone, acknowledged or not, of good sociological thinking. Finding two or more things that are alike in some important way yet differ in other ways, looking for the further differences that create those you first noticed, looking for the deeper processes these surface differences embody – these operations create sociological knowledge of the world and give us the more abstract theories that tell us what to look for the next time out.

Finding things that are alike sounds easier than it is. There are traps. Most commonly, we think two things are alike because they have the same name: all things called schools must be alike, all things called families are the same in all important respects. Why else would we call them by the same name? But, in fact, schools differ in crucial ways and most especially in what they actually do. Some may be engaged in an activity that could charitably called 'education,' but many others are far more custodial in their operation. And other organizations which go by different names – prisons, for example – can easily be seen to do a great deal of educating, both the kind prison officials organize to teach inmates a useful trade and the kind inmates organize to teach each other potentially more useful trades. I leave to you the similar exercise to be done about families.

If we can not take names at face value, how do we find similar things to compare? We can do what Goffman did – in *Asylums* [Goffman, 1961a]: choose a trait that defines the category to investigate and stick with it, no matter how counter-intuitive the collection of cases it produces. But the same problem arises: how to find a trait that identifies a category about which we can make sociological interesting remarks. Goffman's example tells us to choose a trait that constrains social interaction: total institutions, on his definition, prevent the interaction between inmates and staff who live and work in them from interacting with the outside world, and strictly regulate and minimize interaction between these two categories of inhabitants. These characteristics are easy to discover and 'measure,' and provoke no definitional arguments.

Why not? Because they do not coincide with our conventional categories of moral judgment, which make sure to place 'incongruous cases' in their morally relevant slot. We routinely make moral judgments, one way or another, about prisons and mental hospitals, which we conventionally know to be wicked places filled with wicked people (whether we mean the inmates or the custodians), and about places like convents or military training centers, which we conventionally know to be respectable organizations. But we have no such ready-made judgments about a category which contains those four organizations, as well as submarines, ships at sea and all the other varied phenomena Goffman's definition assembles. The morally disparate character (from a conventional point of view) of these organizations which are so clearly alike in their limitation of interaction frees analysis from having to conform to conventional ideas of good and bad.

Having found a category whose interactional similarities promise to produce sociological insight, we then look for other interactionally interesting differences between them. And we look for the conditions of such differences and for their consequences. (Becker: 2010: 1)

However, beginning researchers are unlikely to have the resources to study different cases. Yet this does not mean that comparison is impossible. The constant comparative method involves simply inspecting and comparing all the data fragments that arise in a single case (Glaser and Strauss, 1967).

While such a method may seem attractive, beginning researchers may worry about two practical difficulties involved in implementing it. First, they may lack the resources to assemble all their data in an analysable form. For instance, transcribing a whole data set may be impossibly time consuming – as well as diverting you from data analysis! Second, how are you to compare data when you may have not yet generated a provisional hypothesis or even an initial set of categories?

Fortunately, these objections can be readily overcome. In practice, it usually makes sense to begin analysis on a relatively small part of your data. Then, having generated a set of categories, you can test out emerging hypotheses by steadily expanding your data corpus. This point has been clearly made by Peräkylä using the example of studies based on tape-recorded data:

> There is a limit to how much data a single researcher or a research team can transcribe and analyse. But on the other hand, a large database has definite advantages … a large portion of the data can be kept as a resource that is used only when the analysis has progressed so far that the phenomena under study have been specified. At that later stage, short sections from the data in reserve can be transcribed, and thereby, the full variation of the phenomenon can be observed'. (Peräkylä, 2004a: 288)

I employed this constant comparative method, moving from small to larger data sets, in my study of AIDS counselling (Silverman, 1997). For instance, having isolated an instance of how a client resisted a counsellor's advice, I trawled through my data to obtain a larger sample of cases where advice-resistance was present.

Deviant-case analysis

The comparative method implies actively seeking out and addressing deviant cases. Mehan makes the point:

> The method begins with a small batch of data. A provisional analytic scheme is generated. The scheme is then compared to other data, and modifications made in the scheme as necessary. The provisional analytic scheme is constantly confronted by 'negative' or 'discrepant' cases until the researcher has derived a small set of recursive rules that incorporate all the data in the analysis. (Mehan, 1979: 21)

Mehan notes that this is very different from the sense of 'deviant-case analysis' in quantitative, survey research. Here you turn to deviant cases in two circumstances:

- when the existing variables will not produce sufficiently high statistical correlations
- when good correlations are found but you suspect these might be 'spurious'.

By contrast, the qualitative researcher should not be satisfied by explanations which appear to explain nearly all the variance in their data. Instead, as I have already argued, in qualitative research, every piece of data has to be used until it can be accounted for.

It is important to stress that 'deviant cases' are properly identified on the basis of concepts deriving from a particular model. Thus pieces of data are never intrinsically 'deviant' but rather become so in relation to the approach used. This theoretically defined approach to analysis should also properly apply to the compilation and inspection of data in tabulated form.

However, deviant-case analysis in the context of the constant comparative method, because it involves a repeated to and fro between different parts of your data, implies something much bigger. All parts of your data must, at some point, be inspected and analysed. This is part of what is meant by 'comprehensive data treatment'.

Comprehensive data treatment

Ten Have notes the complaint that, in CA, like other kinds of qualitative research, 'findings ... are based on a subjectively selected, and probably biased, "sample" of cases that happen to fit the analytic argument' (ten Have, 1998: 8).

This complaint, which amounts to a charge of anecdotalism, can be addressed by what ten Have, following Mehan (1979), calls 'comprehensive data treatment'. This comprehensiveness arises because, in qualitative research, 'all cases of data ... [are] incorporated in the analysis' (Mehan, 1979: 21).

Such comprehensiveness goes beyond what is normally demanded in many quantitative methods. For instance, in survey research one is usually satisfied by achieving significant, non-spurious, correlations. So, if nearly all your data support your hypothesis, your job is largely done.

By contrast, in qualitative research, working with smaller data sets open to repeated inspection, you should not be satisfied until your generalisation is able to apply to every single gobbet of relevant data you have collected.

The outcome is a generalisation which can be every bit as valid as a statistical correlation. As Mehan puts it: 'The result is an integrated, precise model that comprehensively describes a specific phenomena [*sic*], instead of a simple correlational statement about antecedent and consequent conditions' (Mehan, 1979: 21).

Such comprehensive data treatment can be aided by the use of *appropriate* tabulations, where the categories counted are derived from theoretically defined concepts.

Using appropriate tabulations

> By our pragmatic view, qualitative research does imply a commitment to field activities. It does not imply a commitment to innumeracy. (Kirk and Miller, 1986: 10)

There are at least two ways in which qualitative researchers can make use of quantitative measures:

- through multi-method studies in which a qualitative case study is combined with some kind of quantitative survey
- by using simple tabulations in an otherwise purely qualitative study.

Multi-method studies have been already discussed in this book (see Section 2.5). In this part of the chapter, I will discuss the second approach of using appropriate tabulations of qualitative data.

I shall try to show that simple counting techniques can offer a means to survey the whole corpus of data ordinarily lost in intensive, qualitative research. Instead of taking the researcher's word for it, the reader has a chance to gain a sense of the flavour of the data as a whole. In turn, researchers are able to engage in comprehensive data treatment by testing and revising their generalisations. In this way, the proper use of simple tabulations can remove the researcher's (and reader's) nagging doubts about the accuracy of their impressions about the data.

There are two broad ways in which simple counting techniques have been used as an aid to validity in qualitative research:

- as an initial means of obtaining a sense of the variance in the data (Type 1)
- at a later stage, after having identified some phenomenon, checking its prevalence (Type 2).

CASE STUDY

As an example of Type 1 tabulations, I will take a study of calls to a child protection hotline already discussed in Section 9.5.1. Hepburn and Potter (2004) discovered that callers to this helpline tended to preface their reports with a reference to their 'concerns'. So a typical call would begin 'I'm concerned about X'.

In order to check the prevalence of this phenomenon, the researchers did a range of simple counts as an aid to understanding the patterning of the way constructions using the terms 'concerned' and 'concern' were used. This is how Hepburn and Potter explain their approach:

it was interesting to consider how specific to the NSPCC data concern constructions were. To check this we did something very simple, which was to compare prevalence in the NSPCC calls with a corpus of everyday phone calls. The terms 'concern' and 'concerned' appear an average of 7 times per call in our material, but only 0.3 times per call in the (everyday) corpus. At a more specific level we were interested in the prevalence of concerns constructions in the call openings, and also how many were initiated by the caller and how many the CPO. About 60% of openings use concerned constructions, about two thirds of these were initiated by the caller, and about a third by the CPO. (2004: 189)

The kind of tabulations described in this case study can only be suggestive. They are not the endpoint but a signpost to further work. As Hepburn and Potter put it:

These counts were certainly interesting, and highlighted some things to follow up. But their implications are not conclusive on their own. Indeed, they are most unclear without considering the specifics of the interaction and how it unfolds.

The course of analysis works through developing ideas about what is going on in some materials ('hypotheses' in rather grander methods speak) and exploring them, seeing how far they make sense. (2004: 189)

What I have called Type 2 tabulations are used at a later stage of the research after a clear phenomenon has been identified. In this context, quantification can neatly tie in with the logic of qualitative research when, instead of conducting surveys or experiments, we count participants' own categories as used in naturally occurring places. The next case study gives you an example of this.

CASE STUDY
Understanding Medical Decision-Making

In the early 1980s (see Silverman, 1987: Chs 1–6) I was directing a group of researchers studying a paediatric cardiology (child heart) unit. Much of our data derived from tape recordings of an outpatient clinic that was held every Wednesday.

We soon became interested in how decisions (or 'disposals') were organised and announced. It seemed likely that the doctor's way of announcing decisions was systematically related not only to clinical factors (like the child's heart condition) but to social factors (such as what parents would be told at various stages of treatment). For instance, at a first outpatients' consultation, doctors would not normally announce to parents the discovery of a major heart abnormality and the necessity for life-threatening surgery. Instead, they would suggest the need for more tests and only hint that major surgery might be needed. They would also collaborate with parents who produced examples of their child's apparent 'wellness'. This step-by-step method of information-giving was avoided in only two cases. If a child was diagnosed as 'healthy' by the cardiologist, the doctor would give all the information in one go and would engage in what we called a 'search and destroy' operation, based on eliciting any remaining worries of the parent(s) and proving that they were mistaken.

By contrast, in the case of a group of children with the additional handicap of Down's syndrome, as well as suspected cardiac disease, the doctor would present all the clinical information at one sitting, avoiding a step-by-step method. Moreover, atypically, the doctor would allow parents to make the choice about further treatment, while encouraging them to dwell on non-clinical matters like their child's 'enjoyment of life' or friendly personality.

This medical focus on the child's *social* characteristics was seen right at the outset of each consultation. I was able to construct a table, based on a comparison of Down's and non-Down's consultations, showing the different forms of the doctor's questions to parents and the parents' answers. This tabulation showed a strong tendency with Down's children for both the doctor and parents to avoid using the word 'well' about the child and this absence of reference to 'wellness' proved to be crucial to understanding the subsequent shape of the clinic consultation.

Moreover, the categories in the table were not my own. I simply tabulated the different questions and answers as actually given (just as Hepburn and Potter tabulated the participants' use of the word 'concern').

(Continued)

(Continued)

At my heart clinic, the most common question that the doctor asked parents was: 'A well child?' However, parents of Down's syndrome children were rarely asked this question. Instead, the most common question was: 'How is he (she)?'

This avoidance of the term 'well' proved to be crucial to understanding the direction which the consultations with Down's syndrome families subsequently took.

The last two case studies show that there is no reason why qualitative researchers should not, where appropriate, use quantitative measures. Simple counting techniques, theoretically derived and ideally based on participants' own categories, can offer a means to survey the whole corpus of data ordinarily lost in intensive, qualitative research. Instead of taking the researcher's word for it, the reader has a chance to gain a sense of the flavour of the data as a whole. In turn, researchers are able to test and to revise their generalisations, removing nagging doubts about the accuracy of their impressions about the data. In Table 11.3, this type of tabulation is called 'autonomous' counting. By contrast, when we simply document our data sources, we engage in 'credentialling' counting.

TABLE 11.3   Two types of counting

- *Autonomous counting*

  The purpose of autonomous counting is to produce numbers that are intended to stand on their own as significant research findings. A key benefit of autonomous counting is that it can enable authors to develop a summary of the entire data set that authors can then scrutinize to discern patterns in the data. For example, Dutton, Ashford, O'Neill, and Lawrence (2001) used autonomous counting in their study of how managers attempted to influence organizational change by 'selling' certain issues to top management. They identified a number of issue selling approaches, and for each one, they counted the number of times managers mentioned that approach in the context of successful issue selling episodes and unsuccessful episodes

- *Credentialling counting*

  The purpose of credentialing counting is to demonstrate why one should have confidence in the findings of a qualitative analysis. This type of counting typically does not produce findings of its own. Instead, it focuses on either (a) documenting counts of data sources, or (b) generating evidence of the analytical honesty of researchers. It is common for qualitative researchers to provide counts of their data sources. For instance, in his study of videos of HIV-counselling, Peräkylä (1995) lists his data sources and explains how he selected particular data for intensive study

Source: Hannah and Lautsch, 2011: 3

TIP

Try not to take a principled stand against all forms of quantification. Providing a study is theoretically well grounded, tabulating data often makes sense. While all scientific work is concerned with the problem of how to generate adequate descriptions of what it observes, qualitative research is especially interested in how ordinary people observe and describe their world. Many of the procedures I have discussed here aim to offer adequate (researcher's) descriptions of (lay) descriptions. Once this is recognised as the central problematic of much qualitative research (at least that informed by a **constructionist** model), then these procedures can be extended to a broad range of social contexts.

EXERCISE 11.5

This exercise is meant to accustom you to the advantages and limitations of simple tabulations. You should return to one of the settings which you have observed in a previous exercise in Chapter 5.

Now follow these steps:

1 Count whatever seems to be countable in this setting (e.g. the number of people entering and leaving or engaging in certain activities).
2 Assess what these quantitative data tell you about social life in this setting. How far can what you have counted be related to any *one* social science theory or concept with which you are familiar?
3 Beginning from the theory or concept selected in step 2, indicate how you might count in terms of it rather than in terms of common-sense categories.
4 Attempt to count again on this basis. What associations can you establish?
5 Identify deviant cases (i.e. items that do not support the associations that you have established). How might you further analyse these deviant cases, using either quantitative or qualitative techniques? What light might that throw on the associations which you have identified?

11.3.3 Validity: a summary

Let me summarise what I have been saying about validity:

- The criterion of *falsifiability* is an excellent way to test the validity of any research finding.
- *Quantitative* researchers have a sophisticated armoury of weapons to assess the validity of the correlations which they generate.
- We should not assume that techniques used in quantitative research are the *only* way of establishing the validity of findings from qualitative or field research.

This third point means that a number of practices which originate from quantitative studies may be *inappropriate* to field research. The following three assumptions are highly *dubious* in qualitative research:

- No social science research can be valid if it is not based on experimental data, official statistics or the random sampling of populations.
- Quantified data are the only valid or generalisable social facts.
- A cumulative view of data drawn from different contexts, so that, as in trigonometry, we can triangulate the 'true' state of affairs by examining where the different data intersect.

All three assumptions have a number of defects. Following the same order as in the list above, I note that:

- Experiments, official statistics and survey data may simply be inappropriate to some of the tasks of social science. For instance, they exclude the observation of '**naturally occurring**' data by ethnographic case studies (see Chapter 5) or by conversation and **discourse analysis** (see Chapter 9).
- While quantification may *sometimes* be useful, it can both conceal and reveal basic social processes. Consider the problem of counting attitudes in surveys. Do we all have coherent attitudes on any topics which await the researcher's questions? And how do 'attitudes' relate to what we actually do – our practices? Or think of official statistics on cause of death compared with studies of the officially organised 'death work' of nurses and orderlies (Sudnow, 1968a) and of pathologists (Prior, 1987). Note that this is *not* to argue that such statistics may be biased. Instead, it is to suggest that there are areas of social reality which such statistics cannot measure.
- Triangulation of data seeks to overcome the context-boundedness of our materials at the cost of analysing their sense in context. For purposes of social research, it may simply not be useful to conceive of an overarching reality to which data, gathered in different contexts, approximate.

So my support for credible qualitative research which takes seriously issues of validity is not based on an uncritical acceptance of the standard recipes of conventional methodology texts or the standard practices of purely quantitative research. I further suggested that data triangulation and **member** validation are usually inappropriate to validate field research. Instead, I have suggested five ways of validating such research:

1 analytic induction
2 the constant comparative method
3 deviant-case analysis

4 comprehensive data treatment

5 using appropriate tabulations.

However, case study research can rarely make any claims about the representativeness of its samples. How far does this mean that we are unable to make generalisations from case studies? Since findings can be valid (or true) but not generalisible to other cases, I now turn to the issue of generalisability.

11.4 GENERALISABILITY

A regular refrain I hear from student researchers is: 'I have so little data, only just one case, how can I possibly generalise about it?'

Generalisability is a standard aim in quantitative research and is normally achieved by statistical **sampling** procedures. Such sampling has two functions. First, it allows you to feel confident about the representativeness of your sample: 'if the population characteristics are known, the degree of representativeness of a sample can be checked' (Arber, 1993: 70). Second, such representativeness allows you to make broader inferences: 'The purpose of sampling is usually to study a representative subsection of a precisely defined population in order to make inferences about the whole population' (Arber, 1993: 38).

Such sampling procedures are, however, usually unavailable in qualitative research. In such studies, our data are often derived from one or more cases and it is unlikely that these cases will have been selected on a random basis. Very often a case will be chosen simply because it allows access. Moreover, even if you were able to construct a representative sample of cases, the sample size would be likely to be so large as to preclude the kind of intensive analysis usually preferred in qualitative research (Mason, 1996: 91).

This give rise to a problem, familiar to users of quantitative methods: 'How do we know ... how representative case study findings are of all members of the population from which the case was selected?' (Bryman, 1988: 88).

For a few writers who see qualitative research as purely descriptive, generalisability is not an issue. For example, Stake (1994: 236) refers to the '*intrinsic case study*' where 'this case is of interest ... in all its particularity and ordinariness'. In the intrinsic case study, according to Stake, no attempt is made to generalise beyond the single case or even to build theories.

This is resisted by many qualitative researchers. As Mason puts it:

> I do not think qualitative researchers should be satisfied with producing explanations which are idiosyncratic or particular to the limited empirical parameters of their study ... Qualitative research should (therefore) produce explanations which are generalizable in some way, or which have a wider resonance. (Mason, 1996: 6)

So, unlike Stake, the problem of 'representativeness' is a perennial worry of many qualitative or case study researchers. How do they attempt to address it? Can we generalise from cases to populations without following a purely statistical logic? Table 11.4 provides some initial answers to such questions.

TABLE 11.4 How to generalise in qualitative research

In qualitative research, we cannot assemble random samples of cases. Instead, we seek to generalise through three kinds of 'theoretical inference':

- *Deductive inference*: choosing a critical or deviant case which can be used (à la Popper) to prove the refutability of an accredited or standard theory
- *Comparative inference*: identifying cases within extreme situations as well as certain characteristics, or cases within a wide range of situations in order to maximise variation; that is, to have all the possible situations in order to capture the heterogeneity of a population. This criterion is used to make generalisations similar to statistical inferences, but without employing probability criteria
- *The emblematic case*: the typical or emblematic case, e.g. single case studies which embody one or more key aspects of social action or social process in particular organisations

Source: adapted from Gobo, 2009: 206

Why does Flyvbjerg (Table 11.5) argue that these five points are misunderstandings? Let us take each point in turn:

TABLE 11.5 Five misunderstandings about case study research

Note: all these assumptions are false

1 General, theoretical (context-independent) knowledge is more valuable than concrete, practical (context-dependent) knowledge
2 One cannot generalize on the basis of an individual case; therefore, the case study cannot contribute to scientific development
3 The case study is most useful for generating hypotheses in the first stage of a total research process, while other methods are more suitable for hypotheses testing and theory building
4 The case study contains a bias toward verification, that is, a tendency to confirm the researcher's preconceived notions
5 It is often difficult to summarize and develop general propositions and theories on the basis of specific case studies

Source: Flyvbjerg, 2004: 421

1 It is a mistake to assume that the further we move away from a specific case, the more valid is our knowledge. Such a view overlooks a key advantage of qualitative research – its ability to give us insight into local practices. As Flyvbjerg puts it:

> For researchers, the closeness of the case study to real-life situations ... is important for the development of a nuanced view of reality, including the view that human behavior cannot be meaningfully understood as simply the

rule-governed acts found at the lowest levels of the learning process, and in much theory. Second, cases are important for researchers' own learning processes in developing the skills needed to do good research. (2004: 422)

2 We should not overvalue formal generalisations. Single cases are crucial in attempting to *refute* initial hypotheses. Flyvbjerg reminds us of Popper's suggestion that the observation of a single black swan would be sufficient to falsify the generalisation that all swans are white. As a consequence:

> falsification is one of the most rigorous tests to which a scientific proposition can be subjected: if just one observation does not fit with the proposition it is considered not valid generally and must therefore be either revised or rejected ... The case study is well suited for identifying 'black swans' because of its in-depth approach: what appears to be 'white' often turns out on closer examination to be 'black'. (2004: 424)

3 The case study is not limited to initial fieldwork but can be used to *test* hypotheses. In particular:

> the typical or average case is often not the richest in information. Atypical or extreme cases often reveal more information because they activate more actors and more basic mechanisms in the situation studied ... random samples emphasizing representativeness will seldom be able to produce this kind of insight. (2004: 425)

4 Preconceptions enter into quantitative studies when one seeks to establish **operational definitions** of some phenomenon at any early stage of the research. By contrast:

> The case study contains no greater bias toward verification of the researcher's preconceived notions than other methods of inquiry. On the contrary, experience indicates that the case study contains a greater bias toward falsification of preconceived notions than toward verification. (2004: 429)

5 We should not worry that case studies are often reported by a complex narrative:

> Good narratives typically approach the complexities and contradictions of real life. Accordingly, such narratives may be difficult or impossible to summarize into neat scientific formulae, general propositions, and theories ... To the case-study researcher, however, a particularly 'thick' and hard-to-summarize narrative is not a problem. Rather, it is often a sign that the study has uncovered a particularly rich problematic. (2004: 430)

> **TIP**
> Flyvbjerg's arguments should make you less defensive about using a case study approach. Apart from the excellent points that he makes, it is worth noting that, as Gobo (2004: 442) suggests, many of the most important, theoretically productive qualitative research studies were based on single cases.

Giampietro Gobo has noted two further arguments which offer more support to Flyvbjerg's position. First, many of the statistical tests that are commonly used in quantitative research do not tell you how strong a relationship found in your sample is in the wider population. In that sense, generalisation is a problem for quantitative researchers (Gobo, 2004: 451). Second, some phenomena are likely to be more pervasive than others. For instance, if you are interested in a native grammar, one informant will be quite adequate (2004: 445).

There remains the issue of how our choice of cases to study can accommodate issues of generalisability. In the rest of this chapter, I will discuss two positive answers to this issue: purposive sampling guided by time and resources theoretical sampling.

11.4.1 Purposive Sampling

Before we can contemplate comparing our case with others, we need to have selected our case. Are there any grounds other than convenience or accessibility to guide us in this selection?

Purposive sampling allows us to choose a case because it illustrates some feature or process in which we are interested. However, this does not provide a simple approval to any case we happen to choose. Rather, purposive sampling demands that we think critically about the parameters of the population we are interested in and choose our sample case carefully on this basis. As Denzin and Lincoln put it: 'Many qualitative researchers employ ... purposive, and not random, sampling methods. They seek out groups, settings and individuals where ... the processes being studied are most likely to occur' (Denzin and Lincoln, 1994: 202).

Stake (1994: 243) gives the example of a study of interactive displays in children's museums. He assumes that you only have resources to study four such museums. How should you proceed? He suggests setting up a typology which would establish a matrix of museum types as in Table 11.6.

The typology set out in Table 11.6 yields six cases which could be increased further by, say, distinguishing between museums located in small and big cities – bringing up the cases to 12. Which cases should you select?

TABLE 11.6 A typology of children's museums

	Type of museum		
	Art	**Science**	**History**
Programme type:			
Exhibitory	1	2	3
Participative	4	5	6

Source: adapted from Stake, 1994: 243

You will be constrained by two main factors. First, there may not be examples to fit every cell. Second, your resources will not allow you to research every existing unit. So you have to make a practical decision. For instance, if you can cover only two cases, do you choose two participatory museums in different locations or in different subjects? Or do you compare such a museum with a more conventional exhibit-based museum?

Provided you have thought through the options, it is unlikely that your selection will be criticised. Moreover, as we see below, how you set up your typology and make your choice should be grounded in the theoretical apparatus you are using. Sampling in qualitative research is neither statistical nor purely personal: it is, or should be, theoretically grounded.

EXERCISE 11.6

Imagine that you have the resources to study *four* cases of the phenomenon in which you are interested. Following my discussion of Stake (Table 11.6), draw up a typology to indicate the universe of cases potentially available. This typology should include between six and twelve possible cases.

Now explain why you propose to select your four cases in terms of the logic of purposive sampling.

11.4.2 Theoretical Sampling

Theoretical and purposive sampling are often treated as synonyms. Indeed, the only difference between the two procedures applies when the 'purpose' behind 'purposive' sampling is not theoretically defined.

Bryman argues that qualitative research follows a theoretical, rather than a statistical, logic: 'the issue should be couched in terms of the generalizability of cases to *theoretical* propositions rather than to *populations* or universes' (1988: 90, my emphasis).

The nature of this link between sampling and theory is set out by Mason:

> theoretical sampling means selecting groups or categories to study on the basis of their relevance to your research questions, your theoretical position ... and most importantly the explanation or account which you are developing. Theoretical sampling is concerned with constructing a sample ... which is meaningful theoretically, because it builds in certain characteristics or criteria which help to develop and test your theory and explanation. (1996: 93–4)

Theoretical sampling has three features which I discuss below:

- choosing cases in terms of your theory
- choosing 'deviant' cases
- changing the size of your sample during the research.

Choosing cases in terms of your theory

Mason (1996: 85) writes about 'the wider universe of social explanations in relation to which you have constructed your research questions'. This theoretically defined universe 'will make some sampling choices more sensible and meaningful than others'. Mason describes choosing a kind of sample which can represent a wider population. Here we select a sample of particular 'processes, types, categories or examples which are relevant to or appear within the wider universe' (1996: 92). Mason suggests that examples of these would include single units such as 'an organization, a location, a document ... [or] a conversation'.

Mason gives the example of a DA study of gender relation as discourses which construct subjects of gender relations. In this approach, as she puts it, 'you are ... unlikely to perceive the social world in terms of a large set of gender relations from which you can simply draw a representative sample of people by gender' (1996: 85).

So in qualitative research the relevant or 'sampleable' units are often seen as theoretically defined. This means that it is inappropriate to sample populations by such attributes as 'gender', 'ethnicity' or even age because how such attributes are routinely defined is itself the *topic* of your research. On the other hand, as Flyvbjerg (2004: 426) notes, your choice of theory can help you to identify *critical* cases.

As an example of theoretically defined sampling, Bryman uses Glaser and Strauss's discussion of 'awareness contexts' in relation to dying in hospital:

> The issue of whether the particular hospital studied is 'typical' is not the critical issue; what is important is whether the experiences of dying patients are typical of the broad class of phenomena ... to which the theory refers. Subsequent research would then focus on the validity of the proposition in other milieux (e.g. doctors' surgeries). (Bryman, 1988: 91)

Further discussion of choosing a case for theoretical reasons is to be found in Silverman (2010: 143–6). Sometimes, however, we will want to choose a case because it appears to be deviant.

Choosing 'deviant' cases

In my discussion of validity, I discussed analysing deviant cases in your data. Here we are concerned with something prior to data analysis – choosing a case to study. Mason notes that you must overcome any tendency to select a case which is likely to support your argument. Instead, it makes sense to seek out negative instances as defined by the theory with which you are working.

For instance, in a study of the forces that may make trade unions undemocratic, Lipset et al. (1962) deliberately chose to study an American printing union. Because this union had unusually strong democratic institutions it constituted a vital deviant case compared with most American unions of the period. Lipset et al.'s union was also deviant in terms of a highly respected theory which postulated an irresistible tendency towards 'oligarchy' in all formal organisations.

So Lipset et al. chose a deviant case because it offered a crucial test of a theory. As our understanding of social processes improves, we are increasingly able to choose cases on such theoretical grounds.

Changing the size of your sample during the research

So far we have been discussing theoretical sampling as an issue at the *start* of a research study. However, we can also apply such sampling during the course of a piece of research. Indeed, one of the strengths of qualitative research design is that it often allows for far greater (theoretically informed) flexibility than in most quantitative research designs. As Mason puts it: 'Theoretical or purposive sampling is a set of procedures where the researcher manipulates their analysis, theory, and sampling activities *interactively* during the research process, to a much greater extent than in statistical sampling' (1996: 100).

Such flexibility may be appropriate in the following cases:

- As new factors emerge you may want to increase your sample in order to say more about them.
- You may want to focus on a small part of your sample in early stages, using the wider sample for later tests of emerging generalisations.
- Unexpected generalisations in the course of data analysis lead you to seek out new deviant cases.

Alasuutari has described this process through using the analogy of an hourglass: 'a narrow case-analysis is broadened … through the search for contrary and parallel cases, into an example of a broader entity. Thus the research process advances, in its final stages, towards a discussion of broader entities. We end up on the bottom of the hourglass' (1995: 156).

Alasuutari illustrates this 'hourglass' metaphor through his own study of the social consequences of Finnish urbanisation in the 1970s. He chose local pubs as a site to observe these effects and eventually focused upon male 'regulars'. This led to a second study even more narrowly focused on a group where drinking was heavier and where many of the men were divorced. As he puts it: 'Ethnographic research of this kind is not so much generalization as extrapolation … the results are related to broader entities' (Alasuutari, 1995: 155).

Table 11.7 offers a summary of my arguments in this section. Taken from a freely available report by the US National Science Foundation, I hope it gives you added confidence to work with small samples.

TABLE 11.7   Generalising from small samples

- *Small Samples Can Sometimes Yield Big Insights*

  If the cases are appropriately chosen with regard to theoretical factors and compared, they can yield unique insights by revealing regularities between categories of cases that may escape large sample studies … by thoroughly examining a small number of cases, the researcher may explore in-depth the contextual dimensions that influence a social phenomenon. Attention to such environmental and situational factors is often downplayed in larger-scale studies that often favor linear analysis and flatten out variegated social patterns even though they may be characteristic of social processes

- *Systematic Sampling Can Still be Scientific, even if it is Not Random*

  Sampling procedures need to be evaluated according to the purpose of the project. Snowball sampling allows the researcher to enter into networks of individuals and identify respondents that they might not otherwise be able to identify. When performing referrals or any other type of targeted sampling, it is essential to ensure that the sample contains enough variation along key demographic and theoretical dimensions to draw conclusions beyond the particular individuals studied

- *Generalizability to Population and Broader Contexts and Processes*

  Although larger-scale qualitative projects may endeavor to generalize to large populations such as nation states or entire ethnic groups, many more seek to inform us about smaller groups or patterns of interaction that can have great significance for our understanding of social processes. Good proposals articulate clearly that the data gathered are meaningful beyond the particular cases, individuals, or sites studied and specify precisely why they are significant, to whom, and to which institutions and processes the findings can be generalized. These can range from subpopulations (i.e., particular minority groups) to types of interactions (i.e., criminal proceedings) to sets of institutions (i.e., admissions committees of elite universities)

Source: Lamont and White, 2005: 11–12

TIP

Quantitative researchers often seek generalisations about *facts*; for example, how many people in a particular city live below the poverty line? In qualitative research, we are often more interested in generalising about *processes*. Small gives a relevant example of a classic qualitative study:

> When Geertz (1973) wrote on the cockfights in a small Balinese village, many expected his *theoretical model* (of how games can embody societal power relations) to be applicable to other sites, but few expected the *empirical findings* to be so applicable – that is, for cockfights to look similar or to follow the same rules in other villages throughout or outside of Indonesia. The latter would be wholly beside the point. (2009: 9)

11.5 CONCLUSIONS

Unless you can convince your audience(s) that the procedures you used to ensure that your methods were reliable and that your conclusions were valid, there is little point in aiming to conclude a research study. Having good intentions, or the correct political attitude, is, unfortunately, never the point. Short of reliable methods and valid conclusions, research descends into a bedlam where the only battles that are won are by those who shout the loudest.

> **TIP**
> Even student reports cannot just rely on the intrinsic interest of their data. Caelli et al. (2003) argue that research reports aiming for credibility must address the following three key areas:
>
> 1 the theoretical positioning of the researcher (e.g. the concepts you are drawing from your discipline and the research model you are using)
> 2 the congruence between methodology and methods (e.g. are your methods appropriate to your research model?)
> 3 the strategies to establish rigour (e.g. are your findings credible?).

Half a century ago, Becker and Geer (1960) recognised that adequate sociological description of social processes needs to look beyond purely qualitative methods. Everything depends, however, on the relation between the quantitative measures being used and the analytic issue being addressed. As Hindess puts it: 'The usefulness of … statistics is a function of the theoretical problematic in which they are to be used and on the use to which they are to be put within it' (1973: 45).

However, I have also shown that quantitative measures are not the only way to test the validity of our propositions. Theoretical sampling and analytic induction, based upon deviant-case analysis and the constant comparative method, offer powerful tools through which to overcome the danger of purely 'anecdotal' quantitative research.

The time for wholesale critiques of quantitative research has passed. What we need to do now is to show the ways in which qualitative research can be every bit as credible as the best quantitative work. Part of that will involve recognising that good-quality research depends upon craft skills that ultimately transcend the kinds of lists of factors that we have been reviewing in this chapter. As Seale has put it:

> I believe there is a lot to be said for a more local conception of social research as a craft skill … good quality work results from doing a research project, learning from the things that did and did not work, and then doing another, better one, that more fully integrates the creativity and craft skills of the researcher, and so on

until a fully confident research style is developed. The issue of constructing abstract, universally applicable criteria for judging whether work is of good quality can happily remain unresolved for such a craftsperson, who is nevertheless continually preoccupied with issues of quality more locally conceived, relevant to the particular research project at hand. (2004a: 410)

> **TIP**
> Try not to be defensive if your data are limited to one or two 'cases'. Instead, seek to understand the logic behind such an approach and work out what you can gain by intensive analysis of limited but rich data.

KEY POINTS

- Social science is credible to the extent that it uses appropriate methods and is rigorous, critical and objective in its handling of data.
- Qualitative research can be made credible if we make every effort to falsify our initial assumptions about our data.
- High reliability in qualitative research is associated with what Seale (1999: 148) calls low-inference descriptors.
- Appropriate methods for validating studies based largely or entirely upon qualitative data include: analytic induction, the constant comparative method, deviant-case analysis, comprehensive data treatment and the use of appropriate tabulations.
- Generalising from case studies is less of a problem than is usually assumed.
- The generalisability of a piece of qualitative research can be increased by purposive sampling guided by time and resources and theoretical sampling

STUDY QUESTIONS

1 What is credibility? Why does it matter?
2 What criteria can be used to assess the credibility of qualitative research studies?
3 What questions can we ask about researchers' choice of data extracts?
4 What is meant by 'anecdotalism'?
5 What is meant by 'critical rationalism'?
6 What is meant by 'reliability'? How can we assess the reliability of any one kind of qualitative data?

7   What is meant by 'validity'? Describe *two* methods you can use to assess the validity of qualitative research studies.
8   When and how does it make sense to quantify qualitative data?
9   In what sense(s) can we generalise from qualitative research?
10 What is meant by 'purposive' and 'theoretical' sampling?

RECOMMENDED READING

Clive Seale's book *The Quality of Qualitative Research* (1999) offers an excellent overall treatment of the issues discussed in this chapter. Shorter but useful discussions are Flyvbjerg (2004), Gobo (2004) and Peräkylä (2011).

For a detailed discussion of 'analytic induction' (AI) see Becker (1998: 197–212). For further discussion of AI, using Bloor's study as an exemplar, see Abrams (1984).

12

Writing Your Report

CHAPTER OBJECTIVES

By the end of this chapter, you will be able to:

- recognise that being scared about 'writing up' is very common
- understand that the earlier you attempt to write, the easier your task will be
- know what your teachers are looking for in your report and be able to tailor it accordingly
- understand the organisational features that characterise a successful research report.

Many students find the prospect of writing a research report highly threatening. Added to the realistic worries of satisfying your teacher seems to be a somewhat irrational fear of the act of writing such a document. Yet, as Amir Marvasti has pointed out, if we think about it, all of us are already experienced writers. As he says:

> Arguably, we are all writers. Letters or emails to friends, memos for our work colleagues, or even grocery lists are all forms of writing. The act of writing, then, is something that all literate people engage in almost daily. However, when it comes to writing research reports, we tend to become afraid and uncomfortable. We put off assignments for weeks and reluctantly turn our attention to the task of writing hours before the work is due. (2004: 119)

Marvasti goes on to provide a set of useful tips for people who tend to freeze when they have to write a research report. I have set a version of these tips in Table 12.1.

TABLE 12.1   Tips to overcome writer's block

- Writing is a craft that involves endless practice and the mastery of techniques. Do not think of writing simply as a unique, creative form of self-expression
- Do not put off writing; write as you go: 'if you don't begin writing until the data collection is complete, your original research question might seem like a needle in a haystack of data. Continuous writing helps you stay on track and focused'
- 'Sometimes, we assume that the sentences we write will make sense to the readers because they are meaningful to us ... when you write, try to visualize your audience. Depending on who this imaginary audience is (an average reader or a learned scholar in your field), ask yourself if your sentences will make sense to them'
- Momentum is all important: 'in the process of moving from vague insights to a coherently articulated text many new ideas are generated'

Source: adapted from Marvasti, 2004: 120–30

The important message we should derive from Table 12.1 is that you cannot write early enough. The very act of writing will make you clarify your work. As Rapley puts it:

> The act of writing is a rich and analytic process as you find yourself not only attempting to explain and justify your ideas but also developing them. It is all very well to think with data in and through internal dialogues with yourself, brief jottings, or conversations with other interested people. However, thinking with data via some brief or extended period, either written or typed, will transform your ideas. Making your ideas 'concrete' enables you to reflect, to see gaps, to explore, to draw other texts in. (2011: 286)

TIP

Kathy Charmaz has some good advice for students who struggle to get their first ideas on to paper. Try thinking about your data in terms of a diagram – this is what she calls *clustering*. As she puts it:

> a major objective of clustering is to liberate your creativity. You write your central idea, category, or process; then circle it and draw spokes from it to circled subtopics to show its defining characteristics and relationships ... Clustering can enable you to define essentials. It allows for chaos and prompts you to create paths through it. You gain a way of sifting and sorting your material while you create a pattern about, around, and through your category(ies). Clustering lets you make what lurks in the background jump into the foreground. Use it to make things explicit and order your topic. A cluster provides a direct visual, as contrasted with a solely mental, image. Hence, you can assess relative importance of the points within your cluster and relationships between them. (2006: 86–7)

In the following case study, based on his research on homelessness, Marvasti shows how it was only when he began to write that he realised that his original research ideas were not working.

CASE STUDY
Writing and Rethinking

[A]t the beginning of my project, I wanted to organize my dissertation around the notion that the homeless are 'the postmodern heroes of our time.' The idea was inspired by interviews with homeless men who had said things like 'It sucks to be a citizen' or 'I feel sorry for the poor bastards who are enslaved by their work. I am free to sleep where I want and go where I want.' I interpreted such statements as clear rejections of the modern, capitalist premise of productive labor. Chatting in coffee shops with fellow students, I would champion the cause of the homeless by quoting their anti-work statements, translating my field notes into political slogans.

Of course, eventually I had to write all of this down into a coherent document. In doing so, I was presented with a serious problem. Namely, I found it impossible to transform a number of catchy statements into a full-length dissertation. Aside from a few banal declarations like 'It appears that some homeless people reject conventional notions of work,' I had nothing else to write on the topic. Given my data and level of expertise, the notion of the homeless as postmodern heroes was a dead end. (Marvasti, 2004: 120)

Fortunately, Marvasti ends this anecdote on an upbeat note. Eventually, after much rewriting, he realised a better path for his report. As he puts it:

> as my writing and analysis progressed, I came across another idea that seemed more in synch with the empirical evidence. In particular, I noticed that the very notion of 'the homeless' was problematic. The men and women on the streets and in shelters viewed their circumstances from many different standpoints. (2004: 120)

TIP

By writing I mean as little as those moments when you are reading or thinking about your data, you have an idea and spend five minutes noting it down, to those moments when you might be spending hours writing. You should get into the habit of writing about anything that might be helpful. An idea may emerge from something you've read, seen, discussed or overheard. It is not only writing, but also working with diagrams, lists, tables, basically, anything that offers you a way to conceptualise your ideas. (Rapley, 2011: 286)

EXERCISE 12.1

As soon as you gather your first data (e.g. one interview, an observation, a text or image), try to write 200 words about it.

Go through the following stages:

- describe in simple terms what you see happening here
- consider how this simple description can be improved by using any one concept with which you are familiar
- note what other data you will need to make your analysis more solid
- think about what further reading you need to do to improve your analysis.

If creativity comes through continued writing, we also need to remember that such creativity should not exist in a vacuum. Writing should always be for a particular *audience*. For instance, as I write this book, I imagine a student perched on top of my computer screen who continually asks me questions such as: How is this going to help me? Why are you using jargon at this point? Can you give me a few, quick tips and references?

Addressing such questions helps remind me that what matters is what you will make of this book. Of course, research reports written by students have a very specific audience – possibly only the professor who teaches the relevant course. So a crucial question to ask yourself is: what is this reader looking for?

The rest of this chapter will offer answers to this question. The various components of a research report will be discussed in this order:

- the beginning stages (title, abstract, list of contents introduction)
- your literature review
- your methodology section
- writing your data chapter(s)
- your conclusion.

For the moment, however, in order to get a quick grasp of what you are aiming for, you should look at the qualities of the good research report listed in Table 12.2.

TABLE 12.2   Features of good student research reports

- Show the importance of the topics and issues to the field of enquiry
- Contribute to existing research and/or theoretical debates
- Exhibit clarity at all stages, e.g. through explicit specification of concepts and theoretical perspectives, clarity of objectives, appropriate treatment of relevant literature, clarity of writing and argumentation
- Display methodological rigour, e.g. through using appropriate methods, appropriate and sufficient data, rigorous and innovative analysis

Source: adapted from Moisander and Valtonen, 2006: 174–82

LINK

The Writing Center, Thesis Writing:

www.rpi.edu/dept/llc/writecenter/web/thesis.html

12.1 BEGINNINGS

Nearly all dissertations begin with four elements:

- a title
- an abstract
- a list of contents
- an introduction.

12.1.1 Your Title

Titles should catch the reader's attention while properly informing them about the main focus of your research. My own preference is for a two-part title: a snappy main title often using a present participle to indicate activity. The sub-title can then be more descriptive.

> TIP
>
> Try to make your main title catch the reader's imagination. To this end, you could use a question as your main title (e.g. Why are Students Disillusioned?). Then you could explain more about your focus in the sub-title (e.g. An Interview Study about Students' Attitudes towards Party Politics).

12.1.2 Your abstract

You will have noticed that journal articles begin with an 'abstract' which offers a brief summary of the aims and results to be described later. It is good professional practice to follow your title page with such an abstract which should succinctly cover the following:

- your research problem
- why that problem is important and worth studying
- your data and methods
- your main findings
- their implications in the light of other research.

There is usually a word limit for abstracts (100 words is common). So, as Punch points out: 'abstract writing is the skill of saying as much as possible in as few words as possible' (1998: 276). Within the word limitations, try to make your abstract as lively and informative as possible.

12.1.3 Your list of contents

You may have noticed that this book is organised into different sections through the use of numbered points. This has been done to allow you to find your way easily between different parts of my book and to pinpoint matters in which you have most interest. The double numbering system used here offers a guide for your own report. So, for instance, your review of the literature chapter (or section) may be listed as:

CHAPTER 3: REVIEW OF THE LITERATURE

3.1   The background studies
3.2   The core readings
3.3   The study closest to my own

12.1.4 Your introduction

Murcott (1997: 1) says that the point of an introduction is to answer the question: what is this report about? She suggests that you answer this question in four ways by explaining:

1 Why you have chosen this topic rather than any other, e.g. either because it has been neglected or because it is much discussed but not properly or fully.
2 Why this topic interests you.
3 The kind of research approach or academic discipline you will utilise.
4 Your research questions or problems.

12.2 YOUR LITERATURE REVIEW

Most research reports contain a review of the literature. By writing this competently, you show that:

- you are able to locate your study within the kind of topics, methods and theories used in your discipline
- you are building on previous research rather than trying to 'reinvent the wheel'.

Every academic has horror stories of literature reviews which were tediously and irrelevantly descriptive. Rudestam and Newton characterise well such failing reviews: '[they consist of] a laundry list of previous studies, with sentences or paragraphs beginning with the words, "Smith found…", "Jones concluded…", "Anderson stated…", and so on' (1992: 46).

By contrast, A. Marvasti (personal correspondence) suggests that a literature review should be a coherent argument for why your particular study is worth doing and not be a litany of everything else that has been done on the topic. By the end of your literature review, the reader should respond in terms like: 'Yes, I can see why this study is important and where it fits relative to what other scholars have done in this field.'

So, when you write your literature review make sure of two things:

- you focus only on those studies that are relevant for defining *your* research problem
- you organise what you say in the form of an *argument* rather than a simple description of other studies.

TIP
Having a continuous 'argument' in your literature review should not mean that you simply criticise other studies. Rather it means that you work to relate such studies to your own research topic and devote much more space to *crucial* studies than to others.

12.3 YOUR METHODOLOGY SECTION

Even modest research reports are supposed to have a section which describes and justifies your research strategy. In particular, your examiner(s) will want to know about:

- your research topic
- the case(s) you have studied
- the research methods you have chosen to use
- how you have analysed your data.

Treat your methodology section as a set of cautious answers to questions that another researcher might have asked you about your work (e.g. why did you use these methods; how did you come to these conclusions?). This means that your methods chapter should aim to *document* the rationale behind your research design and data analysis. Table 12.3 shows how we can use our methodology section (or chapter) to answer a set of questions.

TABLE 12.3   Questions for a qualitative methods chapter

1   How did you go about your research?
2   What overall strategy did you adopt and why?
3   What design and techniques did you use?
4   Why these and not others?

Source: Murcott, 1997

To answer the questions in Table 12.3 will usually mean describing the following:

- the data you have studied
- how you obtained that data (e.g. issues of access and consent)
- what claims you are making about the data (e.g. as representative of some population or as a single case study)
- the methods you have used to gather the data
- why you have chosen these methods
- how you have analysed your data.

12.4 WRITING UP YOUR DATA

We now come to the most crucial part of your report: writing up your data. However competent is the rest of your report, you will primarily be assessed in how well you describe your data analysis.

From the beginning of your research, you should write memos which note down your early ideas about key concepts and processes that emerge from your data analysis. Writing up your data should be viewed as a process of reorganising these memos to integrate them logically and to discard early ideas that no longer work.

> TIP
>
> Memo-writing is much discussed in **grounded theory** (see Section 3.3) but is relevant to all effective research. Here is Charmaz's advice:
>
>> Memos provide the substance for creating first drafts of papers or chapters. Writing memos during each analytic phase prompts you to make the analysis progressively stronger, clearer, and more theoretical. You already have developed categories and titled them in as concrete and specific terms as possible. Now you need to sort and integrate your memos … Sorting and integrating memos seems like simple steps. Each memo on a category may become a section or sub-section of the draft. Integrating the memos may merely reflect the theoretical direction of the analysis, or stages of a process. However, sorting may be more complicated than it appears. Take a memo from your pile and compare it with another, then another. How do the
>
> *(Continued)*

> *(Continued)*
>
> memos compare? Does your comparison spark new ideas? If so write another memo. Do you discern new relationships between memos? What leads do you gain by sorting the memos? If it helps, take your related memos and form quick clusters with them. How do they fit together? What makes most sense? Some sets of memos fit together so well that the answers seem obvious. But for many analyses, you must create the order and make connections for your readers. The first draft of your paper represents how you sort and integrate a set of memos into some kind of coherent order. (2006: 72)

Let us assume you have refined your memos and need to convey your new analysis clearly to your reader(s). What is the best way to do this?

A useful maxim is: never spring anything on your readers. As Becker has cautioned:

> Many social scientists ... think they are actually doing a good thing by beginning evasively. They reveal items of evidence one at a time, like clues in a detective story, expecting readers to keep everything straight until they produce the dramatic concluding paragraph ... I often suggest to these would-be Conan Doyles that they simply put their last triumphant paragraph first, telling readers where the argument is going and what all this material will finally demonstrate. (1986: 51–2)

Following Becker's suggestion that you should clearly lay your cards on the table at the outset, Table 12.4 offers a number of suggestions about how best to set out your data analysis.

'Convince the reader' is the final point in Table 12.4. But your readers will never be convinced unless you have a clear *argument*. What is the main thing you are trying to say about your data? If you are doubtful, one useful mental exercise is to

TABLE 12.4 Design of a data-analysis report

- As a broad rule, no sub-heading should ever appear in a chapter without it having received a prior explanation of its nature and logical place in your argument
- Make one point at a time. If you find yourself veering off in another direction, cut out the offending material and put it in another section. Sometimes this will mean returning to the same data but from a different perspective. Sometimes it will mean getting rid of some data altogether.
- 'Top and tail' each data extract. This means writing a sentence or two before every extract to context it in your argument. This way your readers will know what to look for while they read it. Follow that up with a more detailed analysis of the extract in terms of the single point you are using it to make
- If the extract is inconclusive, then admit to it. Always show that you understand the limitations of both your data and your analysis of them
- Always number your extracts sequentially and use line numbers where appropriate (as in this book)
- Convince the reader. Not only must your readers be able to see why you interpreted your data in the way you did, but also they must be convinced by your interpretation. As Murcott suggests: 'the basis for saying that the data say "x" rather than "y" has to be made apparent' (1997: 2).

TABLE 12.5   Questions to help you find arguments

- What sense of this process or analysis do you want your reader to make?
- Why is it significant (even practised writers often *assume* the significance of their work)?
- What did you tell your reader that you intended to do? Why did you tell them that?
- In which sentences or paragraph do your major points coalesce?
- What are your sub-arguments? How closely aligned are they with your main argument? Can you chop them out without changing it? If so, do so. Pick them up in another piece of work.

Source: adapted from Charmaz, 2006: Ch. 7

imagine that a student in another field has asked you about your research and you have one minute to sum it up! What do you say?

> TIP
>
> Here are Charmaz's suggestions for discovering the central point you want to make (see also Table 12.5):
>
> Most likely, you've buried the argument in the initial drafts. Find it. Get help in finding it. Your actual argument may differ from what you originally set out to do. That's fine. That indicates that you've grown. You will make a more interesting argument now. Go ahead and revise and reorganize your draft around it. Build your argument or purpose into each section, point by point, step by step. Our arguments do not stand like parked cars and wait for us to find them. We seldom begin with an overriding argument that drives our writing. If it happens, appreciate your good fortune. If not, don't stop and wait for an argument to pop up and put the pieces of your analysis together for you.
>
> Instead, work at it. Your argument will emerge. It develops as your thinking progresses. An argument is a product of grappling with the material. You create your argument from points embedded in your analysis. Outlining your paper for the main point in each paragraph can help you identify a nascent argument. Sometimes it may help to begin with a tentative initial argument. Keep refining it; see how it works. But don't commit yourself to it until you know that it accounts for your most important ideas. You may abandon the argument with which you started—that's alright. You'll gain a far more thoughtful argument than you had anticipated through wrestling with the ideas. (2006: 156–7)

EXERCISE 12.2

Ask a fellow student to read through your data analysis in order to answer the following questions:

- Are they convinced by your claims about what the data show?
- If so, why? If not, why not?
- What could you do to make your report more convincing? (Tell your reader that you are not interested in using more jargon to do this but in applying concepts which make sense of your data.)

TABLE 12.6   Suggested contents for your final section

- The relation between the work done, the original research questions and previous work discussed in the literature review chapter
- Some answer to the classic examiner's question: 'if you were doing this study all over again, is there anything you would do differently? Why so?'; that is, the lessons to be learned from the conduct of the study
- Any implications for policy and practice
- Further research that might follow from your findings, methods or concepts

Source: adapted from Murcott, 1997: 3

12.5 YOUR FINAL SECTION

The last thing that you want is for your report to tail off. This will create the very worst impression for your examiner(s) to take away. So avoid writing a final section which simply *reiterates* what you have already written. Apart from anything else, if your report has been well organised, at this stage everything should be crystal clear.

One way of looking at what your final section should contain is an answer to Murcott's question: 'What does the candidate want the reader to make of all this?' (1997: 3). As Table 12.6 shows, the final chapter offers you the opportunity to give your own twist to the wider implications of your research. Such implications must, of course, reflect your own critical sense of what is good and not so good in your own research. Always remember: unless you define your own sense of the limitations (and implications) of your work, your readers will do it for you!

> **TIP**
> To avoid giving the impression of sloppiness, it is important to proofread your report before it is submitted. It can be very useful to get someone else to read your final draft as writers often miss glaring errors in their own text. Also try not to rely on spellchecks (words can be 'right' but inappropriate).

12.6 A SHORT NOTE ON PLAGIARISM

As I wrote this chapter, I noticed a report in a British newspaper about a famous psychiatrist who has been accused of using material written by somebody else without referencing its source. If well-known people can come unstuck this way, imagine what can happen to an ordinary student who does this!

As Bhatt has noted: 'Plagiarism is considered to be cheating and is a very serious academic offence. If you do not cite fully your sources, you may end up presenting other people's ideas and work as if they were your own' (2004: 429).

Table 12.7 suggests how to avoid being charged with plagiarism

TABLE 12.7 How to avoid plagiarism

- Always reference your sources (including Internet sites)
- Discuss your work with other students but never copy from them
- Avoid commercial sites which offer ready-made dissertations

Source: adapted from Bhatt, 2004: 429

> TIP
>
> Amir Marvasti (personal correspondence) suggests to his students that, to avoid plagiarism, they read any source material once or twice and then put it aside and try to rewrite what the author(s) argued without looking at the original source. He also tells them to use direct quotes when necessary.

12.7 SELF-EXPRESSION OR ARGUMENT?

I end this chapter on a note of caution. In some educational quarters, writing is equated with self-expression so that the substance and structure of what you say is less important than whether it expresses your inner feelings and thoughts. Unfortunately, to my mind, this denigration of logic and substance finds its adherents in the **post-modern** turn in qualitative research. Jaber Gubrium warns against a kind of *self-referential* writing – the kind of writing that refers to the personal experience of the researcher, either emphasising their thoughts and feelings over the course of a project or the development of their interpersonal relations with research participants. He comments:

> This definitely has a place especially in the social and behavioral sciences, and now also in social studies of science. The bad habit is that it too can eclipse writing about the subject matter in view. I know that the subject matter can be the experience of the researcher, but what I'm concerned with here is the emphasis this can take in the final written product. If you do aim to feature your place in a project in writing, in particular yourself and your relation with others, then write about how that relates to broader issues of personal and interpersonal experience in the circumstances. Curb this habit so that you offer the reader a way to compare, say, what you went through with themselves and others. Write deliberately with an eye to general understanding of the personal and interpersonal. (2009: 1)

Gubrium's point is underlined by Amir Marvasti. As he argues: 'Writing is typically thought of as a unique, creative form of self-expression, and that myth may be a large part of the problem. Even in its most self-consciously creative manifestations, writing is a craft that involves endless practice and the mastery of techniques' (2011: 384).

LINK

You can find Jay Gubrium's thoughts on self-referential writing at:

www.dur.ac.uk/writingacrossboundaries/writingonwriting/jaygubrium/

KEY POINTS

- Most students find that the act of writing a report very threatening.
- If you delay your writing, you are asking for trouble.
- Writing is the prime way of developing focus for your research.
- Good research reports are well structured and argued.

STUDY QUESTIONS

1. How can you overcome writer's block?
2. List *four* features of a good student report.
3. List *two* principles of a good literature review.
4. List *four* features of a good methodology section.
5. What are the most effective ways to present your data analysis?

RECOMMENDED READING

My book *Doing Qualitative Research* (2010: 311–60) offers a much more detailed account of how to write up a research dissertation. Charmaz (2006) provides a marvellous book-length introductory guide to doing qualitative research – worth reading whether or not you are using grounded theory. Wolcott's (1990) good book on this topic is aimed at US graduate students. Marvasti (2011) and Bhatt (2004: 409–30) offer useful single-chapter guides.

PART FOUR

IMPLICATIONS

13

The Relevance of Qualitative Research

CHAPTER OBJECTIVES

By the end of this chapter, you will be able to:

- distinguish and critically assess three different roles available to the researcher who enters the public realm
- recognise the nature and needs of three different audiences for qualitative research
- understand what research can contribute to each of these audiences.

There are several claims we might like to make about the value of qualitative research to the wider community. Here is one such list:

- it is relatively flexible;
- it studies what people are doing in their natural context;
- it is well placed to study processes as well as outcomes;
- it studies meanings as well as causes. (Hammersley, 1992b: 125)

Although I have made similar claims to both practitioners and research funding bodies, things are, unfortunately, not quite as simple as this list might suggest.

First, as we have already seen (especially in Chapter 1), the status of qualitative research as a naturalistic enterprise, concerned with meanings, is disputable. Second, as Hammersley (1992a) himself points out, non-qualitative approaches can study some of these features (e.g. questionnaire panel studies can examine change over time and thus social processes). Third, as I argued in Chapter 11, the issue of the credibility of qualitative research (its generalisability to larger populations, and the possible anecdotal basis of its claims) is a real one and does not exist just in the minds of policy-makers. Indeed, only recently did systematic reviews of research findings begin to include qualitative studies (see Dixon-Woods, 2011).

Finally, quantitative research tends to define its research problems in a way which makes immediate sense to practitioners and administrators. For instance, unlike many qualitative researchers, quantitative people have few qualms about taking their **variables** (albeit 'operationalised') from current headlines (e.g. 'crime', 'poverty' or 'effective communication') and about speaking a seemingly scientific language of cause and effect.

In the following case study, Alison Brown interviewed researchers using qualitative **methods** in studies commissioned by outside organisations. She reveals a common frustration with applied research.

CASE STUDY
Writing and Reporting Qualitative Findings

Reporting was often the most fraught stage of a commissioned project, and led to further challenges for qualitative methods. Generally, clients sought a brief report, with quantitative results given prominence. Qualitative research lost out because it was more difficult to summarize in a meaningful way. In one case, a team, at the client's request, had to take out of the draft report most of the views of a certain group of respondents (the crucial group, in their view) and published the material separately. On the other hand, clients' lack of interest in qualitative work could be turned to an advantage – to ask additional questions or, in the case of academics, to use the qualitative data for further publications: 'As long as we did still produce the quantitative stuff, they could feel they got these results, we were relatively free to carry on and do this other work. The report to the [client] didn't go into the qualitative in much detail, but when I came to write the book it predominated' (Academic W).

Reporting was constrained by clients' view of 'evidence', distrust of researchers' own analysis, and a view of qualitative research as reportage. Or they ask, 'Can you find a quote?' We sometimes fall into 'make point, provide a quote to illustrate the point, make another point, provide another quote to illustrate that point' – it invalidates the points with no quote. Or they ask, 'is there a respondent who can sum up your conclusion?' And you think, 'No! It's taken me weeks to do that analysis! (Private sector researcher M)'. (Brown, 2010: 239)

Faced with this environment, what can qualitative researchers offer that will be relevant to a wider audience? An example may help to set up my argument. My example comes from the British educational system – although there are several parallel cases in many institutions and countries.

CASE STUDY
British Secondary Education

In the 1960s, there was a lively debate in the UK about the pros and cons of selective education for the 11–18 age group. This debate was heavily influenced by quantitative social surveys which revealed a pool of hidden talent among children who had been unsuccessful in obtaining entry to 'academic' schools at the age of 11. Accordingly, in the late 1960s, the selective element in British secondary education was largely scrapped.

Subsequent research showed that secondary reorganisation did improve overall school performance of this age group. However, this improvement was not as great as many thought it would be. One reason seemed to be that, in non-selective or 'comprehensive' schools, many children were being put into different streams according to their perceived abilities. In some cases, streaming could reproduce the old system of selective education; although children of all abilities attend the same school, some are labelled and, perhaps, discouraged, at the outset.

Now, of course, such streaming could be (and was) turned into a 'variable' to be studied by subsequent survey research. However, the British experience of secondary reorganisation suggests that policy-makers could have gained by paying more attention to non-quantitative research studies. For instance, ethnographic studies of the classroom (e.g. Mehan, 1979) and of educational decision-making (e.g. Cicourel and Kitsuse, 1963) have revealed a great deal about what actually happens inside schools. So, if such studies had been added to more familiar quantitative studies of educational 'outputs', then it is likely that policy-makers would have been much better informed.

This case study fits the qualitative research strategy outlined earlier in this book (see, in particular, Figures 1.1 and 1.2). This strategy involves three arguments:

1 Qualitative research's greatest strength is its ability to analyse what actually happens in naturally occurring settings (unlike quantitative research, which often turns this phenomenon into a 'black box', defined by the researcher at the outset).

2 By refusing to allow their research topics to be defined in terms of the conceptions of 'social problems' as recognised by either professional or community groups and by beginning from a clearly defined academic perspective, qualitative researchers can address such social problems with considerable force and persuasiveness.

3 Qualitative research is not, however, competitive with quantitative work; the proper relationship is a division of labour in which qualitative researchers seek to answer 'how' and 'what' questions and then pass on their findings so that the causes and outputs of the phenomena identified ('why' questions) can be studied by their quantitative colleagues.

These are arguments in need of further demonstration. At the end of the chapter, I will return to the possible relative contributions of qualitative and quantitative research. For the moment, however, I want to move away from the specifics of research to review the wider debate about how all forms of social science stand in relation to social problems.

13.1 THREE ROLES FOR THE SOCIAL SCIENTIST

> The question is not whether we should take sides, since we inevitably will, but rather whose side are we on? (Becker, 1967: 239)

Not all social scientists would agree with Becker's call for moral or political partisanship. Perhaps responding to state apparatuses which are at best suspicious of the purposes of social science, many would go on the defensive. They might find it easier or more acceptable to argue that their concern is simply with the establishment of facts through the judicious testing of competing **hypotheses** and **theories**. Their only slogan, they would say, is the pursuit of knowledge. They would claim to reject political partisanship, at least in their academic work; they are only, they would say, partisans for truth.

I am not, for the moment, concerned to make a detailed assessment of either Becker's statement or the defensive response to it which I have just depicted. I believe both contain dangerous simplifications. As I shall later show, the partisans for truth are mistaken about the purity of knowledge, while Becker's rhetoric of 'sides' is often associated with a style of research which is unable to discover anything because of its prior commitment to a revealed truth (the plight of the underdog, the inevitable course of human history, etc.). Curiously, both positions can be elitist, establishing themselves apart from and above the people they study.

For the moment, however, I want to stress a more positive feature of both arguments. Both recognise that no simply neutral or value-free position is possible in social science (or, indeed, elsewhere). The partisans for truth just as much as the partisans of the 'underdog' are committed to an absolute value for which there can be no purely factual foundation. As Max Weber pointed out during the First World War, all research is contaminated to some extent by the values of the researcher. Only through those values do certain problems get identified and studied in particular ways. Even the commitment to scientific (or rigorous) method is itself, as Weber emphasises, a value. Finally, the conclusions and implications to be drawn from a study are, Weber stresses, largely grounded in the moral and political beliefs of the researcher.

Fifty years afterwards, Gouldner (1962) pointed out how Weber had been grossly misinterpreted by **positivists**. Because Weber had suggested that purely scientific standards could govern the *study* of a research problem, they had used him as the standard-bearer for a value-free social science. They had conveniently forgotten that Weber had argued that the initial choice and conceptualisation of a problem, as well as the subsequent attempt to seek practical implications from its study, were highly 'value-relevant' (to use Weber's term).

The 'minotaur' of a value-free social science which positivists had conjured up from misreading Weber is effectively destroyed by Gouldner. As Denzin (1970) shows, the myth of value-freedom is shattered not only by the researcher's own commitments but by the social and political environment in which research is carried out. Grant-giving bodies will seek to channel research in particular directions: there is no *neutral* money whether one is speaking about the well-meaning 'initiatives' of research councils or the more sinister funding schemes of the tobacco industry or the war machine (Horowitz, 1965). Moreover, organisations that are studied are likely to want some kind of return in terms of 'facts' (assumed to be theory-free and always quantifiable) as well as support for their current political strategy.

Finally, as Robert Dingwall (personal correspondence) has pointed out, governments may sponsor 'window-dressing' research to buy time and to legitimate inaction. So while, as Denzin argues, the researcher may desire nothing more than a publishable paper, this pressure group activity is bound to have an impact on the work.

Given the constraints under which research takes place, how may the researcher respond? To answer this question, three different research roles have been prescribed or adopted. These are presented in summary form in Table 13.1.

It will probably be helpful if I now give a summary presentation of each of these three positions.

TABLE 13.1   Whose side are we on?

Role	Politics	Commitment	Examples
Scholar	Liberal	Knowledge for knowledge's sake protected by scholar's conscience	Weber Denzin
State counsellor	Bureaucratic	Social engineering or enlightenment for policy-makers	Popper Bulmer
Partisan	Radical	Knowledge to support a political theory or practice	Marx Habermas Political research centres

13.1.1 Scholar

In his two famous lectures 'Science as a vocation' and 'Politics as a vocation' (Weber, 1946), Weber enunciated basic liberal principles to a student audience in 1917. Despite the patriotic fervour of the First World War, he insisted on the primacy of the individual's own conscience as a basis for action. Taking the classic position derived from the nineteenth-century German philosopher Immanuel Kant, Weber argued that values could not be derived from facts.

This was not because values were less important than facts (as logical positivists were soon to argue). Rather, precisely because 'ultimate evaluations' (or value choices) were so important, they were not to be reduced to purely factual judgements. The facts could only tell you about the likely consequences of given actions but they could not tell you which action to choose. For Weber, the very commitment to science was an example of an ultimate evaluation, exemplifying a personal belief in standards of logic and rationality and in the value of factual knowledge. Ironically echoing certain aspects of the 'Protestant Ethic' whose historical emergence he himself had traced, Weber appealed to the scholar's conscience as the sole basis for conferring meaning and significance upon events.

Weber's appeal to Protestantism's and liberalism's 'free individual' was fully shared, 50 years on, by Norman Denzin. Denzin (1970) rejects any fixed moral standards as the basis for research. He will not accept, for instance, that sociologists cannot conceal themselves or use disguised research techniques. Nor is he prepared to recognise that research must necessarily contribute to society's own self-understanding. Both standards are, for him, examples of 'ethical absolutism' which fail to respect the scholar's appeal to their own conscience in the varying contexts of research. Denzin's stand is distinctively liberal and individualist: 'One mandate governs sociological activity – the absolute freedom to pursue one's activities as one sees fit' (Denzin, 1970: 332). What 'one sees [as] fit' will take into account that no method of sociological research is intrinsically any more unethical than any other. Citing Goffman (1959), Denzin argues that, since the researcher always wears some mask, covert observation is merely one mask among others.

Denzin does suggest that the pursuit of research in terms of one's own standards should have certain safeguards. For instance, subjects should be told of the researcher's own value-judgements and biases, and should be warned about the kinds of interpretation the research may generate within the community. But he is insistent that the ultimate arbiter of proper conduct remains the conscience of the individual researcher.

Viewed many decades afterwards, Weber's and Denzin's liberal position seems rather unrealistic. Curiously, as sociologists they fail to see the power of social organisation as it shapes the practice of research. For while Denzin acknowledges the role of pressure groups, he remains silent about the privileged authority of the 'scientist' in society and about the deployment of scientific theories by agents of social control as mobilising forms of power/knowledge.

By the beginning of the twenty-first century, Denzin's position was very different. By now Denzin was calling for 'a politics of hope' which 'should criticize how things are and imagine how they could be different' (Denzin, 2000: 916). In order to achieve this, Denzin, following Mills (1959), demands 'a critical intimate ethnography [which] presents the public with in-depth, intimate, stories of problematic everyday life ... These stories create moral compassion and help citizens make intelligent decisions and take public action on private troubles that have become public issues' (2000: 901).

Denzin's new position combines that of the partisan (see Table 13.1) with the kind of commitment to increasing people's options that I discuss below in Section 13.3.2.

13.1.2 State counsellor

Even liberal individualists may occasionally move away from their 'hands-off' attitude towards others. Denzin, for instance, considers the value of the information that sociologists may offer to participants:

> The investigator may open new avenues of action and perception among those studied. Organisational leaders may be ignorant of the dysfunctional aspects of certain programs, and an exposure to the sociologist's findings may correct their misconceptions. (1970: 338)

Notice how, in this early work, Denzin uses 'organisational leaders' as his example of 'those studied'. Just as many sociologists automatically side with the underdog, so also there is a considerable weight of social science work which identifies with the problems and interests of the 'leaders' or 'top dogs'.

One such example is provided by Bulmer (1982). Despite having a general title, *The Uses of Social Research*, his book turns out to be solely a discussion of how social research may be used by 'policy-makers'. It will thus serve as an example of what I have called, in Table 13.1, *bureaucratic* politics, where the researcher adopts the role of state counsellor.

It is at once clear, however, that Bulmer's bureaucrat-cum-researcher is intended to work at arm's length from the administration, offering no simple solutions and preferring to provide knowledge rather than to recommend policies. This is Bulmer's 'enlightenment model' of social research. It is based on a rejection of two other versions of the uses of research – 'empiricism' and the 'engineering model'.

I have set out below how Bulmer depicts each of his three **models**.

Empiricism

This assumes that facts somehow speak for themselves. It reflects the administrative view that research is a neutral tool for the collection of facts for the use of policy-makers. Failing to take account of the post-Weberian consensus that facts can only be recognised in terms of theoretically derived categories, its 'bucket theory of mind' (Popper) is, Bulmer suggests, wholly inadequate. This is not merely a methodological quibble as Bulmer demonstrates. Empiricism fails because it offers no way of: '[bringing] to bear the insights of social science − rather than merely the factual products of social research' (1982: 42).

Bulmer's argument ties in directly with the argument I have been making throughout this book about how research reflects different models of reality which shape how we see 'facts'.

The engineering model

This seems to be based on Popper's (1959) own version of the contribution of research to 'piecemeal social engineering'. Derived from Popper's rejection of attempts at revolutionary social changes, the engineering model takes off from the definition, presumably by the bureaucracy, of a social problem. It then proceeds, in Bulmer's version, through a sequence of four stages:

- the identification of the knowledge that is required
- the acquisition of social research data
- the interpretation of the data in the light of the problem
- a change in the policy.

Bulmer implies that the proponents of the engineering model are politically naive. Bureaucrats often know precisely what policy changes they wish to make and commission research in such a way that the end-product is likely to legitimate their thinking. He also points out that, in large organisations, it is often action rather than research that is needed. Moreover, where problems need to be analysed, the application of common sense is often quite sufficient.

The enlightenment model

This is Bulmer's preferred model. He sees the function of applied research as the provision of knowledge of alternative possibilities. Its role is to enlighten bureaucrats, and not to recommend policies or to choose between administrative options. This means that it *rejects* a number of research aims (Bulmer, 1982: 153–4):

- the provision of authoritative facts (because facts are only authoritative in the context of theories)
- supplying political ammunition (because this is based, Bulmer points out, on the 'sterile' assumption that there are 'left-wing' facts as opposed to 'right-wing' facts)

- doing tactical research, as in government think-tanks (because this reduces the social scientist to a mere technician)
- evaluating policies (because this is based on the rejected engineering model of applied social research).

Instead, Bulmer *proposes* two research aims which are consistent with his enlightenment model:

- interaction – offering mutual contact between researchers and policy-makers
- conceptualisation – the creation of new problems for policy-makers to think about through the development of new **concepts**.

I used to wonder whether Bulmer's enlightenment model was somewhat elitist, defining researchers as a kind of state functionaries. However, my view has changed. As Stewart Clegg (personal correspondence) has pointed out, we may need to call upon the organisational capacities of the state in order to produce real changes. The real problem is that civil servants may misunderstand social research and politicians often choose to ignore it.

This point was made recently by the *Guardian* journalist Polly Toynbee. As she puts it:

> Senior civil servants could do with training in social research. It's a sorry signal that the post of chief social researcher has recently been downgraded and subsumed into the Treasury. There it falls into the hands of economists who can be too determinist to tune into the subtleties of social and behavioural questions. The real value of the new 'nudge' economics is not the blindingly obvious finding that it's easier to use inertia to get people to stay in pension schemes than to get them to volunteer to join. More valuable is the also blindingly obvious discovery that economists' reductionist view of humans as rational economic units is nonsense: people's motivations are just as often not financially motivated, which explains why economists are not very good at predicting even tomorrow's stock market movement, let alone the next crash.
>
> Knowledge about society is invaluable and, in commissioning these new studies, one part of Labour's brain knows it. What's distressing and wasteful is the other part of that brain, which can't resist making populist gestures in defiance of all the research in front of it. Policies on drugs, crime, prisons, faith schools and electoral reform are just a few of those issues where no amount of rock-solid research can shift the politicians' determination to do the wrong thing regardless. (Toynbee, 2008)

11.1.3 Partisan

If the state counsellor is co-opted by administrative interests and scholars delude themselves that they can stand apart from a socially organised world, then the partisan's role would seem to be altogether more defensible. Unlike scholars, partisans do not shy away from their accountability to the world. Unlike the state counsellor, however, they hold the ruling bureaucracy at arm's length. Instead, the partisan seeks to provide the theoretical and factual resources for a political struggle aimed at transforming the assumptions through which both political and administrative games are played.

The danger is that purely partisan social research can be self-confirming. In the same way as the Bible advises 'look and ye shall find', so partisans (Marxists, feminists, Conservatives) look and inevitably find examples which can be used to support their theories.

Dingwall (1980) has noted how such work 'undoubtedly furnishes an element of romance, radical chic even, to liven the humdrum routine of academic inquiry'. He then goes on to suggest that a concern to champion the 'underdog' 'is inimical to the serious practice of ethnography, whose claims to be distinguished from polemic or investigative journalism must rest on its ability to comprehend the perspectives of top dogs, bottom dogs and, indeed, lap dogs' (1980: 874).

Dingwall concludes that social research, whatever its methods, must seek to produce valid generalisations rather than 'synthetic moral outrage' (1980: 874). He has later helpfully described this as 'an ethic of *fair dealing*' where

> the researcher's role is not to sit in judgment but to represent as dispassionately as possible the contribution of each participant to the production of the setting that is being studied. The resulting analysis may be a source for moral outrage but it should not be a vehicle for this: effective reform demands an understanding of how morally outrageous things come to happen, which is rarely the result of deliberate wickedness at all levels. (Miller et al., 2004: 338)

But partisanship need not be inimical to what Dingwall calls 'fair dealing'. In the following case study, Celia Kitzinger shows that, while her feminist position leads her to focus on particular issues, she can do so in a balanced, methodologically rigorous way.

CASE STUDY
Talk as Action: Feminist Conversation Analysis

Listening to women's voices and validating women's experiences remains central to the feminist qualitative research enterprise. But understanding what is involved in such listening is, for many of us, no longer so straightforward.

As feminists we know that women's voices do not always tell 'truths': memories can be fallible, stories can be embroidered, participants may be more interested in creating a good impression than in literal accuracy, speakers contradict themselves and sometimes deliberately lie. From the 'voices' speaking in this research-created context, feminists face the challenge of reconstructing the 'experience' presumed to lie beneath or beyond the talk.

So, for example, if 'coming out' is the research topic, data in which research participants *talk about* coming out (or not coming out) as lesbian or gay require the researcher to make an interpretive leap from these retrospective accounts to the experience they purport to represent – with all of the problems associated with such a leap. By contrast, data in which people actually do (or don't) come out as lesbian or gay give the researcher direct access to this topic. While being committed to methodological pluralism, and to achieving the best possible 'fit' between research objectives and research methods, in my view the study of talk as a form of action in its own right offers the feminist researcher unparalleled opportunities for developing insight into the social world. (Kitzinger, 2004: 128)

Celia Kitzinger's position shows how her feminist ideals are actually strengthened by her commitment to fair dealing. As she puts it in a review of Schegloff's book:

I ... began to grasp the importance of putting aside my own judgement of the ethics and politics of what people are doing in talk at least long enough to be sure that I have understood what they are doing *on their own terms*. Of course, as a lesbian feminist scholar and activist there is much of human action that I want to bewail, to challenge and to change. But those of us who want to challenge sexism, heterosexism, classism, racism etc. need first to understand how they are done before we can figure out whether and how these forms of social interaction can be transformed. (Kitzinger, 2008: 563)

TIP

The problem of partisanship does not mean that you should *avoid* topics about which you feel deeply or have personal experience. But, during your research, try to put your preconceptions on one side. A good test of a successful, fair dealing, study is if you are *surprised* by some of your findings.

EXERCISE 13.1

This exercise gives you an opportunity to think through the various ways social scientists have answered Becker's question: 'Whose side are we on?' You are asked to imagine that research funding is available for whatever topic and research design you prefer.

1 Suggest a research topic and outline a methodology using one or more of the methods set out in Chapters 5–10.
2 Justify the topic and methodology from the point of view of: (a) the scholar, (b) the state counsellor and (c) the partisan.
3 Now select any one article which reports research findings in a social science journal. Which of the positions referred to in question 2 does it adopt?
4 Set out how this position might be criticised from the point of view of (a) the other positions and (b) your own views of the relevance of social science research.

Having taken up Becker's question 'Whose side are we on?' and depicted three roles adopted by social scientists (scholar, state counsellor and partisan), I have found major problems in how these roles have been exercised (for a similar argument, see Bloor, 2011: 411). We would thus seem to be back at square one. Given this, I shall now try to be more positive and indicate the scope for what I believe to be a fruitful relation between qualitative social science and society. The best way to do this is to think about who are the principal audiences for research and what qualitative researchers might have to say to them.

13.2 THE AUDIENCES FOR QUALITATIVE RESEARCH

If you are reading this book as part of a university course, the only audiences relevant to you are your professors, who will grade your papers, and your fellow students, who will listen to your comments in classes. However, members of universities are only one of several potential audiences for qualitative researchers.

This wider audience includes policy-makers, practitioners and the general public. Each group will only want to hear about qualitative research if it relates to their needs. These four audiences and their likely expectations are set out in Table 13.2.

TABLE 13.2   Audiences and their expectations

Audience	Expectation
Academic colleagues	Theoretical, factual or methodological insights
Policy-makers	Practical information relevant to current policy issues
Practitioners	A theoretical framework for understanding clients better; factual information; practical suggestions for better procedures; reform of existing practices
The general public	New facts; ideas for reform of current practices or policies; guidelines for how to manage better or get better service from practitioners or institutions; assurances that others share their own experience of particular problems in life

Source: adapted from Strauss and Corbin, 1990: 242–3

The expectations of academic audiences about both written work and oral presentations are discussed in Silverman (2010: 417–23). The range of other audiences, shown in Table 13.2, may tend to induce despair about the amount of work required to meet their separate expectations and needs. However, it contains a simple, easy-to-follow message: good communication requires focus and yet more focus.

The trick is to combine a recognition of the expectations and needs of such audiences with our own active shaping of our materials. In this context, Gary Marx's concept of 'leverage' is very useful. As he puts it:

Try to leverage your work. The sociological equivalent of a bases-loaded homerun is to take material prepared for a class lecture, deliver it at a professional meeting, publish it in a refereed journal, have it reprinted in an edited collection, use it in a book you write, publish foreign versions and a more popular version and have the work inform a documentary. (Marx, 1997: 115)

Marx reminds us of the range of audiences that await the qualitative researcher. Below, I consider the three non-academic audiences listed in Table 13.1: policy-makers, practitioners and lay audiences. How can qualitative researchers fashion what Marx calls 'a popular version' for such audiences?

13.2.1 The Policy-Making Audience

The idea that social research might influence the policy of public and private organisations provides an inspiration for many young social scientists. In most English-speaking countries, the sad truth is that things have never worked in this way.

Qualitative research has rarely had much appeal to civil servants and managers geared to focus on numbers and the 'bottom line'. The one possible exception, Goffman's (1961a) account of the dehumanising consequences of 'total institutions' in his book *Asylums*, appears merely to have legitimated the cost-cutting frenzy known as 'community care'.

CASE STUDY
Why Commissioners May Reject Qualitative Research

Although some clients are open to critical findings, researchers found often that their qualitative analysis was questioned only if it presented a view the client did not like – the challenge often phrased in terms of 'but how many people said that?' If it's a finding that they're not entirely keen on, they'll say 'but how many said that?' Then they can dismiss it because only one person said it ... It's probably, to be fair, not the research managers ... it's maybe someone else on the advisory group ... But I have had even research managers saying 'can you just give an indication, say "a few" or "many"?' And you argue against it and they say 'I know that's not what it's about, it would just be useful ...' (Private sector researcher M). The only time you'll be questioned ... is if there's a minority view that people don't like, then they will tend to question how many people said this. I answer that by saying it doesn't matter how many said it. I would normally look for other points of view and check that out as well ... I would say if it was a minority view, I think if you are influencing policy, if that's the purpose, that it should be acknowledged, though that shouldn't mean it's given less weight (Academic W). (Brown, 2010: 242)

However, it is arguable that number-crunching researchers have fared little better than the qualitative researchers interviewed in the case study above. As Hadley (1987: 100) has pointed out, 'not being heard' is the common experience of Anglo-American social researchers who attempt to influence public policy.

Among the reasons for this, Hadley cites:

- Research is often commissioned to buy time in the face of public scandal or criticism. This means that 'the customer's motives for commissioning a research project may not necessarily be directly related to an interest in the topic concerned' (1987: 101).
- The time lag between commissioning a study and receiving a report may mean that the customer's interests have shifted.
- Academic researchers who produce unpalatable conclusions can be written off as 'unrealistic' (1987: 102).

Sometimes, however, good research can convince even the most stubborn organisation as the following case study demonstrates.

CASE STUDY
Handicap on the Boston Buses

In 2004, University of Pennsylvania sociologist Ross Koppel was asked by the Greater Boston Legal Services (GBLS) to determine the incidence of abuses to people with disabilities who attempted to use the area's bus system. The Massachusetts Bay Transportation Authority (MBTA) had a long and undistinguished history of mistreating persons with disabilities (e.g. people in wheelchairs, with walkers or canes, and the frail elderly). Stories of driver abuse to people with disabilities (PWDs) were rampant. Drivers were hostile, assistive equipment was erroneously declared broken by drivers and PWDs were passed by – all in violation of the Americans with Disabilities Act and U.S. Department of Transportation regulations. People in wheelchairs would be left in the middle of streets, in traffic, or far from curb cuts; 300-pound wheel chairs were often not secured to the bus, creating a 'missile hazard'.

GBLS had been in a legal battle with the MBTA for five years, costing both sides millions of dollars. GBLS's problem was that all of their reports were anecdotal, and anecdotes were insufficient to prove a court case. Also, everyone knew the disabled community was angry at the bus system. Their anger mitigated the value of their depositions about mistreatment and ride failures.

This is where Koppel's sociological skills came in. He said, 'My first idea was to use observers with hidden cameras on buses. This was a lousy idea for three reasons: One, this was not cost effective, as there are insufficient numbers of PWDs riding buses. Two, there are a few routes with many PWDs on them, for example, routes that passed by hospitals or rehab centers, but the study had to represent the "system," not just a few routes; and three, there was some quirky WWI-era law seemingly outlawing taking photographs on buses.'

Koppel quickly understood that he had to assemble a group of testers/PWDs in wheelchairs, with canes, or using walkers who he would send throughout the bus system with a scientifically designed sampling method. Moreover, because the disabled community would not accept faux-disabled, those testers needed to be genuinely disabled. Also, knowing that the court would not believe reports by PWDs themselves, he realised each tester would have to be accompanied by a trained observer with no prior involvement in these cases.

The project hired 20 teams of PWDs paired with observers, trained them on Koppel's eight-page observation schedule and sent them to pre-selected spots throughout the bus system. Each team measured about 120 aspects of the ride, including, for example, measures of pulling to the curb and positioning the bus so a lift or ramp can be used; operating of the lift, ramp and kneeler; helping the PWD reach the safety area; securing a wheelchair to the bus (there are straps built into the floor), or helping a frail elderly passenger to a seat.

Koppel's team collected almost a thousand observations of PWDs using buses.

In his final report – several hundred pages in length – he combined the parenthetical comments from the observers with the quantitative data from the observation forms. They found MBTA's bus service for people with disabilities evidenced pervasive patterns of non-compliance in most areas of operation. While drivers generally sought to accommodate people with disabilities, the ratios of (reported) failed equipment, seemingly untrained drivers and refusals of service were high. Barriers to public transit use were everywhere.

Koppel anticipated the transit system would continue their legal battle and would hire a battery of statisticians, engineers, etc., to refute his findings. But, that's not what happened. The transit system's leaders and their lawyers read the report and, to Koppel's shock, they called it 'the most definitive study of transportation for the disabled ever conducted'. Then they capitulated entirely, and they put up the funds to fix it – one-third of a billion dollars to buy new buses and to hire managers to oversee the programmes for PWDs. The court-approved agreement also involved new driver training programmes and, critically, monitoring. (Koppel, 2009)

Koppel says he sees this research as an example of the power of social research when applied to real problems. Even the Department of Justice was sufficiently aware of the complex measurement and **sampling** issues that it also promoted this approach. Koppel, who takes both public transportation and jogs daily, added:

> We are all getting older and we are all just one slip away from needing a little help. A bus that can extend a ramp or lower its front step is a reasonable accommodation. If sociological methods can help ensure transit systems comply with the laws, then this is an especially rewarding application of our discipline.

Fashions change. As Koppel's successful study indicates, there is some evidence that public bodies may be starting to take qualitative research more seriously. **Focus groups**, in particular, seem to be 'the flavour of the month', mainly, I think, because they are relatively cheap and quick and give nice 'sound-bites' for politicians and advertisers. However, such changes in fashion do little to affect the natural tendency of policy-makers to redefine the meaning of research 'findings'.

However, as Bloor (2004, 2011) has noted, the policy community is not the sole audience for social research.

13.2.2 The Practitioner Audience

> the real opportunities for sociological influence lie closer to the coalface than they do to head office ... [they] lie in relations with practitioners, not with the managers of practice. (Bloor, 2004: 318)

Taking the example of the sociology of health and illness, Bloor argues that practitioners rather than policy-makers are the most reliable and eager audience for social research:

> Sociologists who have conducted research on sociological aspects of health and medicine ... have long been aware that there is a role for sociologists as participants in debates on public policy, but that there are also other audiences for social research, notably audiences of patients and practitioners (clinicians, nurses and other professionals). (2004: 307)

Bloor suggests that qualitative social researchers can build upon their research relationships with practitioners in order to discuss practical implications. As he puts it:

> qualitative researchers *may* address social problems and that they can address them most effectively by influencing practitioner practice. Qualitative research has a two-fold advantage in these processes of influence: one advantage relates to influencing practitioners who are the researcher's research participants, and the second advantage relates to influencing practitioners who are the wider audience for the research findings. In respect of practitioners who are research participants, qualitative researchers can call upon their pre-existing research relationships with their research subjects as a resource for ensuring an attentive and even sympathetic response to their research findings. In respect of other practitioners (who are not research subjects), the qualitative researcher has the advantage that the research methods allow rich descriptions of everyday practice which enable practitioner audiences imaginatively to juxtapose their own everyday practices with the research description ... Practitioners may not always have the local autonomy to develop new services to new target populations of clients, but all practitioners have the autonomy to modify their everyday work practices. In seeking the chimera of policy influence, sociologists rather neglected how research findings can address social problems through the encouragement of modifications and developments in practitioners' everyday practices. (Bloor, 2011: 412–13)

13.2.3 The General Public

There are at least four reasons why qualitative researchers may become involved in reporting back to the general public:

1 to answer questions asked by your respondents
2 to 'check' provisional findings
3 to provide 'feedback' to organisations and relevant groups
4 to provide information for the media.

The first two points have been considered in Chapters 5 and 11. In particular, you should refer to the section on 'gaining access' (Section 5.2.3) for point 1 and the section on **respondent validation** (Section 11.3.2) for point 2.

Feedback to the general public is usually set up because of your own desire to 'give something back' from your research to ordinary people who, through their taxes, may well have funded your research. The format should vary according to whether your audience are members of an established organisation or simply just a group of people with similar interests or concerns.

CASE STUDY
Feedback to Parents

Following my own research on hospital clinics for children (Silverman, 1987), I gave a talk to the Parents' Association at one of the hospitals I had studied. In this talk, I discussed new facts from my research about doctor–parent communication. I also examined the implications of my findings for reform of current hospital practices. Subsequently, I was invited to write a short piece on my research for the newsletter of a British organisation called the Patients' Association. In this article, I covered much the same ground as well as adding guidelines for how to manage better or get better service from hospitals that treat sick children. Finally, I spoke at a meeting of parents of children with diabetes. My aim here was to stress what my research had revealed about the painful dilemmas experienced by such parents. In this way, I sought to assure them that others share their own experience and that there is no need for them to reproach themselves.

Qualitative researchers only rarely reach a general audience through the mass media. Nearly all social science goes unreported by such media. The cautious way in which researchers are taught to write about their findings runs up against the media's need to pull in audience with sensational stories. So it is always a question of the tension between the media's sense of what is 'newsworthy' and researchers' desire for an accurate, unsensationalised account of their research.

An excellent recent example of this tension arose in a study of computerised physician order entry (CPOE) in US hospitals (Koppel, 2005). This study arose by accident when Ross Koppel was doing a study of the stress experienced by junior house physicians. It turned out that the CPOE system produced not only stress among these doctors but a noteworthy number of errors (although, as Koppel points out, some of these errors may not be experienced as stressful at the time). Moreover, although studies had been completed of how CPOE worked, these were purely quantitative and none were based on interviews and observations of physicians.

CASE STUDY
Medical Errors

To establish the extent of medical errors associated with new software, Ross Koppel constructed a multi-method study which incorporated face-to-face interviews and focus groups with house physicians, shadowing doctors as they entered prescriptions into the system and observing nurses and pharmacists as they received prescriptions, interviews with senior medical and nursing staff and a 72-item questionnaire to a 90 per cent sample of house physicians. The prescribing errors discovered included doctors failing to stop one drug when they prescribed its replacement, confusion over which patient was receiving the drugs and confusing an inventory list for clinical guidelines.

In the United States, it is estimated that medication errors within hospitals kill about 40,000 people a year and injure 770,000. According to Koppel's study, it turned out that CPOE systems can facilitate errors. Ironically, CPOE was most useful at stopping errors with few dangerous consequences. In particular, the way in which CPOE had been programmed had two unfortunate consequences: fragmented data displays meant that physicians had difficulty in identifying the specific patient for whom they were prescribing and that the system did not work in the way that doctors worked and created confusion or extra work to address the ambiguities.

Given the amount of government and industry support for CPOE, it is not surprising that Koppel's findings both were treated as highly newsworthy by the national media and came under immediate attack. Many medical researchers suggested that such qualitative research could not produce 'real data'. The manufacturers of CPOE systems launched a campaign which said that Koppel had 'just talked to people' and reported 'anecdotes'. In particular, the public were told, Koppel's study was faulty because it offered no measure of adverse drug events and had identified no 'real' errors but only 'perceptions of errors' (2005: 200).

Koppel's study is a fascinating example of what can happen when qualitative researchers stumble into what turns out to be a controversial topic. It reveals that the power of vested interests can work to denigrate qualitative research in support of a hidden agenda. In this way, the key strength of such an ethnographic study (its ability to depict what happens *in situ*) is presented as a weakness.

However, feedback to different audiences is only part of the story. To assess fully the relevance of qualitative social research, we need to focus more specifically on what exactly our contribution can be. This is the topic of the next section.

LINKS

The Brookings Institute (United States):

www.brookings.edu

13.3 THE CONTRIBUTION OF QUALITATIVE SOCIAL SCIENCE

As a sociologist, my own strong views on social issues are tempered by an understanding of the ways in which particular practices are relative to certain cultures. Understandably, if you are looking at how things operate in different milieux, you tend to get to the position where it is difficult to take a stand on anything because everything is relative to its particular context – this is what is called **relativism**.

Although sociologists' and anthropologists' stress on the infinite variability of cultures is a useful critique of absolutist notions, if pushed too far, it can be disabling in terms of our relationships to the wider community. For instance, in my own work (Silverman, 1987), I have been forced to question favourite liberal or progressive ideas such as 'patient-centred medicine' – doctors paying more attention to their patient's needs and language rather than looking at everything in a purely organic way. My research suggests that there are traps and power-plays present even within apparently patient-centred medicine.

So a relativist sociology needs to think about how it can present its findings in a way that will seem relevant to people who turn to social science with a naive belief in progress and a positivist version of the role of science. Moreover, as the recent debate on female circumcision shows, there are some practices that even relativist academics will not be able to tolerate.

I want now to tackle the issue of relativism but not head-on because this would deflect us into a philosophical minefield. Instead, I want to show how qualitative social science can overcome relativism simply by making three contributions to society:

1 participating in debates about how organisations function
2 providing new opportunities for people to make their own choices
3 offering a potentially new perspective to practitioners and clients.

Let us consider each contribution in turn.

13.3.1 Reporting on how organisations function

Throughout this book, we have come across examples of how qualitative researchers have come up with intriguing and original knowledge about how organisations function, starting with Dalton's (1959) study of clique structures in management to more recent work on people using photocopy machines (Suchman, 1987) and controlling underground trains on London Transport (Heath and Luff, 2000). Such report not only has interesting findings but contains clear relevance for human resources management and research and development.

Such relevance relates both to organisational structures and to decision-making. Let me take one further example which addresses organisational decision-making in the context of apparently patient-centred medicine. In the paediatric heart clinic discussed in Section 11.3.2, we became interested in how decisions (or 'disposals') were organised and announced (Silverman, 1987). It seemed likely that the doctor's way of announcing decisions was systematically related not only to clinical factors (like the child's heart condition) but to social factors (such as what parents would be told at various stages of treatment).

For instance, at a first outpatients' consultation, doctors would not normally announce to parents the discovery of a major heart abnormality and the necessity for life-threatening surgery. Instead, they would suggest the need for more tests and only hint that major surgery might be needed. They would also collaborate with parents who produced examples of their child's apparent 'wellness'.

This step-by-step method of information-giving was avoided in only two cases. If a child was diagnosed as 'healthy' by the cardiologist, the doctor would give all the information in one go and would engage in what we called a 'search and destroy' operation, based on eliciting any remaining worries of the parent(s) and proving that they were mistaken.

In the case of a group of children with the additional handicap of Down's syndrome (as well as suspected cardiac disease), the doctor would present all the clinical information at one sitting, avoiding a step-by-step method. Moreover, atypically, the doctor would allow parents to make the choice about further treatment, while encouraging them to dwell on non-clinical matters like their child's 'enjoyment of life' or friendly personality.

This medical focus on the child's *social* characteristics was seen right at the outset of each consultation. I was able to construct a table, based on a comparison of Down's and non-Down's consultations, showing the different forms of the doctor's questions to parents and the parents' answers.

At first Table 13.3 looked quite unremarkable – just the sort of questions you would expect a cardiology physician to ask parents at a first consultation. It was only when we compared these questions with the question format with non-Down's children that something striking surfaced.

TABLE 13.3 First history-taking question (Down's syndrome children)

Is he/she well?	0
From your point of view, a well baby?	1
Do you notice anything wrong with him/her?	0
Does he get breathless?	1
She gets a few chest infections?	1
How is he/she?	6
Question not asked	1
Total	10

TABLE 13.4 First history-taking question (random sample from the same clinic)

Is he/she well?	11
From your point of view, a well baby?	2
Do you notice anything wrong with her?	1
From the heart point of view, she's active?	1
How is he/she?	4
Question not asked	3
Total	22

Source: adapted from Silverman, 1981

Tables 13.3 and 13.4 show a strong tendency with Down's children for the doctor to avoid using the word 'well' about the child. At my heart clinic, the most common question that the doctor asked parents was: 'A well child?' However, parents of Down's syndrome children were rarely asked this question. Instead, the most common question was: 'How is he (she)?' Note that the categories in the tables were not my own. I simply tabulated the different questions as actually given (just as Hepburn and Potter tabulated the participants' use of the word 'concern').

Further analysis revealed that parents collaborated with the doctors' choice of words, answering in terms like 'alright' and 'fine' rather than 'well'. This absence of reference to 'wellness' proved to be crucial to understanding the subsequent shape of the clinic consultation.

Having compared medical history-taking with Down's and non-Down's families, we moved on to the final stage of these consultations to examine how treatment decisions were arrived at. In the early 1980s, a child with symptoms of congenital heart disease would usually be recommended for cardiac catherisation, a diagnostic test requiring a brief stay as an inpatient.

In these cases, the doctor would say to the parents something like: 'What we propose to do, if you agree, is a small test.' No parent disagreed with an offer which appeared to be purely formal – like the formal right (never exercised) of the

Queen not to sign legislation passed by the British Parliament. For Down's syndrome children, however, the parents' right to choose was far from formal. The doctor would say things to them like the following:

I think what we would do now depends a little bit on parents' feelings.
Now it depends a little bit on what you think.
It depends very much of your own personal views as to whether we should proceed.

Moreover, these consultations were longer and apparently more democratic than elsewhere. A view of the patient in a family context was encouraged and parents were given every opportunity to voice their concerns and to participate in decision-making.

In this sub-sample, unlike the larger sample, when given a real choice, parents refused the test – with only one exception. Yet this served to reinforce rather than to challenge the medical policy in the unit concerned. This policy was to discourage surgery, all things being equal, on such children. So the democratic form co-existed with (and was indeed sustained by) the maintenance of an autocratic policy (Silverman, 1981).

The research thus discovered the mechanics whereby a particular medical policy was enacted. The availability of tape recordings of large numbers of consultations, together with a research method that sought to develop hypotheses inductively, meant that we were able to develop our data analysis by discovering a phenomenon for which we had not originally been looking – discovery which is far harder to make in more structured quantitative research designs.

'Democratic' decision-making or 'whole-patient medicine' are thus revealed as discourses with no intrinsic meaning. Instead, their consequences depend upon their deployment and articulation in particular contexts. So even democracy is not something that we must appeal to in all circumstances. In contexts like this, democratic forms can be part of a power-play.

Am I still faced with the charge of relativism because I am treating what many of us would hold to be an absolute value (democracy) as having a variable meaning? Well, not necessarily, particularly if I can show that research which questions apparently 'absolute' values, like universal democracy, can have a practical relevance.

Two such practically relevant matters arose from the study of Down's syndrome consultations. First, we asked the doctor concerned to rethink his policy or at least reveal his hidden agenda to parents. We did not dispute that there are many grounds to treat such children differently from others in relation to surgery. For instance, they have a poorer, post-surgical survival rate and most parents are reluctant to contemplate surgery. However, there is a danger of stereotyping the needs of such children and their parents. By 'coming clean' about his policy, the doctor would enable parents to make a more informed choice.

The second practical point, revealed by this research, has already been mentioned. Its relativistic stance about 'patient-centred' medicine rightly serves to discomfit liberal doctors wedded to this fashionable orthodoxy. For, as good practitioners realise, no style of communication is intrinsically superior to another. Everything depends upon its context.

The work I was doing in the paediatric cardiology clinic on the Down's parents already suggests one direction in which that debate could take place. Another example arose from my research on three cancer clinics in which I looked at the practice of a doctor in the British National Health Service (NHS) and compared it with his private practice (Silverman, 1984).

This study was relevant to a lively debate about the NHS and whether there should be more private medicine. I was able to show that, despite these 'ceremonial' gains, patients overall got a better deal when they did not pay, than when they did pay. So this serves as a further example of how qualitative research can contribute to our understanding of how organisations work.

13.3.2 Increasing people's options

Thoughtful qualitative research studies can also, I believe, provide new opportunities which allow people to make their own choices. Our work in the paediatric cardiology unit revealed two aspects of this. First, the study of doctors' decision-making highlighted the need for parents to make their own choices without feeling guilty. Second, the extra clinic that was offered to parents after a first outpatient consultation removed some constraints which allowed all parties to innovate in ways which we could not have predicted.

A further relevant example is the research on the mother talking to a doctor about her worries regarding her diabetic daughter (already discussed in Section 9.4.2). This **naturally occurring** material revealed that this mother is not *intrinsically* 'nagging' or 'irresponsible'. Instead, both are depictions which are *locally* available and *locally* resisted. Conversely, if we had interviewed mothers, the temptation would have been to search for idealised conceptions of their role.

Doctors were interested to learn about the double-binds present in their attention to the autonomy of their young patients. Likewise, parents' groups (largely mothers) of diabetic children found it very helpful to go through material of this kind. It brought out the way in which things they may feel personally guilty about in their relationships with their teenage children are not something that relates to their individual failings. Instead, such problems arise in our culture in the double-binds built into the parent–adolescent relationship.

In all these cases, we contributed to practical matters without imposing any elitist form of social engineering. By attending to the fine detail of interactions, we come to respect the practical skills of the participants. This is shown in the next case study.

CASE STUDY
Unwelcome Sex

Hannah Frith and Celia Kitzinger report a focus group study where young women discussed their experiences of saying 'no' to sex. One typical example is below:

Extract 13.1 [Frith and Kitzinger, 1998: 309]

Carla: I try to think of a way to turn him down without hurting his feelings … Next time I do see him, in a way I make a special effort to talk to him to show that there are no hard feelings.

   The authors point out that it is usually suggested that this is an example of 'emotion work' which involves women adopting a dominant cultural stereotype about how they should act. However, there is an alternative explanation:

> emotion work talk can be heard as a *post hoc* explanation for 'unwanted' sex which avoids using the 'rape' label; or as a justification for 'wanted' sexual behaviour … [indeed] the availability of 'emotion work' as a participant resource may 'cause' women to conduct sexual negotiations in a manner which can subsequently be presented in this way. (1998: 317)

The implication of this research is to recognise that people are *active* subjects who are not simply puppets of cultural codes. This suggests that well-meaning rape-resistance strategies, such as the 'just say no' campaign, may overlook how people actually converse. For instance, 'saying no, is a "dispreferred" activity requiring considerable interactional work' (see my discussion of *preference organisation* in Section 9.2).

As these examples show, the role of the social scientist is not to be more knowledgeable than laypeople but, instead, to analyse how they actually choose between courses of action and, thereby, to increase their options.

13.3.3 Offering a new perspective to practitioners

Bloor has suggested that the detail and transparency of ethnographic data has an appeal to many practitioners:

> the qualitative researcher has the advantage that the research methods allow rich descriptions of everyday practice which allow practitioner audiences imaginatively to juxtapose their own everyday practices with the research description. There is therefore an opportunity for practitioners to make evaluative judgments about their own practices and experiment with the adoption of new approaches described in the research findings. (2004: 321)

Bloor's argument is important because it contests the common assumption that the role of researchers is to find instances of professional failings and then to offer correctives. This assumption draws upon what I have called the 'divine' orthodoxy (Silverman, 1997: 25) which assumes that social scientists can always see better and further than practitioners. By contrast, Bloor offers a vision of qualitative research as the source of good-quality data and rich descriptions which can offer practitioners new resources with which to assess their own practice.

I want to illustrate Bloor's argument with a study of calls to a child protection helpline (Hepburn and Potter, 2004).

CASE STUDY
Calls to a Child Protection Agency

Hepburn and Potter found that nearly all callers prefaced their claims of potential child abuse by a statement of the basis of their knowledge. However, in Extract 13.2, the young caller announces the nature of the abuse early on (line 5).

Extract 13.2 [Hepburn and Potter, 2004: 194] (Two 12-year-old girls)

(CPO = child protection officer)

```
 1   CPO:     Alright Kathryn (.) .hh so wha-what's
 2            goin on:.
 3   Caller:  Well .hh what it i:s: (.) is I've got
 4            a really close friend an: (.) li:ke hhh
 5            (0.3) she's been sexually abu:sed. an (.)
 6   CPO:     Mm↓[mm:, ]
 7   Caller:  [she's] really close to me a-an I
 8            just- (0.1) I wanna tell 'er mum but
 9            I can't bring myself to do it.
10            (0.4)
11   CPO:     tch.hh so:: how did you find out
12            about that.=
```

Hepburn and Potter note that the CPO is now in a difficult position because she needs to ask the caller about the basis of her knowledge (lines 11–12). As they comment: 'although the NSPCC need this information to be able to follow up on a call like this adequately, it is still easily heard as displaying a sceptical stance to the child' (2004: 194).

By providing an analytically grounded account of why problems might appear in calls such as this, Hepburn and Potter are able to offer directions for thinking about how CPOs might counter them. As they suggest:

(Continued)

(Continued)

One of the limitations of training for work of this kind is that it is often based on idealizations or suppositions about the way interaction works … One thing we found with this project was that the initial practical input was rather simple. We were able to provide CPOs with a set of digitised and roughly transcribed calls on a CD that they could play in their own PC (stopping and starting, dipping into and so on). Some of the CPOs found that the facility to reflect on her or his own practice was very helpful. We hope that toward the end of the research we can provide more sophisticated training aids which allow CPOs to step through digitised calls with analytic observations and suggestions about them (e.g. about trouble and its solution). The aim of these kind of practical interventions here is not to tell the CPOs how to do their job better, but to provide one sort of resource that they can draw in their training and practice as is helpful. (2004: 194–5)

EXERCISE 13.2

This exercise offers you an opportunity to address the practical relevance of field research in the context of the **conversation analysis** and **discourse analysis** skills you learned in Chapter 9. It is based on Extract 13.2.

1 Using any of the concepts mentioned in Chapter 9, attempt a further analysis of Extract 13.2.
2 What does your analysis show that is different from or adds to the analysis given above?
3 Imagine you are talking to child protection officers about their work. What kinds of practical implications could you suggest in relation to how they communicate with callers?
4 Imagine you are talking to people who suspect child abuse. What kinds of practical implications could your analysis have for them?

Following this case study, I will conclude this chapter by returning to the argument with which this chapter began.

13.4 SUMMARY

We are all cleverer than we can say in so many words. That is to say, the kinds of skills we are using in everyday settings, from telephone calls to hospital consultations, are much more complicated and require much more analysis than we can actually tell the researcher in an interview study. Yet, by working with naturally occurring material, we can make the skills used by all parties more available for analysis.

By analysing 'common sense' in fine detail, research can often make a direct contribution to professional practice. Moreover, as Hepburn and Potter suggest, the transcripts alone are an excellent resource which professionals can use to examine their own and each other's practice.

I think such research also has an implication for how phenomena can be made available for social science analysis. Researchers too readily assume that some topics, like sexuality, are private matters to which we cannot get direct access – for instance, without putting a tape recorder under everybody's bed or video camera above it. However, this is an example of unclear thinking.

This assumes that sexuality is a unitary phenomenon that only takes place in a certain kind of setting. Instead, I would argue that most phenomena take place in a multiplicity of settings. Why cannot we find sexuality present in soap operas, cartoons or, indeed, in how clients and professionals present versions of themselves and descriptions of their partners and activities (see my discussion of Gubrium and Holstein's work in Section 14.1)?

As I pointed out in the first few pages of Chapter 1, the problem arises from the use by researchers of *essentialist* conceptions of social phenomena. Once we are freed from this common-sense assumption, we can proceed to explicate common-sense practices in order to reveal their fine detail.

My favourite philosopher, Ludwig Wittgenstein, made this point for me. He writes: 'The aspects of things that are most important for us are hidden because of their simplicity and familiarity' (1968, para 129).

Strangely, what we are concerned with in qualitative social science is what is closest to hand. However, because it is so close to hand, both participants *and* researchers may often forget about it. Our common-sense knowledge about the way in which the world is organised is being used all the time by us in the everyday world and also to understand our research findings. But rarely do we topicalise that common-sense knowledge. Wittgenstein draws our attention to this paradox.

13.5 CONCLUSION

> There is a pressing need to show how the practices of qualitative research can help change the world in positive ways. (Denzin and Lincoln, 2000b: x)

Throughout this chapter, I have been arguing that qualitative researchers can best satisfy the 'pressing need' identified by Denzin and Lincoln by resisting directly employing administrators', journalists' or even practitioners' definitions of what is a 'problem'. I have illustrated this point through a number of studies which parallel my own research on outpatient clinics and HIV-test counselling.

In these contexts, I have shown the gains of seeking to understand the local functions of talk rather than directly entering into normative debates about communication styles. Put in another way, this means that we should aim to identify the interactional skills of the participants rather than their failings.

CASE STUDY
Talking Past one Another

David Lodge's novel *Nice Work* is about the relationship between Robyn, a lecturer (at the same university as in all Lodge's books), and Vic, a manager in an engineering firm. She has spent some time with him in order to understand the world of industry. This is, of course, very much a document of the 1980s where one version of 'free market' economics suggested that the value of academic institutions is to be judged in terms of their contribution to the needs of industry.

   Just before the extract below, Robyn, the cultural studies lecturer, had given a highly risqué reading of the cultural symbolism of a cigarette advertisement. Robyn's semiotic analysis of the advertisement is treated by Vic as a display of unnecessary jargon. In this extract, Vic, the manager, speaks first.

Extract 13.3 [Lodge, 1989: 221]

'Why can't you people take things at their face value?'

'What people are you referring to?'

'Highbrows. Intellectuals. You're always trying to find hidden meanings in things. Why? A cigarette is a cigarette. A piece of silk is a piece of silk. Why not leave it at that?'

'When they're represented they acquire additional meanings,' said Robyn. 'Signs are never innocent. Semiotics teaches us that.'

'Semi-what?'

'Semiotics. The study of signs.'

'It teaches us to have dirty minds, if you ask me.'

It seems that Vic and Robyn talk past one another. He does not understand what on earth she is doing. And to her, the world of industry seems to be a world with no morality and little sense. However, at the end of the book they do achieve a dialogue between the world of academia and the everyday world.

   I think such a dialogue, though hard to achieve, should be our aim. In practice, this probably means that both sides will have to give a little. Policy-makers will have to give up their suspicion of research which is not based on statistics and refuses to define its research topic in terms of any obvious social problem. In turn, qualitative researchers will have to demonstrate how their work can be both insightful and valid.

As part of this dialogue, quantitative researchers will have to give up their belief in the stupidity of common-sense ways of acting and be prepared to establish a division of labour with their qualitative colleagues. But, equally, qualitative research-ers will have to question the siren calls of **emotionalism** and its commitment to the transcendent character of 'experience'.

> **TIP**
>
> Workshops for policy-makers or professionals need not always be organised around presentations of your research findings. Alternative points of discussion are often more fruitful (e.g. presentations of 'interesting' raw data or inviting people present to begin by suggesting what they would like to get out of your research – this can also be done prior to the meeting when you send out invitations).

KEY POINTS

- Although no neutral or value-free position is possible in social science, this does not mean that 'anything goes'.

- Researchers can be strongly partisan but still rigorous in their data analysis.

- The wider audience for qualitative research includes policy-makers, prac-titioners and the general public – each will have different expectations.

- Qualitative researchers can attempt to satisfy these expectations by: par-ticipating in debates about public policy; providing new opportunities for people to make their own choices; and by offering a new perspective to practitioners.

STUDY QUESTIONS

1 Why is it difficult to convince policy-makers about the value of the findings of qualitative research?
2 What distinctive topics can qualitative research address?
3 What different answers have been given to the question: 'Whose side are we on?'
4 What kinds of audiences can we seek to interest? What is each audience likely to expect?
5 List *three* contributions our research can make to society.

RECOMMENDED READING

Although almost a century old, Max Weber's lecture 'Science as a vocation' (1946) remains the key reading. Probably the best recent monograph that addresses a practitioner audience is Maynard's (2003) work on news-telling. Roger Hadley's (1987) chapter 'Publish and be ignored: proselytise and be damned' is a vibrant account of the pitfalls of trying to reach a policy audience. Practitioner audiences are very well discussed in Michael Bloor's chapter 'Addressing social problems through qualitative research' in Silverman (2011). Gary Marx's paper (1997) is a lively and extremely helpful guide for the apprentice researcher desiring to make links with a range of audiences. Ian Shaw (1999) provides a helpful, introductory account of the ways in which qualitative research can evaluate programmes and policies.

14

The Potential of Qualitative Research: Eight Reminders

CHAPTER OBJECTIVES

By the end of this chapter you will be able to:

- appreciate the underlying themes of this book
- understand better how the constructionist model can be used in qualitative research.

The author of a textbook is always torn between two different impulses. Naturally, one wants to provide a comprehensive and fair coverage of the field. On the other hand, it is impossible to escape the author's own assumptions, preferences and (dare one say it?) prejudices.

However, providing the reader is given the opportunity to register the intellectual baggage that authors bring to their writing, we should not see such baggage as a drawback. Even if we could imagine a textbook freed from authorial prejudice, it would be a pretty dull affair – rather like those awful book reviews which do little more than list the titles of each chapter.

In this book, I hope that my own intellectual baggage has given flavour and spice to my depiction of the field. Throughout I have tried to be open about the way that this has shaped the route we have followed. In this final chapter, therefore, before setting out my 'reminders', a brief biographical sketch may be helpful.

Forty years ago, I began my research career with a study of the beliefs and values of junior 'white-collar' workers. Influenced by sociological **theories** of class and social status, I wanted to see how far the way you perceived yourself was influenced by where you worked and by your future job prospects.

I used a structured interview schedule and my **methodology** was cast in the standard forms of quantitative research: an initial hypothesis, a two-by-two table and statistical tests (see Silverman, 1968). If I had completed this study, my future career might have taken a completely different path.

However, I started to have nagging doubts about the credibility of my research. Although I could manipulate my data so as to provide a rigorous test of my **hypotheses**, the data were hardly 'raw' but mediated by various kinds of interpretive activities. Not the least of these arose in my administration of the interview schedule.

As I was interviewing my respondents, I was struck by the need to go beyond my questions in various, unforeseen ways so as to obtain the sort of answers I wanted. Perhaps, I thought, I hadn't pre-tested my questions properly. Or, perhaps, how we make sense in conversations necessarily relies on everyday conversational skills that cannot be reduced to reliable techniques (see Antaki and Rapley, 1996).

In any event, I abandoned this study and turned to organisation theory in a work that was to be both my PhD and a successful textbook (Silverman, 1970). I spent the following decade exploring the uses of two contemporary social science theories. An ethnography of the personnel department of a public sector organisation (Silverman and Jones, 1976) was heavily influenced by Garfinkel's (1967) **ethnomethodology** (see Section 5.5). And an analysis of literary texts (Silverman and Torode, 1980) derived from Saussure's (1974) **semiotics** (see Section 10.4). These studies confirmed my belief in the value of theoretically informed research – a belief affirmed throughout the present text.

However, guiding principles tend to be double-edged. So, while we should assert their benefits, we should also be aware of their possible costs. Looking back on this early work, I now feel that is was a trifle over-theorised. Perhaps I had been so enthused by a newly discovered theory that I had not allowed myself to be sufficiently challenged, even surprised, by my data.

Such over-theorisation is an ever-present danger given that many social science disciplines still, I believe, run in fear of being discovered, like the fabled emperor, without any clothes (for a recent valuable exception see Kendall and Wickham's, 1999, fine text on the practical research uses of Foucault's ideas). It is for this reason that what has been called the **post-modern** period of experimental ethnographic writing (Denzin and Lincoln's, 2000b: 17, 'fifth moment') barely figures in this book.

In my later research, I tried to find a better balance between the theoretical 'armchair' and the empirical 'field'. In both an **ethnography** of hospital clinics (Silverman, 1987) and a **conversation analytic** study of HIV-test counselling (Silverman, 1997), I adopted a more cautious approach to my data, inductively establishing hypotheses, using the comparative method, and identifying deviant cases (see Section 8.3.2). In both studies, unlike my earlier work, I explored ways of making my research relevant to a wider, non-academic audience in a non-patronising way (see Chapter 11).

However, these later studies also derived from two related methodological assumptions present in my 1976 study. All three studies were based not on interviews but on **naturally occurring data**. And all of them looked at how the participants talked to one another and focused on the skills they used and the local functions of what they did.

This final chapter gives me the opportunity to pull together these authorial threads. However, it is not meant as an indulgence to myself, still less as a kind of *mea culpa*, where I apologise for my inability to be sufficiently objective. It is one voice in a debate that I believe matters both to social scientists and to our audiences. I hope, therefore, that you will find this chapter worth reading as a way of further stimulating your interest in the potential of qualitative research.

In formulating my ideas as 'reminders', I have followed my favourite philosopher, Ludwig Wittgenstein. Wittgenstein came to reject philosophies based on principles or rules. Instead, he favoured assembling fragments of everyday understandings to serve as reminders of what we know already. For Wittgenstein, these reminders would have a 'hygienic' purpose. They would aim to clear our heads of the babble that sometimes passes as intellectual argument in order to look at the world afresh.

In this chapter, my aims are less grand. I would not, for a moment, claim to have transcended that babble. While much has had to be crammed into a small space, a common thread will emerge which, I hope, will tie together the preceding chapters. For my own position rests firmly on the **models** that have been described in this book as **constructionism** and ethnomethodology. So, in this chapter, I return to the theme of the situated character of accounts and other practices and to the dangers of seeking to identify phenomena apart from these practices and the forms of representation which they embody.

Yet, because I have no time for self-contained 'schools' of social science, I hope that what I have to say will be debated by those researchers with other kinds of preferences and allegiances. Conceived as 'reminders', rather than as rules or dictums, what follows is meant to encourage, rather than stifle, debate.

14.1 TAKE ADVANTAGE OF NATURALLY OCCURRING DATA

I have just referred to my preference for working with naturally occurring data. This seems logical if your interest is in the practices through which phenomena like 'families', 'tribes' or 'laboratory science' are constructed or assembled. Despite this, however, many ethnographers move relatively easily between observational data and data that are artefacts of a research setting, usually an interview. In Chapter 11, I pointed out the difficulties this can create, especially where **triangulation** is used to compare findings from different settings and to assemble the context-free 'truth'.

When it comes to actual research studies, there is hardly an even spread of **methods**. Nor is it the case that ethnography is just one among many methods. Instead of looking, listening and reading, the majority of contemporary qualitative researchers prefer to select a small group of individuals to interview or to place in **focus groups**. In this sense, by assembling a specific research **sample**, linked only by the fact that they have been selected to answer a predetermined research question, such researchers prefer to 'manufacture' their data rather than to 'find' the data in the 'field'. Despite their earnest claims to do something quite different from quantitative research (more 'humanistic', more 'experiential', more 'in-depth'), such manufacture of data to answer a specified research problem is precisely *the* method which quantitative research espouses.

Qualitative researchers' almost Pavlovian tendency to identify research design with interviews has blinkered them to the possible gains of other kinds of data. For it is thoroughly mistaken to assume that the sole topic for qualitative research is 'people'.

C. Seale (personal correspondence) has noted how he seeks to contest this common supposition:

> I find that, in order to counteract the tendency towards wanting to do interviews, it helps to repeatedly make the point that many textbooks assume that when one is going to do a research study one always wants to sample 'people' (rather than, say, documents). This helps [students] realise that al kinds of phenomena can be studied for social research purposes (eg: building design, music lyrics, web sites, small ads etc) and it is then obvious that interviews aren't the only thing to do.

We often falsely assume that there is inherent difficulty in obtaining naturally occurring data because of the supposedly 'private' character of many settings, for example 'family life' or 'sexuality'. However, this assumption trades off a common-sense perception that these are *unitary* phenomena whose meaning is constructed in a single site (e.g. households, bedrooms).

Yet 'family life' is going on all around us – in courtrooms and social security offices as well as households (see Gubrium, 1992). Equally, 'sexuality' is hardly confined to the bedroom; discourses of sexuality are all around us too (see Foucault, 1979).

Given the availability of such naturally occurring data, I share **naturalism**'s enthusiasm to get out 'into the field' to study what participants are doing. Being 'in the field' gives us exposure to the categories that **members** actually use in their day-to-day activities. Categories abstracted from the business of daily life usually impose a set of polarities (or continuums) with an unknown relationship to that business.

Of course, Gubrium and Holstein's arguments apply well beyond family studies. They show that, when researching *any* institution, lack of access should not lead us to assume that interviews are the only way forward.

Following Sacks, we can carry this argument even further than Gubrium and Holstein would probably want to go. Take Jonathan Potter's position on this debate. Potter (1996b; 2002) has roundly criticised researchers who use his own approach (**discourse analysis**) for depending too much on interview data and has argued for a greater use of naturally occurring data. Closely following my concept of 'manufactured' data he shows how interviews, experiments, focus groups and survey questionnaires are all 'got up by the researcher'. Instead, he proposes what he humorously calls *The Dead Social Scientist Test*. As he describes it: 'The test is whether the interaction would have taken place in the form that it did had the researcher not been born or if the researcher had got run over on the way to the university that morning' (Potter, 1996b: 135).

However, there are two dangers in pushing this argument very far. First, we can become smug about the status of 'naturally occurring' data. I have already referred to Hammersley and Atkinson's (1995) observation that there is no 'pure' data; all data are mediated by our own reasoning as well as that of participants (see also Potter, 2002; Speer, 2002). So to assume that 'naturally occurring' data are unmediated data is, self-evidently, a fiction of the same kind as put about by survey researchers who argue that techniques and controls suffice to produce data which are not artefacts of the research setting.

The second danger implicit in the purist response is that it can blind us to the really powerful, compelling nature of interview accounts. Consider, for instance, the striking 'atrocity stories' told by mothers of handicapped children and their appeal to listeners to hear them as 'coping splendidly' (see my discussion, in Section 6.8, of 'moral tales').

This leads me to the problem of how to make the best use of interview data and to the dead-ends identified in Chapter 6.

14.2 AVOID TREATING THE ACTOR'S POINT OF VIEW AS AN EXPLANATION

How could anybody have thought this was the case in social science? How could anybody think that what we ought to do is to go out into the field to report people's exciting, gruesome or intimate experiences?

Yet, judging by the prevalence of what I will call 'naive' interview studies in qualitative research, this indeed seems to be the case. Naive interviewers believe that the supposed limits of quantitative research are overcome by an open-ended interview schedule and a desire to catch 'authentic' experience.

They fail to recognise what they have in common with media interviewers (whose perennial question is 'How do you/does it feel?') and with tourists (who, in their search for the 'authentic' or 'different', invariably end up with more of the same). They also totally fail to recognise the problematic analytic status of interview data which are never simply raw but both situated and **textual** (Mishler,

1986). Such analytic issues, moreover, are not even touched upon in the elegant methodological 'remedies' of survey research.

Of course, the crasser forms of **emotionalism** are restricted to student essays and to some of the speeches of the British ex-Prime Minister Margaret Thatcher ('there is no such thing as society' she once commented). Nevertheless, professional social science often still responds to the emotionalist impulse, particularly in fieldworkers' commitment to the sanctity of what respondents say in open-ended interviews. As we saw in Chapter 6, we are thus sometimes left with the unappetising choice between treating accounts as privileged data or as 'perspectival' and subject to check via the method of 'triangulation' with other observations.

If we reduce qualitative research to the emotionalist interview, we lose much of the thrust of the tradition from which it emerged. As I noted in Chapter 5, you only have to look at interactionist work from the **Chicago School** in the 1930s and 1940s to see the presence of a much more vital approach.

Using their eyes as well as listening to what people were saying, these sociologists invariably located 'consciousness' in specific patterns of social organisation. In their studies of urban life, Park and Burgess showed how the social organisation of the city could be understood in terms of different 'zones' and the movement of population between zones over time (see the beginning of Chapter 5). In this respect, people's behaviour and their accounts are always contexted or situated.

CASE STUDY
Parents' Tales

This issue of the situated nature of people's accounts directly arose in my study of a paediatric cardiology unit (Silverman 1987). When we interviewed parents after their child's first clinic visit, most said that they had a problem taking anything in. They reported that one of their major problems in concentrating properly was caused by the crowded room in which the consultation took place – as a teaching hospital, several other doctors as well as nurses and researchers were present.

Although we could empathise with the parents' response, we thought it worthwhile to go back to our tapes of the encounters they were discussing. It turned out that the number of questions parents asked was directly related to the number of staff present (not inversely related as their interview answers would have suggested).

As is often the case after such a counter-intuitive finding, we found quite a simple explanation. Perhaps when the senior doctor broke off the consultation to ask questions of the junior doctors present, quite unintentionally, this created a space for parents to think about what they had been told so far and to formulate their questions without belonging 'on stage' in direct eye contact with the doctor. This explanation was supported in another unit where parents also asked many questions after they had had some time on their own while the doctor studied clinical data (Silverman, 1987: 91–4).

This took us back to our interview material with the parents. We were not prepared to treat what they had told us ironically, that is as self-evidently mistaken in the light of the 'objective' data.

As already noted, such simple-minded triangulation of data fails to do justice to the embedded, situated nature of accounts. Instead, we came to see parents' accounts as 'moral tales' (Voysey, 1975; Baruch, 1982). Our respondents struggled to present their actions in the context of moral versions of responsible parenthood in a situation where the dice were loaded against them (because of the risks to life and the high-technology means of diagnosis and treatment).

Parents' reference to the problems of the crowded consultation room were now treated not as an explanation of their behaviour at the time but as a situated appeal to the rationality and moral appropriateness of that behaviour.

What we found in the heart hospital was similar to the results of an earlier study of 50 British general practice consultations. Webb and Stimson (1976) noted how patients' accounts of a recent consultation took on a dramatic quality in which the researcher was encouraged to empathise with the patient's difficulties in the consultation.

The usual story was of a highly rational patient who had behaved actively and sensibly. By contrast, doctors were routinely portrayed as acting insensitively or with poor judgement. By telling 'atrocity stories', Webb and Stimson suggest that patients were able to give vent to thoughts which had gone unvoiced at the time of the consultation, to redress a real or perceived inequality between doctor and patient and to highlight the teller's own rationality. Equally, atrocity stories have a dramatic form which captures the hearer's attention – a point which qualitative researchers become aware of when asked to give brief accounts of their findings.

There are powerful cultural forms at work in such 'moral tales'. Consequently, the last thing you want to do is to treat them as simple statements of events to be triangulated with other people's accounts or observations. For the fact is that, as societal members, we can see the 'good sense' of such tales. In many respects, an 'atrocity story' is no less powerful because there is no corroborating evidence. It reveals the 'moral work' involved in displays of 'responsible' parenthood, particularly, as in Baruch's study, where that responsibility had to be demonstrated in the context of potentially unintelligible, high-technology cardiac medicine.

In a certain sense, once again we see how qualitative researchers have come back, in a full circle, to a position held by their quantitative colleagues. Neither wants to take the actor's point of view as an explanation because this would be to equate common sense with social science – a recipe for the lazy qualitative researcher who settles for simply reporting people's 'experiences'. Only when such a researcher moves beyond the gaze of the tourist, bemused with a sense of bizarre cultural practices ('Goodness, you do things differently here'), do the interesting analytic questions begin.

Such questions can be derived from two very different but equally neglected sources. In his later philosophical writing, Wittgenstein (1968) implies that we should not treat people's utterances as standing for their unmediated inner experiences. This is particularly striking in his discussion of statements about pain (paras 244–6, 448–9). Wittgenstein asks: what does it mean when I say I'm in pain? And why is it that we feel unable to deny this assertion when someone makes it about themselves?

In our community, it seems, we talk about pain as if it belongs to individuals. So, in understanding the meaning of someone saying 'I'm in pain' we reveal what our community takes for granted about private experience (but not private experience itself – see Peräkylä and Silverman, 1991). So Wittgenstein makes the point that, in analysing another's activities, we are always describing what is appropriate to a communal 'language-game'.

A second source for understanding the public sense of interview accounts is to be found in Mills's (1940) classic discussion of 'vocabularies of motive'. Mills reminds us that, for sociological purposes, nothing lies 'behind' people's accounts. So when people describe their own or other's motives, the appropriate questions to ask are:

- When does such talk get done?
- What motives are available for people to ascribe in this context?
- What work does 'motive talk' do in the context in which it arises?

As Gilbert and Mulkay were to argue, many years later: 'the goal of the analyst no longer parallels that of the participants, who are concerned to find out what they and others did or thought but becomes that of reflecting upon the patterned character of participants' portrayals of action' (1983: 24).

CASE STUDY
Should We Believe Focus Groups?

Pösö et al. (2008) used focus groups as a tool to study violence in youth residential care; 38 boys and girls in two Finnish reform schools joined single-sex focus groups. However, their responses were not treated as simple reflections of the experiences of violence in care homes. Instead, the researchers reflected upon how the institutional and situational context and the very form of focus groups affected how these young people talked about violence. For instance, talk about their desire to attack staff at the home seemed to function less as a depiction of a 'real' intent and more as a way of generating solidarity among the group (perhaps indicated by the laughter that talk on this topic generated).

As Pösö et al. comment:

> the groups functioned as a means of presenting the issues of youth life and especially residential life to outsiders. The residential life is full of distinctions (e.g. resident vs staff, newcomer vs old resident, child vs adult) to which the focus groups introduced a new dimension of outsiders and insiders to separate the researchers and the residents. This enabled the residents to present themselves as persons who knew something the outsiders were not familiar with. In that respect their accounts had several meanings: they were reports, highlights of long periods of residential life, extremes; possibly they also carnivalized residential life for us. (2008: 77)

Conceived in this sort of way, interview and focus group data become a fascinating topic for analytically sensitive case study work. As I have already suggested, with a little lateral thinking, it is also possible to derive from this approach practical as well as analytic insights.

14.3 STUDY THE INTERRELATIONSHIPS BETWEEN ELEMENTS

The distinctive contribution that qualitative research can make is by utilising its theoretical resources in the deep analysis of small bodies of publicly shareable data. This means that, unlike much quantitative research, we are not satisfied with a simple coding of data. Instead, through comprehensive data treatment, we have to show how the (theoretically defined) elements we have identified are assembled or mutually laminated (see my discussion of Saussure's account of signs in Section 10.4).

Yet there are also similarities between good qualitative and quantitative research. In both, multi-factorial explanation is likely to be more satisfactory than explanations which appeal to what I have called a 'single element'. Just because one is doing a case study, limited to a particular set of interactions, does not mean that one cannot examine how particular sayings and doings are embedded in particular patterns of social organisation.

Despite their very different theoretical frameworks, this is the distinctive quality shared by, say, Whyte (1949) and Moerman's (1974) discussion of a Thai tribe. A further classic case is found in Douglas's (1975) work on a Central African tribe, the Lele (discussed in Section 5.1.1).

Douglas's study of the Lele exemplifies the need to locate how individual elements are embedded in forms of social organisation. In her case, this is done in the manner of **structural anthropology** where behaviour is seen as the expression of a 'society' whlch works as a 'hidden hand' constraining and forming human action.

By contrast, Moerman's work indicates how one can avoid single-element explanations without treating social organisation as a purely external force. In the latter case, people cease to be 'cultural dopes' (Garfinkel, 1967) and skilfully reproduce a moral order.

Saussure provides a message appropriate to both these traditions when he reminds us that no meaning ever resides in a single term. This is an instruction equally relevant to Douglas's structural anthropology and to Garfinkel and Anderson et al.'s ethnomethodology.

So we can take Saussure's message out of context from the kind of linguistics that Saussure himself was doing and use it as a very general methodological principle in qualitative research.

What we are concerned with, as Saussure (1974) showed us, is not individual elements but their relations. As Saussure points out, these relations may be organised in terms of paradigmatic oppositions (ancient Israelites, British sociologists, etc.) or in terms of systems of relations which are organised through what precedes and what follows each item.

An example that Saussure himself gives shows the importance of organisation and sequence in social phenomena. The 8:15 train from Zurich to Geneva remains the 8:15 train even if it does not depart till 8:45. The meaning of the train – its identity – only arises within the oppositions and relationships set out in the railway timetable. The following case study of an auction room illustrates why sequence is so important to understanding how social phenomena work.

CASE STUDY
The Auction Room

Heath (2011) has studied bidding in auctions. Extract 14.1 is a brief fragment from a recent auction of antiquities at a sale-room in London. For convenience, we have simplified and abbreviated the transcript and represented bidding by [B bids], numbering particular bidders [B.1 bids] in the order that they first enter the bidding.

Extract 14.1

(A = auctioneer; B1, B2 and B3 = bidders)

A: Lot one hundred and six. There it is lot one hundred and six Eighty <u>six</u> <u>A</u>: (.) Fi<u>ve</u>: <u>hun</u>dred please::.

A: Eight fifty
      [B.1 bids]
A: Nine hundred
      [B.2 bids]
A: Nine fifty ma<u>d</u>am thank you
      [B.1 bids]
A: A thousand <u>the</u>re:
      (0.4) [B.2 bids]
A: Eleven here
      (.) [B.2 bids]
A: Twelve hundred
      [B.1 bids]
A: Thirteen hundred
      [B.2 bids]
A: Fourteen hundred
      [B.1 bids]
A: Fifteen hundred.

[B3 enters the bidding and B2 increases his bid]

A: Two two:: the standing bidder (0.2) last chance [glances at B.3] (0.2) two thousand two
      hundred pounds:::
      (0.6)
      {knock}

Heath notes that it can be seen that bidding alternates between two principal protagonists, B.1 and B.2. When B.1 withdraws a little later, at £1800, the auctioneer finds a new bidder, and alternates the bidding between B.2 and B.3. This ordering principle is known as the 'run' and is used within almost all auctions of fine art and antiques. The auctioneer establishes two bidders and no more than two bidders at any one time.

Heath comments on how important visible conduct is to 'the run':

- 'turns' at bidding are accomplished through gestures (e.g. a nod or a wave) rather than through talk
- the visible conduct of the auctioneer plays an important part in enabling individuals to know when it is their turn to bid
- bidders and all those present need to know when a bid has been successful and who, at any moment, has bid the highest price. In other words, the organisation of participation during the event, the distribution of opportunities to bid and the rapid escalation of price, rest upon the visible conduct of the auctioneer and potential buyers.

To explore this further, Heath proves some images of the event. Extract 14.2 begins with the auctioneer saying 'eleven here':

(Continued)

Extract 14.2 Transcript and Images

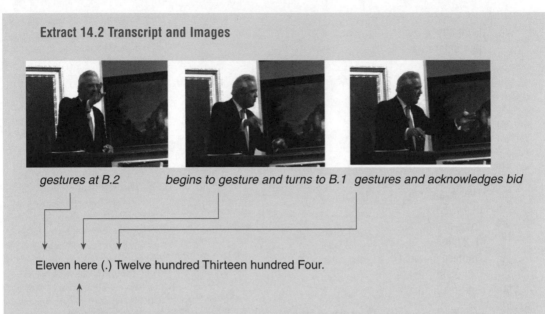

gestures at B.2   begins to gesture and turns to B.1   gestures and acknowledges bid

Eleven here (.) Twelve hundred Thirteen hundred Four.

B.2 nods

As Heath points out:

> From the images, one can see that the auctioneer alternates between gestures with his right hand and gestures with his left. The gestures are accompanied by shifts in his visual alignment in which he turns from the bidder on his right (B.1) to the bidder on his left (B.2). As he begins to announce 'eleven here' (bid by B.1), he turns towards B.2. His gaze arrives with the word 'here'. He withdraws his right hand and starts to raise his left to gesture towards B.2. The moment he looks at and gestures towards B.2, she nods, agreeing to the projected next increment. The visible realignment and the gesture, coupled with the announcement, enables the buyer to know when it is her turn, and the price that she is expected to bid. It also enables the bid to be accomplished through the most minimal of actions – a head nod.

Christian Heath's auction data beautifully demonstrate how participants make sense of what actions mean by recognising a sequence. As he puts it:

> the actions of the participants are accomplished through sequences of actions and these sequences of action inform how people produce their conduct and make sense of the actions of others. For example, the run is dependent upon a social and interactional arrangement that selectively places particular participants under the obligation to respond to an invitation to bid. The invitation is produced through the announcement of a figure, an increment, accompanied by the

auctioneer reorienting and gesturing towards a particular individual. The invitation renders relevant, implicates, an action from a potential buyer, to accept or decline to bid, in this case the acceptance, enabling the auctioneer to immediately invite the protagonist to bid the next increment. The participants actions therefore, and indeed the systematic escalation of price at auction, is accomplished through successive sequences of action, through which particular participants are provided with the opportunity to bid or withdraw. This alternating sequential organisation not only creates successive opportunities for action by particular participants, but also enables an extraordinary economy of behaviour, with turns, bids, accomplished for example through head nods alone; an economy that serves to rapidly establish the value and secure the exchange of goods worth anything from a few pounds to many millions. (2011: 259)

Since participants undeniably attend to sequences, how can qualitative researchers, who want to understand participants' actions, ignore sequential organisation? Whether we are analysing auctions or train timetables, the importance is revealed of avoiding single-element explanations and of focusing upon the processes through which the relations between elements are articulated.

> LINK
> For a recent paper I have written on the importance of studying how different elements are related go to:
>
> www.qualitative-research.net/fqs/fqs-e/inhalt3-05-e.htm

14.4 ATTEMPT THEORETICALLY FERTILE RESEARCH

In any text on social research methodology, there is a danger of reducing analytical questions to technical issues to be resolved by cookbook means, for example good interviewing techniques, simplistic versions of **grounded theory** or the appropriate computer-aided qualitative data-analysis system. I do not wish to criticise these methods but to underline that, as most of their proponents recognise, they are no substitute for theoretically inspired reasoning.

As we have already seen, such theoretical issues lurk behind some apparently technical questions like observing 'private' encounters or interpreting interview data. Following Wittgenstein once more, a touch of 'hygiene' may be useful in clearing our minds about the nature of the phenomena that qualitative researchers attempt to study.

One way of achieving such hygiene is by mobilising the social science discipline in which you have been trained and the models it offers. In Section 2.3.1, I referred to O'Brien's (1993) use of the example of a kaleidoscope as a way to think of how models and theories can inspire the way we think about our data. Let me repeat what O'Brien says about this:

> a kaleidoscope … [is] the child's toy consisting of a tube, a number of lenses and fragments of translucent, coloured glass or plastic. When you turn the tube and look down the lens of the kaleidoscope the shapes and colours, visible at the bottom, change. As the tube is turned, different lenses come into play and the combinations of colour and shape shift from one pattern to another. In a similar way, we can see social theory as a sort of kaleidoscope – by shifting theoretical perspective the world under investigation also changes shape. (1993: 10–11)

I have space for only one example of how O'Brien's kaleidoscope image can be fruitful. How we code or transcribe our data is a crucial matter for qualitative researchers (see Sections 5.2.6 and 9.2). Often, however, such researchers simply replicate the **positivist** model routinely used in quantitative research. According to this model, coders of data are usually trained in procedures with the aim of ensuring a uniform approach. This is a tried and trusted method designed to improve the **reliability** of a research method.

However, ethnomethodology reminds us that 'coding' is not the preserve of research scientists. In some sense, researchers, like all of us, 'code' what they hear and see in the world around them. Moreover, this 'coding' has been shown to be mutual and interactive (Sacks, 1992; Silverman, 1998).

The ethnomethodological response is to make this everyday 'coding' (or 'interpretive practice') the object of enquiry. Alternatively, we can proceed in a more conventional manner but mention and respond to this well-established critique (for an example, see Clavarino et al., 1995, discussed in Section 11.2.5):

> Of course, as I have emphasised throughout, the research 'cake' can be legitimately sliced in many ways – there is no 'correct' kaleidoscope through which to view all data. So I am *not* suggesting that the vast mass of researchers who treat 'coding' as purely an analyst's problem abandon their work. Instead, my minimalist suggestion is that they examine how far the categories they are using can be shown to be used by the participants in their ordinary behaviours.

The example of coding our data shows, I hope, how theory can make our data analysis more fertile. It is also useful because it emphasises my own view of theory-building as being done with data and not from the armchair.

Unfortunately, however, the armchair is a favoured position in much contemporary social science, notably in my own discipline of sociology. One reason for this concentration on armchair thinking is that, unlike many natural sciences, we lack one agreed model of our part of reality.

As the philosopher of science Thomas Kuhn has argued, many social sciences lack a single, agreed set of **concepts** deriving from a common model of 'reality'

(Kuhn, 1970). In Kuhn's terms, this makes social research 'pre-paradigmatic' or at least in a state of competing paradigms. Unfortunately, this has generated a whole series of social science courses which pose different social science approaches in terms of either/or questions.

Such courses are much appreciated by some students. They learn about the paradigmatic oppositions in question, choose A rather than B and report back, parrot fashion, all the advantages of A and the drawbacks of B. It is hardly surprising that such courses produce very little evidence that such students have ever thought about anything – even their choice of A is likely to be based on their teacher's implicit or explicit preferences. This may, in part, explain why so many undergraduate sociology courses actually provide a learned incapacity to go out and do research.

Learning about rival 'armed camps' in no way allows you to confront research data. In the field, material is much more messy than the different camps would suggest. Perhaps there is something to be learned from both sides, or, more constructively, perhaps we start to ask interesting questions when we reject the polarities that such a course markets?

So when I call for theoretically fertile research it is because I believe that theory only becomes worthwhile when it is used to explain something. Becker (1998: 1) reports that the great founder of the Chicago School, Everett Hughes, responded grumpily when students asked what he thought about theory. 'Theory of what?', he would reply. For Hughes, as for me, theory without some observation to work upon is like a tractor without a field.

Theory, then, should be neither a status symbol nor an optional extra in a research study. Without theory, research is impossibly narrow. Without research, theory is mere armchair contemplation.

14.5 ADDRESS WIDER AUDIENCES

To call for more theory in research might seem to drive off our non-academic audiences: policy-makers, practitioners, the general public and others (see Section 11.2). However, by a somewhat roundabout route, our internal debate between theory and data can lead to data sources and findings of great interest to wider audiences. To simplify, I discuss below the policy-making audience.

There are two potentially dangerous orthodoxies shared by many social scientists and by policy-makers who commission social research. The first orthodoxy is that people are puppets of social structures. According to this model, what people do is defined by 'society'. In practice, this reduces to explaining people's behaviour as the outcome of certain 'face-sheet' **variables** (like social class, gender or ethnicity).

We will call this the 'Explanatory Orthodoxy'. According to it, social scientists do research to provide explanations of given problems; for example, why do individuals engage in unsafe sex? Inevitably, such research will find explanations based on one or more 'face-sheet' variables.

The second orthodoxy is that people are 'dopes'. Interview respondents' knowledge is assumed to be imperfect; indeed they may even lie to us. In the same way, practitioners (like doctors or counsellors) are assumed always to depart from normative standards of good practice. This is the 'Divine Orthodoxy'. It makes the social scientist into the philosopher–king (or queen) who can always see through people's claims and know better than they do.

What is wrong with these two orthodoxies? The Explanatory Orthodoxy is so concerned to rush to an explanation that it fails to ask serious questions about what it is explaining.

There is a parallel here with what we must now call a 'post-modern' phenomenon. It seems that visitors to the Grand Canyon in Arizona are now freed from the messy business of exploring the canyon itself. Instead, they can now spend an enlightening hour or so in an multi-media 'experience' which gives them all the thrills in a pre-digested way. Then they can be on their way, secure in the knowledge that they have 'done' the Grand Canyon.

This example is part of something far larger. In contemporary culture, the environment around phenomena has become more important than the phenomenon itself. So people are more interested in the lives of movie stars than in the movies themselves. Equally, on sporting occasions, pre- and post-match interviews become as exciting (or even more exciting) than the game itself. Using a phrase to which we shall shortly return, in both cases, *the phenomenon escapes*.

This is precisely what the Explanatory Orthodoxy encourages. Because we rush to offer explanations of all kinds of social phenomena, we rarely spend enough time trying to understand how the phenomenon works. So, for instance, we may simply impose 'operational definitions' of phenomena, failing totally to examine how such activities come to have meaning in what people are actually doing in everyday (naturally occurring) situations.

This directly leads to the folly of the Divine Orthodoxy. Its methods preclude seeing the good sense of what people are doing or understanding their skills in local contexts. It prefers interviews where people are forced to answer questions that never arise in their day-to-day life. Because it rarely looks at this life, it condemns people to fail without understanding that we are all cleverer than we can say in so many words. Even when it examines what people are actually doing, the Divine Orthodoxy measures their activities by some idealised normative standards, like 'good communication'. So, once again, like ordinary people, practitioners are condemned to fail.

Both kinds of research are fundamentally concerned with the environment around the phenomenon rather than the phenomenon itself. In quantitative studies of 'objective' social structures and qualitative studies of people's 'subjective' orientations, we may be deflected away from the phenomenon towards what follows and precedes it (causes and consequences in the 'objective' approach) or to how people respond to it (the 'subjective' approach).

In both approaches, the phenomenon with which ostensibly we are concerned disappears. In 'Objectivism', it is defined out of existence (by fiat, as Cicourel, 1964, puts it). Equally, what I have called 'Subjectivism' is so romantically attached to the authentic rush of human experience that it merely reproduces tales of a subjective world without bringing us any closer to the local organisation of the phenomena concerned.

How can these theoretically informed reflections aid policy-makers? In the first place, abandoning the Divine Orthodoxy means that we may be able to offer more original suggestions than simply to improve practitioner communication so that it better approximates some idealised model. This point is illustrated in the following case study.

CASE STUDY
Responsible Parenthood

My research in cardiac and diabetic clinics (Silverman, 1987) revealed that parents, particularly mothers, sought ways to display their 'responsible parenthood'. How could this massively recurrent, cultural compunction to treat parenthood as a moral activity be incorporated into medical consultations?

In the study of the paediatric cardiology unit (PCU), it would have been tempting to follow other researchers (e.g. Byrne and Long, 1976) and to suggest that parents' reported problems derive from doctors' inadequate communication skills. Our analysis suggested, however, that the constraints of the setting and of the task at hand (speedy diagnosis and treatment) meant that the first outpatients' clinic had no space for some parental concerns and that, in any event, many parents needed time to come to terms with what they were being told. If time was allowed to pass (when, for instance, parents had faced the questions of other anxious relatives and had consulted popular medical manuals or the family physician) and the family was invited to revisit the hospital, things might turn out differently.

Such a clinic was indeed established at the PCU and the constraints further altered by informing parents in advance that their child would not be examined this time. An evaluation study indicated that, in the eyes of the participants, this was a successful innovation (Silverman, 1987: 86–103).

At no point had we set out to teach doctors communication skills. So the sociological truism – change the constraints of the setting and people will behave differently – had paid off in ways that we had not foreseen. People responded to the new setting in innovatory ways: parents bringing their children along to see the playroom and to discover that the ward was not such a frightening place after all.

This study of a medical clinic indicates the gains of avoiding the Divine Orthodoxy. But what of the Explanatory Orthodoxy? In particular, how are we to satisfy our fellow social scientists, let alone our wider audiences, if we fail to base our research on the study of *causes*? As I argue below, it is all a matter of timing.

14.6 BEGIN WITH 'HOW' QUESTIONS; ONLY THEN ASK 'WHY?'

The kind of detailed ethnographic research discussed above, as well as my con-versation analysis (CA) study of counselling (Silverman, 1997), lays itself open to the charge that it deals 'only' with talk. The implication is that, because it suppos-edly refuses to look beyond the talk, it is unable to offer adequate explanations of its findings. As critics continually reiterate: what about the *context* of your data?

Of course, I have already offered a critical review of this approach in my com-ments on the Explanatory Orthodoxy. Such contexts do not speak for themselves but must be carefully identified in the practices and orientations of the participants.

Nonetheless, I do *not* want to suggest that it is always improper to look beyond talk-in-interaction. Instead, my position is that we are not faced with either/or choices but with issues largely of *timing*.

My assumption is that it is usually necessary to refuse to allow our research top-ics to be defined in terms of, say, the 'causes' of 'bad' counselling or the 'conse-quences' of 'good' counselling. Such topics merely reflect the conceptions of 'social problems' as recognised by either professional or community groups. Ironically, by beginning from a clearly defined analytical perspective, we show how we can later address such social problems with, we believe, considerable force and persuasiveness.

My argument suggests that one's initial move should be to give close attention to how participants locally produce contexts for their interaction. By beginning with this question of 'how', we can then fruitfully move on to 'why' questions about institutional and cultural constraints. Such constraints reveal the functions of apparently irrational practices and help us to understand the possibilities and limits of attempts at social reform.

Using CA, Schegloff (1991) has shown that a great deal depends on the pace at which we proceed:

> the study of talk should be allowed to proceed under its own imperatives, with the hope that its results will provide more effective tools for the analysis of distri-butional, institutional and social structural problems *later on* than would be the case if the analysis of talk had, from the outset, to be made answerable to problems extrinsic to it. (1991: 64, my emphasis)

Quite properly, this will mean delaying what I have called 'why' questions until we have asked the appropriate 'how' questions. But how, eventually, are we to make the link between the two?

A solution is suggested in Maynard's (1991, 2003) account of how paediatricians give diagnostic information to parents. Maynard identifies a 'perspective-display sequence' where doctors invite the parents' views first and then tailor their diag-nostic statements to what they have elicited from parents.

So far, this addresses the 'how' question. However, Maynard then moves on to the 'why' question, relating the 'perspective-display sequence' to the functions of avoiding open conflict over unfavourable diagnoses. In this way, the device serves to preserve social solidarity.

So Maynard's close focus on *how* the parties locally produce patterns of communication ends up by considering the 'functions' of the forms so discovered. The lesson is clear. We cannot do everything at the same time without muddying the water. For policy reasons, as well as from conventional social science concerns, we may well want to ask what I have called 'why' questions. There is no reason not to, providing that we have first closely described how the phenomenon at hand is locally produced. If not, we are limited to an explanation of something that we have simply defined by fiat.

This means that there is nothing wrong with the search for explanations, providing that this search is grounded in a close understanding of how the phenomena being explained are 'put together' at an interactional level. It follows that, wherever possible, one should seek to obtain 'naturally occurring' data in order to obtain adequate understanding, leading to soundly based policy interventions.

14.7 STUDY 'HYPHENATED' PHENOMENA

When we attempt to unravel the 'black box' of social phenomena, we invariably start to see the multiple ways in which apparently uniform phenomena are locally constructed. This emphasises that a botanist classifying a plant is engaged in a less problematic activity than an anthropologist classifying a tribe (see my discussion of Moerman's research on the Lue in Section 2.2.3).

Let me take some examples of research which disabuses us of our common-sense assumptions about the stable realities of particular collectivities. As we saw in Section 9.4.2, Gilbert and Mulkay's (1983) study of scientists' accounts of their work showed that there are better research questions than 'what is science?' Instead, it is more fruitful to ask questions like: 'How is a particular scientific discourse invoked? When is it invoked? How does it stand in relation to other discourses?' In this way, Gilbert and Mulkay lead us to see that 'science', like other social institutions, is a **hyphenated phenomenon** which takes on different meanings in different contexts.

So scientists, treated as a collectivity having stable goals and practices, also escaped in Gilbert and Mulkay's work. As I noted above (Section 14.2), 'patients', conceived as a stable phenomenon, escaped in the Webb and Stimson study just as 'care home residents with stable views on violence' disappeared from Pösö et al.'s (2008) focus group study.

A second example of hyphenated phenomena, drawn from Steve Woolgar's account of 'artificial intelligence', is given below.

CASE STUDY
Where is 'Real' Science?

Woolgar (1985) notes how participants themselves may be reluctant to treat their own activities as instances of particular idealised phenomena. Like Gilbert and Mulkay, Woolgar was interested in the sociology of science. Yet, he reports, that, when he tried to get access to laboratories to study scientists at work, each laboratory team would uniformly respond that, if he was interested in science, this really was not the best place to investigate it. For whatever reason, what was going on in this laboratory did not really fit what scientific work really should be. On the other hand, the work being done at some other place was much more truly scientific.

Curiously, Woolgar tells us that he has yet to find a laboratory where people are prepared to accept that whatever they do is 'real' science. He was perpetually being referred to some other site as the home of 'hard' science.

Like 'science', Woolgar also found that 'artificial intelligence' (AI), conceived as an indisputably 'real' phenomenon, was also perceived to be 'elsewhere'. As each new test of what might constitute 'real' AI appeared, grounds were cited to find it inadequate. The famous Turing test, based upon asking subjects whether they can tell if the communication they are hearing is from a person or a machine, is now largely rejected.

Even if a hearer cannot tell the difference between human reasoning and AI, a machine may be held to be only 'simulating intelligence' without being 'intelligent'. Even machines which successfully switch off televisions during commercials will not be recognised as an example of AI since, it is held, this is a response to changes in the broadcast signal rather than in programme content. Hence the search for 'genuine' AI, Woolgar argues, has generated a seemingly endless research programme in which the phenomenon always escapes.

These kinds of studies point to the way in which idealised conceptions of phenomena become like a will-o'-the-wisp on the basis of systematic field research, dissolving into sets of practices embedded in particular milieux. Nowhere is this clearer than in the field of studies of the 'family'. As Gubrium and Holstein (1987) note, researchers have unnecessarily worried about getting 'authentic' reports of family life given the privacy of the household. But this implies an idealised reality – as if there were some authentic site of family life which could be isolated and put under the researcher's microscope. Instead, discourses of family life are applied in varying ways in a range of contexts, many of which, like courts of law, clinics and radio call-in programmes, are public and readily available for research investigation.

If 'the family' is present wherever it is invoked, then the worry of some qualitative researchers about observing 'real' family life looks to be misplaced. Their assumption that the family has a unitary reality looks more like a common-sense way of approaching the phenomenon with little analytic basis.

Finding families is, of course, is no problem at all for laypeople. In our everyday life, we can always locate and understand 'real' families by using the documentary method of interpretation (Garfinkel, 1967) to search beneath appearances to locate the 'true' reality. In this regard, think of how social workers or lawyers in juvenile or divorce courts 'discover' the essential features of a particular family.

Yet, for social scientists, *how* we invoke the family, *when* we invoke the family and *where* we invoke the family become central analytic concerns. Because we cannot assume, as laypeople must, that families are 'available' for analysis in some kind of unexplicated way, the 'family', conceived as a self-evident phenomenon, always escapes.

Note that this wholly fits with my earlier argument about the disappearing phenomenon in 'objectivist' and 'subjectivist' social science. The phenomenon that *always* escapes is the 'essential' reality pursued in such work. The phenomenon that can be made to *reappear* is the practical activity of participants in establishing a phenomenon-in-context – the *hyphenated phenomenon*.

14.8 TREAT QUALITATIVE RESEARCH AS DIFFERENT FROM JOURNALISM

My final reminder will be brief. Presupposed in all I have written is an appeal to treat qualitative research as different from journalism. This is *not* because I have no regard for the skills (as well as the sins) of journalists. It is simply because, contrary to how much qualitative research is written, I believe that if qualitative research has anything to offer it is because we possess different (not better) skills to those of journalists.

The skills of journalists are related to the ephemeral nature of their products. They pursue stories which are 'newsworthy'. Their interest (and that of their readers) is in what can be treated as 'new'. However, many things can be 'new' without being 'newsworthy' (for instance, I would not expect my purchase of a new pullover to be reported in a newspaper!).

Because of this, journalists seek the 'new' in what can be seen as previously 'hidden' or 'concealed'. In this regard, particular powerful journalistic motifs are ironic contrasts (say between the public statements and private lives of celebrities) or 'in-depth' accounts of the experiences and feelings of ordinary people who have found themselves in extraordinary situations (falling off a cliff, winning a lottery).

Of course, this is a very crude account of journalism which fails to do justice to the range of media outlets or to the audience sought. Nonetheless, even at this level, the similarities with much qualitative research, I believe, speak for themselves. For instance, ironic contrasts and 'in-depth' accounts are the meat and drink of many of our research findings.

By contrast, I suggest that qualitative researchers make use of quite different skills. These skills should allow us to:

- avoid the assumption that research is only newsworthy if it reveals what is hidden or secret
- recognise that what is usually of most interest is what is *unremarkable* to participants

- avoid ironic comparisons between what people say and what we (think we) we know about what they do
- recognise that 'experience' is not more or less 'authentic' but narrated in ways that are open to lively investigation.

EXERCISE 14.1

Select any qualitative research report with which you are familiar. Now proceed as follows:

1　Apply to it the eight 'reminders' discussed in this chapter.
2　Consider how well it stands in relation to each.
3　In the light of your reading, assess how the research could be improved to satisfy any *one* of these reminders.
4　Assess whether, in the light of your analysis, any of these reminders needs to be modified or rejected.

14.9 CONCLUDING REMARKS

Despite the *negative* form of some of my comments, I have intended throughout this chapter to convey a sense of the good things that research can do. I tried to show this in the examples of successful case studies and, above all, in my implicit appeal to lateral thinking. If, as I heard somebody say the other day, the world is divided into two sorts of people, those who make such a statement and those who don't, then I am firmly with the latter group.

Perhaps, as Douglas implies, we have something to learn from the Lele. Part of what we might learn is living with uncertainty. Curiously, the critics of such apparently disparate theorists as Garfinkel and Saussure and their heirs have one argument in common. If everything derives from forms of representation, how can we find any secure ground from which to speak? Are we not inevitably led to an infinite regress where ultimate truths are unavailable (see Bury, 1986)?

Three responses suggest themselves. First, is it not a little surprising that such possibilities should be found threatening when the natural sciences, particularly quantum physics, seem to live with them all the time and adapt accordingly, even ingeniously? Second, instead of throwing up our hands in horror at the context-boundedness of accounts, why not marvel at the elegant solutions that societal members use to remedy this? For practical actors, the regress becomes no problem at all. Finally, like members, why not use practical solutions to practical problems? For instance, as I argued in Chapter 11, even sophisticated qualitative analysis can find practical solutions to the problem of **validity** (counting where it makes sense to count, using the constant comparative method, and so on).

The worse thing that contemporary qualitative research can imply is that in this post–modern age, anything goes. The trick is to produce intelligent, disciplined work on the very edge of the abyss.

KEY POINTS

This chapter draws together the arguments present in the rest of my book. These arguments are offered not as self-evident truths but as one voice in a debate that I believe matters both to social scientists and to our audiences. To this end, I provided eight reminders:

1   Take advantage of naturally occurring data.
2   Avoid treating the actor's point of view as an explanation.
3   Study the interrelationships between elements.
4   Attempt theoretically fertile research.
5   Address wider audiences.
6   Begin with 'how' questions; then ask 'why?'
7   Study 'hyphenated' phenomena.
8   Treat qualitative research as different from journalism.

STUDY QUESTIONS

1   What is meant by 'naturally occurring data'? Why are such data so inviting for qualitative research?
2   What problems arise if we treat the actor's point of view as an explanation?
3   Why should 'how' questions usually precede 'why' questions in qualitative research?
4   What is meant by 'hyphenated phenomena'? How can an understanding of such phenomena help us in conducting research?

RECOMMENDED READING

State-of-the-art accounts of qualitative research which fit the reminders presented in this chapter are to be found in David Silverman (editor), *Qualitative Research:*

(Continued)

(Continued)

Theory, Method and Practice (Third Edition, 2011) and Clive Seale, Giampietro Gobo, Jaber Gubrium and David Silverman (editors) *Qualitative Research Practice* (2004). These books can be contrasted with the wider range of positions in Martyn Hammersley's *Questioning Qualitative Inquiry* (2008) and Norman Denzin and Yvonna Lincoln's *Handbook of Qualitative Research* (Third Edition, 2006).

Good treatments of theoretically inspired but rigorous qualitative research are: Pertti Alasuutari, *Researching Culture: Qualitative Method and Cultural Studies* (1995); Jennifer Mason, *Qualitative Researching* (1996); Amanda Coffey and Paul Atkinson, *Making Sense of Qualitative Data* (1996); and Anselm Strauss and Juliet Corbin, *Basics of Qualitative Research* (1990).

The various theoretical traditions that comprise qualitative research are skilfully dissected in Jaber Gubrium and James Holstein, *The New Language of Qualitative Method* (1997). Gary Marx's paper, 'Of methods and manners for aspiring sociologists: 37 moral imperatives' (*American Sociologist*, Spring 1997, 102–25) is a lively and extremely helpful short guide for the apprentice researcher.

Appendix: Simplified Transcription Symbols

[	C2: quite a [while Mo: [yea	Left brackets indicate the point at which a current speaker's talk is overlapped by another's talk.
=	W: that I'm aware of = C: =Yes. Would you confirm that?	Equal signs, one at the end of a line and one at the beginning, indicate no gap between the two lines.
(.4)	Yes (.2) yeah	Numbers in parentheses indicate elapsed time in silence in tenths of a second.
(.)	to get (.) treatment	A dot in parentheses indicates a tiny gap, probably no more than one-tenth of a second.
_____	What's up?	Underscoring indicates some form of stress, via pitch and/or amplitude.
::	O:kay?	Colons indicate prolongation of the immediately prior sound. The length of the row of colons indicates the length of the prolongation.
WORD	I've got ENOUGH TO WORRY ABOUT	Capitals, except at the beginnings of lines, indicate especially loud sounds relative to the surrounding talk.

.hhhh	I feel that (.2) .hhh	A row of h's prefixed by a dot indicates an inbreath; without a dot, an outbreath. The length of the row of h's indicates the length of the in- or outbreath.
( )	future risks and ( ) and life ( )	Empty parentheses indicate the transcribers inability to hear what was said.
(word)	Would you see (there) anything positive	Parenthesised words are possible hearings.
(( ))	confirm that ((continues))	Double parentheses contain author's descriptions rather than transcriptions.

Glossary

ANALYTIC INDUCTION (AI)   is the equivalent to the statistical testing of quantitative associations to see if they are greater than might be expected at random (random error). Using AI, the researcher examines a case and, where appropriate, re-defines the phenomenon and re-formulates a hypothesis until a universal relationship is shown (Fielding, 1988: 7–8).

ANECDOTALISM   is found where research reports appear to tell entertaining stories or anecdotes but fail to provide an analytic or methodological framework with which to convince the reader of their scientific credibility.

CHICAGO SCHOOL   is a form of sociological ethnography usually assumed to have originated in the 1920s when students at the University of Chicago were instructed to put down their theory textbooks and to get out onto the streets of their city and use their eyes and ears. It led to a series of studies of the social organisation of the city and of the daily life of various occupational groups.

COGNITIVE ANTHROPOLOGY   seeks to understand the structures that organise how people perceive the world. This leads to the production of ethnographies, or conceptually derived descriptions, of whole cultures, focused on how people communicate.

CONCEPTS   are clearly specified ideas deriving from a particular model.

CONSTRUCTIONISM   is a model which encourages researchers to focus upon how phenomena come to be what they are through the close study of interaction in different contexts. It is opposed to NATURALISM and EMOTIONIALISM.

CONTENT ANALYSIS   involves establishing categories, systematic linkages between them and then counting the number of instances when those categories are used in a particular item of text.

CONTEXTUAL SENSITIVITY   involves the recognition that apparently uniform social institutions (e.g. 'tribes', 'families', 'crime') take on different meanings in different contexts.

CONVERSATION ANALYSIS (CA)   is based on an attempt to describe people's methods for producing orderly talk-in-interaction. It derives from the work of Sacks (1992).

CRITICAL RATIONALISM   is a concept deriving from the work of the philosopher of science Karl Popper. It demands that we must seek to falsify assumed relations between phenomena. Then, only if we cannot falsify the existence of a certain relationship, are we in a position to speak about 'objective' knowledge. Even then, however, our knowledge is always provisional, subject to a subsequent study which may come up with disconfirming evidence.

DEVIANT-CASE ANALYSIS   in qualitative research involves testing provisional hypotheses by 'negative' or 'discrepant' cases until all the data can be incorporated in an explanation (see ANALYTIC INDUCTION).

DIACHRONIC   analysis is a linguistic method concerned with historical changes in language (see ETYMOLOGY). It is opposed to SYNCHRONIC analysis.

DISCOURSE ANALYSIS (DA)   is the study of the rhetorical and argumentative organisation of talk and texts.

EMIC ANALYSIS   is a term mainly used by anthropologists to describe culture based on subjects' own concepts and descriptions (see ETIC ANALYSIS)

EMOTIONALISM   is a model of social research in which the primary aim is to generate deeply authentic insights into people's experiences. Emotionalists draw from ROMANTIC perspectives and favour open-ended interviews (see Gubrium and Holstein, 1997a).

ETHNOGRAPHY   puts together two different words: 'ethno' means 'folk' or 'people', while 'graph' derives from 'writing'. Ethnography refers, then, to highly descriptive writing about particular groups of people.

ETHNOMETHODOLOGY   is the study of folk's – or members' – methods. It seeks to describe methods that persons use in doing social life. Ethnomethodology is not a methodology but a MODEL closely linked to CONSTRUCTIONISM.

ETIC ANALYSIS   is a term used mainly by anthropologists to describe concepts and descriptions based on the researcher's own concepts (as opposed to those of research subjects).

ETYMOLOGY   is the study of historical changes in the meanings of words.

FOCUS GROUPS   are group discussions usually based on visual or verbal stimuli provided by a researcher.

FORMAL THEORY   is a theory which relates findings from one setting to many situations or settings (see Glaser and Strauss, 1967).

FRAME   is a term applied by Goffman (1974), using the metaphor of a picture frame, to reference how people treat what is currently relevant and irrelevant. Such treatment defines the frame through which a setting is constituted.

GATEKEEPER   is someone who is able to grant or deny access to the field.

GROUNDED THEORY   involves three stages: an initial attempt to develop categories which illuminate the data; an attempt to 'saturate' these categories with many appropriate cases in order to demonstrate their relevance; and trying to develop these categories into more general analytic frameworks with relevance outside the setting.

HYPHENATED PHENOMENA   is a concept which refers to the way in which apparently stable social phenomena (a 'tribe' or a 'family') take on different meanings in different contexts. Thus a family-as-seen-by-the-oldest-child takes on a different meaning than a family-as-seen-by-the-youngest (see CONSTRUCTIONISM).

HYPOTHESES   are testable propositions.

IMPRESSION MANAGEMENT   is how people manage the impressions they give, for instance by how they dress or how they furnish their houses. This concept derives from the early work of Erving Goffman.

INTERPRETATIVE REPERTOIRES   are 'systematically related sets of terms that are often used with stylistic and grammatical coherence and often organized around one or more central metaphors' (Potter, 1996b: 131) (see DISCOURSE ANALYSIS).

LABORATORY STUDY   is a method sometimes used in quantitative research in which subjects are placed in an artificial environment and their responses to various stimuli are measured.

LOW-INFERENCE DESCRIPTORS   seek to record observations 'in terms that are as concrete as possible, including verbatim accounts of what people say, for example, rather than researchers' reconstructions of the general sense of what a person said, which would allow researchers' personal perspectives to influence the reporting' (Seale, 1999, 148) (see RELIABILITY).

MEMBER   is a term used by Garfinkel (1967) to refer to participants in society or particular social groups. It is a shorthand term for 'collectivity member' (see ETHNOMETHODOLOGY).

MEMBERSHIP CATEGORISATION DEVICE (MCD)   is a collection of categories (e.g. baby, mommy, father = family; male, female = gender) and some rules about how to apply these categories (further definitions of MCD concepts are found in Section 8.5).

METHODOLOGY   refers to the choices we make about appropriate MODELS, cases to study, methods of data gathering, forms of data analysis, etc., in planning and executing a research study.

METHODS   are specific research techniques. These include quantitative techniques, like statistical correlations, as well as techniques like observation, interviewing and audio recording.

MODELS   provide an overall framework for how we look at reality. They tell us what reality is like and the basic elements it contains ('ontology') and what is the nature and status of knowledge ('epistemology').

NARRATIVES   are the organisation of stories (beginning, middle and end; plots and characters) which makes these stories meaningful or coherent in a form appropriate to a particular context.

NATURALISM   is a model of research which seeks to minimise presuppositions in order to witness subjects' worlds in their own terms. It is particularly associated with early forms of ETHNOGRAPHY.

NATURALLY OCCURRING DATA   derive from situations which exist independently of the researcher's intervention (e.g. everyday conversations but not interviews).

OPERATIONAL DEFINITION   is a working definition which allows quantitative researchers to measure some variable.

PARTICIPANT OBSERVATION   is a method that assumes that, in order to understand the world 'firsthand', you must participate yourself rather than just observe it at a distance. This method was championed by the early anthropologists but is shared by some ethnographers (e.g. the CHICAGO SCHOOL).

POSITIVISM   is a model of the research process which treats 'social facts' as existing independently of the activities of both participants and researchers. For positivists, the aim is to generate data which are valid and reliable, independently of the research setting.

POST-MODERNISM   is a contemporary approach which questions or seeks to deconstruct both accepted concepts (e.g. the 'subject' and the 'field') and scientific method (see CRITICAL RATIONALISM). Post-modernism is both an analytical model and a way of describing contemporary society as a pastiche of insecure and changing elements.

RELATIONAL   views of language analyse the system of relations between words; they do not assume a simple correspondence between individual words and their meanings (cf. Saussure).

RELATIVISM   is a value position where we resist taking a position because we believe that, since everything is relative to its particular context, it should not be criticised.

RELIABILITY refers to 'the degree of consistency with which instances are assigned to the same category by different observers or by the same observer on different occasions' (Hammersley, 1992a: 67) (see VALIDITY).

RESEARCHER-PROVOKED DATA are data which are actively created and, therefore, would not exist apart from the researcher's intervention (e.g. interviews, focus groups).

RESPONDENT VALIDATION (sometimes appears as 'member validation') involves taking one's findings back to the subjects being studied. Where these people verify one's findings, it is argued, one can be more confident of their validity.

REWRITING HISTORY is a term used by Garfinkel (1967) to refer to the way in which an account retrospectively finds some reason for any given outcome.

ROMANTIC(ISM) is an approach taken from nineteenth-century thought in which authenticity is attached to personal experiences (see EMOTIONALISM).

SAMPLE, SAMPLING are statistical procedures for finding cases to study. Sampling has two functions: it allows you to estimate the representativeness of the cases you study and thereby the degree of confidence in any inferences you draw from them.

SCRIPTS are members' devices used to invoke the routine character of described events in order to imply that they are features of some (approved or disapproved) general pattern (see DISCOURSE ANALYSIS).

SEMIOTICS is the study of signs (from speech, to fashion to Morse code).

SHADOWING is an ethnographic method where the researcher follows someone during their day-to-day tasks (Czarniawska, 2007).

STRUCTURAL ANTHROPOLOGY is only interested in single cases insofar as they relate to general social forms, while cognitive anthropology is usually content with single case studies of particular peoples. Structural anthropologists draw upon French social and linguistic theory of the early twentieth century, notably Ferdinand de Saussure and Emile Durkheim. They view behaviour as the expression of a 'society' which works as a 'hidden hand' constraining and forming human action (see Levi-Strauss, 1967).

SUBSTANTIVE THEORY is a theory about a particular situation or group; used as a basis for developing GROUNDED THEORY.

SYNCHRONIC analysis is ahistorical; it is concerned with any language's present functioning. It treats language as a complete system whose meaning derives not from history but from the relation of each of its parts to others.

TEXT(UAL) data consist of words and/or images which have become recorded without the intervention of a researcher (e.g. through an interview).

THEMATIC ANALYSIS   attempts to locate themes in qualitative data. Sometimes used with focus group data.

THEORIES   arrange sets of concepts to define and explain some phenomenon.

THICK DESCRIPTION   is a term from anthropology and ETHNOGRAPHY used to describe research reports which analyse the multiple levels of meaning in any situation (see Geertz, 1973).

TRIANGULATION   involves comparing different kinds of data (e.g. quantitative and qualitative) and/or different methods (e.g. observation and interviews) to see whether they corroborate one another.

VALIDITY   is 'the extent to which an account accurately represents the social phenomena to which it refers' (Hammersley, 1990: 57). Researchers respond to validity concerns by describing 'the warrant for their inferences' (Fielding and Fielding, 1986: 12) (see RELIABILITY).

VARIABLES   are factors which in research are isolated from one another in order to measure the relationship between them (a term usually used only in quantitative research).

References

Abrams, P. (1984) 'Evaluating soft findings: some problems of measuring informal care', *Research Policy and Planning*, 2 (2): 1–8.

Adler, P.A. and Adler, P. (1994) 'Observational techniques'. In N. Denzin and Y. Lincoln (eds), *Handbook of Qualitative Research*. Thousand Oaks, CA: Sage, pp. 377–92.

Agar, M. (1986) *Speaking of Ethnography*, Qualitative Research Methods Series, Volume 2. London: Sage.

Agar, M. and MacDonald, J. (1995) 'Focus groups and ethnography', *Human Organization*, 54 (1): 78–86.

Alasuutari, P. (1990) 'Desire and craving: studies in a cultural theory of alcoholism', University of Tampere, Finland.

Alasuutari, P. (1995) *Researching Culture: Qualitative Method and Cultural Studies*. London: Sage.

Ali, S. (2004) 'Using visual materials'. In C. Seale (ed.), *Researching Society and Culture*, Second Edition. London: Sage, pp. 265–78.

Altheide, D.L. and Johnson, J. M. (1994) 'Criteria for assessing interpretive validity in qualitative research'. In N. K. Denzin and Y. S. Lincoln (eds), *Handbook of Qualitative Research*. Thousand Oaks, CA: Sage, pp. 485–99.

Anderson, R., Hughes, J. and Sharrock, W.L. (1987) 'Executive problem finding: some material and initial observations', *Social Psychology Quarterly*, 50 (2): 143–59.

Antaki, C. and Rapley, M. (1996) '"Quality of life" talk: the liberal paradox of psychological testing', *Discourse & Society*, 7 (3): 293–316.

Arber, S. (1993) 'The research process'. In N. Gilbert (ed.), *Researching Social Life*, London: Sage, pp. 32–50.

Ashmore, M. (1989) *The Reflexive Thesis: Wrighting Sociology of Scientific Knowledge*. Chicago: University of Chicago Press.

Atkinson, J.M. (1978) *Discovering Suicide*. London: Macmillan.

Atkinson, J.M. and Drew, P. (1979) *Order in Court*. London: Macmillan.

Atkinson, J.M. and Heritage, J.C. (eds) (1984) *Structures of Social Action*. Cambridge: Cambridge University Press.

Atkinson, P. (1990) *The Ethnographic Imagination*. London: Routledge.

Atkinson, P. (1992) 'The ethnography of a medical setting: reading, writing and rhetoric', *Qualitative Health Research*, 2 (4): 451–74.

Atkinson, P. and Coffey, A. (2002) 'Revisiting the relationship between participant observation and interviewing'. In J. Gubrium and J. Holstein (eds), *Handbook of Interview Research*. Thousand Oaks, CA: Sage, pp. 801–1.

Atkinson, P. and Coffey, A. (2004) 'Analysing documentary realities'. In D. Silverman (ed.), *Qualitative Research*, Second Edition. London: Sage, pp. 56–75.

Atkinson, P. and Coffey, A. (2011) 'Analysing documentary realities'. In D. Silverman (ed.), *Qualitative Research*, Third Edition. London: Sage, pp. 77–92.

Atkinson, P. and Hammersley, M. (1994) 'Ethnography and participant observation'. In N. Denzin and Y. Lincoln (eds), *Handbook of Qualitative Research*. Thousand Oaks, CA: Sage, pp. 248–261.

Atkinson, P. and Silverman, D. (1997) 'Kundera's *Immortality*: the interview society and the invention of self', *Qualitative Inquiry*, 3 (3): 324–45.

Austin, J.L. (1962) *How To Do Things with Words*, Oxford: Clarendon Press.

Back, L. (2004) 'Politics, research and understanding'. In C. Seale et al. (eds), *Qualitative Research Practice*. London: Sage, pp. 261–75.

Baddeley, A. (1979) 'The limitations of human memory: implications for the design of retrospective surveys'. In L. Moss and H. Goldstein (eds), *The Recall Method in Social Surveys*. London: University of London Institute of Education.

Baker, C. (1997) 'Membership categorization and interview accounts'. In D. Silverman (ed.), *Qualitative Research*. London: Sage, pp. 130–43.

Baker, C.D. (1982) 'Adolescent-adult talk as a practical interpretive problem'. In G. Payne and E. Cuff (eds), *Doing Teaching: The Practical Management of Classrooms*. London: Batsford, pp. 104–25.

Baker, C.D. (1984) 'The search for adultness: membership work in adolescent–adult talk', *Human Studies*, 7: 301–23.

Bales, R.F. (1950) *Interaction Process Analysis*. Cambridge, MA: Addison-Wesley.

Bamberg, M. (1997) 'A constructivist approach to narrative development'. In M. Bamberg (ed.), *Narrative Development – Six approaches*. Mahwah, NJ: Lawrence Erlbaum, pp. 89–132.

Barbour, R. (2007) *Doing Focus Groups*. London: Sage.

Barthes, R. (1967) *Elements of Semiology*. London: Cape.

Barthes, R. (1973) *Mythologies*. London: Cape.

Barthes, R. (1977) *Image, Music, Text*. London: Fontana.

Barthes, R. (1981) *Camera Lucida: Reflections on Photography*. New York: Hill and Wang.

Baruch, G. (1981) 'Moral tales: parents' stories of encounters with the health profession', *Sociology of Health and Illness*, 3 (3): 275–96.

Baruch, G. (1982) 'Moral tales: interviewing parents of congenitally ill children'. PhD thesis, Goldsmiths College, University of London.

Basso, C. (1972) '"To give up on words": silence in western Apache culture'. In P.-P. Giglioli (ed.), *Language and Social Context*. Harmondsworth: Penguin.

Bateson, G. and Mead, M. (1942) *Balinese Character: A Photographic Study*. New York: New York Academy of Sciences.

Bauer, M. (2000) 'Classical content analysis: a review'. In M. Bauer and D. Gaskell (eds), *Qualitative Researching with Text, Image and Sound: A Practical Handbook for Social Research*. London: Sage, pp. 131–51.

Becker, H.S. (1953) 'Becoming a marihuana user', *American Journal of Sociology*, 59: 235–42.

Becker, H.S. (1967) 'Whose side are we on?', *Social Problems*, 14: 239–48.

Becker, H. (1981) *Exploring Society Photographically*. Chicago: University of Chicago Press.

Becker, H. (1986) *Writing for Social Scientists*. Chicago: University of Chicago Press.

Becker, H.S. (1998) *Tricks of the Trade: How To Think about Your Research while Doing It*. Chicago and London: University of Chicago Press.

Becker, H.S. (2010) 'The art of comparison: lessons from the master, Everett C. Hughes', *Sociologica*, 2: www.sociologica.mulino.it/main.

Becker, H.S. and Geer, B. (1960) 'Participant observation: the analysis of qualitative field data'. In R. Adams and J. Preiss (eds), *Human Organization Research: Field Relations and Techniques*, Homewood, IL: Dorsey.

Berelson, B. (1952) *Content Analysis in Communicative Research*. New York: Free Press.

Bhatt, C. (2004) 'Doing a dissertation'. In C. Seale (ed.), *Researching Society and Culture*, Second Edition. London: Sage, pp. 409–30.

Billig, M. (1992) *Talking of the Royal Family*. London: Routledge.

Billig, M. (1995) *Banal Nationalism*. London: Sage.

Birdwhistell, R. (1970) *Kinesics in Context: Essays on Body Motion Communication*. Philadelphia: University of Philadelphia Press.

Blaxter, M. (1983) 'The causes of disease: women talking', *Social Science & Medicine*, 17: 59–69.

Bloor, M. (1978) 'On the analysis of observational data: a discussion of the worth and uses of inductive techniques and respondent validation', *Sociology*, 12 (3): 545–57.

Bloor, M. (1983) 'Notes on member validation'. In R. Emerson (ed.), *Contemporary Field Research: A Collection of Readings*. Boston, MA: Little Brown.

Bloor, M. (2004) 'Addressing social problems through qualitative research'. In D. Silverman (ed.), *Qualitative Research*, Second Edition. London: Sage, pp. 305–24.

Bloor, M. (2011) 'Addressing social problems through qualitative research'. In D. Silverman (ed.), *Qualitative Research*, Third Edition. London: Sage, pp. 399–415.

Bloor, M., Frankland, J., Thomas, M. and Stewart, K. (2000) *Focus Groups in Social Research*, Introducing Qualitative Methods Series. London: Sage.

Blumer, H. (1956) 'Sociological analysis and the "variable"', *American Sociological Review*, 21: 633–60.

Boden, D. (1994) *The Business of Talk*. Cambridge: Polity Press.

Boje, D.M. (1991). 'Organizations as storytelling networks: a study of story performance in an office-supply firm'. *Administrative Science Quarterly*, 36: 106–26.

Brannen, J. (2004) 'Working qualitatively and quantitatively'. In C. Seale et al. (eds), *Qualitative Research Practice*. London: Sage, pp. 312–26.

Brekhus, W., Galliher, J. and Gubrium, J. (2005) 'The need for thin description', *Qualitative Inquiry*, 11 (6): 861–79.

Brenner, M. (ed.) (1981) *Social Method and Social Life*. London: Academic Press.

Brewer, J. (2000) *Ethnography*. Buckingham: Open University Press.

Brown, A. (2010) 'Qualitative method and compromise in applied social research', *Qualitative Research*, 10 (2): 229–48.

Bryman, A. (1988) *Quantity and Quality in Social Research*. London: Unwin Hyman.

Bulmer, M. (1982) *The Uses of Social Research*. London: Allen & Unwin.

Burgess, R. (ed.) (1980) *Field Research: A Sourcebook and Field Manual*. London: Allen & Unwin.

Burton, L. (1975) *The Family Life of Sick Children*. London: Routledge.

Bury, M. (1986) 'Social constructionism and the development of medical sociology', *Sociology of Health and Illness*, 8: 137–69.

Buscatto, M. (2008) 'Who allowed you to observe? A reflexive overt organizational ethnography', *Qualitative Sociology Review*, IV (3), 29–48: www.qualitativesociologyreview.org/ENG/archive_eng.php.

Buscatto, M. (2011) 'Using ethnography to study gender'. In D. Silverman (ed.) *Qualitative Research*, Third Edition. London: Sage, pp. 35–52.

Byrne, B. (2004) 'Qualitative interviewing'. In C. Seale (ed.), *Researching Society and Culture*, Second Edition. London: Sage, pp. 179–92.

Byrne, P. and Long, B. (1976) *Doctors Talking to Patients*. London: Her Majesty's Stationery Office.

Caelli, K., Ray, L. and Mill, J. (2003) Clarity in generic research. *International Journal of Qualitative Methods*, 2 (2): 1–24.

Cain, M. (1986) 'Realism, feminism, methodology and law', *International Journal of the Sociology of Law*, 14: 255–67.

Cantor, M. and Pingree, S. (1983) *The Soap Opera*. London: Sage.

Charmaz, K. (2006) *Constructing Grounded Theory*. London: Sage.

Charmaz, K. and Bryant, A. (2011) 'Grounded theory and credibility'. In D. Silverman (ed.), *Qualitative Research*, Third Edition. London: Sage, pp. 291–309.

Charmaz, K. and Mitchell, R. (2001) 'Grounded theory in ethnography'. In P. Atkinson et al. (eds), *Handbook of Ethnography*. London: Sage, pp. 160–74.

Charteris-Black, J. (2005). *Politicians and Rhetoric: The Persuasive Power of Metaphor*. Basingstoke: Palgrave Macmillan.

Cherry, N. and Rodgers, B. (1979) 'Using a longitudinal study to assess the quality of retrospective data'. In L. Moss and H. Goldstein (eds), *The Recall Method in Social Surveys*. London: University of London Institute of Education.

Cicourel, A. (1964) *Method and Measurement in Sociology*. New York: Free Press.

Cicourel, A. (1968) *The Social Organization of Juvenile Justice*. New York: Wiley.

Cicourel, A. and Kitsuse, J. (1963) *The Educational Decision-Makers*. New York: Bobbs-Merrill.

Clark, J.A. and Mishler, E.G. (1992) 'Attending to patients' stories: reframing the clinical task', *Sociology of Health and Illness*, 14: 344–70.

Clavarino, A., Najman, J. and Silverman, D. (1995) 'Assessing the quality of qualitative data', *Qualitative Inquiry*, 1 (2): 223–42.

Clayman, S.C. (1992) 'Footing in the achievement of neutrality: the case of news-interview discourse'. In P. Drew P. and J.C. Heritage (eds), *Talk at Work*. Cambridge: Cambridge University Press, pp. 163–98.

Coffey, A. and Atkinson, P. (1996) *Making Sense of Qualitative Data*. London: Sage.

Cortazzi, M. (2001) 'Narrative analysis in ethnography'. In P. Atkinson et al. (eds), *Handbook of Ethnography*. London: Sage, pp. 384–94.

Cuff, E.C. and Payne, G.C. (eds) (1979) *Perspectives in Sociology*. London: Allen & Unwin.

Culler, J. (1976) *Saussure*. London: Fontana.

Czarniawska, B. (1997). *Narrating the Organization: Dramas of institutional identity*. Chicago: University of Chicago Press.

Czarniawska, B. (1998) *A Narrative Approach to Organization Studies*. London: Sage.

Czarniawska, B. (2003) *Narratives in Social Science*. London: Sage.

Czarniawska, B. (2007) *Shadowing and Other Techniques for Doing Fieldwork in Modern Societies*. Copenhagen: Liber.

Dalton, M. (1959) *Men Who Manage*. New York: Wiley.

Deegan, M. (2001) 'The Chicago School of ethnography'. In P. Atkinson et al. (eds), *Handbook of Ethnography*. London: Sage, pp. 11–25.

Delamont, S. (2004) 'Ethnography and participant observation'. In C. Seale et al. (eds), *Qualitative Research Practice*. London: Sage, pp. 217–29.

Denzin, N. (1970) *The Research Act in Sociology*. London: Butterworth.

Denzin, N. (1991) *Images of Postmodern Society*. Newbury Park, CA: Sage.

Denzin, N. (1995) *The Cinematic Society: The Voyeur's Gaze*. Thousand Oaks, CA: Sage.

Denzin, N. (2000) 'The practices and politics of interpretation'. In N. Denzin and Y. Lincoln (eds), *Handbook of Qualitative Research*, Second Edition. Thousand Oaks, CA: Sage, pp. 897–922.

Denzin, N. and Lincoln, Y. (1994) 'Introduction'. In N. Denzin and Y. Lincoln (eds), *Handbook of Qualitative Research*. Thousand Oaks, CA: Sage, pp. 1–20.

Denzin, N. and Lincoln, Y. (2000a) 'The discipline and practice of qualitative research'. In N. Denzin and Y. Lincoln (eds), *Handbook of Qualitative Research*, Second Edition. Thousand Oaks, CA: Sage, pp. 1–28.

Denzin, N. and Lincoln, Y. (eds) (2000b) *Handbook of Qualitative Research*, Second Edition. Thousand Oaks, CA: Sage.

Denzin, N. and Lincoln, Y. (eds) (2006) *Handbook of Qualitative Research*, Third Edition. Thousand Oaks, CA: Sage.

Dey, I. (2004) 'Grounded theory'. In C. Seale et al. (eds), *Qualitative Research Practice*. London: Sage, pp. 80–93.

Dingwall, R. (1980) 'Ethics and ethnography', *Sociological Review*, 28 (4): 871–91

Dingwall, R. (1992) 'Don't mind him – he's from Barcelona: qualitative methods in health studies'. In J. Daly et al. (eds), *Researching Health Care: Designs, Dilemmas, Disciplines*. London: Routledge.

Dixon-Woods, M. (2011) 'Systematic reviews and qualitative methods'. In D. Silverman (ed.), *Qualitative Research*, Third Edition. London: Sage, pp. 331–46.

Douglas, M. (1975) 'Self-evidence'. In M. Douglas, *Implicit Meanings*. London: Routledge.

Drew, P. and Heritage, J.C. (eds) (1992) *Talk at Work*. Cambridge: Cambridge University Press.

Duncombe, J. and Marsden, D. (1993) 'Love and intimacy', *Sociology*, 27: 221–41.

Dutton, J., Ashford, S., O'Neill, R. and Lawrence, K. (2001) 'Moves that matter', *Academy of Management Journal*, 44 (4): 716–36.

Eberle, T. and Maeder, C. (2011) 'Organizational ethnography'. In D. Silverman (ed.), *Qualitative Research*, Third Edition. London: Sage, pp. 53–74.

Edwards, D. (1995) 'Two to tango: script formulations, dispositions, and rhetorical symmetry in relationship troubles talk', *Research on Language and Social Interaction*, 28: 319–50.

Edwards, D. (1997) *Discourse and Cognition*. London: Sage.

Eldridge, J. and Murcott, A. (2000) 'Adolescents' dietary habits and attitudes: unpacking the "problem of (parental) influence"', *Health*, 4 (1): 25–49.

Emerson, R.M., Fretz, R.I. and Shaw, L.L. (1995) *Writing Ethnographic Fieldnotes*. Chicago: University of Chicago Press.

Emmison, M. (1988) 'On the interactional management of defeat', *Sociology*, 22: 233–51.

Emmison, M. (2004) 'The conceptualization and analysis of visual data', In D. Silverman (ed.), *Qualitative Research*, Second Edition. London: Sage, pp. 246–65.

Emmison, M. (2011) 'Conceptualizing visual data'. In D. Silverman (ed.), *Qualitative Research*, Third Edition. London: Sage, pp. 233–49.

Emmison, M. and McHoul, A. (1987) 'Drawing on the economy: cartoon discourse and the production of a category', *Cultural Studies*, 1 (10): 93–112.

Emmison, M. and Smith, P. (2000) *Researching the Visual*, Introducing Qualitative Methods Series. London: Sage.

Engebretson, J. (1996) 'Urban healers: an experiential description of American healing touch groups', *Qualitative Health Research*, 6 (4): 526–41.

Estroff, S.E. (1995) 'Whose story is it anyway?' In K.S. Toombs et al. (eds), *Chronic Illness: From Experience to Policy*. Bloomington: Indiana University Press.

Fielding, N. (1982) 'Observational research on the national front'. In M. Bulmer (ed.), *Social Research Ethics: An Examination of the Merits of Covert Participant Observation*. London: Macmillan.

Fielding, N.G. (ed.) (1988) *Actions and Structure*. London: Sage.

Fielding, N.G. and Fielding, J.L. (1986) *Linking Data*, Qualitative Research Series No. 4. London: Sage.

Filmer, P., Phillipson, M., Silverman, D. and Walsh, D. (1972) *New Directions in Sociological Theory*. London: Collier Macmillan.

Finch, J. (1984) '"It's great to have someone to talk to": the ethics and politics of interviewing women'. In C. Bell and H. Roberts (eds), *Social Researching*. London: Routledge.

Flyvbjerg, B. (2004) 'Five misunderstandings about case-study research'. In C. Seale et al. (eds), *Qualitative Research Practice*. London: Sage, pp. 420–34.

Fontana, A. and Frey, J. (2000) 'The interview: from structured questions to negotiated text'. In N. Denzin and Y. Lincoln (eds), *Handbook of Qualitative Research*, Second Edition. Thousand Oaks, CA: Sage, pp. 645–72.

Foucault, M. (1977) *Discipline and Punish*. Harmondsworth: Penguin.

Foucault, M. (1979) *The History of Sexuality*, Volume 1. Harmondsworth: Penguin.

Frake, C. (1964) 'Notes on queries in ethnography', *American Anthropologist*, 66: 132–45.

Frake, C. (1972) 'How to ask for a drink in Subanun'. In P.-P. Giglioli (ed.), *Language and Social Context*. Harmondsworth: Penguin.

Frith, H. and Kitzinger, C. (1998) '"Emotion work" as a participant resource: a feminist analysis of young women's talk-in-interaction', *Sociology*, 32 (2): 299–320.

Gabriel, Y. (2000). *Storytelling in Organizations*. Oxford: Oxford University Press.

Garfinkel, E. (1967) *Studies in Ethnomethodology*. Englewood Cliffs, NJ: Prentice Hall.

Gatrell, C. (2009) 'Safeguarding subjects? A reflexive reappraisal of researcher accountability in qualitative interviews', *Qualitative Research in Organizations and Management*, 4 (2): 110–22.

Geertz, C. (1973) *The Interpretation of Cultures*. London: Fontana.

Gilbert, N. (ed.) (1993) *Researching Social Life*. London: Sage.

Gilbert, N. and Mulkay, M. (1983) 'In search of the action'. In N. Gilbert and P. Abell (eds), *Accounts and Action*. Aldershot: Gower.

Gladwin, T. (1964) 'Culture and logical process'. In W. Goodenough (ed.), *Explorations in Cultural Anthropology*. New York: McGraw-Hill.

Glaser, B. and Strauss, A. (1967) *The Discovery of Grounded Theory*, Chicago: Aldine.

Glaser, B. and Strauss, A. (1968) *Time for Dying*. Chicago: Aldine.

Glassner, B and Loughlin, J. (1987) *Drugs in Adolescent Worlds: Burnouts to Straights*. New York: St. Martin's Press.

Gobo, G. (2004) 'Sampling, representativeness and generalizability'. In C. Seale et al. (eds), *Qualitative Research Practice*. London: Sage, pp. 435–456.

Gobo, G. (2008) *Doing Ethnography*, Introducing Qualitative Methods Series. London: Sage.

Gobo, G. (2009) 'Re-conceptualizing generalization: old issues in a new frame'. In P. Alasuutari, L. Bickman and J. Brannen (eds), *The SAGE Handbook of Social Research Methods*. London: Sage, pp. 193–213.

Gobo, G. (2011) 'Ethnography'. In D. Silverman (ed.), *Qualitative Research*, Third Edition. London: Sage, pp. 15–35.

Goffman, E. (1959) *The Presentation of Self in Everyday Life*. New York: Doubleday Anchor.

Goffman, E. (1961a) *Asylums*. New York: Doubleday Anchor.

Goffman, E. (1961b) *Encounters: Two Studies in the Sociology of Interaction*. Indianapolis, IN: Bobbs-Merrill.

Goffman, E. (1974) *Frame Analysis*. New York: Harper & Row.

Goffman, E. (1979) *Gender Advertisements*. Cambridge, MA: Harvard University Press.

Goffman, E. (1981) *Forms of Talk*. Oxford: Basil Blackwell.

Gouldner, A. (1962) '"Anti-minotaur": the myth of a value-free sociology', *Social Problems*, 9: 199–213.

Grahame, P. (1999) 'Doing qualitative research: three problematics', *Graduate Program in Applied Sociology*, Volume 2 (Fall): 1, 4–10. Boston, MA: University of Massachusetts.

Greatbatch, D. (1992) 'On the management of disagreement among news interviewers'. In P. Drew and J.C. Heritage (eds), *Talk at Work*. Cambridge: Cambridge University Press, pp. 268–301.

Greimas, A.J. (1966) *Semantique Structurale*. Paris: Larousse.

Guba, E. and Lincoln, Y. (1994) 'Competing paradigms in qualitative research'. In N. Denzin and Y. Lincoln (eds), *Handbook of Qualitative Research*. Thousand Oaks, CA: Sage, pp. 105–17.

Gubrium, J. (1986) *Oldtimers and Alzheimer's: The Descriptive Organization.of Senility*. Greenwich, CT: JAI Press.

Gubrium, J. (1988) *Analyzing Field Reality*, Qualitative Research Methods Series No. 8. Newbury Park, CA: Sage.

Gubrium, J. (1992) *Out of Control: Family Therapy and Domestic Disorder*. London: Sage.

Gubrium, J. (1997) *Living and Dying in Murray Manor*. Charlottesville, VA: University Press of Virginia.

Gubrium, J. (2005) 'Narrative environments and social problems', *Social Problems*, 52 (4): 525–8.

Gubrium, J. (2009) 'Curbing self-referential writing', Durham University, Anthropology Department: www.dur.ac.uk/writingacrossboundaries/writingonwriting/jaygubrium/.

Gubrium, J. (2010) 'A turn to narrative practice', *Narrative Inquiry*, 20 (2): 387–91.

Gubrium, J. and Buckholdt, D. (1982) *Describing Care: Image and Practice in Rehabilitation*. Cambridge, MA: Oelschlager, Gunn & Hain.

Gubrium, J. and Holstein, J. (1987) 'The private image: experiential location and method in family studies', *Journal of Marriage and the Family*, 49: 773–86.

Gubrium, J. and Holstein, J. (1990) *What is Family?* Mountain View, CA: Mayfield.

Gubrium, J. and Holstein, J. (1997a) *The New Language of Qualitative Method.* New York: Oxford University Press.

Gubrium, J. and Holstein, J. (1997b) 'The active interview'. In D. Silverman (ed.), *Qualitative Research.* London: Sage, pp. 113–291.

Gubrium, J. and Holstein, J. (eds) (2002) *Handbook of Interview Research.* Thousand Oaks, CA: Sage.

Gubrium, J. and Holstein, J. (2004) 'The active interview'. In D. Silverman (ed.), *Qualitative Research,* Second Edition. London: Sage, pp. 140–61.

Gubrium, J. and Holstein, J. (2008) 'Narrative ethnography'. In S. Hesse-Biber and P. Leavy (eds), *Handbook of Emergent Methods.* New York: Guilford Press, pp. 241–64.

Gubrium, J. and Holstein, J. (2009) *Analyzing Narrative Reality.* Thousand Oaks, CA: Sage.

Gubrium, J. and Holstein, J. (2011) 'Animating interview narratives'. In D. Silverman (ed.), *Qualitative Research,* Third Edition. London: Sage, pp. 149–67.

Hadley, R. (1987) 'Publish and be ignored: proselytise and be damned'. In G.C. Wenger (ed.), *The Research Relationship: Practice and Politics in Social Policy Research.* London: Allen & Unwin, pp. 98–110.

Haldar, M. and Wærdahl, R. (2009) 'Teddy Diaries: A method for studying the display of family life', *Sociology,* 43 (6): 1141–50.

Halfpenny, P. (1979) 'The analysis of qualitative data', *Sociological Review,* 27 (4): 799–825.

Halkier, B. (2010) 'Focus groups as social enactments: integrating interaction and content in the analysis of focus group data', *Qualitative Research,* 10 (1): 71–89.

Hall, E. (1969) *The Hidden Dimension.* London: Bodley Head.

Hammersley, M. (1990) *Reading Ethnographic Research: A Critical Guide.* London: Longman.

Hammersley, M. (1992a) *What's Wrong with Ethnography? Methodological Explorations.* London: Routledge.

Hammersley, M. (1992b) *Research and Policy.* Lewes: Falmer Press.

Hammersley, M. (2008) *Questioning Qualitative Inquiry.* London: Sage.

Hammersley, M. and Atkinson, P. (1995) *Ethnography: Principles in Practice.* London: Tavistock.

Hannah, D. and Lautsch, B. (2011) 'Counting in qualitative research: why to conduct it, when to avoid it, and when to closet it', *Journal of Management Inquiry,* 20 (1): 14–22.

Hart, C. (1998) *Doing a Literature Review: Releasing the Social Science Imagination.* London: Sage.

Hart, C. (2001) *Doing a Literature Search.* London: Sage.

Hawkes, T. (1977) *Structuralism and Semiotics.* London: Methuen.

Hay, I. and Israel, M. (2006) *Research Ethics for Social Scientists.* London: Sage.

Heath, C. (2004) 'Analysing face-to-face interaction'. In D. Silverman (ed.), *Qualitative Research,* Second Edition. London: Sage, pp. 266–82.

Heath, C. (2011) 'Embodied action: video and the analysis of social interaction'. In D. Silverman (ed.) *Qualitative Research,* Third Edition. London: Sage, pp. 250–70.

Heath, C. and Luff, P. (2000) *Technology in Action.* Cambridge: Cambridge University Press.

Heath, C., Hindmarsh, J. and Luff, P. (2010) *Video in Qualitative Research.* London: Sage.

Heath, S. (1981) *Questions of Cinema.* London: Macmillan.

Hepburn, A. and Potter, J. (2004) 'Discourse analytic practice'. In C. Seale et al. (eds), *Qualitative Research Practice.* London: Sage, pp. 180–96.

Heritage, J. (1984) *Garfinkel and Ethnomethodology.* Cambridge: Polity Press.

Heritage, J. (2011) 'Conversation analysis: practices and methods'. In D. Silverman (ed.), *Qualitative Research*, Third Edition. London: Sage, pp. 208–30.

Heritage, J. and Sefi, S. (1992) 'Dilemmas of advice: aspects of the delivery and reception of advice in interactions between health visitors and first time mothers'. In P. Drew and J.C. Heritage (eds), *Talk at Work.* Cambridge: Cambridge University Press, pp. 359–417.

Hindess, B. (1973) *The Use of Official Statistics in Sociology.* London: Macmillan.

Holstein, J. and Gubrium, J. (1995) *The Active Interview.* Thousand Oaks, CA: Sage.

Holstein, J. and Gubrium, J. (2004) 'Context: working it up, down and across'. In C. Seale et al. (eds), *Qualitative Research Practice.* London: Sage, pp. 297–311.

Holstein, J. and Gubrium, J. (2008) 'Constructionist impulses in ethnographic fieldwork'. In Holstein, J. and Gubrium, J. (eds), *Handbook of Constructionist Research.* New York: Guilford Press, pp. 373–95.

Holstein, J. and Gubrium, J. (2011) 'Animating interview narratives'. In D. Silverman (ed.), *Qualitative Research*, Third Edition. London: Sage, pp. 149–67.

Hookway, N. (2008) '"Entering the blogosphere": some strategies for using blogs in social research', *Qualitative Research*, 8 (1), 91–113.

Hornsby-Smith, M. (1993) 'Gaining access'. In N. Gilbert (ed.), *Researching Social Life.* London: Sage, pp. 52–67.

Horowitz, I.L. (1965) 'The life and death of Project Camelot', *Transaction*, 3: 44–7.

Hughes, E. (1958) *Men and their Work.* Glencoe, IL: Free Press.

Hughes, E. (1971) *The Sociological Eye.* Chicago: Aldine Atherton.

Humphreys, L. (1970) *Tearoom Trade: Impersonal Sex in Public Places.* Chicago: Aldine.

Kelly, M. and Ali, S. (2004) 'Ethics and social research'. In C. Seale (ed.), *Researching Society and Culture*, Second Edition. London: Sage, pp. 115–28.

Kendall, G. and Wickham, G. (1999) *Using Foucault's Methods*, Introducing Qualitative Methods Series. London: Sage.

Kendon, A. (1991) *Conducting Interaction: Patterns of Behaviour in Focussed Encounters.* Cambridge: Cambridge University Press.

Kent, G. (1996) 'Informed consent'. In *The Principled Researcher.* Social Science Division, The Graduate School, University of Sheffield, pp. 18–24.

Kiely, R., McCrone, D. and Bechhofer, F. (2005) 'Whither Britishness? English and Scottish people in Scotland', *Nations & Nationalism*, 11 (1): 65–82.

Kirk, J. and Miller, M. (1986) *Reliability and Validity in Qualitative Research*, Qualitative Research Methods Series, Volume 1. London: Sage.

Kitzinger, C. (2004) 'Feminist approaches'. In C. Seale et al. (eds), *Qualitative Research Practice.* London: Sage, pp. 125–40.

Kitzinger, C. (2006) 'After post-cognitivism', *Discourse Studies*, 8 (1): 67–83.

Kitzinger, C. (2007) 'Editor's introduction: the promise of conversation analysis', *Feminism & Psychology*, 17 (2): 133–48.

Kitzinger, C. (2008) 'Review essay: Emanuel A. Schegloff, "Sequence Organization in Interaction: A primer in conversation analysis, Volume 1"', *Discourse and Society*, 19 (4): 560–7.

Kitzinger, C. and Frith, H. (1999) 'Just say no? The use of conversation analysis in developing a feminist perspective on sexual refusal', *Discourse and Society*, 10 (3): 293–316.

Kitzinger, J. and Miller, D. (1992) '"African AIDS": the media and audience beliefs'. In P. Aggleton et al. (eds), *AIDS: Rights, Risk and Reason.* London: Falmer Press.

Koppel, R. (2005) 'Role of computerized physician order entry systems in facilitating medical errors', *Journal of American Medical Association*, 293 (10): 1197–1202.

Koppel, R. (2009) 'Reprise of a battle won: sociologist monitors Boston Transit System's treatment of the disabled', American Sociological Association, *Footnotes*, February.

Kuhn, T.S. (1970) *The Structure of Scientific Revolutions*, Second Edition. Chicago: University of Chicago Press.

Kvale, S. (1996) *InterViews*. London: Sage.

Laclau, E. (1981) 'Politics as the construction of the unthinkable', Paper trans. from the French by D. Silverman, mimeo. Department of Sociology, Goldsmiths College.

Lamont, M. and White, P. (2005) *Interdisciplinary Standards for Systematic Qualitative Research*. Arlington, VA: National Science Foundation.

Landsberger, H. (1958) *Hawthorne Revisited*. Ithaca, NY: Cornell University Press.

Lawton, J. (2001) 'Gaining and maintaining consent: ethical concerns raised in a study of dying patients'. *Qualitative Health Research*, 11 (5): 693–705.

Levinson, S.C. (1983) *Pragmatics*. Cambridge: Cambridge University Press.

Levi-Strauss, C. (1967) *Structural Anthropology*. New York: Basic Books.

Linders, A. (2008) 'Documents, texts, and archives in constructionist research'. In J. Holstein and J. Gubrium (eds), *Handbook of Constructionist Research*. New York: Guilford Press, pp. 467–90.

Lipset, S.M., Trow, M. and Coleman, J. (1962) *Union Democracy*. Garden City, NY: Anchor Books, Doubleday.

Livingston, E. (1987) *Making Sense of Ethnomethodology*. London: Routledge.

Llewellyn, N. and Hindmarsh, J. (eds) (2010) *Organization, Interaction and Practice*. Cambridge: Cambridge University Press.

Lodge, D. (1989) *Nice Work*. London: Penguin.

Loseke, D.R. and Kusenbach, M. (2008) 'The social construction of emotion'. In J. Holstein and J. Gubrium (eds), *Handbook of Constructionist Research*. New York: Guilford Press, pp. 511–30.

Lynch, M. (1984) *Art and Artifact in Laboratory Science*. London: Routledge.

Lyons, R.F., Sullivan, M.J.L., Ritvo, P.G. with Coyne, J.C. (1995) *Relationships in Chronic Illness and Disability*. Thousand Oaks, CA: Sage.

Macnaghten, P. and Myers, G. (2004) 'Focus groups'. In C. Seale et al. (eds), *Qualitative Research Practice*. London: Sage, pp. 65–79.

Malinowski, B. (1922) *Argonauts of the Western Pacific*. London: Routledge.

Mann, C. and Stewart, F. (eds) (2000) *Internet Communication and Qualitative Research: A Handbook for Researching Online*. London: Sage.

Markham, A. (2004) 'Internet communication as a tool for qualitative research'. In D. Silverman (ed.), *Qualitative Research,* Second Edition. London: Sage, pp. 95–124.

Markham, A. (2011) 'Internet research'. In D. Silverman (ed.), *Qualitative Research*, Third Edition. London: Sage, pp. 111–28.

Marsh, C. (1982) *The Survey Method*. London: Allen & Unwin.

Marshall, C. and Rossman, G. (1989) *Designing Qualitative Research*. Sage: London.

Marvasti, A (2004) *Qualitative Research in Sociology*. London: Sage.

Marvasti, A. (2011) 'Three aspects of writing qualitative research: practice, genre and audience'. In D. Silverman (ed.), *Qualitative Research*, Third Edition. London: Sage, pp. 383–96.

Marx, G. (1997) 'Of methods and manners for aspiring sociologists: 37 moral imperatives', *American Sociologist*, Spring: 102–25.

Maseide, P. (1990) 'The social construction of research information'. *Acta Sociologica*, 33 (1): 3–13.

Mason, J. (1996) *Qualitative Researching*. London: Sage.

Mason, J. and Davies, K. (2009) The Living Resemblances Project: www.reallifemethods. ac.uk/research/resemblances/.

Maynard, D. (1989) 'On the ethnography and analysis of discourse in institutional settings', *Perspectives on Social Problems*, 1: 127–46.

Maynard, D. (1991) 'Interaction and asymmetry in clinical discourse', *American Journal of Sociology*, 97 (2): 448–95.

Maynard, D. (2003) *Bad News, Good News: Conversational Order in Everyday Talk and Clinical Settings*. Chicago: Chicago University Press.

Maynard, D. and Clayman, S. (1991) 'The diversity of ethnomethodology', *Annual Review of Sociology*, 17: 385–418.

McKeganey, N. and Bloor, M. (1991) 'Spotting the invisible man: the influence of male gender on fieldwork relations', *British Journal of Sociology*, 42 (2): 195–210.

Mcnaghten, P. and Myers, G. (2004) 'Focus groups'. In Seale et al. (eds), *Qualitative Research Practice*. London: Sage, pp. 65–79.

Mehan, H. (1979) *Learning Lessons: Social Organization in the Classroom*. Cambridge, MA: Harvard University Press.

Mercer, K. (1990) 'Powellism as a political discourse'. PhD thesis, Goldsmiths College, University of London.

Miles, M. and Huberman, A. (1984) *Qualitative Data Analysis*. London: Sage.

Milgram, S. (1963) 'Behavioural study of obedience', *Journal of Abnormal and Social Psychology*, 67: 371–8.

Miller, G., Dingwall, R. and Murphy, E. (2004) 'Using qualitative data and analysis: reflections on organizational research'. In D. Silverman (ed.), *Qualitative Research*. London: Sage, pp. 325–41.

Miller, J. (2001) *One of the Guys: Girls, Gangs and Gender*. New York: Oxford University Press.

Miller, J. and Glassner, B. (1997) 'The "inside" and the "outside": finding realities in interviews'. In D. Silverman (ed.), *Qualitative Research*. London: Sage, pp. 99–112.

Miller, J. and Glassner, B. (2004) 'The "inside" and the "outside": finding realities in interviews'. In D. Silverman (ed.), *Qualitative Research*, Second Edition. London: Sage, pp. 125–39.

Miller, R.L. (2000) *Researching Life Stories and Family Histories*, Introducing Qualitative Methods Series. London: Sage.

Mills, C.W. (1940) 'Situated actions and vocabularies of motive', *American Sociological Review*, 5: 904–13.

Mills, C.W. (1959) *The Sociological Imagination*. New York: Oxford University Press.

Mishler, E.G. (1986) *Research Interviewing: Context and Narrative*. London: Harvard University Press.

Moerman, M. (1974) 'Accomplishing ethnicity'. In R. Turner (ed.), *Ethnomethodology*. Harmondsworth: Penguin.

Moisander, J. and Valtonen, A. (2006) *Qualitative Marketing Research: A Cultural Approach*, Introducing Qualitative Methods Series. London: Sage.

Molotch, H. and Boden, D. (1985) 'Talking social structure: discourse, domination and the Watergate Hearings', *American Sociological Review*, 50 (3): 273–88.

Mulkay, M. (1984) 'The ultimate compliment: a sociological analysis of ceremonial discourse', *Sociology*, 18: 531–49.

Murcott, A. (1997) 'The PhD: some informal notes', School of Health and Social Care, South Bank University, London.

Murray, L. (2009) 'Looking at and looking back: visualization in mobile research', *Qualitative Research*, 9 (4) 469–88.

Nash, J. (1975) 'Bus riding: community on wheels'. *Urban Life*, 4: 99–124.

Nash, J. (1981) 'Relations in frozen places: observations on winter public order', *Qualitative Sociology*, 4: 229–43.

Neisser, U. (1994) 'Self-narratives: true and false'. In U. Neisser and R. Fivush (eds), *The Remembering Self: Construction and Accuracy in the Self-narrative*. Cambridge: Cambridge University Press, pp. 1–18.

Nelson, B. (1984) *Making an Issue of Child Abuse*. Chicago: University of Chicago Press.

Noaks, L. and Wincup, E. (2004) *Criminological Research: Understanding qualitative methods*. London: Sage.

Oakley, A. (1981) 'Interviewing women: a contradiction in terms'. In H. Roberts (ed.), *Doing Feminist Research*. London: Routledge.

Oboler, R. (1986) 'For better or for worse: anthropologists and husbands in the field'. In T. Whitehead and M. Conway (eds), *Self, Sex and Gender in Cross-Cultural Fieldwork*. Urbana, IL: University of Illinois Press, pp. 28–51.

O'Brien, M. (1993) 'Social research and sociology'. In N. Gilbert (ed.), *Researching Social Life*. London: Sage, pp. 1–17.

O'Dochartaigh, N. (2007) *Internet Research Skills*. London: Sage.

O'Malley, C. (2005) 'Supporting structured observational analysis of multimodal records'. Talk given at Video, Social Research and Technical Innovations Colloquium, Department of Management, King's College, London, 23 March.

Peräkylä, A. (1989) 'Appealing to the experience of the patient in the care of the dying', *Sociology of Health and Illness*, 11 (2), 117–34.

Peräkylä, A. (1995) *AIDS Counselling*. Cambridge: Cambridge University Press.

Peräkylä, A. (2004a) 'Reliability and validity in research based upon transcripts'. In D. Silverman (ed.), *Qualitative Research*. London: Sage, pp. 283–304.

Peräkylä, A. (2004b) 'Conversation analysis'. In C. Seale et al. (eds), *Qualitative Research Practice*. London: Sage, pp. 165–79.

Peräkylä, A. (2011) 'Validity in research on naturally-occurring interaction'. In D. Silverman (ed.), *Qualitative Research*, Third Edition. London: Sage, 365–82.

Peräkylä, A. and Silverman, D. (1991) 'Owning experience: describing the experience of others', *Text*, 11 (3): 441–80.

Phelps, R., Fisher, K. and Ellis, A. (2007) *Organizing and Managing Your Research: A Practical Guide for Postgraduates*. London: Sage.

Pink, S. (2004) 'Visual methods'. In C. Seale et al. (eds), *Qualitative Research Practice*. London: Sage, pp. 361–76.

Pollner, M. (1987) *Mundane Reason: Reality in Everyday and Sociological Discourse*. Cambridge: Cambridge University Press.

Popper, K. (1959) *The Logic of Scientific Discovery*. New York: Basic Books.

Pösö, T., Honkatukia, P. and Nyqvist, L. (2008) 'Focus groups and the study of violence', *Qualitative Research*, 8 (1): 73–89.

Potter, J. (1996a) 'Discourse analysis and constructionist approaches: theoretical background'. In J. Richardson (ed.), *Handbook of Qualitative Research Methods for Psychology and the Social Sciences*. Leicester: BPS Books, pp. 125–40.

Potter, J. (1996b) *Representing Reality: Discourse, Rhetoric and Social Construction*. London: Sage.

Potter, J. (1997) 'Discourse analysis as a way of analysing naturally-occurring talk'. In D. Silverman (ed.), *Qualitative Research*. London: Sage, pp. 144–60.

Potter, J. (2002) 'Two kinds of natural', *Discourse Studies*, 4 (4): 539–42.

Potter, J. (2004) 'Discourse analysis as a way of analysing naturally-occurring talk'. In D. Silverman (ed.), *Qualitative Research*, Second Edition. London: Sage, pp. 200–21.

Potter, J. (2011) 'Discursive psychology and the study of naturally occurring talk'. In D. Silverman (ed.), *Qualitative Research*, Third Edition. London: Sage, pp. 187–207.

Potter, J. and Hepburn, A. (2005) 'Qualitative interviews in psychology: problems and possibilities', *Qualitative Research in Psychology*, 2: 281–307.

Potter, J. and Hepburn, A. (2008) 'Discursive constructionism'. In J. Holstein and J. Gubrium (eds), *Handbook of Constructionist Research*. New York, Guilford Press, pp. 275–93.

Potter, J. and Wetherell, M. (1987) *Discourse and Social Psychology: Beyond Attitudes and Behaviour*. London: Sage.

Prior, L. (1987) 'Policing the dead: a sociology of the mortuary', *Sociology*, 21 (3): 355–76.

Prior, L. (1988) 'The architecture of the hospital: a study of spatial organization and medical knowledge', *British Journal of Sociology*, 34 (1): 86–113.

Prior, L. (2003) *Using Documents in Social Research*. London: Sage.

Prior, L. (2004) 'Doing things with documents'. In D. Silverman (ed.), *Qualitative Research*, Second Edition. London: Sage, pp. 76–94.

Prior, L. (2007) 'Talking about the gene for cancer: a study of lay and professional knowledge of cancer genetics', *Sociology*, 41 (6): 985–1001.

Prior, L. (2011) 'Using documents in social research'. In D. Silverman (ed.), *Qualitative Research*, Third Edition. London: Sage, pp. 93–110.

Procter, M. (1993) 'Analysing survey data'. In N. Gilbert (ed.), *Researching Social Life*. London: Sage, pp. 239–54.

Propp, V.I. (1968) *Morphology of the Folktale*, Second Revised Edition, ed. L.A. Wagner. Austin: University of Texas Press.

Puchta, C. and Potter, J. (2004) *Focus Group Practice*. London: Sage.

Puchta, C., Potter, J. and Wolff, S. (2004) 'Repeat receipts: a device for generating visible data in market research focus groups', *Qualitative Research*, 4 (3): 285–309.

Punch, K. (1998) *Introduction to Social Research: Quantitative and Qualitative Approaches*. London: Sage.

Punch, M. (1994) 'Politics and ethics in fieldwork'. In N. Denzin and Y. Lincoln (eds), *Handbook of Qualitative Research*. Thousand Oaks, CA: Sage, pp. 83–97.

Radcliffe-Brown, A.R. (1948) *The Andaman Islanders*. Glencoe, IL: Free Press.

Rapley, T. (2004) 'Interviews'. In C. Seale et al. (eds), *Qualitative Research Practice*. London: Sage, pp. 15–33.

Rapley, T. (2007) *Doing Conversation, Discourse and Document Analysis*. London: Sage.

Rapley, T. (2011) 'Some pragmatics of qualitative data analysis'. In D. Silverman (ed.), *Qualitative Research*, Third Edition. London: Sage, pp. 273–90.

Rathje, N. and Hughes, T. (1975) 'A garbage project as a non-reactive approach: garbage in, garbage out?' In H.W. Sinaiko and L.A. Broedling (eds), *Perspectives on Attitude Assessment: Surveys and Their Alternatives*, Manpower and Advisory Services, Technical Report No. 2. Washington, DC: Smithsonian Institute.

Reason, P. and Rowan, J. (1981) *Human Inquiry: A Sourcebook of New Paradigm Research*. Chichester: Wiley.

Richardson, L. (1990) *Writing Strategies: Reaching Diverse Audiences*. Newbury Park, CA: Sage.

Riessman, C. (1990) *Divorce Talk: Women and Men Make Sense of Personal Relationships*. New Brunswick, NJ: Rutgers University Press.

Riessman, C. (1993) *Narrative Analysis*. Newbury Park, CA: Sage.

Riessman, C. (2004) 'Exporting ethics: a narrative about narrative research in South India'. *Health* (Special Issue on Informed Consent, Ethics and Narrative), 9 (4): 73–90.

Riessman, C.K. (2008) *Narrative Methods for the Human Sciences*. London: Sage.

Riessman, C.K. (2009) 'Considering grounded theory: categories, cases, and control'. *Symbolic Interaction*, 32 (4): 390–3.

Riessman, C.K. (2011) 'What's different about narrative inquiry? Cases, categories and contexts'. In D. Silverman (ed.), *Qualitative Research*, Third Edition. London: Sage, pp. 310–30.

Rudestam, K. and Newton, R. (1992) *Surviving Your Dissertation*. Newbury Park, CA: Sage.

Ryen, A. (2004) 'Ethical issues'. In C. Seale et al. (eds), *Qualitative Research Practice*. London: Sage, pp. 217–29.

Ryen, A. (2011) 'Ethical issues'. In C. Seale et al. (eds), *Qualitative Research Practice*. London: Sage, pp. 217–29.

Ryen, A. and Silverman, D. (2000) 'Marking boundaries: culture as category-work', *Qualitative Inquiry*, 6 (1): 107–28.

Sacks, H. (1972a) 'On the analysability of stories by children'. In J. Gumperz and D. Hymes (eds), *Directions in Sociolinguistics*. New York: Holt, Rinehart & Winston.

Sacks, H. (1972b), 'Notes on police assessment of moral character'. In D. Sudnow (ed.), *Studies in Social Interaction*. New York: Free Press, pp. 280–93.

Sacks, H. (1974) 'On the analyzability of stories by children'. In R. Turner (ed.), *Ethnomethodology*. Harmondsworth: Penguin, pp. 216–32.

Sacks, H. (1984) 'On doing "being ordinary"'. In J.M. Atkinson and J. Heritage (eds), *Structures of Social Action: Studies in Conversation Analysis*. Cambridge: Cambridge University Press, pp. 513–29.

Sacks, H. (1992) *Lectures on Conversation*, Volumes I and II, ed. Gail Jefferson with an introduction by Emmanuel Schegloff. Oxford: Blackwell.

Sacks, H., Schegloff, E.A. and Jefferson, G. (1974) 'A simplest systematics for the organization of turn-taking in conversation', *Language*, 50 (4): 696–735.

Saussure, F. de (1974) *Course in General Linguistics*. London: Fontana.

Scheflen, A.E. (1964) 'The significance of posture in communication systems', *Psychiatry*, 27: 316–31.

Schegloff, E.A. (1968) 'Sequencings in conversational openings', *American Anthropologist*, 70: 1075–95.

Schegloff, E.A. (1982) 'Discourse as an interactional accomplishment: some uses of "uh huh" and other things that come between sentences'. In D. Tannen (ed.), *Georgetown University Round Table on Language and Linguistics: Analyzing Discourse: Text and Talk*. Washington, DC: Georgetown University Press, pp. 71–93.

Schegloff, E.A. (1991) 'Reflections on talk and social structure'. In D. Boden and D. Zimmerman (eds), *Talk and Social Structure: Studies in Ethnomethodology and Conversation Analysis*. Cambridge: Polity Press, pp. 44–70.

Schegloff, E.A. (1992a) 'On talk and its institutional occasions'. In P. Drew and J.C. Heritage (eds), *Talk at Work*. Cambridge: Cambridge University Press, pp. 101–36.

Schegloff, E.A. (1992b) 'Repair after next turn: the last structurally provided defense of intersubjectivity in conversation', *American Journal of Sociology*, 98: 1295–1345.

Schegloff, E.A. (1997) 'Whose text? Whose context?', *Discourse and Society*, 8: 165–87.

Schegloff, E.A. (2007) *Sequence Organization in Interaction: A Primer in Conversation Analysis*. Cambridge: Cambridge University Press.

Schreiber, R. (1996) '(Re)defining my self: women's process of recovery from depression', *Qualitative Health Research*, 6 (4): 469–91.

Schwartz, H. and Jacobs, J. (1979) *Qualitative Sociology: A Method to the Madness*. New York: Free Press.

Seale, C. (1999) *The Quality of Qualitative Research*, Introducing Qualitative Methods Series. London: Sage.

Seale, C.F. (2002) 'Cancer heroics: a study of news reports with particular reference to gender', *Sociology*, 36 (1): 107–26.

Seale, C. (2004a) 'Quality in qualitative research'. In C. Seale et al. (eds), *Qualitative Research Practice*. London: Sage, pp. 409–19.

Seale, C. (ed.) (2004b) *Researching Society and Culture*, Second Edition. London: Sage.

Seale, C.F. (2006) 'Gender, cancer experience and internet use: a comparative keyword analysis of interviews and online cancer support groups', *Social Science & Medicine*, 62 (10): 2577–90.

Seale, C. (2010) 'Using computers to analyse qualitative data'. In D. Silverman (ed.), *Doing Qualitative Research*, Third Edition. London: Sage, pp. 251–67.

Seale, C. (ed.) (2011) *Researching Society and Culture*, Third Edition. London: Sage.

Seale, C., Gobo, G., Gubrium, J. and Silverman, D. (eds) (2004) *Qualitative Research Practice*. London: Sage.

Seale, C., Ziebland, S. and Charteris-Black, J. (2006) 'Gender, cancer experience and internet use: a comparative keyword analysis of interviews and online cancer support groups', *Social Science & Medicine*, 62 (10): 2577–90.

Searle, J. (1969) *Speech Acts*. Cambridge: Cambridge University Press.

Selltiz, C., Jahoda, M., Deutsch, M. and Cook, S. (1964) *Research Methods in Social Relations*. New York: Holt, Rinehart & Winston.

Sharples, M., Davison, L., Thomas, G. and Rudman, P. (2003) 'Children as photographers: an analysis of children's photographic behaviour and intentions at three age levels', *Visual Communication*, 2 (3): 303–30.

Shaw, I. (1999) *Qualitative Evaluation*, Introducing Qualitative Methods Series. London: Sage.

Silverman, D. (1968) 'Clerical ideologies: a research note', *British Journal of Sociology*, XIX (3): 326–33.

Silverman, D. (1970) *The Theory of Organizations*. London: Heinemann (New York: Basic Books, 1971).

Silverman, D. (1973) 'Interview talk: bringing off a research instrument', *Sociology*, 7 (1): 31–48.

Silverman, D. (1975) 'Accounts of organizations: organizational structures and the accounting process'. In J. McKinlay (ed.), *Processing People: Cases in Organizational Behaviour*. London: Holt, Rinehart & Winston.

Silverman, D. (1981) 'The child as a social object: Down's syndrome children in a paediatric cardiology clinic', *Sociology of Health and Illness*, 3 (3): 254–74.

Silverman, D. (1984) 'Going private: ceremonial forms in a private oncology clinic', *Sociology*, 18: 191–202.

Silverman, D. (1985) *Qualitative Methodology and Sociology*. Aldershot: Gower.

Silverman, D. (1987) *Communication and Medical Practice*. London: Sage.

Silverman, D. (1989a) 'Telling convincing stories: a plea for cautious positivism in case-studies'. In B. Glassner and J. Moreno (eds), *The Qualitative–Quantitative Distinction in the Social Sciences*. Dordrecht: Kluwer.

Silverman, D. (1989b) 'The impossible dreams of reformism and romanticism'. In J. Gubrium and D. Silverman (eds), *The Politics of Field Research: Sociology Beyond Enlightenment*. London: Sage.

Silverman, D. (1991) 'Unfixing the subject: viewing "bad timing"', *Continuum: An Australian Journal of the Arts*, 5 (1): 9–31; reprinted in C. Jenks (ed.) (1993) *Cultural Reproduction*. London: Routledge.

Silverman, D. (1997) *Discourses of Counselling: HIV Counselling as Social Interaction*. London: Sage.

Silverman, D. (1998) *Harvey Sacks and Conversation Analysis*, Polity Key Contemporary Thinkers Series. Cambridge: Polity Press; New York: Oxford University Press.

Silverman, D. (2005) *Doing Qualitative Research: A Practical Handbook*, Second Edition. London: Sage.

Silverman, D. (2007) *A Very Short, Fairly Interesting, Reasonably Cheap Book about Qualitative Research*. London: Sage.

Silverman, D. (2010) *Doing Qualitative Research*, Third Edition. London: Sage.

Silverman, D. (2011) *Qualitative Research*, Third Edition. London: Sage.

Silverman, D. and Jones, J. (1976) *Organizational Work: The Language of Grading/The Grading of Language*. London: Collier Macmillan.

Silverman, D. and Torode, B. (1980) *The Material Word: Some Theories of Language and its Limits*. London: Routledge.

Simmel, G. (1950) *Sociology*. Glencoe, IL: Free Press.

Singleton, R., Straits, B., Straits, M. and McAllister, R. (1988) *Approaches to Social Research*. Oxford: Oxford University Press.

Skelton, J.R., Wearn, A.M. and Hobbs, F.D. (2002) 'A concordance-based study of metaphoric expressions used by general practitioners and patients in consultation', *British Journal of General Practice*, 52 (475): 114–18.

Slater, D. (1989) 'Corridors of power'. In J. Gubrium and D. Silverman (eds), *The Politics of Field Research: Sociology Beyond Enlightenment*. London: Sage.

Small, M. (2009) '"How many cases do I need?" On science and the logic of case selection in field-based research', *Ethnography*, 10 (1): 5–38.

Smith, D. (1996) 'The relations of ruling: a feminist inquiry', *Studies in Cultures, Organizations and Societies*, 2: 171–90.

Speer, S. (2002) '"Natural" and "contrived" data: a sustainable distinction?', *Discourse Studies*, 4 (4): 511–25.

Spicer, N. (2004) 'Combining qualitative and quantitative methods'. In C. Seale (ed.), *Researching Society and Culture*, Second Edition. London: Sage, pp. 293–304.

Spradley, J.P. (1979) *The Ethnographic Interview*. New York: Holt, Rinehart & Winston.

Stake, R. (1994) 'Case studies'. In N. Denzin and Y. Lincoln (eds), *Handbook of Qualitative Research*. Thousand Oaks, CA: Sage, pp. 236–47.

Stanley, L. and Wise, S. (1983) *Breaking Out: Feminist Consciousness and Feminist Research*. London: Routledge.

Stimson, G. (1986) 'Place and space in sociological fieldwork', *Sociological Review*, 34 (3): 641–56.

Strauss, A. and Corbin, J. (1990) *Basics of Qualitative Research*. Thousand Oaks, CA: Sage.

Strauss, A. and Corbin, J. (1994) 'Grounded theory methodology: an overview'. In N. Denzin and Y. Lincoln (eds), *Handbook of Qualitative Research*. Thousand Oaks, CA: Sage, pp. 273–85.

Strong, P. (1979) *The Ceremonial Order of the Clinic*. London: Routledge.

Stubbs, M. (1981) 'Scratching the surface'. In C. Adelman (ed.), *Uttering, Muttering: Collecting, Using and Reporting Talk for Educational Research*. London: Grant McIntyre.

Suchman, L. (1987) *Plans and Situated Actions: The Problem of Human–Machine Communication*. Cambridge: Cambridge University Press.

Sudnow, D. (1968a) *Passing On: The Social Organization of Dying*. Englewood Cliffs, NJ: Prentice Hall.

Sudnow, D. (1968b) 'Normal crimes'. In E. Rubington and M. Weinberg (eds), *Deviance: The Interactionist Perspective*. New York: Macmillan.

ten Have, P. (1998) *Doing Conversation Analysis: A Practical Guide*. London: Sage.

ten Have, P. (2007) *Doing Conversation Analysis*, Second Edition, Introducing Qualitative Methods Series. London: Sage.

Tesch, R. (1991) *Qualitative Research: Analysis Types and Software Tools*. Lewes: Falmer Press.

Thomas, W. and Znaniecki, F. (1927) *The Polish Peasant in Europe and America*. New York: Alfred Knopf.

Thornberg, R. (2008) 'School children's reasoning about school rules', *Research Papers in Education*, 23 (1): 37–52. http://dx.doi.org/10.1080/02671520701651029.

Toynbee, P. (2008) 'Labour is bound to bypass the lessons of the 58ers', *Guardian*, 18 August.

Venkatesh, S. (2008) *Gang Leader for a Day*. London: Allen Lane.

Voysey, M. (1975) *A Constant Burden*. London: Routledge.

Walsh, D. (2004) 'Doing ethnography'. In C. Seale (ed.), *Researching Society and Culture*. London: Sage, pp. 217–32.

Warren, A. (1988) *Gender Issues in Field Research*, Qualitative Research Methods, Volume 9. Newbury Park, CA: Sage.

Warren, A. and Rasmussen, P. (1977) 'Sex and gender in fieldwork research', *Urban Life*, 6: 359–69.

Watson, R. (1997) 'Ethnomethodology and textual analysis'. In D. Silverman (ed.), *Qualitative Research*, London: Sage, pp. 80–98.

Weatherburn, P. and Project SIGMA (1992) 'Alcohol use and unsafe sexual behaviour: any connection?'. In P. Aggleton et al. (eds), *AIDS: Rights, Risk and Reason*. London: Falmer Press.

Webb, B. and Stimson, G. (1976) 'People's accounts of medical encounters'. In M. Wadsworth (ed.), *Everyday Medical Life*. London: Martin Robertson.

Weber, M. (1946) 'Science as a vocation'. In H. Gerth and C.W. Mills (eds), *From Max Weber*. New York: Oxford University Press.

Weber, M. (1949) *Methodology of the Social Sciences*. New York: Free Press.

Wetherell, M. (1998) 'Positioning and interpretative repertoires: conversation analysis and post-structuralism in dialogue', *Discourse Society*, 9 (3): 387–412.

Wetherell, M. and Potter, J. (1992) *Mapping the Language of Racism: Discourse and the Legitimation of Exploitation*. Brighton: Harvester/Wheatsheaf; New York: Columbia University Press.

Whyte, W.F. (1949) 'The social structure of the restaurant', *American Journal of Sociology*, 54: 302–10.

Whyte, W.F. (1980) 'Interviewing in field research'. In R. Burgess (ed.), *Field Research: A Sourcebook and Field Manual*. London: Allen & Unwin.

Widdicombe, S. and Wooffitt, R. (1995) *The Language of Youth Subcultures: Social identity in action*. London; Harvester/Wheatsheaf.

Wilkinson, S. (2011) 'Focus group research'. In D. Silverman (ed.), *Qualitative Research*, Third Edition. London: Sage, pp. 168–84.

Wilkinson, S. and Kitzinger, C. (2000) 'Thinking differently about thinking positive: a discursive approach to cancer patients' talk', *Social Science and Medicine*, 50: 797–811.

Wilkinson, S. and Kitzinger, C. (2003) 'Constructing identities: a feminist conversation analytic approach to positioning in action'. In R. Harre and F. Moghaddam (eds), *The Self and Others: Positioning Individuals and Groups in Personal, Political and Cultural Contexts*. New York: Prager/Greenwood.

Wittgenstein, L. (1968) *Philosophical Investigations*. Oxford: Basil Blackwell.

Wolcott, H. (1990) *Writing Up Qualitative Research*, Qualitative Research Methods Series 20. Newbury Park, CA: Sage.

Woolgar, S. (1985) 'Why not a sociology of machines? The case of sociology and artificial intelligence', *Sociology*, 19 (4): 557–72.

Yarrow, M.R., Campbell, J.D. and Burton, R.V. (1970) 'Recollections of childhood: a study of the retrospective method', *Monograph of the Society for Research in Child Development*, 35 (5).

Zimmerman, D. (1974) 'People work and paper work'. In R. Turner (ed.), *Ethnomethodology*. Harmondsworth: Penguin.

Zimmerman, D. (1992) 'The interactional organization of calls for emergency assistance'. In P. Drew and J.C. Heritage (eds), *Talk at Work*. Cambridge: Cambridge University Press, pp. 418–69.

Zimmerman, D. and West, C. (1975) 'Sex roles, interruptions and silences in conversations'. In B. Thorne and N. Henley (eds), *Language and Sex*. Rowley, MA: Newbury House, pp. 105–29.

Author Index

Subject Index

DOING QUALITATIVE RESEARCH

Third Edition

David Silverman *Visiting Professor in the Business School, University of Technology, Sydney*

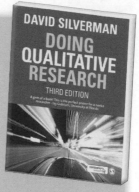

Written in a lively, accessible style, **Doing Qualitative Research, 3rd Edition** provides a step-by-step guide to all the questions students ask when beginning their first research project. Silverman demonstrates how to learn the craft of qualitative research by applying knowledge about different methods to actual data. He provides practical advice on key issues such as: defining 'originality' and narrowing down a topic; keeping a research diary and writing a research report; and presenting research to different audiences.

This hugely popular textbook is essential reading for anyone planning their own research project.

2009 • 472 pages
Cloth (978-1-84860-033-1) • £88.00
Paper (978-1-84860-034-8) • £27.99
Electronic (978-1-84920-790-4) • £88.00

QUALITATIVE RESEARCH

Third Edition

Edited by **David Silverman** *Visiting Professor in the Business School, University of Technology, Sydney*

This hugely successful textbook has been fully updated and revised to make it even more accessible and comprehensive than previous editions. New chapters have been added on a range of key topics, including grounded theory, research ethics and systematic review.

This book draws on a stellar list of leading qualitative researchers, each of whom is writing on their own specialized area in qualitative research, but doing so in a way that is clear and accessible to students and those new to the field of qualitative methods.

This is a comprehensive and accessible first text on qualitative methods that boasts a who's who of leading qualitative methodologists and is a must-have book for any student involved in doing research.

2010 • 464 pages
Cloth (978-1-84920-416-3) • £75.00
Paper (978-1-84920-417-0) • £26.99

ALSO FROM SAGE